T0332559

Non–Functional Properties in Service Oriented Architecture:

Requirements, Models and Methods

Nikola Milanovic
Model Labs – Berlin, Germany

INFORMATION SCIENCE REFERENCE

Hershey · New York

Senior Editorial Director:	Kristin Klinger
Director of Book Publications:	Julia Mosemann
Editorial Director:	Lindsay Johnston
Acquisitions Editor:	Erika Carter
Development Editor:	Joel Gamon
Production Coordinator:	Jamie Snavely
Typesetters:	Keith Glazewski & Natalie Pronio
Cover Design:	Nick Newcomer

Published in the United States of America by
Information Science Reference (an imprint of IGI Global)
701 E. Chocolate Avenue
Hershey PA 17033
Tel: 717-533-8845
Fax: 717-533-8661
E-mail: cust@igi-global.com
Web site: http://www.igi-global.com

Library of Congress Cataloging-in-Publication Data

Non-functional properties in service oriented architecture : requirements,
models, and methods / Nikola Milanovic, editor.
       p. cm.
  Includes bibliographical references and index.
  Summary: "This book offers a selection of chapters that cover three
important aspects related to the use of non-functional properties in SOA:
requirements specification with respect to non-functional properties, modeling
non-functional properties and implementation of non-functional properties"--
Provided by publisher.
  ISBN 978-1-60566-794-2 (hardcover) -- ISBN 978-1-60566-795-9 (ebook) 1.
Service-oriented architecture (Computer science) 2. Non-functional
requirements (Systems engineering) I. Milanovic, Nikola.

  TK5105.5828.N66 2011
  004.6'54--dc22

                          2010033600

British Cataloguing in Publication Data
A Cataloguing in Publication record for this book is available from the British Library.

All work contributed to this book is new, previously-unpublished material. The views expressed in this book are those of the authors, but not necessarily of the publisher.

Table of Contents

Section 1
Requirement Specification in SOA

Section 2
Modeling Non-Functional Properties in SOA

Section 3
Methods for Implementing Non-Functional Properties in SOA

Detailed Table of Contents

Section 1
Requirement Specification in SOA

Bode and Riebisch present a novel architectural design method supporting specification of non-functional requirements in the design phase and, more importantly, traceability: mapping of requirements to software solutions. In that way, not only specification, but also implementation of non-functional properties is architecturally supported. The case study is presented where a manufacturing execution system has been reengineered to SOA and integrated with an ERP system using this methodology.

Gross, Yu, and Song argue that the true challenge of modeling non-functional properties is how to support them in different platforms or application domains. For that purpose the authors present a platform and a development method supporting goal and scenario oriented modeling and analysis of non-functional properties. Special attention is given to such variations as domains specific meaning of non-functional properties, different terminologies, load and configuration settings.

Chapter 3

    Hanane Becha, University of Ottawa, Canada
    Gunter Mussbacher, University of Ottawa, Canada
    Daniel Amyot, University of Ottawa, Canada

Becha, Mussbacher, and Amyot present an aspect-oriented approach for analyzing non-functional requirements in SOA applications. They describe how to apply User Requirements Notation (URN) together with aspect-oriented extensions for that purpose. The proposed notation enables quantitative specification of non-functional properties and thus provides the foundation for service discovery, selection, and composition. In the accompanying case study, cost, response time, reliability, and availability are the non-functional properties which are explicitly illustrated.

Chapter 4

    Jesús Rodríguez, University of Castilla – La Mancha, Spain
    Eduardo Fernández-Medina, University of Castilla – La Mancha, Spain
    Mario Piattini, University of Castilla – La Mancha, Spain
    Daniel Mellado, National Competition Commission, Spain

Rodríguez et al. present a novel tool for capturing security requirements in software product lines. It facilitates management of complex security requirements by providing the possibility to specify those requirements in the early development stage, manage and visualize them, as well as enable variability and traceability in the implementation phase. Furthermore, the tool can integrate existing security standards.

Section 2
Modeling Non-Functional Properties in SOA

Chapter 5

    Nicolò Perino, University of Lugano, Switzerland
    Marco Massarelli, Universitá degli Studi di Milano-Bicocca, Italy
    Daniele Cammareri, Universitá degli Studi di Milano-Bicocca, Italy
    Claudia Raibulet, Universitá degli Studi di Milano-Bicocca, Italy
    Francesca Arcelli, Universitá degli Studi di Milano-Bicocca, Italy

Perino et al. provide an overview of non-functional properties in SOA. The authors propose the basic set of non-functional properties (policy, security, transaction, and management), each with the corresponding set of attributes. The main challenges are then discussed, such as modeling, dependencies and conflicts, management through Service Level Agreements, and service compositions. Finally, future trends and promising approaches for modeling non-functional properties in SOA are presented.

Moayerzadeh and Yu argue that although widely used, basic SOA principles such as abstraction, discoverability, reusability, and composability are rarely collected and systematically organized. They propose a goal-graph representation of SOA principles which can be used in system design. Non-functional properties are automatically extracted from the text-based description (knowledge base) and then formalized. Goal-graphs thus obtained can be then used in different phases of system design.

Chapter 7

Achilleos, Yang and Georgalas describe a model-based framework for engineering non-functional properties in the context of pervasive service creation. High dynamicity of pervasive services requires new approaches for their specification, development, and management. The authors propose a context modeling language which can be used to generate platform independent context models describing non-functional properties. These models are then transformed into platform specific source code. The approach is illustrated with a case study showing all steps of this process, from the context model definition to code generation.

Chapter 8

Shekhovtsov et al. present an approach of using non-first-normal-form tables for modeling quality of service in SOA. They argue that it is very suitable for communicating application design issues to stakeholders with the business background. They show how to use such tables as an intermediate step between requirements specification and system design to define functional and quality requirements of services and business processes (service orchestrations).

Chapter 9

Ortiz and Hernández argue that combining model-driven and aspect-oriented methods provides a useful foundation for development of high-quality SOA systems. The authors provide a method for integrating non-functional properties into SOA model-driven development process using aspect-oriented methods, thus separating non-functional properties from the code. They demonstrate how application of this method increases modularity and reduces implementation and maintenance complexity.

Miladi et al. address the problem of dynamic deployment for services that need to adapt their behavior based on the changes in requirements or context. The authors propose a generic model called unified deployment and management model of distributed software architectures. It is described how to use this model to enable dynamic deployment in both SOA and traditional component-based applications.

Section 3
Methods for Implementing Non-Functional Properties in SOA

Salinas and Salinas describe non-functional properties as the major complexity factor in software product lines (SPL) of SOA, as they are difficult to manage being found in many contexts with varying concerns and crosscut multiple concerns across the entire lifecycle. Furthermore, existing variability methods concentrate on functional properties only. The authors present and apply an extended version of an aspect-oriented framework for SPLs that exploits aspect-oriented software development techniques in order to model variability of NFRs in SPLs of SOAs from early development stages.

Satoh et al. discuss the problem of very late and missing specification of security properties in SOA development, because of which, developers in the downstream development phases must manage different security requirements and configurations ad-hoc and manually. The authors then propose a model-driven process which can be extended to multiple specification and development phases for definition of various security properties, such as business security requirements or platform security properties. Finally, a model-driven tool for security configuration, implementing the proposed methodology, is described and demonstrated.

Chapter 13

Diao, Hellerstein and Parekh discuss scalability of SOA applications. They argue that scaling SOA applications requires a systematic approach to resource management to achieve service level objectives (SLO). They propose a methodology for scaling SOAs based on the control engineering theory and demonstrate the benefits achieved in an industrial setting.

Stantchev and Tamm argue that, with massively distributed architectures becoming more prevalent, the assurance of availability and dependability for distributed applications becomes an even more challenging and nontrivial task. The authors describe an approach for addressing non-functional properties in SOA based on reference models such as ITIL and the SOA life cycle model, which has been already applied in several industrial setting in the telecommunications sector.

Liu et al. provide an illustrative case study of applying functional and QoS properties in the field of SOA-based biomedical multimedia processing applications. They adapt the concepts of requirements elicitation of Software Engineering as well as a training set of machine learning to analyze functional and QoS properties of biomedical multimedia data. Two medical education projects are introduced as case studies to illustrate the usage of functional and QoS semantics extracted to improve the performance of subsequent classification and search.

Foreword

Computing services have evolved from their erstwhile emphasis of specific functionalities with dedicated implementation schemas and on dedicated platforms. As computing has expanded to wide scale growth of applications, platforms and service requirements, these have entailed an increasing sophistication of operations and correspondingly increasing complexity of the (software) realization. Subsequently with current Web scale systems, the needs for adaptable and scalable services and also the progression to non-specific platforms/technologies has only added to the complexity of realizing computing services. As classical computing paradigms face limitations to handle complexity, the concepts of service oriented architectures (SOA) offer architectural approaches towards simplification of complex software designs by advocating modular building blocks for services that could be interconnected to realize the desired (complex) services. Consequently, SOA offers a fundamentally richer abstraction of specifying service functionality sans a mandated implementation. This decoupling of services from dedicated implementations has helped evolve the modular and composable Web model of interactions, and also offers developers diverse implementation choices of (interoperable) programming languages and implementation components. The popularity of the cloud computing model is a natural progression both building upon and supporting the SOA paradigms.

While the SOA concepts provide the essence of "service on demand" across the service providers and service consumers, the realized value of SOA gets enhanced when the contracted services also incorporate extra-functional properties. These include services delivered in a secure, reliable and timely manner, transparent to the occurrence of component coupling, transparent to the occurrence of perturbations, and of a granularity matching the service needs and similarly related service quality attributes. It is this group of "extra-functional" or "non-functional" SOA features that significantly determines the actual value of an SOA approach. At the same time, the provisioning of these non-functional attributes is not easy. SOA obtains its core value from an "open system" design philosophy that includes facets of modularity, evolving composition via loose coupling of functional blocks, variety of programming schema, lack of embedding of calls across modules, among other aspects. On the other hand, the provisioning of non-functional attributes such as dependability or security or timeliness attributes work best with a complete systems view, having a well structured (and controlled) operational structure and usage of specifically advocated implementation mechanisms. Unfortunately this is also often counter to the SOA approaches making the integration of non-functional aspects in SOA to be non-trivial.

While there exists an abundance of SOA design approaches, this key consideration of "non-functional" attributes is often conspicuous by its absence. It is this explicit and dedicated coverage of "non-functional aspects in SOA" that distinguishes this book. Its systematic coverage of the requirements, models and approaches help set proper foundations to addressing non-functional attributes in SOA. I applaud Nikola

Milanovic for his exemplary initiative in addressing this hard, but much needed SOA challenge area. I am positive that the readers will find the book to offer a high value, high impact exposition of SOA.

Neeraj Suri
TU Darmstadt, Germany

Neeraj Suri *received his PhD from the University of Massachusetts at Amherst. He currently holds the TU Darmstadt Chair Professorship in "Dependable Embedded Systems and Software" at TU Darmstadt, Germany. His earlier appointments include the Saab Endowed Professorship, faculty at Boston University and sabbatical at Microsoft Research. His research interests focus on design, analysis and assessment of distributed-dependable systems and software. His research emphasizes composite issues of dependability and security for SW/OS, verification/validation of protocols and especially "trusted/secure systems by design". His group's research activities have garnered support from the European Commission, NSF, DARPA, ONR, Microsoft, Hitachi, IBM, NASA, Boeing, Saab, Volvo, SSF, Vinnova, and Daimler Chrysler among others. He is also a recipient of the NSF CAREER award and the 2008 IBM Faculty Award. Suri serves as the associate Editor in Chief for IEEE Transactions on Dependable and Secure Computing, on the editorial boards for: IEEE Transactions for Software Engineering, ACM Computing Surveys, Journal of Security and Networks, and has been an editor for the IEEE Transactions on Parallel and Distributed Systems. He is a member of IFIP WG 10.4 on Dependability, and a member of Microsoft's Trustworthy Computing Academic Advisory Board. More professional details are available at: http://www.deeds.informatik.tudarmstadt.de/suri/activities/activities.html.*

Preface

Service Oriented Architecture (SOA) is the paradigm for software and system specification, design, implementation and management, that pretends to shape and dominate IT and business landscapes in the near future. SOA has departed from the initial hype phase and ceased to be a simple buzzword long time ago, while entering a relatively mature phase with numerous companies offering SOA products and services. The scientific community has kept apace and continues to explore creative and inspiring approaches at an astonishing pace that further enrich this approach.

SOA initially promised and also thereafter successfully delivered several basic functionalities: unified and standardized description, discovery, communication, and binding of autonomous and self contained software entities, called services, at an unprecedented scale. They have furthermore enabled dynamic and complex enterprise interactions, previously unthinkable or commercially unattainable, and at the global level.

However, very soon it also became clear that functional interoperability offered by the first generation of SOA standards and products failed to satisfy several important requirements, such as efficient discovery and matching of business and/or technical requirements between service requestors and service providers. The increasing number of offered services further exacerbated this problem: it was not clear how to choose adequate interaction partners (services) among many of them offering approximately "the same" functionality; how to select optimal partners according to a given criteria or their combination (e.g., price or performance); or how to be able to specify "soft" or "non-functional" requirements on the requestor side and match them with provided properties on the service side. In other words, the issues of specifying a whole range of properties orthogonal to pure functional description (what the service should do) remained generally unaddressed.

Parallel to these developments, the decade-old idea of a component marketplace was brought to life once again as the service marketplace under the umbrella of emerging SOA standards. Here also, very soon it was only too clear that matching and searching for composition partners or building an application based on third party services depends heavily on many other properties beside the pure functional ones.

The properties which are orthogonal to functional properties (**what** is the service doing) and describe the nature, mechanism, or context of the service execution (**how** and **under which conditions** is the service doing), have been given different names in different disciplines and by different people, including "non-functional properties", "extra-functional properties", "quality of service properties" or "service level agreement properties." In this book, the term non-functional properties will be mostly used, although other designations may also appear. Notable examples of non-functional properties are security, reliability, availability, timeliness, location, price, performance, et cetera.

This book offers a selection of chapters that cover three important aspects related to the use of non-functional properties in SOA: requirements specification with respect to non-functional properties, modeling non-functional properties, and implementation of non-functional properties.

Each software project begins with requirements specification phase. Hidden, unspecified requirements present a constant source of errors, frustrations, and costly workarounds required to fix them. This problem is further exacerbated in heterogeneous and dynamic SOA environment, where frequent changes of processes and technologies dictate adaptive and tool supported requirement specification. In the first section of the book, four approaches for capturing non-functional requirements in SOA will be presented. They build a foundation for successful modeling and execution of complex SOA projects. In Chapter 1, Bode and Riebisch present a novel architectural design method supporting specification of non-functional requirements in the design phase and, more importantly, traceability: mapping of requirements to software solutions. Gross, Yu, and Song argue in Chapter 2 that the true challenge of modeling non-functional requirements is how to support them in different platforms or application domains. For that purpose the authors present a platform and a development method supporting goal and scenario oriented modeling and analysis of non-functional requirements. In Chapter 3, Becha, Mussbacher, and Amyot present an aspect-oriented approach for analyzing non-functional requirements in SOA applications. Finally in Chapter 4 Rodríguez et al. describe a novel tool for capturing security requirements in software product lines.

Modeling non-functional properties is the critical step for achieving successful realization of complex SOA projects. Issues of reliability, availability, security, or quality of service are often subsumed under the general term of Service Level Agreements (SLA). The second section of the book discusses approaches for formal and tool supported modeling of SLAs containing non-functional properties. In Chapter 5, Perino et al. provide an overview of non-functional properties in SOA. The authors propose the basic set of non-functional properties (policy, security, transaction and management), each with the corresponding set of attributes. Moayerzadeh and Yu argue in Chapter 6 that although widely used, basic SOA principles such as abstraction, discoverability, reusability, and composability are rarely collected and systematically organized. They propose a goal-graph representation of SOA principles which can be used in system design. In Chapter 7, Achilleos, Yang, and Georgalas describe a model-based framework for engineering non-functional properties in the context of pervasive service creation. Shekhovtsov et al. present in Chapter 8 an approach of using non-first-normal-form tables for modeling quality of service in SOA. They argue that it is very suitable for communicating application design issues to stakeholders with the business background. Ortiz and Hernández argue in Chapter 9 that the combination of model-driven and aspect-oriented methods provides useful foundation for development of high-quality SOA systems. The authors propose a method for integrating non-functional properties into SOA model-driven development process using aspect-oriented methods.

The final, third section of the book discusses practical application of methods for implementing non-functional properties in SOA environments. Methods such as aspect oriented programming (AOP), model driven architecture (MDA) or control theory are presented and applied to diverse properties (e.g., security) in various domains (e.g., biomedicine). In Chapter 11 Salinas and Salinas present and apply an extended version of an aspect-oriented framework for software product lines that exploits aspect-oriented software development techniques in order to model variability of non-functional properties in SOA from early development stages. Satoh et al. discuss in Chapter 12 the problem of very late and missing specification of security properties in SOA development, because of which developers in the downstream development phases must manage different security requirements and configurations ad-hoc and manually. The authors then propose a model-driven process which can be extended to multiple specification and development phases for definition of various security properties, such as business security requirements or platform security properties. In Chapter 13 Diao, Hellerstein and Parekh explore scalability of SOA applications. They propose a methodology for scaling SOAs based on the control engineering theory and demonstrate the benefits achieved in an industrial setting. Stantchev and Tamm argue in Chapter 14 that, with massively distributed architectures becoming more prevalent, the assurance of availability and dependability for distributed applications becomes an even more challenging and nontrivial task. The authors describe an approach for addressing non-functional properties in SOA based on reference models such as ITIL and the SOA life cycle. Finally, in Chapter 15 Liu et al. provide an illustrative case study of applying functional and QoS properties in the field of SOA-based biomedical multimedia processing applications.

The book will thus gradually guide the reader through all steps of SOA application development, starting with requirement specification, over non-functional property modeling, to their implementation. Focusing state-of-the art research results in one place, the book can serve both as a practical reference manual as well as advanced scientific source. Finally, the authors discuss open issues, and propose future exciting questions yet to be explored.

Nikola Milanovic
Model Labs - Berlin, Germany

Section 1
Requirement Specification in SOA

Each software project begins with requirements specification phase. Hidden, unspecified requirements present a constant source of errors, frustrations and costly workarounds required to fix them. This problem is further exacerbated in heterogeneous and dynamic SOA environment, where frequent changes of processes and technologies dictate adaptive and tool supported requirement specification. In this section four approaches for capturing non-functional requirements in SOA are presented. They build a foundation for successful modeling and execution of complex SOA projects.

Section 1
Requirement Specification in
SOA

Chapter 1
Tracing the Implementation of Non-Functional Requirements

Stephan Bode
Ilmenau University of Technology, Germany

Matthias Riebisch
Ilmenau University of Technology, Germany

ABSTRACT

A software architecture has to enable the non-functional properties, such as flexibility, scalability, or security, because they constitute the decisive factors for its design. Unfortunately, the methodical support for the implementation of non-functional requirements into software architectures is still weak; solutions are not generally established. Recently, there are only few approaches that actually deal with non-functional requirements during design; even fewer take advantage of traceability, which supports a mapping of requirements to solutions through the development process. Therefore, in this chapter the new architectural design method TraGoSoMa is presented, which supports these issues. The method uses a so-called Goal Solution Scheme, which guides the design activities, supports conflict resolution, decision-making, and the classification of solutions. For illustration purposes the chapter uses a case study from a reengineering project for a Manufacturing Execution System (MES) that is restructured according to the SOA principles and integrated with an Enterprise Resource Planning (ERP) system.

INTRODUCTION

Motivation

Performance, scalability, flexibility, security and other so-called non-functional requirements or

DOI: 10.4018/978-1-60566-794-2.ch001

quality properties are crucial for the success of nearly every software project. They bear even more risk than functional requirements, because they can hardly be implemented after making the major design decisions. The software architecture has to enable these non-functional requirements, because they constitute the decisive factors for its design. Several architectural methods emphasize the analysis of non-functional requirements (Hofmeister et al., 2000) and the design considering them (Bosch, 2000; Bass et al., 2002). Furthermore, in the field of requirements engineering functional and non-functional requirements and their interdependencies are modeled using some mature and established goal-oriented approaches (Chung et al., 2000; Yu, 1995; Amyot, 2003). Therefore, some development steps of requirements engineering and architectural design are strongly related with each other. However, bridging the gap between these two research areas is still a critical issue (Galster et al., 2006) especially in the case when non-functional requirements change.

Service-oriented architectures are frequently applied for business-critical purposes. For these systems a long life expectancy constitutes an important concern, during which they have to be adjusted to a high number of changes to maintain their operation and their business value. Thus, evolvability is an important issue for this type of systems.

Traceability links support changes, and therefore the evolution of software systems, by expressing relations between artifacts in different phases of software development (Letelier, 2002). They facilitate program comprehension by expressing dependencies explicitly. They relate design decisions to constraints, and they are used to trace dependencies for checking the completeness of changes. These benefits can be achieved from fine-grained traceability links on the level of design elements and design decisions.

There is a considerable amount of research for managing traceability and for maintaining their accuracy during changes, which is for example discussed in (Mäder et al., 2006). However, the tracing of non-functional requirements usually requires a very high number of links, since typically a high number of a system's components depend on one such requirement.

There are some critical issues that make the whole process complex: for example (a) the mapping of high-level non-functional requirements to their low-level solutions and mechanisms, as well as (b) detecting and solving conflicts among non-functional requirements resulting in trade-offs, and further (c) the missing structuredness of existing methodologies or even their complete absence.

The management of traceability links, and with them the non-functional properties, requires a high human effort, first because of the high number of links and second because of missing rules inhibiting effective tool support. In order to reduce the effort for establishing, maintaining, and validating the traceability links, our work presents contributions to facilitate tool support, and hence, traceability of non-functional requirements, in several ways, which are described in the next sections.

Challenges

The proper treatment of non-functional requirements is a very important part of architectural design. Unfortunately, the methodical support for the implementation of non-functional requirements is still lacking even if this book addresses it. The absence of a consolidated set of solutions for non-functional requirements, the abstraction gap between requirements and design as well as the many influencing factors on design decisions reduce the applicability of detailed design instructions.

From the point of view of software architectural design there are only few methods that lead to an improved design process by especially considering non-functional requirements: for example the QASAR method (Bosch, 2000) or the Attribute-Driven Design (ADD) method (Bass et al., 2002). On the other hand, in requirements engineering there are adequate approaches for dealing with non-functional requirements in a goal-oriented way: for example the NFR framework (Chung et al. 2000), the i* framework (Yu, 1995), or the Goal-oriented Requirement Language (GRL) (Amyot, 2003). Although efforts are made to push these goal-oriented methods towards support for architectural design, and therefore some overlapping in the development steps can be observed, further research has to be done to bridge the gap. The goal-oriented techniques are valuable for dealing with the interdependencies and the refinement of functional and non-functional requirements, and to some extent are able to map high-level solutions to those goals. However, despite some research on their support for architectural design, (e.g., Grau & Franch, 2007 or Liu & Yu, 2001), on their own they are rather unsuitable and insufficient for the whole architectural design process. Therefore, from our point of view, we have to adjust and integrate these techniques into the software architectural methodologies and publish this knowledge to software architects. This will help them as a means for going from the problem space to the solution space and for choosing and evaluating proper architectural solutions especially for non-functional requirements.

As another aspect, traceability promises strong benefits for the design and evolution of service-oriented architectures and applications especially if traceability links are available on a fine-grained level. However, this leads to a very high number of traceability links. Thus, the complexity of the link structure and a high overhead effort for its maintenance constitute hampering factors. This holds especially for the traceability of non-functional properties, since usually a high number of design elements depend on each non-functional requirement, and this results in a high number of traceability links related to these requirements.

The integration and application of the above-mentioned methods provides the potential for an improved traceability. However, the traceability concepts have to be integrated within these methods, and vice versa the methods have to be adapted to make use of traceability. As a next step after integration, a proper tool support for the management of the traceability links has to be built, covering the establishment, the maintenance, the validation, and the exploitation of the links.

Objectives and Contribution

In this work we present the design method TraGoSoMa (an acronym for Traceability-driven Goal Solution Mapping) for a proper treatment of non-functional requirements during architectural design. The method is intended to give a better support and guidance for architectural design activities while dealing with non-functional goals. It supports the conflict resolution between competing goals and a classification of solutions to the goals they are derived from, as well as a systematic selection based on methodical decision-making. TraGoSoMa clearly is a software architectural design method, even if it partly integrates requirements engineering activities and goal-oriented techniques for modeling non-functional requirements. With its Goal Solution Scheme as a core concept the method maps non-functional goals and subgoals to architectural principles, which are essential criteria for finding the right architectural design, and it maps them further to the functional and technical solutions. Therefore, it enables an accumulation of architectural know-how. Beyond, the application of the method facilitates traceability link establishment, and thus, a better maintainability of the software. The method is illustrated in the next sections with the help of a case study.

BACKGROUND

In this section we briefly investigate the contributions of state-of-the-art methods for non-functional design. Therefore, we discuss Bosch's Quality Attribute-based Software Architectural (QASAR) method (Bosch, 2000) and the Attribute-Driven Design (ADD) method (Bass et al. 2002). We express how our approach is influenced by the goal-oriented approaches from requirements engineering, such as the Non-Functional Requirements (NFR) framework of Chung et al. (2000) and the i* framework which was introduced by

Yu (1995). Moreover, we relate our traceability framework for non-functional requirements to other works concerning traceability.

The Design Method QASAR

A frequently performed way of constructing a software architecture for both kinds of requirements is described by Bosch's QASAR method (Bosch, 2000). QASAR considers non-functional requirements by architectural transformations. The method describes three phases. In the first phase, the functional requirements are implemented by functional components with the Functionality-based Architectural Design (FAD) method. FAD uses core abstractions of functional concepts—the so-called archetypes—to derive architectural components by functional decomposition. In the second phase, the developed architecture is assessed in order to decide whether the non-functional requirements are fulfilled or not. Different approaches for the assessment of the non-functional requirements can be used in this phase, e.g., scenario-based evaluation, simulation, mathematical modeling, or objective reasoning. Once the non-functional properties of the architecture are assessed, in the third phase the architecture is transformed to satisfy the non-functional requirements specifications. This transformation leads to suitable functional structures and components, which are developed for the implementation of as many as possible non-functional requirements. All remaining non-functional requirements are implemented by changing all affected components. In this phase the changes are scattered over the system.

We consider QASAR as a very important method of architectural design and we will use its core concept—the fulfilling of non-functional requirements by functional solutions—in our TraGoSoMa method. The drawback of QASAR, the scattered implementation of the remaining non-functional requirements, results from its third phase. The scattering is accompanied with a demand for a very high number of traceability links

and hampers maintainability. We want to address this issue in the TraGoSoMa method by a careful consideration of the non-functional properties.

Attribute-Driven Design

The ADD method of Bass et al. (2002) is a step-by-step method for designing software architectures. ADD considers non-functional requirements at least as important as functional ones and takes them as input together with other constraints. The non-functional requirements, or quality attributes, have to be specified as quality attribute scenarios before. Then, with ADD the requirements are transformed into a conceptual architecture by a recursive refinement, which is applied in several design steps.

First, an architectural element is chosen to be refined, beginning with the system itself. Next, those requirements that influence the architecture the most have to be determined. These architecturally significant requirements—called architectural drivers—are quality, business, or functional goals and can be identified by prioritization. In a further step, architectural styles and patterns are chosen that satisfy the architectural drivers. In this third step, for the one architectural element that is to be refined and its high-prioritized architectural drivers, the most appropriate solution has to be chosen. The fourth step is about the actual refinement. The chosen style is instantiated and corresponding architectural elements are created. The new elements are assigned with functionality they are responsible for, and their interfaces are specified for information flow. In the fifth step, the refinement of the child elements is prepared by verifying and refining their requirements descriptions. Finally, all steps are repeated for further decomposition until all architectural drivers are fulfilled.

ADD, just as QASAR, achieves the fulfilling of quality goals by allocating functional components. Its strength is that it concentrates on the most significant architectural drivers for choosing a proper functional solution utilizing appropriate architectural styles and patterns. We will use this concept in our TraGoSoMa method by prioritizing requirements. However, ADD also has its drawbacks. First, the method ends with only a conceptual architecture and no concrete components; hence, the design process has to be continued by other means. Furthermore, ADD does not exactly describe how to identify the architectural drivers. This step is apparently left for the requirements engineer. Additionally, due to its recursive nature, the capability of the ADD method to evaluate alternative solutions for the overall architecture is limited. If an architectural element is refined once and the method continues with the child elements, there is no possibility to consider an alternative for the previous decision. Besides, there is nothing about traceability support with ADD, which is an important issue we want to address with our TraGoSoMa method.

Goal-Oriented Approaches

In the field of requirements engineering goal-oriented approaches are a popular way to elicit and model requirements. The Non-Functional Requirements (NFR) framework by Chung et al. (2000) constitutes one of these approaches for dealing with non-functional requirements. The framework uses the concept of so-called softgoals that represent non-functional requirements. Softgoals are goals that have no clear-cut definition or criteria for their satisfaction. Development decisions often contribute only partially to or even against these goals within acceptable limits. Because softgoals are accomplished rather partially than completely or not at all, they are considered as fulfilled, and then called *satisficed*, if an adequate level of the criteria is reached. The interdependencies between softgoals can be categorized into several contribution types according to their weak or strong positive or negative influence on satisfying a softgoal.

The NFR framework describes several interleaving and iterative activities to arrange softgoals with their interdependencies in a Softgoal Interdependency Graph. First NFR softgoals are established and refined into subgoals by decomposition. Then, different architectural solutions are developed as so-called operationalizations for the softgoals. Furthermore, softgoals can be refined by so-called argumentations, which model domain characteristics and developers' expertise. Beyond, during the refinement, decisions about the criticality of different goals can be made. Performing these activities, different alternative solutions and corresponding design trade-offs are elaborated in a well-founded way. Implicit interdependencies among softgoals are detected and documented together with design rationale. Alternative solutions are evaluated regarding their contribution to the non-functional requirements. Finally, an adequate solution is selected based on the evaluation.

Another important goal-oriented method is the i* framework, which was presented by Yu (1995). Akin to the NFR framework, i* uses the notation of goals and softgoals to model system requirements. In addition, it contains further elements, e.g., tasks, resources, and actors, and it uses different types of links, as for example contribution, decomposition, and means-end. Therefore, it can be utilized to not only describe the system's requirements but also the organizational context.

In 2008 the User Requirements Notation (URN) (Amyot, 2003) was approved as an international standard as ITU-T Recommendation Z.151. URN consists of the Goal-oriented Requirement Language (GRL), which is based on NFR and i*, and Use Case Maps (UCM), which are used for scenario modeling. GRL as an elaborate notation can be used especially to model non-functional requirements as goals.

We consider the described goal-oriented approaches as appropriate means for modeling non-functional requirements. By explicitly considering non-functional requirements right from the beginning and providing a well-defined evaluation process, they can help to design software architectures. Therefore, our TraGoSoMa method builds on them and uses their notation of softgoals for non-functional requirements and contribution links for the interdependencies.

However, the approaches focus on the refinement of non-functional requirements and their analysis from a requirements engineering point of view. From an architectural point of view, despite some works also dealing with architectural design as for example the one of Grau and Franch (2007), further design activities and notations have to be used. We argue that there are several drawbacks. For example, in the goal-oriented approaches, architectural constraints from the environment as well as interdependencies with technical solutions are not considered. They cannot assure that a selected solution can be implemented with a specific technology. Furthermore, the goal-oriented approaches do not consider general design principles in their decomposition and refinement, although they are very important for choosing proper solutions during architectural design. Beyond, the comprehension of the quality goals' background is an important issue for architectural design. That is way giving only goal models as input to software architects as a means for description is rather insufficient. Therefore, we integrate these techniques in a context of further design steps. Furthermore, in the work of Chung et al. (2000) they only concentrate on accuracy, performance, and security requirements—on the last one in a rather outdated way—and are not concerned with traceability issues. We will later discuss traceability and also some security aspects, when describing our TraGoSoMa method, in more details.

Traceability

Traceability is a concept to relate artifacts from different development stages, such as requirements analysis, design, and implementation via links. The use of traceability links is advantageous even if additional effort is required. Traceability links facilitate system comprehension by providing information about dependencies between artifacts and entities. Requirements traceability enables to trace back the origin of a requirement to its elicitation and to document every change made to it. Important works in this field are the ones of Gotel and Finkelstein (1994), Pohl (1996), Ramesh and Jarke (2001), Letelier (2002) as well as Pinheiro (2004). Other approaches for traceability link establishment consider links between requirements and test cases, for example the scenario-driven approach by Egyed (2001) and the approach by Olsson and Grundy (2002).

In the scope of our work, traceability links can be used to trace design decisions during the development process. Approaches regarding traceability from requirements to design and between various design artifacts have to be considered. Traceability links for design shall be established and adapted while building or manipulating models or other development activities. Therefore, the steps of link establishment have to be embedded into the steps of design methods. We have to state that—to the best of our knowledge—there are no approaches of this kind. For establishing traceability links regarding non-functional requirements and design artifacts there is the probability-based retrieval approach by Clelang-Huang et al. (2005) called Goal-Centric Traceability. Their user evaluation step to discard incorrectly retrieved links to increase precision is valuable. However, they can only identify links that are incidentally included in the descriptions of artifacts that were elaborated regardless of traceability. They cannot identify links, if the investigated artifacts do not cover the relations. Therefore, the completeness and correctness of the links can never be optimal. The incremental approach of Latent Semantic Indexing by Jiang et al. (2007) aims at the identification of related elements with link recovery. It can be helpful for finding links in existing designs and maintaining their change, but it cannot provide all links.

For the definition of relations between design activities and traceability links, a standardized definition of the syntax and semantics of the traceability links is necessary. Unfortunately, the definition of a standard set of traceability link types is still an unresolved issue. Due to different research goals, a high number of traceability link types has been defined, for example in (Pohl, 1996) or (Ramesh & Jarke, 2001). As a step towards simplification and abstraction, we will later restrict ourselves on a small set of types.

For an exploitation of the traceability links, they have to be established on a detailed level, for example to generate test cases; they have to connect model elements and expressions. As a result, the number of links and the complexity of traceability information are high. The issue of maintaining and checking the links leads to a high effort and thus tool support is essential. An overview of research topics, results, and open issues in the field of traceability is discussed in (Mäder et al. 2006) and (Winkler & von Pilgrim, 2010).

There is already support for traceability by requirements management tools, e.g., Requisite Pro or Doors, and by goal-modeling tools, such as jUCMNav (Roy et al. 2006). However, their support for linking other artifacts than requirements is limited. Mäder et al. (2008) present an approach that tackles the problem of automated traceability for UML-based development. Their *traceMaintainer* is a rule-based prototype tool for traceability link maintenance. Nonetheless, there is a need for further work, because the tool does not cover initial link establishment and tool support should not be limited to UML models as well. For an automated link establishment, the definition of proper rules is an important issue. Therefore, as a first step, in (Bode & Riebisch, 2009) we already described in detail, how traceability links can be established during several development steps and between different design artifacts using the example of the category-based design methodology Quasar (Siedersleben, 2004).

In the next section we illustrate our design method TraGoSoMa for tracing the implementation of non-functional requirements. We establish traceability links between non-functional requirements, architectural principles, and functional solutions. Therefore, we present a set of link types and their semantics, and we explain how they are applied while performing the several design activities according to our Goal Solution Scheme. With the help of these traceability links according to the Goal Solution Scheme, especially the comprehension of the transformation of non-functional requirements to solutions is supported. The design-decisions are traced and rationale for the decisions can be connected to the links. Furthermore, with the help of the links and an evaluation of the decisions, the completeness of solutions for the non-functional requirements can be checked.

ARCHITECTURAL DESIGN PROCESS OF THE TRAGOSOMA METHOD

In this section we present the design method TraGoSoMa, named by an acronym for Traceability-driven Goal Solution Mapping. We first give a short overview of the method; afterwards we introduce our case study, which illustrates the design activities, and the Goal Solution Scheme, which constitutes a core concept and drives our method. Further, traceability issues are discussed and the phases of the design method are explained in detail.

TraGoSoMa Method Overview

The method TraGoSoMa represents an architectural design method with focus on non-functional properties. It starts after elicitation, analysis, and specification of the requirements and consists of different phases and steps illustrated in Figure 1. First of all, a functional decomposition of the sys-

Figure 1. Phases and steps of the TraGoSoMa method related to requirements engineering

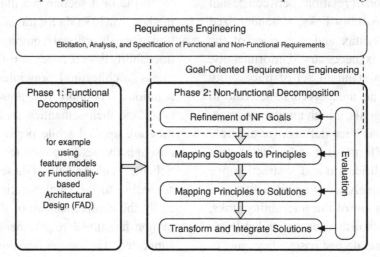

tem is performed akin to QASAR's FAD method. This could be done using different approaches, such as feature models or function trees, and results in candidates for architectural components, the responsibilities of which are determined by functional requirements. We propose to perform decomposition according to the functional requirements first, because this is for example necessary to determine the security-relevant parts of the system; see (Bode et al. 2009) for details. However, designing for the non-functional goals is even more important, but less understood today. So, in the second phase of our method especially the design for non-functional requirements is handled.

This second phase is strongly connected to the Goal Solution Scheme. The first step is performed, if not already provided from the requirements specification. The soft, imprecise, mostly vague, ambiguous, and competing non-functional requirements, such as flexibility, scalability, or security, are modeled as goals and refined into subgoals. This enables the resolution of conflicts between the goals by prioritizing the subgoals accordingly. In this step, we utilize the goal-oriented approaches discussed before, instead of pure scenario-based techniques as proposed by most architectural design methods. In a second step, these subgoals are mapped to the design

principles, which support the subgoals. We introduce this mapping, which is not performed in the goal-oriented approaches, because general design principles are very important for choosing proper solutions during architectural design. Additionally, the architect has to be involved in this modeling process since only providing goal models as input for further design is not enough. In the third step, possible functional solutions and technical components, as so-called solution instruments that support specific principles and subgoals are identified, and traceability links are established accordingly. In this second and third step several architectural decisions have to be made about which principles and solutions are considered for design of the software architecture with regard to trade-offs and synergies between different subgoals. These decisions are significant, because the effect of the relations between subgoals can be mutual enhancement or reduction. A final fourth step in the second phase further combines the functional decomposition of the first phase with the findings from the second.

As a result of the second phase, the architectural components are defined according to functional and non-functional responsibilities, and functional solutions are elaborated for non-functional responsibilities. The solutions and technical components established in the second phase with the help of the Goal Solution Scheme are integrated into the software architecture. Therefore, adequate architectural transformations have to be performed akin to the third phase of QASAR. The kind of these transformations, and how they are applied, is discussed in a later section. All activities in the second phase of the TraGoSoMa method have to be subject to an early assessment within an iterative design process. With the evaluation all decisions and the contributions of the solutions to the non-functional requirements are checked. We deal with this issue in an extra section.

In the following sections we assume the requirements specification and functional decomposition to be done and concentrate on the second phase of the architectural design process dealing with the non-functional properties. We also explain how this approach facilitates design traceability.

Service-Oriented MES Case Study

For the illustration of the TraGoSoMa method we use a case study from a reengineering project for a Manufacturing Execution System (MES) that is restructured according to the SOA principles. A MES manages the manufacturing in modern flexible plants (VDI, 2007). It is connected to Enterprise Resource Planning (ERP) systems, which handle manufacturing plans and actions and represent a business perspective, while the MES is able to manage the manufacturing actions on a more fine-grained level. An MES has access to the abilities and the limitations of the real manufacturing processes and, therefore, it is able to optimize them, and simultaneously provides an increased flexibility. The MES covers tasks, such as detailed scheduling and process control, the management of machines, material, and personnel, etc. For the case study we focus on the integration between ERP and MES. The requirements to the interface between both are defined by the ANSI standard ISA-95 (ISA, 2000). As the platform for the MES interface the Enterprise Service Bus (ESB) (Chap-

Figure 2. Overview of the integration interface

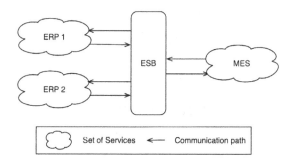

pell, 2004) has been chosen, in a style similar to a middleware. Figure 2 shows the integration interface and its environment.

There are some non-functional properties an MES has to fulfill: a high flexibility and scalability, time behavior as well as security. As an example for a security requirement we mention the information flow control. In our case it is important to protect the business-critical private information of the customer 1 from an unauthorized access by its competitor customer 2. Even if both give manufacturing tasks to the producer, no details about the order must be disclosed to the competitor through the ESB or the MES, for example details concerning amount, specification, and technological process. Flexibility is necessary regarding different planning algorithms, control principles, and regarding the integration with a variety of machines and ERP systems. The requirements for scalability arise from the need for mastering complex manufacturing tasks with a high number of variants and elements, and for the interoperation with multiple different ERP systems due to outsourcing.

Goal Solution Scheme

The Goal Solution Scheme was developed to guide the designer to deal with non-functional properties while designing the architecture, to ease resolving conflicts between competing goals and design principles, and to facilitate decision-making.

Figure 3. Structure of the Goal Solution Scheme

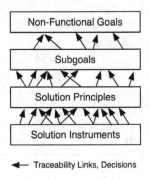

◄── Traceability Links, Decisions

It has some similarities with goal-graphs from requirements engineering. However, the scheme extends it by the explicit consideration of design principles and a classification of functional and technical solutions. As indicated in Figure 3, the Scheme maps non-functional requirements to their subgoals, to solution principles supporting these goals, and further to solution instruments, such as technical solutions and components, for an implementation of the principles. The mapping is represented by traceability links, which are visualized in Figure 3 by the arrows. From top to bottom the scheme represents possible refinements and decisions during the implementation of non-functional requirements. The traceability links carry the information about the design decisions. By providing guidance the scheme refines the design methods and facilitates the establishment and maintenance of traceability links related to the design activities.

The scheme guides the activities within analysis and design and represents them by transitions between the layers. The upper transition supports the resolution of conflicting non-functional properties by a refinement to subgoals. Such a specification and refinement of non-functional goals can also be provided by the goal-oriented approaches we discussed above, e.g., the NFR framework, i*, or GRL. However, we included this transition step because this kind of specification of non-functional goals is seldom provided to software architects in practice. The comprehen-

sion of this transition is necessary for the software architects as well, because they have to contribute to the prioritization of the non-functional goals and they have to implement the goals by selecting proper principles. Since we do not want to reinvent the wheel, we adopt the goal-oriented notation for softgoals and the contribution links, even if this leads to an overlapping with requirements engineering models.

The next transition of the scheme guides the designer from non-functional goals to solution principles, which is a novelty step regarding the design progress towards a solution in comparison to the goal-oriented requirements engineering approaches. In the lower transition of the scheme, technical solutions and existing components are mapped as solution instruments to the principles, making decisions on how to implement the goals and principles by solutions. A similar concept is used for the Factor-Strategy Models of Marinescu and Ratiu (2004) who use design rules and principles to map metrics to quality goals.

As a major contribution the scheme facilitates the prioritizing for decision-making. Furthermore, the scheme supports the resolution of conflicting non-functional requirements by an identification of potential trade-offs and synergies. It provides a fine-grained sequence of design steps. In this way, the scheme represents a refinement of the design activities, which are represented by traceability links. A reduction of the traceability link complexity is achieved, since one or a few principles and solution instruments implement one subgoal. In an ad-hoc design non-functional requirements are implemented in a scattered manner leading to a much higher number of links, for example 10 or 100 times higher.

The Goal Solution Scheme constitutes the central concept for the simplification of the traceability links. It facilitates the traceability in several ways:

- Significant reduction of the number of links,

- Guidance for the designer by sequences of proposed design activities, which enables tool-supported decisions and automation,
- Simplification of link checks for accuracy, completeness, and consistency by a comparison between chosen solutions and relations within the Goal Solution Scheme.

As a result, the scheme provides an alignment of solution principles and solution instruments, it classifies them according to their impact on non-functional properties, and it provides a stock of reusable solution instruments to the architect and the designer. The solution instruments serve as a source of proposals for design alternatives during decision-making.

The scheme is not a design artifact that requires additional maintenance and effort. It rather is a data structure on a meta-level, which indicates and guides how the architectural design steps should be performed in the TraGoSoMa method. If traceability links are established appropriately and managed in a repository, the organization of the repository reflects the Goal Solution Scheme. Beyond, a software architect can use the scheme as a knowledge base, where solution instruments are mapped to principles and goals.

Traceability Links

As mentioned previously, traceability links connect artifacts in the sequence the developer has built or accessed them. Furthermore, they carry the information about the design decisions that lead to the related solution instruments, such as components. For the link tracking, evaluation, and exploitation, the type of the traceability link is important, because it determines a link-semantics as mentioned in the background section; the number of link types should be small.

Additional information can be stored attached to the link, e.g., design decisions. Important elements an explicit traceability link comprises are:

- a unique identifier for its recognition and to avoid ambiguity,
- a start element as source of the link, including type and context of this element,
- an end element as destination of the link, including type and context,
- the type of the link.

For the decision-making, traceability links are advantageous because they make decisions explicit and comprehensible. Alternatives can be estimated. Software architecture design decisions should always be documented with their design rationale (Clements et al. 2003). Therefore, they are recently seen as first class entities. Duenas and Capilla (2005) for example introduced a decision view for software architectures. The Goal Solution Scheme facilitates the tracing of such decision entities to their related artifacts. Therefore, a link may contain additional information:

- a reference to a design rule for this specific activity,
- the decision connected with the development activity, including the goal of the decision, alternatives, the rating of the alternatives and the choice,
- the link status concerning the certainty of correctness (e.g., after changes of the connected elements or during reverse engineering activities),
- the creator of the link,
- a temporary priority to control the tracking of the links.

As introduced by earlier works (Mäder et al., 2007), we distinguish four different link types, which are sufficient for the most design situations:

- *refine* – for an activity increasing the level of detail, either by specialization or by decomposition including the AND and OR types.

- *realize* – represents a step towards the solution (e.g., between a non-functional goal and a design principle or between a principle and a solution)
- *verify* – compares the behavior and the properties of requirements and of the developed solution or its parts (e.g., between a use case and a test case) and
- *define* – relates the establishment of an identifier and its usage.

Additional link types can be introduced for dependency types from utilized models as for example UML models. In order to be able to handle the goal models and their contribution links we added the link type

- *contribution* – which can express degrees of positive or negative influence between model elements.

With the help of the contribution links an evaluation of alternatives can be achieved, for example in relation to the goal models. However, positive contributions can also be linked as realizations, when a solution is chosen. The realization links then enable tracing which path was taken from the problem space to the solution space and how the goals are achieved by the implemented solution.

Traceability links can be tracked in both directions, regardless of the direction that is defined by the link type. Besides, a distinction between implicit and explicit links is necessary. Explicit traceability links are established, while a developer performs a software development activity. Implicit traceability represents existing associations between elements of the system model using identifiers, for example between an analysis and a design artifact. These traceability links are references, but they are evaluated if traceability links are tracked during their utilization.

The type of the traceability links is defined according to the TraGoSoMa design activities. The transitions in the Goal Solution Scheme represent these activities. In the first transition the non-functional goals are decomposed and thus linked to the subgoals by links of the type *refine*. In the second and third transition the positive and negative influence has to be represented. Therefore, links of the type *contribution* are established. In addition to the influences, these transitions represent steps towards solutions. Consequently, the link type *realize* is used to express this aspect. A possible decomposition on each level of the Goal Solution Scheme, for example a decomposition of solutions, can also be traced by links of the type *refine*.

Goal Refinement and Elaboration

The several non-functional requirements for a product are often competing and conflicting in their interdependencies. As a solution they have to be prioritized. If this is not possible on the top-level, a resolution is attempted after a refinement. By refining the requirements vague interdependencies can be concretized and previously hidden dependencies can be made explicit. To determine the mutual impact of the relations and to detect conflicts and synergies, the requirements or goals can be classified in dominating (fundamental) and supporting (instrumental) ones (Wohlfarth, 2008).

The refinement of the non-functional goals is covered by the first transition in the Goal Solution Scheme. This is the first step in the second phase of our design approach. The refinement of the non-functional properties is necessary for their comprehension and makes them more specific. It can be performed according to the abovementioned goal-oriented approaches, e.g., the NFR framework.

For the refinement standards can help, for example the ISO 9126 (ISO, 2001). This standard for instance provides subgoals for maintainability, namely analyzability, changeability, stability, testability, and maintainability compliance. Furthermore, the Goal Question Metrics (GQM) method can be applied to identify subgoals. This

Figure 4. First transition of the goal solution scheme (cut-out from the case study)

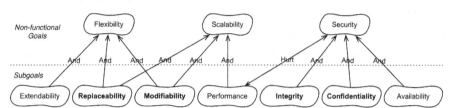

structured querying technique helps to analyze influences on a goal (Basili et al., 1994). The Factor-Strategy Model of Marinescu and Ratiu (2004) uses a similar principle for mapping quality goals to metrics.

According to the NFR framework (see section *Background*) non-functional requirements have a type and a topic. As an example, the requirement "Security of accounts" has the type "security", which indicates the specific NFR, and the topic "accounts", which targets at the subject. Non-functional requirements can be refined regarding type or topic. The refinement of maintainability mentioned above is a refinement regarding the type of the NFR.

In our case study the top-level non-functional requirements are *flexibility*, *scalability*, and *security*. According to the ADD method they constitute architectural drivers. After a consideration of their relationships on this level we can assume that flexibility and scalability are in a rather synergetic relation to each other, because they both deal with change, while security might be conflicting to the others, because it implies restrictions of the information flow and the data access. This guess has to be proven in the next steps. For a precise analysis and a solution for our MES project, a refinement has been performed. Figure 4 shows parts of the results. The refinement is presented using the i* notation for softgoals and links.

For flexibility, there is a definition in the IEEE standard glossary of software engineering terminology (IEEE, 1990), although a detailed discussion of its subgoals is missing. Regarding flexibility some discussion can be found in the literature

(Zeng & Zhao, 2002; Nelson et al., 1997; Eden & Mens, 2006; Morgan, 2006). We elaborated the subgoals *extendability* (IEEE, 1990), *replaceability* (ISO, 2001), and *modifiability* (Bengtson et al., 2004) for our example. We focus on the latter two because of their high priority.

Scalability is lacking a definition by a standard; however, some works discuss this quality attribute (Hill, 1990; Bondi, 2000; Duboc et al., 2006; Duboc et al., 2007). Scalability is always concerned with *performance,* or efficiency in terms of the ISO 9126 (2001), and how well a solution to a problem will work when the size of the problem increases. However, if a system performs well it is not necessarily scalable, too. Therefore, we considered replaceability and modifiability as subcharacteristics of scalability as well. If an MES has to face changes for example due to an increasing complexity of the manufacturing tasks, modifications are necessary. Moreover, it should be easy to replace parts of the whole system with more efficient ones, if this is necessary to scale up and retain a high performance.

For security there are several definitions from the International Organization for Standardization (ISO), e.g., (ISO, 2001; ISO, 2005), and Chung et al. (2000) comprehensively discuss its refinement in their NFR framework. The most important subgoals are *integrity*, *confidentiality*, and *availability*.

Before the refinement, we already mentioned our assumption for a synergetic relation between flexibility and scalability, as well as the possible conflict between scalability and security. The conflict could neither be verified nor solved on the top level, because both scalability and security are essential. However, after the refinement of the non-functional goals illustrated in Figure 4, we can try to solve the conflict and verify the synergetic interdependency between flexibility and scalability. The latter could be verified by the mutual positive influence of replaceability and modifiability on both top-level goals. Beyond, a negative interdependency between performance and security was detected, because security mechanisms, as for example encryption, require extra operations, often are time consuming, and can hamper performance. This confirms the conflict; however, for a resolution a further refinement to principles is necessary. For the further design process of our case study we will concentrate on the subgoals replaceability, modifiability, as well as integrity, and confidentiality because of their high priority.

The abovementioned refinements are expressed using *and*-contribution links according to the i* notation. In the Goal Solution Scheme they are represented by traceability links of the type refine. The *hurt*-contribution can be traced with links of the type contribution if necessary.

Decision about Solution Principles

After the first step of the second phase of TraGo-SoMa, the top-level goals are refined into subgoals and are more specific. But, they are still non-functional and still cannot be implemented directly. In the second step, the transition from the subgoals to the design principles is performed, as presented by the Goal Solution Scheme.

As a step from the problem space to the solution space, in this second step, design principles and guidelines are assigned to the subgoals. These principles and guidelines give hints or advice for the functional solutions. Of course, lots of principles exist and even more relations between non-functional goals and these principles are imaginable. Therefore, the designer has to analyze the subgoals and to decide on suitable principles.

It is always the case, that there are different non-functional goals that have symbiotic relations or in contrary compete with each. In order to resolve conflicts, knowing about the interdependencies between the different subgoals is important. A goal model contains these dependencies and the trade-offs.

For illustration an example for a decision is discussed here. The principle of high encapsulation supports changeability. On the other hand, a strong encapsulation has a negative influence on testability, because inaccessible attributes are hard to control. Because of the refinement from the first step, both changeability and testability are known to be subgoals of maintainability and contribute to it. Now, by assigning encapsulation to these subgoals the trade-off becomes visible and can be considered. Frequently, multiple different principles contribute to the same subgoal. In these cases a decision can be made, which principle is applicable or how to prioritize them.

Trade-offs between different non-functional subgoals and solution principles often are still not tangible enough. Then, they have to be elaborated further on the solution instruments level of the Goal Solution Scheme. This is necessary to be able to decide with clear rationale, which principle to choose to achieve the highest degree of goal fulfillment. In this case, the principles are mapped further to solution instruments and the decision-making is postponed to the next step, when the criteria for adequate solution instruments are more precise than those for the principles. Based on the solution instruments' contributions to the principles and the non-functional goals, the different alternatives can be weighed and the decisions, which alternatives to choose, can be made. For the goal-oriented approaches some evaluation techniques exist, anyway, it is always reasonable to decide as soon as possible to reduce further effort.

For our case study, the second transition of the Goal Solution Scheme is partly shown in Figure 5. The subgoals result from the refinement in the

Figure 5. Cut-out of the transition from subgoals to principles for the case study

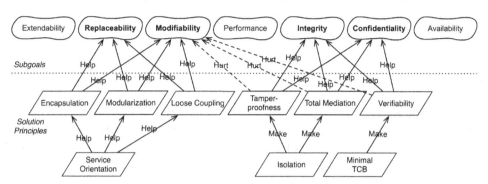

previous step of TraGoSoMa. Starting from the higher prioritized subgoals, appropriate solution principles are chosen. For the subgoals replaceability and modifiability, we decide in favor of the architectural design principles *encapsulation, modularization* and *loose coupling*. These principles are well known to support changes. Already Parnas (1972) discussed the importance of modularization for changeability and flexibility, which is one of our most important non-functional goals. Moreover, *service orientation* was identified to support encapsulation, modularization, and loose coupling. A service-oriented architecture obviously can help in this scenario, because loose coupling is one of its core principles. It further helps encapsulation and modularization. In addition to the contribution links shown in Figure 5, the mentioned principles are explicitly related to the subgoals replaceability and modifiability by traceability links of the type realize. This type of links is established, because the principles represent a step towards the solution of the non-functional goals, and to document the design decisions for choosing service orientation.

The security subgoals integrity and confidentiality are discussed as another example. To integrate such requirements, security policies have to be applied, as a comprehensive set of rules that are designed to achieve the system's security goals (Goguen & Meseguer, 1982). Security policies are applied to determine a so-called *trusted com-*

puting base (TCB) (Lampson et al. 1992). The TCB comprises the functional parts of a system that enforce and protect the security policy. For the implementation of a security policy and a trusted computing base, there are fundamental principles that refer to the so-called reference monitor concept (Anderson, 1972). A reference monitor must be tamperproof, always invoked and small enough to be analyzable and verifiable, which is represented by the principles *tamperproofness, total mediation,* and *verifiability*. These reference monitor principles are further supported by *isolation* and a *minimal TCB* as principles for the architectural design. Isolation of the security relevant functions in the security architecture of a system is a necessary consequence to be able to realize a tamperproof reference monitor that cannot be bypassed (Gasser, 1988). Correctness and completeness are additional necessary properties not further discussed here (Department of Defense, 1985). These decisions and the causes are again documented by traceability links of the type realize.

However, in this design step, conflicting relations between the security principles and the subgoal modifiability were identified as well. They are shown as *hurt*-contribution links. Modifications in the software architecture can have a negative influence on the minimality of the trusted computing base and vice versa. The other security principles are affected by changes as well. Tamperproofness can easily be breached if a modification is performed in a wrong way. Therefore, changes should only be made on those architectural parts that have not to be isolated due to security reasons.

These conflicts confirm our earlier assumption that security is in conflict with flexibility and scalability. However, at the principles level their interdependencies have been clarified and we have a much better understanding of the conflict than on the goal or the subgoal level. Anyway, the conflict between the fundamental security principles and the subgoal modifiability cannot be resolved in this transition of the Goal Solution Scheme. The conflict resolution has to be postponed to the next design step, when a related solution can be analyzed more precisely than the principles.

Decision about Solution Instruments

In the third design step the actual transformation of the non-functional properties to a functional solution is performed. This step is closely related to the third step of the QASAR method (Bosch, 2000). A similar mapping of solution instruments to goals can also be found in the NFR framework and the i* framework, where operationalizations, or tasks respectively, are assigned to decomposed softgoals.

In our method solution instruments can be functional concepts or even existing technical components, which either support the realization of non-functional goals or completely fulfill some of them. In this third design step a large number of solution instruments is possible. In order to find the most adequate ones, the designer weights the different alternatives, akin to the last step.

The explicit linkage from goals to principles and solution instruments classifies the latter ones according to their contributions to the non-functional goals. The Goal Solution Scheme serves as a knowledgebase, which enables the incremental collection and the reuse of the solutions in a goal-oriented way.

Of course, the decisions are also influenced by other technical or organizational requirements and constraints. For example the technical component JGoodies (2008) explicitly facilitates usability with its subgoal user satisfaction by an easy alignment and balancing of visual elements. However, it cannot be chosen, if the project demands for the C++ programming language, because JGoodies is based on Java and Swing. To consider such architectural constraints, a two-stage process can be applied. In a first step, all solutions that are inappropriate are ignored. In a second step, the remaining ones are ranked according to their satisfaction of the goals to find the best solution.

Figure 6 shows a part of the Goal Solution Scheme for the transition from principles to solution instruments for our case study. To realize service orientation, and thus the principles encapsulation, modularization, and loose coupling, the solution instruments *Web Services* and *Enterprise Service Bus* (ESB) for the integration of the MES and ERP are chosen. The reason for these decisions is that well-defined web services according to the Service-Oriented Architecture (SOA) paradigm inherently reinforce those principles (Erl, 2007). A component-based Common Object Request Broker Architecture (CORBA), for example, could have been an alternative for a service-oriented architecture. However, for our case study a CORBA infrastructure was not available.

As an example from our case study, one realized service shall be mentioned. The service *MachineAvailability* can be used for the interaction of the detailed planning of an MES and the general planning of an ERP. Using this service the ERP can request status information about machines, such as their availability. When implementing the web services, architectural and design patterns, such as *Service Layers* (Fowler, 2003; Erl, 2008), *Service Facade*, or *Legacy Wrapper* (Erl, 2008), contribute to the realization of the principles, and hence, to the non-functional goals.

The application of a reference monitor solves the integration of the security aspects. The se-

Figure 6. Cut-out of the transition from principles to solutions for the case study

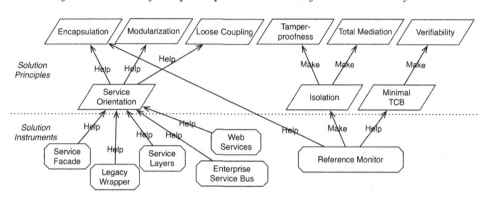

curity principles are integrated with the help of the ESB to gain control of the communication between the MES and ERP system and to isolate the security-relevant architectural parts. Aside, it must be considered to keep the TCB as small as possible. A discussion on the integration of security with web services can be found in (Fischer & Kühnhauser, 2008). With this kind of solution the conflict between the security principles and the subgoal modifiability, which was detected in the last design step, cannot be resolved completely. However, it can be implemented in a controlled way by controlling access to the security relevant functionality. Hence, the realization of a reference monitor not only positively contributes to the reference monitor principles, but also helps encapsulation, and therefore, even modifiability despite the conflicts.

As an alternative to the reference monitor, in an ad-hoc approach or according to the discussion by Chung et al. (2000), one could have considered only multiple single solution instruments, such as encryption mechanisms, or roles and rights, for security purposes. Of course, these solution instruments can contribute to confidentiality and maybe availability and integrity. However, as a drawback, without considering the reference monitor principles the system would be much more vulnerable.

In this step of the TraGoSoMa design method again all decisions about solution instruments

for the solution principles are made explicit by traceability links. As shown in Figure 6 all solution instruments are mapped to the corresponding solution principles. The chosen solution instruments, such as the patterns Service Layers, Service Facade, and Legacy Wrapper, are traced with links of the type realize. Additionally, elaborated alternatives not discussed here can also be linked with the type contribution and may be reused later. Figure 6 depicts only the mentioned solution instruments. Actually, much more solution instruments are contained, and the architect can easily extend them by additional ones.

Merging the Functional Solutions

In the fourth step of TraGoSoMa's second phase the solution instruments from both origins have to be merged, from functional goals and from non-functional ones. In this step a balancing between both types of requirements has to be performed (Harrison & Avgeriou, 2007). The functional requirements—the first type—have been elaborated into candidates for functional components as in phase 1 (see Figure 1) by a functional decomposition, for example following the FAD method by QASAR. For non-functional goals—the second type—solution instruments in the form of components are integrated, which are developed according to the Goal Solution Scheme in the second phase.

The merge can be performed by architectural change operations of different types. The simplest case is to only *add* the functional components that implement non-functional requirements from the second phase to the components of the first phase. A second type of transformation is to *replace* functional components. For example, if a functional component from phase one is insufficient in fulfilling the non-functional requirements, it is replaced by the solution instruments elaborated in the second phase. A third type of transformation is to *remove* a previously decomposed functional component to enable the realization of a non-functional goal. Baldwin and Clark (2000) mention three more elementary types of changes called modular operators: *split* a component into two, *port* a component for extraction to a new one, and *inversion of hierarchy* for moving components from a lower position in a hierarchy to a higher one. As another example, we mention the implementation of security goals. To solve this task by the reference monitor concept (Anderson, 1972) a separation of security-relevant and security-irrelevant functional components is performed to achieve a minimal Trusted Computing Base applying the *inversion of hierarchy* operation (for more details see Bode et al., 2009). In the case security-relevant and security-irrelevant functions are covered by one component, it has to be *split* or partly *ported*.

As the result of the merge a software architecture has been developed. Its components are functional ones, which can be implemented directly. All responsibilities that are due to functional and non-functional requirements are assigned to these components.

Evaluation of the Decisions

For an early assessment of the architectural design any iteration should include an evaluation. The assessment technique depends on the characteristics of the assessed products and on the criteria to be evaluated.

There are several well-established assessment techniques for software architectures. Two types are especially suitable—questioning and measuring techniques. The techniques of the first type, for example structured scenario-based inspections with the Architecture Tradeoff Analysis Method (ATAM) (Kazman et al., 2000), are performed by experts. Based on the assessment criteria, the scenarios are established, for example an intrusion scenario for an evaluation regarding security or an extension scenario regarding maintainability. Evaluations of this type can be performed early, even if the architecture is not complete. Performing the evaluation in a structured, formally defined way by external experts can reduce the disadvantage of the subjective nature of the result.

The measuring techniques provide objective, quantitative results. However, they require formal models and well-defined evaluation criteria. Examples for this type are metrics for architectural quality, e.g., for modularity by relating the number of all inner dependencies of a component to the outer ones. In (Brcina & Riebisch, 2008) traceability links between model elements are evaluated for evolvability, and for example the effects of tangled or scattered components are assessed as criteria for architectural quality.

FUTURE RESEARCH DIRECTIONS

The consideration of non-functional properties constitutes a long-term goal for architectural development, even beyond SOA. Further work is needed to close the gap between requirements engineering and architectural design regarding integration of methods. Maybe aspect-oriented techniques can help regarding this issue as well. Moreover, there is a special need for integrating the mentioned concepts with the Model-Driven Architecture (MDA) approach.

The need for a rigor specification of non-functional requirements can be fulfilled only for some categories, e.g., security. Many others, e.g., usability, flexibility, and scalability, are specified by informal or semi-formal descriptions. Ontologies can help to analyze the semantics of these descriptions based on the terms and their relations.

For the early evaluation of the results of architectural decisions, a prototyping is necessary in some cases, for example for requirements regarding efficiency and scalability. The generation of the necessary prototypes shall be based on the architectural decisions and documents to minimize the additional effort.

CONCLUSION

In this paper the architectural design method TraGoSoMa has been presented, which provides improved support and guidance for the architect to consider non-functional properties. The method aims at the definition of components and their implementation illustrated with a SOA example. As an important element the method introduces the Goal Solution Scheme, which represents the alignment between non-functional goals, their subgoals, the applied solution principles, and the solution instruments for implementing the required properties. By using this scheme, the conflict resolution between competing goals is supported, the solution principles and the solution instruments are classified according to the non-functional goals supported by them, and the systematic selection of solution instruments during architectural decisions is facilitated. Furthermore, the Goal Solution Scheme supports the accumulation of architectural know-how by a stepwise extension of the classification and the solution instruments. The scheme expresses traceability links in an explicit way, while the method facilitates their establishment, and thus, supports the maintainability of the software. Especially important is the traceability between non-functional goals, such as scalability, efficiency, and security, and the chosen solution instruments.

Regarding state-of-the-art methods, the contributions of the method can be compared to the QASAR method as well as to the works of Chung et al. and Yu as discussed in the background section. The QASAR method is extended by enhancing its second design phase by a systematic procedure for non-functional properties, which reduces the effort for transformations, and by improving the third phase by reducing the scattering of the changes to the design. In comparison to the goal-oriented approaches from requirements engineering, we consider architectural constraints from the environment as well as interdependencies with technical solution instruments. Furthermore, as a novelty step, we map non-functional goals to solution principles and integrate the goal-oriented activities in the context of an architectural design method. We use a design decision process, especially considering well-known solution principles to find conflicts, synergies, and solution instruments. Beyond, we include the establishment of traceability links into our method.

The method is applied for the redesign of a Manufacturing Execution System (MES) in order to integrate it into a service-oriented environment of business systems in manufacturing. With the help of this case study, we illustrate the several design steps, and therefore, show the importance of such a methodical design and its relevance for industrial use.

REFERENCES

Amyot, D. (2003). Introduction to the user requirements notation: Learning by example. *Computer Networks*, *42*(3), 285–301. doi:10.1016/S1389-1286(03)00244-5

Anderson, J. P. (1972). *Computer security technology planning study* (Tech. Rep. ESD-TR-73-51), L. G. Hanscom Field, Bedford, MA, USA: U.S. Air Force, Electronic Systems Division, Deputy for Command and Management Systems, HQ Electronic Systems Division (AFSC).

Baldwin, C. Y., & Clark, K. B. (2000). *Design rules: The power of modularity* (*Vol. 1*). Cambridge, MA: MIT Press.

Basili, V. R., Caldiera, G., & Rombach, H. D. (1994). The goal question metric approach. In Marciniak, J. (Ed.), *Encyclopedia of software engineering*. Wiley.

Bass, L. J., Klein, M., & Bachmann, F. (2002). Quality attribute design primitives and the attribute driven design method. In F. van der Linden (Ed.) *Software product-family engineering, 4th International Workshop, PFE 2001, Revised Papers,* (pp. 169-186). Berlin: Springer.

Bengtsson, P., Lassing, N., Bosch, J., & van Vliet, H. (2004). Architecture-level modifiability analysis (ALMA). *Journal of Systems and Software, 69*(1-2), 129–147. doi:10.1016/S0164-1212(03)00080-3

Bode, S., Fischer, A., Kühnhauser, W., & Riebisch, M. (2009). Software architectural design meets security engineering. In *Proceedings of the 16th Annual IEEE International Conference and Workshop on the Engineering of Computer Based Systems (ECBS).* (pp. 109-118). USA: IEEE.

Bode, S., & Riebisch, R. (2009). Tracing quality-related design decisions in a category-driven software architecture. In Liggesmeyer, P., Engels, G., Münch, J., Dörr, J., & Riegel, N. (Eds.), *Proceedings of Software Engineering 2009* (pp. 87–98). Bonn, Germany: Köllen.

Bondi, A. B. (2000). Characteristics of scalability and their impact on performance. In *Proceedings of the 2nd International Workshop on Software and Performance (WOSP '00),* (pp. 195-203). New York: ACM.

Bosch, J. (2000). *Design and use of software architectures.* New York: Addison Wesley.

Brcina, R., & Riebisch, M. (2008). Architecting for evolvability by means of traceability and features. In *Proceedings of the 4th International ERCIM Workshop on Software Evolution and Evolvability (Evol'08) at the 23rd IEEE/ACM International Conference on Automated Software Engineering,* (pp. 235-244). USA: IEEE.

Chappel, D. A. (2004). *Enterprise service bus.* USA: O'Reilly Media.

Chung, L., Nixon, B. A., Yu, E., & Mylopoulus, J. (2000). *Non-functional requirements in software engineering.* Norwell, MA: Kluwer Academic Publishing.

Cleland-Huang, J., Settimi, R., BenKhadra, O., Berezhanskaya, E., & Christina, S. (2005). Goal-centric traceability for managing non-functional requirements. In *Proceedings 27th International Conference on Software Engineering,* (pp. 362-371). New York: ACM.

Clements, P., Bachman, F., Bass, L., Garlan, D., Ivers, J., & Little, R. (2003). *Documenting software architectures: Views and beyond.* Amsterdam: Addison-Wesley Longman.

Department of Defense (1985). *Trusted computer system evaluation criteria.* DoD 5200.28-STD.

Duboc, L., Rosenblum, D., & Wicks, T. (2006). A framework for modelling and analysis of software systems scalability. In *Proceedings of the 28th International Conference on Software Engineering ICSE '06,* (pp. 949-952). New York: ACM.

Duboc, L., Rosenblum, D., & Wicks, T. (2007). A framework for characterization and analysis of software system scalability. In *Proceedings of the 6th Joint Meeting of the European Software Engineering Conference and the ACM SIGSOFT Symposium on The Foundations of Software Engineering ESEC-FSE '07,* (pp. 375-384). New York: ACM.

Dueñas, J. C., & Capilla, R. (2005). The decision view of software architecture. In *Proceedings of the 2nd European Workshop on Software Architecture* (LNCS 3527), (pp. 222-230). Berlin: Springer.

Eden, A., & Mens, T. (2006). Measuring software flexibility. *IEE Proceedings. Software*, *153*(3), 113–125. doi:10.1049/ip-sen:20050045

Egyed, A. (2001). A scenario-driven approach to traceability. *In Proceedings of the 23rd International Conference on Software Engineering ICSE'01,* (pp. 123-132). Washington, DC: IEEE.

Erl, T. (2007). *SOA: Principles of service design*. Upper Saddle River, NJ: Prentice Hall.

Erl, T. (2008). *SOA design patterns*. Upper Saddle River, NJ: Prentice Hall.

Fischer, A., & Kühnhauser, W. E. (2008). Integration von Sicherheitsmodellen in Web Services. In P. Horster (Ed.), *D.A.CH security 2008*. Hannover, Germany: eMedia.

Folmer, E., & Bosch, J. (2003). Usability patterns in software architecture. In *Proceedings of the 10th International Conference on Human-Computer Interaction HCII2003 vol. I,* (pp. 93-97).

Fowler, M. (2003). *Patterns of enterprise application architecture*. Boston: Addison Wesley.

Galster, M., Eberlein, A., & Moussavi, M. (2006). Transition from requirements to architecture: A review and future perspective. In *Proceedings Seventh ACIS International Conference on Software Engineering, Artificial Intelligence, Networking, and Parallel/Distributed Computing (SNPD'06),* (pp. 9-16). USA: IEEE.

Gasser, M. (1988). *Building a secure computer system*. New York: Van Nostrand Reinhold Co.

Goguen, J. A., & Meseguer, J. (1982). Security policies and security models. In *Proceedings IEEE Symposium on Security and Privacy,* (pp. 11-20). Washington, DC: IEEE.

Gotel, O. C. Z., & Finkelstein, A. C. W. (1994). An analysis of the requirements traceability problem. In *Proceedings of the First International Conference on Requirements Engineering,* (pp. 94-101). USA: IEEE.

Grau, G., & Franch, X. (2007). A goal-oriented approach for the generation and evaluation of alternative architectures. In F. Oquendo (Ed.), *Software architecture, Proceedings First European Conference, ECSA 2007.* (pp. 139-155). Berlin: Springer.

Harrison, N., & Avgeriou, P. (2007). Pattern-driven architectural partitioning: Balancing functional and non-functional requirements. In *Proceedings Second International Conference on Digital Telecommunication (ICDT'07),* (pp. 21-26). USA: IEEE.

Hill, M. D. (1990). What is scalability? *SIGARCH Computer Architecture News*, *18*(4), 18–21. doi:10.1145/121973.121975

Hofmeister, C., Nord, R., & Soni, D. (2000). *Applied software architecture*. New York: Addison Wesley.

ISA. (2000). *ISA–95.00.01–2000 Enterprise-control system integration. Part 1: Models and terminology*. North Carolina: ISA.

ISO. (2001). ISO/IEC 9126-1 International standard. Software engineering–product quality –part 1: Quality models.

ISO. (2005). ISO/IEC 27001:2005 Information technology–security techniques–information security management systems–requirements.

JGoodies. (2008). *JGoodies: Java user interface design*. Retrieved October 13, 2008, from http://www.jgoodies.com/

Jiang, H., Nguyen, T. N., Chang, C. K., & Dong, F. (2007). Traceability link evolution management with incremental semantic indexing. In *Proceedings 31st Annual International Computer Software and Applications Conference (COMPSAC 2007),* (pp. 309-316). USA: IEEE.

Kazman, R., Klein, M., & Clements, P. (2000). *ATAM: Method for architecture evaluation.* (Tech. Rep. CMU/SEI-2000-TR-004). Pittsburgh: Carnegie-Mellon University, Software Engineering Institute.

Lampson, B., Abadi, M., Burrows, M., & Wobber, E. (1992). Authentication in distributed systems: Theory and practice. *ACM Transactions on Computer Systems*, *10*(4), 265–310. doi:10.1145/138873.138874

Letelier, P. (2002). A framework for requirements traceability in UML-based projects. In *1st Int. Workshop on Traceability in Emerging Forms of SE (TEFSE'02),* (pp. 32-41). Edinburgh, UK.

Liu, L., & Yu, E. (2001). From requirements to architectural design–using goals and scenarios. In *From Software Requirements to Architectures Workshop (STRAW 2001),* (pp. 22-30). Toronto, Canada.

Mäder, P., Gotel, O., & Philippow, I. (2008). Rule-based maintenance of post-requirements traceability relations. In *Proceedings of the 2008 16th IEEE International Requirements Engineering Conference (RE '08),* (pp. 23-32). USA: IEEE.

Mäder, P., Philippow, I., & Riebisch, M. (2007). Customizing traceability links for the unified process. In *Proceedings of the Third International Conference on the Quality of Software-Architectures (QOSA2007)* (LNCS 4880). (pp. 47-64). Berlin: Springer.

Mäder, P., Riebisch, M., & Philippow, I. (2006). Traceability for managing evolutionary change. In *Proceedings of the 15th International Conference on Software Engineering and Data Engineering (SEDE-2006),* (pp. 1-8). USA: ISCA.

Marinescu, R., & Ratiu, D. (2004). Quantifying the quality of object-oriented design: The factor-strategy model. In *Proceedings 11th Working Conference on Reverse Engineering (WCRE 2004),* (pp. 192-201). USA: IEEE.

Morgan, G. (2006). *Design for flexibility.* Retrieved October 13, 2008, from http://blogs.msdn.com/gabriel_morgan/archive/2006/10/03/Design-for-Flexibility.aspx

Nelson, K., Nelson, H., & Ghods, M. (1997). Technology flexibility: Conceptualization, validation, and measurement. In *Proceedings of the Thirtieth Hawaii International Conference on System Sciences, Vol. 3,* (pp. 76-87). Washington, DC: IEEE.

Nielsen, J. (1993). *Usability engineering.* Boston: Academic Press.

Ollson, T., & Grundy, J. (2002). Supporting traceability and inconsistency management between software artifacts. In *Proceedings of IASTED International Conference on Software Engineering and Application.*

Parnas, D. L. (1972). On the criteria to be used in decomposing systems into modules. *Communications of the ACM*, *15*(12), 1053–1058. doi:10.1145/361598.361623

Pinheiro, F. A. C. (2004). Requirements traceability. In Leite, J. C. S. P., & Doorn, J. (Eds.), *Perspectives on software requirements* (pp. 91–113). Norwell, MA: Kluwer Academic Publishers.

Pohl, K. (1996). PRO-ART: Enabling requirements pre-traceability. In *Proceedings of the Second International Conference on Requirements Engineering ICRE'96,* (pp. 76-84). Washington, DC: IEEE.

Ramesh, B., & Jarke, M. (2001). Toward reference models for requirements traceability. *IEEE Transactions on Software Engineering*, *27*(1), 58–93. doi:10.1109/32.895989

Roy, J., Kealey, J., & Amyot, D. (2006). Towards integrated tool support for the user requirements notation. In R. Gotzhein & R. Reed (Eds.), *System analysis and modeling: Language profiles.* (pp. 198-215). Fifth International Workshop, SAM 2006. Berlin: Springer.

Shneiderman, B. (1992). *Designing the user interface: Strategies for effective human-computer interaction* (2nd ed.). Boston: Addison-Wesley.

Siedersleben, J. (2004). *Moderne Software Architektur: Umsichtig planen, robust bauen mit Quasar.* Heidelberg, Germany: dpunkt.verlag.

Standards Coordinating Comittee of the Computer Society of the IEEE. (1990). *IEEE standard glossary of software engineering terminology.* IEEE Std 610.12-1990.

VDI. (2007). *VDI 5600: Fertigungsmanagementsysteme. Manufacturing Execution Systems (MES).* Berlin: Beuth.

Winkler, S., & von Pilgrim, J. (2010). A survey of traceability in requirements engineering and model-driven development. In *Software and Systems Modeling*, 9(4), 529-565.

Wohlfarth, S. (2008). *Entwicklung eines rationalen Entscheidungsprozesses für Architekturentscheidungen.* Unpublished doctoral dissertation, Ilmenau University of Technology, Germany.

Yu, E. (1995). *Modelling strategic relationships for process reengineering.* Unpublished doctoral dissertation, Dept. of Computer Science, University of Toronto, Ontario, Canada.

Zeng, D., & Zhao, J. (2002). Achieving software flexibility via intelligent workflow techniques. In *Proceedings of the 35th Annual Hawaii International Conference on System Sciences, HICSS,* (pp. 606-615). Washington, DC: IEEE.

KEY TERMS AND DEFINITIONS

Architectural Design Method: A systematic approach with analysis, synthesis, and evaluation activities to create a software architectural description from functional as well as non-functional requirements taking organizational and technological constraints into account.

Enterprise Resource Planning: The complex task to efficiently use all resources of an enterprise, such as financial assets, production facilities, or personnel, to control and optimize business processes.

Manufacturing Execution System: A software system responsible for the organization and execution of the production process in a factory with numeral scopes of duty as management of all required activities within the production process or the exchange of information with the environment as to ERP systems (for a comprehensive definition see (VDI, 2007) for a comprehensive definition).

Non-Functional Requirement: Also quality requirement, quality attribute, or quality goal – a software requirement that describes not what a software system has to do, but how it should be done and under which constraints, and therefore, defines its quality (for a comprehensive discussion see (Chung et al., 2000) for a comprehensive discussion).

Software Architecture: The description of the organizational structure of a software system, its architectural elements, their properties, interfaces, relations, and behavior, as well as a set of decisions and guidelines for the design of the system.

Software Quality: The totality of characteristics of a software product that bear on its ability to satisfy specified requirements (cf. ISO, 2001)).

Traceability: The capability to track and recover in both a forwards and backwards direction the development steps of a software system and the design decisions made during on-going refinement and iteration in all development phases by relating the resulting artifacts of each development step to each other (based on (Gotel & Finkelstein, 1994)).

Chapter 2
Developing Non-Functional Requirements for a Service-Oriented Application Platform:
A Goal and Scenario-Oriented Approach

Daniel Gross
University of Toronto, Canada

Eric Yu
University of Toronto, Canada

Xiping Song
Siemens Corporate Research, USA

ABSTRACT

The challenges in developing non-functional requirements (NFRs) for an application platform go much beyond those for a single application system. To derive platform NFRs from NFR specifications of different domain applications, requirements analysts must deal with much variation of domain specific NFRs, with different deployment configurations and load conditions, with different NFR related trade-offs, as well as with different terminology and metric definitions. This chapter presents a platform NFR development method that supports dealing with the aforementioned challenges. The presented method offers a goal- and scenario-oriented modeling and analysis technique that supports dealing with qualitative and quantitative NFRs during platform NFR development in an integrated way. The platform NFR development method was used to develop NFRs of a service-oriented application platform for three different application domains in an industrial setting.

DOI: 10.4018/978-1-60566-794-2.ch002

INTRODUCTION

Large software development organizations with software product offerings across multiple markets and industries usually have core competences that underpin diverse product offerings. Identifying and formalizing those core competences provides development organizations with opportunities to create common application platforms to support their products development efforts across markets and industries.

Shared application platforms significantly increase reuse of software assets, reduce time to market and cost, and improve software quality. Service orientation offers additional benefits including enterprise-wide standardized reusable software assets, increased interoperability, and ease of extension, evolution and adoption of new services-based functionalities and features.

Specifying the requirements, and in particular the non-functional requirements (NFRs) for an application platforms is however challenging. Application platforms aim to support a large number of domain specific applications in meeting functional and non-functional requirements. While common functionality can be identified from shared core competencies across different domain applications, the non-functional requirements across domains can still vary greatly, which makes it hard to pin down which NFRs a common platform should support. In industrial settings, the following main challenges have been identified (Song et al., 2009):

Varying domain-specific needs: Different application domains give rise to different NFRs. For example, a solution system that supports automation in manufacturing, which often requires meeting tight hard real time constraints, and a solution system that provides building security in factories, where real time requirements are much less demanding, have quite distinct NFRs, even if both systems involve much of the same control functionalities.

Varying deployment configurations and load conditions: Solution systems can be deployed and operated in different configurations and under different load conditions. For example, a common platform may need to support an application that is deployed and operated as an embedded standalone system responding to several hundred events per minute. The same platform may however also need to support an application deployed as an integrated multi-site system of dedicated servers responding to tens of thousands events per second. What non-functional platform requirements should be specified so that once implemented the platform can be deployed on an embedded standalone system or on dedicated servers, and respond well for both types of loading conditions?

Terminology and metrics mismatch: During the development of NFRs for the platform, requirements analysts must deal with a wide range of concepts, terminology and metrics used in different application domains. For example, in one industrial domain, a performance requirement could be specified in events per seconds, while in another in alarms per minute. Platform developers must translate such differences in terminology and metrics into common platform terminology and metrics before compatible platform requirements can be specified.

Dealing with NFR trade-offs: Developing an application platform in general and adopting service orientation in particular requires the implementation of specific design principles, such as modularity, loose coupling, service statelessness, service autonomy, service contracting, etc. (Erl, 2007), which help achieve non-functional benefits, such as reusability, interoperability, consistency and extensibility, associated with application platforms and service orientation. However implementing such design principles comes with a price and requires developers to make trade-offs with other non-functional requirements such as performance and increased upfront development costs. Platform developers must evaluate the importance of each NFR to the success of domain application. Such evaluation determines whether the NFRs are inconsistent with service-oriented design principles. If so, they must determine what trade-offs to platform NFRs and/or to NFRs of the domain application must be made, when establishing a service-oriented application platform, and when adopting the platform for domain applications.

This chapter presents a systematic analysis method to support requirements analysts in dealing with aforementioned challenges during the development of NFRs for application platforms in the control system domain. in earlier work, the Platform NFR Developed Method (PND) (Song et al., 2009) provided guidelines for developing platform NFRs. The method presented in this chapter include the introduction of a systematic trade-off analysis by use of a goal- and scenario-oriented modeling and analysis techniques. We thus, refer to this new method as GS-PND.

Introducing goal and scenario-oriented modeling affords benefits including an integrated treatment of quantitative (Keller, Kahn et al. 1990) and qualitative NFRs (Mylopoulos, Chung et al. 1992; Chung 1993; Chung, Nixon et al. 2000), support for different types of automated consistency checking across NFRs, the ability to take into account already existing, as well as anticipate future key requirements and design choices during the development of NFRs, as well as systematic trade-off analysis.

The background section introduces industrial control systems – the domain area in which the analysis method was developed and applied, elaborates on platform NFRs and discusses related work. Section three presents an overview of the analysis method, illustrates the offered modeling and analysis techniques, and how these are used to represent and model the adoption of service orientation as part of the platform architecture strategy. Section four applies the analysis method by deriving platform NFRs from three industrial control system solutions. Section five discusses

future trends, while section six concludes and points to future work.

BACKGROUND

Industrial Control Systems

The Goal and Scenario-oriented Platform NFR Development Method (GS-PND) was developed while analyzing non-functional requirements of three existing industrial control systems to derive non-functional requirements for a common application platform. Each control system was developed for a different application domain – automation technology (AT), building technology (BT), and transportation technology (TT), and each system exhibits distinct NFRs.

The purpose of an industrial control system is to control systems or processes in its environment (Sperling and Lutz 1997; Speck 2003). Essentially, a control system continuously reads input data from a number of input sensors, and the input data is fed into controlling algorithms to calculate appropriate control data. Control data is then sent as output to actuators, which effects appropriate physical change to the controlled system or process, which in turn is reflected in new input data read from input sensors (see Figure 1). Control systems also include processes to support displaying data captured and calculated from sensors, and to support user input to configure the systems and its components.

Figure 1. Context diagram of control systems

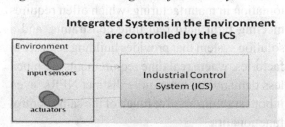

Figure 2. Anatomy of typical control system

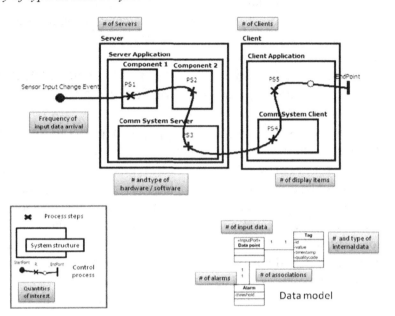

Industrial control systems usually have a large number of input sensors and actuators connected, requiring them to continuously read and process a large number of input data. A key non-functional requirement of such systems is that inputs must be processed and outputs generated under real time constraints. A key design goal of industrial control systems is therefore to achieve sufficient processing throughput of input data.

For example, in one application (TT) a key throughput requirement is that the system is capable of detecting, processing and responding to 3000 changes of input value on its input sensors per second, while in another one (AT) a similar non-functional requirement is to process 30,000 changes of values per second.

Apart from providing sufficient processing throughput, the commercial success of an industrial control system however also depends on meeting other important non-functional requirements. Developers of industrial control systems must address non-functional requirements such as cost of ownership, usability of the operators user interface, availability, reliability and interoperability of the control systems, as well as reusability,

scalability and flexibility to changing controlling environments and customer needs. Industrial Control systems must also often be implemented on system hardware with limited capabilities.

A key concern when addressing such aforementioned NFRs, such as by adopting a service-oriented platform development approach, is whether hard real time constraints can be met, if all else is kept equal, and if not, what trade-offs to make.

Figure 2 illustrates typical internals and several quantitative characterizing measures of industrial control systems, using the UCM notation (Buhr & Casselman 1996). A "wiggled line" represents a control process. In the UCM notation an "x" on a wiggled line represents computational responsibility. In Figure 2 each "x" represents a control process steps. Boxes represent architectural elements such as applications, Operating system processes, components and the like. Together all wiggled lines and boxes in Figure 2 define a use case map (UCM). The purpose of a UCM is not to provide a complete description of a computational process, but to support capturing at a higher level of abstract essential computational structures and responsibilities.

Control systems are usually client/server systems where servers are connected to input sensors and actuators, while clients provide user interfaces to the system's operators (Figure 2). Clients are connected to servers via a communication system. Standalone control systems combine client and server functionality in one device.

Important parameters that characterize control systems include the number of input sensors, and the frequency these must be read and processed, the number of clients each server has connected, and so forth. Figure 2 shows a typical control process that reads data from an input sensor, performs some processing, then outputs control data as well as status information to clients. Internally, control systems maintain a data model which stores data items such as data read, alarms identified and processed, as well as information about connected clients. Industrial control systems typically adopt architectural features such as modularization and layering to address non-functional requirements such as reusability, maintainability and extensibility (Speck, 2003).

Broadly speaking, the specification of non-functional requirements for industrial control systems involves several kinds of trade-offs. The number of data points and hard real time requirements establish baseline processing throughput needs for processing input data, such as detecting and processing 3000 changes of input values per second. To address other relevant NFRs, such as usability, scalability, and interoperability requires additional system and software processes and structures which add processing overhead to the baseline.

To achieve additional throughput requirements requires specifying additional and/or more powerful processors, and more memory which however increases the cost of ownership. To reduce cost of ownership, developers must either sacrifice some relevant NFRs, or reduce system throughput needs, by reducing the number of input data processing

needs – the latter can for example be achieved by positioning the product in a less demanding market niche.

NFRs of Platform, Platform Application and Domain Application

Application platforms offer common runtime facilities and programming interfaces to application program developers. Successful application platforms are usually developed by analyzing already existing domain applications to identify common reusable functionality and features. Platform NFR specifications should thus be derived from NFR specifications of already existing domain applications.

To specify platform NFRs, an important distinction we make is between deployed application system and application (see Figure 3). A deployed application system, or deployed application in short, is an application deployed according to one of its predefined deployment configurations. For example, consider a building security application, which can be deployed as a small standalone embedded system, for small homes, or as a larger distributed client/server system for larger office buildings. We say that the building security application has two deployment configurations: an embedded configuration and a client/server configuration, and that the building security application can therefore be deployed as two types of systems: an embedded system, or a client server system.

Making this distinction is important, since some NFRs such as load conditions (e.g. alarms per second that must be processed), are only meaningfully defined for deployed application systems. For example, the building security application when deployed as a client/server system can deal with a much greater number alarms per second, than when deployed as an embedded system.

According to this distinction, developing platform NFRs includes developing two types of

Figure 3. Defining NFR specifications

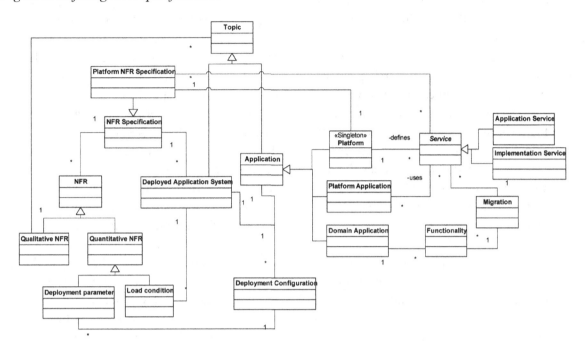

NFRs (a) the developing of NFRs that are defined independently of a deployment configuration, and (b) developing NFRs for the deployed platforms, where the platform is deployed according to one or more predefined deployment configurations. In this chapter, unless indicated otherwise, we will just say platform NFR to NFRs of either type.

Figure 3 further shows that a Deployment configuration is defined by one or more Deployment parameters, such as number and types of Servers, number of Clients, number of input sensors, number of configurable alarms, and so forth. Deployment parameters which characterize deployment configurations are NFRs specified for an Application.

Another important distinction we make is between Quantitative and Qualitative NFRs. Distinguishing between Quantitative and Qualitative NFRs enables us to use different techniques during the development of platform NFRs. Deployment parameters and load conditions are both Quantitative NFRs, NFRs specified in terms of countable quantities (Keller, Kahn et al. 1990; Kazman,

Klein et al. 2000). In contrast to Quantitative NFRs, Qualitative NFRs are NFRs such as usability, security, interoperability, which are hard or impossible to formalize or count (Mylopoulos, Chung et al. 1992; Chung 1993; Chung, Nixon et al. 2000). In a subsequent section we will further see that in the context of a qualitative NFR analysis technique, a Quantitative NFR, such as processing throughput, can also be treated as a Quality NFR.

Chung (1993) suggests analyzing qualitative NFRs into type and topic. A type such as Scalability is applied to a topic, such as *System* defining the qualitative NFRs *Scalability of System*. In Figure 3, Topic captures the fact that Qualitative NFRs are defined over Applications or Deployed Application systems (type is not separately shown). A subsequent section will further clarify the difference between Quantitative and Qualitative NFRs, and elaborate on other type and topic distinctions.

Figure 3 indicates that the Platform defines Services. A Platform Application is an application that uses the Platform's services. We distinguish between two types of services: Application Services and Implementation Services. Application services are services that can directly be used by applications to add required functionality. Implementation Services are, on the other hand, similar to programming libraries, and support implementing functionality of an application. Finally, Figure 3 also shows that migrating Domain Applications to the Platform requires migrating functionality of Domain Applications to platform Services.

The structural relationships between the different types of Applications allow us to point out an important relationship between NFRs specifications:

1. NFRs of platform applications are dependent on NFRs of the platform, since platform applications make use of platform services.
2. When developing NFRs for the platform a key success factor is that important NFRs of domain applications should as much as possible be preserved, when selected functionality of domain applications is migrated to make use of platform services

To develop platform NFRs such that migrated domain applications retain their important NFR properties requires trade-offs, since platforms, and in particular service-oriented platforms, have distinct architectural features. The best that can usually be achieved is to support retaining some of the important NFRs, by sacrificing less important ones. Such trade-offs could, for example, involve the development of several Platform, each resulting from different kind of NFR trade-offs, and offering different subsets of platform Services to platform applications. Figure 3 captures such an approach by defining an association link between the Platform NFR Specification and the Services provided by the Platform.

Related Work

A qualitative treatment of NFRs was first suggested by Mylopoulos and Chung (Chung, 1993;

Mylopoulos, Borgida et al. 1997; Chung, Nixon et al. 2000) who proposed a process-oriented approach that treats NFRs as goals that are achieved during a requirements and architectural design modeling and analysis process. Nixon specialized this work to specifically dealing with the performance NFR during information system design (Nixon, 1994). Nixon does however not deal with throughput requirement, or with relating the proposed qualitative analysis to a quantitative analysis of performance.

Based on Mylopoulos and Chung's work Cai and Yu (2002) outlined an approach for dealing with the performance NFR in conjunction with Use Case Maps (UCMs) (Buhr & Casselman, 1996). UCMs are a scenario modeling approach for representing high level system structures and behaviors. The approach presented in this chapter has similarities with Cai and Yu's approach in that it also makes use of scenario modeling. However Cai and Yu focus on a qualitative performance analysis of architecture choices during which Scenario modeling supports capturing the results of goal-oriented reasoning and decision making. The method presented in this chapter further utilizes scenario modeling to support a quantitative analysis of throughput and to linking the qualitative and quantitative analyses of throughput via scenario models to support an integrated analysis approach.

The work most closely related to GS-PND is by Pourshahid et. al. (2007). Pourshahid et al. extend the User Requirements Notation (URN) (ITU-T 2008) a recent requirements analysis and specification standard, that supports representing, capturing and analyzing qualitative NFR and linking these to UCM scenario modeling. While Pourshahid et. al. applies and extend URN to represent and evaluate business processes in organizations, the GS-PND adapts and extends URN to specifically deal the development of NFRs for a control systems' application platform.

There has been much interest in recent years related to dealing with NFRs in relation to service orientation (see for example, (NFPSLA-SOC'07) and (MNPSC'08)). Much of the work however relates to quantitative methods, models and techniques to support the specification, discovery, matching and selection of services, to best meet client's quantifiable non-functional needs. Little work deals with Qualitative NFRs or with NFRs (both Qualitative and Quantitative) during the design of service-oriented software systems in general, or software system platform, in particular.

One notable exception is Liu et. al. (Liu, Zhu et al. 2008), which offers a method for modeling and evaluating the performance overhead when service-oriented business processes are deployed across different organizations. Liu et al. offers a quantitative performance modeling and analysis approach to evaluate how different deployment topologies affect process performance. However, no treatment of qualitative NFRs is provided. Furthermore, Liu's et al. approach is applied in the business process domain and does not deal with the development of NFRs for an application platform.

The relationship between non-functional requirements and service orientation is informally explored by Erl (2007). While Erl provides important insights into the non-functional driving forces behind the adoption of service orientation, no systematic modeling and analysis approach is provided. Erl's work is however a useful source for identifying relevant service-oriented NFRs during qualitative modeling and analysis.

ANALYZING PROCESSING THROUGHPUT AND PROCESSING CAPACITY

A key NFR for industrial control systems is to achieve sufficient processing throughput of input data so that all hard real time performance requirements are fully met. Processing throughput is a quantitative requirement that specifies the volume of data a deployed control system must process within a unit of time under a specified loading condition. For example, a throughput requirement could be specified to support the processing of 3000 Change of Input Values (COVs) per second which specifies the throughput requirement during normal system operation or 50,000 Change of Input Values which specifies a peak load condition.

A control system usually has many types of throughput requirements specified. For example, additional throughput requirements are Alarms per second to process during normal operation or during maximum load conditions.

We defined processing capacity as the number of instructions a deployed system can processes per second. Processing capacity is directly related to the systems hardware capabilities. The more hardware or the more powerful the hardware, if all else is equal for a deployed system (such as amount of memory, operating system, etc.), the higher the processing capacity.

Intuitively, the more processing throughput required, the more processing capacity is needed. This intuition leads us to the key analysis questions underlying the development of platform NFRs:

- What factors impact total processing throughput of a deployed system
- How much processing capacity is needed to achieve required processing throughput requirements of different deployed systems, given the factors that impact each system's processing throughput

To systematically address these questions, GS-PND offers a goal-and scenario-oriented analysis technique:

Goal-oriented analysis technique: helps identifying how the throughput NFR is qualitatively interpreted, refined and addressed, as well as the design techniques that are introduced to address other qualitative NFRs and the impact these techniques have on the throughput NFR, as well as other relevant qualitative NFRs. A goal-oriented graph developed during a goal-oriented

Figure 4. Qualitative analysis of throughput requirements

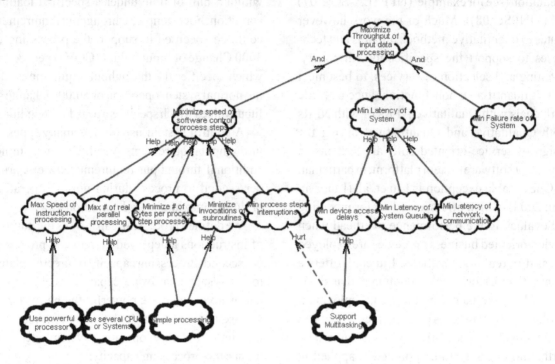

analysis of NFRs is a "top down" *representation* of quality NFRs that supports requirements trade-offs analysis (Mylopoulos, Chung et al. 1992; Chung, Nixon et al. 2000). The goal graph supports clarifying the operational meaning of qualitative NFRs, helps justify design choices and trade-offs and represents a trace of the reasoning about how Qualitative NFRs are achieved.

Scenario-oriented analysis technique: helps identifying the processing capacity needed to meet required load conditions of deployed applications. Scenario's captured using the UCM notation (Amyot and Mussbacher 2003) represent high level system processes and structures are adapted according to the results obtained during goal-oriented analysis.

Goal-Oriented Analysis Technique

Figure 4 illustrates an NFR goal graph that captures a goal-oriented analysis of the processing throughput NFR. Although processing throughput

can be measured quantitatively (such as number of inputs processed per second), during goal-oriented analysis processing throughput is analyzed in a qualitative manner.

Figure 4 indicates that to identify the factors that affect throughput, we first state the goal to *Maximize throughput of input data processing*. This goal is achieved by three sub goals: *Maximize speed of software control process steps*, by *Minimizing latency of the System* and by *Minimizing Failure rate of the System*. The "and" contribution link specifies that we expect those three sub goals, once addressed, to sufficiently address their parent goal. No other sibling goal needs to be identified.

Each sub goal in turn is then analyzed to identify additional sub goals. Goals are decomposed into sub goals, until one can identify particular requirements or design techniques that address the lowest level goals. The *Maximize speed of software control process steps* NFR goal is further decomposed into *Maximize speed of instruction processing, Maximize Speed each instruction is processed, Maximize number of real (i.e. not virtual) parallel processing, Maximize number of bytes per process step that is performed, Minimize number of invocations of subroutines, Minimize number of interruption of process steps* NFR goals. The "help" contribution link between the sub goals and the parent goal indicate that each sub goal independently contributes ("helps") to some extend achieving their parent goal, although other contributing sibling goals could further be identified. The *Maximize speed of instruction processing* is then further decomposed into a known design technique, to the *Use powerful processors* operationalization, which helps M*aximize the speed of instruction processing*, and *Use several CPUs or Systems* operationalization to *Maximize the number of real parallel processing*. Operationalization goals refer to requirements or design techniques that help address NFR goals.

Figure 4 further illustrates that introducing *Support Multitasking* operationalization, which comes to help *minimize device access delays,* which in turn contributes *Minimize the latency of the system*, has as a negative "side effect", shown by the dotted "hurt" correlation link, on *Minimizing process step interruption* NFR goal. Introducing multitasking is thus a trade-off between latency and speed of processing of the control software. Other trade-offs, not shown in Figure 4, can be identified, such as the use of several CPUs increases "hurts" to minimize total cost of ownership. Finally, Figure 4 shows that the operationalization *Simple processing*, to keep the processing algorithms and data structures simple helps minimize number of bytes per process step as well as minimize number invocation of subroutines. In other words, simple data and system structures and processes help reduce computational overhead.

Figure 5 expands the NFR goal graph to include additional NFR goals, which are analyzed in conjunction with Processing Throughput, such as *Usability, Cost of Ownership*, as well as *Interoperability*, a key design goal that motivates

the use of service-orientation, and shows additional related trade-offs.

Figure 5 schematically illustrates how some of the design techniques (captured as operationalizations) are factors that negatively impact throughput. The graph at the bottom of Figure 5 (which however is not part of the goal graph notation) shows that with the selection of different operationalizations, processing overhead is incurred on top of a baseline level of processing needs. For example, the inclusion of a high level object model in addition to a basic control data model into the control system helps improve usability (since it supports defining control data at an abstraction level closer to the system's users), incurs a processing overhead. Similarly, the use of web services, which helps achieve *Interoperability* incurs additional processing overhead. The NFR goal graph in Figure 5 helps answer the first question: "What factors impact processing throughput of each deployed system?"

A goal graphs aims to assist in capturing domain knowledge. The validity of the goal graph must continuously be reviewed to identify whether additional information must be added to make the requirements and design information and knowledge more accurate and complete. Capturing requirements and design knowledge by use of goal graphs also supports developing knowledge based approaches, where existing goal graph templates can be used to validate and further complete other goal graphs under development (Mylopoulos, Chung et al. 1992; Chung 1993; Yu & Mylopoulos 1996; Chung, Nixon et al. 2000).

Scenario-Oriented Analysis Technique

To answer the second question: "How much processing capacity is needed to achieve required processing throughput requirements of different deployed systems, given the factors that impact each system's processing throughput", we turn to a scenario-oriented analysis technique.

Figure 5. Qualitative NFR reasoning linked to quantitative processing overhead estimation

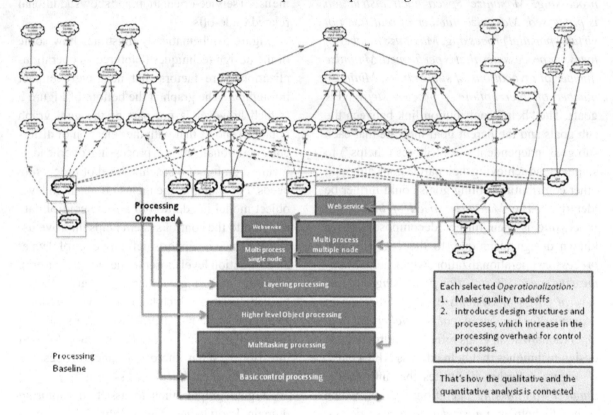

Goal and Scenario modeling complement each other. Goal modeling assists in identifying a selection of operationalizations that help address important qualitative NFRs, while making acceptable qualitative NFR trade-offs. Scenario-oriented analysis support estimating for each selected operationalization the related capacity requirements and thus ultimately the total cost of ownership. If total cost of ownership exceeds acceptable limits, it prompts analysts to return to the goal models and seek different quality NFR trade-offs that have reduced overhead footprints.

During scenario-oriented analysis we construct an abstract processing model of an industrial control system (see Figure 6) which we use to estimate processing capacity needs. The model adapts and extends the Use Case Map notation (Buhr & Casselman 1996) to captures a high level description of control processes in terms of processing steps and high level structural elements.

Figure 6 captures baseline processing steps for two key control processes, the Change of Value (COV) process, and the Alarm process. The Change of Value process is invoked whenever a change in an input data point is detected. The changed value is then read from the input sensor and sent to subscribing system clients. The Alarm process is invoked by the Change of Value process to check if the changed value exceeds a threshold. If the threshold is exceeded alarm data is sent to subscribing clients. The model also captures key system structures such as a Server, Client as well as, a Communication System. To capture baseline processing needs no overhead structures and processes are included in Figure 6. The process model in Figure 6 thus corresponds to selecting the *Simple Processing* operationalization.

Each control process is further associated with key supporting data structures. For example Figure 6 shows that to check if a change of value

Figure 6. abstract processing model of industrial controller

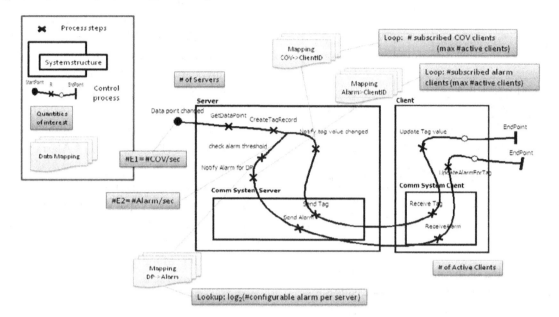

has exceeded a threshold, a lookup data structure is used that maps between input data points and Alarm entities that store respective threshold values for input data points. Figure 6 also shows two "looping" data structures that support the COV process, and Alarm process in sending messages to all subscribed clients. These data structures capture COV and Alarm subscribers.

Finally, the control process model is annotated with relevant quantitative variables derived from deployment parameters and loading conditions NFRs (see Figure 3). For example, the number of Change of Values per second or the number of Alarms per second the control system is expected to process. Each data structure is also associated with related deployment parameters. For example, the number of configurable alarms determines the number of mapping from data points to alarms, which in turn also determines the processing needed to look up one mapping – which is usually the $\log_2$ (size of the mapping table). Once a processing model is established, and relevant quantitative variables linked to the control processes, a mathematical function is derived for calculating processing capacity needs. This function is then

used to estimate the processing capacity needs of different deployment configurations of existing domain applications. Deriving the processing capacity function involves three steps:

1. Capture processing capacity needs for each processing step
2. Capture processing capacity needs for single invocations of each control process
3. Capture processing capacity needs for multiple invocations of each control process per unit of time

Table 1 summarizes the first analysis step for the processing model in Figure 6. Each process step is analyzed in terms of processing capacity needs. The processing capacity needs are identified as follows:

A processing step that has no quantitative variable associated requires a constant factor of high level instructions. A processing step that has a loop mapping table requires a constant factor times the maximum possible number the loop can be performed. A processing step that has a lookup mapping table requires a constant factor times

Table 1. processing capacity formula for single invocation of processing steps

Capacity Variable	Process step	Processing capacity Formula
P1	Get data point value	F_1 – a constant
P2	Create Tag record	F_2 – a constant
P3	Notify Tag value changed	F_3 x *ActiveClients*
P4	Check for Alarm threshold	F_4 * Log_2 (*ConfigurableAlarms*)
P5	Notify Alarm for Data Point	F_5 x *ActiveClients*
P6	Send Tag	F_6 * *ActiveClients*
P7	Send Alarm	F_7 * *ActiveClients*

the base two log of the size of the lookup table to perform one lookup. Finally, the processing steps that are shared amongst two control processes are scored separately for each control process because they execute separately.

Once the processing capacity of each processing step is identified, an aggregate formula for each control process is derived. According to Figure 6 and Table 1 the Change of Value control process includes processing steps: P1, P2, P3 and P6, while the Alarm control process includes the steps: P4, P5 and P7.

Finally, we identify for each process its associated maximum load condition to capture processing capacity for multiple invocations of each control process per unit of time. For example if we designate with COV the maximum number of change of values per second requirement, and with ALARM the maximum number of alarms per

second that same industrial controller must processes. Then the total processing capacity for the Change of Value process is calculated by the sum total of individual processing steps for one control process invocation, times the number of times the control process is invoked per second. This yields the following formula: (P1+P2+P3+P6)* COV, for the total capacity requirement of the Change of Value process (P4 + P5 + P7) * Alarm for the Alarm process.

Substituting the capacity variables (P1, P2, etc.) with processing capacity formula they designate, the total capacity formula according to the processing model in Figure 6 is as follows (tagged factors are sums of individual factors, such as F_1' $= F_1 + F_2$) in Box 1.

The equation captures the total processing capacity needed as a function of deployment parameters: *Active Clients* and *Configurable Alarms*, and loading conditions: *Change of Values per second* and *Alarms per second*. Since the scenario model is a baseline model the function constructed from the scenario model specifies baseline processing needs with no processing overhead.

Analyzing Service Orientation Processing Overhead

Figure 7 illustrates reasoning structures related to interoperability, a key service-oriented NFR. *Interoperability of the System* is decomposed into *Interoperability of Device Access* and *Interoperability of Messaging*, indicating that to achieve Interoperability of the control system we need to

Box 1.

$$TotalProcessingCapacityNeed(ActiveClient, ConfigurableAlarm, COV, ALARM)$$
$$= (F_1^{'} + F_2^{'} \times ActiveClients) \times COV$$
$$+ (F_2^{'} + \log_2 ConfigurableAlarm + F_3^{'} \times ActiveClient) \times ALARM$$

Figure 7. NFR goal graph fragment to analyze interoperability and related NFR trade-offs, showing use of web services vs. direct processing

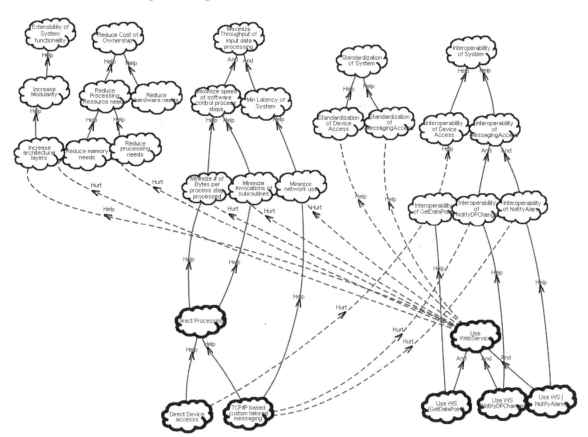

deal with interoperability for those processing steps that access external devices, and those that access the messaging systems. To deal with these interoperability sub goals we further decompose them into *Interoperability of Get Data Point*, *Interoperability of Notify Data Point Change* and *Interoperability of Notify Alarm* sub goals. Finally, we further decomposed into the *use web services* operationalization to help achieve the respective interoperability NFRs.

Figure 7 further shows that the web service operationalization introduces positive as well as negative effects on other quality NFRs. For example, the use of web services helps achieve *Standardization* and *Extensibility*, and hurts achieving the *Throughput* and *Cost of Ownership*.

Choosing to adopt web services thus adds overhead to the baseline.

Once we select the web services operationalizations we can annotate the processing steps that are web service enabled process model. Figure 8 shows the annotated process model. Annotations are shown below processing tasks as two parallel lines with "WS" initials. The process model now shows that the *Get Data Point Value*, the *Notify Tag Change Value* as well as the *Notify Alarm for Tag* process steps utilize a web service based approach in its design. These annotations are used when determining processing capacity requirements for each processing step.

Figure 9 shows how web service annotations are expanded into a processing model fragment that helps estimate processing capacity require-

Figure 8. Processing model annotated with web services indicators

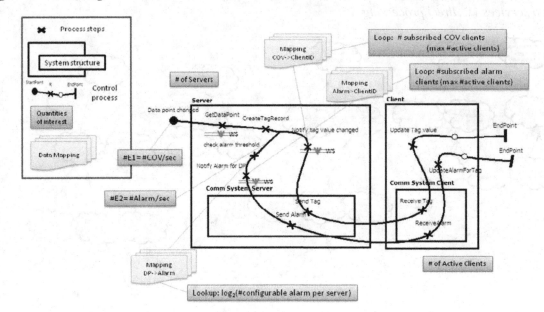

ment for process steps implemented as web services. More specifically, each web service annotation specifies the execution of the several additional processing steps, including encoding data as web service messages, sending web service messages and decoding web service messages to extract included data. From a capacity needs point of view of the control server, we find that each web service enabled processing steps adds a constant factor F_{ws} of processing steps. Table 2

captures how the additional processing overhead is included in the processing capacity formulas when web service enabled processing steps are introduced.

It is noteworthy that the UCM notation supports a notion of UCM plug-ins, where a single responsibility can be expanded into another UCM. The notion of expansion of an annotation is a generalization of the plug-in concept, which is useful when detailed processes and structures do

Figure 9. Expansion of WS annotation into more detailed structures and processes

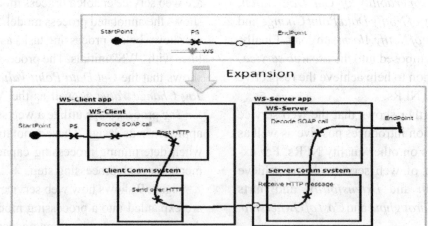

Table 2. Processing capacity formula for single invocation of processing steps with web service overhead

Capacity Variable	Process step	Processing capacity Formula
P1	Get data point value	$F_1 + F_{ws}$
P2	Create Tag record	F_2
P3	For each *COV*-subscribed Client notify Tag value changed	$(F_3 + F_{ws}) \times Active\text{-}Clients$
P4	Check for Alarm threshold	$F_4 \times Log_2$ (*ConfigurableAlarms*)
P5	For each alarm-subscribed Client notify Alarm for Tag	$(F_5 + F_{ws}) \times Active\text{-}Clients$
P6	Send Tag	$F_6 \times ActiveClients$
P7	Send Alarm	$F_7 \times ActiveClients$

not encapsulate well within single UCMs. Figure 9 for example illustrates that expansions occur both on the Client and on the Server.

Based on table 2 we modify the Total Processing Capacity Needs equation (see Box 2). To use the equation we need to set the constants included in the equation to some specific numbers. For the purpose of our analysis we estimate the number of high level instructions each steps would require. Since we want to compare different deployment

configurations we can further simplify and just estimate a relative weight of each step to each other. We estimate as follows: Each processing step is weighted as "1". If, however, a processing step is decomposed, then its weigh, is the total weight of its components. Based on that formula we find that all constants are weighted with "1" while FWS is weighted with "5", since it is expanded into 5 additional processing steps (see Box 3).

The modified Total Processing Capacity Needs formula now captures the increased processing capacity need a control server requires. Taken together the NFR goal graph model in Figure 7 and the processing model in Figure 8 helps identify for what purpose and where within industrial control processes web service are introduced, and what kind of processing overhead the introduction of web services would cause.

The goal model supports identifying the design choices for achieving qualitative NFRs, and helps to point out qualitative NFRs trade-offs. In the goal models, design approaches under consideration are expressed as operationalizations. As illustrated in this section, operationalizations in turn introduce additional design elements in scenario models, thereby adding processing overhead. Stated differently, processing overhead

Box 2.

$$TotalProcessingCapacityNeed\_WS(ActiveClient, ConfigurableALARM)$$
$$= (F_1' + F_{WS}(F_2' + F_{WS}) \times ActiveClents) \times COV$$
$$+ (F_2' + \log_2 ConfigurableAlarm(F_3' + F_{WS}) \times ActiveClients) \times ALARM$$

Box 3.

$$TotalProcessingCapacityNeed\_WS(ActiveClient, ConfigurableAlarm, COV, ALARM)$$
$$= (6 + 6 \times ActiveClients) \times COV$$
$$+ (1 + \log_2 ConfigurableAlarm + 6 \times ActiveClients) \times ALARM$$

introduced is justified by the achievement of stated qualitative NFRs. Analysts must therefore carefully select which of the stated NFRs to address, while trading off increased processing overhead and increased costs. While the goal and scenario oriented techniques does not support optimizing requirements and design choices, they do support identifying requirements and design choices that are good enough for the purposes specified. It is noteworthy that goal and scenario modeling supports the systematic modeling and analyzing of processing overhead incurred for the selection of any kinds of quality NFR, not only those relevant to service orientation.

DERIVING PLATFORM NFRS FROM NFRS OF EXISTING CONTROL SYSTEMS

The problem the goal and scenario oriented analysis helps address is as following: there exist several control applications defined for distinct problem domains. Each control application has three deployment configurations defined: small, medium and large. Each deployment configuration is characterized by distinct deployment parameters: the number of (active) clients that a

particular server running the control application can concurrently handle, and the number of alarms that can be configured per server. The larger the deployment configuration, the more active clients and configurable alarms are supported. Each deployment configuration is associated with different loading conditions: the number of Change of Values (COVs) per second and the number of alarms per second a server can process. The analysis questions are as follows:

a. what deployment configurations should be defined for a shared application platform;

b. what deployment parameters and what loading conditions should each platform deployment configuration support; and

c. what effect does service-orientation have on defining deployment configurations for the shared application platform?

We answer these questions using the mathematical functions derived earlier, and from particular input data (deployment parameters and loading conditions) provided for each deployment configuration of the existing control applications. Table 3 captures deployment configurations (top two tables) and loading conditions (bottom two tables) of three different control applications, for

Table 3. Deployment and loading conditions

	Small	Medium	Large			Small	Medium	Large
AT	1	8	50		AT	8000	18000	160000
BT	8	30	150		BT	1100	12000	45000
TT	2	3	6		TT	1000	2000	4000
Number of Active Clients per Server					**Number of Configurable Alarms per Server**			
	Small	Medium	Large		Small	Medium	Large	
AT	12500	35000	91000		AT	7	10	3500
BT	50	250	340		BT	12	20	45
TT	1450	3200	4800		TT	120	300	350
Max possible COV/sec per Server					**Max possible Alarms/sec per Server**			

Automation Technology (AT), Building Technology (BT) and Transportation Technology (TT) domain. Each application has a small, medium and large deployment configuration defined. Table 3 shows the deployment parameters *"number of active clients attached per Server"*, and *"number of configurable alarms per Server"* that characterize the size of a deployment configuration, as well as the required loading conditions *"Max possible COV/sec per Server"* and *"Max possible Alarms/sec per Server"* for each deployment configuration.

Using the Total Processing Capacity Needs for Web Services formula we now calculate actual processing needs, including the processing overhead incurred by utilizing web services. Table 4 captures the total capacity needs when applying this formula for each deployment configuration of each domain application. The table is sorted by capacity needs. The *Power increase* column captures the ratio between two adjacent capacity needs, such as 33446 instructions per second, for BT/Small, divided by 3955 Instructions per second, for TT/Small, which equals to 8.46. The power increase column shows how much more processing power hardware must offer to provide sufficient processing capacity.

The processing needs in table 4 help identifying the cost each deployment configuration types incurs when supported by the platform. For example, we could define a small and cost effective deployment configuration which supports domain applications up to the processing capacity of BT/Small. A medium deployment configuration that would support a processing capacity up to AT/Medium, a large one that supports processing capacity up to AT/Medium, and finally a very large deployment configuration that supports processing capacity of up to AT/Large.

Table five compares the processing needs of a service oriented and non-service oriented platforms. According to table 5 the use of web services increases the processing capacity needs by a factor of 5 to 7 across all deployment configurations. Since processing capacity needs is proportional to cost of ownership, requirements analysis can thus expect that a lowest end deployment configuration without service-orientation (such as BT/Small) costs about 6 times less than the same deployment configuration that is service oriented. Cost of ownership considerations may suggest offering two low cost deployment configurations, one non-web service enabled that offers a particularly small processing foot print with minimal capacity needs, which however is trades-off with Interoperability and Standardization; and a web service enabled one, which does offers the benefits of service-orientation, however at a higher cost of ownership.

While the above analysis focused on qualitative NFRs related to the adoption of service-orientation, other NFRs such as Modularity, Extensibility and the like can be analyzed in a similar manner. Requirements and/or design techniques addressing these NFRs can be identified and captured using goal graphs, and scenario models can be developed to identify and calculate relevant overhead.

Although not illustrated in this chapter, selected sets of operationalizations and related scenario models can be clustered together, to support dealing with groups of related requirements and design decisions (ITU-T 2008).

Table 4. Total processing capacity needs -- ranking

	Deployment	Instructions	Power
Application	**Configuration**	**per second**	**increase**
BT	Small	3955	
TT	Small	33446	8.46
BT	Medium	58741	1.76
TT	Medium	99490	1.69
AT	Small	175147	1.76
TT	Large	254438	1.45
BT	Large	407371	1.60
AT	Medium	2205711	5.41
AT	Large	33776007	15.31

Table 5. Comparing WS and non-WS enabled capacity needs

Application	Deployment Configuration	With WS Instructions per second	No WS Instructions per second	Power Ratio
BT	Small	3955	679	5.82
TT	Small	33446	5906	5.66
BT	Medium	58741	8641	6.80
TT	Medium	99490	17290	5.75
AT	Small	175147	25105	6.98
TT	Large	254438	40238	6.32
BT	Large	407371	58831	6.92
AT	Medium	2205711	315231	7.00
AT	Large	33776007	4880007	6.92

Progressively more Detailed Levels of Analysis

The above goal and scenario analysis used only two process models to describe control processes of all domain applications, and of the platform. One process model captured base line control processes, and another annotated process model included structures and process steps associated with web services. The analysis assumed that all domain applications as well as the platform are composed of essentially identical internal control structures and processes. In cases where such assumptions are not appropriate, a more detailed level of analysis can be performed. This section outlines several levels of capacity analysis supported by GS-PND.

Basic capacity analysis: focuses on scenario-oriented analysis by identifying common processing capacity requirements across different domain applications, while assuming simple uniform architectural structures and processes across all control system applications and for the application platform. All platform services are assumed to be application services (see Figure 3).

While this level of analysis simplifies the structure and processes of individual domain applications, and disregards platform specific

processing overhead, it does provide a first cut view of processing capacity needs across different domain applications, which offers a first cut estimations of processing capacity needs for the application platform.

Intermediate capacity and platform overhead analysis: focuses on scenario and goal-oriented analysis to support basic processing overhead estimation and reasoning. Although simple and uniform architectural structures and processes are assumed across all domain applications, additional overhead structures and processes for the application platform are identified and evaluated both in terms of capacity overhead and in terms of trade-offs amongst quality NFR.

While this level of analysis also makes simplifying assumptions about structure and processes of individual domain applications, it does adjust results to include platform specific overhead introduced by platform specific NFRs.

This level of analysis offers more accurate capacity estimations, and additionally supports deriving in conjunction with variability analysis (discussed further below) estimations for different NFR trade-off and capacity overhead scenarios. This level of analysis is best suited when differences in architectural structures and processes of individual domain applications can be disregarded

Detailed capacity and overhead analysis: focuses on scenario and goal-oriented analysis to support detailed processing overhead estimation and reasoning. At this level of analysis for each domain application a process and goal model is developed capturing for each domain application the processing capacity and overhead estimations. Architectural structures and processes are further justified by NFR goal graphs establishing the qualitative NFR trade-offs included in each domain application.

Process and goal models of individual applications are then used to develop a global process and goal model for the application platform, where the process model is adjusted in accordance with different NFR trade-offs that are made when migrating from individual domain application's architectural structures and processes to the application platform.

Once all process and goal models are completed, processing capacity analysis can be performed by discounting or transferring domain specific architectural processes and structures to platform specific overhead structures. Also at this detailed level of capacity and overhead analysis variability analysis can be performed to identify capacity estimations for different NFR trade-offs, and related different capacity overhead scenarios.

This level of analysis is most time consuming, it does however, support developing the most accurate capacity estimations when structures and processes of individual domain applications exhibit significant differences both in terms of capacity overheads and addressed quality NFRs.

Variability analysis: focuses on identifying platform structures and processes (including platform services), which can be added, removed or exchanged to support different qualitative NFRs and quantitative capacity requirements under varying deployment and load conditions. This type of analysis supports creating systems that adapt during runtime to offer different processing capacities while adjusting the selection of quality NFR actively addressed by the system.

For example, variability analysis can support identifying different selections of platform services, or different selections of platform services configurations, to offer or activate, under different loading conditions, thereby varying overhead factors and related quality NFRs addressed. Under normal load conditions all platform services could be activated, while under burst load conditions, some platform services could be deactivated so that additional processing capacity is made available.

Standardizing Terminology and Metrics

The previous sections illustrated how goal and scenario-oriented modeling and analysis techniques support developing platform NFRs from NFRs specifications of individual domain application. The development method presented so far assumed that terminology and metrics of NFRs are standardized across all domain applications. This section overviews a terminology and metrics meta-model (figure 10) that supports standardizing terminology and metrics of NFRs across different domain applications.

Figure 10 shows a meta-model a terminology and metrics meta-model. The meta model was developed to address terminology and metric requirements which were identified during earlier work on the PND method (Xiping Song, Beatrice Hwong et al. 2009). The meta-model captures terms of domain applications as *PhenomenonTypes*.

For example, *AlarmThroughput* or *ChangeOfValueThrougput* are both PhenomenonTypes. Each PhenomenonType is associated with a *Unit*. For example, in one domain application, AlarmThroughput can be associated with a Unit of *Alarm per Second*, while in another domain application in Alarms per minute. *Conversion Ratio* supports specifying how units relate to each another, thereby establishing different unit conversion schemes for different metrics.

Figure 10. Terminology and metrics meta-model

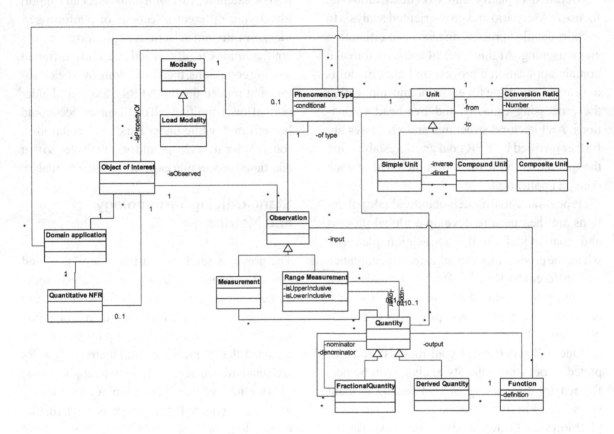

Each *PhenomenonType* is associated with an *ObjectOfInterest* over which phenomenon types are identified. For example, the control system as a whole is an *ObjectOfInterest* over which phenomenon types such as *ChangeOfValueThrougput* and *AlarmThroughput* are defined. One can be more specific and specify the alarm control process as *ObjectOfInterest* to define the AlarmThrougput PhenomenonType over that particular control process.

Other concepts support dealing with ranges of throughput requirements (Range Measurement), as well as dealing with fractional quantities such as 500 alarms in 10 milliseconds (Fractional Quantity). Finally Load Modality supports specifying whether throughput requirement are specified for Maximum load or Normal load conditions.

Figure 11 provides a simplified view of the GS-PND method using an IDEF0 process representa-tion. It illustrates each method steps and related inputs and outputs. The series of steps conveyed in the diagram merely represents the flow of in-put and output data among method steps, while no specific order of method steps is prescribed.

A first step in the methodology is the develop-ment of a standardized terminology for quantita-tive and qualitative NFRs. Standardized NFRs are then utilized during goal and scenario analy-sis. Figure 11 further illustrates that goal-model-ing is performed in preparation for goal and scenario analysis. During basic capacity analysis goal modeling and analysis is omitted.

FUTURE TRENDS

With functionality of systems becoming more pervasive and commoditized the non-functional

Figure 11. IDEF0 diagram of Analysis method steps overview

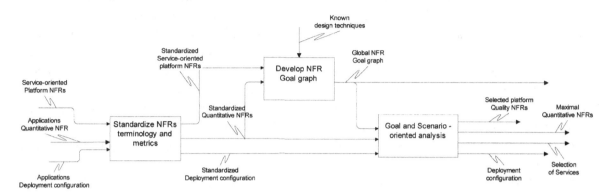

aspects of products and services, such as cost, time to market, quality, as well as extensibility and interoperability are becoming key competitive advantages. While in the past much emphasis has been put on developing methodologies and tools that support delivering functionality, the future will likely see a much increased focus on support for modeling, evaluation and reasoning about quantitative and qualitative NFRs during the development and deployment of products and services.

Also, with the tremendous growth of economies in developing countries, companies who want to participate in those important emerging markets must develop low cost solution that fit the cost profiles for those regions. Future product portfolio offerings will need to not only include solutions that efficiently scale up to meet growing demands, but also efficiently scale down to meet much more restricted budgetary constraints.

The efficient development of successful application platforms that support product portfolios with significantly diversified application NFRs may thus well be an important success factor for future organizations who participate in a global market place.

The platform NFR development method presented in this chapter is a step towards dealing with competing NFRs originating from multiple applications during the development of platform NFRs. The GS-PND method supports analysts in

evaluating the kind of trade-offs they must make during platform NFR development, and offers them some guidance when developing product portfolio that overcome inherent NFR related inconsistencies across product offerings. GS-PND also support dealing with changing NFRs needs, when market demands change and evolve, when new products are developed and/or when existing products are adapted for new markets. GS-PND thus provides organizations with some support to compete not only by identifying a better selection of functionality, but also by meeting or exceeding the non-functional expectations of their customers.

CONCLUSION

Developing non-functional requirements for a service-oriented platform that supports industrial control systems in different domains requires dealing with various requirements challenges. Requirements analysts must deal with varying needs among the different domain applications both in terms of hard real time constraints and in terms of product viability in the market place.

This chapter presented a NFR platform developed method that systematically supports dealing with such diverse requirements and offers analytical support in arriving at viable product NFR specifications. The presented approach was applied to analyze NFRs of three control systems that were developed in different domain, and recommendations for platform NFRs were developed, and positive feedback was received.

The emphasis of this chapter on throughput as a key quantitative and qualitative NFR that drive the design of industrial control systems appear specific to industrial system's real time domain. Furthermore, the manner how deployment parameters and load conditions interrelate when determining throughput capacity in scenario models also appear specific to the problem domain at hand. At the same time the goal-oriented modeling and analysis technique is not specific to dealing with throughput. Other qualitative NFRs can be captured, developed, and different kinds of links between the goal models and process models captured and analyzed.

Validation of the GS-PND method is ongoing. The method has been derived based on a real-life industrial problem, reflecting complexities found in actual practice. The method was reviewed by stakeholders in the platform development domain, who found the GS-PND method in principle appropriate to the problems at hand. Additional validation of the method is in progress.

Future work will focus on further developing and evaluating the more detailed capacity analyses, and variability analysis. Future work will also focus on extending the performance modeling approach and analysis approach in directions of SOA Governance similar to Liu et al. (Liu, Zhu et al. 2008) as well as for dealing with performance measures that include probabilistic system behavior, such as probabilistic cache hit behavior, and maximum sustainable throughput in percentage of time.

Additional work will focus on tool support for collecting qualitative and quantitative NFRs from product's stakeholders, as well as on standardization of NFR terminology across different domain application.

Another area of future research is to extend GS-PND towards an agent-oriented modeling and analysis (Yu 1994; Yu 2001), to support reasoning about functional and non-functional requirements and design decision making that is performed by

different development organization stakeholders (Gross and Yu 2001). Including agent-oriented analysis support into the GS-PND method appears particular useful, since the design success of the application platform will much depends on how well design decisions included in the platform facilitates the achievement of functional and non functional design goals of the different business units responsible for developing platform based product offerings.

REFERENCES

Amyot, D., & Mussbacher, G. (2003). *URN: Towards a new standard for the visual description of requirements*. 3rd SDL and MSC Workshop (SAM02), (pp. 21-37).

Buhr, R. J. A., & Casselman, R. S. (1996). *Use case maps for object-oriented systems*. Prentice Hall.

Cai, Z., & Yu, E. (2002). *Addressing performance requirements using a goal and scenario-oriented approach*. International Conference on Advanced Information Systems Engineering, (pp. 706-710).

Chung, L. (1993). *Representing and using non-functional requirements for Information System development: A process-oriented approach*. Unpublished doctoral thesis, Department of Computer Science, University of Toronto.

Chung, L., & Nixon, B. (2000). *Non-functional requirements in software engineering*. Boston: Kluwer Academic.

Erl, T. (2007). *SOA principles of service design*. Prentice Hall.

Gross, D., & Yu, E. (2001). Evolving system architecture to meet changing business goals: An agent and goal-oriented approach. *Proceedings of the First International Workshop From Software Requirements to Architectures (STRAW 2001) at the International Conference of Software Engineering*. Toronto, Canada.

ITU-T. (2008). *User Requirements Notation (URN) language definition.* Geneva, Switzerland: International Telecommunications Union.

Kazman, R., & Klein, M. (2000). *ATAM: Method for architecture evaluation. Software Engineering Institute.* SEI.

Keller, S. E., & Kahn, G. H. (1990). Specifying software quality requirements with metrics. In Thayer, R. H., & Dorfman, M. (Eds.), *Tutorial: System and software requirement engineering* (pp. 145–163). IEEE Computer Society Press.

Liu, Y., Zhu, L., et al. (2008). *Non-functional property driven service governance: Performance implications.* ICSOC Workshop on Non Functional Properties and Service Level Agreements in Service Oriented Computing.

Mylopoulos, J., Borgida, A., et al. (1997). *Representing software engineering knowledge.* Automated Software Engineering.

Mylopoulos, J., & Chung, L. (1992). Representing and using nonfunctional requirements: A process-oriented approach. *IEEE Transactions on Software Engineering, 18*(6). doi:10.1109/32.142871

Nixon, B. (1994). Representing and using performance requirements during the development of Information Systems. *Proceedings of the 4th international conference on extending database technology: Advances in database technology,* (p. 187).

Pourshahid, A., Chen, P., et al. (2007). Business process monitoring and alignment: An approach based on the user requirements notation and business intelligence tools. 10th International Workshop on Requirements Engineering. (pp. 149-159).

Song, X., Hwong, B., et al. (2009). *Experiences in developing NFRs for the service-oriented software platform.* Technical Report.

Speck, A. (2003). Reusable industrial control systems. *IEEE Transactions on Industrial Electronics, 50*(3). doi:10.1109/TIE.2003.812274

Sperling, W. & Lutz, P. (1997). Enabling open control systems: An introduction to the OSACA system platform. *Robotics and Manufacturing, 6.*

Yu, E. (1994). *Modeling strategic relationships for process re-engineering.* Unpublished doctoral thesis, Department of Computer Science, University of Toronto.

Yu, E. (2001). Agent-oriented modelling: Software versus the world. *Agent-Oriented Software Engineering AOSE-2001 Workshop Proceedings.*

Yu, E. & Mylopoulos, J. (1996). Using goals, rules, and methods to support reasoning in business process reengineering. *Intelligent Systems in Accounting, Finance and Management, 5*(1-13), 1-13.

Chapter 3
Modeling and Analyzing Non-Functional Requirements in Service Oriented Architecture with the User Requirements Notation

Hanane Becha
University of Ottawa, Canada

Gunter Mussbacher
University of Ottawa, Canada

Daniel Amyot
University of Ottawa, Canada

ABSTRACT

Non-functional properties (NFPs) represent an important facet of service descriptions, especially in a Service Oriented Architecture. Yet, they are seldom explicitly described, and their use in service selection and composition is still limited. This chapter presents the User Requirements Notation (URN) as a means to model and analyze functional and non-functional service requirements. Aspect-oriented extensions to URN (AoURN) enable the modeling and modularization of different concerns, including non-functional requirements, which can crosscut services or service components. The chapter also proposes a taxonomy of NFPs used to annotate services and service compositions modeled with AoURN. These annotations enable the specification of quantitative non-functional values for services, guide service selection, and support the computation of the NFP (e.g., the quality of service) of their composition. This approach is illustrated with a simple yet realistic composite service (BookItWell), with an emphasis on four types of NFPs, namely service cost, response time, reliability, and availability.

DOI: 10.4018/978-1-60566-794-2.ch003

INTRODUCTION

In a *Service Oriented Architecture* (SOA), applications are designed as business processes and realized using services and service composition. A *service* is a mechanism that enables access to one or more capabilities offered by a provider for use by one or many consumers. Service providers and service consumers may be part of different organizations. *Service composition* is the capability of combining loosely-coupled (atomic or composite) services, residing in the network and accessible via standardized protocols, into a larger composite service by defining when and under which conditions the composite service invokes the services of which it is built. If concrete services are selected at design time, then the composition is called *static* composition. Otherwise, the composition is *dynamic* and is based on abstract services until runtime, at which point concrete services are selected. An abstract service is only a description of the functionality of the service and is not associated with any specific concrete service. Due to the dynamic nature of the SOA environment, as services are replaced or upgraded and new services are developed, dynamic composition becomes more effective than static composition. It enables business processes to be implemented from the latest existing services and those implementations to be adjusted quickly to meet changing business requirements and an ever evolving context.

Although many such requirements target the functionalities of desired services, it is also essential to consider the non-functional requirements in order to satisfy the relevant goals of the parties involved. *Goals* are high-level objectives of the business, stakeholders, or system. They are often used to discover, select, evaluate, and justify requirements for a service. Whereas functional requirements define the functions of the service, *non-functional requirements* (NFRs) characterize service properties and qualities, such as expected performance, reliability, availability, usability, and cost. Goals and NFRs capture essential (and often conflicting) system concerns and have a huge impact throughout the development process. In comparison with traditional software engineering, managing NFRs is even more difficult in a service engineering context due to the highly distributed nature of SOA applications where services are used in different business domains and under different contexts by a variety of stakeholders with little control over the services.

This chapter presents the *User Requirements Notation* (URN) as a means to model and analyze functional and non-functional service requirements. URN, a language standardized by the International Telecommunications Union (ITU-T), combines modeling concepts and notations for goals and intentions (mainly for non-functional requirements, quality attributes, and reasoning about alternatives) and scenarios (mainly for operational requirements, functional requirements, and performance and architectural reasoning) (Amyot, 2003; ITU-T, 2003; ITU-T, 2008a). In this chapter, we will tackle the modeling and analysis of NFRs for SOA from three perspectives, which can be used standalone or preferably combined:

a. The use of **standard URN** for modeling service goals and functions in an integrated way, hence enabling the analysis of NFRs in context. Current tool-supported techniques for scenario execution, strategy evaluation, and performance analysis will be briefly summarized.

b. The use of **aspect-oriented extensions** to URN (AoURN) to better modularize in individual units called *concerns*, different NFRs that can crosscut services or service components.

c. The use of new **NFR-oriented annotations** for service composition. These scenario annotations, based on a taxonomy also introduced in this chapter, enable the specification of quantitative NFR values for services and the computation of the NFR characteristics (e.g., the quality of service) of their composition.

The background section of this chapter provides an overview of URN's and AoURN's basic concepts and notation as well as of SOA. This is followed by a section discussing NFRs including a taxonomy of non-functional properties (NFPs) as well as composition operators and functions for select NFPs. The next section focuses on the use of AoURN-based modeling of composite services, URN-based modeling of NFRs, as well as URN-based analysis techniques for service engineering. URN metadata is employed to define NFR-oriented annotations for service composition, with an emphasis on cost, response time, availability, and reliability. Service composition can be achieved through annotated URN models, which in turn provide the operators needed to compute the quality of composite services. This type of analysis allows modellers to assess compliance with service-level agreements and enables dynamic selection/adaptation of services. The chapter concludes with a discussion of related work, conclusions, and an overview of future work. The simple yet realistic BookItWell composite service will be used throughout the chapter for illustration.

BACKGROUND

User Requirements Notation

URN combines two complementary visual languages: the *Goal-oriented Requirement Language* (GRL) for business goals, (non-functional) requirements, alternatives, decisions and rationales, and the *Use Case Map* (UCM) visual scenario notation for causal flows of behavior superimposed on architectural components. GRL's intentional elements include goals, softgoals, resources, beliefs, and tasks, which can contribute positively or negatively to each other and can be decomposed

in a connected graph. These elements can also be allocated to stakeholders, who may have dependencies as well as conflicting concerns requiring appropriate trade-offs as a result. UCMs model scenarios and use cases related to GRL elements by expressing relationships between responsibilities (such as sequencing, alternatives, concurrency, and decomposition). These responsibilities represent activities that need to be done, and they can be allocated to components describing actors, roles, software modules, network elements, etc. UCM components can be decomposed into subcomponents. Various links between GRL and UCM elements are supported in URN to specify traceability and refinement. URN elements can also be annotated with *metadata*, which are name-value pairs.

GRL and UCMs have successfully been used to model and analyze requirements for various types of systems (e.g., telecommunication, wireless, object-oriented, reactive systems, embedded, agent-base, operating, Web-based, e-business, and e-health), and have more recently been used for business processes modeling, patterns formalization, reverse-engineering, performance engineering, test generation, and architecture evaluations. The URN Virtual Library (2008) offers more than 200 papers and theses reporting on these experiences. The Eclipse plug-in *jUCMNav* (2008) is a graphical editor for URN models that supports the evaluation of GRL goal graphs according to different strategies and the execution or extraction of scenarios in UCMs (Kealey & Amyot, 2007; Roy, Kealey, & Amyot, 2006). The tool enables the combined use of these analysis techniques to help reach suitable tradeoffs among conflicting goals in service engineering, not only at design time (Weiss, Esfandiari & Luo, 2006) but also at runtime (Amyot, Becha, Bræk, & Rossebø, 2008). The notation and the tool also support performance annotations on UCMs that enable the generation of performance models through an intermediate format (Petriu & Woodside, 2005; Petriu & Woodside, 2007). jUCMNav and URN have also

Figure 1. Aspect-oriented use case maps

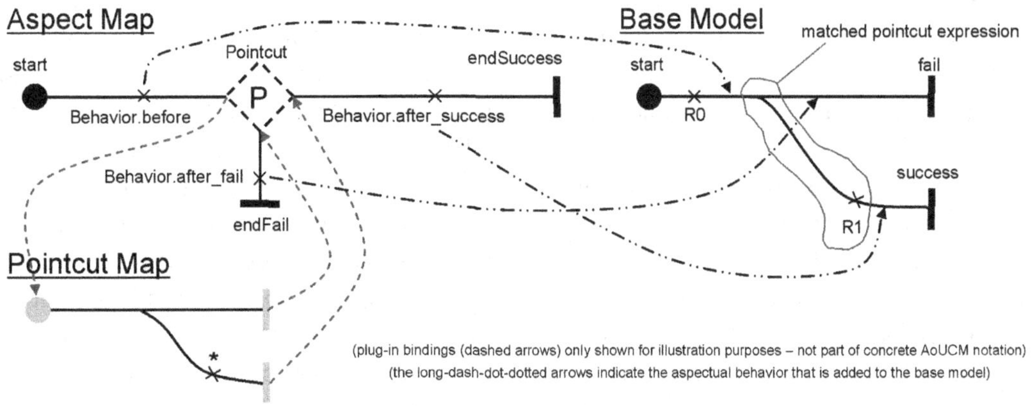

been shown to be suitable for the modeling and management of business process modeling. In particular, extensions to GRL enable the definition of *Key Performance Indicators* (KPIs) that can be used to monitor running business processes and assess whether or not their goals are met (Pour-shahid *et al.*, 2009). The UCM view also exhibits interesting benefits over many other workflow notations, including BPMN and UML activity diagrams (Mussbacher & Amyot, 2008). URN models can also be imported and linked to other types of requirements in a requirements management system (e.g., Telelogic DOORS); this also enables one to assess and maintain compliance with legislation (an important yet often forgotten source of non-functional requirements).

Aspect-Oriented User Requirements Notation

The *Aspect-oriented User Requirements Notation* (AoURN) is a modeling framework that extends URN with aspect-oriented concepts (Mussbacher, 2008). In AoURN, an *aspect* encapsulates cross-cutting concerns by grouping relevant aspectual properties such as goals, behavior, and structure, as well as pointcut expressions and supplementary attributes needed to apply new goal and scenario elements to a base model or to modify existing

elements. A pointcut expression is a pattern that must be matched if the aspect is to be applied. AoURN uses GRL and UCM diagrams to describe pointcut expressions. AoURN adds aspect concepts to views, leading to Aspect-oriented GRL (AoGRL) (Mussbacher *et al.*, 2007a) and Aspect-oriented UCMs (AoUCM) (Mussbacher, Amyot, & Weiss, 2007; Mussbacher *et al.*, 2007b). Concerns and aspects are first-class modeling elements in AoURN. AoURN employs an exhaustive aspect composition technique that can fully transform URN models. With aspects, NFRs can more easily be encapsulated in their own modules and selectively composed.

Our approach makes use of AoUCM which is therefore explained in more detail in Figure 1. UCM pointcut expressions define the pattern to be matched with a *pointcut map*. For example, the pointcut stub in Figure 1 contains one pointcut map that matches against all maps that contain an OR-fork followed by a responsibility on at least one branch. Grey start and end points are not included in the match but only denote the beginning and end of the pointcut expression.

The aspectual properties are shown on a separate *aspect map*. The aspect map is linked to the pointcut expression with the help of a *pointcut stub* (indicated by the P in the dynamic stub symbol). Pointcut stubs are structurally the same as dynamic stubs but have a slightly different semantic meaning. While dynamic stubs contain sub-maps called plug-in maps that further describe the structure and behavior of a system, pointcut stubs contain pointcut maps that visually describe pointcut expressions.

The causal relationship of the pointcut stub and the aspect's properties visually defines the composition rule for the aspect, indicating how the aspect is inserted in the base model (such as before, after, instead of, in parallel, interleaved, or anything else that can be expressed with the UCM notation). For example, the model in Figure 1 defines that the aspectual behavior Behavior. before is added to the base model before the matched pointcut expression.

Service Oriented Architecture

As defined in the OASIS reference model for *Service Oriented Architecture* (SOA), "SOA is a paradigm for organizing and utilizing distributed capabilities that may be under the control of different ownership domains. It provides a uniform means to offer, discover, interact with and use capabilities to produce desired effects consistent with measurable preconditions and expectations" (OASIS, 2006, p. 29). SOA is not tied to any specific technology and does not rely on any particular implementation, although it is commonly implemented using Web Services, being primarily developed by the Organization for the Advancement of Structured Information Standards (OASIS, 2008) and the World Wide Web Consortium (W3C, 2008).

SOA is an architectural style that promotes sharing and reusing software components (i.e. published services). Services are discoverable as service providers publish their services' descriptions in registries. Service consumers can then discover, select, and compose these published services to meet their business process needs.

Services are opaque, that is, service consumers do not have to develop or even understand the underlying logic and implementation details of services they use. Services abstract underlying logic, which means they share nothing but a formal contract that contains only the information required by service consumers to determine whether a given service is appropriate for their needs (including functional and non-functional properties of the service) and the information necessary to interact with the service such as service interfaces, behavior and location.

Services are also composable. As shown in Figure 2, each service may be used to create other services allowing different service granularity and abstraction layers. Ideally, services have to be stripped of specific business logic or usage in order to be generic enough to be reused in different contexts and business domains by different stakeholders. Service composition (or service orchestration) is this capability of combining atomic or composite services into larger composite services. This is achieved by defining the sequence and conditions in which one higher-level service invokes other services in order to realize a more complex business function. In a SOA, an application is developed as a composition of shared services selected and combined to satisfy a given business process. Whenever a required service does not exist within and outside of the organization, its functionality may be added as part of service composition or a new service may be created for others to reuse.

Adoption of SOA brings the promise of increased interoperability, agility, and flexibility. The ability to reuse services either internally developed or provided by third parties often speeds up applications' development time in comparison with present long-established, tightly-coupled, monolithic environments. SOA is based on standardized messaging protocols between services decoupled from the computing platforms, which eases the integration of disparate computing systems.

However, SOA raises new challenges including SOA governance, the granularity level of services

Figure 2. Composition of services

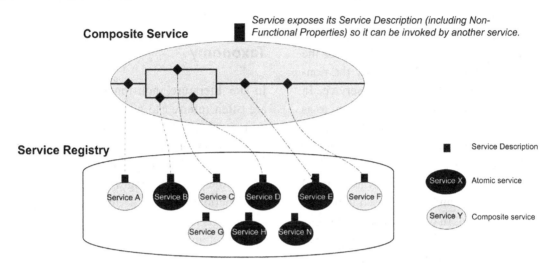

(i.e., fine-grained services cause too many message exchanges, coarse-grained services hinder reusability), standards compliance, explicit Service Level Agreements (SLAs), SLA negotiation, SLA monitoring, and testing.

Using externally developed services, provided and managed by third parties, is of a particular interest. This allows service providers to offer new functionalities for which resources and expertise are not necessarily available internally. On the other hand, the ability to predict the behavior and characteristics of the resulting composite service without resorting to tight binding to the underlying services can be difficult. Hence, it is essential to establish SLAs to guarantee the quality of third parties' services. The following section focus on the non-functional properties of services.

NON-FUNCTIONAL PROPERTIES

This section first gives an overview of *non-functional properties* (NFPs) in the context of Service Oriented Architecture. Then, a taxonomy of sixteen NFPs is introduced to describe common non-functional characteristics that a service should expose as part of its description for SLA

establishment. The definitions are adapted from various sources, including software quality standards. Also, we have introduced our specific definitions to facilitate the understanding of these terms in the context of this chapter's problematics. Furthermore, our framework for handling NFPs of atomic and composite services defines common composition operators in the context of SOA as well as composition functions for each composition operator and NFP.

Overview

Non-functional requirements are of critical importance and, at times, functional requirements might be sacrificed to meet them (Galster & Bucherer, 2008). In general, dealing with NFRs is difficult since it is often hard to determine whether they are met, and they often contradict each other and impact functional requirements when conflicts are solved.

In the SOA context, NFRs are even more difficult to handle than in traditional software engineering due to the highly distributed nature of SOA applications. In traditional software engineering, stakeholders play an important role in expressing explicitly or implicitly the NFRs of their application, and then verifying and validating the implementation of these requirements at various stages of the application's life-cycle. In service-based applications, the NFRs of the application are directly influenced by the non-functional properties (NFPs) of the service. In the literature, NFPs are quite often referred to as Quality of Service (QoS) criteria. In SOA, services consumers are often not involved in any stage of the development phase of the services. Services are used as black boxes (i.e., services are opaque) and their behavior cannot be assessed until they are actually invoked. In contrast with traditional application development processes, these NFPs are not applied to and assessed against an application as a whole but against multiple independent distributed services, leading to additional challenges.

NFPs play an important role in each stage of the SOA process lifecycle such as in the discovery, selection, and substitution of services. This is due to the accessibility of multiple services that can deliver the same functionality, with their NFPs as only differentiators. Consequently, the ability of service consumers to choose services based on their NFPs is crucial.

In a composite service, the services used in the composition, their NFPs, and the manner in which they are composed have a direct effect on the NFPs of the composite service. The relationship between NFPs of a composite service and the services of which it is built can be complex. For example, it is not true that if all of the services in a composite service have 90% availability, then the resulting availability of the composite service is 90%.

Proper handling of NFPs of services in SOA implies, first, that atomic services need to expose a number of NFPs and, second, that these NFPs be composable since service composition is at the heart of SOA's services sharing and reusing principle. Composition techniques should ensure a proficient atomic service selection and adequate NFPs computation of the composite service. Without first-class citizens' treatment of NFPs,

SOA cannot easily be adopted in mission critical applications.

Taxonomy

In the literature, non-functional requirements are often referred to as qualities of an application. Other terms often used for non-functional requirements include "constraints", "quality attributes", "quality goals", and "quality of service requirements". Building applications satisfying the functional as well as the non-functional requirements is vital for the success of applications in many domains.

In service-based applications, NFPs of services drive the design of the composed applications and the selection of the concrete services of which they are composed. NFPs when defined clearly and well managed benefit both services providers and services consumers. Service providers that handle the NFPs of their services well will contribute positively to an increased use of their offered services and, consequently, to a better reputation and larger financial gain. For service consumers, relying on services with well handled NFPs will impact directly the quality and hence the success of their applications and systems.

Service providers supply an SLA for each service, where they guarantee the service consumers a certain level of service in return for a specified payment. A SLA includes the conditions of the outsourcing service to be provided, the quality of service, how this quality is measured, and the penalties to the provider if the service quality is not met. A SLA has to address not only the functional but also the non-functional aspects of the service. When a service-based application is developed, it must take into account various tradeoffs of NFPs.

The aim of the following taxonomy is to define a list of generic NFPs to be considered when SLAs are developed in SOA. Specific business rules will drive the selection of appropriate NFPs to be considered out of the ones that we propose below. Additional domain-specific properties might also be needed. The focus is on what services should expose as part of their descriptions to guarantee a certain NFP level of the service-based applications as a whole. Hence, the NFPs at the network infrastructure level are out of scope. We assume that other service contracts govern the network usage between the provider and the consumer. In other words, the service provider-consumer contract is dependent on the networking service contracts and enforceability is conditional on the network service contracts.

Our taxonomy is composed of the following concepts. The first four are explained in more detail as they will be used in our service composition example, whereas the others are more briefly described due to space constraints:

a. **Cost** is the fee that the service consumer has to pay for invoking a given service. This amount can be fixed or, more likely, calculated by a function based on the input (e.g., when a "back-up storage" service is called, the total cost could be calculated based on the number or the size of files that this service is invoked against. A second example of input is "location" for the "make a call" service). Other business models are possible such as "all you can use" for a monthly or yearly payment. Price can vary based on the quality of the service including response time, method of payment etc.

b. **Performance** represents how fast a service provider responds to requests. The performance property can be described in quality sub-factors such as *response time* (e.g., process queries in less than 30 seconds 95% of the time), *throughput* (e.g., on average 15 requests processed per minute), *threshold* quality (e.g., maximum number of messages exchanged per minute), and *timeliness* (e.g., the guarantee to process a request within a deterministic amount of time units). Response time is the most important aspect to be added to the service description

since the service consumer can verify it. In addition, the response time depends on the throughput, threshold, and other relevant qualities. Response time is the number of time units reflecting the duration of the execution of a given service calculated starting at the moment the service consumer invokes the service and terminated when the service's desired real effect takes place. Response time can be estimated as a bounded interval taking into account the invoked service's input (e.g., response time could be estimated based on the size of files that the "back-up storage" service is invoked against) and the transmission time (e.g., latency and throughput of the communication links).

c. **Availability** is the probability of an item to be in a state to perform a required function at a given instant of time or at any instant of time within a given time interval, assuming that the external resources, if required, are provided (ITU-T, 2007). Often reported in terms of probability that a service is accessible and operational when required for use, the value of service availability is computed by dividing the number of units (i.e., time or number of invocations) in which the service was available during the last Δ units (time or invocations) by Δ, where Δ is a constant that depends on the domain.

d. **Reliability** is the ability of a system or component to perform its required functions under stated conditions for a specified period of time (ITU-T, 2008b). Often reported in terms of probability that a system operates correctly (i.e., without failure or unacceptable degradation of performance) under given conditions for a specified period of time. We focus on the reliability of the services, as the reliability of the network is out of the scope for this chapter. Service reliability is the success execution rate of a given service based on its past invocations. Whenever a given service fails, the failure mode (i.e., how to handle the failure best, defined below) of the service comes into play. Service reliability can be linked to service trust. Note that a service can have low reliability but have high availability and vice-versa. The value of service reliability is computed by dividing the number of successful executions by the total number of invocations for a given period of time.

e. **Trust** is a measurement of the reputation (i.e., overall quality) of a given service. It mainly depends on the level of satisfaction of previous users.

f. **Usability** is a measure of the quality of a service consumer's experience including the ease-of-use (i.e., required input format for invoking and interacting with the service) and the reuse of the services (i.e., service granularity for business suitability).

g. **Accuracy** is the degree of correctness with which the function is performed. The function may or may not be performed with the desired speed or precision.

h. **Standards compliance** is the list of standards to which the service claims to comply (e.g., reliable messaging or security standards).

i. **Scalability** captures the number of simultaneous service instances that can be supported without degradation of the service level below an agreed level.

j. **Failure mode** is a description of what is done when something goes wrong. Different classes of failure modes for services are needed since there is no single failure mode that will be adequate for every domain. Services have to publish a) the failure and recovery type (e.g., crash-only (Hobbs, Becha, & Amyot, 2008)), b) whether the service is idempotent (i.e., a service, when invoked multiple times, has no further effect on its subject after the first time it is performed), c) rollback capability, and d) the anticipated (modeled or measured) failure distribution.

k. **Security** includes the measures of privacy, confidentiality, authenticity, and integrity (i.e., information is not corrupted). Services should address the following functionalities: data privacy and confidentiality, authorization, authentication, data integrity, auditing, user identity management, single sign-on, password policy, and non-repudiation.

l. **Execution Model**: The service should expose whether it a) supports a transactional model with automated roll-back on error execution, b) uses a publish/subscribe model, or c) uses a request/reply model.

m. **Jurisdiction**: With the ever-increasing need for systems to comply with regulatory legislation, services should expose their countries of jurisdiction to reflect the presumably respected legal obligations (e.g., privacy laws).

n. **Life-cycle updates**: The SOA registry (see service registry in Figure 2) is continually evolving. A service should therefore expose whether future updates will cause changes to its interface.

o. **Penalty rate**: Whenever the contract is breached by a consumer, a penalty is charged to his account (e.g., cancelling a hotel reservation 48 hours before the intended arrival date).

p. **Compensation rate**: Whenever a service provider was not up to the promise stated in the SLA, compensation is added to the consumer's account (e.g., an airline will pay 100 EUR for baggage missing on arrival at destination).

Composition Operators

The following five composition operators are commonly found in the description of composite services (Figure 3 shows the UCM notational elements that represent these operators, where services are captured with *stubs* visualized with

Figure 3. Visual representation of composition operators in UCM

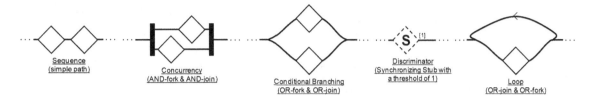

diamond symbols; note that all of these operators can be combined):

1. **Sequence:** All services placed in series are invoked and the result of each service is needed (i.e., the failure of any service results in the failure of the composite service).

2. **Concurrency:** Two or more services placed in parallel are invoked concurrently and the results of all services are needed. Usually these services have different but complementary tasks – hence the need for synchronization.

3. **Conditional branching:** Only one service out of two or more services is invoked depending on the result of branching conditions.

4. **Discriminator:** Two or more equivalent services are invoked in parallel to achieve a given task but only one is required to finish before proceeding with the composite service. We presume that these services are equivalent in terms of functionalities but different from the perspective of their NFPs. The results of the first service to finish are used while the results of the remaining invoked services are ignored. At least one service of the invoked services must succeed for the composite service to succeed. The UCM notational symbol used to model a discriminator is the synchronizing stub (ITU-T, 2008a) as indicated by the S in the stub symbol in Figure 3. A synchronizing stub executes all of its plug-in maps in parallel and continues when as many plug-in maps have

finished as defined by the threshold of the stub's exit. In the case of the discriminator, this threshold needs to be set to 1.

5. **Loop:** One or more services can be part of a "cycle" in the composite service. These services will be invoked as many times as needed until a given loop condition is satisfied. All invoked services that are part of the loop must succeed as many times as they are invoked for the composite service to succeed. For composition of NFPs, the maximum number of invocations must be known.

Composition of Cost, Response Time, Reliability, and Availability

For the sake of simplicity of our example, we have chosen four properties from our taxonomy to illustrate our framework. These properties are generic enough to be applied in different domains but sufficiently complicated to illustrate trade-offs between NFPs. For each of the four properties, we now define its composition function in Table 1 for each of the previously defined composition operators.

For our example, we assume that the *cost* is a fixed amount of dollars per service invocation. *Response time* is a bounded interval but we will rely only on the upper bound as we take a pessimistic view. *Reliability* and *availability* are expressed as percentages, between 0 and 1 inclusively. In general, the composition functions take a pessimistic view of the composite service.

Table 1. Composition functions for NFPs

	Cost	Response Time	Reliability	Availability
Sequence	$\sum_{i=1}^{n} C_i$	$\sum_{i=1}^{n} T_i$	$\prod_{i=1}^{n} R_i$	
Concurrency	$\sum_{i=1}^{n} C_i$	$\max(T_1 \dots T_n)$	$\prod_{i=1}^{n} R_i$	
Conditional branching	$\max(C_1 \dots C_n)$	$\max(T_1 \dots T_n)$	$\min(R_1 \dots R_n)$	Same as reliability but with A_i instead of R_i
Discriminator	$\sum_{i=1}^{n} C_i$	$\max(T_1 \dots T_n)$	$1 - \prod_{i=1}^{n}(1 - R_i)$	
Loop (m is the max. nr. of iterations)	$m * \sum_{i=1}^{n} C_i$	$m * \sum_{i=1}^{n} T_i$	$(\prod_{i=1}^{n} R_i)^m$	

n is the number of services composed with the composition operator.
C_i, T_i, R_i, and A_i are the metrics for the ith service composed with the composition operator.

The sequence operator requires us to take all individual services into account (cost and response time need to be added but the percentages of reliability and availability need to be multiplied). The reliability and availability of a composite service are equal to the product of the reliabilities and availabilities of its underlying services, respectively. This is similar to determining the probability of rolling double sixes with dice. The first service corresponds to the probability of rolling a six from the first die (1/6) and the service corresponds to the probability of rolling a six from the second die (1/6). Since both must happen, they are in a sequence configuration with a probability of 1/36. Services are assumed independent of each other, and can each fail independently at their respective reliabilities rate.

The concurrency operator also needs to take all individual services into account except for response time for which the maximum is taken. The conditional branching operator only has to take the chosen service into account. It assumes that the worst case occurs, and therefore selects the service with the highest cost, longest response time, and lowest reliability as well as availability. The discriminator operator adds cost since all individual services are invoked and assumes

that only the individual service with the longest response time succeeds (the worst case). Reliability and availability are calculated as the chance of all individual services failing and then taking the complement of it, because this is similar to determining the probability of rolling a six on either die, when rolling two dice. This is calculated easiest by determining the probability of not rolling a six at all and taking the complement of that. The first service corresponds to the probability of not rolling a six from the first die (5/6) and the second service corresponds to the probability of not rolling a six from the second die (5/6). Since both must happen, the probability is 25/36 and the complement is then 11/36.

Finally, the loop operator is the same as the sequence operator except multiplied by or to the power of the maximal number of iterations.

URN-BASED SERVICE SELECTION AND COMPOSITION

This section introduces step-by-step our approach to service selection and service composition based on the User Requirements Notation (URN) and the framework for measuring and composing various non-functional properties (NFPs) as introduced in the previous section. The approach is illustrated with an example of a composite service called BookItWell, adapted from the example of Hobbs and Storrie (2007), and provided by DriveALot Inc. BookItWell endeavors to book accommodation for a subscriber based on the subscriber's geographic location, today's weather forecast, and the subscriber's planned activities for today and tomorrow. DriveALot has orchestrated the underlying services into a business process. Each of the underlying services may themselves be composed of lower-level services, but this is of no interest to DriveALot. BookItWell is both a provider (to DriveALot's subscribers) and a consumer (of other providers' services). Although the service and company are fictitious, all of the components exist and several related services are already available from various service providers.

Our approach consists of the seven following steps, after which aspect-oriented extensions are presented that better modularize crosscutting concerns. At the end of this section, the automation of these steps is discussed.

Model Composite Service with UCM (1)

In the first step, a composite service is modeled based on its required abstract services with the Use Case Map (UCM) notation. Abstract services are represented as static stubs (diamonds) that are composed with each other using the UCM-equivalents of the composition operators defined earlier. As shown in Figure 4, the BookItWell composite service is built by combining six services provided independently by different companies: location, weather forecasting, calendar, hotel booking, motel booking, and route calculation.

First, the location of the user is determined with the help of a Location service. Given the location, a Weather Forecast service is invoked for today's forecast. In parallel, the Calendar service of the user is queried to retrieve location

Figure 4. The BookItWell composite service

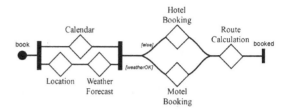

and time information of any planned activities for today and the next day. Based on the weather forecast and the schedules, BookItWell will either book a more expensive hotel or a cheap motel. The Hotel Booking service is used if the weather does not allow any scheduled outdoor activities. The Motel Booking service is used if the weather permits the planned activities. In both cases, the locations of the planned activities are taken into account when booking accommodation. Finally, the Route Calculation service provides directions to the planned activities and the chosen accommodation.

At this point, the modeler may consider adding additional functionality to the composite service, e.g., for integrity checks before and after the booking services, for billing functionality, for after-the-fact auditing features, and for redundancy in case of potentially unavailable services as described in the next step.

Model Additional Functionality with UCM (2)

Figure 5 shows the complete model of the composite service including additional functionality. Integrity checks were added for the Hotel and Motel Booking services. First, a snapshot of the system state (mem) is taken and then compared against the system state after the service completed (che). If the check fails, the matched service is reset before retrying at the most three times. Billing functionality (add) is required after each service to add the service fee to the service provider's account and to the bill of the user. Just before the

Figure 5. The complete BookItWell composite service

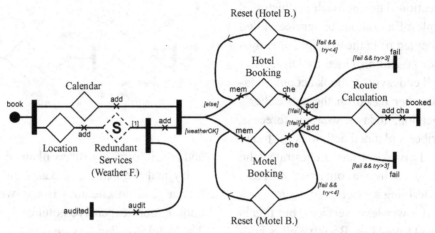

Abbreviations: add … both addTo… responsibilities from Billing; cha … chargeUser; che … check; mem … memento

end of the composite service, the user is charged (cha) the amount added to the user's bill (plus a margin of course).

Furthermore, some services may be known to be not sufficiently reliable. This applies to the Weather Forecast service in our example, and it is therefore changed to a redundant service with the help of a synchronizing stub (i.e., several concrete Weather Forecast services will be started in parallel to ensure quality of service). In addition, a concurrent audit service (audit) is added after the Weather Forecast service to ensure that not too much money is spent on running several Weather Forecast services in parallel). At this point, neither the actual concrete services nor their NFPs are captured by the UCM model. The next step takes care of this.

Populate Abstract Services with Concrete Services (3)

Based on the description of services in registries, the abstract services in the UCM model can be augmented with the concrete offerings for each abstract service. As abstract services are modeled with stubs in the UCM model, the concrete services for an abstract service are modeled as plug-in maps

for the stub. The example in Figure 6 shows that three concrete Location services were found in the registry. A stub with more than one plug-in map is called *dynamic* and shown with a dashed outline. In addition, each plug-in map (i.e., each concrete service) is annotated with the metrics of its NFPs as retrieved from the registry. Metadata in the form of name/value pairs is used to capture the NFPs (e.g., <<cost = 3>> is attached to the first plug-in map in Figure 6). Each plug-in map has a condition which must evaluate to true for the plug-in map to be selected when its stub is reached in the composite service. By default, the condition of a plug-in map of a dynamic stub is set to false for all concrete services. The condition of a plug-in map for a static stub is set to true because only one plug-in map exists for a static stub (i.e., there is only one option for the service which will have to be selected).

The concrete services of all abstract services of the BookItWell example are listed with their NFPs in Table 2. Since more than one Location and Hotel Booking service exists, the static stubs that model these two services are now changed to dynamic stubs. The Calendar, Motel Booking, and Route Calculation stubs, however, remain static because only one concrete service exists for

Figure 6. Concrete services for the abstract location service

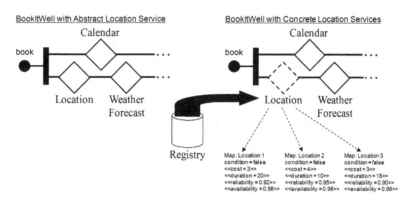

each one of them. The question that remains at this point is which one of the concrete services to choose if there is a choice (e.g., it is not clear which one of the three location services is the best choice)? For this purpose, the NFPs of the service candidates need to be evaluated because the functionalities of the candidates are equivalent.

Model NFPs with GRL (4)

In the fourth step, a goal model is created with the Goal-oriented Requirement Language (GRL). The goal model describes the impact of NFP metrics on high-level goals of the stakeholder of

the composite service (see Figure 7), thereby facilitating tradeoffs between high-level goals. In this GRL model, *intentional elements* are linked together using contribution links. Elements are called intentional because they carry stakeholder intentions. Contribution links indicate the impact of intentional elements on each other – in this case, positive qualitative contributions are shown. Two types of intentional elements have been used in this model. Soft goals (�, e.g., Cost) describe something to be achieved that cannot be measured quantitatively but is of a qualitative nature, while Key Performance Indicators (KPIs) (⬡, e.g., Metric: Response Time) indicate metrics of the

Table 2. Summary of concrete services

Concrete Service	Cost	Response Time	Reliability	Availability
Location L1	3	20	0.92	0.98
Location L2	4	10	0.95	0.98
Location L3	3	15	0.90	0.98
Calendar C1	3	10	0.90	0.98
Weather Forecast WF1	3	20	0.80	0.70
Weather Forecast WF2	3	20	0.90	0.60
Weather Forecast WF3	5	33	0.95	0.40
Weather Forecast WF4	6	18	0.95	0.20
Hotel Booking HB1	3	15	0.90	0.92
Hotel Booking HB2	2	10	0.90	0.90
Motel Booking MB1	2	13	0.95	0.90
Route Calculation RC1	3	10	0.90	0.95

Figure 7. The GRL model of NFPs

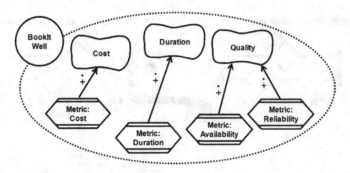

system. *Intentional elements* may be assigned to stakeholders called *actors* (⌒, e.g., BookItWell).

The BookItWell example is rather simplistic as it only shows the cost metric influencing the high-level cost goal, the response time metric influencing the high level response time goal, and both, reliability and availability metrics, influencing the high-level quality goal. Arguably, GRL graphs are not required for a model like this. However, besides the metrics based on our framework for measuring and composing various NFPs, other factors that impact high-level goals may be modeled with GRL. These extensions will be investigated in future work (see last section). To decide which particular service to choose, the BookItWell actor needs to be evaluated given the metrics for the particular service. This is discussed in the next step.

Each metric is modeled as a Key Performance Indicator (KPI) in the GRL model. KPIs allow metrics to be normalized to the scale ranging from -100 to 100 that is used by the GRL model. For each metric, a target value (the best possible) and a worst value must be defined as well as a threshold value that lies somewhere between the target and the worst value and identifies the 0 value in the scale used by GRL. These values have to be established based on the requirements of the company providing the composite service. For the BookItWell example, the values in Table 3 were defined for the four chosen NFPs.

Evaluate NFPs of Concrete Services with GRL (5)

In the fifth step, the goal model is evaluated with the GRL evaluation mechanism that propagates initial satisfaction values of the KPIs defined in a GRL strategy to satisfaction values of goals and eventually actors. GRL strategies are created for each abstract service with multiple concrete service options. One GRL strategy describes one possible configuration of concrete services. This enables the evaluation of each concrete service and the comparison of concrete services. One GRL strategy is created per concrete service of a dynamic stub, as only one out of the possible concrete services is to be selected for the composite service. For synchronizing stubs, however, one GRL strategy is created per combination of concrete services, as a group of concrete services out of the possible services is to be selected for the composite service. Therefore in the BookItWell example, three GRL strategies are created for the three location services (i.e., one for each service),

Table 3. KPI target, threshold, and worst case values

NFP (unit)	Target	Threshold	Worst
Cost ($)	0	5	15
Response Time (sec)	1	20	35
Reliability (%)	0.99999	0.9	0.8
Availability (%)	0.99999	0.9	0.8

Figure 8. Evaluated GRL model for the first location service

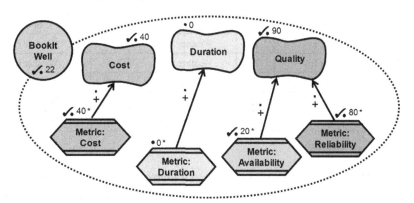

two strategies are created for the two hotel booking services (i.e., one for each service), and 15 GRL strategies are created for the four weather forecasting services to cover all possible combinations (i.e., 4 strategies with one service each, 6 strategies with two services each, 4 strategies with three services each, and 1 strategy with all four services). This is feasible since the number of service is not expected to be in the dozens.

For example, the GRL strategy for the first location service in the BookItWell example sets the satisfaction value for the KPI Cost to 40 (given 3 for the NFP cost defined in Table 2 and since the target value of 0 and the threshold value of 5 defined in Table 3 are mapped to 100 and 0, respectively, by the normalization of KPI values). Analogously, the satisfaction value for the KPI Response Time is set to 0 (given 20 for the NFP response time), for the KPI Reliability to 20 (given 0.92 for the NFP reliability), and for the KPI Availability to 80 (given 0.98 for the NFP availability). See KPIs marked with * in Figure 8. For the strategies based on a combination of services as is the case for the weather forecast services, the NFPs of the individual services first have to be combined using the composition functions defined earlier – in this case, the functions for the discriminator. Given the satisfaction values for the KPIs, the GRL evaluation mechanism then calculates the values of the goals and the actor (22

in the example). GRL also allows for an importance attribute to be specified for the high-level goals of an actor which influences the final evaluation of the actor. In the BookItWell example, however, all goals have the same importance.

The results of the evaluation of all location services, all hotel booking services, and all combinations of weather forecasting services are shown in Table 4 with the best choice for each service highlighted. The services or combination of services with an X as the result are below the worst case for one of the NFPs and are therefore not even considered (e.g., the first weather forecasting service has an availability of 0.70 which is beyond the specified worst value of 0.80; similarly, the combination of all four weather forecasting services has a cost of 3+3+5+6=17 which is beyond the specified worst value of 15).

Select Concrete Services (6)

Step 6 uses a shortest path approach to select concrete services (i.e., each stub in the composite service is addressed individually one after the other). A static stub does not require any decision because only one concrete service exists in this case. The conditions of plug-in maps of dynamic and synchronizing stubs, however, need to be defined based on the results of the evaluation from the fifth step. Setting the condition of a plug-in

Table 4. Evaluation results (ER) for location, hotel booking, and weather forecasting services

Services	ER	Services	ER	Services	ER	Services	ER
Location 1	22	Weather F. 1	X	Weather F. 1/3	-18	Weather F. 1/2/3	-9
Location 2	27	Weather F. 2	X	Weather F. 1/4	X	Weather F. 1/2/4	3
Location 3	24	Weather F. 3	X	Weather F. 2/3	X	Weather F. 1/3/4	-20
Hotel B. 1	14	Weather F. 4	X	Weather F. 2/4	X	Weather F. 2/3/4	-28
Hotel B. 2	19	Weather F. 1/2	8	Weather F. 3/4	X	Weather F. 1/2/3/4	X

map to true essentially selects the concrete service the plug-in map represents (e.g., Location 2, Hotel Booking 2, and Weather Forecast 1 and 2).

Calculate NFPs for the Composite Service (7)

The final step of our approach calculates the NFP metrics for the composite service from the selected individual services. This is a straightforward process if the UCM model of the composite service is well-structured. If it is not, as is the case for the BookItWell example, heuristics have to be employed to be able to parse the UCM model and get the composition formula. Based on UCM slicing techniques in Hassine, Dssouli, & Rilling (2005), the approach taken in this case is to start exploring from the expected end of the composite service (the booked end point) and traverse the UCM model in a backward direction until the start point book is reached. Fail cases and spawned off parallel branches that do not impact the end result of the composite service are not traversed and therefore avoided. The resulting formula derived by parsing the sliced UCM is:

Result = Sequence (Part1, Part2, Part3);
Part1 = Concurrent {C1, Sequence [L2, add, Discriminator (WF1, WF2), add]};
Part2 = Conditional Branching (Branch1, Branch2);
Branch1 = Sequence [mem, HB2, che, Loop$_2$ (Reset-HB2, mem, HB2, che), add];

Branch2 = Sequence [mem, MB1, che, Loop$_2$ (Reset-MB1, mem, MB1, che), add];
Part3 = Sequence (RC1, add, cha);

Finally, the NFP metrics of the selected concrete services are plugged into this formula and the overall NFP metrics for the composite service are established based on the computation functions in Table 1. The following is the formula for reliability and availability:

Result = $\prod$ (Part1, Part2, Part3);
Part1 = $\prod$ {C1, $\prod$ [L2, add, 1 - $\prod$ (1-WF1, 1-WF2), add]};
Part2 = min (Branch1, Branch2);
Branch1 = $\prod$ [mem, HB2, che, ($\prod$ (Reset-HB2, mem, HB2, che))^2, add];
Branch2 = $\prod$ [mem, MB1, che, ($\prod$ (Reset-MB1, mem, MB1, che))^2, add];
Part3 = $\prod$ (RC1, add, cha);

The calculation of the NFPs for the composed service requires NFPs to be defined for the responsibilities introduced in step 2 by annotating the responsibilities with metadata. As the company in our example has total control over these responsibilities, the values of these NFPs are more easily established. In our example, each one of the responsibilities add, cha, che, and mem is deemed to have a cost of 0, a response time of 1, 0.99999 reliability, and 0.99999 availability. Resetting a service is also assumed to have the same NFP values. Therefore, given the individual NFPs defined in Table 2 for the concrete services selected

Figure 9. Crosscutting concerns for the BookItWell composite service

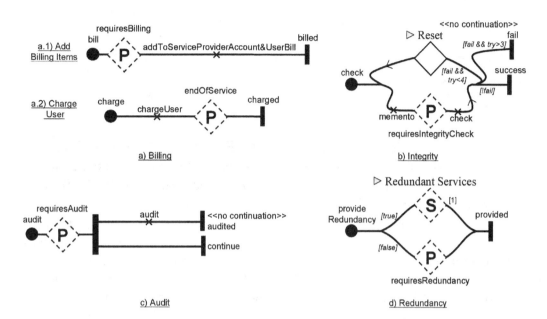

in step 6, the NFP cost for the overall composite service is 22, response time is 72, reliability is 0.54967, and availability is 0.58523.

AO Extension: Model Crosscutting Concerns with AoUCM (A1)

In the second step, integrity checks, billing functionality, auditing features, and redundancy features were added explicitly to the URN model in the same way as abstract services in Figure 4, but their crosscutting nature makes them perfect candidates for aspect-oriented modeling with the help of Aspect-oriented UCM (AoUCM) as described in steps A1 to A3. These steps replace the second step and model each identified crosscutting concern with the Aspect-oriented UCM (AoUCM) notation. In the case of the BookItWell example, the required crosscutting concerns are Billing, Integrity, Audit, and Redundancy as shown in Figure 9. These crosscutting concerns are modeled in a generic way and are therefore applicable to many different composite services. The pointcut stubs (the diamonds with the P inside) represent

in a generic way abstract services in a composite service that meet certain matching criteria. In the next step of the aspect-oriented extensions to our approach, the matching criteria are customized to BookItWell, thus applying the crosscutting concerns to our example.

The Billing aspect (Figure 9a) consists of two sub-aspects. The first adds functionality after a service requiring billing. The fee for the service charged by the service provider is added to the service provider's account and the same amount is added to the bill of the user. The second adds further functionality before the end of the composite service to charge the user the amount added to the user's bill (plus a margin of course).

The Integrity aspect (Figure 9b) takes a snapshot of the system state (memento) before a service requiring an integrity check and then compares the snapshot against the system state (check) after the service completed. If the check fails, the matched service is reset before retrying at the most three times (note how the matched service is reused by the Integrity aspect with the help of a URN link indicated by the small shaded

Figure 10. Pointcut expressions for the crosscutting concerns

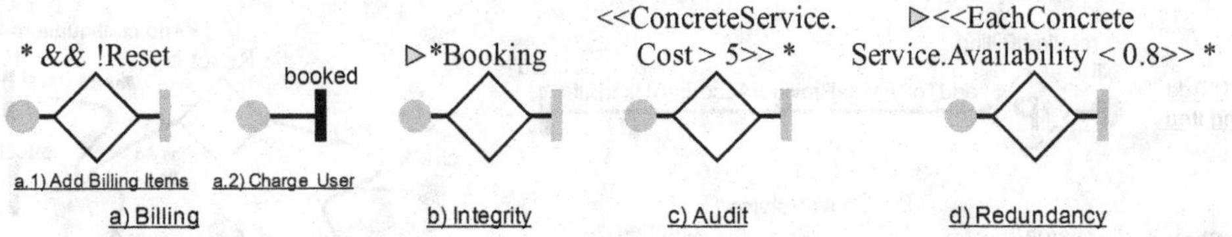

triangle; the Reset keyword indicates that the reset functionality of the matched service is invoked instead of the actual matched service). The loop counter is initially zero and increased by one by the memento responsibility. After the third try, the service fails and the composite service stops at the end point as indicated by <<no continuation>>.

The Audit aspect (Figure 9c), an internal process of DriveALot, starts the Audit service in parallel to the composite service and after the service requiring an audit. The Audit service aims to investigate selections of high-cost services after-the-fact to avoid them in the future. The end point of the branch with the Audit service is tagged as <<no continuation>>, since the composite service does not continue at this point but at the other end point. Note that an improved Audit aspect could verify upon completion of an individual service if the service provider violated its SLA.

Finally, the Redundancy aspect (Figure 9d) starts a number of redundant services as indicated by the discriminator stub on the true branch instead of the service requiring redundancy (as it is located on the false branch). The true and false branches are AoUCM's way of modeling replacement (i.e., an aspect replaces existing behavior with its own behavior). When the Redundancy aspect is applied, the false branch is often not shown as it represents the replaced behavior and will never be traversed. Similar to the Integrity aspect, the Redundancy aspect reuses the matched service with the help of the URN link to indicate that the matched abstract service needs to be composed in a redundant way.

AO Extension: Model Pointcut Expressions for Crosscutting Concerns with AoUCM (A2)

A pointcut expression makes a generic aspect specific to the composite service under design by describing the matching criteria as shown in Figure 10. The third step of our approach requires pointcut expressions to be defined for each crosscutting concern applicable to the composite service under design.

For the BookItWell example, the pointcut expression for the requiresBilling pointcut stub of the Billing aspect matches against any abstract service except those named Reset (since the wildcard * matches against any name). Therefore, after all services except one the billing functionality defined by the Billing aspect is performed. The pointcut expression for the endOfService pointcut stub matches against the end point booked. Therefore, the user is charged just before the end of the composite service. The pointcut expression of the Integrity aspect matches against any abstract service with a name ending in Booking. Therefore, the preconditions and postconditions of the Hotel Booking and the Motel Booking services can be verified to ensure that correct amounts have been charged for the booking. The URN link ensures that the matched booking service is reset if the integrity check fails.

The pointcut expressions of the Audit and Redundancy aspects illustrate another dimension of the matching capabilities of AoUCM by using the non-functional properties (NFPs) of services for the match. The Audit aspect matches against any abstract service if the NFP cost of at least one of its concrete services is greater than five units. The Redundancy aspect, on the other hand, matches against any abstract service if the NFP availability for each of its concrete services is less than 0.8 units (80%). The URN link ensures that the matched services are used in the discriminator in the Redundancy aspect. These pointcut expressions are formulated with concrete services and their NFPs in mind and codify the reasons for adding Audit and Redundancy features to the composite service instead of relying on the modelers knowledge and intuition as in step 2.

AO Extension: Apply Aspects to the Composite Service (A3)

As the pointcut expressions make use of the NFPs of concrete services, the aspects need to be applied to the composite service after step 3 as only this step introduces concrete services into the UCM model. The aspects also need to be applied before the evaluation in step 5 since aspects may add further services and functionalities to the composite service or even restructure the composite service. Step A3 uses the aspect composition algorithm of AoURN to apply the aspects to the composite service given the pointcut expressions. The end result is identical to the complete model in Figure 5 (except that the Location and Hotel Booking stubs are dynamic because step 3 has already been executed). As aspects may interact with each other in undesirable ways, an ordering of aspect defines which aspect is applied when. For the BookItWell example, the Redundancy aspect must be applied first and the Integrity aspect applied last. Therefore, the Weather Forecast stub was replaced by the RedundantServices stub in the resulting composite service (see Figure 5) because all concrete Weather Forecast services have an NFP availability of less than 0.8. Note that the RedundantServices stub now contains the same concrete services as the Weather Forecast stub. Billing functionality is included after each

stub except when resetting a service (i.e., after Location, Calendar, RedundantServices, Hotel Booking, Motel Booking, and Route Calculation), and additional billing functionality is added just before the booked end point. The parallel Audit service is added after the RedundantServices stub because it contains the fourth concrete Weather Forecast service which has an NFP cost greater than five. Finally, the loop of the Integrity service is added around the Hotel Booking and Motel Booking stubs.

The composed system showcases the powerful aspect composition mechanism of AoUCM. For example, instead of adding the billing functionality explicitly after each service, a simple pointcut expression achieves the same effect but allows individual maps to remain simple. Furthermore, the UCM model can be visualized in an aspect-oriented way that does not require the complicated composed model in Figure 5 (not shown here due to space constraints, see Mussbacher (2008)).

Automation of URN-Based Approach to Service Selection and Composition

The first three steps as well as the sixth step (modeling the composite service and the GRL model) only need to be done once, while the remaining steps should be redone on a regular basis to take into account the dynamic nature of the registry. Steps 1, 2, 3, and 6 cannot be automated but the remaining steps can be. Current tool support by jUCMNav, however, does not allow full automation of our approach at this point. The following extensions to jUCMNav are required:

1. retrieving concrete services from the registry to create plug-in maps for them in the UCM model (step 4),

2. the application of aspects is at a prototyping stage and not yet released in the official version of jUCMNav (step 5),

3. establishing GRL strategies and initial satisfaction values based on the annotations of plug-in maps (step 7),
4. setting the condition of plug-in maps to true based on the evaluation of GRL strategies (step 8), and
5. parsing the UCM model to get the formula for the NFPs of the composite service and calculating the NFPs for the composite service (step 9).

RELATED WORK AND FUTURE TRENDS

Galster and Bucherer (2008) recognize the critical importance and the difficulties associated with handling NFPs in general and the fact that they are even more difficult to handle in the SOA context. The authors attempt to provide an extensive generic checklist of various NFPs to be considered when atomic or composite services are under development. However, they do not provide any operational representations or metrics to evaluate these NFPs. In addition, they do not investigate the composability of these NFPs.

Milanovic, Milic, and Malek (2008) focus on modeling business process availability. They map dependencies between Information and Communications Technologies (ICT) components, services, and business process (the process is expressed in terms of communication paths, reliability of the services, the routers, and the switches). However, if we assume that the services are opaque, then we know neither how they are implemented nor what they use internally. In this chapter, we aim to solve the problem of composing the NFPs of the services directly, without having to map them to the ICT components that they depend on.

Wada *et al*. (2008a) propose an optimization framework called E3 (Evolutionary multiobjective sErvice composition optimizEr) to address the QoS-aware service composition problem. E3 defines a multiobjective genetic algorithm, called E3-MOGA, which assumes that services have three QoS attributes: throughput, latency, and cost. While the cost is fixed, the two other criteria can vary at runtime obeying probability distributions known from historical data. E3 considers running multiple service instances in parallel to improve the availability and performance. E3 determines (1) which concrete services to use and (2) how many instances of each concrete service to use. This paper also addresses the problem of aggregating the NFPs of resulting composite service. However, the set of NFPs considered is not yet as extensive as ours, and the composition patterns are simpler too (e.g., no clear treatment for conditional branches).

Hughes and Hillman (2006) have proposed a tool, *QoS Explorer*, which shares many of our objectives. QoS Explorer is an interactive tool that predicts quality of service of a workflow from the QoS characteristics of its constituents. Interestingly, this tool supports the processing of entire statistical distributions and probabilistic states (instead of the simple numeric constants used in our examples) to model NFPs that could be varying, such as response time. Composition operators include sequence, concurrency, conditional branching, and a simple version of the discriminator, but loops are not covered. QoS Explorer, however, targets optimizations at design time; dynamic service selection is not really addressed. Also, unlike AoURN, the workflow language does not offer any aspect-oriented modeling concept for composition and does not include any relationships to goals for evaluations.

Choi, Her, and Kim (2007) have identified unique features of SOA and then derived six quality attributes and their respective metrics to measure each attribute. The proposed set of attributes is intended to be used by service providers to ensure that a qualified service is published. Again however, the set of NFPs considered is limited, and the composability of these attributes was not addressed either.

Hobbs, Becha, and Amyot (2008) recognize that there are serious gaps in the semantics of published service descriptions and that these hinder the adoption of SOA in mission-critical applications. They identify some of these lacunae and propose a foundation for resolving one of them, namely service failure. The technique of crash-only failure is proposed as a useful first step for building a taxonomy of service's failure behavior in SOA. Crash-only failure is a software design approach based on the assumption that it is easier to restart quickly in a known state than to clean up and rebuild to recover from an error. This failure mode NFP was however not characterized in a quantifiable way.

Zeng *et al*. (2004) have defined QoS-aware middleware for atomic and composite web services. The list of NFPs is again limited, and several issues can be observed with success rate and availability in particular. For QoS composition, the authors define as *critical services* the services that belong to the critical path, which is the path that has the longest total sum of weights labeling its nodes. In this paper, the weight is the execution duration of the service. The authors compute the QoS composition taking into account the critical services path only, which is a simplistic treatment of the services that are part of parallel or conditional branches. Also, the approach assumes that when the execution of a non-critical service is not successful, the task can be re-executed without delaying the whole composite service execution, which is often an incorrect assumption. The selection mechanism does not return the service with the best tradeoffs and does not investigate the possibility of using multiple services or multiple instances of the same service to best accommodate the user's constraints.

The idea of using aspects to represent NFPs crosscutting multiple services in a business process is not new and was explored, for example, by Wada, Suzuki and Oba (2008b). This approach takes advantage of the Ark transformation tool to weave NFP aspects into a base business process

model and even to generate code. Our approach, however, enables goals and processes to be combined and used in pointcut expressions and aspects, and for NFP criteria to be used in matching expressions. Our aspects can also be used in a context where dynamic selection and composition of services is performed.

We are observing trends in the formalization and standardization of quantifiable NFPs in SLAs and of composition operators, which will be usable for service selection and composition and also to measure the extent of SLA satisfaction. The use of aspect-oriented models also shows great potential for separating non-functional concerns properly and re-composing them in a dynamic service-oriented environment. The use of goal-oriented models not only enables the evaluation of trade-offs during selection but it can do so in a much more generic way than what was shown in this chapter's example (Figure 7). For instance, the use of information from the external world was explored with context-aware GRL models by Amyot, Becha, Bræk, and Rossebø (2008) for Next-Generation Network service engineering. In a SOA environment, such information could take the form of current security threat levels, market stock trends, user complaint levels, etc., which are not modeled as services but could impact positively or negatively several goals (such as those in Figure 7) and hence influence the dynamic selection of suitable services.

DISCUSSION AND CONCLUSION

In SOA, managing non-functional properties of services is crucial to compare and select concrete services in dynamic composition and to establish and monitor SLAs in general. In this chapter, we have presented a modeling framework for dynamic service composition and NFP-aware service selection. URN, with aspect-oriented extensions, has been successfully used to model composite services using abstract services, to compare and select the appropriate concrete services to be populated at runtime based on the NFPs of existing functionally-equivalent services and on desired non-functional requirements, and to compute the NFPs of the resulting composite service. The composite service BookItWell was used throughout the chapter as a case study to illustrate and validate our nine-step service selection and dynamic composition approach, the proposed taxonomy, and the NFP aggregation functions. As future work, we will evaluate our approach using a real-world case study.

For the NFP-aware selection of services, we have defined a generic taxonomy of sixteen non-functional properties of services in SOA. Our taxonomy is extensible since we can define as many new NFPs as needed without impacting our methodology or the UCM notation. For four of them and for five common composition operators, we have defined functions to compute the NFPs of the composite service. We are working towards completing the definition of such functions for the remaining NFPs described in our taxonomy. Some existing functions will also be revisited. For example, the aggregation function of the loop operator is based on the assumption that the maximum number of invocations of the services is known, which is not always the case. In addition, our proposed functions take a pessimistic view of the composite service; we always assume the worst case for service invocations, whereas we could also report on the best case and the average case, or use a probabilistic approach for service invocations.

The UCM notation was used to model composite services based on their required abstract services. Aspect-oriented UCMs enable the modeling and the weaving of additional functionality (or internally developed services) to the composite service such as integrity checks, billing, after-the-fact auditing, and redundancy in case of potentially unavailable services. Plug-in maps could also specify the behavior of the concrete service, allowing for more fine-grained estimates of composite NFPs. Aspects may also be used to describe other services and add them to the composite service.

GRL models were used to assess the impact of the NFPs of different functionally-equivalent services on the NFPs of the composite service, hence facilitating the selection of a concrete service with the best NFPs or tradeoff. In the future, we could also extend the goal model to consider non-functional requirements beyond the NFPs of the services to take non-technical issues into account such as the financial status of the company, Internet virus threat levels, overloaded networks, and customer satisfaction.

The nine steps of our approach were defined and illustrated with the BookItWell service. Several modeling steps are obviously manual (albeit supported by tools), but the others are amenable to automation. Our main tool (jUCMNav) does not yet support these steps entirely, but required prototype functionalities are being developed.

In our example, the final results for reliability and availability in step 9 may be considered too low (although they are realistic given the complexity of that composite service). This situation could be improved by taking the overall composite service into account in step 8 instead of a shortest path approach. This is feasible for static composition, however this may not be possible if highly dynamic composition is required.

REFERENCES

W3C. (2008). *Homepage information*. Retrieved October 2008, from http://www.w3.org/

Amyot, D. (2003). Introduction to the user requirements notation: Learning by example. *Computer Networks*, *42*(3), 285–301. doi:10.1016/S1389-1286(03)00244-5

Amyot, D., Becha, H., Bræk, R., & Rossebø, J. E. Y. (2008). *Next generation service engineering.* ITU-T Innovations in NGN Kaleidoscope Conference, Geneva, Switzerland.

Bass, L., & John, B. E. (2003). Linking usability to software architecture patterns through general scenarios. *Journal of Systems and Software, 66*(3), 187–197. doi:10.1016/S0164-1212(02)00076-6

Choi, S. W., Her, J. S., & Kim, S. D. (2007). *QoS metrics for evaluating services from the perspective of service providers.* IEEE International Conference on e-Business Engineering (ICEBE 2007), Hong Kong, China. IEEE Computer Society, (pp. 622-625).

Galster, M., & Bucherer, E. (2008). *A taxonomy for identifying and specifying non-functional requirements in service-oriented development.* International Workshop on Methodologies for Non-functional Properties in Services Computing (MNPSC), Honolulu, USA. IEEE CS, (pp. 345-352).

Hassine, J., Dssouli, R., & Rilling, J. (2005). Applying reduction techniques to software functional requirement specifications. *Proceedings of System Analysis and Modeling - Fourth International SDL and MSC Workshop, SAM 2004*, Ottawa, Canada. (LNCS 3319), (pp. 138-153). Springer.

Hobbs, C., Becha, H., & Amyot, D. (2008). *Failure semantics in a SOA environment.* 3rd Int. MCeTech Conference on eTechnologies, Montréal, Canada. IEEE Computer Society, (pp. 116-121).

Hobbs, C., & Storrie, J. (2007). Time-sensitive Service-Oriented Architectures. *Nortel Technical Journal, 5*, 20–32.

Hughes, C., & Hillman, J. (2006). *QoS Explorer: A tool for exploring QoS in composed services.* International Conference on Web Services (ICWS'06), Chicago, USA. IEEE Computer Society, (pp. 797-806).

ITU-T. (2003). *User Requirements Notation (URN)–language requirements and framework.* Geneva, Switzerland.

ITU-T. (2007). *Framework and methodologies for the determination and application of QoS parameters.* Geneva, Switzerland.

ITU-T. (2008a). *User Requirements Notation (URN)–language definition.* Geneva, Switzerland.

ITU-T. (2008b). *Definitions of terms related to quality of service*, Geneva, Switzerland. jUCMNav. (2008). *Version 3.2.* University of Ottawa. Accessed October, 2008, from http://jucmnav.softwareengineering.ca/jucmnav/

Kealey, J., & Amyot, D. (2007). *Enhanced use case map traversal semantics.* 13th SDL Forum (SDL'07), Paris, France. (LNCS 4745), (pp. 133-149). Springer.

Milanovic, N., Milic, B., & Malek, M. (2008). *Modeling business process availability.* International Workshop on Methodologies for Non-functional Properties in Services Computing (MNPSC), Honolulu, USA. IEEE CS, (pp. 315-321).

Mussbacher, G. (2008). Aspect-oriented user requirements notation. In Giese, H. (Ed.), *Models in software engineering: Workshops and symposia at MODELS 2007. (LNCS 5002)* (pp. 305–316). Springer.

Mussbacher, G., & Amyot, D. (2008). Assessing the applicability of use case maps for business process and workflow description. *3rd International MCeTech Conference on eTechnologies Proceedings*, Montréal, Canada. IEEE Computer Society, (pp. 219-222).

Mussbacher, G., Amyot, D., Araújo, J., Moreira, A., & Weiss, M. (2007a). *Visualizing aspect-oriented goal models with AoGRL.* Second International Workshop on Requirements Engineering Visualization (REV'07), New Delhi, India.

Mussbacher, G., Amyot, D., & Weiss, M. (2007). Visualizing early aspects with use case maps. In Rashid, A., & Aksit, M. (Eds.), *Transactions on Aspect-Oriented Software Development III* (pp. 105–143). Springer. doi:10.1007/978-3-540-75162-5_5

Mussbacher, G., Amyot, D., Whittle, J., & Weiss, M. (2007b). *Flexible and expressive composition rules with Aspect-oriented Use Case Maps (AoUCM)*. 10th International Workshop on Early Aspects (EA 2007), Vancouver, Canada. (LNCS 4765), (pp. 19-38).

OASIS. (2006). *Reference model for Service Oriented Architecture 1.0*. OASIS Standard. Retrieved October 2008, from http://www.oasis-open.org/specs/index.php#soa-rmv1.0

OASIS. (2008). *Homepage information*. Retrieved October 2008, from http://www.oasis-open.org/home/index.php

Petriu, D. B., & Woodside, M. (2005). Software performance models from system scenarios. [Elsevier.]. *Performance Evaluation*, *61*(1), 65–89. doi:10.1016/j.peva.2004.09.005

Petriu, D. B., & Woodside, M. (2007). An intermediate metamodel with scenarios and resources for generating performance models from UML designs. [Springer.]. *Software and Systems Modeling*, *6*(2), 163–184. doi:10.1007/s10270-006-0026-8

Pourshahid, A., Chen, P., Amyot, D., Forster, A. J., Ghanavati, S., & Peyton, L. (2009). Business process management with the user requirements notation. [Springer.]. *Electronic Commerce Research*, *9*(4), 269–316. doi:10.1007/s10660-009-9039-z

Roy, J.-F., Kealey, J., & Amyot, D. (2006). Towards integrated tool support for the user requirements notation. *Proceedings of SAM 2006: Language Profiles - Fifth Workshop on System Analysis and Modelling*, Kaiserslautern, Germany. (LNCS 4320), (pp. 183-197). Springer.

URN Virtual Library. (2008). *Case maps*. Retrieved October 2008, from http://www.usecase-maps.org/pub/

Wada, H., Champrasert, P., Suzuki, J., & Oba, K. (2008a). Multiobjective optimization of SLA-aware service composition. *Proceedings of the International Workshop on Methodologies for Non-functional Properties in Services Computing (MNPSC)*, Honolulu, USA. IEEE CS, (pp. 315-321).

Wada, H., Suzuki, J., & Oba, K. (2008b). *Early aspects for non-functional properties in service oriented business processes*. 2008 IEEE Congress on Services - Part I, Honolulu, USA. IEEE CS, (pp. 231-238).

Weiss, M., Esfandiari, B., & Luo, Y. (2005). Towards a classification of Web service feature interactions. *Proceedings of the International Conference on Service-Oriented Computing (ICSOC)*, Amsterdam, Netherlands. (LNCS 3826), (pp. 101-114). Springer.

Zeng, L., Benatallah, B., Ngu, A. H. H., Dumas, M., Kalagnanam, J., & Chang, H. (2004). QoS-aware middleware for Web services composition. *IEEE Transactions on Software Engineering*, *30*(5), 311–327. doi:10.1109/TSE.2004.11

Chapter 4

A Security Requirements Engineering Tool for Domain Engineering in Software Product Lines

Jesús Rodríguez
University of Castilla – La Mancha, Spain

Eduardo Fernández-Medina
University of Castilla – La Mancha, Spain

Mario Piattini
University of Castilla – La Mancha, Spain

Daniel Mellado
National Competition Commission, Spain

ABSTRACT

The concepts of Service-Oriented Architectures and Software Product Lines are currently being paid a considerable amount of attention, both in research and in practice. Both disciplines promise to make the development of flexible, cost-effective software systems possible and to support high levels of reuse, and may sometimes be complementary to each other. In both paradigms, security is a critical issue, although most of the existing product line practices do not comprise all the security requirements engineering activities or provide automated support through which to perform these activities, despite the fact that it is widely accepted that the application of any requirements engineering process or methodology is much more difficult without a CARE (Computer-Aided Requirements Engineering) tool, since it must be performed manually. Therefore, this chapter shall present a tool denominated as SREPPLineTool, which provides automated support through which to facilitate the application of the security quality requirements engineering process for software product lines, SREPPLine. SREPPLineTool simplifies the management of security requirements in product lines by providing us with a guided, systematic and intuitive manner in which to deal with them from the early stages of product line development, thus

DOI: 10.4018/978-1-60566-794-2.ch004

simplifying the management and the visualization of artefact variability and traceability links and the integration of security standards, along with the management of the security reference model proposed by SREPPLine.

INTRODUCTION

As software complexity grows and customers demand higher and higher quality software, non functional requirements can no longer be considered to be of secondary importance (Cysneiros & Yu, 2005). The tendency towards larger systems that are distributed over the Internet, such as those based on SOA (Service Oriented Architecture), has simultaneously introduced many new security threats (Opdahl & Sindre, 2008);. Present-day information systems are therefore vulnerable to a host of threats and cyber-attackers, such as malicious hackers, code writers, cyber-terrorists, etc. (Choo et al., 2007).

Furthermore, there is currently an increase both in the demand for and the complexity of the software needed. Thus, in order to obtain high-quality systems along with higher productivity, software product line (SPL) based development has become the most successful approach in the reuse field, since it can help to significantly reduce both time-to-market and development costs (Bosh, 2000; Clements & Northrop, 2002), by increasing the reuse of all types of artefacts, thanks to the combination of coarse-grained components with a top-down systematic approach in which software components are integrated into a high-level structure. Moreover, existing SOA techniques can be used as an infrastructure on which increasingly complex software product line systems can be built with the aim of facilitating the emergence of a concurrent market in which atomic products from supplier product lines can be automatically integrated into a larger product line (Trujillo et al., 2008). This scenario, in which a product line consumes products that are supplied from third-party product lines, is called Service-Oriented

Product Line (SOPL), an example of which might be web portals of portlets (Trujillo et al., 2008).

The complexity and the extensive nature of the SPL also make security and requirements engineering much more important for SPL based development, (particularly if this is a SOPL), than for the development of the information system since a security breach or vulnerability on the line can cause major long-term problems both to all SPL products and to third-party SPLs if the product in question was a SOPL.

Nevertheless, despite the fact that many requirements engineering practices must be appropriately tailored to the specific demands of product lines (Birk & Heller, 2007), SPL engineering software engineering methodologies and standard proposals have traditionally ignored security requirements and security variability issues. Thus, although several works dealing with security requirements management tools, similar to SREPPLineTool exist, none of them are either sufficiently specific or are tailored to the SPL development paradigm, mainly because they do not deal with security requirements variability.

This chapter will describe a security requirements management tool called SREPPLineTool which has been developed with the aim of providing SREPPLine (security requirements engineering process for software product lines) (Mellado et al., 2008c) with an automated support. This tool will facilitate the development of secure software product lines and could be applied to the development of secure service-oriented product lines, since the security requirements engineering concepts for SPL that SREPPLine manages do not change for this type of SPL, which is based on SOA techniques.

SREPPLineTool will provide a guided, systematic and intuitive manner in which to apply SREPPLine, along with a simple integration with the remaining requirements and the different stages of the SPL development lifecycle. It will additionally facilitate the integration of the Common Criteria (CC) (ISO/IEC, 2005a) and the ISO/IEC 27001 (ISO/IEC, 2006) into the software development process, and will fulfil the IEEE 830:1998 standard (IEEE, 1998). To do so, it is assisted by the functionalities offered by 'IBM Rational RequisitePro' (a CARE tool which is extended by SREPPLineTool). This prototype also assists in the development of products and SPLs which conform to the aforementioned security standards with regard to the management of security requirements, thus removing the necessity for a perfect knowledge of these standards, and therefore reducing the participation of security experts to achieve this aim. In other words, it improves SREPPLine efficiency. Furthermore, the Security Variability Model and the Security Requirement Decision Model implemented within SREPPLineTool, facilitate both the management and the visualization of the artefacts' variability and traceability links and the reusability of the security artefacts, thus successively improving quality.

The remainder of the chapter is organized as follows: In section 2, we shall summarize some of the basic characteristics of SREPPLine with the aim of understanding the later explanation of the tool. In section 3 we shall go on to describe the most important characteristics of the SREPPLineTool and how it automates the application of SREPPLine. In section 4 we shall then present related work and the main contributions of SREPPLineTool. Finally, our conclusions, future trends and future work will be set out in section 5.

SREPPLINE: SECURITY REQUIREMENTS ENGINEERING PROCESS FOR SOFTWARE PRODUCT LINES

Product Line Requirements Engineering

A software product line is a set of software-intensive systems sharing a common, managed set of features (Kang et al., 1990) which satisfy the specific needs of a particular market segment or mission and which are developed from a common set of core assets in a prescribed way (Clements and Northrop, 2002). Exploiting commonalities between different systems is at the heart of Software Product Line Engineering. These commonalities and differences are described by using the core concept in Software Product Line Engineering: variability. Variability describes the variations in (both functional and non-functional) features along the product line: features are either a commonality or a variation.

The software product line engineering paradigm differentiates two processes: domain engineering and application engineering (Pohl et al., 2005). On the one hand, domain engineering is the process of SPL engineering in which the commonality and variability of the product line are defined and performed. According to (Pohl et al., 2005) the domain requirements engineering sub-process encompasses all activities for eliciting and documenting the common and variable requirements of the product line. On the other hand, application engineering is the process of SPL engineering in which the applications of the product line are built by reusing domain artefacts and exploiting product line variability.

Product line requirements define the products and their common and variable features in the product line. Requirements common to the entire family, which constitute product line requirements and are an important core asset, should be managed separately from those requirements that are particular to a subset of the products (or to a single product), which must also be managed. The SPL scope binds the products included in the product line: product line requirements refine the scope by more precisely defining the characteristics of the products in the product line. Both concepts are tightly coupled and evolve together (Clements and Northrop, 2002).

Overview of SREPPLine

SREPPLine (Mellado et al., 2008c), is an evolution of our previous "generic" security requirements engineering process (SREP) (Mellado et al., 2006, 2007), and is an add-in of activities which can be incorporated into an organization's SPL development process model providing it with a security requirements engineering approach. It could also be used to identify and specify reusable security services in SOA, based on security features for developing a service-oriented product line. It is a security features or security goals based process which is driven by risk and security standards (concretely ISO/IEC 27001 (ISO/IEC, 2006) and Common Criteria (ISO/IEC, 2005a)) and deals with security requirements and their related artefacts from the early stages of SPL development in a systematic manner which has been especially tailored to SPL based development. It is based on the use of the latest and widely validated security requirements techniques, such as security use cases (Firesmith, 2003a) or misuse cases (Opdahl & Sindre, 2008), along with the integration of the Common Criteria (CC) components and the ISO/IEC 27001 controls in the SPL lifecycle in order to facilitate SPL products security certification. Moreover, our proposed process suggests the use of a method to carry out risk assessment which conforms to ISO/IEC 13335 (ISO/IEC, 2004a); it concretely uses Magerit (Ministry for Public Administration of Spain, 2005) for both SPL risk assessment and SPL products risk assessment.

Furthermore, SREPPLine has the aim of minimizing both knowledge of the necessary security standards and the participation of security experts during SPL product development.

To this end, it provides a Security Core Assets Repository to facilitate security artefacts reuse and to implement the security variability model and the security requirements decision model, which assist in the management of the variability and traceability of the security requirements related artefacts of the SPL and its products. These models are the basis used by SREPPLine activities to capture, represent and share knowledge concerning security requirements for SPL and to help certify them in compliance with security standards. In essence, it is a knowledge repository with a structure to support security requirements reasoning in SPL.

Our process is composed of two sub processes, as is shown in Fig. 1: the Product Line Security Domain Requirements Engineering (PLSecDomReq) subprocess and the Product Line Security Application Requirements Engineering (PLSecAppReq) subprocess. These subprocesses cover the four basic phases of requirements engineering according to (Kotonya & Sommerville, 2000): requirements elicitation; requirements analysis and negotiation; requirements documentation; and requirements validation and verification.

Security Requirements Variability Management

The security requirements artefacts variability management in SREPPLine, which is explained in detail in (Mellado et al., 2008b), is supported by two models. Firstly, the Security Variability Model is used to assist in the management of the variability and traceability of both the security requirements related artefacts and the security standards certification of the SPL and its products. Secondly, the Security Requirements Decision

Figure 1. SREPPLine framework

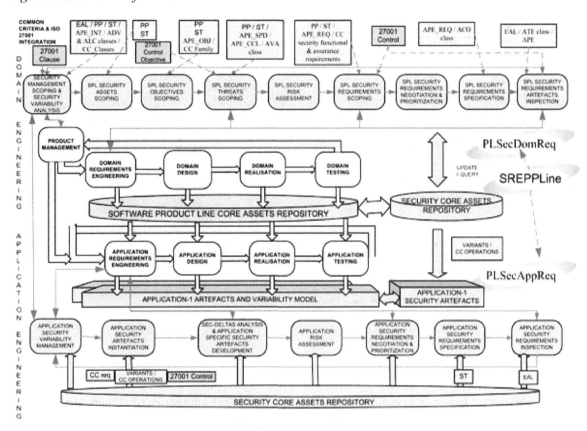

Model supports capture, specification and reasoning with regard to security requirements and their artefacts for SPL members. It also supports the development of a security requirements protection profile for the system's security goals, and is additionally helpful in the process of determining the most appropriate security requirements artefacts and security standards.

Security Variability Model

Our proposed Security Variability Model, which is shown in Fig. 2, is based on the Reusable Assets Specification (RAS), adopted as an OMG standard (OMG_(Object_Management_Group), 2004) and extends the orthogonal variability model of Pohl et al.(Pohl et al., 2005). It is also part of the Security Requirement Decision Model. This variability model relates the defined variability to

other software development models such as feature models, use case models, design models and test models, thus providing a cross-cutting view of the security requirements variability across all security development artefacts and assisting in keeping the different views of the variable security requirements artefacts consistent.

In order to relate the variability defined in the variability model to the software artefacts specified in other models, the meta-model depicted in Figure 2 contains the class 'artefact' which represents any kind of development artefact. Particular development artefacts are sub-classes of the 'artefact' class, such as 'security artefact' which is a specialization of an artefact. A development artefact can but does not have to be related to one or several variants, but a variant must be related to at least one development artefact. Furthermore, a development artefact can but does

Figure 2. Security variability meta-model

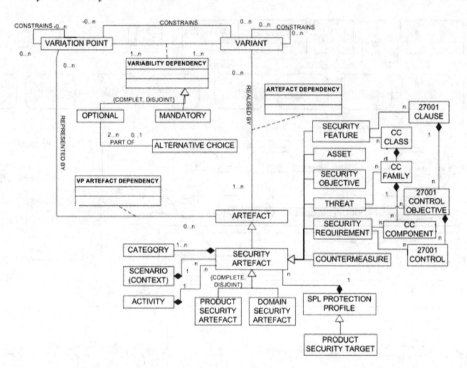

not have to be related to one or several variation points and vice versa. In addition, as is depicted in Figure 2, a security artefact can but does not have to be categorized. The 'category' class helps to avoid semantic problems and assists in the reuse of security artefacts, and even in applying security patterns. It is a key class for the security requirement decision model, because it guides us through the categories, thus allowing us to identify the security requirements artefacts systematically. The 'security artefact' class also has 'version' as a mandatory attribute in order to facilitate the traceability and variability of security artefacts versions, as products with different versions of the same security artefacts might exist (due to the variability in time and in space). Finally, in Figure 2 we have represented the security standards variability, by integrating the Common Criteria (CC) elements and the ISO/IEC 27001 controls into the security variability model. These security standards elements are

related to the categories of certain particular security artefacts (security features, threats and security requirements) with the aim of assisting in the certification of these standards in SPL or SPL products, and making their reasoning easier.

Security Requirements Decision Model

We treat security requirements artefacts as a natural source of variability among products or SPL artefacts. In order to capture and manage knowledge related to security requirements in SPL, we propose a security requirement decision model for SPL engineering, which will be shown in a different figure (Figure 3) in order to facilitate its understanding. This model facilitates both security requirements related artefacts reasoning and security standards conformance. It supports the capture, specification and reasoning of security requirements for both SPL and SPL members.

Figure 3. Security requirements decision model

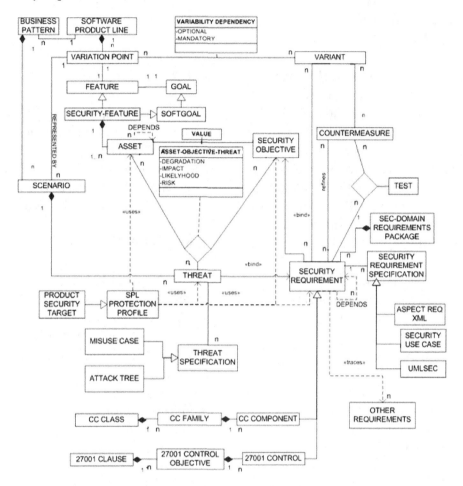

As a starting point we have used the goals/soft-goals (Chung et al., 2000) and feature models and their correlations in order to take into consideration functional and non-functional requirements, concretely security requirements. Both goal models and feature models can be used to express the intentions of a system, and these will, in most cases, define similar information (Pohl et al., 2005). Our interest in using a goal/soft goal model as a starting point therefore lies in the fact that it allows us to decide (if the traceability links are carefully established) which security features are needed to achieve the selected security goals and what the optimal set of security features/goals of a determined priority is in the context of the different scenarios of the SPL that provides the rationale of the selection. This supposes a rise in the abstraction level of the variants selection process. The selection will thus be made at the requirements level rather than at the design level. In this model we additionally characterize an SPL as being a set of 'variation points' which are represented by 'features' or 'goals'. Each goal can be achieved in many concrete ways, which are represented as 'scenarios'. Security features are those features that describe the security characteristics of the system which correspond to the security goals that the system under consideration should achieve.

Product Line Security Domain Requirements Engineering Sub Process

As the current version of SREPPLineTool supports this sub-process of SREPPLine, this section will provide a more detailed explanation of SREPPLineTool in order to improve its understanding. The main goals of this sub-process are: to develop common and variable security requirements which conform to IEEE 830:1998 (IEEE, 1998); their precise documentation in a Protection Profile (PP) adapted document by following the standard ISO/IEC 15446 (ISO/IEC, 2004b); to facilitate the conformance of the SPL to ISO/IEC 15408 (ISO/IEC, 2005a) and ISO/IEC 27001 (ISO/IEC, 2005c); and to develop their common and variable related security requirements artefacts.

Activity A1.1: Security Management Scoping

This activity comprises the following tasks: security core assets repository improvement (up-to-date artefacts and links); identification of specific stakeholders; security definitions agreement; security environment identification (security policy, security standards, laws, constraints, stakeholders' security needs and security acceptance criteria along with the evaluation assurance level (EAL) of the CC); identification of the relevant type/categories of assets and security goals; security features identification (commonalities and variability); and security cost impact and superficial risk estimations.

Activity A1.2: Security Assets Scoping

This activity comprises the following tasks: security assets identification for each asset (or group of assets) and for the environment; security assumptions; security asset scoping which aims to identify particular components to be developed for reuse, common and variable assets; and the identification of dependences between security assets.

Activity A1.3: Security Objectives Scoping

This activity comprises the following tasks: security objectives identification (commonality and variability analysis) for each asset; security objectives modelling and specification in XML (APE_OBJ CC class); and assets valuation as regards their related security objectives.

Activity A1.4: Security Threats Scoping

This activity comprises the following tasks: identification of potential vulnerabilities in public domain sources; identification of the attack tree associated with the business pattern or SPL domain; identification of the misuse cases and threats for each security objective and asset (commonality and variability analysis); threats modelling and specification (misuse cases or aspect-oriented XML); validation of security goals as regards threats and assets and their variability model.

Activity A1.5: Security Risks Assessment

This activity comprises the following tasks in order to achieve 100% risk acceptance: assessing whether the threats are relevant according to the security level specified by the security objectives; estimating the security risks based on the relevant threats, their likelihood and their potential negative impact, depending on the variation points. To do this, we propose the use of Magerit (Ministry_for_Public_Administration_of_Spain, 2005), which conforms to ISO/IEC 13335 (ISO/IEC, 2004a), and will soon conform to ISO/IEC 27005. This standard was, moreover, recognised by both NATO (at the 9th NATO cyber defence workshop) and by the OECD (OECD, 2005).

Activity A1.6: Security Requirements Scoping

This activity comprises the following tasks: security requirements elicitation (the appropriate CC security functional requirements and the ISO/IEC 27001 control objectives should also be selected), the selection of suitable security requirements or the suitable package of security requirements with which to mitigate threats at the necessary levels with regard to the risk assessment; the identification of common security requirements according to the elicited requirements and through the previously performed risk analysis; the definition of variable requirements and variability dependencies; security requirements modelling; the definition of the permitted CC operations (iteration, assignment, selection or refinement); and the validation of security requirements as regards security goals and business goals.

Activity A1.7: Security Requirements Negotiation and Prioritization

This activity comprises the following tasks: interdependences with other functional and non-functional requirements and trade-offs in the security requirements decision model; balancing the risk with the economic impact of implementing countermeasures.

Activity A1.8: Security Requirements Specification

This activity comprises the following tasks: security requirements modelling and specification (security use cases or aspect-oriented XML (Kuloor and Eberlein, 2003) or UMLsec (Jürjens, 2002a; Jürjens, 2002c)); the definition of the security test/metric and countermeasure for each security requirement. Once this activity has been completed in accordance with ISO/IEC 27001, both the functional, assurance and organizational security requirements, and the security requirements for IT development and operational environment should therefore have been specified.

Activity A1.9: Security Requirements Artefacts Inspection

This activity comprises the following tasks: (i) to verify whether the security requirements satisfy the stakeholders' security needs and the SPL security goals, and also whether a risk assessment outlined to obtain the residual risks has been performed; (ii) to verify whether the security requirements conform to ISO/IEC 27001 control objectives, to CC (ISO/IEC 15408) assurance requirements and to the IEEE 830-1998 standard since, according to this standard, a quality requirement must be correct, unambiguous, complete, consistent, ranked by importance and/or stability, verifiable, modifiable, and traceable; (iii) to use CMMI DEV+SAFE (SEI, 2007) in order to assist in the evaluation of the product line security engineering process in the Domain Testing sub-process; (iv) to verify the fulfilment of the previously approved EAL and the CC evaluation.

SREPPLINETOOL

Characteristics

We have developed a prototype of a CARE (Computer Aided Requirements Engineering) tool, called SREPPLineTool, which is a first approximation to assist us in obtaining experience in the problem through its application in real case studies, with the purpose of refining it and obtaining a definitive version. The SREPPLineTool prototype allows us to apply the SREPPLine process to an SPL development by providing its activities with automated support.

This tool implements the Security Variability Model and the Security Requirement Decision Model (explained in (Mellado et al., 2008b)) by means of dynamic repositories of security artefacts, and guides us in the execution of the process in a sequential manner. It is thus able to propose security artefacts related to each of the SREPPLine process activities, according to the domain categories of the SPL project artefacts and related CC (Common Criteria) and ISO/IEC 27001 security artefacts, and it also imports security features from IBM Rational RequisitePro. The tool therefore conforms to the most important security standards related to security requirements management, and avoids the need for an in depth knowledge of security standards, thus reducing the involvement of security experts.

In addition, SREPPLineTool uses wizard windows to facilitate the management and the visualization of the artefacts' variability and traceability links, the generation of SPL security documents, which could be generated in XML, and integration with other functional and non-functional requirements and features. In this version of the prototype, we have implemented the Product Line Security Domain Requirements Engineering Sub process, but for a future version we hope to include both the domain sub process and the product sub process.

Technology

This prototype has been developed with.NET technology and implemented with C#, using an SQL Server 2005 database. It is linked to the IBM Rational RequisitePro tool by means of a Visual Basic.NET interface (as is described in Figure 4) in order to retain the advantages of this requirements management tool, thus enabling it both to read the requirements and features from a RequisitePro project and to send the documents it has generated to a RequisitePro project.

In addition, and with the objective of helping other tools to use this prototype, SREPPLineTool allows us to export the tools' variability model in XML format to a file so that this information can be used by other applications in a simple manner.

Having taken into account the characteristics of the SREPPLine process and the objectives of its application, we considered it appropriate to extend an existing tool and to focus our search within the field of CARE tools, since we believe that a major success factor for practical security requirements engineering in SPL will be the seamless integration of existing tools rather than the need for special purpose tools. The INCOSE survey (INCOSE, 2008) was used as a basis to carry out an initial selection of tools that fulfilled the majority of the key functions of a CARE tool. We eventually decided to extend RequisitePro as a support for our prototype, principally due to the following factors:

- RequisitePro allows us both to access the data stored in it (project, requirements, attributes, etc.) and to control the RequisitePro user interface and Microsoft Word documents.
- Automated integration with the remaining life cycle activities. This is due to the fact that RequisitePro is integrated into the "Rational Suite Analyst Studio".

Figure 4. SREPPLineTool architecture

- RequisitePro permits the creation of traceability relationships between different types of requirements; and a certain amount of reuse through the use of document patterns.

SREPPLine Automation

The tool automates the security requirements engineering process for software product lines (PLSecDomReq), but we hope that in a future version of the prototype, it will also support the product process (PLSecAppReq). The prototype automates and assists the user in SREPPLine execution by giving him/her a step by step guide to the nine stages of the process.

IBM Rational RequisitePro Interface

SREPPLineTool projects are synchronized with RequisitePro projects; this means that one project cannot exist without the existence of the other, since both use the same name in their representation. SREPPLineTool uses its communication interface with RequisitePro to import requirements (such as features) and send documents containing SPL security information. The tool initially requires that there be an open project in Rational RequisitePro, although this project may initially be empty. RequisitePro uses the Features table, which can be used in a SREPPLinetool project,

in which those Features to be added to the variability model can be selected.

Security Resources Repository

The Security Resources Repository (SRR) allows us to propose various kinds of artefact sets that may interest the user, thus providing him/her with a simpler and more agile definition of the SPL.

As Figure 5 shows, the SRR implements four different sub repositories:

- **ISO/IEC 27001 Repository:** This repository proposes ISO/IEC 27001 Clauses to be used at the Security Management Scoping stage (i.e. Security Features). At the Security Threats Scoping stage, it will propose the ISO/IEC 27001 Control Objectives belonging to the Clauses that were added earlier. Finally, and always maintaining traceability, at the Security Requirements Scoping stage, it will propose the ISO/IEC 27001 Controls that are related to the Control Objectives (Threats) to be added, such as Security Requirements.
- **Common Criteria Repository:** Firstly, the addition of CC Classes (i.e. Security Features) is proposed. Then, at the Security Threats Scoping stage, the repository proposes the Families belonging to the Classes that were added earlier. Finally, it is possible to add the proposed Components that are related to the threats Families, such as Security Requirements.
- **Domain Artefacts Repository:** This sub-repository will show the artefacts related to each domain at each stage, depending on the domains that the SPL project is related to.
- **Project Artefacts Repository:** This repository allows us not only to reuse the artefacts that have been created at each stage of an SPL project but also to restore the artefacts that have been removed or

Figure 5. Security resources repository diagram

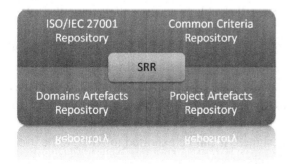

Figure 6. Variability identification sub-activity

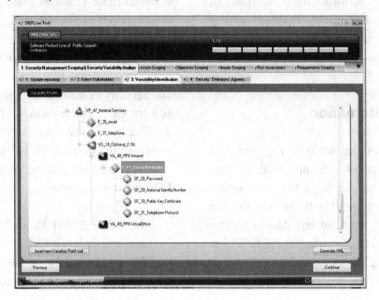

disassociated, thus maintaining a constant traceability without losing any artefact in the process.

We shall now explain how SREPPLineTool automates each stage of the process; the artefacts that are used as examples are based on the application of the tool in a case study in (Mellado et al., 2009)

Activity 1: Security Management Scoping

The tool first opens a Rational RequisitePro project. If the user's identification in the project is correct, SREPPLineTool will load all the data from the project and will show the first step of the first activity. This step is the Features Update in which stakeholders may change the security artefacts (Features and Security Features) that flow from each variation point or variant. Security Features or Features can be added or removed by using the contextual menu that appears when the artefact with which we wish to work is clicked. A Feature can be added from different sources: from the Project Repository, from the Domains

Repository or from the imported features of the Rational RequisitePro project. A Security Feature can be linked to a Feature through the following manners of selection: Adding a new Security Feature by entering its details, referencing one previously used in the project, or adding one from the Domains Repository, from ISO/IEC 27001 Clauses or from the Common Criteria Classes.

We can thus make the changes demanded by other users of the project (there is a list of requests to add, change or eliminate artefacts). The user can remove a request once it has been checked.

The next sub-activity is the Stakeholders' Selection, in which the project manager selects the users and their roles from a list according to the available Human Resources previously introduced in the Security Resources Repository. These users are thus able to access and develop the SPL.

The third sub-activity is that of Variability Identification (Figure 6) which shows the features variability tree implemented by the SPL variability model; finally we can see the related artefacts that were added in the previous sub-activity. In addition, once the variability model has been designed, it can be exported to XML to be used by other tools.

The artefacts shown are the following:

 Variation Points.

 Variants.

 Variability Dependencies.

 Features.

 Security Features.

It is possible to work directly with the Variability Tree, adding or removing artefacts by using contextual menus; it is specifically also possible to add or remove variation points and variants, and Variability Dependencies can be added over these artefacts. We may also add more Variations Points or Variants over one Dependency, and so on. The Variation Points or Variants can be added from the security resources repository, or new ones can be added by entering their data. If we wish to add a Variability Dependency we must first decide whether it will be mandatory or optional, and if it is optional, we must specify the minimum and maximum amount of variability elements that may be selected; this will be helpful in describing the common and variable elements of a specific SPL product.

The last sub-activity of the first activity is the Definitions Agreements in which SREPPLineTool assists us in reaching an agreement upon a common set of security definitions such as: Information security, threat, confidentiality, etc., by providing us with the definitions of these concepts according to ISO/IEC 17799:2005 (ISO/IEC, 2005b) and ISO/IEC 27001. SREPPLineTool additionally allows us to define both new standards and their concepts, which will be registered in the repository. It also allows us to state the evaluation assurance level (EAL) of the Common Criteria.

Activity 2: Security Assets Scoping

In this activity, we identify the security assets for each security feature, and the dependences between assets. Moreover, we add a value to each asset which describes how important or critical the asset is; higher rated assets represent more importance and a greater degradation of the product in the event of the appearance of a security breach in the asset. Additionally, SREPPLineTool allows us to define dependencies between assets, signifying that the value will be propagated throughout the assets dependency tree.

Whenever an asset is selected, all information concerning it will be shown in the assets editor, whose upper and lower dependencies can be modified in order to modify the value / importance of the asset and insert a description of it. When an asset is added, the values of other assets may be modified, since the final value of an asset is the highest value of the assets upon which it depends. Furthermore, the Security Resources Repository assists us in the task of security assets identification and categorization. The SRR allows us to reference assets from the Domain Repository or from other assets of the same Project Repository.

Activity 3: Security Objectives Scoping

In this activity we select the Security Objectives for each Asset; the tool shows the available security objectives and the current relationships between Assets and Security Objectives, and also the value for each pair (Asset, Security Objective) which represents how important it is to fulfil the Security Objective for an asset; the value scale is proposed in MAGERIT (Ministry_for_Public_Administration_of_Spain, 2005) (from 0 (min) to 10 (max)).

The Security Objectives/Security Dimensions are the following:

- Integrity (I).
- Confidentiality (C).
- Availability (D).

Figure 7. Security threats scoping activity

- Authenticity of service users (A_S).
- Authenticity of data origin (A_D).
- Accountability (or traceability) of service use (T_S).
- Accountability of data access (T_D).

Activity 4: Security Threats Scoping

The Security Threats Scoping activity is responsible for specifying and associating the security objectives with the potential security threats that may create a security breach (Figure 7). The SRR of SREPPLineTool allows us to select the Security Threats from the followings sources: threats previously used in the project, the domain classes repository, ISO 27001-Control Objectives and Common Criteria-Families. When a new threat is created, it is possible to specify a set of Misuse Cases and Attack-trees which define the behaviour of a Threat against a Security Objective.

Activity 5: Security Risk Assessment

After having identified the Threats in the previous activity, the risk assessment is carried out, as is shown in Fig. 8. In order to perform this

task, SREPPLineTool uses a technique proposed by the MAGERIT guide to techniques which is based on a quantitative analysis. First, and with the assistance of stakeholders, for each set of (Asset, Security Objective, Threat) we estimate the Likelihood (in terms of frequency of occurrence from 0 to 100: 100 for very frequent, daily; 10 for frequent, monthly; 1 for normal, annually; 0'1 for infrequent, every few years) that each threat will take place, and the Degradation of the value of an Asset caused by a Threat (expressed as a percentage).

Finally, the tool uses these data to automatically calculate the Impact and the Risk over an Asset; higher values indicate a higher Impact or Risk.

- Impact = Asset_Value * Degradation/100.
- Risk = Impact * Likelihood.

Activity 6: Security Requirements Scoping

Security requirements are derived by analyzing each security objective for possible relevance, together with those threats that imply a greater

Figure 8. Security risk assessment activity

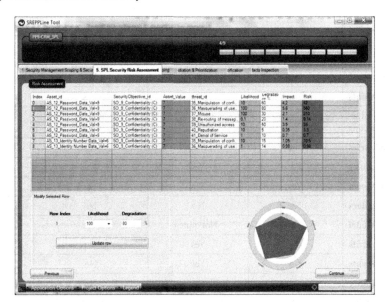

risk, in order to select the suitable security requirements or the suitable package of security requirements that will mitigate the threats at the necessary levels with regard to the result of the risk assessment activity.

Once the threats relevant to the project have been selected, we select those security requirements that are necessary according to the user. The following options can be used to do this:

- Selecting a Security Requirement previously used in the project (Project Repository).
- Selecting a Security Requirement from one of the Domain Classes of the Repository (Domain Repository).
- Selecting a Security Requirement from ISO 27001: Controls list or Common Criteria: Components list. (ISO 27001 & CC Repositories).
- Creating a new Security Requirement/ Requirements Package/Generic Security Requirement/Security Test.
- Selecting one of the requirements packages/test and within that package/test, the desired requirements.

Activity 7: Security Requirements Negotiation and Prioritization

The purpose of this activity is to automate the security requirements prioritization according to the risk of the threats that have been mitigated and the dependences between other functional and non-functional requirements. A priority level (from 1 to 10) is selected for each security requirement established in the project, and SREPPLineTool then sorts the security requirements list from greatest to least priority.

Activity 8: Security Requirements Specification

In this activity, SREPPLineTool facilitates the task of verifying that the security requirements conform to IEEE 830:1998 and ISO/IEC 15408; SREPPLineTool thus facilitates the security requirements verification and validation tasks by checking those threats for which we have not specified security requirements in the project, together with the assurance requirements that have not been added to the project according to the assurance level defined in activity 1.

Table 1. Comparison of CARE tools for product lines

Tools Requirements	FAMA FW	Requiline	Pure::variants	SREPPLineTool
Hierarchical Goals/Features	Yes	Not quite	Yes	Yes
Variation Points/Variants	Yes	Yes	Yes	Yes
Mandatory, Optional, Alternative Relations	Yes	Yes	Yes	Yes
Dependencies	Yes	Yes	Yes	Yes
Cardinalities	Yes	Yes	No	Yes
Variability Model	Yes	Yes	Yes	Yes
Stakeholders	No	No	No	Yes
Business Model	Yes	Not quite	Yes	Yes
Fuctional Requirements	No	Yes	No	Yes
Non Fuctional Requirements	No	Yes	No	Yes
Traceability	Not quite	Not quite	No	Yes
Security Requirements	No	No	No	Yes
Security Use Cases	No	No	No	Yes
Misuse Cases	No	No	No	Yes
Attack Trees	No	No	No	Yes
ISO 27001 Integration	No	No	No	Yes
Common Criteria Integration	No	No	No	Yes
Security Repository	No	No	No	Yes

Activity 9: Security Requirements Artefacts Inspection

SREPPLineTool allows us to select those security artefacts modified/generated in the last iteration which are considered sufficiently important to introduce into the SRR.

Finally, in this activity, the tool generates the SPL Protection Profile Document conforming to the Common Criteria (ISO/IEC 15408) which integrates all the information related to the remaining artefacts generated by SREPPLineTool in the previous activities.

RELATED WORK

The aim of this section is to obtain an overview of the SPL tools related to SREPPLineTool, a sum-

mary of which will be shown in Table 1 (FAMA Framework (Trinidad et al., 2008), Requiline (Maßen & Lichter, 2004) and Pure::variants (Pure_Systems, 2008)). Each tool will then be compared to SREPPLineTool.

The parameters that will be evaluated for each tool are those that allow the execution of the SREPPLine process to take place correctly, that is, features for supporting security requirements engineering in SPL: support for variability models, support for security artefacts in variability models, support for security requirements, and integration with major security standards such as ISO / IEC 27001 and Common Criteria, etc.

These tools provide almost all the needs required for a CARE tool. However, none of them cover all the needs to support SREPPLine. In fact, some of their limitations are critical to a successful implementation of SREPPLine. Among other weaknesses found, we can highlight the fact that none of the tools provide adequate techniques for the specification of security requirements, security use cases, misuse cases, and so on. Moreover, these tools do not provide any methodological support for automated security requirements management and for fundamental activities, such as risk evaluation, and neither do they provide compliance with the security standards regarding security requirements which are currently most relevant (such as Common Criteria (ISO / IEC 15408), ISO / IEC 27001).

In brief, the main contributions of SREP-PLineTool with regard to the former proposals are as follows:

- SPL has become the most successful approach in the reuse field (Laguna and Gonzalez-Baixauli, 2005), therefore SREPPLineTool is a reuse-based tool based on a security reference model implemented by dynamic repositories of security artefacts, signifying that threats and requirements and their specifications, security features, security objectives, assets, countermeasures and tests, are reused. Thus, the quality of these artefacts is successively increased in each new product or new version of the SPL products.

- It facilitates both the management and the visualization of the artefacts variability and traceability, and the automated integration of the security requirements with the remaining security artefacts and lifecycle activities in the SPL development paradigm, not only with the other requirements but also with other artefacts of the SPL lifecycle (such as features or goals).

- SREPPLineTool is a standard-centred tool. It assists in the development of ISs which conform to the most important current security standards in various activities of the requirements engineering process. It integrates the CC (ISO/IEC 15408) se-

curity functional requirements within the elicitation of security requirements and it also introduces the CC security assurance requirements into the requirements inspection. In addition, it conforms to ISO/IEC 13335 (GMITS) in carrying out risk assessment and facilitates conformance to those sections of ISO/IEC 17799:2005 (sections: 0.3, 0.4, 0.6 and 12.1) and ISO/IEC 27001:2005 (sections: 4.2.1, 4.2.3, 4.3, 6.a, 6.b and A.12.1.1) which concern security requirements.

- SREPPLineTool integrates the latest security requirements specification techniques (such as security use cases (Firesmith, 2003b), misuse cases and attack trees (Sindre & Opdahl, 2005; Opdahl & Sindre, 2008), and UMLsec (Jürjens, 2002a), which will be included in the next version of our tool).

- It automates report generation.

The SREPPLine process, together with the SREPPLineTool, therefore cover a wider area, and support Software Product Lines architecture with the elicitation and specification of security requirements.

CONCLUSION AND FUTURE TRENDS

Software security is currently generating a growing interest, particularly in SPL and SOA, due to the fact that security requirements issues are extremely important in both paradigms and because a weakness in security can cause problems in all the products of a product line or in all the products that use a vulnerable service. Although there have been several attempts to fill the gap between requirements engineering and SPL requirements engineering, a systematic approach or tool support with which to define security quality requirements and manage their variability and the security artefacts related to SPL models is not yet available. Designing Software Product Lines based on a Service-Oriented Architecture with the possibility of replacing or extending existing functionality by services offered by third-party providers simultaneously opens a very promising path towards Enterprise Component Platforms.

While traditional requirements management tools are not able to directly support the aforementioned security requirements management in SPL engineering, we have shown in this paper that it is possible to create a seamless integration of security requirements engineering concepts and SPL engineering or service-oriented product line engineering, together with the latest security requirements specification techniques (such as security use cases (Firesmith, 2003a), misuse cases and attack trees (Opdahl & Sindre, 2008), UMLSec (Jürjens, 2002a) in the next version) and along with the most relevant security standards with regard to the management of security requirements (such as ISO/IEC 15408 or ISO/IEC 27001) in these tools.

Tools such as SREPPLineTool are thus a critical enabler for the industrial uptake of security requirements engineering in SPL development, as was shown in the real case study of a CRM (Customer Relationship Management) product line based on SOA which was carried out in the Spanish Social Security (Mellado et al., 2008c), or in the case study of a Public Registry Online Product Line of a Spanish Public Administration (Mellado et al., 2008a).

Finally, a set of aspects is planned for the future of this prototype that will allow us to increase the level of automation of SREPPLine application and thus better the efficiency of organizations' requirements engineering processes in SPL engineering. Among them, we can highlight the following: to extend the type of supported requirements specifications in order to support UMLSec (Jürjens, 2002b); to refine the integration with IBM Rational RequisitePro and to extend the tool for it to be supported in other CARE tools; to automate the creation of security use cases by using misuse cases created in SREPPLine PLSecDomReq activity 4; and to improve the graphical interface of SREPPLineTool for the security variability definition in order to make it more intuitive.

ACKNOWLEDGMENT

This paper is part of the ESFINGE (TIN2006-15175-C05-05) project of the Ministry of Science and Innovation (Spain), and of the MELISA (PAC08-0142-335) and QUASIMODO (PAC08-0157-0668) projects of the Castilla - La Mancha Regional Government and the FEDER.

REFERENCES

Birk, A., & Heller, G. (2007). Challenges for requirements engineering and management in software product line development. International Conference on Requirements Engineering, (pp. 300-305).

Bosh, J. (2000). *Design & use of software architectures*. Pearson Education Limited.

Choo, K.-K. R., Smith, R. G., & McCusker, R. (2007). *Future directions in technology-enabled crime: 2007–09*. (p. 78).

Chung, L., Nixon, B., Yu, E., & Mylopoulos, J. (2000). *Non-functional requirements in software engineering*. Kluwer Academic Publishers.

Clements, P., & Northrop, L. (2002). *Software product lines: Practices and patterns*. Addison-Wesley.

Cysneiros, L. M., & Yu, E. (2005). Non-functional requirements elicitation. In Leite, J. C. S. P., & Doorn, J. H. (Eds.), *Perspectives on software requirements: An introduction* (pp. 115–138).

Firesmith, D. G. (2003a). Engineering security requirements. *Journal of Object Technology, 2*(1), 53–68. doi:10.5381/jot.2003.2.1.c6

Firesmith, D.G. (2003b). Security use cases. *Journal of Object Technology,* 53-64.

IEEE. (1998). Recommended practice for software requirements specifications.

INCOSE. (2008). *The INCOSE requirements management tools survey.* Retrieved from http://www.incose.org

ISO/IEC. (2004a). Security techniques-management of information and communications technology security.

ISO/IEC. (2004b). Security techniques-guide for the production of protection profiles and security targets.

ISO/IEC. (2005a). *Security techniques-evaluation criteria for IT security.*

ISO/IEC. (2005b). *Security techniques-code of practice for information security management.*

ISO/IEC. (2005c). *Security techniques-information security management systems requirements.*

ISO/IEC. (2006). *Security techniques-information security management systems requirements.*

Jürjens, J. (2002a). *Automated verification of UMLsec models for security requirements* (pp. 365–379).

Jürjens, J. (2002b). *UMLsec: Extending UML for secure systems development.* (LNCS 2460), (pp. 412-425).

Jürjens, J. (2002c). *Using UMLsec and goal trees for secure systems development* (pp. 1026–1030).

Kang, K., Cohen, S., Hess, J. A., Novak, W. E., & Peterson, S. A. (1990). *Feature-Oriented Domain Analysis (FODA) feasibility study.* Software Engineering Institute, Carnegie-Mellon University.

Kotonya, G., & Sommerville, I. (2000). *Requirements engineering process and techniques.* John Willey & Sons.

Kuloor, C., & Eberlein, A. (2003). Aspect-oriented requirements engineering for software product lines. *Proceedings of the 10th IEEE International Conference and Workshop on the Engineering of Computer-Based Systems* (ECBS'03).

Laguna, M. A., & Gonzalez-Baixauli, B. (2005). *Goals and MDA in product line requirements engineering.* Department of Computer Science, University of Valladolid.

Maßen, T. d., & Lichter, H. (2004). *RequiLine: A requirements engineering tool for software product lines.* (pp. 168-180).

Mellado, D., Fernández-Medina, E., & Piattini, M. (2006). *Applying a security requirements engineering process.* 11th European Symposium on Research in Computer Security (ESORICS 2006). (LNCS 4189), (pp. 192-206). Springer.

Mellado, D., Fernández-Medina, E., & Piattini, M. (2007). A common criteria based security requirements engineering process for the development of secure Information Systems. *Computer Standards & Interfaces, 29*(2), 244–253. doi:10.1016/j.csi.2006.04.002

Mellado, D., Fernández-Medina, E., & Piattini, M. (2008a). *Security requirements engineering process for software product lines: A case study.* The Third International Conference on Software Engineering Advances (ICSEA 2008), (pp. 1-6).

Mellado, D., Rodríguez, J., Fernández-Medina, E., & Piattini, M. (2009). *Automated support for security requirements engineering in software product line domain engineering.* The Fourth International Conference on Availability, Reliability and Security (ARES 2009).

Mellado, M., Fernández-Medina, E., & Piattini, M. (2008b). *Security requirements variability for software product lines*. Symposium on Requirements Engineering for Information Security (SREIS 2008) co-located with ARES 2008, (pp. 1413-1420).

Mellado, M., Fernández-Medina, E., & Piattini, M. (2008c). Towards security requirements management for software product lines: A security domain requirements engineering process. *Computer Standards & Interfaces*, *30*, 361–371. doi:10.1016/j. csi.2008.03.004

Ministry for Public Administration of Spain. (2005). *Methodology for Information Systems risk analysis and management.*

OECD. (2005). The promotion of a culture of security for Information Systems and networks in OECD countries.

OMG. (2004). *Reusable Assets Specification.* RAS.

Opdahl, A.L. & Sindre, G. (2008). *Experimental comparison of attack trees and misuse cases for security threat identification.*

Pohl, K. Böckle, G. & Linden, F.v.d. (2005). *Software product line engineering. Foundations, principles and techniques*. Berlin, Heidelberg: Springer.

Pure Systems. (2008). *Pure variants*. Retrieved from http://www.pure-systems.com/Variant_Management.49.0.html

SEI. (2007). *A safety extension to CMMI-DEV V1.2*. Software Engineering Institute, Carnegie Mellon University.

Sindre, G., & Opdahl, A. L. (2005). Eliciting security requirements with misuse cases. *Requirements Engineering*, *10*(1), 34–44. doi:10.1007/s00766-004-0194-4

Trinidad, P., Benavides, B., Ruiz-Cortés, A., Segura, S., & Jimenez, A. (2008). *FAMA framework*. Software Product Line Conference, 2008. SPLC '08. 12th International. (pp. 359-359).

Trujillo, S., Kästner, C., & Apel, S. (2008). Product lines that supply other product lines: A service-oriented approach. In S. Cohen & R. Krut (Eds.), *Proceedings of the First Workshop on Service-Oriented Architectures and Software Product Lines*.

Section 2
Modeling Non–Functional
Properties in SOA

Modeling non-functional properties is critical step for achieving successful realization of complex SOA projects. Issues of reliability, availability, security or quality of service are often subsumed under the general term of Service Level Agreements (SLA). This section discusses approaches for formal and tool supported modeling of SLAs containing non-functional properties.

Chapter 5
A Look on Engineering Non-Functional Properties in Service Oriented Architectures

Nicolò Perino
University of Lugano, Switzerland

Marco Massarelli
Universitá degli Studi di Milano-Bicocca, Italy

Daniele Cammareri
Universitá degli Studi di Milano-Bicocca, Italy

Claudia Raibulet
Universitá degli Studi di Milano-Bicocca, Italy

Francesca Arcelli
Universitá degli Studi di Milano-Bicocca, Italy

ABSTRACT

Service-oriented architectures (SOA) aim to define a common approach for both the providers and consumers of services by introducing the mechanisms necessary to publish services, to search for services, and to request the execution of services. The proliferation of the providers of services offering identical or similar services has led customers to choose services based on information behind their functionality. This type of information may regard issues such as quality, performance, response time, security, availability, and reliability. In the scientific literature, such information is known under the name of non-functional properties or non-functional requirements.

Usually, non-functional requirements are not explicitly addressed during the analysis and design of Information Systems, even if they are fundamental for the architectural or technological decisions. Hence, they are neither traceable nor documented. However, in recent years, the engineering of non-functional properties together with the functional ones is gaining more and more the attention of software engineers. There are various proposals for the specification of non-functional features which range from informal textual specification to extensions of the Unified Modelling Language.

DOI: 10.4018/978-1-60566-794-2.ch005

The aim of this chapter is to provide an overview on non-functional issues in service oriented architectures. First, it introduces the non-functional requirements which should be addressed in service-oriented architectures and the challenging issues they raise (i.e., specification, conflicts, run-time management). Second, it presents the available approaches related to the engineering of non-functional issues. Third, it discusses the possible future trends regarding this topic.

INTRODUCTION

The development of information systems focuses on the functionalities systems should provide to the users. Craig Larman sustains that one of the most common and successful iterative development approaches for software applications is *use-case driven* (Larman, 2004). Essentially, use case diagrams model the functional (behavioural) requirements of a system. This means that the analysis, design, implementation and testing phases are all driven by use-cases. In the same book, Larman indicates as non-functional "everything else" related to a system and not indicating a functional requirement. He mentions that non-functional properties are usually related to the quality of a software system, but this book lacks in providing detailed information on addressing non-functional requirements during the development life-cycle of an information system.

Ian Sommerville defines non-functional properties as "constraints on the services or functions offered by a system" (Sommerville, 2004). Non-functional requirements may be related to the reliability, reparability, security, usability of a system. Sommerville discusses the importance of being able to identify and consider them both during the development and the execution phases. This is because they address critical aspects which determine the usability of a system. These critical aspects may be more important than individual functional requirements. For example, users may find alternative ways to use a system function which does not respond exactly to their needs. But if a real-time control system fails to meet the performance requirements, the control component is not reliable and thus it cannot be used (Sommerville, 2004). Furthermore, Sommerville asserts that non-functional properties may be more complex than the functional ones because they regard the entire system rather than a single component, service, or function. They may be related not only to the software product, but they may influence the development process of a system (i.e., the specification of the quality standards that should be used in a process). From this point of view, non-functional issues may be considered of two types: *product-oriented* and *service-oriented* (Franch, 1998; Mylopoulos, Chung, & Nixon, 1992; Sommerville, 2004).

Taylor, Medvidović, and Dashofy define non-functional properties as "constraints on the manner in which the system implements and delivers its functionalities" (Taylor, Medvidović, & Dashofy, 2009). They identify at least three main types of non-functional properties: structural, behavioural, and interactional. Furthermore, they focus on the multi-dimensional characteristic of non-functional properties, as well as on the challenge to measure them due to their more qualitative rather than quantitative nature. It is also stressed that the software engineering methodology claims to perform the correct steps from the beginning of the software development: hence, non-functional properties should be considered from the first analysis of the requirements of a system in order to save later development and maintenance costs. Taylor, Medvidović, and Dashofy discuss on the tight link between the software architecture and the non-functional properties of a system: through software architectures engineers may address explicitly and trace further non-functional properties such as efficiency, scalability, availability, security, or fault-tolerance. Usually, the systems which are not based on a well-defined architectural model, and which address non-functional properties later in the development process have significant difficulties to achieve non-functional goals.

The complexity and the quality of a software system are given both by its functional and non-functional properties. Functional requirements represent the reason why a system should exist, while non-functional requirements influence its development (being determinant in taking decisions and selecting the most appropriate solution) and its usability (being determinant for its quality and performance).

The service-oriented paradigm (Erl, 2005) represents one of the modern approaches of developing today's information systems. The main advantages it provides derive from the decoupling of service consumption from service implementation in terms of platform, location, availability, and versions (Nano & Zisman, 2007). This separation between service providers and consumers raises challenging issues regarding the non-functional properties. Such issues derive from the dynamic composition and negotiation of services, as well as from the exploitation of services by various types of applications in different contexts. Due to the proliferation of service providers it is fundamental that non-functional features (i.e., the quality (Aagedal, 2001; OMG, 2004) or the performance) of services are determined at run-time and consumers are bound to the most appropriate services for their current needs and contexts (Wada, Suzuki, & Oba, 2006, 2007). This is tightly related to the trade-offs among various non-functional properties required by the consumers such as costs, execution time, and reliability which should be addressed at run-time (Singhera, 2004).

Further issues are raised by the adaptivity feature of the service-oriented approaches. Essentially, adaptivity (Cheng, de Lemos, Giese, Inverardi, & Magee, 2009; Raibulet, 2008) is related to the ability of a service to have a dynamic behaviour while maintaining its interface intact and its policies consistent (Padmanabhuni, Majumdar, Chawla, & Mysore, 2006). Due to its adaptivity feature, a service may be provided with

different non-functional properties (essentially qualities) in different contexts and to different providers.

To summarize, the service-oriented approach represents a more and more exploited solution for developing today's information systems in which non-functional requirements have a fundamental role both in their development process and during their execution.

This chapter aims to provide an overview on the non-functional properties of service-oriented systems by focusing on their role, as well as on their identification, specification and run-time exploitation. It is fundamental to understand their importance in the development and usage of service-oriented systems in order to address them explicitly. To achieve this objective the chapter is organized as following. The Main Features of SOA Section introduces the service-oriented architecture concept, as well as its main functional and non-functional design issues. The Non-Functional Properties in SOA Section provides several definitions of non-functional requirements in general and of SOA in particular. Furthermore, it discusses the available approaches for their specification. The possible conflicts which may occur between functional and non-functional requirements, as well as among non-functional properties of a SOA-based system are addressed in the Requirements Interconnections Section. The Non-Functional Modelling Approaches in SOA presents several of the available solutions for the design and implementation of non-functional requirements. The Related Work Section mentions several articles which aim to offer a survey on various aspects of SOA. The chapter ends with a list of several main future trends in SOA.

MAIN FEATURES OF SOA

The definition provided by Newcomer and Lomow (2005) mention that a "service-oriented architecture (SOA) is a style of design that guides all the aspects of creating and using business services throughout their lifecycle (from conception to retirement), as well as of defining and provisioning the IT infrastructure that allows different applications to exchange data and participate in business processes regardless of the operating system or programming languages underlying those applications". Also Erl (2005) sustains that "a SOA establishes an architectural model that aims to enhance the efficiency, agility, and productivity of an enterprise by positioning services as the primary means through which solution logic is represented in support of the realization of strategic goals associated with service-oriented computing".

What do these definitions imply? The first important concept is that SOA is not just a software architecture: it is extended to other domains of a business organization, ranging from the business level to the department level. The main goal of this architecture, citing Newcomer and Lomow (2005) again, is to align the IT infrastructure to the business goals of its company. This is one of the most important concepts to understand and to apply when designing a SOA: the IT architecture should be driven by the business model, adapt to it and support it, and not the contrary. To achieve this, IT services should be modeled to match existing business services, so that the IT and business infrastructures are aligned among them.

To further stress this concept we use the vision given by Nicholas Carr (2004) on this topic and synthesized in Geet (2008): IT is turning from a competitive advantage into a commodity and thus into a cost. It happened the same with the electricity in the last decades: the advantages gained by the latest technology fade away so quickly that often they do not even repay their investment. Therefore, attention must be shifted to obtaining a reliable and cost-effective IT infrastructure to support daily business: only by focusing to a company's core business, which is not the IT for most enterprises, real competitive advantage is gained.

IT executives have been trying to surmount the challenges in overcoming costs and maximize utilization of existing technology assets and, at the same time, better serve the customers, be more competitive and be able to face changes in the business environment. Heterogeneity and change (Endrei, Ang, Arsanjani, Chua, Comte, Krogdahl, Luo & Newling, 2004) are the two themes that still drive the IT personnel's efforts: they have to cope with different existing system applications and architectures, coming from different time periods and being implemented with different technologies, and they have to be ready for unforeseen evolution of their working environment. The concern about existing systems is that they have to be well integrated and a vendor-specific approach to the problem is not an option: while granting a certain degree of stability and ease of deployment it lacks in the required flexibility and interoperability properties. The second problem comes from globalization and e-business, which leads to fierce competition, and also from the fact that different offers and the widespread availability of product information make customers' needs and requirements change more quickly, thus posing the problem of change for enterprises and IT executives as well. Technology advance is not keen on those professionals and companies alike, since continuous evolution promises to enhance productivity while diminishing costs: changes would then be required to take full advantage of these possibilities, but it should also not alter the way services were provided in the past, granting backward compatibility to consumers.

Therefore, software architectures have evolved alongside with enterprises' business, reaching the current generation of Service Oriented Architecture, as shown in Figure 1. SOA tries to overcome heterogeneity, integration and change in customers and business needs along with technology advances, it propose a solution to these problems by providing a platform that supports application services, which are the second important concept expressed by the aforementioned SOA definitions.

Figure 1. Evolution of software architecture

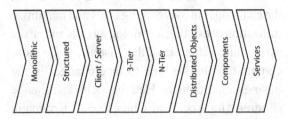

Figure 2. Architectural elements of a SOA

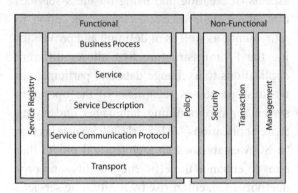

From the perspective of OASIS SOA Reference Model TC (MacKenzie, Laskey, McCabe, Brown & Metz, 2006), any design for a system that adopts the SOA approach should: (1) have entities that can be identified as services as defined by this reference model; (2) be able to identify how visibility is established between service providers and consumers; (3) be able to identify how interaction is mediated; (4) be able to identify how the effect of using services is understood; (5) have descriptions associated with services; (6) be able to identify the execution context required to support interaction.

Following again the definitions presented in Endrei et al. (2004), services are software elements mapped directly to business functions, which are identified in the process of business analysis. They interact with applications and other services by means of a communication model which is described as loosely coupled and message based. A service has a well-defined interface, called its contract, which allows it to be published, discovered and invoked. Services may be published internally within the organization or externally to business partners.

Loose coupling is one of the important design goals for services (Newcomer & Lomow, 2005). This term has a broad meaning and may refer to interface, technology and process coupling. Interface coupling measures the dependencies that the provider imposes on the requester; loose coupling here means that the requester should know the details of a service implementation when requesting the service to the provider because service usage should be possible just by exploiting

the published service contract (its interface) and service-level agreement. Technology coupling measures the dependencies of a service on specific technologies; loose coupling here means that the requester of a service is not forced to use the same IT technology of the provider, such as language, platform or operating system. Process coupling measures how much a service is dependent on a particular business process and by being loose it means that the service may be reused in different applications or businesses process: this should enable developers to compose and orchestrate new services based on smaller ones.

SOA focuses not only on functional aspects of services, but also on their non-functional qualities, such as Quality of Service (QoS). Currently, well-established SOA elements cover most of the functional elements, while non-functional ones are emerging and still not well-defined and widespread. Figure 2 shows all these elements and their role in SOA, following the view given in Endrei et al. (2004).

Functional issues include:

- **Transport** – It is related to the delivery of service requests and responses between the requester and the provider.
- **Service Communication Protocol** – A well-defined mechanism used by the requester and provider of a service to communicate with each other.

- **Service Description** – A schema which defines what a service is, how it should be requested and what data is required to invoke it successfully.
- **Service** – Describes an actual service that is made available for use.
- **Business Process** – A set of services invoked in a particular sequence, to meet a business requirement.
- **Service Registry** – A repository of service and data descriptions which is used by providers to publish their services and by consumers to find them.

Non-functional properties include:

- **Policy** – A set of rules under which a service provider makes its service available to consumers. They may be related both to functional and non-functional properties of a service and thus being located in both areas.
- **Security** – A set of functionalities which enable authentication, authorization, and access control to a service.
- **Transaction** – A set of attributes which may be applied to a group of services to deliver a consistent result.
- **Management** – A set of attributes which may be applied to manage the services provided or consumed.

Through SOA companies have a number of benefits that help them deal with concerns like quick change and cost reduction. Adaptation to internal factors such as acquisitions and restructuring, and external factors such as customer requirements and competitive forces, is a key ability that an enterprise has to have in order to remain ahead of its competitors.

SOA grants a way to leverage existing assets, by exposing them as services that can be used in new applications and contexts both by the company itself and its partners, thus eliminating the need to start from scratch its development. Migration becomes easier and complexity can be managed more effectively, since services are defined by their interface and not by their implementation. This means that changes in technology and organization are completely transparent from a functional point of view; integration is easier because of the provisioning of an interface for existing assets and resources distributed on different systems, hence, complexities are isolated. The modularity and the ability to build composite services on top of existing ones shortens time-to-market and response time to new customers' requirements. Since business functions are exposed in a loosely coupled way as services, they are reusable, reducing cost and duplication of resources. Through SOA, companies are better prepared to address future requirements, because they gain flexibility and responsiveness.

However, SOA is not a solution for all problems: the migration to such an architecture cannot be done overnight. The first and main challenge is to ensure adequate staff training and discipline in order to develop reusable services conceived for the long-term benefit. Citing Newcomer and Lomow (2005), "the existence of an individual service isn't much of a value unless it fits in a larger collection of services that can be consumed by multiple applications, and out of which multiple new applications can be composed. In addition, the definition of a reusable service is very difficult to get right the first time". Services may be built upon existing assets, reducing development costs and better leveraging previous investments; as good as it might sound, exposing existing applications as services usually means that some modifications have to be done in order to let those resources participate in SOA. Another challenge is managing short-term cost, since migrating to SOA or building it from scratch is far from being cheap. SOA shows its value over time, therefore a way to mitigate expenses might be to incrementally adopt this architecture in areas where it will have the greatest business impact.

Figure 3. Architectural elements of a SOA

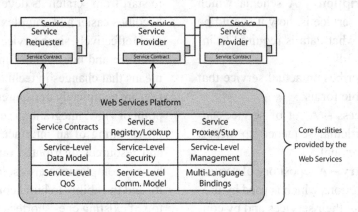

When considering SOA and its implementation examples, the Web Services approach should be mentioned. While it is commonly accepted that SOA does not mean Web Services, it is also clear that the second is a good way to implement the first. A SOA based on Web Services has a series of advantages (Newcomer & Lomow, 2005): it is standard-based, ensures interoperability and supports integration at various levels, thus adhering to the SOA model. Also a Web Services platform is based to the greatest extent possible on open standards like WSDL, SOAP, UDDI or WS-*and it contains basic and extended features necessary to support a SOA, along with an Enterprise Service Bus (ESB) to connect the services. A view of the basic Web Services platform (Newcomer & Lomow, 2005) is presented in Figure 3.

NON-FUNCTIONAL PROPERTIES IN SOA

The complexity of today's information systems is determined not only by their functionalities, but also by their non-functional requirements such as cost, performance, availability, reliability, security, scalability. While functional aspects describe *what* a system does, the non-functional ones define *how* these functionalities are fulfilled. The market of systems and services is increasing with the demand

for software which implements the requested functionalities and moreover, addresses a set of the above mentioned features.

In general, systems are considered as a whole when evaluating functional and non-functional requirements satisfaction; in a SOA architecture, both types of requirements are achieved with the use of a set of services, each of them implementing a part of the business logic that is requested. This means that each service has a direct impact on the system ability to achieve its requirements, most importantly the non-functional ones. Let's think about a financial system that must give exchange rates for a given currency in a timely fashion and it is implemented using a SOA architecture: if the system implements the requested business logic by using a currency conversion service, it binds its ability to achieve the non-functional requirement of "timeliness" to the capability of the service to respond in a short interval of time. Because each service concurs in the achievement of functional requirements in a SOA architecture, since it is part of the system's business logic, it is also directly responsible for the system ability to achieve non-functional requirements, since its non-functional properties have in general a direct impact on the system performance.

To help the understanding and the schematization of non-functional properties we can refer to the classification made by Sommerville (2004) for non-functional requirements. This classification was intended for software systems in general, and not specifically for SOA architectures, but it is never the less valid to guide the characterization of services properties. Sommerville classifies non-functional requirements into three categories (Sommerville, 2004):

- *Product* requirements, which are related to the behavior of the final product; examples of such requirements include performance, reliability, portability, usability aspects; this type of requirements has its roots in the users' needs.
- *Organizational* requirements, which are determined by the customer's and developer's organization procedure; examples of such requirements include design methodologies, competences in using programming languages, documentation support; this type of requirements is a consequence of the internal organization of the IT companies.
- *External* requirements, which do not concern the software product or its development process; examples of such requirements include interoperability, legislative, ethical aspects.

Each non-functional requirement can be considered as the need for a specific level of performance on a specific field, while non-functional properties express the level of performance on a specific field that can be delivered by a system or a service. We can consider that requirements and properties are the two faces of the same coin, thus explaining why Sommerville classification is very helpful in characterizing non-functional properties in SOA architectures. It should be made clear that this classification is also intended to be general and abstract, since each specific domain needs a finer division and a proper prioritization of non-functional requirements that are important for that domain. A further classification of non-functional

requirements, for example, may divide them into those which can be observed at run-time, such as performance and usability, and those which regard static features, such as maintainability or scalability. To help the engineering and the maintenance of non-functional requirements in SOA, it is possible to use some specific UML profile to graphically specify non-functional aspects in an implementation independent manner, such as the one proposed in Wada, Suzuki and Oda (2006).

Engineering non-functional requirements for a SOA architecture may also take advantage of the notions contained in Sommerville's work, since they are intended for general software systems, but they also need some additional considerations in order to tackle some specific problems that arise in such an architecture. In Xiping (2007), the author identifies several non-functional characteristics that describe SOA platforms, such as the flexibility of deployment in different scenarios and domains or the service sharing among different stakeholders. The large number of deployment variations and the user's needs will have repercussions on non-functional requirements and will make the task of collecting, formalizing and designing such requirements harder, more complex and expensive. The development and service life-cycle can also influence non-functional requirements, making more difficult to test them in the development environment. In Reiff-Marganiec, Yu and Tilly (2007) the authors propose a methodology to obtain non-functional requirements and capture non-functional properties for individual services in a SOA implemented via web services. The methodology is based on the assignment of each operation offered by a service to one or more categories at registration time. A category associates to a certain set of criteria (non-functional properties) which are defined during generation of the categories and it is used in the process of service ranking during the service selection phase of the SOA architecture.

Because non-functional properties of a service are essential to evaluate that service ability to fulfill some non-functional requirement, it becomes clear that in the service-oriented domain those properties should be considered as an essential part of a service description (O'Sullivan, Edmond & ter Hofstede, 2002). The authors sustain that a service description is complete only after the specification of non-functional properties and that an accurate and complete description of services is useful to address their discovery, substitution, composition and management.

Specification of Non-Functional Properties

The non-functional properties of a system play a critical role in the life-cycle of a software because the experience shows that they are the most difficult and expensive to deal with and to correct. A famous example of critical failures due to non-compliance of non-functional requirements is the case of the deactivation of the London Ambulance System just after its deployment, because of several problems, many of them related to non-functional requirements such as performance, robustness and conformance with standards (Finkelstein & Dowell, 1996; Cysneiros & Leite, 2002).

A correct managing of non-functional properties must be made as early as possible and they must be considered during the whole software development process in order to take correct decisions and avoid costly failures. Non-functional properties are in fact related to architectural and design decisions of a system and their non-compliance can lead to costly changes.

Primarily, the management of non-functional properties consisted in writing them in the software requirements document in natural languages. Today's research in software engineering is focusing more and more on approaches that explicitly model and address them during the development phases of a system.

In this context, the non-functional properties of a system may be described through a Software Requirements Specification (SRS). IEEE Std-830-1998 (IEEE Std, 1998) proposes a standard for writing a good document in which are described both functional and non-functional requirements. A SRS is a specification for a particular software product which addresses the following aspects: the functionalities of a system, the definition of external interfaces, performance, system's attributes (intended as additional non-functional properties not considered in other sections) and design constraints. A SRS does not address neither project requirements, nor design details.

A well-written SRS should be (IEEE Std, 1998):

- *correct*: the software system shall meet every requirement that is in the SRS. Verifying the correctness of a SRS is not an automatic procedure and can be addressed by traceability.
- *unambiguous*: every requirement must have only one interpretation. Non-functional requirements must be unambiguous both for who writes them and for who reads them. Because they are written in a natural language, it is recommended to make a review of the SRS by a third party, and to keep a glossary in which all ambiguous terms are explained. To help in avoiding ambiguity, languages and tools for their semi-formal or formal representation should be used.
- *complete*: the SRS should contain all the significant requirements.
- *internal consistent*: no contradiction should arise from requirements.
- *ranked by importance and/or stability*: in order to distinguish between critical and desirable requirements, there must be indicated their importance.
- *verifiable*: there must exist a cost-effective process by which we can determine if requirements are satisfied.

- *modifiable*: the requirements must have a structure that permits to change and evolve them easily.
- *traceable*: the origin of the requirements must be clear and there must be possible to correctly reference them.

In the template proposed by the standard, non-functional properties are below the functional ones and are organized as follows: three separated sections for performance requirements, design constraints and standard compliance, and a macro-section for additional non-functional properties (called system's attributes) like availability, security and so on.

The standard gives also recommendations for the process of writing a SRS. It must be written by both a developer and a user, because a user does not have skills to write an effective SRS while the developer must understand users' needs in detail.

A critical aspect in defining non-functional properties is that they must be verifiable. Where possible, it is important to describe them in a measurable way, because it must be possible to interpret them correctly during the development phase and objectively verify them. Sommerville remarks that there are several properties, such as the response time or memory occupation which are objectively measurable, while others such as usability which are not objectively measurable (because it depends on the user who tests the system). Furthermore, non-functional properties such as maintainability cannot be measured. Examples of measures are: transactions per second or response time for performance, training time for usability, mean time between failures for reliability.

Zscahler proposes a framework for the specification of non-functional properties in a composition-based system (Zscahler, 2004). Again, measurability is the most relevant aspect in the definition of a non-functional property. First, there are defined measurements of a non-functional dimension of a system and then constraints over them are introduced. The author makes the dis-

tinction between extrinsic measurements, which describe a dimension that is applicable to the service and is relevant from a user perspective (e.g. response time) and intrinsic measurements, which refer to components implementation and describe the properties of an actually existing property independently of the implementation details (e.g. execution time of an operation).

During the last years different approaches to deal with non-functional requirements were defined. The traditional approach is product-oriented. Product-oriented requirements engineering is typically a quantitative approach. Its objective is to define non-functional requirements in a way that it is possible to evaluate how (or better how much) the system meets them. The principal activity is to define metrics by which non-functional requirements can be measured.

A qualitative approach to non-functional requirements is considered process-oriented. Mylopoulos, Chung and Nixon (1992) define non-functional requirements in order to motivate design decisions during the software development cycle. As we may have different alternatives to consider as possible solutions during the software design, non-functional requirements can be viewed as a determinant indication to choose the most appropriate one.

In the context of goal-oriented engineering (Regev & Wegmann, 2005), requirements are modeled as goals to be achieved by a design of a system. Examples of goals include security, privacy for non-functional requirements, authentication and billing for functional ones. An analysis of the goal-oriented approaches is given in Lamsweerde (2001). Goals are objectives of a system whose satisfaction requires cooperation of agents in the software or in the environment. Goals may refer to a functional requirement, and are used for defining models such as use cases, or a system quality, and are used in order to choose between different design alternatives. A possible model is the goal-graph, that shows all the goals and how they interact. Goal-oriented approaches lead to various advantages, such as the possibility to automatically reason over them, or to verify if they are completed through the generation scenarios covered by goals, as remarked in Lamsweerde (2001).

Another approach that has emerged in the last years is the aspect-oriented requirements engineering (Sousa & Castro, 2003), and it is related to the use of Aspect Oriented Programming (AOP). AOP tries to achieve separation of concerns by modeling the cross-cutting issues of a system, that often refer to non-functional properties, such as security, separated from the provided functionalities. The objectives of aspect-orientation is to address these cross-cutting issues in the early stage of development process in a way that it is natural to map them down in AOP.

A Closer Look to Non-Functional Properties in SOA

The non-functional requirements previously presented apply to all software systems. However, it is obvious that various types of such requirements are more important in specific domains. Examples of the most important systems qualities in different application areas are presented in Ghezzi, Jazayeri and Mandrioli (2003). For instance, the most relevant non-functional properties in real-time system are response time, reliability, security, while in a informative system are transactions per second, usability, data integrity, security and availability.

Non-functional properties that are relevant in service-oriented solutions are discussed in O'Sullivan, Edmond and ter Hofstede (2002). Based on a research related to the existing commercial service-oriented solutions, nine important non-functional properties have been identified:

- *Temporal availability*, which refers to the temporal constraints related to a service, meaning the time when a service is available.

- *Spatial availability*, which refers to the spatial constraint of a service, intended as where a service is available.
- *Channel*, which refers to a description of how a service is used in terms of endpoints, information being transmitted and interaction patterns.
- *Charging styles*, which refers to how to pay for a service. Three kinds of charging styles are mentioned: a payment for the service delivery, a payment by unit of measure and granularity, and a payment on a percentage of some aspects of the service.
- *Settlement*, which refers to mutual obligations of the provider (usually related to the delivery of a service) and requestor (usually considered the payment for a service). Two types of settlement models are identified: transactional and rental. The first is a delivery for payment, while the second implies a long term relationship.
- *Payment obligation*, which refers to the description of the various payments which must be performed during some stage of the delivery of a service.
- *Service quality*, which refers to the difference between expected and actual service provision. Authors outline that this is a complex and domain-specific property.
- *Security and trust*, security refers to the identity, privacy, alteration and repudiation of information exchanged, while trust is determined by the reputation of the service providers and requestors.
- *Ownership and rights*, which refers to the degree of control of the requestor over the consumption of the service. The authors identify the following rights: to comprehend the service (by questioning the provider), to retract the request, to terminate a service prematurely, the right to suspend and resume a service.

Most of these properties can be defined in a Service Level Agreement (SLA) (Jin Machiraju & Sahai, 2002). A SLA is a contract between the requestor and the provider of a service, which can include penalties for the non-compliance of one or more properties. A SLA defines every aspect of a service delivery. A typical template of a SLA contains the following parts: purpose, parties, validity period, scope, restrictions, service-level objectives, penalties, optional services, exclusions, and administration details (Jin Machiraju, & Sahai, 2002). Service qualities are without any doubt the most user-perspective critical requirements in the service delivery. With the proliferation of services users can choose between several services with the same functionalities that differ by the qualities related to their delivery. If a user chooses and pays for a service, he wants to be sure that it will be compliant to the requested features, otherwise, he wants to be refunded. The part of a SLA that addresses service qualities is the Service Level Objectives (SLO) section. The SLO is an agreement between the requestor and the provider on how to measure the qualities of a service in order to decide if the service delivery is compliant with users' needs.

Security is another important property when dealing with services and software engineering in general. Security, as other non-functional issues, can have a fundamental role in the final architecture of the system. In the Web Services domain there is a standard for addressing security: WS-security, a protocol dealing with the integrity and confidentiality in Web Services messaging. The standard includes authentication mechanisms based on, for examples, the X.509 or Kerberos standards and confidentiality and integrity mechanisms, such as XML encryption and XML signature (Larrucea & Alonso, 2008). These mechanisms are achieved through headers of SOAP messages. In comparison with other security methods such as those based on a transport layer protocol (e.g., SSL), WS-security guarantees the security over the whole route of messages, providing an end-to-end security approach.

Management of Non-Functional Properties in SOA through SLA

Service Level Agreements (SLA) are contracts negotiated between the requester and the provider of a service. These contracts define the functional and non-functional requirements expressed by a client and agreed by a provider for a specific service or a set of services.

Sturm, Morris and Jander (2000) give detailed structure of a SLA that is composed by the following components:

- *Purpose*: describes the motivation for creating the SLA.
- *Parties*: defines the two (or more) groups, and their respective roles, which are involved in the definition of the SLA.
- *Term*: defines the period of time in which the SLA is valid.
- *Scope*: defines all the services covered in the agreement.
- *Limitations*: qualifies the services defined in the *scope* section by indicating reasonable restrictions on the use of the services by the consumer.
- *Service level objectives*: are the agreed levels of services that providers assure to deliver/respect. Usually levels refer to availability, performance, reliability and so on.
- *Service level indicators*: every *service level objective* must be measurable thus, the indicators, are the measure of objectives.
- *Non-performance*: describes the penalties that are applied to the provider in the case it was not able to provide the agreed level of services.
- *Optional services*: describes additional services that should be needed by the consumer, but they are not normally provided.

- *Exclusions*: specifies what is not included in the agreement and not covered in the SLA.

- *Administration*: describes how the measures of levels of services are checked and what processes are created to meet the needs.

Modeling SLA is an important task to achieve in order to assure the quality of services between consumers and providers. Building SLA models automatically can improve the process of defining services and the monitoring process of the level of quality. Many researchers have focused their research on programmatically modeling an SLA. Chau *et al.* (2008) propose a technique for modeling and monitoring SLA with an event-based approach. The proposed model is based and refines the WSLA specification and consists of multiple service level objectives (SLO); metrics are also used to indicate different measurement aspects of a process. SLA are monitored with an event-based approach so this allows to define action handlers that can be raised and can react when SLO are violated. In this approach, the state of the current process is contained in the events that are emitted by the business process.

An alternative way to model SLA is proposed by Lamana *et al.* (2003). They introduce SLAng, a language for modeling SLA that extends existing business process languages which provides a format for the negotiation of quality of service (QoS) properties and a language for describing QoS-aware adaptive middleware. In SLAng, a SLA is defined as a set of QoS parameters that the target server must support in order to provide a service's i-th defined specification.

Several authors try to address the problem of modeling and monitoring SLA from the Web Services point of view. Sahai *et al.* (2002), for example, introduce an own language to specify service level agreements, and present an engine to monitor them automatically.

Keller *and* Ludwig (2003) propose an XML-based schema for SLA modeling that allows, for example, to express complex metrics and SLO as a composition of a number of other metrics. The schema also allows hierarchical relationships creation/definition between metric and SLO that increment the extensibility of the model.

REQUIREMENTS INTERCONNECTIONS

In the software development often arise conflicts which involve non-functional requirements. These conflicts may be between non-functional requirements or between the non-functional and functional ones. Typical examples are conflicts between performance and cost aspects or between the system quality, development cost and time-to-market. In bank applications which are reachable through the Web, users are requested to provide authentication information in different phases and places. Users may be annoyed of this repetition. Hence, this can be considered a conflict between the security and usability non-functional properties.

The cross-cutting nature of non-functional properties over the functional ones causes interactions between them (Weiss & Esfandiari, 2004). These interactions can lead to conflicts. Consider the example of a search file system in which it is introduced periodically the automatic indexing of files. This is a useful functionality, but it may have a significant impact on the system's performance.

In SOA, the conflicts' problem is divided into two sub-problems. The first is verified during the service-development, when conflicts between requirements may arise. This is common to other software development processes. The second is related to the conflicts which arise in the services composition. One of the objectives of SOA, in fact, is to permit services composition and interaction through orchestration and choreography. During these operations attention must be paid in order to avoid undesirable conflicts between the functionalities and the qualities of services.

Requirements Conflicts in Software Development

The problem of requirements conflicts in software development may be addressed during the specification step through requirements negotiation. This is analyzed in Ruhe and Eberlein (2003), and the solution proposed consists in a framework for the requirements selection. The problem of selecting the wrong subset of requirements may have a disastrous impact in the software development. The conflicts between requirements arise mainly due to the different views and priorities that the different stakeholders have on the system. Moreover, requirements are often imprecise and incomplete in the early stages of the development process and evolve later. The solution is to make a compromise among the requirements, by establishing appropriate trade-offs. The framework proposed by authors, called WinWin, helps in balancing different stakeholders' needs and in selecting the most appropriate subset of requirements. Hence, the main objective is to balance these three conflicting non-functional variables: effort of the developing team, time-to-market, and qualities of the system.

A frequent problem which may raise conflicts is related to the fact that even if the architecture design and requirements negotiations are very coupled activities, they are often performed separately (Kazman In & Chen, 2005). This causes uncertainty in requirements selection with costly consequences. Authors propose an enhanced version of WinWin, called WinCBAM, that joins Win-Win and CBAM (Cost-Benefit Analysis Method) to create a more effective framework. The result is a eight-step process in which each stakeholder elicits their winning conditions through a deep evaluation and selection.

In software development, the analysis and negotiation of requirements have to be addressed as early as possible, in order to avoid costly changes to the system. Analytical methods for dealing with these aspects, such as the ones we presented above, can help in achieving this task.

Requirements Conflicts in Services Compositions

In SOA, it is possible to compose services in order to create new higher-level services. Moreover, it is possible to implement business processes invoking a certain sequence of services, through, for example, the WS-BPEL (Oasis, 2007) standard. This is a very desirable feature, but it introduces also several challenges due to the interaction among services.

The composition of services is much more than a simple composition of their functionalities: their non-functional properties should also be considered and the composition of the last may be even more complex than the functional ones (O'Sullivan, Edmond & ter Hofstede, 2002). How composition of services causes feature (intended as functional and non-functional properties) interactions that have to be considered is shown in Weiss and Esfandiari (2004). Authors identify three types of composition of Web Services. The first is the explicit interaction in which services are intentionally composed. The other two are different kinds of implicit compositions, intended as non-intentional interactions among Web Services. There are parallelisms among Web Services, which can lead to interactions such as contention of resources and side-effects that regard interactions between services through other services they intentionally interact with. Seven possible causes of conflicts among Web Services are identified (Weiss & Esfandiari, 2004):

- *Goal conflict*: it arises when two Web Services address different and conflicting goals of a stakeholder. The example explained by authors consists in a conflict between privacy and usability due to distribution of users' data to other services providers in order to have a unique point of authentication.

- *Deployment and ownership*: the decision of who provides a service (ownership) and where the service is executed (deployment) can avoid or create a conflict. For example, deploying a service on different hosts can avoid resources' contentions and can increase system's scalability and performance.
- *Information hiding:* it consists in exposing only the interface of a service. A user that exploits a service does not know anything about its implementation. Conflicts in Web Services composition can arise from possible hidden calls of services involved in the composition.
- *Invocation order:* it occurs when the execution does not follow the correct flow of message exchange. The example given by authors is a user that cancels an order just before the payment is processed. If the message arrives after the payment is completed, but before the product is shipped, the result is that the user has paid for a product that will never be shipped. The solution for these problems can be the use of a transaction system.
- *Resource contention*: it occurs when two services claim from the same resource, which can be, for example, a hardware resource or another service.
- *Violation of assumptions*: it occurs when a third party service is invoked by an intermediary one with incorrect or incomplete arguments.
- *Policy conflict*: it occurs when there are two or more possible conflicting policies to access a service. The example given by authors is an e-commerce Web site where a user has two different discount policies, but only one can be used when an order is processed.

The most interesting issue to address when dealing with non-functional requirements is without any doubt the goal conflict. Any non-functional requirement is, in fact, related to a goal of a stakeholder. A methodology to detect and address a Web Service feature interaction is shown in Weiss and Esfandiari (2004). It is composed of three steps: the first one is to model a goal graph, the second is to analyze it in order to relieve conflicts among goals and the third is to resolve the interaction through various strategies.

When dealing with composition of services, we have to take into consideration all possible interactions and side-effects of both functional and non-functional requirements. An approach for dealing with these aspects is provided in Weiss and Esfandiari (2004), but the authors stress that this is not a methodology, but a reference framework. Accurate analyses and experience can further help in detecting and avoiding these types of conflicts.

NON-FUNCTIONAL MODELLING APPROACHES IN SOA

The approaches addressing the modelling of non-functional properties in SOA range from informal to UML-based solutions. It is fundamental to understand the benefits they offer in order to exploit them properly, and their limitations in order to enhance them. This section provides an overview of various approaches addressing this issue.

A framework to analyze decisions regarding implementations of SOA by assessing their business value through the measurement of costs, efforts and benefits is introduced in Lagerström and Öhrström (2007) and Öhrström (2007). The framework is based on a modeling language called Extended Influence Diagrams (EID) (Johnson Lagerstrom Narman & Simonsson, 2006; Johnson & Ekstedt, 2007; Johnson Lagerström & Narman, 2007) that helps IT-decision makers to analyze what decisions to take in order to achieve specific goals. Thus, it provides support to evaluate the business value of SOA. The framework defines the business of a SOA-based solution as a combination of two components: the modifying effort of making the change to become service oriented and the specific benefits of SOA. The first uses the definition provided in Oman, Hagemeister and Ach (1992) to estimate the effort of change. The definition has two parts: the modifiability of the system, measured by attributes such as system complexity, analyzability, age of system, and the complexity of the change, measured through the size of change, number of components, experience. The second component related to the benefits of SOA is measured by the degree of increased revenues, degree of decreased costs within the organization and the level of positive internal organizational effects.

A general purpose UML profile for service-oriented architectures which handles different aspects of SOA and both functional and non-functional issues is described in Amir and Zeid (2004). This meta-model consists of five different profiles: the resource profile, which is intended for modeling any resource by identifying a main key or identifier of the resource; the service profile, which extends the previous one and describes how to model a service with a controller and how to package all these elements in a service component; the message profile, which describes how each message exchanged by the service should be modeled as a component; and the agent profile, which shows how to introduce agents. The service policy profile describes the modeling of the policies, and therefore non-functional properties, which should be applied to the service usage. It is composed of six elements: audit guard, permission guard, policy, permission, obligation, and policy interface.

On the other hand Wada, Suzuki and Oba (2006) present a UML profile to graphically design non-functional properties and maintain them independent of any implementation detail. This UML profile provides five key model elements defined as stereotypes: service, message

exchange, message, connector and filter. The service stereotype represents a network service. The message exchange element represents a pair of a request and reply messages. These messages are described by the message stereotype. The connector element represents a link between services and defines the semantics of message transmissions and processing. The filter stereotype customizes the semantics of the message transmission and message processing in a connector.

Web Services and Agent-Oriented Services may be considered fulfillments of Service-Oriented Computing (SOC). Two different agent-based approaches to address QoS issues and the dynamic selection of services are proposed in Shah *et al.* (2008) and Maximilien and Singh (2004).

The framework for service-oriented applications described in Shah, Iqbal, James and Iqbal (2008) monitors and achieves the requested level of QoS through agents. Each service has its own monitoring agent and every communication between the provider and consumer takes place through a QoS monitoring agent. The agents are able to detect any abnormality because QoS agreements and commitments between a producer and a consumer are translated into rules used by agents to monitor the QoS. Agents are also equipped with the knowledge of exceptions, symptoms, and causes which may occur during the delivery of a service. The QoS monitoring agent is composed of two components: the detection module and the diagnostic capability. The detection module monitors all service's interactions and detects all the potential abnormalities; when an exception is detected, the module offloads the event to the diagnostic capability. The last applies the Heuristic Classification (Clancy, 1985) approach to uncover the cause of a symptom.

A framework for the dynamic service selection via agents coupled with a QoS ontology which allows to determinate services' qualities in a collaborative environment is presented in Maximilien and Singh (2004). The dynamic selection is based on autonomous agents, which can represent autonomous services as well as collaborate to reconfigure dynamically service-based applications by gathering, storing and aggregating QoS information. The implementation of the agent-based architecture is called Web Services Agent Framework (WSAF) and uses QoS ontologies that allow providers and consumers to expose and match their offered and required quality. Agents provide interfaces, which are able to capture clients' QoS preferences, identify the suitable solution and let consumer rank services, too.

An evaluation framework that includes a meta-model to formalize the QoS and a decisional model to allow a systematic approach for comparing services through two different components is presented in Casola, Fasolino, Mazzocca and Tramontana (2007). The first component consists of a SLA policy meta-model providing an approach to define and formalize QoS criteria by policies. The meta-model supports a hierarchical view of QoS which allows the decomposition of each quality characteristic into lower level measurable ones. The second component is a decision-making process which automates the selection of the most appropriate service based on providers' offers and customers' requests. To achieve this task, authors propose to use the Analytic Hierarchy Process (Saaty, 1990; Zhu, Aurum, Gorton & Jeffery, 2005).

Adaptivity (Cheng, de Lemos, Giese, Inverardi & Magee, 2009) is an important issue which addresses the needs of consumers requesting different and customized sets of contexts and preferences related to the quality of the services. Erradi, Maheshwari and Padmanabhuni (2005) present a framework that aims to improve the dynamic services composition to provide a greater degree of configurability and quality of Web Services. The proposed framework, namely AdaptiveBPEL, can easily adapt to changes in business rules, policies and services interactions. Moreover, it provides different levels of functional and QoS offerings. The idea is to extend the functionalities of existing Web Services composition engine in order to provide new functionalities like check constraints defined in SLA, add debugging features, encryption and decryption, trap and redirect all messages from and to different services. With this approach, all these features can be made at runtime and services can reconfigure themselves by altering the process and data flows. AdaptiveBPEL is based on Aspect-Oriented Software Development (AOSD) (AOSD, 2008) and on a policy-driven core. Using AOSD, the framework can dynamically extend and customize the functional and non-functional behavior of services, adapt to changes of services and provide various levels of QoS. The adaptation process is the core of the framework. It is policy driven and it declaratively defines the adaptive service behavior through selective and dynamic injection of functional and non-functional extensions into a core service. This allows on-demand service instance adaptation and the provisioning of differentiated service levels from the same service implementation/composition. Thus, components responsible of adaptivity and non-functional concerns need to be encapsulated into a set of aspects, then there is the need to identify the joint points for service composition and finally AdaptiveBPEL drives the aspects of the core service composition.

One of the most important non-functional issues concerns security. A security model built for applications may become insecure after its migration to a service-oriented solution. Candolin (2007) proposes a security framework as a part of a security architecture that can manage this non-functional issue both from services and users prospective. A user must be able to authenticate and trust a service, while providers must be sure that users are legitimated to use their services. In Candolin (2005), security is considered at three levels: content, communication and network. The protection of the content level corresponds to the application layer of the IP stack and here is where SOA security is handled. At this level several protocols in different architectural stacks are used and the security framework relies on this structure. The framework needs to meet several requirements such as service and user authentication, access control, confidentiality, integrity, availability, privacy and trust. The SOA security standards are able to handle authentication and access control. The Content Based Information Security model (CBIS) (Candolin & Kiviharju, 2007) makes confidentiality and integrity secure. Availability is divided into two classes: availability of the network resources which can be ensured via the Packet Level Authentication architecture, and availability of the service, which can be ensured by puzzle based authentication schemes. The Packet Level Authentication adds an extension header to the IPv6 stack which contains a cryptographic key, while a puzzle based authentication is based on several not trivial schemes which a client must solve before using the service. For the privacy, the framework uses standards already built-in in other security services. Trust is another complex issue and the framework imports the results from Nikander (1999).

Another approach to secure services is provided by Amouzegar, Mohammadi, Tarokh and Hidaji (2008), which proposes a security model for interactive stateful services based on automata. An automaton is a self-operating machine (Amouzegar Mohammadi Tarokh & Hidaji, 2008). One of the features of automata-based programming is the ability to relegate business logic to event handlers where the automata can interact among them by calling each other with the help of the state numbers interchange. From this point of view, there are three types of security needs: preventing unsecured entrances, finding unsecured inside threats and unsecured threats should not finish any data transaction. This approach maps these three issues to three states of a finite state machine: start, middle and final. Thus, if a client needs a service, he should have a key to enter the service, the appropriate identity to go through the middle states, and then he should have the key to commit the transaction, too.

Usually, the modeling of SOA is addressed from the services providers' point of view. An alternative approach considering a Consumer-Centric SOA (CCSOA) is presented in Tsai, Xiao, Chen and Paul (2006). The basic idea behind this solution is to allow consumers to publish the services and the applications they need and to allow providers to produce and suggest their services. When a consumer publishes an application, he can specify the application workflow, the service description and the acceptance criteria for the service related to both functional and non-functional properties. This approach supports the search of services and enables the consumers to check if there is already a service matching their requests. A service may be integrated with other applications, too. Hence, CCSOA provides a framework for collaboration-oriented service specification, registration, discovery, matching, verification, validation and composition. Applications can be built using BPEL, SCA/SDO or PSML-S and may include workflow, service, acceptance criteria specifications and application templates. Consumers should check if their application templates are reasonable and qualified in order to permit providers to produce services; this can be performed using a Distributed Dynamic Service-Oriented Simulation (DDSOS) (Tsai Fan & Chen, 2006) to simulate and evaluate the soundness of the applications design. To enable the discovery and matching of application templates, CCSOA provides a collaboration ontology. Once a provider builds a service for an application, before registering, the service must be verified and validated by the service broker through the service acceptance criteria. This is done by a service verification and validation agent, which can retrieve the test cases supplied by the application builder. After the service passes all the testing requirements, it is registered to the application template, CCSOA can maintain the link between the application and service implementations, because a service can be an implementation of many different applications and, vice-versa, an application can have many different service implementations. Thus, CCSOA is able to manage and store multiple one-to-many links between services implementations and application templates.

RELATED WORK

The SOA and its related issues are subject of different surveys available in the scientific literature. In this section we mention the ones which are closer to the subject of this chapter.

A survey on the development issues which should be addressed in SOA is presented in Papazoglou and van den Heuvel (2006). The authors provide details on the characteristics of services' development life cycle methodology and present a Web Services case study based on a design and development methodology exploiting models like the Rational Unified Process, the Component-Based Development and the Business Process Modeling. This work outlines the principles of the service-oriented design and development centered on business processes such as coupling, cohesion and granularity. The detailed methodology proposed by the authors for the design and development of SOA, is divided into nine phases, which include planning, analysis, service design, service test, service construction, service deployment, service execution, service management and service monitoring. The paper mentions also several of the main non-functional properties (e.g., security and authorization concerns), which should be addressed in each phase, even if it is concentrated on the functional properties of SOA.

Perrey and Lycett (2003) attempt to discuss services in SOA by unifying different definitions and views used in practice. It defines services in terms of components, interfaces and Internet enabled applications. Thus, it gives two different perspectives on services: the point of view of the business participants and of the technical participants. The paper does not mention the role played by non-functional properties in the context of the service definition.

The highly distributed feature of SOA together with its related design and implementation issues is addressed in Papazoglou and van den Heuvel (2007). The authors provide a description of the basic concepts in SOA (e.g., services, methodologies and technologies), as well as a technological review of several approaches exploiting the event-based programming. Attention is focused on the Enterprise Service Bus (ESB), which defines an integration platform based on available standards and supports a wide range of communication approaches. The management of the ESB is performed though a event-driven methodology. The paper lacks in considering the non-functional properties of SOA.

A survey of patterns used in SOA is presented in Zdun Hentrich and Van Der Aalst (2007). Attention is focused on the description of a basic service architecture together with the contracts and interfaces for services. The paper presents a list of patterns for the SOA layers, for adaptivity (regarding both service providers and consumers adaptation), for business services (starting from high-level patterns and going through integration between services and processes) and for ESB. The most important non-functional issue addressed in this work is adaptivity.

FUTURE TRENDS IN SOA

Service-Oriented Architecture is a vast and enormously complex subject, spanning through different domains and embracing different technologies. This intricacy comes from the need of integrate so many different issues, from the basic levels of service provisioning and discovery to the more advanced levels of SOA engineering and governance. Due to these difficulties, SOA is still spreading in the business world and successful and well-designed implementations of this model are emerging in various forms. Even if the basic concepts are still being understood, there is already a dynamic research activity in many areas that might be the future of the Service-Oriented Architecture.

Semantic SOA

Among the most promising and useful innovations are the ones connected to the semantic world, which promises to enable a wide range of new solutions for current SOA's issues and make new levels of automation possible (McIlraith, Plexousakis & Harmelen, 2004). A SOA that uses semantics to enhance its benefits and to extend its functionality is often called a Semantic Service-Oriented Architecture (SSOA). Typical services in a SOA environment aim to be self-describing so that they may be as loose coupled as possible: accepted standards exist to define a service interface and its data model enabling a requester to know how to invoke that service.

While these principles are widespread and well-understood, there are a growing number of technologies that try to set a new standard for semantic enabled services. Using languages such as the DARPA Agent Markup Language (DAML) family, Ontology Inference Layer (OIL), or Web Ontology Language, it is possible to build a service definition or contract that offers machine understandable semantics. Such descriptions would contain, for example, information about what the service can do, thus enabling more precise and meaningful categorization in service registries. Automatic service discovery becomes possible and useful when such data is available in a SOA environment: a consumer does not need to know exactly which service providers are available for the task he needs to complete, since he may just search them using a natural language query such as "book airline ticket from A to B" and then receive a list based on the semantic meaning of what he just asked.

Automatic service execution is another process that can benefit from semantic enabled services. As we stated before, there are standards to define a service interface and data model, so that a human

may know how to use services in an appropriate way. Such descriptions are, however, oblivious to non-intelligent software and do not provide enough meaningful information to enable automatic invocation; input data, for example, needs to be identified manually in order to be correctly associated with required parameters, while using semantics it is possible to automatically parse a consumer query to find data and then match it with the correct input parameters.

Automatic service composition is another open issue in SOA: a developer has to know exactly what steps need to be taken in order to achieve a given goal, then map these steps to a precise sequence of service invocations and finally, select the correct providers for each service. Semantic reasoning gives a mean for software to understand simple or complex objectives and then build a workflow of services that may accomplish them. To do all these tasks, the automatic service composition needs not only intelligent reasoning on given goals, but also automatic service discovery, to find the appropriate services and providers, and to automate the service invocation, in order to autonomously map data to input parameters and correctly execute such services.

Service Level Agreements

We have stated that semantics would help the automatic service discovery, invocation and composition, but we have not yet discussed the field in which semantics would prove invaluable: Service-Level Agreements (SLA) and Quality of Service (QoS). When requesting a business service in the real world, companies form contracts that state their commitment, describing precisely the terms of an agreement, such as what kind of service is considered, what non-functional qualities it should possess, what policies for failure are defined and the period in which the service provisioning is valid. This gives a mean to both the consumer and provider parties to monitor how well the job is performed and take precautions or countermeasures to overcome shortfalls or problems.

In the SOA world, SLA can be used to define a framework of data for service invocation: a semantic-enriched SLA may contain a service description, requested QoS, scheduled execution and policies for client adaptation to unfulfilled quality requests. Each of these elements would be less effective or useful without the aid of semantic annotations: QoS, for example, would have to be defined statically and uniformly between each provider and consumer. Providing the number of possible variations of service types and their associated qualities, it is unthinkable to propose a valid and definitive solution to the problem using static logics. Semantics come in handy as they are flexible enough and give insights on what quality request means in a specific context and in an unambiguous way, thus enabling negotiation between parties that may not share a common vision on the same domain.

By enabling the availability of non-functional data on provided services and the ability to parse non-functional goals requested by a consumer and correctly reason on them, the automatic service composition may be enriched and empowered by these functionalities. The architecture may be able to identify a number of different workflows that achieve a given goal and then select the best one among them, optimizing cost, time or a set of constraints.

Trust Management

We have also stated that a SOA is based on the concept that a service is published in a network and then invoked and used in new applications. This poses a great concern on trust between the requester and provider when they do not know each other. When building a business application using external services, the developers usually trust providers that they already know because of trade agreements or past interactions. Nobody wants to take risks by choosing an unknown provider,

especially if the service will be used in a business application.

The lack of trust between companies or service providers is the reason why the UDDI registers are mainly used internally in enterprises or federation of companies. For SOA to thrive in the future and to be able to offer its maximum advantage to businesses that rely on it, it is necessary to evolve the tools to represent trust and its evaluation (Wu & Weaver, 2007). Since the trust problem is defined as an homonymy, which means that a label encompasses different concepts, formal languages or protocol need to be defined to precisely represent trust factors of interest, such as credential, intention and behavior. Using the two definitions given by McKnight and Chervany (2000) on this topic, the Trusting Intention may be defined as "the extent to which one party is willing to depend on the other party in a given situation with a feeling of relative security, even though negative consequences are possible", while the Trusting Behavior as "the extent to which one party voluntarily depends on another party in a specific situation with a feeling of relative security, even though negative consequences are possible". When this data is ready there is a need for a secure channel, on which to transfer that information, which deals with privacy, integrity and interoperability issues. Establishment and enforcement of trust between domains need a flexible architecture, with strong privacy protection and the capability to maintain the correct relationship between trust intentions and behaviors of such domains. The same architecture should also provide a storage system that can effectively protect credential, policies and trust-related information.

Design Patterns

The more the SOA model is implemented and used by companies, the more insight developers and researchers will have on its issues and problems during the design and implementation phases. When object-oriented programming spread into the business world and was adopted in a number of different projects, there were recurring problems that needed to be addressed effectively with a solution that was in line with the principles of object-orientation. By studying the solutions adopted by different companies, it was possible to define design patterns that aimed to ease the work of developers by synthesizing the best answers to those common problems.

As in the case of object-orientation, patterns are being searched and solutions are being provided. The problem is that there are still a few and early publications on this topic at the moment this chapter is being written at the best of the authors' knowledge. Most of the patterns fall into the domain of Enterprise Application Integration and focus on message and data exchange, which is a wider domain than SOA. In the future we will see appropriate design patterns for SOA implementations, such as in a work by Thomas Erl, which hopefully will contain a coherent and complete collection of design patterns for SOA development which is currently under the publication process.

REFERENCES

Aagedal, J. O. (2001). *Quality of service support in development of distributed systems*. Unpublished doctoral dissertation, University of Oslo, Norway.

Adopted Specification, O. M. G. (2004). *UML profile for modeling quality of service and fault tolerance characteristics and mechanisms*. Retrieved from http://www.omg.org

Amir, R., & Zeid, A. (2004). A UML profile for Service Oriented Architectures. In *Proceedings of the 19th Annual ACM SIGPLAN Conference on Object-oriented Programming Systems, Languages, and Applications*, (pp. 192-193).

Amouzegar, H., Mohammadi, S., Tarokh, M. J., & Hidaji, A. N. (2008). A new approach on interactive SOA security model based on automata. In *Proceedings of the Seventh IEEE/ACIS International Conference on Computer and Information Science*, (pp. 667-671).

AOSD. (2008). *Homepage information*. Retrieved from http://www.aosd.net.

Candolin, C. (2005). *Securing military decision making in a network-centric environment*. Unpublished doctoral dissertation, Helsinki University of Technology.

Candolin, C. (2007). A security framework for Service Oriented Architectures. In *Proceedings of the IEEE Military Communications Conference*, (pp. 1-6).

Candolin, C., & Kiviharju, M. (2007). A roadmap towards content based information security. In *Proceedings of the Eight European Conference on Information Warfare and Security*.

Carr, N. G. (2004). *Does IT Matter? Information Technology and the corrosion of competitive advantage*. USA: Harvard Business School Press.

Casola, V., Fasolino, A. R., Mazzocca, N., & Tramontana, P. (2007). A policy-based evaluation framework for quality and security in Service Oriented Architectures. In *Proceedings of IEEE International Conference on Web Services*, (pp. 1181-1190).

Chau, T., Muthusamy, V., Jacobsen, H., Litani, E., Chan, A., & Coulthard, P. (2008). Automating SLA modeling. In *Proceedings of the 2008 Conference of the Center for Advanced Studies on Collaborative Research*, (pp. 126-143). Ontario, Canada.

Cheng, B.H.C., de Lemos, R., Giese, H., Inverardi, P. & Magee, J. (2009). *Software engineering for self-adaptive systems*. (LNCS 5525).

Clancy, W. J. (1985). Heuristic classification. [Elsevier Science Publishers.]. *Artificial Intelligence, 27,* 289–350. doi:10.1016/0004-3702(85)90016-5

Cysneiros, L., & Leite, J. (2002). Non-functional requirements: From elicitation to modelling languages. In *Proceedings of the 24th International Conference on Software Engineering,* (pp. 699-700).

Endrei, M., Ang, J., Arsanjani, A., Chua, S., Comte, P., Krogdahl, P., et al. (2004). *Patterns: Service Oriented Architecture and Web services.* USA: WebSphere Software, IBM RedBooks.

Erl, T. (2005). *Service-Oriented Architecture: Concepts, technology and design.* USA: Prentice Hall PTR.

Erradi, A., Maheshwari, P., & Padmanabhuni, S. (2005). Towards a policy-driven framework for adaptive Web services composition. In *Proceedings of the International Conference on Next Generation Web Services Practices,* (p. 33).

Finkelstein, A., & Dowell, J. (1996). A comedy of errors: The London ambulance system case study. In *Proceedings of the Eighth International Workshop on Software Specification and Design,* (p. 2).

Franch, X. (1998). Systematic formulation of non-functional characteristics of software. In *Proceedings of the Third International Conference on Requirements Engineering,* (pp. 174-181).

Geet, J. V. (2008). Reverse engineering in the world of enterprise SOA. In *Proceedings of the 15ᵗʰ Working Conference on Reverse Engineering,* (pp. 311-314).

Ghezzi, C., Jazayeri, M., & Mandrioli, D. (2003). *Fundamentals of software engineering.* USA: Prentice Hall.

IEEE. (1998). *Standard for software requirements specification.* Retrieved from http://ieeexplore.ieee.org/stamp/stamp.jsp?arnumber=720574&isnumber=15571

Jin, L.-J., Machiraju, V., & Sahai, A. (2002). *Analysis on service level agreements of Web services.* (Technical Report HPL-2002-180). HP Laboratories Palo Alto.

Johnson, P., & Ekstedt, M. (2007). *Enterprise architecture: Models and analyses for Information Systems decision making.* Studentlitteratur.

Johnson, P., Lagerström, R., & Narman, P. (2007). Extended influence diagram generation. In *Enterprise Interoperability II* (pp. 599–602). New Challenges and Approaches.

Johnson, P., Lagerstrom, R., Narman, P., & Simonsson, M. (2006). Extended influence diagrams for enterprise architecture analysis. In *Proceedings of the 10th IEEE International Annual Enterprise Distributed Object Computing Conference,* (pp. 3-12).

Kazman, R. (2005). From requirements negotiation to software architectural decisions. *Journal on Information and Software Technology, 47*(8), 511–520. doi:10.1016/j.infsof.2004.10.001

Keller, A., & Ludwig, H. (2003). The WSLA framework: Specifying and monitoring service level agreements for Web services. *Journal of Network and Systems Management, 11*(1), 57–81. doi:10.1023/A:1022445108617

Lagerström, R., & Ohrstrom, J. (2007). A framework for assessing business value of Service Oriented Architectures. In *IEEE International Conference on Services Computing,* (pp. 670-671).

Lamanna, D., Skene, J., & Emmerich, W. (2003). SLAng: A language for defining service level agreements. *Proceedings of The Ninth IEEE Workshop on Future Trends of Distributed Computing Systems.*

Lamsweerde, A. (2001). Goal-oriented requirements engineering: A guided tour. In *Proceedings of the Fifth International Symposium on Requirements Engineering*, (pp. 249-262).

Larman, C. (2004). *Applying UML and patterns, an introduction to object-oriented analysis and design and iterative development*. USA: Prentice Hall PTR.

Larrucea, X., & Alonso, R. (2008). ISOAS: Through an Independent SOA Security Specification. In *Proceedings of the Seventh Composition-Based Software Systems*, (pp. 92-100).

MacKenzie, C.M., Laskey, K., McCabe, F., Brown, P. & Metz, R. (2006). *Reference model for Service-Oriented Architecture 1.0*. OASIS Public Review Draft 1.0.

Maximilien, E. M., & Singh, M. P. (2004). A framework and ontology for dynamic Web services selection. *IEEE Internet Computing*, *8*(5), 84–93. doi:10.1109/MIC.2004.27

McIlraith, S. A., Plexousakis, D., & van Harmelen, F. (2004). The Semantic Web. In *Proceedings of the Third International Semantic Web Conference*. (LNCS 3298), Springer.

McKnight, D. H., & Chervany, N. L. (2000). *The meanings of trust*. MISRC Working Papers Series.

Mylopoulos, J., Chung, L., & Nixon, B. (1992). Representing and using non-functional requirements: A process-oriented spproach. *IEEE Transactions on Software Engineering*, *14*(6), 483–497. doi:10.1109/32.142871

Nano, O., & Zisman, A. (2007). Realizing service centric software systems. *IEEE Software*, *24*(6), 28–30. doi:10.1109/MS.2007.166

Newcomer, E., & Lomow, G. (2005). *Understanding SOA with Web services*. USA: Addison-Wesley Pfrofessional.

Nikander, P. (1999). *An architecture for authorization and delegation in distributed object-oriented agent systems*. Unpublished doctoral dissertation, Helsinki University of Technology.

O'Sullivan, J., Edmond, D., & ter Hofstede, A. (2002). What's in a service? Towards accurate description of non-functional service properties. *Journal on Distributed and Parallel Databases*, *12*(2-3), 117–133. doi:10.1023/A:1016547000822

OASIS. (2007). *OASIS Web services business process execution language*. Retrieved from http://www.oasis-open.org/committees/tc_home.php?wg_abbrev=wsbpel

Öhrström, J. (2007). *Business value using Service Oriented Architecture*. Unpublished Master thesis, Royal Institute of Technology.

Oman, P., Hagemeister, J., & Ach, D. (1991). *A definition and taxonomy for software maintainability* (pp. 91–108). Software Engineering Test Lab, University of Idaho.

Padmanabhuni, S., Majumdar, B., Chawla, M., & Mysore, U. (2006). A constraint satisfaction approach to non-functional requirements to adaptive Web services. In *Proceedings of the International Conference on Next Generation Web Services Practices*, (pp. 109-116).

Papazoglou, M. P., & van den Heuvel, W. J. (2006). Service-oriented design and development methodology. *International Journal of Web Engineering and Technology*, *2*(4), 412–442. doi:10.1504/IJWET.2006.010423

Papazoglou, M. P., & van den Heuvel, W. J. (2007). Service Oriented Architectures: Approaches, technologies, and research issues. *The VLDB Journal*, *16*(3), 389–415. doi:10.1007/s00778-007-0044-3

Perrey, R., & Lycett, M. (2003). Service-Oriented Architecture. In *Proceedings of the Symposium on Applications and the Internet Workshops*, (pp. 116-119).

Raibulet, C. (2008). Facets of adaptivity. In *Proceedings of the 2ⁿᵈ European Conference on Software Architecture*, (LNCS 5292), (pp. 342-345).

Regev, G., & Wegmann, A. (2005). Where do goals come from: The underlying principles of goal-oriented requirements engineering. In *Proceedings of the 13th IEEE International Requirements Engineering Conference*, (pp. 353-362).

Reiff-Marganiec, S., Yu, H.Q. & Tilly, M. (2009). *Service selection based on non-functional properties*. Service-Oriented Computing - ICSOC 2007 Workshops: ICSOC 2007.

Ruhe, G., & Eberlein, A. (2003). Trade-off analysis for requirements selection. *International Journal of Software Engineering and Knowledge Engineering*, *13*(4), 345–366. doi:10.1142/S0218194003001378

Saaty, T. L. (1990). How to make a decision: The analytic hierarchy process. *European Journal of Operational Research*, *48*(1), 9–26. doi:10.1016/0377-2217(90)90057-I

Sahai, A., Machiraju, V., Sayal, M., Moorsel, A. P., & Casati, F. (2002). Automated SLA monitoring for Web services. In M. Feridun, P.G. Kropf & G. Babin (Eds.), *Proceedings of the 13th IFIP/IEEE International Workshop on Distributed Systems: Operations and Management: Management Technologies For E-Commerce and E-Business Applications* (October 21 - 23, 2002). (LNCS 2506), (pp. 28-41). London: Springer-Verlag.

Shah, N., Iqbal, R., James, A., & Iqbal, K. (2008). An agent based approach to address QoS issues in Service Oriented Applications. In *Proceedings of 12th International Conference on Computer Supported Cooperative Work in Design*, (pp 317-322).

Singhera, Z. U. (2004). Extended Web services framework to meet non-functional requirements. In *Proceedings of the International Symposium on Applications and the Internet Workshops*, (pp. 334-340).

Sommerville, I. (2004). *Software engineering*. USA: Pearson Addison-Wesley.

Sousa, G. I., & Castro, J. (2003). Adapting the NFR framework to aspect-oriented requirement engineering. In *Proceedings of the XVII Brazilian Symposium on Software Engineering*.

Sturm, R., Morris, W., & Jander, M. (2000). *Foundations of service level management*. Indianapolis: Sams.

Taylor, R. N., Medvidović, N., & Dashofy, E. M. (2009). *Software architecture: Foundations, theory, and practice*. John Wiley & Sons, Inc.

Tsai, W. T., Fan, C., & Chen, Y. (2006). DDSOS: A Dynamic Distributed Service-Oriented Simulation framework. In *Proceedings of the 39th Annual Simulation Symposium*, (pp. 1-8).

Tsai, W. T., Xiao, B., Chen, Y., & Paul, R. A. (2006). Consumer-centric Service-Oriented Architecture: A new approach. In *Proceedings of the Fourth IEEE Workshop on Software Technologies For Future Embedded and Ubiquitous Systems, and the Second international Workshop on Collaborative Computing, integration, and Assurance*, (pp. 175-180).

Wada, H., Suzuki, J., & Oba, K. (2006). Modeling non-functional aspects in Service Oriented Architecture. In *Proceeding of the IEEE International Conference on Service Computing*, (pp. 222-229).

Wada, H., Suzuki, J., & Oba, K. (2007). A feature modeling support for non-functional constraints in Service Oriented Architecture. In *Proceeding of the IEEE International Conference on Service Computing*, (pp. 187-195).

Weiss, M., & Esfandiari, B. (2004). On feature interactions among Web services. In *Proceedings of the IEEE International Conference on Web Services*, (pp. 88-95).

Wu, Z., & Weaver, A. C. (2007). Requirements of federated trust management for Service-Oriented Architectures. In *Journal of Information Security*, *6*(5), 287–296. doi:10.1007/s10207-007-0027-9

Xiping, S. (2007). Developing non-functional requirements for a service-oriented software platform. In *Proceedings of the 31st Annual International Computer Software and Applications Conference*, (pp. 495-496).

Zdun, U., Hentrich, C., & Van Der Aalst, W. M. P. (2006). A survey of patterns for Service-Oriented Architectures. In *International Journal of Internet Protocol Technology*, *1*(3), 132–143.

Zhu, L., Aurum, A., Gorton, I., & Jeffery, R. (2005). Tradeoff and sensitivity analysis in software architecture evaluation using analytic hierarchy process. *Software Quality Journal*, *13*(4), 357–375. doi:10.1007/s11219-005-4251-0

Zscahler, S. (2004). Towards a semantic framework for non-functional specifications of component-based systems. In *Proceedings of the EUROMICRO Conference*, (pp. 92-99).

Chapter 6
A Goal–Oriented Representation of Service–Oriented Software Design Principles

Alireza Moayerzadeh
University of Toronto, Canada

Eric Yu
University of Toronto, Canada

ABSTRACT

Service-oriented architecture (SOA) embodies a set of principles including service abstraction, composability, discoverability, and reusability, among others. Although these principles are widely circulated by SOA technology vendors, there have been few efforts to collect, organize, and elaborate on these principles for the purpose of guiding system design. This chapter explores how service-oriented design principles can be organized in a goal-graph representation complementary to original text and used in system design. The approach builds upon the NFR framework for treating non-functional requirements in software engineering. The chapter proposes a method to extract SOA design principles from textually represented service-oriented knowledge sources. The method is applied to an SOA knowledge source, extract an SOA design knowledge-base organized by design principles and presented by goal-graphs, and the chapter then explores application of such knowledge-base.

INTRODUCTION

Service-oriented architecture (SOA) is an architectural model that aims to enhance the agility and cost-effectiveness of an enterprise while reducing

DOI: 10.4018/978-1-60566-794-2.ch006

the overall burden of IT on an organization. It accomplishes this by positioning services as the primary means of providing functionality. A service is a unit of potentially independent logic which contributes to providing required functionality in a solution designed with service-orientation in mind. SOA promises that proper use of services as building blocks of business applications will bring about benefits such as increased intrinsic interoperability, increased business agility, and reduced IT burden within an organization. As a result, SOA is being embraced by the software community.

Like any other architectural model, using SOA in system design requires following a set of design principles such as service abstraction, service autonomy, and service discoverability. Implementing such designs, in turn, needs appropriate technologies such as WebService standards and middleware servers. While the mentioned principles are promoted by vendors providing the necessary technology, the main focus is usually on the technology rather than the concept and rationale of design principles. Such introduction of design principles from a perspective relevant to technology keeps designers from gaining an objective and complete understanding of principles which ultimately leads to poor vendor-biased designs.

There have been few efforts to collect, organize, and elaborate on these principles for the purpose of guiding system design. When these principles are elaborated, there are complementary as well as conflicting aspects that can be uncovered. Recently, more comprehensive attempts to articulate these design principles have emerged in the literature. However, while the textual format is necessary for the exposition and explanation of concepts, it does not lend itself easily for visualizing the relationships and interactions among inter-related concepts and principles.

To address the mentioned issues, we propose to use a goal-oriented modeling method to model non-functional requirements and represent design knowledge in SOA as a complement of the original text. Also, we propose to use well-developed goal-oriented analysis techniques to provide analysis support and guide system design. Finally, we propose to organize SOA knowledge from different sources into an integrated knowledge-base.

First, we present our knowledge extraction and modeling method and discuss it further by going through details of extracting knowledge from a textually represented SOA knowledge source and representing it using goal-oriented concepts. By SOA knowledge source we mean any source that contains expressed knowledge about Service Orientation. Books, articles, or internet websites about SOA are all valid examples of an SOA knowledge source. After introducing our method we show the result of using that method on a reference book of SOA design and argue how the result serves as a knowledge-base we can integrate more SOA knowledge upon. Then we demonstrate applications of such extracted knowledge in system design. Next, we show how to use our method on other SOA knowledge sources in order to integrate more sources into our knowledge-base. Finally, we present conclusions and lessons learned and explain how structure of a knowledge source affects the extracted knowledge.

In summary, this chapter has two distinct contributions: First contribution is a knowledge-base of SOA knowledge which serves as a base to integrate knowledge from various SOA knowledge sources. Second contribution is a method which is used to construct the knowledge-base from a selected SOA knowledge source and can be used to integrate more sources into the knowledge-base.

BACKGROUND

SOA Knowledge Sources

We plan to organize SOA knowledge in a navigable and useful knowledge-base. Below is a list of related efforts to organize SOA knowledge.

Erl (2005) provides an in-depth overview of service-orientation, its history, and its fundamental characteristics and concepts. It also covers key web-service related specifications and technologies such as WS-* family of standards. It then provides a comprehensive overview of service-orientation support in .NET and J2EE.

Erl (2007) discusses fundamental concepts involved in service-oriented architecture. Then, it elaborates on design principles involved in building an effective service-oriented system while trying to stay away from any specific SOA-related technology. Finally, it provides a comparison of service-orientation and alternative methodologies.

Endrei et al. (2004) talk about using patterns for e-business purposes and then list and elaborate on patterns used in implementing e-business systems using web-services, the most prominent form of service orientation. They continue with chapters on available technology options covering IBM's service-oriented middleware offerings, and IBM's vision of an on-demand service-orientation architecture.

Knowledge Representation and Reasoning

We model design knowledge using a custom goal-oriented framework in order to support design-time analysis of non-functional requirements. What follows is a list of work related to our method.

Mylopoulos (1992) introduces NFR, a framework for representing and using non-functional requirements during the development process. Central to NFR is the notion of *goal-graph* which consists of softgoals connected with links. A *softgoal* is a concept which represents a goal without a clear-cut definition of whether it is satisfied or not, so it provides a means to model the qualitative aspects of a system such as its non-functional requirements. Relations among various softgoals are modeled with *links*. For instance, a negative contribution link from one softgoal to another indicates that meeting the former has a negative effect on meeting the latter. However, since softgoals are not satisfied like regular goals, NFR talks about *satisficing* a softgoal to emphasize the difference. Finally, NFR supports an evaluation process which allows designers to propagate effects of choosing

to satisfice or deny a set of softgoals on the rest of a given goal-graph. As described later on in "Representational Framework" subsection, we use the softgoal concept and a subset of NFR links to model non-functional requirements. We also demonstrate a trade-off analysis based on NFR's evaluation process.

Yu (1996) presents i*, a full-fledged framework for modeling the organizational context and rationale that lead up to various requirements in the system. i* includes concepts of NFR framework but also contains advanced constructs to gain more expressive power. In addition, i* supports a well-defined process for evaluating design alternatives which is explored in great detail by Horkoff (2006). Of all the new constructs, we use the concept of *task* to get the expressive power we require and leave all other elements of i* in favor of simplicity. i* is later standardized as Goal-oriented Requirements Language (GRL) to support modeling and reasoning for non-functional requirements.

The mentioned representation methods are used to model and provide reasoning for various knowledge areas in the same way we use goal-models to model and reason about SOA design principles:

Gross and Yu (2001) use NFR models to describe patterns and document the rationale behind using them in various design situations. They propose a systematic way to model patterns expressed in textual format using NFR. The design patterns from Gamma et al. (1995) are used as the source knowledge area.

Mussbacher et al. (2007) use User Requirements Notation (URN), a combination of GRL and a notation to model scenarios as causal flows of responsibilities called Use Case Maps (UCM), to formalize design patterns and enable trade-off analysis among patterns. Their purpose is comparable to our extraction method which formalized SOA design principles using a simpler goal-oriented framework. However, compared to our method, Mussbacher et al. (2007) have a more formal process for trade-off analysis based on GRL and UCM.

Chung et al. (2002) propose a process to capture both functional and non-functional requirements in an integrated use case driven model. This model is then used to get a complete picture of functional and non-functional goals. These goals are then operationalized using architectures and design patterns, and realized using UML class diagram and sequence diagram. In our method, however, we mainly focus on non-functional requirements while using tasks and low-level softgoals instead of UML diagrams to operationalize NFRs.

Weiss et al. (2007) employ URN to model WebService features as goal-graphs similar to what we do for design principles. However, they use the more advanced links present in GRL to model interactions among WebServices and then find conflicts through the presence of "Breaks" links in analysis result. UCM is then used to explore various resolutions suggested by GRL models and to resolve the conflicts. In contrast, since we don't use the full power of GRL we don't have this type of formal conflict resolution policy but rather rely on expert knowledge to resolve the conflicts.

Knowledge Extraction

Dardenne et al. (1993) describe KAOS, a goal-oriented approach to software requirements acquisition. They describe a method to extract such elements from textual representation of requirements by scanning text and presenting information using the semantics of KAOS. Our method of extracting bits of goal-graphs from text is based on this method except we use our own representational framework to present knowledge.

Anton (1997) introduces a method for identification and refinements of goals into operational requirements. Her method is based on four sets of heuristics, guidelines, and recurring question types to identify, classify, refine, and elaborate goals. The identifying set of heuristics introduced in her work relate closely to our extraction method since

these heuristics are designed to detect information containing expressed knowledge about goals.

Darimont and Lemoine (2006) stress on the similarity between requirement documents and regulation documents. Then they use an extraction method based on that of Dardenne et al. to extract the regulations. Their overall method is therefore quite similar to our extraction method except that they directly use KOAS to represent knowledge.

Finally, Cleland-Huang et al. (2006) introduce an algorithm to detect and classify NFRs in textual documents. Their method is interesting since it is automatic and therefore can greatly improve the speed of the extraction process. However, it has precision, recall, and knowledge representation issues which prevent its direct usage in our manual extraction method.

KNOWLEDGE EXTRACTION METHOD

In order to enable analysis support, we need a well-devised method to extract knowledge and represent it using goal-oriented concepts. In this section we introduce the method we used in detail including our expectations, anticipated problems and proposed workarounds for them, and representational framework used to visualize knowledge.

Expectations

We expect the method to support the following list of features:

1. **An Integrated view of the knowledge area:**
    An integrated view of the knowledge area is a representation of design knowledge, for instance in form of a graph or a table, that presents design information contained in a knowledge subarea, for instance a book chapter, in a single and easy to navigate view. Such views can help designers to easily review and navigate important points

involved in design of a feature related to that part of the knowledge area.

2. **Analysis support:** The representation framework should enable algorithmic analysis on the extracted knowledge. Such support is necessary to guide system design by enabling designers to investigate the effects of picking different design alternatives on various aspects of their software system including non-functional requirements.

3. **Relating detailed decisions to the big picture:** Each software project has its own specific goals not necessarily discussed in the knowledge area in question. The representational framework should provide a means to relate such project-specific goals to the design knowledge extracted from the knowledge area, because meeting such specific goals is the ultimate purpose of software systems after all.

4. **Structuring knowledge according to different criteria:** It is often desirable to structure and present the same body of knowledge according to different information types present in a knowledge area. For instance, a book on enterprise software design may contain information on both design principles of enterprise systems and common architectural patterns used in enterprise software. A flexible representational framework allows the knowledge area to be structured and presented according to both formats.

To achieve the items listed above, as mentioned before, we use a goal-oriented representational framework that is completely explained in "Representational Framework" section later on. Considering the fact that SOA knowledge areas are most likely large sources such as books or online knowledge bases, and having in the mind the general knowledge extraction process of introduced goal-oriented methods, we expect

that the following problems will arise during the process of applying our method:

1. **Managing size of extracted knowledge:** A large knowledge area naturally contains a large amount of design knowledge. However, since the extracted knowledge is initially not integrated, approaching such large knowledge areas without a careful plan leads to an unmanageable integration surface. To address this problem, it is recommended that the knowledge area be divided into smaller and more manageable subareas. Integration should be performed first on the subarea level and then on the all subareas to create an integrated view of the whole knowledge area. It is obvious that each subarea can be further divided to reach a manageable size for knowledge extraction and integration. It should be noted that since divided areas need to be integrated later, dividing excessively may result in extra effort in integration.

2. **Complex goal-graphs:** Large knowledge areas lead to large and complex graphs. This problem, however, is somewhat present in all goal modeling frameworks. Since this problem is similar in nature to the first problem, dividing subareas and presenting graphs for each subarea can help in reading and following the graphs.

3. **Naming inconsistency:** Since extraction is a manual process, it is easy to introduce inconsistency to names of extracted elements. For instance, it is possible that a different name be assigned to information about the same softgoal extracted from various parts of text. Such inconsistencies lead to serious integration problems. Since un-integrated knowledge is not usable by its own, it limits the explicitly expressed knowledge and thus the whole usefulness of the model. To fix this problem, set of names used for softgoals and tasks needs to be normalized. Normalization should preferably be performed by someone

with expertise on the knowledge area since modeling different softgoals as similar softgoals introduces false information into the extracted knowledge.

4. **Missing links:** Sometimes integrating knowledge from a subarea results in a number of disconnected graphs rather than a complete connected graph that is not suitable for analysis. Such situations can happen due to insufficient extracted knowledge, so the first way to resolve them is to search for text containing information about elements from various disconnected graphs. Such situations also happen due to poor naming of graph element, but as mentioned before normalizing names can fix the problem in such cases. It is also possible that there is information in other subareas that can connect the disconnected part. This situation suggests that subareas are not divided properly since information in subareas is not coherent enough to allow integration. Finally, information connecting the disconnected parts might be assumed implicitly in the context but not expressed explicitly in the text. In such cases it is safe to add the implicit information to graph in order to facilitate the integration. However, extra care should be taken to prevent addition of false and fabricated information to the graph.

5. **Traceability:** Since goal-graphs are only complementary to the main knowledge source, it is often desirable to refer to the part of text a link or a softgoal is extracted from. In order to do so, a reference to the extraction place should be maintained. Depending on the knowledge area page numbers, URLs, or other resource identifiers might be used to represent such information. Also, links that are added through other means such as adding implicit information should be marked to document their origin. Maintaining such information combined with appropriate tool support can provide a navigable view of the knowledge area.

6. **Conflicts and errors:** Since extraction and integration processes are manual, it is likely that conflicting and bogus information is extracted. This problem has a number of causes such as bogus knowledge extraction, incorrect normalization, assuming false context information and adding it to the integrated graph, or even conflicting information in the original text. However, by dividing knowledge area into smaller subareas, such errors can be detected more easily. It is a good idea to check integrated graph of each subarea for such errors before integrating the subareas together since such errors will propagate to higher level graphs if they are ignored.

Procedure

Considering the anticipated problems in the previous section, in order to create integrated views representing information in a given knowledge area a three-step method is proposed: dividing the knowledge area, extracting information from text of each subarea and making a goal-graph using our representational framework, and integrating information obtained from previous steps.

Step 1: Dividing the Knowledge Area

The first step is to break up the knowledge area into manageable subareas. Each subarea will later be studied to have its design knowledge extracted. Thus, division should be performed so that each subarea contains information about the same subject matter.

Step 2: Extracting Knowledge from Text

The second step is to extract design information from text in each subarea. To achieve this, a process similar to extraction process of Dardenne et al. (1993) is used. To get design information, text should be searched for sentences and paragraphs containing desired information. More specifically, sentences which show support or denial of various goals should be found and modeled by contribution links. Also, sentences that show various ways involved in completing tasks should be found and modeled with task decomposition links. For example, consider the following text snippet from http://msdn2.microsoft.com/en-us/library/bf9xhdz4(VS.71).aspx (an ASP.NET reference):

Because data stored in application state is not durable, it is lost if the host containing it is destroyed. If you want state to survive these types of failures, you should store it in a database or other durable store.

Converting this snippet using task and softgoal concepts from our representational framework (see next section):

Employ[DurableStore] task contributes positively to Durability[ApplicationStateInfo] softgoal.

Moreover, it is easy to show the information above as a simple graph with two elements and a positive contribution link using notation and semantics of our representational framework. Also, the extracted piece should be marked with its extraction place, in this case the page number, to enable further references to the text.

Step 3: Integrating Extracted Knowledge

The third step is to combine all simple graphs resulted from previous steps. Integration is performed on two or more levels depending on how the knowledge area is divided. First, all graphs from each subarea are combined to create a graph representing design knowledge of that same subarea. Later on, all subarea graphs are combined to create a comprehensive graph for the whole knowledge area.

The integration process is fairly simple. For each subarea, all of the small two node graphs are considered together, and same softgoals and tasks are found and represented by one symbol instead of using a symbol for each occurrence. In models where one type of element appears more frequently than the other, it helps to integrate the more frequently appearing element type first and then integrate the other element type.

Normalization of Naming

Adopting a consistent naming convention can facilitate normalization. For softgoals, we recommend the naming convention of NFR described in Chung et al. (1999). This convention expects names in the form of Type[Topic]. *Type* indicates the general category of the element and *Topic* further specializes that type. For instance, LowCost[Development] and LowCost[Hardware] are two softgoals with different topics. A rule of thumb for a conforming softgoal name is that it should convey "Type of Topic". For instance, LowCost[Development] indicates "LowCost of Development". For a task, Type is usually a verb and Topic is its object. Employ[DurableDataStore] is an example of a good task name.

Representational Framework

We use a representational framework with semantics mostly same as semantics of the NFR framework while borrowing some concepts from the i* framework. To be more specific, we model knowledge using *softgoals* and *tasks*, with softgoals having the same semantic as in NFR and i* and tasks having the same semantics as in i*. Softgoals are connected to each other using positive and negative contribution links. Tasks can be connected to each other using decomposition links. Finally, tasks can be connected to softgoals using positive and negative contribution links. Semantics of all links and elements are same as their equivalent counterparts in NFR and i* framework.

Figure 1. Symbols used

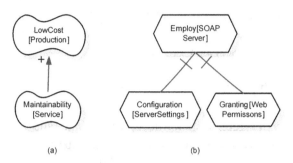

Figure 1 shows the symbols used to presents softgoals, tasks, and various links in our representational framework, which is same as symbols of the i* framework. Figure 1 (a) shows two softgoals connected using a positive contribution link, and expresses the fact that Maintainability[Service] softgoal contributes positively to LowCost [Production] softgoal. Figure 1 (b) shows Employ[SOAPServer] task decomposed into two alternative tasks Configuration[ServerSettings] and Granting[WebPermission].

Our representational framework is intentionally this simple. By choosing only the bare minimum concepts required to achieve our expectations we will have a simpler and therefore more approachable framework compared to traditional frameworks such as i* or GRL, especially for users with limited expertise on academic goal-oriented concepts. We anticipate that the described representational framework is expressive enough to support modeling and reasoning on knowledge to the extent required to meet our expectations. However, it should be noted that our framework will not capture all knowledge presented in a given knowledge source. For instance, it has no support to capture details such as priority of softgoals or sequence of tasks. Some of these issues such as integrating work on priority-supporting evaluation processes with our method are candidates for further work. Other issues, such as capturing sequence of tasks, are not significant since our framework is intended to capture answers to 'Why' questions instead of 'How' questions. It is designed to be used as a complementary representation to help alleviate problems of just using text. It can model rationale behind various design alternatives with accuracy on par with that of the NFR framework and express goal-graphs consistent with the content of the knowledge area.

KNOWLEDGE EXTRACTION

From the knowledge sources introduced in "Background" section, we choose Erl (2007) to illustrate our method and its usefulness. This knowledge source has the most systematic approach to organizing service-oriented design knowledge. More importantly, it is almost free from technology-related content and contains discussions about the real knowledge involved in designing service-oriented systems. Therefore, it makes the most suitable starting point for constructing a goal-oriented knowledge-base of SOA design knowledge. In this section, we will elaborate on the process of applying our method to this source.

Structure of the Knowledge Source

Erl (2007) is composed of three main parts: The first part is an introduction on service-oriented and the fundamental knowledge to start with SOA. The second part contains detailed explanation on eight principles of service design. The last part contains supplemental information such as supporting practices and comparing service-orientation to other design paradigms.

The second part contains most of the design knowledge we are trying to extract about SOA design principles. It consists of eight chapters, starting from chapter 6: Service Contracts, Service Coupling, Service Abstraction, Service Reusability, Service Autonomy, Service Statelessness, Service Discoverability, and Service Composability. Each chapter contains detailed information on the design principle in question.

The book also contains eight design patterns (not to be confused with object-oriented design patterns introduced by Gamma et al. (1995) that help applying the service design principles. These design patterns are mentioned in the text whenever it is relevant to the principles, so information about them is brief and scattered in various chapters.

We built goal-graphs from extracted design knowledge based on both design principles and design patterns. Principle-based graphs show the design knowledge organized based on design principles and pattern-based graphs present the design knowledge organized based on patterns.

Extracting Design Principle Information

To divide the knowledge area, we use the chapter-structure of Erl (2007) described earlier because the book organizes knowledge according to design principles. Therefore, each chapter in part II of the

book can serve as a separate subarea. We demonstrate the process of knowledge extraction and integration for the Chapter 6 of the book which is about Service Contracts.

Softgoals

Textual representation needs to be scanned and the results need to be integrated. To get better results, we further divide the subarea into smaller parts and then assemble the results into one graph. Also, due to having relatively more softgoals compared to tasks in our source, we first integrate softgoals and add tasks later on. This practice helps in having consistent softgoals across a subarea.

Figure 2 shows the graph that results from normalizing and putting together softgoal-only knowledge extracted for Service Contracts principle. Relation arrows with number annotations are extracted directly extracted from one or more snippets in text and the number on arrow indicates

Figure 2. Integration of softgoal only knowledge for service contract design principle

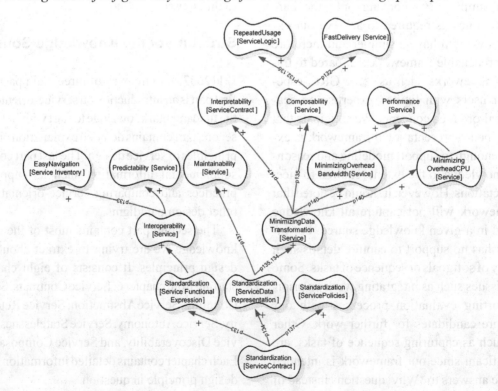

the corresponding page number in text. Relation arrows without a number are added by interpreting implicit knowledge in text. For instance, using information provided in the introduction chapter of text we can argue that standardizing the functional expression of services in service inventory increases interoperability between services because parameters of service capabilities are standardized, so services can interoperate more easily. Thus, St andardization[ServiceFunctionalExpression] can be connected to Interoperability[Service] with a positive contribution link.

This example shows how to make implicit knowledge explicit by adding it to the graph. It should be noted that there shouldn't be any guess-

work or biased interpretation involved in the newly added knowledge. Otherwise, it leads to false information and potential conflicts in the integration process.

The Rest of Design Knowledge

The goal-graph in the previous part only contains information about links with softgoals on each side. Integrating task-task and goal-task relations to Figure 2 leads to the complete graph for Service Contract design principle shown in Figure 3. Page numbers are omitted for reducing clutter.

Figure 3. Final graph for service contracts design principle

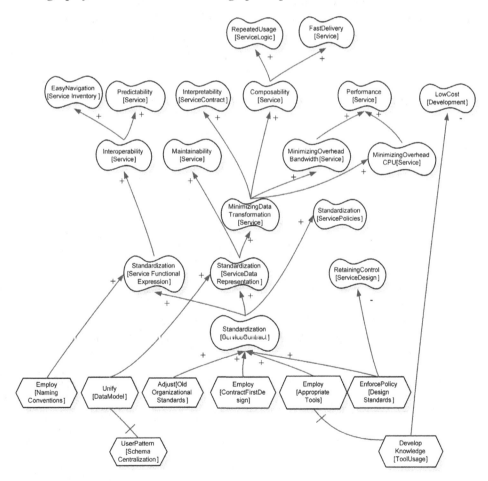

Integrating Design Principle Goal-Graphs

Although having design information of each design principle chapter summarized in one graph is useful by its own, it helps designers to get a better understanding of the knowledge area if all of graphs were integrated so that the relation of principles would be clear.

To make the integration more manageable, first we combine softgoal-only graphs of each chapter and then add the rest of design information. For instance, if we extract the softgoal-only graph of Service Autonomy principle and integrate it with softgoal-only graph of Service Contracts principle around the common softgoals we get the goal-graph in Figure 4.

Softgoals from Service Contracts principle are on the left side, with dotted outline, softgoals from Service Autonomy principle are on the right side, with dashed outline, and common softgoals are the ones with bold outline.

Integration helps to reveal the knowledge about the softgoals that can only be seen when considering subareas together. For instance, in the graph of service autonomy there is a positive contribution from Performance[Service] to Composability[Service] which if the text is looked up, comes from the fact that high performance is required for services that need to participate in a large number of service compositions. However, although both softgoals are also present in graph of Service Contracts principle, this relation was not documented in Figure 2.

Also, in the Service Contracts graph, there is a positive contribution link from MinimizingDataTransformation[Service] to Composability[Service]. In the integrated graph, there is a path of positive contribution links starting from Minimizing Data Transformation [Service] passing thru MinimizingOverheadBandwidth[Servi

Figure 4. Softgoal integration of service contracts and service autonomy principle goal-graphs

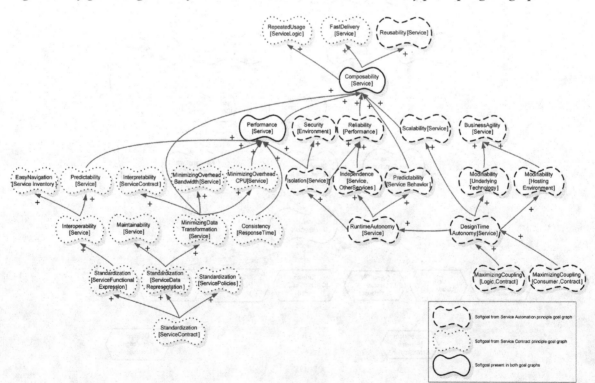

ce] and Performance[Service] and finishing at Composability[Service]. This path describes contribution of MinimizingDataTransformation[Service] softgoal to Composability[Service] softgoal in more detail. In other words, it explains the nature and the reason of relation between these two softgoals in a way that is only achievable by looking at the information scattered across various chapters of the text. It also partly validates the correctness of Service Contract graph since it shows that the extracted design knowledge is consistent with the more detailed Service Autonomy graph. Finally, the contribution link from MinimizingDataTransformation[Service] to Composability[Service] can be removed since a more descriptive path is already present.

The rest of design information can be integrated using the same process. The result of integrating all design information for two chapters is presented in Figure 6. More design information can be induced as a result of integration. For instance, a new LowCost[Production] softgoal is created to represent and aggregate all of cost-reducing softgoals such as LowCost[Development] and LowCost[Hardware]. More softgoals of this kind are encountered as more subareas are integrated.

SOA DESIGN KNOWLEDGE

In this section, we present SOA design knowledge extracted from Erl (2007) in form of goal-graphs. Then, we show how to use these goal-graphs to support system design.

Resulting Goal-Graphs

The main result of applying the extraction method is a goal-graph for each design principle. Design knowledge about each principle is summarized in one goal-graph. Also, to demonstrate how our method can be used to organize knowledge area according to an alternative perspective, a goal-graph is extracted for each design pattern. However, it is

important to note that since Erl (2007) is focused on design principles principle-based goal-graphs are more complete compared to pattern-based goal-graphs when considering the completeness of extracted knowledge.

An example of a principle goal-graph was presented in Figure 3. Using the same method, design information about design patterns can be assembled into a goal-graph. The only difference between pattern and principle graphs is how the knowledge area is divided in the first step. Figure 5 shows the goal-graph for Contract Centralization design pattern. All results of applying the extraction method on Erl (2007) which includes design principle and design pattern goal-graphs are available at http://www.cs.toronto.edu/~alireza/erl-graphs/.

Also, principle graphs can be integrated to provide a complete view of the knowledge area and reveal more design knowledge (as discussed). Figure 6 provides an example of such integration. If we integrate all design principles in one graph we get a comprehensive view of all design knowledge in one graph. Figure 8 shows the high-level goals of such integration (checkmarks, X marks and extra project-specific goals will be explained later).

Analyzing Design Alternatives using Goal-Graphs

A benefit of having each design principle represented by a goal-graph is that the consequences of choosing various design alternatives on other softgoals can be analyzed using the evaluation process of the NFR framework (Chung et al.. 1999). In this method, each alternative is represented by selecting a set of tasks. Mutually exclusive tasks can be selected simultaneously, and in the case of decomposed tasks all of its decomposed sub-tasks should be selected too since performing a decomposed tasks involves performing all of its sub-tasks. As an example of evaluation, consider the bottom row tasks in goal-graph of Service

Figure 5. Goal-graph for contract serialization design pattern

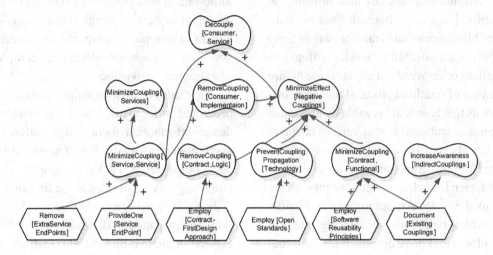

Figure 6. Full graph of integrating service contracts and service autonomy principles

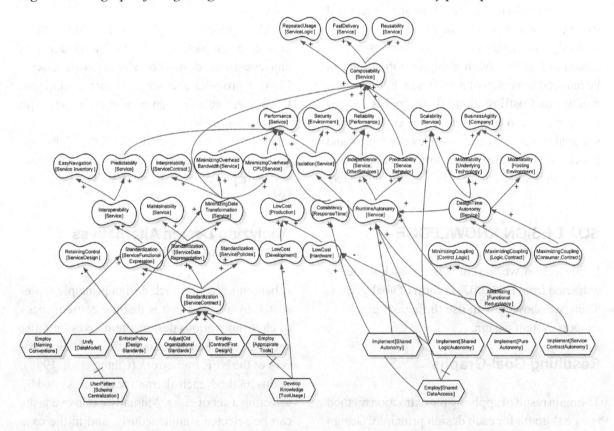

Autonomy principle in Figure 7 which show four ways to satisfice RuntimeAutonomy[Service] softgoal represented by Implement[ServiceContractAutonomy], Implement[SharedAutonomy], Implement[SharedLogicAutonomy], and Implement[PureAutonomy] tasks (the first one does so indirectly by satisficing MinimizingFunctionalRedundancy[Service] softgoal). It is possible

Figure 7. Effect of choosing shared logic autonomy

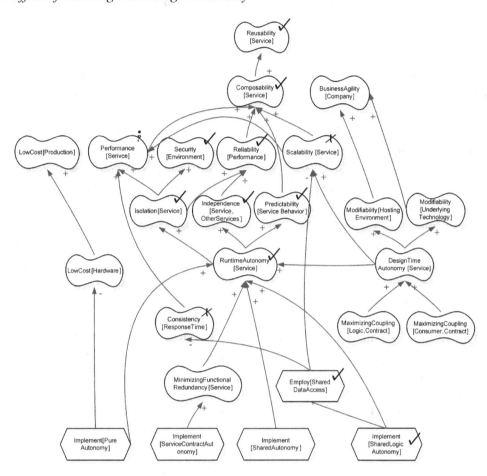

to analyze effects of implementing each alternative using a simplified version of evaluation process described by Chung et al. (1999). Figure 7 shows the effects of implementing Service Autonomy using shared logic method. In this graph, a check mark indicates that a softgoal is satisfied. It also indicates that a task is chosen. An X indicates that a softgoal is denied. It also indicates that a task is not chosen. A question mark indicates that the outcome is not clear. Also, elements without any marks are those elements that their usage or satisficing is not affected by propagating the initial state of the evaluation. Finally, since we used a subset of links available in the NFR framework we only used the subset of propagation rules that contain positive and negative contribution links.

Simply put, a positive contribution link propagates the same satisficing state at its starting endpoint while a negative contribution negates it. (see Horkoff, 2006 for a more detailed version of the evaluation procedure)

For instance, if in an evaluation process RuntimeAutonomy[Service] is satisficed, Predictability[ServiceBehavior] is also satisficed since there is a positive contribution link from the former to the latter. Also, if Employ [Shared-DataAccess] is chosen, Consistency [Response-Time] will be denied due to the negative contribution link between these elements. There are also cases in which both positive and negative input contribution links are present. In real-world scenarios, the result of such a propagation case depends on importance of individual links and their contribution to satisficing the softgoal in question. As a result, the best approach is to let the designers themselves resolve such issues. Although doing so may reduce the evaluation from an automatic process (as in the NFR framework) to a semi-automatic one, there is still a step by step structure to the process, which can be facilitated using appropriate tool support.

Figure 7 reveals that although using shared-logic autonomy satisfices RuntimeAutonomy[Service] it denies Scalability[Service] which means that it has a negative impact on scalability. Also, its effect on Performance[Service] is undecided. We can perform the evaluation process for a new alternative by selecting another task, such as Implement[PureAutonomy]. The evaluation graph for pure autonomy is omitted to avoid clutter, but if we perform the evaluation we will observe that choosing pure autonomy helps satisficing Performance[Service], has a negative effect on LowCost[Production], while its effect on Scalability[Service] is undecided.

Relation of Design Principles

Looking at goal-graphs of various design principles can reveal the relation of design principles with each other especially in terms of common middle-level and high-level softgoals. For instance, examining goal-graphs of Service Autonomy and Service Contracts principles shows that they mostly have high-level softgoals in common which suggests that these principles are loosely coupled. If Service Coupling principle is also included in the graph, a close relationship between service coupling and service autonomy will be observed since these two principles have a number of common softgoals at lower levels. Some of these coupling-related goals can be seen at the lower right side of Figure 6.

Project-Specific Goals

As mentioned before, Figure 8 shows the high-level part of the integrating all principle graphs (it also shows evaluation results for an application example later on). Apart from these high-level goals, each project has a set of specific organizational goals of its own. The high-level softgoals can be used to relate design elements to these project-specific organizational goals. From an organizational standpoint, it is desirable to analyze effects of various design decisions on such goals. Increased return of investment, increased vendor diversification options, and reduced IT burden are examples of such project-specific goals. Integrating these goals into the graph of high-level softgoals is fairly straightforward since such goals usually have fairly noticeable relations with high-level softgoals of Figure 8. For instance, there is already a ReturnOfInvestment[Company] softgoal which is exactly the same as the first example. Some of LowCost softgoals such as LowCost[Hardware] and LowCost[Development] as well as Maintainability[Serivce] obviously result in reduced IT burden, and finally, increased vendor diversification can be related to Modifiability[HostingEnvironment] and Modifiability[UnderlyingTechnology] softgoals. Having project-specific softgoals enables designers to see the effects of their decisions all the way to the high-level goals of their specific project at hand using the same kind of analysis described before. However, it is argued that the specific design situations of each project can change the nature of contributions of design principles to the project-specific goals. Therefore, result of project-specific analyses should be interpreted while having specific properties of the project at hand in mind.

Application Example

In this part we look at the analysis in context of a real world example of Cutit Saws Ltd adopted

Figure 8. Evaluation of choosing shared-logic autonomy level on high-level goals

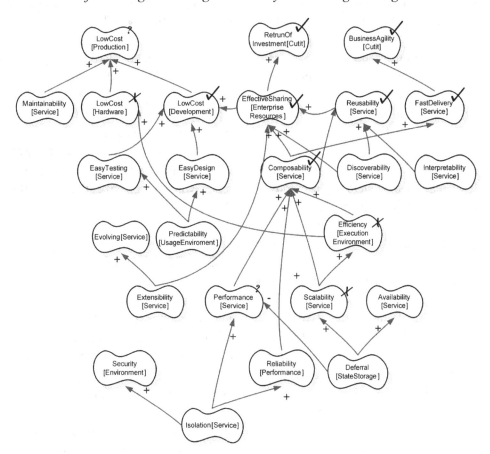

from Erl (2007). Cutit Saws is a manufacturer and reseller of high-end hydraulic diamond chainsaws. Recently, they have released a new chain model that caught the eye of their business community, and they received orders from everywhere. However, Cutit Saws has not been able to keep up with the demand due to outdated IT infrastructure among other reasons. As a result, they decided to use service-orientation to build their new IT system to address the needs of this growing company for the next five years. They built various web-services to support their business processes. Now, they are looking at various service capabilities to make sure their services will provide desirable performance required for the anticipated growth of the next five years.

The original example provides a review of current implementation of services and recommends implementing a higher level of autonomy for a specific service capability but doesn't compare applicable autonomy levels. It also provides a brief and textual analysis of effects of the proposed implementation on other aspects of the system. Here, we use our analysis technique to compare various applicable autonomy levels and visualize their effect on other softgoals including project-specific goals.

Since we have extracted the graph for Service Autonomy principle, it is possible to evaluate effects of implementing each available autonomy level on the other softgoals using the same analysis explained before for alternative analysis. The result of evaluation for the case which shared logic level is selected is shown in Figure 8. However, as mentioned before about the evaluation process for real world examples, for each service capability results may be different from those figures since on each step the designers themselves need to determine if a softgoal is satisfied.

Moreover, by connecting high-level goals to project-specific goals the designers can find out about the effects of implementing each alternative on project-specific goals. Cutit Saws' main goal is to be able to react fast to changes in market demands and make its IT department a facilitating tool rather than an obstacle of their growth. Cutit is also interested in decreasing IT costs and in getting the most value out of their investment in upgrading the IT department. These goals translate to BusinessAgility[Cutit], LowCost[Production], and ReturnOfInvestment[Cutit] softgoals respectively, all of which are already present in Figure 8. Assuming that for a given service capability evaluation process finishes as Figure 7, we can continue the evaluation process to see the effect of choosing shared-logic autonomy level on project-specific goals (Figure 8).

If we apply the same analysis for pure autonomy level, continuing evaluation up to high-level and project-specific goals and then compare the results to Figure 8, we will observe that the only difference between the two is the effect on Scalability[Service] which is negative contribution in case of choosing shared-logic autonomy and it is undecided in case of choosing pure autonomy. The collective conclusion suggests that for the service capability in question, implementing pure-logic autonomy provides better benefits compared to the alternative.

However, there is more to the results than this analysis reveals. If we consider how Composability[Service] is satisfied, we see that in case of shared logic autonomy this softgoal is satisfied despite the negative contribution from Performance[Service] softgoal, while in case of pure autonomy the goal is satisfied by only receiving positive contributions. It can be argued that

the softgoal in question is satisficed more strongly in the second case. There is, unfortunately, no such notion in our representational framework, so we can not take relative strengths on which a goal is satisficed or denied into account. Since BusinessAgility[Cutit] is the main softgoal in our example, the difference in strength might worth the extra cost incurred by choosing the pure autonomy level. This is a kind of decision only designers with enough field expertise can make, which emphasizes the role of designers in the evaluation process.

A SECOND KNOWLEDGE SOURCE

In order to demonstrate how nature of information in a knowledge source affects the resulting goal-graphs, we show the results of applying goal-graph extraction process on another knowledge source.

Structure of the Knowledge Source

The second knowledge source is a combination of a book and an online website. The book, Endrei et al. (2004), discusses common e-business scenarios, proven patterns to address them, and guidelines on how to implement such patterns using SOA and specially Web Services. The website is "IBM's Patterns collection for e-business" (available at http://www.ibm.com/developerworks/patterns/) that is an online repository of patterns. The book starts with introducing e-business patterns, various pattern types and their usage. Then, it introduces SOA and describes an approach to develop service-oriented applications.

To understand the structure of pattern repository, various types of patterns should be introduced first. The book recognizes the following types of patterns on various design levels:

- **Business patterns:** Business patterns are high-level constructs that can be used to describe the key business purpose of a solution. They are the fundamental building blocks of most e-business solutions, and describe the interaction between the main participants in an e-business solution which are *users*, *businesses*, and *data*. For instance, *Self-Service* or *User-to-Business* pattern addresses cases that internal and external users interact with enterprise transactions and data.

- **Integration patterns:** Integration patterns span multiple participants in an e-business solution to provide solutions that can not be built based on a single business pattern.
- **Composite patterns:** Composite patterns represent frequently used combinations of business and integration patterns. For instance, *e-Marketplace* is a composite pattern for applications that facilitate trading goods for communities of buyers and seller and promote business communities among trading partners.
- **Application patterns:** Application patterns provide a conceptual layout which describes interactions and relations of various application components and data within an integration or business pattern.
- Runtime patterns: Runtime patterns define logical middleware structure that supports an application pattern. They also define role of each middleware node and interfaces between nodes.

At the time of this writing, the repository contains 10 top level patterns and a few custom patterns:

- **Business patterns:***Self-service* or user-to-business pattern, *Collaboration* or user-to-user pattern, *Information aggregation* or user-to-data pattern, and *Extended enterprise* or business-to-business pattern.
- **Integration patterns:***Access integration* and *Application integration*.

- **Composite patterns:***Electronic commerce*, *e-Marketplace*, *Portal*, and *Account Access*.
- **Custom patterns:** Patterns that fall under none of three categories mentioned above are put here. The important high-level pattern in this category is *Non-functional requirements*.

For each high-level pattern, application patterns that can be used to realize the high-level pattern are listed. Moreover, runtime patterns that can realize each application pattern are listed and discussed for each specific application pattern. To sum up, pattern repository uses a three level hierarchy of patterns:

1. High-level patterns at top level.
2. Application patterns for each high-level pattern at middle-level.
3. Runtime patterns for realization of each application pattern at the bottom.

Each application pattern includes a short description, a conceptual diagram showing various components of the pattern and their interactions, key features, business and IT drivers, special consideration, and limitations. Each runtime pattern includes description of the pattern and diagrams showing middleware required to realize the associated application pattern.

The only exception to the hierarchy structure is *Non-functional requirements* high-level pattern. For this pattern, the notion of non-functional requirement replaces the application pattern. It means non-functional requirements are listed at middle-level and runtime patterns are listed for each non-functional requirement. Currently, there are only two non-functional requirements available in the repository: *High Availability*, and *High Performance*. This set is pretty limited compared to non-functional requirements that Erl (2007) addresses.

Comparing the mentioned design knowledge structure with design knowledge structure of Erl's book leads to a few interesting points:

- **Basis of structure:** The most prominent difference between two structures is the subject each source uses as a basis. For the patterns, the main subject is the business scenario and it reveals itself by having business patterns, whose aims are to address such scenarios, appear at top level. For the principles, the main subject is desired qualities and it is apparent since subareas are directly devoted to qualities such as discoverability and autonomy.
- **Hierarchical vs. flat structure:** The patterns repository uses a hierarchical structure to organize more that 40 application patterns and even more runtime patterns. As we go down in the hierarchy technical details are introduced more frequently, and technical details are about 'How's rather than 'Why's. So it is expected to extract more task-based information as we go down the hierarchy. On the other hand, Erl's book uses a flat structure and is expected to have more expressed design knowledge.

Resulting Goal-Graphs

The first step of the extraction process is to figure out the partitioning of the knowledge into subareas. Considering the categorization of patterns explained above, a two level partitioning is suggested. First, each business, integration, and composite pattern is considered as a separate subarea. Then, each application pattern is treated as a separate subarea inside its top level subarea.

The following figure shows the resulting goal-graph for the *Access Integration: Single Sign-On* application pattern from the *Access Integration* high-level subarea. We extracted goal-graphs for other Access Integration patterns but we were

unable to integrate them all due to insufficient common elements.

Comparing goal-graphs extracted here to goal-graphs extracted from Erl (2007) results in a number of interesting points:

- **Alternative design information source:** In extracting goal-graphs from "IBM's Patterns collection for e-business" we noticed that some pieces of design information such as information about components of an application pattern and interactions among them is expressed using architectural diagrams rather than plain text. Such pieces are important parts of extracted design information and can be extracted by a simple technique of expressing information using sentences and applying the normal process on these sentences. Usage of this technique however should be supervised by knowledge experts as well in order to prevent the introduction of bogus information into graphs. Also, the diagram number or the page number of the diagram may be used to mark the source of the extracted information.
- **Nature of the knowledge area and its effect on extracted knowledge:** Goal-graphs extracted from "IBM's Patterns collection for e-business" contain more tasks compared to the ones extracted from Erl (2007), particularly when compared to principle goal-graphs. This outcome, however, is not surprising since IBM's patterns collection is naturally about solving common e-business problems and the bulk of its information is about configurations of components which solve those problems. It aims to provide designers with proven solutions to satisfy immediate requirements but it does not offer much about effects of choosing each component on various software qualities. Such information, if present, is usually presented by a list as a

Figure 9. Goal-graph of access integration: Single sign-on pattern

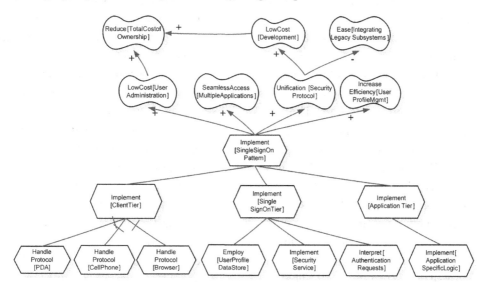

whole result of implementing a pattern. As a result, reasons behind design decisions and more importantly the effects of low-level design decisions on high-level goals can not be analyzed properly. This is the expected result of nature of information in "IBM's Patterns collection for e-business".

- **Structure of the knowledge area and integration:** As mentioned earlier, lack of enough common softgoals and tasks in the extracted goal-graphs for application patterns prevents effective integration of those graphs into a high-level graph for Access Integration pattern. While various Access Integration sub-patterns help designers provide a single and consistent access to various features in the system, each pattern, on its own, is a relatively separate problem. So, it results in separate extracted design information, particularly when focus is on the implementation of solutions. In other words, gaps between various sub-areas are a result of original structure of the knowledge area. When information is organized to address different concrete

problems then lack of enough common softgoals to integrate around is anticipated.

CONCLUSION

We introduced service-oriented architecture and discussed the need for organizing and analyzing SOA design knowledge to support system design. Subsequently, we demonstrated how to extract design knowledge from Erl's SOA design book. In particular, the contributions of this study were the following:

1. **SOA design knowledge:** The result of applying our knowledge extraction method is a set of graphs which visualize design knowledge about various principles of service-oriented design using goal-oriented concepts. We presented goal-graphs for a few principles and demonstrated how to use these goal-graphs in various design scenarios including design alternative and project-specific goal analysis. We believe the collective set of goal-graphs constitutes a concrete knowledge-base of SOA design knowledge in a compact and analyzable

format which facilitates designing effective service-oriented systems. It can be used as a foundation to gather and integrate SOA design knowledge from various sources. Moreover, it serves as a vendor-agnostic learning resource of SOA design.

2. **Knowledge extraction method:** The extraction method used to extract SOA design knowledge from Erl (2007) and "IBM's Patterns collection for e-business" has general applicability. Although this method is designed to extract SOA design knowledge, there is nothing to prevent using it on knowledge areas other than SOA. The main intended application of this method, however, is to treat more SOA sources to enhance SOA design knowledge we extracted here.

Here is a review of a few important points we observed during the course of this study:

1. **Expectations:** All of the initial expectations are met to an acceptable degree. Goal-graphs present an integrated view of their corresponding subareas. They also support semi-automatic analysis of design alternatives and their effects on other softgoals in the system. Low-level goals and tasks are related to project-specific goals as illustrated. Also, knowledge can be categorized according to different criteria as demonstrated by extracting design principle and design pattern goal-graphs from the same knowledge area. Finally, our proposed representational framework proved to be expressive enough to support the mentioned expectations particularly for rationale-intensive knowledge sources (as opposed to task-intensive knowledge sources).

2. **Dividing the knowledge area:** Since breaking up the knowledge area is a step which affects all other activities, it should be performed in a way that there is no significant overlap among the resulting subarea. Such

overlaps lead to extra unnecessary work in extraction and integration steps. Also, it should completely cover the knowledge area as leaving some parts uncovered leads to incompleteness of extracted information and complicates the integration step since the information explaining the relations among softgoals might reside in the uncovered parts. These hints are more important when knowledge area is divided according to a categorization other than its original structure.

3. **Normalizing Names:** Normalizing names of softgoals is essential to integrating the extracted knowledge. However, extra care should be taken in performing normalization. Grouping semantically different softgoals as one leads to incorrect information. On the other hand, inflexible normalization results in graphs that are hard or even impossible to integrate. In general, the normalization policy needs to be adjusted for the knowledge area at hand.

4. **Filling in implicit knowledge:** Some information about the knowledge area is implied and can be deduces from the context. Doing so not only increases the explicitly expressed information about the knowledge area, but also facilitates the integration process by providing the missing links between elements. However, this method should be used only when there is no ambiguity about the information being added. Otherwise, it leads to incorrect information added to result graphs. Therefore, it is recommended that such information be added by experts on the knowledge area. Other sources of extra information are diagrams and graphs, as explained in "A second knowledge source" section. Such information can be used to find the required links to integrate currently extracted pieces of information or it can be just viewed as extra information used

to increase the completeness of extracted knowledge.

5. **Revealing extra information:** Our method helps to expose knowledge about the design objectives that may only be extracted when subareas are integrated together. Integration of two or more subareas enables goal-graphs of various subareas to complete missing links of one another in order to form a richer goal-graph. An example is further explained in "Integrating design principle goal-graphs" section and demonstrated in Figure 4.

6. **Corroborating goal-graphs:** A sign of a good integration process is that information extracted from one graph corroborates information extracted from other graphs. This happens when information from one graph provides more detail about a contribution link in current graph during the integration process. For instance, as explained in "Integrating design principle goal-graphs" section, integration reveals more details about the link from MinimizingDataTransformation[Service] to Composability[Service]. Such corroborating knowledge serves as validation for extracted knowledge, which increases the certainty and accuracy of graphs.

7. **High-level integration:** Another sign of good normalization is that high-level soft-goals are easy to integrate since high-level goals are shared among various subareas. It should be noted that information in each subarea is dependent on how the knowledge area is divided in the first place and how frequently high-level goals appear in various subarea graphs.

8. **Benefits over text form:** As seen throughout the chapter, using goal-graphs to represent SOA knowledge have many benefits: Goal-graphs provide a navigable, concise, and integrated view of the knowledge area and enable structured analysis of knowledge. They enable connecting of high-level project goals to design knowledge. Finally, they enable integration of knowledge from various sources while revealing supporting as well as conflicting relations among them. All these claims are validated thorough various discussions especially in "Integrating design principle goal-graphs" subsection as well as an example of a fictitious company in "Application Example" subsection.

9. **Organization of the knowledge source:** As explained in "A second knowledge source" section, original organization of the knowledge area is an important factor of effective integration and analysis support. Organizing information based on solutions results in naturally separated and hard to integrate subareas while organizing information based on desired qualities and principles results in more conceptually connected subareas. This, in turn leads to better analysis support and reveals complementary characteristics and goals of various subareas.

10. **Mindset of knowledge source authors:** As a curious reader might notice, in our graphs positive contribution links appear considerably more frequently than negative contribution links. This issue is a direct result of type of information available in our chosen knowledge sources. We observed that typical SOA knowledge sources usually discuss various principles and methods while mainly focusing on the problems they solve rather than thoroughly discussing both positive and negative effects of the method at hand. As a result, using extraction on such knowledge areas results in substantially more positive contributions. The issue is even more noticeable on knowledge areas focusing on technology such as "IBM's Patterns collection for e-business". This unbalance makes trade-off analysis less effective and models less useful. However, we hope that studies like this one can help change the mindset of service-oriented community towards writ-

ings that explore both sides of issues rather than focusing on just one side.

11. **Completeness:** A valid concern about completeness is that some bits of knowledge are not presented in the graph due to human error or insufficient expressiveness of the representational framework. This issue is inherent in all manual extraction methods, and it is the reason that attention to details is of such importance in extracting process. Also, it is worth mentioning again that the completeness issue is why graphs are only complementary to the original text and why they maintain traceability link to the original text for every bit of knowledge they represent.

Limitations

We introduced an SOA knowledge-base, demonstrated its usefulness, and discussed our method of constructing such a knowledge-base. However, both the knowledge-base and the extraction method have limitations of their own:

1. **Usc of few knowledge sources:** Although Erl (2007) is a comprehensive and well-structured SOA knowledge source, the fact remains that SOA design knowledge in our work is extracted primarily from only one source. To make a complete knowledge-base of SOA design knowledge more SOA sources should be integrated with this work. However, since the extraction method is explained in detail, we hope that with help form the community the SOA design knowledge-base will grow into a complete and mature source of SOA information.

2. **Tediousness and expertise requirements:** As demonstrated, extracting and integrating design information requires considerable effort. Moreover, it is highly recommended that people involved in extraction and especially integration be familiar with the knowledge

area, since the process of choosing consistent names for softgoals and tasks and the process of adding new knowledge based on current extracted knowledge need familiarity with the area.

3. **Scalability of models:** A noticeable problem with our representation framework is that as the amount of knowledge increases, graphs become more complicated and harder to manage and navigate. To make our models scalable, we need to introduce means to modularly manage the size of our models. Reusable goal modules, separate views, and aspects-oriented models are a few methods that can help make our graphs, especially results of integrating smaller graphs, more manageable.

4. **Traceability:** In our method we only established the bare minimum traceability links. Although these links provide a means to trace various bits of knowledge back to their original knowledge sources, the method doesn't have a clear stand on how to manage these links. Adopting a solid stand on traceability by using a traceability framework or a traceability management tool facilitates managing these links and provides the necessary means for SOA experts to resolve possible conflicts among knowledge sources by tracing back conflicting bits of knowledge and interpreting them properly.

5. **Dependency on structure:** As explained before, the effectiveness of the extraction method is related to the structure of design knowledge. Knowledge sources which focus on solutions rather than design qualities and principles usually do not yield useful goal-graphs unless a complementary source such as knowledge of an expert is used.

Future Work

Future research directions of this work can be categorized into three groups:

1. **Improving SOA design knowledge:** Although the set of goal-graphs we extracted is a good start for documenting and organizing SOA design knowledge, there is more SOA design knowledge out there. Applying our extraction method to new SOA knowledge sources and integrating the results will improve the completeness and quality of SOA design knowledge-base. We believe that with proper contribution from the community it is possible to collect SOA design knowledge scattered in the literature and create an analyzable goal-oriented knowledge-base of such design information.

2. **Knowledge extraction related research:** Next research path is improving the knowledge extraction process itself. For instance, since applying this method is fairly time-consuming, it is helpful to devise techniques to automate the process. The use of human-aided techniques for performing semi-automated extraction and integration process and the developing supporting design tools are interesting research paths.

3. **Supporting system design:** This research path concerns with finding new applications for the extracted design knowledge. One possible application involves goal-prioritization in real world projects. Real world projects always have limited budget and development time. As a result, not all high-level softgoals can be satisficed. The common solution is to prioritize goals and optimize development efforts to satisfice as many high priority softgoals as possible. Having an integrated graph, designers can describe a proposed solution by assigning initial values to lower level goals and use the evaluation process to find out which high-level softgoals are satisficed. Backed up with a supporting tool such as OpenOME (http://www.cs.toronto.edu/km/openome/), this method can help designers find the optimal solution given the project goals, budget, and time limitations.

REFERENCES

Antón, A. (1997). *Goal identification and refinement in the specification of software-based Information Systems*. Unpublished doctoral dissertation, Georgia Institute of Technology, Atlanta, GA, USA.

Chung, L., Nixon, B. A., Yu, E., & Mylopoulos, J. (1999). *Non-functional requirements in software engineering*. Springer.

Chung, L., Supakkul, S., & Yi, A. (2002). *Good software architecting: Goals, objects, and patterns*. Information, Computing & Communication Technology Symposium (ICCT- 2002), UKC'02. Seoul, Korea.

Cleland-Huang, J., Settimi, R., Zou, X., & Solc, P. (2006). *The detection and classification of nonfunctional requirements with application to early aspects* (pp. 36–45).

Dardenne, A., van Lamsweerde, A., & Fickas, S. (1993). Goal-directed requirements acquisition. *Science of Computer Programming, 20*(1-2), 3–50. doi:10.1016/0167-6423(93)90021-G

Darimont, R., & Lemoine, M. (2006). *Goal-oriented analysis of regulations*. REMO2V06: Int. Workshop on Regulations Modelling and their Verification & Validation, Luxemburg.

Endrei, M., Ang, J., Arsanjani, A., Chua, S., Comte, P., Krogdahl, P., et al. (2004). Patterns: Service-Oriented Architecture and Web services. IBM Red books.

Erl, T. (2005). *Service-Oriented Architecture; Concepts, technology, and design*. Prentice Hall PTR.

Erl, T. (2007). *SOA principles of service design*. Prentice Hall PTR.

Gamma, E., Helm, R., Johnson, R., & Vlissides, J. (1995). *Design patterns*. Addison-Wesley Professional.

Gross, D., & Yu, E. (2001). From non-functional requirements to design through patterns. *Requirements Engineering Journal*, *6*(1), 18–36. doi:10.1007/s007660170013

Horkoff, J. (2006). *Using i* models for evaluation*. MSc thesis, Toronto, Ont, Canada.

Mussbacher, G., Amyot, D., & Weiss, M. (2007). *Formalizing patterns with the user requirements notation* (pp. 304–325). Hershey, PA: IGI Global.

Mylopoulos, J., Chung, L., & Nixon, B. (1992). Representing and using nonfunctional requirements: A process-oriented approach. *IEEE Transactions on Software Engineering*, *18*(6), 483–497. doi:10.1109/32.142871

Weiss, M., Esfandiari, B., & Luo, Y. (2007). Towards a classification of Web service feature interactions. *Computer Networks*, *51*(2), 359–381. doi:10.1016/j.comnet.2006.08.003

Yu, E. S. (1996). *Modelling strategic relationships for process reengineering*. PhD thesis, Toronto, Ont., Canada.

Chapter 7
Model–Driven Engineering of Non–Functional Properties for Pervasive Service Creation

Achilleas Achilleos
University of Cyprus, Cyprus

Kun Yang
University of Essex, UK

Nektarios Georgalas
Centre of Information and Security Systems Research, UK

ABSTRACT

Pervasive services are highly customizable and personalized services that must have the capability to run anytime, anywhere, and on any device with minimal user attention. The creation of these dynamic services using application level approaches becomes a daunting task for the software engineering community. This necessitates changes to the way services are designed and implemented, in order to simplify and increase the agility of the service creation process. In this chapter, a model-driven development process and an environment that facilitates pervasive service creation using an abstract platform independent approach are described. Using this approach, a context modelling language is defined in the form of a metamodel and a context modelling framework is generated. The framework facilitates the definition of platform independent context models that describe the non-functional requirements of pervasive services. Subsequently, context models are mapped and transformed via the use of the generic environment's capabilities to implementation specific service code. Finally, a pervasive museum case study is presented to demonstrate the effectiveness of the approach for the definition of a context model and the generation of the service implementation.

DOI: 10.4018/978-1-60566-794-2.ch007

INTRODUCTION

In the context of software engineering, *services* are generally considered to be software applications that can be deployed and executed on a *specific* device and platform to accomplish conventional computing tasks. However, the notion of *pervasive* services is characterised by a larger degree of flexibility in that they refer to software applications capable of running *anytime, anywhere and on any device* with minimal user attention (Yang et al., 2005). Such services should be capable of operating in a dynamic environment and provide users with a specialized and personalized behaviour that allows performing dynamic computing tasks. This means in particular that the service must be able to adapt dynamically on the basis of changing context information and in accordance to certain predefined rules. Furthermore, the service must take into account individual user preferences in order to aid the user and undertake appropriate actions on behalf of the user with increased probability of correctness.

Service creation is a complex process that involves multiple tasks for the rapid analysis, design, implementation and validation of services (Adamopoulos et al., 2002; Glitho et al., 2003). The process supports the development of services commonly via the use of a high-level service creation environment. A variety of high-level service creation environments have been developed (Glitho et al., 2003; Lennox & Schulzrinne, 2000), which attempt to simplify the service creation process. The technology-specific complexities introduced though by these kinds of environments hinder slightly the realisation of this objective. According to our views a high-level service creation environment should steer clear of implementation specific technologies. Hence, an abstract model-driven development environment, as the one proposed in (Achilleos et al., 2007), is required in order to provide solutions to these open issues.

Context-awareness is the key characteristic feature of pervasive services that indicates the requirement to adapt the service behaviour on the basis of input context information and certain predefined rules. Typically in conventional services information is acquired mainly as input from the user and this profiled information drives the service execution. On the contrary when dealing with pervasive services input information must be acquired from a variety of context sources; e.g. repositories, sensors, users. Consequently, the complexity of the service creation process is further augmented due to the necessity to represent and manage effectively the information obtained from diverse input context sources.

The term context has been interpreted in many different ways during the course of research (Dey & Abowd, 2000). In our work we define context as: *"Any information relevant to the interaction of the user with the service where both the user and the application's environment are of particular interest"*. Context commonly refers to information such as the identity, time, location and activity of the user, together with additional information that are specific to a particular pervasive service. Therefore, understanding which information is termed as context, how to represent them and manage them, is crucial in order to simplify the pervasive service creation process and realize the overall objective of service adaptability.

Pervasive service creation has been studied during the course of research following two complementary directives, namely: (i) infrastructure-level approaches and (ii) application-level approaches. The primary directive focuses on building an infrastructure that provides the capability to sense, gather and process low-level context information required by pervasive services (McFadden et. al., 2004). Although this directive is important, our work aligns with complementary approaches that tackle pervasive service creation at the application level (Strang & Linnhoff-Popien, 2004). This is due to the fact that pervasive service creation requires an abstract model-driven approach, in order to avoid implementation specific complexities. Furthermore, a model-driven approach provides the capability to address issues such as portability and adaptability of pervasive services.

These approaches are commonly termed as context modelling techniques. They deal with management related tasks such as representation, administration and distribution of context information to pervasive services to achieve their adaptation. The principal requirement is the representation of context information at the application level, in a format that can be realised and utilised by pervasive services. Generally the representation of context information is conveyed in the form of a context model. The context model depicts the non-functional properties required for the creation of pervasive services. These non-functional requirements introduced into the context model ensure that the functionality of the service is kept to the desired level. They define the non-functional aspects of the pervasive service, which are namely context validity, context quality and context privacy. These aspects are essential in order to ensure that the context information provided to the service is valid, is of the best quality possible and access is restricted in accordance to the defined conditions.

The diversity of input context sources is the main contributing factor that introduces the non-functional requirements of the service (Henricksen & Indulska, 2006). For instance information acquired from a static repository is usually of superior quality than information captured from a sensor (Henricksen & Indulska, 2002; Simons & Wirtz, 2007). Furthermore, different context information requires to be treated differently in terms of privacy. For instance a user might want to keep its profile information accessible to all users of the service. Opposed to this, some context information such as credit card details must not be accessible to other users. Hence, different permissions should be set on each context source to restrict accordingly the access to context information.

An ideal context model shall go head to head with the service creation environment into which is to be implemented. A common software engineering technology that underpins both context modelling and pervasive service creation can naturally bring context-awareness into pervasive services at the service compilation stage; i.e. prior to service execution. The Model Driven Architecture (MDA) (Frankel 2003; Kleppe et al., 2005) paradigm introduced by the Object Management Group (OMG MDA, 2003) comprises such a technology. In our previous wok, a preliminary MDA-based service creation environment has been proposed and verified (Achilleos et. al., 2008). The work presented in this chapter follows on our previous research outcomes to tackle context-awareness and support the engineering of non-functional properties of pervasive services. This is performed using a model-driven technology, in particular, OMG's MDA. MDA's many advantageous features such as high-level abstraction and platform independence simplify the context modelling and implementation tasks associated with pervasive service creation.

The chapter promotes the thought of incorporating context-awareness into pervasive services at the static compile time, i.e. service creation stage. These non-functional mechanisms defined into context models at the service creation stage will be triggered at the service execution phase to provide inherent and therefore much enhanced service adaptability. This is in complementation to the main-stream service adaptation methodology that is largely based on a complicated middleware infrastructure. The main technical contributions introduced in this chapter lie in twofold. Primarily, a model-driven methodology is proposed, which is based on the MDA paradigm and facilitates the service creation process. We utilise the methodology for context modelling and consider context modelling as an integral part for pervasive service creation. Secondly, we practise the methodology to design and generate a Context Modelling Framework (CMF), which is integrated into the

MDA-based service creation environment as one of its components to support the design, validation and implementation of pervasive services. Finally, the effectiveness of the integrated environment is showcased and evaluated via a pervasive service case study.

The rest of the chapter is structured as follows: Section 2 presents related research work on pervasive service creation. Section 3 introduces the model-driven methodology and presents the architecture of the generic MDA-based environment. In Section 4 we extract the requirements of the context modelling domain and introduce the proposed CMF. The CMF is then integrated into the generic environment to comprise the Pervasive Service Creation Environment (PSCE). Section 5 presents the creation of pervasive museum service and performs a preliminary evaluation of the approach using selected software metrics. In Section 6 we present the conclusions and identify future work on pervasive service creation.

BACKGROUND

Recent research work on pervasive service creation focuses on an application based solution to the problem. Several approaches have been proposed that illustrate the divergence in modelling and utilising context information for diverse application domains (Strang & Linnhoff-Popien, 2004). These approaches are commonly termed as context modelling techniques and can be categorized in accordance to the representation proposed for modelling context information. Furthermore these modelling techniques identify the non-functional properties of context-aware services that are namely context quality, context validity and context privacy. These non-functional requirements are intuitively captured in the context model proposed by different context modelling techniques.

Initially Schilit et al. (1994) introduce such an approach, in an attempt to model context

information using key-value pairs. Key-value models represent context in the form of a value of context information that is delivered to the application as a variable. The proposed approach is characterised by its simplicity in representing context information, something that benefits the technique in terms of its applicability. The simple representation of context information is therefore a plus from the functional management viewpoint but it is a downside if quality, validity and privacy of this information are considered.

Bauer (2003) makes use of the Unified Modelling Language (UML), to model context information relevant to air traffic management in the form of a UML extension. The strength of the approach relies on the use of graphical models for modelling context information, which makes it easy to comprehend and transform the context models. Another major benefit is the use of the very well known and widely accepted UML modelling language. Despite these benefits, Bauer's context model does not address explicitly context validity and context privacy.

In a similar approach Simons and Wirtz (2007) defined a UML based Context Modelling Profile (CMP) that allows to model context information for mobile distributed systems. UML stereotypes have been defined for the context modelling domain and Object Constraint Language (OCL) (OMG OCL, 2005) constraints are enforced to ensure the correctness of models. In this work context quality, validity and privacy are addressed via the definition of temporal constraints and the classification of diverse context sources. Consequently, these non-functional aspects are defined accordingly in the proposed CMP. In overall the approach benefits from the use of the widely accepted UML, since the CMP can be used in various UML tools. Despite that fact, these tools do not provide a standard way to access model stereotypes and enforce constraints (Simons & Wirtz, 2007). Hence, constraints are imposed and enforced in this approach using the Eclipse Modelling Framework (EMF) (EMF, 2008). Moreover, mapping context models to an implementation, which enforces non-functional requirements during the service execution, is considered as future work.

Henricksen and Indulska (2004, 2006) propose an infrastructure and a framework to gather, manage and disseminate context to services. Context modelling concepts are introduced that facilitate the generation of a context management system from models. These are namely the context modelling language, the situation abstraction, the preference, branching and programming models. The approach is mainly based on the taxonomy of context sources used in this work. The taxonomy presents a clear-cut classification that segregates context sources as static, profiled, sensed or derived. In particular it is denoted that information obtained from a static source is usually of superior quality than information acquired from a dynamic source (profiled, sensed, derived). Moreover it is stated that dynamic context sources usually provide information that is outdated in comparison to static sources, which are commonly more reliable. Context privacy is also addressed in the approach. Furthermore, formality of models is considered and validation capabilities are provided. The approach is slightly hindered by the absence of a context modelling editor and the degree of automation provided for software generation.

The absence of a clear cut approach that follows the MDA paradigm as defined by the OMG

increases the service creation overheads in terms of cost and effort required to develop new services (Azmoodeh et al., 2005). In this chapter we propose a model-driven approach that is strictly based on the MDA paradigm and provides a higher level of automation in software generation. Via the use of the generic MDA-based service creation environment we facilitate the semi-automatic generation of service creation environments for different application domains. Using this approach the CMF is semi-automatically generated in the form of an Eclipse plug-in. The plug-in is then integrated into the generic service creation environment, comprising a new software capability of the resulting PSCE. Consequently, via the use of the PSCE the definition and validation of context models can be effectively carried out. In addition the capability to transform the context models to different implementations is also provided. This simplifies the process and enables the rapid creation of pervasive services.

MODEL DRIVEN METHODOLOGY FOR PERVASIVE SERVICE CREATION

The model-driven development process presented in this section aims to provide a systematic methodology, which facilitates primarily the generation of service creation environments (Achilleos et al., 2008) and supports in overall the service creation process. Table 1 shown below illustrates the mapping between the MDD process phases and the service creation phases. The mapping demonstrates how each phase of the MDD process can be effectively used to perform the task associated with the corresponding phase of the service creation process. In this chapter we make explicit use of the methodology to facilitate the pervasive service creation process.

Table 1. Mapping the MDD process to service creation

MDD process	Service creation process
Domain specific language definition	Service analysis
Domain model definition	Service design
Domain model validation	Service validation/testing
Domain model-to-model transformation	Service implementation/management
Domain model-to-code generation	Service implementation

Figure 1. Domain specific language definition; service analysis

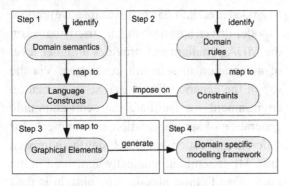

Domain Specific Language Definition

The domain specific language definition phase reflects fully the service analysis phase. In the service analysis phase a requirements analysis is performed to identify the semantics of the domain and provide an overall understanding of the service to be implemented. Correspondingly, as illustrated in Figure 1, during the domain specific language definition phase the domain semantics are identified and mapped to language constructs (step 1). These language constructs are defined in the form of a metamodel that comprises the abstract syntax of the domain specific language (DSL). Furthermore, domain rules that govern the language need to be identified and mapped to corresponding OCL constraints. The constraints are then imposed onto the language definition (metamodel) to restrict the language and allow the definition of valid model instances (step 2). The constraints are most commonly applied separately of the domain metamodel definition, but it is the case that some constraints are implicitly stated in the definition.

Correct definition of the modelling language and successful imposition of constraints allows defining complete and unambiguous models. Since subsequent phases of the development process rely heavily on these models, it is crucial that the language allows the definition of coherent models.

This saves considerably on time and minimises costs, since it does not require performing heavy testing and applying extensive corrections onto the generated implementation. Domain models definition requires a graphical modelling framework, which should consist part of the overall service creation environment. Implementing a modelling framework from scratch is often cumbersome and costly. Especially its maintenance introduces quite an overhead on the development process and subsequently increases costs. Therefore the capability to generate service creation environments for different application domains must be essentially provided.

The generic service creation environment provides the capability to map the metamodel definition to graphical elements comprising the language's concrete syntax (step 3). This is performed by automatic interpretation of the metamodel elements and relationships to visual constructs (graphical metamodel) of the domain specific modelling framework. Moreover, the domain metamodel artefacts are translated in an automatic manner to components (tooling metamodel) that form the palette of the modelling framework. Subsequently, the domain, graphical and tooling metamodels are merged into a common mapping metamodel that facilitates generation of a domain specific modelling framework (step 4).

Besides the definition of a new modelling language the potential to utilise and customise accordingly existing modelling languages is addressed in the methodology. Given that the existing modelling language can be represented using the standard based XML Metadata Interchange (XMI) format then the capability to import it into the generic service creation environment is effectively provided. The XMI standard comprises of an XML like syntax that is utilised for exchanging models in the form of metadata information. Consequently, each modelling language represented using an XMI format can be imported into the environment. This provides the capability to

Figure 2. Domain model definition and validation; service design and validation

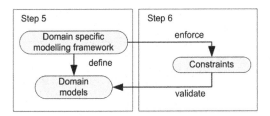

Figure 3. Model-to-model transformation; service implementation/management

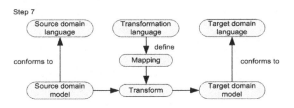

perform the subsequent steps (step 2, 3 and 4) of the language definition and generate a domain specific modelling framework for the language. Furthermore, the framework is integrated to the generic service creation environment to support the following phases of the MDD process.

Domain Model Definition and Validation

The second phase of the MDD process facilitates the definition of domain models via the use of the generated domain specific modelling framework; as illustrated in Figure 2. The framework comprises of a modelling editor with drag and drop capabilities used for the design of domain models on the basis of the modelling language (step 5). This phase corresponds to the service design phase since models can resemble services; if the DSL(s) targets the application domain of services.

The third phase involves domain models validation against the rules imposed during the language definition phase. Figure 2 illustrates that via the use of the generated modelling framework the defined OCL constraints are enforced to validate the domain models (step 6). This is performed in order to ensure that only non erroneous implementations can be automatically generated from these models. Models validation reflects the service validation/testing phase if again we consider that the domain models defined resemble services.

Model-to-Model Transformation

The model-driven development process entails a model-to-model transformation phase (step 7), which assists either the service implementation or the service lifecycle management. As illustrated in Figure 3, via the use of the transformation language the mapping of the source language to the target language is defined. The transformation takes as input a model conforming to a metamodel and produces an output model conforming to another metamodel. In the case of the service implementation phase the transformation accepts as input a platform independent model (PIM) and generates an output platform specific model (PSM). The PSM includes implementation specific details and conforms to a metamodel, which reflects the operational semantics of a programming language. Besides the service implementation phase, transformations can be used for the configuration management of services when porting from one service version to another version; PIM to PIM transformation.

Model-to-Code Generation

The final phase is model-to-code generation (step 8), which corresponds to the service implementation phase. In case the intermediary PIM to PSM transformation phase is omitted, implementation specific details are hard-coded within the code generator. The implementation is obtained via a semi-automatic process that transforms the models (PIM or PSM) to code. Figure 4 illustrates

Figure 4. Model-to-code generation; service implementation

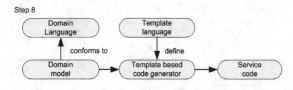

Figure 5. Generic service creation environment architecture

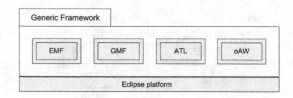

the definition of the code generator in the form of templates, via the use of a template language. The code generator accepts as an input the domain model defined in accordance to the language and generates the corresponding software application code.

GENERIC SERVICE CREATION ENVIRONMENT ARCHITECTURE

In order to apply the methodology in practice a generic MDA-based service creation environment is required. The proposed service creation environment is composed by existing model-driven frameworks integrated together on top of the Eclipse platform. The platform provides an extensible component-based architecture for the environment that supports the integration of additional modelling frameworks in the form of Eclipse plug-ins. The core components integrated into a common generic framework (Achilleos et. al.; 2008) are namely the *Eclipse Modelling Framework (EMF)* (EMF, 2008), the *Graphical Modelling Framework (GMF)* (GMF, 2008), the *Atlas Transformation Language (ATL)* (ATL, 2008) and *openArchitectureWare (oAW)* (oAW, 2008). Figure 5 presents the Eclipse platform as the foundation and the container of the combined modelling frameworks.

The Eclipse Modelling Framework is the core software component of the generic environment that interlinks and enables the functionality of the additional frameworks. This means in particular

that these software components rely on EMF, to perform their individual operations. For instance transformations written in the ATL language are defined on the basis of the EMF-based domain metamodel. Similarly, template-based code generators are defined in accordance to the EMF-based domain metamodel. Therefore, EMF acts as the bridge and ensures horizontal integration of the environment's individual frameworks.

In this work we utilise the capabilities of the generic framework to define the Context Modelling Language (CML) and generate in a semi-automatic manner it's supporting Context Modelling Framework. The CMF is the new software component generated as an Eclipse plug-in, which is integrated with the main frameworks to deliver the Pervasive Service Creation Environment (PSCE). It provides its own context modelling capabilities for the definition and validation of non-functional requirements for pervasive services. Moreover, it makes use of the software capabilities of the existing components to execute the rest of the phases of the MDD process.

CONTEXT MODELLING

Non-Functional Properties of Context Information

Context-awareness is the main characteristic feature of pervasive applications that denotes the requirement to adapt to dynamic changes in context information. This dynamic nature arises from the diversity of context sources from which context information can be obtained. Although early research on context-awareness focused mainly on sensed context sources current work identified and defined a taxonomy of context sources (Henricksen & Indulska, 2006). According to the taxonomy the nature of the context source determines the persistence of context information. In particular the class of the context source depicts the soundness of the acquired information and can be considered as a measure of context *quality* (Simons & Wirtz, 2007). For instance sensed context sources are commonly recognised as error prone due to sensing errors that can occur and subsequently these sources can provide imperfect or improper information to the user. On the other hand information stored within a repository is generally considered as reliable. Consequently the overall *quality* of the service is affected by the quality of context information obtained from the context source and supplied to the user.

Another non-functional property that also arises from the dynamic nature of context information is context *validity* (Simons & Wirtz, 2007). Context might refer to information that is constantly changing through time, such as the current location of the user of the service. Other pieces of information are rather static and changes are very infrequent; for example a person's date of birth never changes. Therefore, it can be realised that the validity of the information that refers to the current location of the user is generally lower than the validity of static information. In particular context validity denotes the reliability and the accuracy of context information obtained from diverse context sources.

Privacy of context information is an additional issue that must be addressed in order to gain the acceptance of pervasive services by users (Simons & Wirtz, 2007). The protection of the users' privacy indicates another important non-functional property that must be addressed in the context model. Once again the context source provides the target where access restrictions to context information must be applied. Consequently each context source linked to particular information must be assigned a permissions property in order to control and restrict the access to this information. For instance a user of a calendar service might require keeping his work schedule open to all users but he would like to keep his personal schedule restricted to family members.

On the basis of the context sources diversity, the aforementioned non-functional requirements are identified and addressed in this work. Context model associations (sources) are enriched with properties that provide the capability to incarcerate the non-functional requirements within the service implementation. These properties incorporated in the context model support merely the decision making for selecting different context sources. This is performed in order to provide to the user the best information available for a particular pervasive service.

Requirement Analysis

The pervasive service creation process relies heavily on context-awareness, which is considered the principal feature of pervasive services. Context-awareness is a dynamic feature that depicts the capability of devices to detect changes in context information and react accordingly to adapt the service execution. Different categorisations of context information have been defined during the course of research. We acknowledge and build upon the categorisation defined by Dey and Abowd (2000) that enumerate context information as *Identity, Time, Location and Activity*. In addition to these categories of context information we introduce also the *Preference* category. This particular context information is of significant importance since it depicts user preferences that facilitate the personalisation, customisation and adaptation of the service behaviour.

Moreover, by denoting user preferences as explicit context information we can monitor and provide a rating to individual preferences in order to enable the service to undertake the cor-

Figure 6. Context categories hierarchy

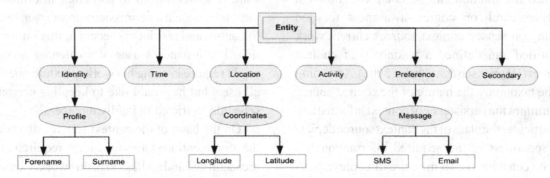

rect actions on behalf of the user. For instance, by monitoring how a user contacts a particular user (e.g. telephone, email, SMS), the service can realise at a later stage and recommend the appropriate communication channel between the two users. Furthermore, by recording and providing a rating to user preferences the pervasive service can undertake appropriate actions with increased probability of correctness (Henricksen & Indulska, 2006).

Apart from the primary context categories, explicit information that is specific to a context-aware service is introduced in the context model. This context information is termed in this work as secondary categories. Secondary categories describe information specific to a service such as the details of a restaurant; e.g. name, address, and telephone. Both primary and secondary categories are composed by simple properties that are mainly described as primitive datatypes. For instance, if a person's *Identity* is known we can realise primitive context information about that individual such as his *name, email and gender*.

In accordance to the aforementioned categorisation a hierarchy for modelling context categories associated to a particular entity has been defined. Figure 6 illustrates this hierarchy presenting at the top level the *Entity* element that represents any type of real world object (e.g. Person, Device), which can be associated with particular context information. For example a *Person* has an *Identity*,

which is successively specialised by the *Profile* complex datatype. The complex datatype is also refined into primitive datatypes such as *Forename and Surname*. A similar context hierarchy is also depicted in the case of the *Location* category. Furthermore, categories can be specialised via an enumeration rather than a complex datatype. For instance, in this example the *Preference* category is refined by the *Message* enumeration, which contains two enumeration literals namely *SMS and Email*.

Context information for pervasive services is acquired typically from different input sources (e.g. repositories, sensors), in contrast to conventional services where information is obtained mainly as input from the user. Consequently, apart from context categorisation a classification of context sources is essential, to extract and define the non-functional properties of pervasive services in the context model. The classification defined by Henricksen and Indulska (2006) and presented next provides a clear-cut taxonomy for context sources:

- **Static:** information of high persistence (e.g. date of birth).
- **Profiled:** user-supplied information.
- **Sensed:** information captured from sensors.
- **Derived:** derived on the basis of other context information.

The primary non-functional requirement addressed by this classification is *context validity*, which can be determined by the persistence of context information. Persistence defines the frequency with which context information is subject to change, which is essentially different for diverse context sources. Conventionally, static context sources disclose a permanent correlation between the entity and its associated context information. Profiled sources reveal infrequent (seldom) context changes since information remain fixed over long periods of time; unless altered by the user. Conversely, sensed and derived context sources denote information that change frequently and are extremely unstable (frequent or volatile). This is because context obtained from sensors or derived from other information is highly unpredictable. Furthermore, context validity can be defined in the context model using temporal constraints, which are either set as comparative or absolute time constraints. Comparative constraints define a valid expiration time for context information acquired from a context source. On the other hand, absolute temporal constraints designate both the starting and expiring time for context information. Temporal constraints are of prime importance since they designate when information becomes outdated.

The second non-functional requirement that is determined via the sources classification is *context quality*. Typically static information contained within a repository is of superior quality than profiled information inputted by the user. This is due to the fact that a user might neglect to input or update the necessary context information. Respectively, sensed information is of inferior quality than profiled information since context information obtained from sensors is generally inaccurate (or erroneous) and thus unreliable. Moreover, context information derived on the basis of other information is considered of the lowest quality. This is because derived information quality is based on the quality of other information and on the defined derivation rule. For example,

potential restaurants for dining can be derived from the food preference of the person.

Context privacy is another important non-functional property that must be depicted in the context model, in order to achieve the acceptance of pervasive services by users. Different permissions must be set to restrict access to different context information and preserve the privacy of individual users. For example, a user should be able to limit access to personal context information such as his credit card details but on the other hand keep his profile information open to all users of the service. Consequently, different access restrictions must be imposed on each context source to restrict the access to context information in accordance to the user's requirements.

In addition to context information and non-functional properties, contextual situations are crucial for the development of pervasive services. These situations depict explicit actions that should be executed when a context event occurs. For instance the change of context information related to a person (*e.g. location*) results in the alteration of the person's situation (*e.g. in office or at a meeting*). If the person is currently at a meeting its mobile phone device must be set automatically to silent mode in accordance to the occurring contextual situation. Therefore, it can be realised that contextual situations are imperative for modelling explicit behaviours, which are valuable to the interaction between the user and the service.

The definition of context categories, non-functional properties and contextual situations facilitate the mapping of the context model and the generation of the corresponding pervasive service implementation. Primarily categorisation supports the generation of information classes in accordance to the requirements of each distinct category. Moreover, context classification aids the generation of different context management classes for dealing with non-functional properties as required in a distributed environment. Also the definition of contextual situations supports the generation of distinct situation classes that

Figure 7. Creating the context modelling framework

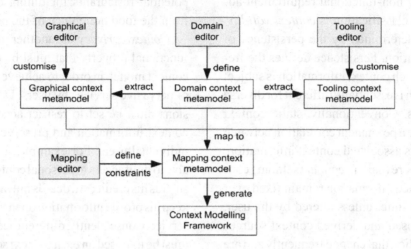

handle explicit service behaviours. Via the generated classes the developer can query, obtain and distribute context information to the pervasive service to achieve its adaptation. Hence, the generated implementation aids and simplifies the pervasive service creation process.

PERVASIVE SERVICE CREATION ENVIRONMENT

Context Modelling Language Definition

The requirements analysis facilitates the identification of the necessary properties of the context modelling domain for accomplishing the domain specific language definition phase. Figure 7 presents the definition of the CML and the generation of the CMF in accordance to steps 1-4 (Figure 1) of the proposed model-driven development process. The creation of the CMF is delivered via the use of the software components of the generic service creation environment. The CMF component is then integrated to the service creation environment to compose the Pervasive Service Creation Environment.

The model-driven development process defines that the semantics identified during the requirement analysis must be mapped to language constructs (step 1 – Figure1). In practice this denotes the definition of the CML in the form of a context metamodel that captures the abstract syntax of the modelling language. The context metamodel is defined on the basis of the Meta Object Facility (MOF) (OMG MOF, 2005) formal specification. Given that the MOF specification does not contribute any software tools to support the metamodel and the concrete syntax definition, the Ecore meta-modelling language of the EMF component is used instead. The motive for selecting EMF as the core of the generic environment is its one-to-one mapping with MOF (Gerber & Raymond, 2003; Mohamed et al., 2007). Furthermore, both EMF and GMF influenced heavily the MOF 2.0 specification towards the critical direction of software tools integration to achieve the overall objective of model-driven development. The context metamodel definition can be performed either using the EMF or the GMF based editor. The GMF domain editor is preferred, as shown in Figure 7, since it facilitates the context metamodel definition using a comprehensible graphical representation.

Figure 8. Context modelling language

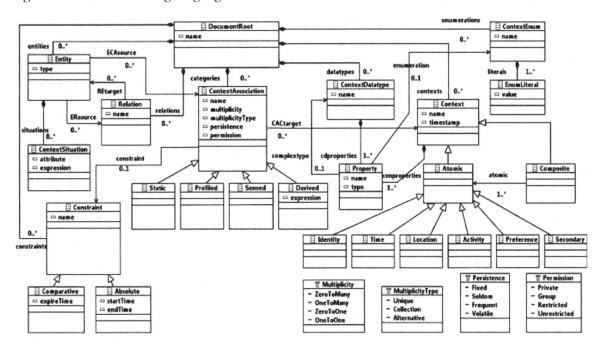

The metamodel describes the elements (*e.g. Entity*), properties (*e.g. multiplicity*) and relationships (*e.g. ECAsource*) of the context modelling domain as identified during the requirement analysis. Figure 8 illustrates the *DocumentRoot* metaclass as the container of the elements of the context model. Its aggregation associations (*e.g. contexts*) define the containment relationships with the rest of the elements.

The *Entity* metaclass represents objects that can be associated via the *ContextAssociation* metaclass to a variety of context information. The object type (*e.g. Person, Device*) can be defined via the *type* property designated in the metaclass. Entities can contain one or more situations defined by the *ContextSituation* metaclass. Contextual situations are defined via the *attribute* and *expression* properties of the *ContextSituation* metaclass. The *attribute* property describes a Boolean variable. In accordance to the expression defined as an OCL constraint the variable value is evaluated either to true or false, which denotes the occurrence or not of the contextual situation. Finally

an entity can be associated to other entities via the *Relation* metaclass and the *ERsource* and *Retarget* associations. Conceptually the *Relation* metaclass denotes a relationship between two entities and it is interpreted as a specific behaviour bound to the two entities; e.g. *Person → owns → Device*.

ContextAssociation is defined as an abstract parent metaclass from which the *Static, Profiled, Sensed and Derived* metaclasses inherit their properties. These metaclasses depict the classification between context sources and facilitate the definition of non-functional requirements in the context metamodel. The primary property depicts the name of the context source. Secondly the *multiplicity* property designates a collection of information and can be assigned the values defined by the *Multiplicity* enumeration. Moreover, the *multiplicityType* property determines the number of simultaneous valid occurrences of context information and obtains its values from the *MultiplicityType* enumeration. The *persistence* property is bound to the *Persistence* enumeration, which describes the frequency with which context is subject to change. Finally the *permission* property discloses the access restrictions imposed upon context information. The values defined via the *Permission* enumeration show the access restrictions that can be imposed on context information in order to safeguard the privacy of the user. In addition to the properties of the parent metaclass, the *Derived* metaclass includes an *expression* property that is used to define the dependence of context information on other context information via an OCL constraint.

Additionally each context source is associated via the *constraint* relationship to the abstract *Constraint* metaclass, which defines a temporal constraint for the specific context source. This constraint ensures the validity of context information by establishing a valid expiration time for the context source or by designating an absolute time interval indicating both the starting and expiration time. The time constraints imposed onto the context source provide the capability to denote when this information was acquired and for how long information is valid.

Context information is defined as an instance of the *Context* abstract metaclass and can be either *Atomic* or *Composite*, in accordance to the inheritance relationship. The *Atomic* context contains simple properties, which represent the lowest level of context information. The *Composite* context contains both simple properties and atomic context. Moreover, the *Atomic* context is also defined as an abstract metaclass since it is extended by the context categories. Properties can be defined as primitive datatypes or even complex datatypes via the *complextype* association. Additionally a property can be associated to an enumeration (instead of a context datatype) as depicted by the *enumeration* relationship.

The context metamodel definition provides the abstract syntax of the modelling language but does not restrict the designer from defining invalid context models; metamodel instances. In order to guarantee the correctness of the context models

certain domain rules need to be identified and mapped to OCL constraints. These constraints are subsequently imposed onto the context metamodel definition using the GMF mapping editor and the OCL capabilities provided by the generic service creation environment. This is performed in accordance to step 2 of the model-driven development process; Figure 1. Following we present some example OCL constraints imposed onto the metamodel to signify their importance for the context modelling language.

Domain Element Target: Entity::EClass
- *Entity.allInstances()->forAll(e1, e2 | e1 <> e2 implies e1.type <> e2.type)*
- *Entity.allInstances()->forAll(e1, e2 | e1<>e2 implies e1.ERsource <> e2.ERsource)*

Domain Element Target: Context::EClass
- *self.conproperties->forAll(p: Property | p.type = 'char' or p.type = 'String' or p.type = 'boolean' or p.type = 'Integer' or p.type = 'double' or p.type = 'float' or p.type = 'long' or p.type = 'short' or p.type = p.complextype.name or p.type = p.enumeration.name)*
- *self.conproperties->forAll(p1: Property, p2: Property | p1 <> p2 implies p1.name <> p2.name)*

The two OCL constraints defined for the *Entity* metaclass restrict the definition of entities so that duplicate entity instances cannot be defined and cyclic relationships between entities are not permitted. The first constraint defines precisely that for all instances of the *Entity* metaclass the *type* property cannot be identical. Moreover the second constraint defines that for all instances of the *Entity* metaclass, no two instances of the *ERSource* association can be identical. The second group of OCL expressions targets the *Context* metaclass and ensures that the definition of context properties is restricted to valid *Property* instances. The first

Figure 9. PSCE software components and tools

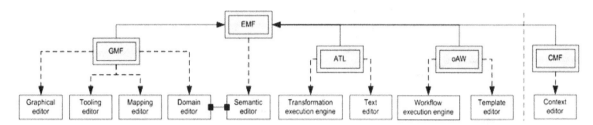

constraint restricts the context model definition and ensures that the *type* property of the *Property* metaclass is set to one of the following: (i) primitive datatype, (ii) complex datatype, (iii) enumeration. Moreover, the second rule complements the first since it prevents the definition of the same *name* property for distinct context properties.

The definition of the context modelling language and the imposition of OCL constraints provides a coherent abstract syntax for the definition of context models. Following step 3 of the model-driven development process (Figure 1) the metamodel abstract syntax is mapped to the corresponding concrete syntax. Figure 7 illustrates the automatic interpretation of the metamodel and the extraction of the graphical and tooling context metamodels; concrete syntax. The graphical metamodel defines the graphical components that will be used to define visually the context model within the modelling editor. Likewise, the tooling metamodel defines the palette components that enable the drag-and-drop functionality of the modelling editor. Both metamodels can be customised using the graphical and tooling editors to optimise the appearance of the CMF.

Figure 7 illustrates how the three distinct metamodels are merged automatically into a mapping metamodel that enables the generation of the CMF (step 4 – Figure 1). The framework is generated as an Eclipse plug-in using the capability provided by the existing Java Emitter Templates (JET) generators of the EMF component. These template-based generators define the mapping of the combined metamodel to the Java implementa-

tion and drive the generation of the framework code. The CMF comprises of the Context Modelling Language as its core constituent and a context modelling editor with drag and drop capabilities for the definition and validation of context models. Figure 9 illustrates the architecture of the Pervasive Service Creation Environment, which comprises of the generated CMF component integrated with the core components of the generic framework. The software tools of each component that support the pervasive service creation process are also illustrated in the figure.

Context Model Definition and Validation

The definition and validation of context models is imperative for the correct execution of the remaining steps of the pervasive service creation process. Consequently, the designer must be assisted in the definition of precise and coherent context models. Figure 10 presents the context model as the key input for the model-to-model transformation and model-to-code generation phases. The context (modelling) editor facilitates the model definition (step 5 – Figure 2) and prohibits implicitly the designer from defining an invalid context model. Moreover, the editor supports the validation of the context model (step 6 – Figure 2), according to the OCL constraints imposed during the CML definition phase. The validation exposes any model definition inconsistencies and informs the designer using descriptive information messages. Subsequently, the designer undertakes the neces-

Figure 10. Context model definition, validation, transformation and code generation

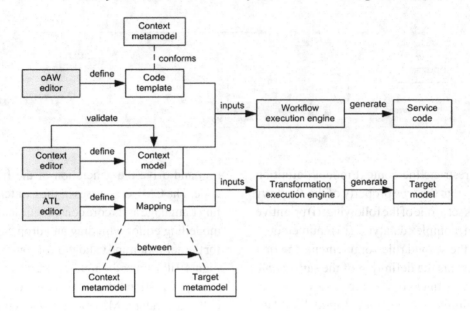

sary steps to rectify the errors before proceeding to the subsequent phases of the process.

Context Model-to-Model Transformation

The coherent definition of the context models enables the model-to-model transformation phase of the process (step 7 – Figure 3). This phase is performed using the ATL component of the PSCE, as shown in Figure 10, which comprises as its core constituent the Atlas Transformation Language. The language provides the capability of writing transformations in the form of a mapping. The ATL editor facilitates the textual definition of the mapping between the semantics of the CML and the semantics of the target modeling language. Subsequently, the context model and the mapping are accepted as the inputs of the transformation execution engine that drives the translation of the context model, e.g. to a relational model. In many cases the transformation phase is performed in order to aid the model-to-code generation by transforming a platform independent model (e.g. context model) to a platform specific model. The

PSM includes implementation specific details that ease the generation of the required implementation code. Most commonly, transformations are used to support the translation (extension) of existing PIMs to improved PIMs versions, rather than aiding the code generation process. This is performed by defining a mapping between the current version of the mctamodel and an extended version of the metamodel. The procedure is known as software (model) configuration management and supports the service evolution.

Context Model-to-Code Generation

The model-to-code generation phase facilitates the transformation of PIM or PSM models (e.g. context models) to implementation code (step 8 – Figure 4). In the case that PIM models are interpreted directly to code, implementation specific details are hard-coded within the code generator. The proposed model-driven development process currently supports this approach where the implementation specific details are included in the generator. Therefore the mapping of the context models is defined using a template-based approach to the corresponding programming language. Although the implementation is not generated fully, a considerable portion of the pervasive service implementation is obtained from the context models. This includes information classes, context management classes and contextual situations classes. In this work we assume that low-level architectural components (e.g. widget, interpreters) for acquiring, processing and distributing raw data from sensors either exist or require to be implemented manually. Moreover, graphical user interfaces and complex computations must be also implemented manually.

The oAW component of the PSCE is utilised to accomplish the model-to-code generation phase. Primarily the code generators are defined in the form of templates, using the oAW component's editor. These advanced code generators are defined on the basis of the context metamodel, using the xPand scripting language, to facilitate the transformation of context models to any implementation technology. This means in particular that the artefacts of the CML are mapped to the operational semantics of the corresponding programming language. Figure 10 illustrates the context model and the code templates, which are accepted as inputs of the workflow execution engine. The engine is responsible to execute the workflow and drive the transformation of models to service implementation code.

PERVASIVE MUSEUM SERVICE

Museum Tourist Guiding Service

In this section we present a case study for the creation of pervasive museum service. We utilise the PSCE to carry out the steps 5-8 (Figures 2-4) of the model-driven development process. The pervasive service aids the visitors touring experience by providing historic and other helpful information on the museum sites and facilities. This information is delivered dynamically to the user of the service due to the occurrence of a context event or because the user has explicitly requested the information. For instance, when a user enters a museum virtual zone a proximity sensor detects his presence. The occurrence of this contextual situation denotes that the user should be presented with information on historic sites available within this virtual zone. The primary aim is to provide to the user context information of the best quality possible (e.g. information is not erroneous) and ensure that this information delivered to the user is also valid (e.g. information is not outdated).

The CMF component of the PSCE is used initially to design the context model illustrated in Figure 11. The model defines both the functional and non-functional properties required for the creation of the pervasive museum service. In the context model the main element is the *Person* entity that signifies the user of the service. Each person is associated to relevant context information via the context source elements, which are defined as instances of the *ContextAssociation* metaclass. For instance each user is associated via the *identity* association to the *Identity* context information, which defines a simple user profile.

The *identity ContextAssociation* describes the necessary properties of the context source from which profile information is acquired. The type of the context source is defined as *Static*, something that denotes that profile information is stored within a context repository. Moreover, the type of the context source depicts that the acquired context quality is very high. In addition the persistence property, which is defined as *fixed*, ensures that the validity of the context information is also very high. This is due to the fact that information stored within a database remains the same for large periods of time. In addition the multiplicity property designates that only a single profile exists for each user. Furthermore, the multiplicity-Type property is defined as *unique* and the permission property is set as *private*. These properties determine correspondingly that a distinct profile exists for each user and only the user can access

Figure 11. Pervasive museum service context model

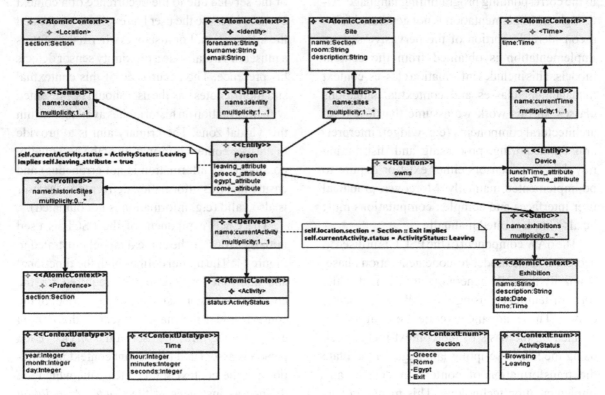

this context information. The profile properties are defined as *String* primitive datatypes and are named accordingly as *forename, surname and email*.

The *sites* and *exhibitions* associations denote two additional static sources defined in the context model. These designate once again static repositories that contain correspondingly information on historic sites of the museum and exhibitions taking place at the museum within the current calendar month. Each historic site is defined as a *Site* secondary context, which comprises of the *name, room* and *description* properties. Both the room and description properties are defined as *String* primitive datatypes. In contrast the name property is defined as an enumeration and can be assigned the literal values defined by the *Section* enumeration (ContextEnum). Furthermore, the *Exhibition* secondary context comprises the *name* and *description String* primitive datatypes

and the *date* and *time* complex context datatypes (*ContextDatatype*).

Apart from the static context sources, a sensed source is defined in the context model. The *location* source defines the association to the *Location* context, which describes the current position of the user within the museum. For this case study we have separated the museum premises into four virtual zones, which are defined by the *Section* context enumeration. These virtual zones define the possible locations of the user within the museum, which are obtained and processed via the use of proximity sensors. The type of the source is defined as sensed.

Moreover, the *historicSites* profiled association determines a context source that obtains input information directly from the users. This input context information denotes preferences on historic sites of the museum, which are of particular interest to the user. These preferences are defined

Figure 12. Activity context association properties view

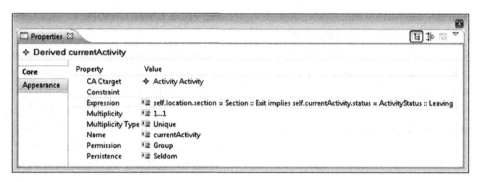

via the *section* property of the *Preference* context, which derives its values also on the basis of the *Section* enumeration.

The example model includes also the *currentActivity* context source, which determines the derived *Activity* context information on the basis of the *Location* context. This denotes in particular the current activity of the user in accordance to his current location. It is expressed in the context model in the form of an OCL constraint defined using the *expression* property, which describes the derivation rule for this conceptual fact. The OCL expression[1] shown next illustrates the following derived fact: "If a user is located at the exit of the museum this denotes that he is currently leaving the museum premises". Consequently, if the user is located at any other virtual zone (e.g. Greece, Rome) apart from the exit zone, it means that he is still browsing the museum historic sites.

```
self.location.section = Section::
Exit implies
    self.currentActivity.status =
    ActivityStatus:: Leaving
```

Figure 12 illustrates the properties view of the *currentActivity* derived source, which comprises of the defined properties that guide the generation of the required functionality (implementation). The properties view defines the target of the context source, which is the *Activity* context information.

Accordingly the multiplicity is set to *1...1* and the multiplicityType is set as *Unique* to denote that a person can be engaged in one distinct activity at any given time. Moreover the permission property is set to *Group*, something that defines that only a group of people can access this context information. For instance the security personnel of the museum might require having access and being able to identify the current activity (or location) of the user. The persistence of the source is defined as *Seldom* to depict the infrequent change of the activity context information; user is either *Browsing* or *Leaving*. Finally the expression property defines the textual derivation rule of the conceptual fact, which can be validated for consistency using the Interactive OCL console of the PSCE.

The final context source depicted in the model associates the user's *Device* to the corresponding *Time* context information. This information is profiled by the user on its own device (e.g. mobile, laptop) and can be acquired and managed in accordance to the properties defined for the *currentTime* context source. The set of context associations introduced in the model and their individual properties, realize the main prerequisite to distinguish between diverse classes of context information and manage differently this information.

In addition to entities, sources and context information the model comprises of contextual situations, which are defined for each entity. One of the contextual situations defined in the context model determines the following: "As soon as the user leaves the museum premises details of forthcoming exhibition tours within the current calendar month should be presented to the user". This proactive behaviour is determined by the OCL constraint illustrated next, which depicts a contextual situation defined for the *Person* entity.

```
self.currentActivity.status = Activi-
tyStatus:: Leaving
     implies self.leaving_attribute
     = true
```

The expression defines that if the person activity status changes from *Browsing* to *Leaving* this means that the user is currently leaving the museum. Therefore, in accordance to the evaluated logical expression the value of the *Boolean* variable *leaving_attribute* becomes true. Consequently, monitoring the state (true or false) of the attribute using different instances of the contextual situation provides the capability to detect the context event and react accordingly. Likewise, each attribute defined in the context model (*e.g. greece_attribute, closingTime_attribute*) is accompanied by an OCL expression, which describes every contextual situation that must be depicted in the model.

Following the model definition phase, the validation of the museum context model is performed using the CMF capabilities in accordance to the imposed metamodel level constraints. This prevents the developer from attempting to transform or generate implementations out of erroneous context model definitions. In the case that an inconsistency is detected in the context model a corresponding error message is displayed suggesting possible resolutions using an informative description. Subsequently, the designer can undertake the necessary actions to rectify the problems discovered in the model definition.

Pervasive Museum Service Evaluation

The implementation phase is carried out primarily by means of context model-to-code generation. For this purpose we have defined the mapping between the context metamodel and the operational semantics of two programming languages. The mapping was defined in the form of code templates to facilitate the transformation of context models (e.g. museum context model) to the Java and J2ME implementation technologies.

Appendix A illustrates an extract of the template mapping defined for transforming context associations to J2ME implementation code. From the mapping (lines 6-8), we can observe that for each context source defined in the context model a corresponding class is being generated. Furthermore, the conditional statements defined at lines 15 and 17 drive the generation of the required implementation in accordance to the multiplicity property depicted in the context source. Another important section of the mapping is presented in lines 10-13 where each property of the context source is mapped accordingly to a corresponding class variable. Accordingly, helper functions are defined that allow accessing these variables from other classes to facilitate and simplify the implementation of the required functionality.

Appendix B illustrates the helper functions defined for the association properties, using the extension language of the oAW component. The extension language facilitates the definition of rich libraries of functions, which can be accessed within code templates to aid the code generation process. These helper functions are imported in the code template definition via the Extensions statement defined at line 1 and accessed via the «ecas.SourceHelperFunctions()» statement defined at line 19 of Appendix A.

The implementation generated from the context model eradicates the requirement to manually implement repetitious code such as information and context management classes (Henricksen &

Table 2. Pervasive museum service evaluation

Implementation	Metric	Generated service code		Overall service code	
		Overall	*Per Module*	*Overall*	*Per Module*
J2ME	Number of modules	40	-	53	-
	Lines of Code	1768	44.200	2330	43.962
	Cyclomatic Number	128	3.200	181	3.415
	Lines of Comment	560	14.000	648	12.226
Java	Number of modules	33	-	53	-
	Lines of Code	1282	38.848	1859	35.075
	Cyclomatic Number	49	1.485	101	1.906
	Lines of Comment	543	16.455	564	10.642

Indulska, 2006). This simplifies and enables the rapid creation of context-aware services. Despite that fact, complex computations and graphical user interfaces require to be manually implemented by extending or modifying the generated service code. Table 2 demonstrates an evaluation of the developed pervasive museum service according to selected software metrics. The analysis results are obtained via the use of the CCCC analysis tool (Littlefair, 2001). The selected metrics for the evaluation are: (i) Lines of Code (LOC) and (ii) McCabe's cyclomatic complexity (Bhansali, 2005). The analysis shows the effectiveness of the approach in minimising the cost, time and effort required to implement the pervasive service.

Table 2 illustrates the analysis results for both the J2ME and Java implementation of the museum context-aware service. Primarily, the LOC metric shows the number of non-comment and non-blank lines of code. From the table it is calculated that 75.879% of the J2ME service code and 68.96% of the Java service code is generated from the context model. The percentages calculated in this case study provide the capability to derive the necessary conclusions but do not serve in any case as an explicit baseline for future case studies. These analysis results indicate simply that the effort required for the implementation of the pervasive museum guiding service has been significantly reduced.

Code complexity is another valuable metric, which denotes the degree of code understandability and indicates the code amenability to modification. Moreover it's a dominant indicator of the code testability (Bhansali, 2005). From the table it is clear that the complexity of the generated code (indicated by the cyclomatic number) is lower than that of the overall service code. This indicates that the generated code can be easily modified and be subjected to testing. Furthermore, it is realised that the mapping can be optimized further to decrease the generated service code complexity. Conversely, it is very difficult to achieve optimization and reduce the code complexity when manual implementation is involved.

Figure 13 illustrates the pervasive museum service running on a J2ME device emulator and a Java enabled laptop device. The screen capture on the top left of the figure shows the historic sites preference selection list. In accordance to the user's preferences the service retrieves and loads the appropriate information on historic sites, as illustrated onto the second screen capture. Following, onto the next screen capture we can observe the occurrence of the leaving contextual situation, which causes a list of upcoming exhibitions tours to be displayed to the user. Moreover, we have the occurrence of the location contextual situation, which signifies that the user has entered the virtual zone of Egypt. Consequently, the user is

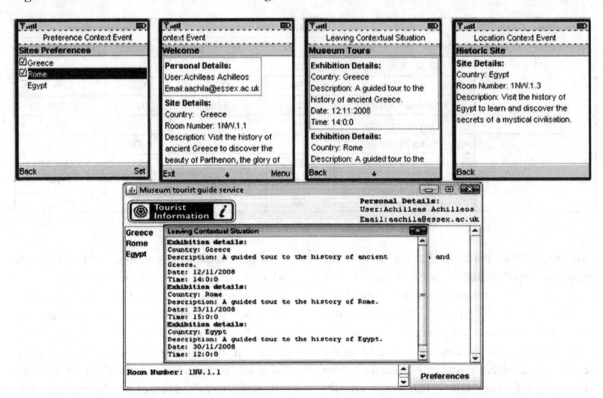

Figure 13. Pervasive museum service running on a J2ME device emulator

presented with information on historic sites located in this virtual zone, as illustrated onto the fourth screen capture. Finally, the screenshot shown at the bottom of the figure presents respectively the occurrence of the leaving contextual situation, while the service is running on the Java enabled laptop device.

CONCLUSION

In this work we propose a model-driven development methodology that supports the service creation process and utilise the process for the creation of pervasive services. The generic service creation environment developed guides the process and provides the capability to define and generate domain specific modelling frameworks. Each generated framework can be effectively integrated into the generic environment to comprise

a service creation environment that addresses a particular services domain (e.g. pervasive services, web services). Consequently, via the composed environment the service creation process is accomplished, starting from service modelling to service implementation.

The chapter deploys the methodology for the development of a Context Modelling Framework that addresses the definition of non-functional properties in the form of context models. The CMF comprises a new component of the generic service creation to compose the Pervasive Service Creation Environment, which supports efficiently the pervasive service creation process. In particular the PSCE facilitates the definition of context models that describe mainly the non-functional properties required for the creation of pervasive services. Moreover, via the use of the environment context models can be validated to ensure their correctness and support respectively the model-to-code generation phase. The generation of the pervasive service implementation from the context models provides the capability to enforce the defined non-functional requirements during the service execution stage.

The Pervasive museum service developed in this work provides the capability to evaluate the efficiency of the methodology. According to the results obtained from the analysis performed using the Lines of Code and the Code Complexity software metrics the effort required for the implementation of the pervasive service is significantly reduced. Moreover, the development cost is also drastically decreased since it is proportional to the time consumed to undertake the implementation. The results presented on Table 2 illustrate that for 40 modules of the generated J2ME code the Cyclomatic Complexity number computed is 128. In contrast the increase of the Cyclomatic Complexity number with merely 13 manually implemented J2ME modules is 52. This denotes an increase of 8.12% in code complexity when manual implementation is involved.

Consequently, by optimising the context modelling language and the model-to-code generator the complexity of the generated service implementation can be minimised. This is performed as part of an iterative process that aims to refine and enhance both the modelling language and the generator. As part of future work we aim is to address this issue by carrying out further case studies that will provide the capability to detect and rectify any deficiencies in the modelling language and the code generator.

REFERENCES

Achilleos, A., Georgalas, N., & Yang, K. (2007). *An open source domain-specific tools framework to support model driven development of OSS.* (LNCS 4530), (pp. 1-16).

Achilleos, A., Yang, K., & Georgalas, N. (2008). *A model-driven approach to generate service creation environments*. IEEE Globecom, Global Telecommunications Conference, (pp. 1 – 6).

Adamopoulos, D. X., Pavlou, G., & Papandreou, C. A. (2002). Advanced service creation using distributed object technology. *IEEE Communications Magazine, 40*(3), 146–154. doi:10.1109/35.989777

ATL. (2008). *Homepage information.* Retrieved from http://www.eclipse.org/m2m/atl

Azmoodeh, M., Georgalas, N., & Fisher, S. (2005). Model-driven systems development and integration environment. *British Telecom Technical Journal, 23*(03), 96–110.

Bauer, J. (2003). *Identification and modelling of contexts for different information scenarios in air traffic*. Diplomarbeit, Faculty of Electrical Engineering and Computer Sciences, Technische Universitat Berlin.

Bhansali, P. V. (2005). Complexity measurement of data and control flow. *ACM SIG-SOFT Software Engineering Notes, 30*(1), 1–2. doi:10.1145/1039174.1039191

Dey, A. K., & Abowd, G. D. (2000). *The context toolkit: Aiding the development of context-aware applications*. ICSE Workshop on Software Engineering for Wearable and Pervasive Computing.

EMF. (2008). *Homepage information.* Retrieved from http://www.eclipse.org/modeling/emf/

Frankel, D. S. (2003). *Model Driven Architecture: Applying MDA to enterprise computing.* Indianapolis: Wiley Publishing Inc.

Gerber, A., & Raymond, K. (2003). MOF to EMF: There and back again. In *Proceedings of the OOPSLA Workshop on Eclipse Technology eXchange,* (pp. 60–64).

Glitho, R. H., Khendek, F., & De Marco, A. (2003). Creating value added services in Internet telephony: An overview and a case study on a high-level service creation environment. *IEEE Transactions on Systems, Man and Cybernetics. Part C, Applications and Reviews, 33*(4), 446–457. doi:10.1109/TSMCC.2003.818499

GMF. (2008). *Graphic Modelling Framework.* Retrieved from http://www.eclipse.org/gmf/

Henricksen, K., & Indulska, J. (2004). A software engineering framework for context-aware pervasive computing. *Proceedings of the 2nd IEEE International Conference on Pervasive Computing and Communications,* (pp. 77 – 86).

Henricksen, K., & Indulska, J. (2006). Developing context-aware pervasive computing applications: Models and approach. *Pervasive and Mobile Computing Journal, 2*(1), 37–64. doi:10.1016/j.pmcj.2005.07.003

Henricksen, K., Indulska, J., & Rakotonirainy, A. (2002). *Modeling context information in pervasive computing systems.* (LNCS 2414), (pp. 79 – 117).

Kleppe, A., Warmer, J., & Bast, W. (2005). *MDA explained: The Model Driven Architecture: Practice and promise.* Boston: Addison-Wesley.

Lennox, J., & Schulzrinne, H. (2000). *Call processing language framework and requirements.* Retrieved from http://www.ietf.org/rfc/rfc2824.txt

Littlefair, T. (2001). *An investigation into the use of software code metrics in the industrial software development environment.* Unpublished doctoral dissertation, Faculty of Communications, Health and Science, Edith Cowan University.

McFadden, T., Henricksen, K., & Indulska, J. (2004). Automating context-aware application development. In *Proceedings of UbiComp, 1st International Workshop on Advanced Context Modelling, Reasoning and Management,* (pp. 90 – 95).

Mohamed, M., Romdhani, M., & Ghedira, K. (2007). EMF-MOF alignment. *Proceedings of the 3rd International Conference on Autonomic and Autonomous Systems,* (pp. 1–6).

oAW. (2008). *User guide v4.3.1.* Retrieved from http://www.openarchitectureware.org/pub/documentation/4.3.1/openArchitectureWare-4.3.1-Reference.pdf.

OMG. (2003). *Model Driven Architecture (MDA) specification guide v1.0.1.* Retrieved from http://www.omg.org/docs/omg/03-06-01.pdf

OMG. (2005). *Meta Object Facility (MOF) core specification v2.0.* Retrieved from http://www.omg.org/docs/formal/06-01-01.pdf

OMG. (2005). *Object Constraint Language (OCL) specification v2.0.* Retrieved from http://www.omg.org/docs/formal/06-05-01.pdf

Schilit, B., Adams, N., & Want, R. (1994). Context-aware computing applications. In *Proceedings of the IEEE Workshop on Mobile Computing Systems and Applications,* (pp. 85 – 90).

Simons, C., & Wirtz, G. (2007). Modelling context in mobile distributed systems with the UML. *Journal of Visual Languages and Computing, 18,* 420–439. doi:10.1016/j.jvlc.2007.07.001

Strang, T., & Linnhoff-Popien, C. (2004). A context modelling survey. In *Proceedings of UbiComp, 1st International Workshop on Advanced Context Modelling, Reasoning and Management,* (pp. 34–41).

Yang, K., Ou, S., Azmoodeh, M., & Georgalas, N. (2005). Policy-based model-driven engineering of pervasive services and the associated OSS. *British Telecom Technical Journal, 23*(3), 162–174.

KEY TERMS AND DEFINITIONS

Context Modelling: A modelling technique that deals with the design of an advanced information model that captures the context-awareness characteristic of pervasive services. From this model the implementation is automatically generated that handles representation, administration and distribution of context information to pervasive services to achieve their adaptation.

Context-Awareness: Describes the key characteristic of pervasive services that defines the capability to obtain, process and utilise context information in order to adapt software applications.

Metamodelling: The process that guides the definition of a metamodel, which describes the elements, properties and relationships of a particular modelling domain.

Model-Driven Development: A software development methodology that focuses on the design and implementation of software applications at an abstract platform-independent level.

Non-Functional Requirements: Properties that define how applications must behave and evaluate the operation of these applications. Typical non-functional requirements are: quality, validity, security, privacy, etc.

Pervasive Computing: Defines a software engineering paradigm that deals with the development of highly adaptive software applications that can run anywhere, anytime and on any particular device (mobile or stationary) with limited or no user attention.

Pervasive Service Creation: Describes a service creation process that deals with the analysis, design, validation and implementation of pervasive services.

ENDNOTE

[1]   The OCL expressions defined for the case study are in a simplistic form to aid the understanding of the proactive behaviour.

APPENDIX A

1.   «**EXTENSION** extensions::functions»
2.   «**DEFINE** Root **FOR** cml::DocumentRoot»
3.   «**EXPAND** Entity **FOREACH** entities»
4.   «**ENDDEFINE**»
5.   «**DEFINE** Entity **FOR** cml::Entity»
6.   «**FOREACH this**.ECAsource **AS** ecas-»
7.   «**FILE** ecas.ext1()+".java"»
8.   public class «ecas.ext1()»{
9.   private static final String atomic_context = "« **this**.ext2()+""+ecas.CACtarget.first().ext3()»";
10. private static final String multiplicity = "«ecas.multiplicity»";
11. private static final String multiplicityType = "«ecas.multiplicityType»";
12. private static final String persistence = "«ecas.persistence»";
13. private static final String permission = "«ecas.permission»";
14.
15. «**IF** ecas.multiplicity == "0...1" || ecas.multiplicity == "1...1"»
16.
17. «**ELSEIF** ecas.multiplicity == "0...*" || ecas.multiplicity == "1...*"»
18.
19. «ecas.SourceHelperFunctions()»
20.
21. «**FOREACH** ecas.CACtarget.conproperties **AS** cp-»
22. public static String «cp.get1()»() {
23. return «cp.name»;
24. }
25. «**ENDFOREACH**»
26. }
27. «**ENDFILE**»
28. «**ENDFOREACH**»
29. «**ENDDEFINE**»

APPENDIX B

1: String SourceHelperFunctions(ContextAssociation ca):
2: 'public static String getMultiplicity() {
3: return multiplicity;
4: }
5: public static String getMultiplicityType() {
6: return multiplicityType;
7: }
8: public static String getPersistence() {
9: return persistence;
10: }
11: public static String getPermission() {
12: return permission;
13: }';

Chapter 8
Relational Service Quality Modeling

Vladimir A. Shekhovtsov
National Technical University "Kharkiv Polytechnic Institute", Ukraine

Roland Kaschek
Information Science Research Center, New Zealand

Christian Kop
Alpen-Adria-Universität Klagenfurt, Austria

Heinrich C. Mayr
Alpen-Adria-Universität Klagenfurt, Austria

ABSTRACT

The paper argues that using non-first-normal-form (NF^2) tables for requirements modeling is a suitable approach for communicating application system issues to stakeholders who have a business background. In particular, such tables are used in an intermediate predesign step residing between requirements elicitation and conceptual design for modeling functional and quality requirements of services and business processes. This approach extends to quality requirements of business processes used for service orchestration.

CONTEXT AND MOTIVATION

Our work focuses on the elicitation and modeling of service and business process quality requirements within the context of Service-Oriented Architecture and Process-aware Information Systems (PAIS) (Dumas, Van der Aalst, & ter

Hofstede, 2005) that are facilitated by computer applications such as BPM engine (workflow management system).

Requirements concerning system quality are often referred to as *non-functional requirements* in order to distinguish them from what traditionally is just called *requirements* in the realm of information systems and only covers functional system aspects. We consider quality requirements

DOI: 10.4018/978-1-60566-794-2.ch008

regarding a system under development (SUD) as a specification of the quality that the SUD is expected to have in order to be fit for use. Thus, featuring the right functionality, i.e. implementing the functional requirements, might be one quality aspect among others. Within the context of SOA, quality requirements are related to both individual services and orchestrations thereof, i.e. business processes.

Elicitation and modeling of quality requirements is important and challenging because:

1. System development is often driven by stated requirements rather than stakeholder needs; inappropriate quality requirements likely are going to waste resources spent for development.
2. Requirements engineering is about system branding, i.e., conceptually shaping or working out the related SUD. Using abstract design-time notions (classes, attributes, activities etc.) at that stage of the development lifecycle for describing system qualities might compromise that branding, as the chosen concepts might be inappropriate for stakeholder understanding and validation.
3. In future, automated service selection, based on automated negotiations, is likely to take place. These negotiations involve service quality characteristics such as performance, security, cost, risk, and similar. That approach obviously has the potential to fundamentally change the way web applications are created.

Our approach is built on the predesign technique described in (Kop & Mayr, 2002; Mayr & Kop, 1998; Shekhovtsov, Kop, & Mayr, 2008) which is about modeling functional requirements for information systems. Our approach aims at quality requirements as opposed to functional ones, and focuses on services and business processes. For empowering stakeholders to cope with service and business process quality issues we propose using a simple but sufficiently expressive semantic model for addressing the relevant concepts. That model is represented as a *non-first-normal-form* (NF^2) relational model (Schek & Pistor, 1982) permitting repetition groups and nested relations. In the present context we call a NF^2 table *glossary*. Its advantage is that it allows for the specification of any relationship between any number of given concepts. In mathematics such a definition of concepts in terms of each other and relationships among them is called an *implicit definition* or *axiomatization*.

Experience from practice suggests that stakeholders having a business background with relative ease understand predesign models because they come along in the well-known shape of tables (Galle, Kop, & Mayr, 2008; Janicki, Parnas, & Zucker, 1997). The conceptual predesign model also is suitable for model mapping. For static and dynamic aspects it was shown that predesign modeling notions can be mapped into class diagrams, activity diagrams and state charts (Kop & Mayr, 2002; Mayr & Kop, 1998) or modeling notions of business process models can be derived from them (Mayr, Kop, & Esberger, 2007). The aim is to guarantee such a mapping flexibility also for quality requirements. Our approach, as suggested by (Mayr, 2006; Pastor, 2006), thus enables both: focusing on requirements and stakeholders' needs, and model mapping onto design notation such as UML and further onto executable code.

In addition, using a unified tabular (relational) representation for requirements allows users to perform relational queries over requirements repositories using a domain-specific SQL-like language. This will be illustrated by examples later in the chapter.

The chapter is organized as follows: in the next section we discuss the foundations of our work and rationalize in favor of our approach. Then we apply our approach to capture service and process quality requirements. The paper is completed with a discussion of the related work and a conclusion.

MODELING SERVICE AND BUSINESS PROCESS QUALITY

We consider quality of an artifact as that artifact's fitness for a specified kind of use. Thus, when a particular kind of use is considered we aim at defining quality characteristics which aid in discussing that particular fitness for use. Our quality requirements model therefore builds on the concept of service or business process quality.

For working out a conceptual framework of requirements models we briefly look into quality requirements metamodels. The paper (Jureta, Herssens, & Faulkner, 2008) has suggested a related metamodel. We reuse that paper's quality requirements metamodel, add a number of metamodel characteristics that have been missed out by that paper, and adapt the terminology to our purposes. We call these quality requirement metamodel characteristics *quality model parameters* because they affect the quality model without being an explicit part of it.

We identify the following quality model parameters:

1. **Context:** the considered circumstances of a service or process execution request.
2. **Dependency:** the permitted relationships between different quality characteristics.
3. **Priority:** the importance of quality characteristics.
4. **Schema:** the kind of organization of the quality characteristics (taxonomy, ontology etc.).
5. **Scoring:** the concepts and rules for scoring requirements.
6. **Stakeholder:** the stakeholders whose requirements are to be considered.
7. **Status:** a given requirement model's life cycle phase.
8. **Polymorphy:** whether or not a quality requirement's metamodel is fixed.
9. **Version:** a given requirement model's version number.

Service and Business Process Quality Models

To describe service quality issues, the concept of Quality of Service (QoS) is widely used. It roots in the research on network-related service delivery performance and reliability. Currently it is usually understood in broader sense – as a synonym for service quality in general.

Service and Business Process Quality Taxonomies

The number of service quality models that employ a taxonomy of quality characteristics (possessing the *schema* parameter value of taxonomy) is quite large and we discuss only a small subset of them. Most taxonomy-based models addresses QoS (Dobson, 2004; Evans & Filsfils, 2007). The models in (Chaari, Badr, Biennier, BenAmar, & Favrel, 2008; Galster & Bucherer, 2008; Ran, 2003) utilize QoS. (Al-Masri & Mahmoud, 2008; Andreozzi, Montesi, & Moretti, 2003; O'Sullivan, Edmond, & ter Hofstede, 2002; Zeng et al., 2004) refer to a general notion of quality with application to services. We will not make further distinctions between these two categories of models.

A number of efforts address the standardization of service quality models. For example, OASIS published the Web Services Quality Model (WSQM) (E. Kim & Lee, 2005; Lee & Yeom, 2007). It is intended to serve all the associated bodies. There are models utilizing existing quality model standards, such as the SQuaRE series of quality standards (ISO/IEC 250xx) (Abramowicz, Zyskowski, Suryn, & Hofman, 2007). In our further examples, we will use WSQM as an example of comprehensive service quality model. The approach of (Lee & Yeom, 2007) adds the concept of quality chain to WSQM for addressing *dependency* quality model parameter. The *stakeholder* parameter is addressed by WSQM as it allows for detailed treatment of the abilities of stakeholders to express different quality requirements.

Most of the quality models for business processes are taxonomies of quality characteristics (Aburub, Odeh, & Beeson, 2007; Guceglioglu & Demirors, 2005). Low-level quality characteristics are accompanied with metrics (Lee, Bae, & Shin, 2005; Vanderfeesten, Cardoso, Mendling, Reijers, & van der Aalst, 2007).

Mostly, regarding *polymorphy,* the value *fixed* is employed, i.e. the resp. models do not allow to define additional characteristics or metrics. (Liu, Ngu, & Zeng, 2004) propose a model which employs the parameter value *float*. It permits to obtain numerical scores for the requirements model quality. Changing the requirements model metamodel is guaranteed by uniformity of QoS calculation which does not depend on particular quality characteristic.

Service Quality Ontologies

Quality can also be conceptualized as an ontology. Most related approaches draw from semantic web services concepts; we will describe them together with a discussion of the possible mapping of our predesign model into such conceptualization in the "related work" section. In this section, we briefly mention several ontologies not directly connected to the Semantic Web.

A set of requirements for two unified ontologies: specific QoS ontology and Service-Level Agreement ontology (including, among others, notions for QoS requirements) is presented in (Dobson & Sanchez-Macian, 2006). An ontological approach for QoS representation introduced in (Zhou, Niemelä, & Savolainen, 2007) is based on two levels of ontologies: an upper-level QoS ontology introducing such domains as entity, people, process, property and means and lower-level ontologies for these domains (with an example of QoS property lower-level ontology actually conceptualizing the quality model). Another ontology representing QoS requirements (subdivided into

requirement, measurement, traceability, and quality management system ontologies) is presented in H. M. Kim, Sengupta, and Evermann (2007).

PREDESIGN CONCEPTS

The proposed technique merges two mutually supplementing approaches: an approach to model functional requirements for services and business processes and an approach to model quality requirements: In this section, we outline the common properties of these approaches; approach-specific concepts will be covered in the subsequent sections.

Predesign Process

We propose a five step *predesign process* for requirements elicitation and modeling. Note that the first two steps are drawn from requirements engineering and only the remaining steps are predesign specific. Therefore we will not step into much detail of the first two steps but concentrate on the remaining ones (3 to 5) instead. Note that not all approaches to perform Step 3 depend on performing the previous steps. The predesign process steps are supposed to be iterated, as long as no more need for change is felt:

Step 1: Identify the relevant actors, tasks and quality concerns. Before any elicitation of requirements can start the right *tasks* and *actors* have to be decided upon. The identification of actors is an iterative task itself since the requirements engineer typically has to start with persons nominated by management and then to find out other relevant people, i.e., stakeholders who might provide relevant information about important tasks or for a task at hand: e.g., persons who are interested that the project will become a success, opinion leaders for the project, or persons affected by the execution of the task. During each interview, the meta question should be asked: "whom else can I interview to certain aspects of what you have told me?" thus establishing iteration. Among others this is a simple rule of thumb to get in contact with candidates for actors.

Examples of actors are humans and organizational units. Actors and tasks will later be related to each other by the association "is responsible for". We provide special tables, in particular "organizational unit/task" and "task/information provider" to help in organizing this step.

Step 2: Establish a requirements elicitation plan. For questioning actors, a kind of schedule and guideline should be worked out. This, in our opinion, will be quite project specific, nevertheless, it is good practice to start at the management level going to the operative level next. Managers can draw an overview of the planned system's aims and concerned people although will not utter many operative details (functionality of the system). Besides, early decision maker participation makes them feeling responsible which may substantially strengthen the requirements engineer's position.

Furthermore it has to be decided on requirements priorities from indispensable to "nice to have". This will help to avoid getting lost in detail discussions about unnecessary features.

Step 3: Collect detailed requirements according to the elicitation plan. The conventional technique is to elicit requirements via interviews or brainstorm sessions. This way, free-form or structured answers to interview questions will be obtained as raw input data for predesign. In addition to that even entire free-text specifications may be used and transformed (semi)- automatically into glossary entries using natural language processing techniques (see, e.g., (Fliedl, Kop, Mayerthaler, Mayr, & Winkler, 2002)). All entries will be indexed by task, stakeholder, organizational unit, date, etc., and, if necessary, manually revised (finding implicit information, eliminating redundancies, etc.).

Collecting requirements based on specification texts is convenient only if these texts can be obtained easily. Concerning quality requirements we have to encounter that the known

problem stakeholders usually have with uttering requirements without experiencing the system even grows. Without such experience they are forced to be speculative and, as a result, formulate requirements that need to be further refined and corrected. To solve this problem (Kaschek, Kop, Shekhovtsov & Mayr, 2008) proposed a tool-supported approach providing stakeholders with a means for experiencing software qualities in a simulated working environment as early as possible, and assessing these simulated qualities using some defined scale. This approach will also provide requirements engineers with a means for eliciting quality requirements out of such assessments.

Step 4: Organize the elicited requirements. We propose a specific **predesign model** to organize the elicited requirements. It consists of a set of **predesign glossaries** representing a small set of modeling concepts that are intuitively understandable and verifiable by stakeholders; this is enhanced by the tabular glossary representation which is well-known to our intended audience, i.e., business people. After verification, the requirements glossaries have to be mapped onto a design-time representation (predesign mapping step) which will be discussed in detail in this chapter.

Step 5: Transformation to conceptual schema or update of actors, tasks, requirements, and requirements elicitation plan. According to whatever respective need is found during steps 1 to 4 the requirements collected in the predesign model are, if necessary, validated, updated and refined, and finally transformed to a conceptual schema. Note, that this process might be iterative in case of more sophisticated information systems.

A graphical summary of the process can be seen in Figure 1.

Predesign Metamodeling Hierarchy

The predesign process runs along a model hierarchy consisting of three layers: object-model (M1),

Figure 1. The predesign process

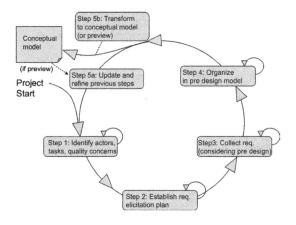

meta-model (M2) and NF² or meta-metamodel (M3).

The object model layer allows defining particular models that describe the requirements for the case at hand. These predesign models consist of a small set of concepts, can be verified by stakeholders and later mapped into design. The predesign concepts represent things in a real world or their attributes or operations etc. Higher in the metamodel hierarchy, the predesign model is defined via a predesign metamodel which is an object-oriented depiction of predesign concepts (a concept corresponds to a metaclass). On top, the predesign meta-metamodel layer describes the way of representing the metamodeling structures. We propose to use the Non-First-Normal Form (NF²) relational notion for this layer.

We define a predesign glossary as a NF²-table view over our metamodel populated with data. This approach is valid due to the following observations (along the lines of Codd, 1979):

1. Within the relational context, any object identity can be modeled by a tuple identifier.
2. Object methods can be modeled by tables that on request will be joined with the table holding the object's basic data.
3. Each of the metamodel diagrams can have a relational representation.

Different predesign glossaries will be defined in detail subsequently.

Example Requirements Specification

Our further description of predesign techniques will be based on a simple example of both service and business process requirements specifications which include functional and quality requirements. For brevity, implementation constraints are not included, and the number of requirements is kept rather small. We list the requirements for a set of order processing services: (Figure 2).

1) Order processing services should allow the order department to perform:
   (S1) order acceptability check;
   (S2) relating the items to the order;
   (S3) order confirmation;
   (S4) order rejection; and
   (S5) order postponing.
2) Order processing services should allow the stock clerk to perform:
   (S6) stock item top-up;
3) Authorization services should allow the bookkeeping department to perform:
   (S7) payment authorization;
4) Authorization services should allow the order processing services to perform:
   (S8) user authorization check.
5) The order processing services must have the following qualities:
   (S9) The response time to user actions related to orders and order items is below 0.5 sec.
   (S10) The response time to any payment authorization is below 0.3 sec.
   (S11) The response time to any stock items top-up for dialup connection requests is below 2 sec for a load up to 500 users and below 5 sec for a higher load; it is below 0.5 sec for all other requests.

Figure 2. Requirements displayed on predesign object model, metamodel and NF² meta-metamodel level

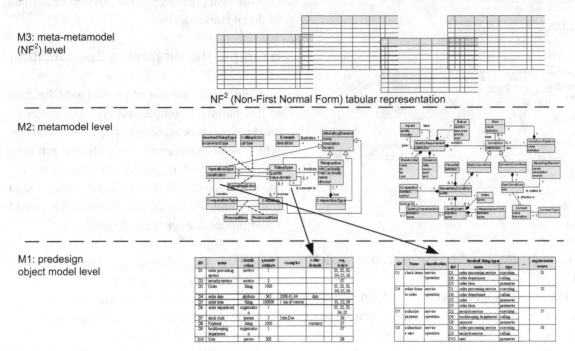

(S12) Any operation performed by the order department has highest possible availability.

(S13) Stock item top-up has second highest availability.

(S14) Only authorized users can use the order processing service.

6) The business process for order processing is defined as follows (Fowler, 2005):

(S15) The order comes in.

(S16) The order department for each ordered item checks its availability on stock.

(S17) If each ordered item is on stock, then the order department relates that item to the order.

(S18) If the item quantity on stock is below the threshold, then the stock clerk orders this item for the stock.

(S19) If the order comes in, the bookkeeping department checks the payment.

(S20) If the payment is authorized and all ordered items are on stock, then the order department confirms the order.

(S21) If payment is authorized and some items are not on stock, then the order department marks the order as pending.

(S22) If the payment is not authorized, then the order department must reject the order.

7) The business process for order processing must have the following qualities:

(S23) The availability of all the operations performed if order comes in must exceed 99%.

(S24) The activities performed if the order is rejected must have the response time below 0.3 sec.

In the next two sections, we will describe how the proposed predesign technique allows for modeling functional and quality requirements. These two parts of the predesign process must be performed together to form the common predesign model using the appropriate metamodel. We will describe the metamodels for these two kinds of

Figure 3. Part of the predesign metamodel describing the model for functional requirements

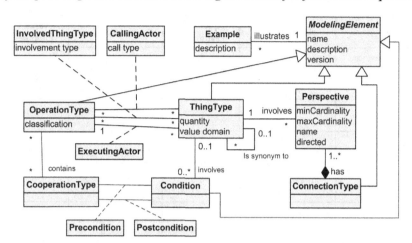

requirements separately but actually they are both parts of the same predesign metamodel.

RELATIONAL PREDESIGN OF FUNCTIONALITY

The predesign technique for functionality presented in this paper is based on a technique described in (Kop & Mayr, 2002; Mayr & Kop, 1998). The corresponding part of the predesign metamodel is shown on Figure 3.

The most general concept of functionality predesign is *ModelingElement*. It permits referring to any phenomena and, among others, is specialized into thing-type and connection-type. The concept *ThingType* generalizes conceptual notions such as class, entity, attribute, or value. The instances of the concept *ConnectionType* are relationships between instances of thing-types. Any such relationship is considered as a set of *Perspectives*. Each perspective of a relationship models the contribution instances of the resp. involved thing-type have in that relationship. Typical instances of thing-types are natural or juristic persons, material or immaterial objects, abstract notions. In textual requirements specifications they are usually referred to by noun phrases.

Predesign models include a *statics* and a *dynamics* submodel, having operation invariant and dependent information, respectively. Thing-types and connection-types constitute the statics predesign submodel. The dynamics submodel consists of *OperationTypes* (defining the permitted operations) and *CooperationTypes* including pre and post-conditions for operation execution (Kop & Mayr, 2002; Mayr et al., 2007).

The metamodel includes (among others) the "is synonym to" link permitting the use of synonyms. Examples can be specified for all predesign concepts; this is represented via "illustrate" link. Concept versioning is supported with a "version" attribute of ModelingElement.

Glossary-Based Modeling Using Thing-Types and Connection-Types

First two kinds of predesign glossaries are thing-type and connection-type glossaries. They are NF^2 representations of the metamodels for the corresponding predesign notions.

We need to introduce thing-types and connection-types present in our domain, as we will use these types throughout the example model. The corresponding glossaries are shown on Table 1.

Table 1a. Thing-type and connection-type

id#	name	classification	quantity estimate	examples	value domain	req. source
D1	order pocessing service	service	1			S1, S,S3, S4, S5, S6
D2	security service	service	2			S7
D3	Ordr	thing	1000			S1, S, S3, S4, S5, S6
D4	order date	attribute	365	2008-01-04	date	
D5	order iem	thing	100000	1 ton o cement		S1, S2, S6
D6	order department	organization	1			S1, S2, S3, S4, S5
D7	stock clerk	person	5	John Do		S6
D8	Payment	thing	1000		currec	S7
D9	bookkeeping department	organization	1			S7
D10	User	person	200			S8

Using Operation-Types to Model Service Functional Requirements

Following (Mayr et al., 2007) we model software services using the concept of operation-type. The corresponding metamodel is shown in Table 2. Every operation-type is related to its executing actor, originating actor(s), and resources such as operation subject and auxiliary or associated materials (operation parameters). These are referred to as involved thing-types.

The requested operation-types are to be collected into an *operation-type glossary* (see Table 2).

Using Cooperation-Types to Model Business Process Functional Requirements

The business process functionality is the set of permitted service flows as specified via the business process definition.

Following (Mayr et al., 2007) our organization modeling concepts are: *Organization*, the whole entity such as a tax office or municipal administration; *Department* and/or *Project Group*, i.e., functioning subunits of an organization; *Position*, atomic organization subunits which are occupied by a set of actors; *Citizen, Customer, Supplier* – organization external actors interacting with

Table 1b. Thing-type glossary examples

c-id#	name	...	Perspective				requirements source
			p-id#	involved thing-type	name		
C001	containent		p001a	D3, order	contains		S1, S2, S6
			p001b	D5, order item	is contained in		
C002	attribute possessing		p002a	D3, Order	has an attribute		
			p002b	D4, order date	is an attribute of		

Table 2. Example operation-type glossary

id#	Name	classification	involved thing-types			requirements source
			id#	name	type	
O1	check iems	service operation	D1	order processing service	executing	S1
			D6	order department	calling	
			D5	order item	parameter	
O4	relate items to order	service operation	D1	order processing service	executing	S2
			D6	order department	calling	
			D3	order	parametr	
			D5	order item	parameter	
O7	authorize payment	service operation	D2	security service	executing	S7
			D9	bookkeeping department	calling	
			D8	payment	parameter	
O8	authenticate user	service operation	D1	order processing service	executing	S8
			D2	security service	calling	
			D10	user	parametr	

it; *Resource* and *Document*, used during task execution. They are materialized as thing-type instances. Any such instance providing or using a service occupies the role of actor executing or initiating that service, respectively. In addition, we use the concepts of *Task* and *Service Flow*, i.e., elementary and composite activity in favor of the organization's goals. Any service flow of an organization is described as network of tasks each of which is executed by a position. Any task may have inputs and outputs.

To generalize service flow modeling notions, (Kop & Mayr, 2002; Mayr et al., 2007) introduce the concept cooperation-type. A *cooperation-type* C is a triple (–C, C(O), C+) of pre- and post-condition sets –C and C+, respectively, and the set C(O) of operation-types contained in C. For two cooperation-types C and D the *concurrent composition* of operation-types C(O) and D(O) is defined for –C = –D and C+ = D+. The *sequential composition* C(O) before D(O) is defined for C+ = –D.

Tasks and positions are modeled as operation-type and task executing actor, respectively. To any task set there is thus associated a set of pre- and post

conditions, respectively. Task inputs and outputs are modeled as thing-types related to operation-types as parameters. Any business process phases are modeled as cooperation-types. An excerpt from a cooperation-type glossary is shown on Table 3. Among other tabular requirements modeling approaches, the closest counterpart of this glossary is a mode transition table used in SCR method (Heitmeyer, 2007).

RELATIONAL PREDESIGN OF QUALITY

A part of the common meta-model describing the predesign model for service and business processes quality requirements is shown on Figure 4. For obtaining it we have used the papers (Aburub et al., 2007), (Kassab, Ormandijeva, & Daneva, 2008), and (Jingbai, Keqing, Chong, & Wei, 2008).

A quality requirement is essentially an utterance declaring that something should be in a particular and specified way. The metamodel depicts this via the metaclass *QualityRequirement*. Quality requirements may impact each other. Each

Table 3. Example cooperation-type glossary

id#	Pre-condition			Operation			Post-condition			req. source
	id#	name	involved types	id#	name	involved types	id#	name	involved types	
E1	C1	order comes in	D3, Order	O7	check payment	D2, security service D9, bookkeeping department D8, Payment	C2	payment is authorized	D8, Payment	S15, S19
							alternate			
							C3	payment is not authorized	D8, Payment	
				in parallel						
				O1	check all items	D1, order processing service D6, order department D5, Order	C4	all articles are in stock	D3, Order	S15, S16
							alternate			
							C5	not all articles are in stock	D3, Order	
E2	C3	payment is not authorized	D8, Payment	O5	reject order	D1, order processing service D9, bookkeeping department D3, Order	C6	order is rejected	D3, Order	S22

Figure 4. Part of the predesign metamodel describing the model for quality requirements

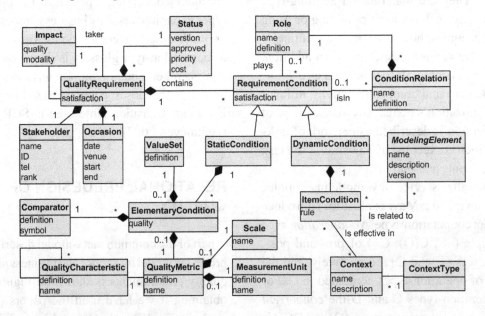

such impact has a number of givers and takers. The attributes of an impact are quality and modality. Quality means supporting or hindering to achieve the satisfaction of the quality requirement. Modality means the extent to which achieving of

that requirement's satisfaction can be supported or hindered. A quality requirement's satisfaction can be scored as a value in {0,1}, [0,1], or different. For simplicity we avoid including into that metamodel a facility for specifying the escalation of requirements satisfaction from sub-requirements to super requirement and vice versa. Quality requirement is a composite of *Stakeholder* (representing the person responsible for verifying the requirement), *Occasion* (representing the information related to the specific case of eliciting the requirement), the requirement *Status* (its meta-attributes include version, priority reflecting its importance, cost of non-meeting the requirement reflecting its urgency etc), and *Requirement-Condition*, i.e., the one which is actually requested by the requirement.

We propose to employ two kinds of condition: static and dynamic ones. Furthermore, conditions can be in *Relations* to other conditions. A condition relation is defined as the composite of a number of *Roles*. If a condition is in a relation to another condition that it can play (in that relation) only play roles that are defined for that relation.

Dynamic Conditions: Connecting Quality and Functionality

At the instance level, dynamic conditions include a number of *functional item* conditions connecting this requirements with artifacts defined in the functionality-related part of the predesign model. We consider three kinds of functional items: *activity* (represented via operation-type), *event* (represented via cooperation-type), and *actor* (represented via thing-type). These three kinds of conditions allow us to represent the set of requirements for both services and business processes.

To describe this relationship, we show a connection between a *DynamicCondition* and a *ModelingElement*. This connection reflects the *scope* of a quality requirement, i.e., the set of functional model elements it affects. It is easy to conclude that in our model, the scope of a quality requirement is a set of functional items (actors, operations, and events). This set is formed based on the set of the item conditions (depicted via the *ItemCondition* metaclass) belonging to this requirement.

Calling Contexts

Services can be called in different contexts and that *calling context* may impact the required or possible quality (Wada, Suzuki, & Oba, 2006). To reflect this fact, for each functional item condition a *Context* can be specified and a rule that applies to an item instance of that kind if the context is the specified one. For example, consider an event such as "the order arrives" then this way we can specify that another event must take place and can even specify alternative responses by distinguishing different contexts. Context belongs to a specific *ContextType* (such as "connection" or "load"), for example "dialup" and "broadband" contexts belongs to a context type "network connection". We can also have a *default* or *void context* for the cases when the specification indicates that the rule always applies to that item instance.

Among the rules, we distinguish *conditional* (if-then-else) rules, and *negative rules* (permitting to specify that events must not occur under certain circumstances). Actors have a portfolio of operations they are entitled to perform under specified circumstances. *item condition* allows to change that portfolio for specified contexts.

Static Conditions: Integrating the Quality Model

A static condition is assumed to be a composite of elementary conditions each of which has specified parts and each of which has a quality, i.e., can be required to take place or be prohibited. The specified parts of such condition include a *QualityMetric* (described below), a *Comparator* and the *ValueSet* that describes a threshold for the given requirement. For example, requirement S11 above employs the comparator *below* and the threshold value *2 sec*.

Table 4. Excerpt from quality model predesign glossary representing WSQM

Quality model				WSQM (E. Kim & Lee, 2005) adaptation for the order processing domain					
Quality category		Quality characteristic		Quality metric					
id#	name	id#	name	id#	name	definition	unit	order	scale
Q1	Business value								
Q2	Service measure-ment	Q3	Performance	Q4	Response time	time taken to send a request and receive the response	sec	mini-mize	absolute
				Q5	Maximum throughput	max number of services to be processed for a unit time		maxi-mize	…
		Q6	Stability	Q7	Availability	the ratio of time period in which a service is ready		maxi-mize	ratio
				Q8	Accessibility	the ratio of acknowledge-ments to the requests		maxi-mize	ratio

Glossary Representation of the Quality Model and Software Metrics

Our metamodel allows for a flexible representation of the composite elements related to quality measurement. Every elementary condition can refer to a quality metric which is used by this condition. The treatment of this metric can vary; in our metamodel, we show a simplified representation. However, a more complicated fragment of the metamodel (such as the metamodel corresponding to the measurement ontology described in (Bertoa, Vallecillo, & Garc¡a, 2006)) can be integrated instead. A corresponding glossary fragment is shown on Table 4, which uses table nesting to represent relationships between quality characteristics and metrics.

Glossary Representation of Quality Requirements

Scope expressions and operation-type specifications are specified in a requirement scope glossary shown in Table 5. This glossary corresponds to

Table 5. Defining requirement scope expressions in a requirement scope glossary

id#	name	classification	scope		…	req. source
QS1	all operations involving orders or order items	expression	D3, Order	parameter		S9
			OR			
			D5, Order item	parameter		
QS2	authorize operation	enumeration	O7, authorize			S10
QS3	order items operation	enumeration	O3, order items			S11
QS4	all operations called by order department	expression	D6, Order department	calling		S12
QS5	all order processing service operations	Expression	D1, Order processing service	executing		S14
QS6	all operations performed if the order comes in	Condition	C1, order comes in			S23
QS7	all operations performed if the order is rejected	Condition	C6, order is rejected			S24

Table 6. Service and business process quality requirements in a quality requirements glossary

| id# | quality characteristic | Scope | Context information | | ... | threshold | description | req. source |
			context type	context				
C1	Q4, Response time	QS1, all operations involving orders or order items				0,5		S9
C2	Q4	QS2				0,3		S10
C3	Q4	QS3, order items operation	T1, connection	dialup		2		S11
			T2, load	<500 users				
			T1, connection	dialup		5		S11
			T2, load	>500 users				
			T1, connection	non-dialup		0,5		S11
C4	Q7, Availability	QS4, all operations called by order department					highest possible	S12
C5	Q7	QS3					second highest	S13
C6	Q9, Authentication	QS5, all order processing service operations						S14
C7	Q7	QS6				99		S23
C8	Q4	QS7				0,3		S24

the target for the metaassociation between *Item-Condition* and *ModelingElement* metaclasses in a metamodel (Figure 4). To represent the requirement scope, the glossary contains what we call *scope expressions*. The parameters of an *elementary scope expression* P(T,I) are an involved thing-type *T* and involvement type *I* for the operation-types in question. For example, for requirement S14 above (which refers to all operations of OPS the order processing service) a scope expression will accept *T = "Order processing service"* and *I = "provides for execution"* so the resulting requirement scope will contain all the operation-types provided for execution by the OPS. Elementary scope expressions can be chained together using logical operators to form *complex scope expression*.

Table 6 shows a fragment of a quality requirements glossary related to our example. C4 and C5 are imprecise constraints, C3 is a context dependency. C1, C2, and C6 represent refined requirements. It corresponds to both dynamic conditions and calling contexts in a metamodel.

Our metamodel allows us to easily extend the quality modeling notation to business process quality requirements. It is easy to see that the dynamic condition for the quality requirements (represented by its scope in glossaries) can refer, among others, to cooperation-types as a whole, as well as to their pre- and post-conditions. As a result, it becomes possible to capture the semantics of quality requirements applied to any point in a workflow: both cooperation-types and operation-types in general.

Quality requirements may influence each other (a fact reflected by the *Impact* metaclass on Figure 4). That association can be specified in a related glossary (*requirement impact glossary*). For brevity, we omit this glossary here.

PREDESIGN ADVANTAGES AND USAGE EXAMPLES

Reasons for choosing the predesign approach to model service requirements are the following:

1. The approach applies a simple semantic model, and a representation that is well-known to the intended audience: business stakeholders. A glossary (tabular representation) may be used like a check list (Galle et al., 2008) which is particularly useful during requirements elicitation. Tabular representations complement elicitation whenever a graphical model is not adequate or would lead - if used - to numerous topological revisions (i.e. elicitation phase).

2. The approach is user-centered, participative, and restricts itself to a small set of modeling concepts.

3. The relational model (minus queries) encoded form of requirements predesign provides a definition of key concepts which allows to interpret these concepts as well in terms of the application domain as well as software items. This justifies an easy way of creating a first system prototype by simulating the application domain concepts as functionality chunks.

4. The definitions above show that application domain experts do not have to treat their domain in terms of formal or even implementation concepts. This is important because most of them are not educated for this and thus would be overstrained. Moreover, they would be ruled out from validation in case of un-familiar formalisms.

5. The approach is integrated into a rich set of requirements analysis techniques utilizing natural language processing (Fliedl et al., 2002) and interactive simulation of the system under development (Kaschek et al., 2008)

6. A rich set of mapping techniques allows the predesign model to be mapped into other semantic models (design-time) such as UML or Semantic Web Services languages.

7. Using the NF^2 meta-metamodel allows for performing complex relational queries over

Table 7a. Tradeoff-supporting query

thing-type	involvement	constraint
		id#
D1, order processing service	executing	C1
		C3
		...
		C6

the predesign model. We will discuss this below.

Relational and Dimensional Queries over Glossaries

We will look in more detail at one particular advantage of our relational predesign: *that all quality information is contained in glossaries, i.e., models of similar structure*. We think that generic queries can be worked out and issued against glossary sets that calculate the impact of any quality requirement on required functionality or quality characteristics. That would make it possible to estimate the effect of any requirements changes on selected quality characteristics or functionality.

Assume, for example, that we want to consider the effect of any requirements changes to OPS the "order processing service". Then we need to know all the requirements that have OPS in their scope (see Table 7a). It is not difficult to design a query that would do the job. Something like "SELECT id# FROM RSG WHERE OPS IN scope" will essentially do if RSG is the requirements scope glossary in Table 4.

Relational predesign could simplify to make tradeoffs between different quality characteristics. Suppose that we want, with the given resources, at a time to ensure minimal response time and maximal availability. By issuing a query for each constraint against CIG the constraint impact glossary (not included in this paper) we can identify those operation-types that impact the constraint positively (towards the optimum) or negatively

Table 7b. Maintenance-supporting query

Context information		operation-type	
context type	context	id#	name
T1, connection	dialup	O3	order items
		...	

(away from the optimum). This allows us (by investigating the scopes of impacting requirements) at least to identify those operations the implementation of which aids at the same time meeting both requirements. We also can identify those operations that are counter-productive with respect to achieving the two requirements.

Relational predesign also can play a role in system maintenance as changed requirements could be related to those parts of programs that need to be changed. For example assume that we plan a system upgrade from using dialup lines to more recent communication media. We might then have to find the functionality affected by the requirements related to "dialup". The query corresponding to this request has to find the set of requirements referring to the "dialup" context and then identify the operation-types belonging to the scopes of these requirements. Resulting glossary can be seen on Table 7b. It is also possible to explore the query further using functionality-related part of the predesign model, e.g. finding all services providing these operations for execution or all the thing-types calling these services.

Interesting query possibilities can be also opened by exploring the obvious similarity between the metamodel for quality requirements (Table 4) and data schemas commonly used in dimensional data modeling (Kimball & Ross, 2002) such as a star or snowflake schema. Using the terminology of dimensional modeling, we can state that the requirements glossary can be seen in a way similar to a *fact table* while quality model glossary and, to less degree, scope and context (thing-type) glossaries can be treated similarly to *dimension tables* (quality, functionality and context dimensions, respectively). Exploiting this similarity further, we can state that many query and presentation techniques originated in dimensional modeling and OLAP communities can be exploited this way. For example, if we take a look at the Quality dimension we can see that its hierarchical organization allows implementing the "drill down" operation: for advancing from high-level quality characteristic down to lower-level ones narrowing the sets of requirements received along the way – up to pointing to the set of characteristics affected to the particular low-level metric (Figure 5). Aggregate functions like *count* of relevant requirements, their *average* impact, or the *smallest* established threshold can be calculated as well instead of receiving the lists of requirements. As an example, consider an analyst who would like to see the largest throughput required for all operations in a system in order to make sure that the set of requirements is compliant to the current hardware capabilities. To do this, it is possible to drill from "Service Measure-

Figure 5. Example of drilling down the quality dimension

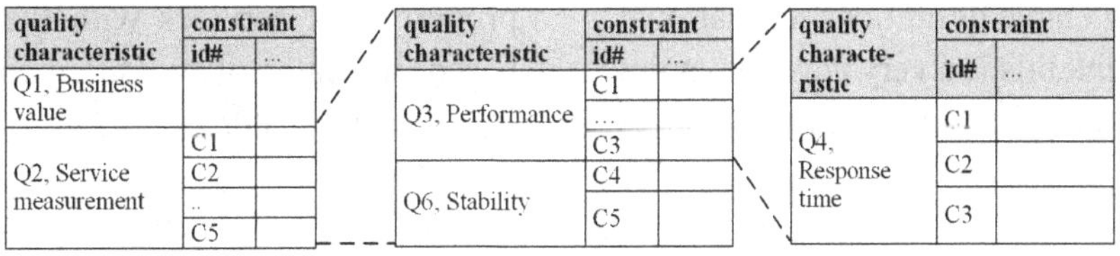

Table 8. Requirements grouped by quality scope, quality characteristic and context

quality scope	constraint			quality characteristic	constraint			context information		constraint	
	id#	...			id#	...		context type	context	id#	...
QS1	C1				C1			T1, connection	dialup	C3	
QS2	C2			Q4, Response time	C2				non-dialup	C3	
QS3	C3				C3			T2, load	<500 users	C3	
	C5				C4					...	
QS4	C4			Q7, Availability	C5			default		C5	
QS5	C6			Q9, Authentication	C6					C6	

ment" high-level characteristic down to the "maximum throughput" metric and to obtain the value of the aggregate function "MAX(threshold)".

Another dimension of drilling down can be the functionality. Here one can proceed from the coarser-grained functional artifacts (such as thing-types representing services) down to fine-grainer ones (such as particular service operations).

The "slice and dice" operation can be performed as well. In this operation, the information can be presented from several points of view on the user's request. For example, the quality requirements in a glossary can be grouped by affected functionality (starting from quality scope), quality characteristic and context (Table 8).

Similarities between Business Processes and Data-Centric Information Systems

Our approach allows us to highlight and try to exploit the analogon between our notion of business process (as PAIS backed by BP engine enacting NF^2 definitions of business processes) and data centric information systems that are facilitated by DBMS "enacting" table definitions in relational databases. We think this is a very new viewpoint that helps better understand BP quality.

RELATED WORK

Modeling Service Quality Requirements

Song (2007) discusses three challenges related to developing quality requirements for service-oriented applications: flexibility of service deployment, sharing services among stakeholders, and a more complex cost structure. (Wada et al., 2006) provides UML stereotypes for conceptualizing service, message exchange, message, connector and filter for modeling non-functional service attributes in a service-oriented application. The key elements of that approach, as listed above, correspond to the low-level (technical) aspects of service implementation, which are not well suited for end-user verification. That model was enhanced in (Wada, Suzuki, & Oba, 2007) with a feature modeling technique from (Czarnecki & Eisenecker, 2000) to represent the requirements. That technique allows a detailed treatment of interdependencies among quality characteristics that are treated as features of the service under development. Another metamodel for non-functional properties of services with their classification based on scales of measurement was proposed in (Hündling, 2005).

(Jingbai et al., 2008) provides an approach to modeling quality service requirements. A domain process model (DPM) is introduced that includes dynamic system behavior aspects with notions similar to operation-types and cooperation-types. Integration of quality-related information into DPM is explained. That paper deals with the non-functional context of the service invocation on the metamodel level. That has actually influenced our solution. The differences between our approaches are, however, quite significant. In particular, we have worked out the business process model much further. Also their approach does not include inter-dependencies between quality requirements and tasks. The invocation context, though similar in meaning, is simpler in structure and allows only textual representation.

Modeling Business Process Quality Requirements

Quality requirements to business processes are similar in organization to the traditional quality requirements. Among the modeling efforts (Pavlovsky & Zou, 2008) introduced the notion and graphical representation of so called quality constraint condition which can be applied to different steps of the process. Several papers use aspect-oriented techniques for expressing quality requirements and quality attributes of business processes. In (Wada et al., 2006) and (Wada et al., 2007) a method is specified for modeling non-functional business processes characteristics. (Wada, Suzuki, & Oba, 2008) uses the language of aspect-orientation for discussing crosscutting relationships. That approach, however, is not well suited for expressing relationships between quality and such process functionality that can be verified by business stakeholders. An aspect-oriented approach to introduce QoS into BPEL utilizing WS-Policy ("Web Services Policy Framework," 2006) for QoS policy description is (Charfi, Khalaf, & Mukhi, 2007).

(Aburub et al., 2007) is devoted to establishing an approach to represent quality requirements to business processes; in particular, it proposes the corresponding quality model. The problems with this paper are connected with the fact that it equates without further discussion the quality of the process they have studied with the quality of the data that process obtains. This may be in line with the requirements of the related project. We think that was not really clear from that paper. For example, it is obviously an important process quality aspect beyond the data quality how much running one process instance costs and how long it takes to do so. These quality characteristics were ignored in the paper.

Service Quality for the Semantic Web Services Framework

Predesign modeling of service requirements is closely related to the Semantic Web Services approach. (Cappiello, Pernici, & Plebani, 2005) introduce a general semantic model that features the quality dimension (actually a metamodel for some quality model) and provide an integration with service representation describing the QoS. Possible ways of representing this model using OWL are discussed too. Another approach aimed at creating a QoS ontology suitable for integration in any web services description ontology is presented in (Tondello & Siqueira, 2008), this ontology is called QoS-MO.

A comprehensive comparison of OWL-S and WSMO is done in (Lara et al., 2005). It considers, among others, the possibility to incorporate QoS-related information into the related ontologies. Some specific approaches to achieve this goal are known. In particular, an approach to enhance WSMO with QoS ontology is introduced in (Toma, Foxvog, & Jaeger, 2006; Wang, Vitvar, Kerrigan, & Toma, 2006). A techniques for enhancing OWL-S with information based on UML Profile for QoS is discussed in (Celik & Elci, 2008; Kritikos & Plexousakis, 2007; Schröpfer, Schönherr, Offermann, & Ahrens, 2007). Defining quality-related characteristics through policies on the level of BPEL-defined processes is described in Baresi, Guinea, and Plebani (2007).

The predesign approach and Semantic Web Services are, in our view, complementary and can be integrated. That requires: (1) representing service ontologies using the predesign model in a way similar to domain ontologies (Kop, Mayr, & Zavinska, 2004); (2) Integrating quality-related information into these ontologies; and (3) mapping semantic service information into a specific service description language.

CONCLUSION

In this chapter, we have proposed an extension of the predesign model initially defined in Kop and Mayr (2002), Mayr and Kop (1998), and Shekhovtsov et al. (2008). By strictly employing NF^2-tables we progressed to *Relational Predesign*. That extension is for modeling quality requirements for services and business processes. We showed that it flexibly integrates specific or standard quality models for both services and business processes, separates functional and quality-related concerns and flexibly describes the requirements semantics through relationships between these concerns.

Predesign can contribute to improved requirements quality because it is integrated, as technology exists for mapping predesign models onto UML and other conceptual languages. It is open, as new elicitation techniques can be easily integrated into the predesign. It is participative, since our targeted audience easily can comprehend and manage its models. Predesign employs only few modeling concepts and thus is easy to learn. It is sound, as technology exists for analyzing predesign models. We consider predesign as stakeholder centered, because it empowers stakeholders to drive the requirements process.

REFERENCES

Abramowicz, W., Zyskowski, D., Suryn, W., & Hofman, R. (2007). SQuaRE based Web services quality model. In [IAENG.]. *Proceedings of IMECS, 08,* 827–835.

Aburub, F., Odeh, M., & Beeson, I. (2007). Modelling non-functional requirements of business processes. *Information and Software Technology, 49*(11), 1162–1171. doi:10.1016/j.infsof.2006.12.002

Al-Masri, E., & Mahmoud, Q. H. (2008). Toward quality-driven Web service discovery. *IT Professional, 10*(3), 24–28. doi:10.1109/MITP.2008.59

Andreozzi, S., Montesi, D., & Moretti, R. (2003). Web services quality. In [IEEE Press.]. *Proceedings of CCCT, 03,* 252–257.

Baresi, L., Guinea, S., & Plebani, P. (2007). Policies and aspects for the supervision of BPEL processes. In *Proceedings of CAiSE'07,* (LNCS 4495), (pp. 340-354). Springer.

Bertoa, M., Vallecillo, A., & Garcia, F. (2006). An ontology for software measurement. In Calero, C., Ruiz, F., & Piattini, M. (Eds.), *Ontologies for software engineering and software technology* (pp. 175–196). Springer. doi:10.1007/3-540-34518-3_6

Cappiello, C., Pernici, B., & Plebani, P. (2005). Quality-agnostic or quality-aware semantic service descriptions? In *Proceedings of W3C Workshop on Semantic Web Service Framework.*

Celik, D., & Elci, A. (2008). Semantic QoS model for extended IOPE matching and composition of Web services. In [IEEE CS Press.]. *Proceedings of COMPSAC, 08,* 993–998.

Chaari, S., Badr, Y., Biennier, F., BenAmar, C., & Favrel, J. (2008). Framework for Web service selection based on non-functional properties. *International Journal of Web Services Practices, 3*(1-2), 94–109.

Charfi, A., Khalaf, R., & Mukhi, N. (2007). QoS-aware Web service compositions using non-intrusive policy attachment to BPEL. In *Proceedings of ICSOC'07,* (LNCS 4749), (pp. 582-593). Springer.

Codd, E. F. (1979). Extending the database relational model to capture more meaning. *ACM Transactions on Database Systems, 4*(4), 397–434. doi:10.1145/320107.320109

Czarnecki, K., & Eisenecker, U. (2000). *Generative programming: Methods, tools and applications.* Addison-Wesley.

Dobson, G. (2004). *Quality of Service in Service-Oriented Architectures.* Dependability Infrastructure for Grid Services Project.

Dobson, G., & Sanchez-Macian, A. (2006). Towards unified QoS/SLA ontologies. In [IEEE CS Press.]. *Proceedings of SCW, 06,* 169–174.

Dumas, M., Van der Aalst, W., & ter Hofstede, A. (2005). *Process-aware Information Systems.* Wiley-IEEE. doi:10.1002/0471741442

Evans, J., & Filsfils, C. (2007). *Deploying IP and MPLS QoS for multiservice networks: Theory and practice.* Morgan Kaufmann.

Fliedl, G., Kop, C., Mayerthaler, W., Mayr, H. C., & Winkler, C. (2002). The NIBA approach to quantity settings and conceptual predesign. In *Proceedings of NLDB'01.*

Galle, D., Kop, C., & Mayr, H. C. (2008). A uniform Web service description representation for different readers. In [IEEE CS Press.]. *Proceedings of ICDS, 08,* 123–128.

Galster, M., & Bucherer, E. (2008). A taxonomy for identifying and specifying non-functional requirements in service-oriented development. In *Proceedings of 2008 IEEE Congress on Services - Part I,* (pp. 345-352). IEEE CS Press.

Guceglioglu, A. S., & Demirors, O. (2005). Using software quality characteristics to measure business process quality. In *Proceedings of BPM'05,* (LNCS 3649), (pp. 374-379). Springer.

Heitmeyer, C. L. (2007). Formal methods for specifying, validating, and verifying requirements. *Journal of Universal Computer Science, 13*(5), 607–618.

Hündling, J. (2005). Modelling properties of services. In *Proceedings of 1st European Young Researchers Workshop on Service Oriented Computing.*

Janicki, R., Parnas, D. L., & Zucker, J. (1997). Tabular representations in relational documents. In Brink, C., Kahl, W., & Schmidt, G. (Eds.), *Relational methods in computer science.* Berlin: Springer.

Jingbai, T., Keqing, H., Chong, W., & Wei, L. (2008). A context awareness non-functional requirements metamodel based on domain ontology. In *Proceedings of IEEE International Workshop on Semantic Computing and Systems,* (pp. 1-7). IEEE CS Press.

Jureta, I.J., Herssens, C. & Faulkner, S. (2008). A comprehensive quality model for service-oriented systems. *Software Quality Journal.*

Kaschek, R., Kop, C., Shekhovtsov, V. A., & Mayr, H. C. (2008). Towards simulation-based quality requirements elicitation: A position paper. In *Proceedings of REFSQ 2008,* (LNCS 5025), (pp. 135-140). Springer.

Kassab, M., Ormandijeva, O., & Daneva, M. (2008). A traceability metamodel for change management of non-functional requirements. In *Proceedings of International Conference on Software Engineering Research, Management, and Applications,* (pp. 245-254). IEEE CS Press.

Kim, E., & Lee, Y. (2005). *Quality model for Web services 2.0.* OASIS.

Kim, H. M., Sengupta, A., & Evermann, J. (2007). MOQ: Web services ontologies for QoS and general quality evaluations. *International Journal of Metadata. Semantics and Ontologies, 2*(3), 195–200. doi:10.1504/IJMSO.2007.017612

Kimball, R., & Ross, M. (2002). *The data warehouse toolkit: The complete guide to dimensional modeling* (2nd ed.). Wiley.

Kop, C., & Mayr, H. C. (2002). Mapping functional requirements: From natural language to conceptual schemata. In. *Proceedings of SEA, 02,* 82–87.

Kop, C., Mayr, H. C., & Zavinska, T. (2004). Using KCPM for defining and integrating domain ontologies. In *Proceedings of Web Information Systems - WISE 2004 Workshops,* (LNCS 3307), (pp. 190-200). Springer.

Kritikos, K., & Plexousakis, D. (2007). OWL-Q for semantic QoS-based Web service description and discovery. In *Proceedings of SMRR'07.*

Lara, R., Polleres, A., Lausen, H., Roman, B., de Bruijn, J. & Fensel, D. (2005). *A conceptual comparison between WSMO and OWL-S.* (WSMO Deliverable 4.1).

Lee, Y., Bae, J., & Shin, S. (2005). Development of quality evaluation metrics for BPM (Business Process Management) system. In [IEEE CS Press.]. *Proceedings of ICIS, 05,* 424–429.

Lee, Y., & Yeom, G. (2007). A research for Web service quality presentation methodology for SOA framework. In [IEEE CS Press.]. *Proceedings of ALPIT, 07,* 434–439.

Liu, Y., Ngu, A. H. H., & Zeng, L. (2004). QoS computation and policing in dynamic Web service selection. In [ACM Press.]. *Proceedings of WWW, 04,* 66–73.

Mayr, H. C. (2006). Conceptual requirements modeling–a contribution to XNP (eXtreme Non Programming). In *Proceedings of APCCM'06,* (CRPIT, Vol. 53). Australian Computer Society.

Mayr, H. C., & Kop, C. (1998). Conceptual predesign-bridging the gap between requirements and conceptual design. In [IEEE CS Press.]. *Proceedings of ICRE, 98,* 90–100.

Mayr, H. C., Kop, C., & Esberger, D. (2007). Business process modeling and requirements modeling. In *Proceedings of ICDS'07,* (p. 8). IEEE CS Press.

O'Sullivan, J., Edmond, D., & ter Hofstede, A. (2002). What's in a service? Towards accurate description of non-functional service properties. *Distributed and Parallel Databases, 12,* 117–133. doi:10.1023/A:1016547000822

Pastor, O. (2006). From extreme programming to extreme non-programming: Is it the right time for model transformation technologies? In *Proceedings of DEXA'06,* (LNCS 4080), (pp. 64-72). Springer.

Pavlovsky, C. J., & Zou, J. (2008). Non-functional requirements in business process modeling. In *Proceedings of APCCM'08 - Vol 79,* (pp. 103-112). Australian Computer Society.

Ran, S. (2003). A model for Web services discovery with QoS. *ACM SIGecom Exchanges, 4*(1), 1–10. doi:10.1145/844357.844360

Schek, H., & Pistor, P. (1982). Data structures for an integrated database management and information retrieval system. In. *Proceedings of VLDB, 82,* 197–207.

Schröpfer, C., Schönherr, M., Offermann, P., & Ahrens, M. (2007). A flexible approach to service management-related service description in SOAs. In *Emerging Web Services Technology, Part II.* (pp. 47-64). Basel: Birkhäuser.

Shekhovtsov, V. A., Kop, C., & Mayr, H. C. (2008). Capturing the semantics of quality requirements into an intermediate predesign model. In *Proceedings of SIGSAND-EUROPE'2008 Symposium,* (pp. 25-37). GI.

Song, X. (2007). Developing non-functional requirements for a service-oriented software platform. In [IEEE CS Press.]. *Proceedings of COMPSAC, 07,* 495–496.

Toma, I., Foxvog, D., & Jaeger, M. C. (2006). Modeling QoS characteristics in WSMO. In *Proceedings of MW4SOC'06* (pp. 42–47). ACM Press. doi:10.1145/1169091.1169098

Tondello, G. F., & Siqueira, F. (2008). The QoS-MO ontology for semantic QoS modeling. In *Proceedings of 2008 ACM Symposium on Applied Computing,* (pp. 2336-2340). ACM Press.

Vanderfeesten, I., Cardoso, J., Mendling, J., Reijers, H. A., & van der Aalst, W. (2007). Quality metrics for business process models. In *2007 BPM and Workflow Handbook,* (pp. 179-190). Future Strategies Inc.

Wada, H., Suzuki, J., & Oba, K. (2006). Modeling non-functional aspects in Service Oriented Architecture. In *Proceedings of SCC'06,* (pp. 222-229). IEEE CS Press.

Wada, H., Suzuki, J., & Oba, K. (2007). A feature modeling support for non-functional constraints in Service Oriented Architecture. In *Proceedings of SCC'07,* (pp. 187-195). IEEE CS Press.

Wada, H., Suzuki, J., & Oba, K. (2008). Early aspects for non-functional properties in service oriented business processes. In *Proceedings of 2008 IEEE Congress on Services - Part I,* (pp. 231-238). IEEE CS Press.

Wang, X., Vitvar, T., Kerrigan, M., & Toma, I. (2006). A QoS-aware selection model for Semantic Web services. In *Proceedings of ICSOC'06,* (LNCS 4294), (pp. 390-401). Springer.

Web Services Policy Framework. (2006). *Policy outline.* Retrieved from http://www.w3.org/Submission/WS-Policy/

Zeng, L., Benatallah, B., Ngu, A. H. H., Dumas, M., Kalagnanam, J., & Chang, H. (2004). QoS-aware middleware for Web services composition. *IEEE Transactions on Software Engineering, 30*(5), 311–327. doi:10.1109/TSE.2004.11

Zhou, J., Niemelä, E., & Savolainen, P. (2007). An integrated QoS-aware service development and management framework. In *Proceedings of WICSA'07.* IEEE CS Press.

Chapter 9
Model–Driven Development of Non–Functional Properties in Web Services:
An Aspect–Oriented Approach

Guadalupe Ortiz
University of Extremadura, Spain

Juan Hernández
University of Extremadura, Spain

ABSTRACT

For the last few years, model-driven architecture, aspect-oriented software development and Web service engineering have become widely accepted alternatives for tackling the design and building of complex distributed applications; however, each of them addresses the principle of separation of concerns from their own perspective. When combined appropriately, both model-driven and aspect-oriented software development complement each other to develop high-quality Web service-based systems, maintaining non-functional properties separate from models to code. This chapter provides a methodology that integrates non-functional properties into Web service model-driven development, increasing the systems' modularity and thus reducing implementation and maintenance costs.

INTRODUCTION

Service-Oriented Architectures (SOA) provide a successful way of letting distributed applications communicate, in a platform-independent and loosely coupled manner, providing systems with great flexibility and easier maintenance. Web services have become one of the best known implementations of SOA, in which academy and industry try to maintain each specific development aspect independent through the use of encapsula-

DOI: 10.4018/978-1-60566-794-2.ch009

tion and different WS-* standard specifications. Focusing on the main advantages of Web services, we can mention, first of all, at a very high level, that developing applications with Web services results in implemented applications with a very loosely coupled environment; loosely coupled applications are normally easier to scale, manage and extend and less susceptible to errors when modifications are required. At a low level, we can highlight two significant advantages: their interoperability and the use of Internet standard protocols for transport. Interoperability is acquired thanks to the use of XML for message creation and service description, being common to all platforms and service developers. The use of Internet standard protocols, such as HTTP, will permit easier communication through the net, avoiding problems with firewalls and letting us take advantages of its wide infrastructure. Thus, Web services provide a unique technology for the integration of business in and outside firewalls, which allows companies to integrate internal applications, to publish active applications for other companies and to use third-party applications.

On the other hand, the software engineering community is currently moving on to application development based on models rather than technologies. Model-driven development allows us to focus on essential aspects of the system, delaying the decision of which technology to use in the implementation for a later step. Models may be used in multiple phases of development, from the initial system specification to its testing. Each model will address one concern, independently of the remaining issues involved in the system's development, thus allowing the separation of the final implementation technology from the business logic achieved by the system. Transformations between models enable the automated development of the system from the models themselves; therefore, model definition and transformation become key parts of the process.

Although Web service implementation is properly achieved by development middlewares,

non-functional properties have not been given due consideration in the named implementations in such a way that a loosely coupled environment, characteristic from the SOA scope, is maintained. In these systems the functionality which does not perform main but added value system objectives –which is called in this chapter non-functional properties- is scattered and tangled all over the main functionality code. Consequently, there is a lack of tools for earlier stages of Web service development in which non-functional properties and WS-* standards integration are considered. This problem was already solved by other disciplines at code level through the use of aspect-oriented techniques, which allow us to encapsulate and modularize transversal concerns in the systems, thus improving the decoupleness of software systems and reducing maintenance costs. In regard with their models, it is desirable to have a graphical notation which facilitates the developer tasks, especially when integrating the property models into the already existent system models. Thus, when trying to solve the non-functional gap both at code and model levels, we arrive at the use of model-driven development in conjunction with aspect-oriented techniques and assert that the aforementioned methodologies may complement each other to develop high quality software systems. Model-Driven Architecture (MDA) and Aspect-Oriented Software Development (AOSD) provide good support for software evolution through an appropriate separation of concerns; AOSD has focused on modeling cross-cutting concerns whereas MDA concentrates on the explicit separation of platform-independent from platform-specific concerns and model-driven generation processes.

This chapter describes a methodology that integrates non-functional properties into Web service model-driven development, where services and properties remain separated during all stages of development –from platform-independent models to code- and property traceability across all these phases is maintained.

For this purpose, a non-functional property profile has been developed, which allows us to identify the different properties through the use of stereotypes at a platform-independent level. In this sense, properties are defined as model elements, thus allowing them to be added to services during modeling. Then, this platform-independent model can be converted into a platform-specific one and the latter into code, automatically, through the application of a set of predefined transformation rules.

Concerning platform-specific models, we have defined and implemented suitable metamodels for non-functional properties within the service-oriented scope. In this case the scope will limit, on the one hand, the number of ways in which properties can be integrated into the developed services: given the nature of Web services, the functionality provided by properties can only be injected on service operations' execution or invocation. On the other hand, additional attributes will be required in order to provide a description of the properties, so that the essential Web service characteristic of auto-description be maintained. In this regard we propose an aspect-oriented metamodel and a policy description-based one, respectively.

Finally, we will show how an aspect-oriented implementation of the properties' functionality, automatically generated from platform-specific models, provides us with a decoupled development appropriate for such properties, which can be perfectly integrated with the services' implementation. Furthermore, an XML-based description of the properties will also be automatically obtained from these models and attached to the corresponding services.

To conclude the chapter we will evaluate the resulting approach through a series of metrics and we will prove how the aspect-oriented implementation provides good modularization and encapsulation of the system. Besides, we will analyze the benefits of the generated code on the system, which will contribute to its optimum

implementation and maintenance, thus reducing development costs and maintaining property traceability at all stages of development, whilst reducing development workload.

BACKGROUND

In the scope of SOA, we note that most proposals where non-functional properties are considered are not based on modeling standards such as UML. In fact, most of the approaches which consider non-functional properties in their models are mainly based on XML-based standard proposals (such as WS-Policy and Web Service Level Agreement (WSLA)) or on semantic expressions. Although they are useful property description proposals for other stages of development, none of these approaches can be considered as a standard graphical way to model non-functional properties as we will show in the following subsections, where one representative approach of each of these two trends, XML-based and semantics, are described.

XML for Non-Functional Requirements

Considering properties separately from the main functionality in service models (Papazoglou, 2006) is regarded as mandatory. In this sense, WS-Policy (Hirsch, 2007) provides a general purpose model and XML syntax to describe policies in Web Services. In this proposal a policy is defined as a collection of policy alternatives and each policy alternative as a collection of policy assertions. Policy assertions, which may be general or domain-specific, define service requirements and capabilities. The following lines show an example of policy which specifies two encryption methods from which only one has to be followed (extracted from Hirsch, 2007). (Box 1)

WS-Policy does not define how the policy has to be attached to the service; this may be done by using WS-PolicyAttachment (Orchard, 2007).

Box 1.

```
<wsp:Policy
 xmlns:sp="http://schemas.xmlsoap.org/ws/2005/07/securitypolicy"
 xmlns:wsp="http://schemas.xmlsoap.org/ws/2004/09/policy" >
 <wsp:ExactlyOne>
     <sp:Basic256Rsa15 />
     <sp:TripleDesRsa15 />
 </wsp:ExactlyOne>
</wsp:Policy>
```

The attachment description could be done internally to the WSDL (although WS-PolicyAttachment elements are not standard elements from the WSDL for the time being) or can be provided in a separate document. In this case, we could have an additional file indicating which policy is going to be applied to which service (or part of [this] service). The code below shows an example in which the policy in the URI provided in PolicyReference is applied to the service whose name, port type and endpoint location are referenced (extracted from Orchard, 2007). (Box 2)

Therefore, WS-Policy supplies the non-functional description, whereas a WSDL document provides the main functional description for a specific service. We can highlight three major reasons for separating non-functional property description from the main functional one in Web service development (Weerewarana, 2005):

- First of all, it is currently beneficial to separate concerns, avoiding their being mixed and providing good system modularization. As previously mentioned, the WSDL document provides service functional description; when talking about non-functional capabilities, we are referring to an additional functionality unrelated to the main one, and therefore it would be expected that the new functionality be described in an aside document. This is WS-Policy's main purpose.

- Secondly, policies should be applicable to the different service elements, such as an operation, a message and a port; therefore they are expected not to be centred on a WSDL document as the latter makes reference to a service endpoint. Thus, as long as we keep the policy description modularized and independent from the service to

Box 2.

```
<wsp:PolicyAttachment>
  <wsp:AppliesTo>
   <wsa:EndpointReference>
   <wsa:Address>http://www.example.com/acct/wsa:Address>
   </wsa:EndpointReference>
  </wsp:AppliesTo>
  <wsp:PolicyReference
   URI="http://www.example.com/policies#RmPolicy" />
 </wsp:PolicyAttachment>
```

which it is attached, it may be reused wherever necessary.

- Thirdly, whilst maintaining policies separate from the functional behavior of the service and its main description, these non-functional capabilities will be susceptible to addition at any stage of development.

However, even though WS-Policy is an excellent way of describing policies at implementation level, it is not suitable for a modeling stage, in which we would like to depict the main and non-functionality of our services graphically. The same can be said of the multiple extensions or variations of WS-Policy or about any other XML-based description of properties which may be found in the literature.

Semantic Modeling for Non-Functional Requirements

Web Service Modeling Ontology (WSMO) provides ontological specifications for the elements of semantic Web services by combining semantic Web technologies and Web services (Lausen, 2005). The Web service element of WSMO provides a metamodel for describing all the aspects of a Web service, including its non-functional properties, its functionality, and the interfaces to access it. A WSMO Web service is a computational entity which is able (by invocation) to meet the user's needs. In WSMO the interaction with a service can be accomplished by using Web services based on the WSDL document. These interactions are not restricted to WSDL services, since there are other alternatives for them.

The Web Service Modeling Framework (WSMF) (Fensel, 2002) consists of four different main elements: ontologies that provide the terminology used by other elements, goal repositories that define the problems that should be solved by Web services, Web service descriptions that define different aspects of a Web service and mediators which provide interoperability between services.

In their framework, ontologies are utilized to define the terminology to be used by other elements of WSMF specifications. A goal specification consists of two elements: pre-conditions describe what a Web service expects to receive in order to provide its functionality and post-conditions describe what a Web service returns in response to its invocation.

Since WSMO is used in this framework to define services, non-functional properties can be described by the XML syntax provided by WSMO for this purpose. They may also be modeled as pre- or post- conditions, following the goal syntax. Both alternatives are possible, but none of them follows the UML syntax.

MODELING AND IMPLEMENTING NON-FUNCTIONAL PROPERTIES IN WEB SERVICES

The Gap in Modeling

As we have mentioned before, simplicity and a loosely coupled environment are remarked by many approaches to be important characteristics models should follow. We have seen how there are several approaches which intend to include non-functional properties in Web services, mainly based on textual description, whether based on XML-based description standards or semantic-based ones. Emerging XML or semantic-based standards are appropriate for a different level of service description, but not for a platform-independent model for which it is desirable to have a graphical notation to be integrated into the general system model, even particularly positive if based on UML.

There is not a determined and fixed defined standard for modeling Web services, however there are several approaches in which UML is used in different ways to model them. Thus, we could say that the tendency is to evolve towards a standard based on software modeling standards, such as

UML. There are two main trends in UML Web service modeling, one which defends that UML Web service modeling is to be done by representing each element in the WSDL file in the UML model, specifically by creating a stereotype for these elements, and another one which claims that interface and operations are the core of Web service modeling and there is no need to include such a large number of elements in the model which could induce to confusion. We cannot infer which will be the standard for Web service modeling in the future, however we can affirm that, whichever is the preferred option interfaces and operations will be an important part of these models, since Web services, by definition, provide an interface with the offered operations. This information -offered interface and operations- is the relevant information for the approach presented in this chapter. As a conclusion, we can say that a graphical notation for non-functional properties in the sphere of Web service development is necessary and it should be easily used in conjunction with Web service model-driven development approaches.

In this chapter we provide a model-driven approach which allows us to introduce non-functional properties into Web service development without impairing the loosely coupled environment (Ortiz, 2005). In this sense, first of all, a UML profile is provided to facilitate loosely coupled non-functional property modeling at PIM level. Then, using a set of transformation rules, the platform-independent model turns into platform-specific ones. Finally, the appropriate code is obtained by applying the corresponding transformation rules to the platform-specific models. This code consists of an aspect-oriented implementation for property functionality development and a policy based one for property description.

Modeling Non-Functional Properties at Platform-Independent Level

Consequently, a way to integrate non-functional properties into Web service development is necessary from different steps of their lifecycle and this is the reason why we provide this approach, which may be used to integrate properties in a model-driven development of Web services.

Platform-Independent Metamodel For Non-Functional Properties

In order to maintain our system loosely coupled when adding non-functional properties to the model at platform-independent level, we propose the profile in Figure 1, whose elements will be explained.

Figure 1. Non-functional property profile

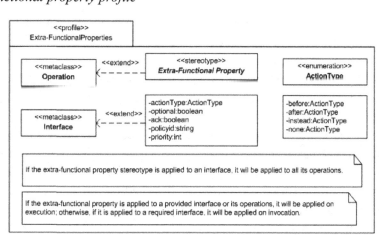

199

To start with, we define the abstract stereotype called *extra-functional property* in order to reflect that non-functional properties are parts of the system which do not constitute the main service functionality, but provide additional value to it. This stereotype will extend *operation* metaclass or *interface* metaclass, which are the elements necessary to represent the service functionality, as previously explained. This means that the stereotype may be applied to an operation – then the specified property would be applied to the stereotyped operation – or to an interface –, in which case the property will be applied to all the operations which form the stereotyped interface. The non-functional property provides five attributes, which will be defined as definition tags of the stereotype: the first one is *actionType*, which is needed to indicate whether the property functionality will be performed *before, after* or *instead* of the stereotyped operation's execution depending on the requirement of the property– or if no additional functionality is needed it will have the value none, only possible in the client side. Secondly, the attribute *optional* will allow us to indicate whether the property is performed optionally –the client may decide if it is to be applied or not– or compulsorily –it is applied whenever the operation is invoked. Then, a third attribute, *ack*, is included: when *false* it means that it is a domain-specific property and so only the skeleton code can be generated. Otherwise it will have the value *true* indicating it is a well-known property whose full functionality code can be generated. Next, we have one more attribute, *policyID*, which will contain the name to be assigned to the created policy. Finally, the attribute *priority* will let us establish which properties have to be considered first at execution time, when more than one is affecting the same operation, if necessary.

In order to define *actionType*, an enumeration is provided with four alternative values: *before, after, instead* or *none*. These different values relate to the different options available to perform the properties at implementation time, as they may include new behaviour before the stereotyped operation execution, after it or they can even replace the operation's functionality by a different one. The *none* value, as mentioned before, is only used at the client side.

It is also specified in the profile that if the property is applied in an offered interface, then it will be implemented when the stereotyped operations are executed (as the point from where it is invoked is out of scope). On the other hand, if the property is applied in a required interface, it will be performed when the operations are invoked, as the execution point is out of the service scope. In this case the service is acting as a client and this will not be explained in this paper, since we will focus on the service side.

The non-functional property stereotype will be specialized into different stereotypes related to well-known properties or to domain-specific ones in the particular systems modeled. Each property may have additional attributes, represented as tagged values, related to their specific functionality.

Platform-Independent Model for Non-Functional Properties

Once established what the platform-independent metamodel is, the developer will define the system model using a case tool. The developer designs the service component model, then extends the abstract stereotype extra-functional property with the specific non-functional properties desired for this system and finally stereotypes the operations in question with the selected properties. Afterwards the model is exported to XMI.

Therefore, the elements which may appear in the platform-independent model are those described in the previous metamodel and those which are originally part of the UML syntax; a simple generic example follows. We have said that the first step is to extend the non-functional property profile with the specific desired property. Let us say our service provides *property_x* (i.e.

Figure 2. Generic example of service and property PIM model

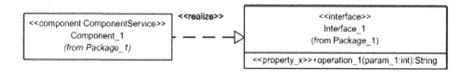

log property*)*; this would imply the extension of the abstract stereotype by a new specific stereotype –*property_x*, for which we have supposed no additional attributes are required.

Once defined *property_x*, it may be applied to any operation or interface offered by a service. In Figure 2, we see *Component_1*, stereotyped as a *ComponentService*, offering an interface, *Interface_1*, with one operation, *operation_1*, which is stereotyped with *property_x*.

Figure 3 shows the values taken by the tagged values in *property_x*, which can be seen when clicked on *operation_1*. We see that *actionType* is *instead*, which means that the functionality provided in *property_x* will replace the one provided by *operation_1*; *optional* is *true* and therefore the client may choose its application or not; *ack* is *false* and thus we cannot generate the complete property code, but only the skeleton, *policyId* is *xName*, this is the policy name and no *priority* has been assigned.

Modeling Non-Functional Properties at Platform-Specific Level

Once we have our platform-independent model with its non-functional properties included, we

Figure 3. Property_x attributes and their values

Owner Stereotype	Label	Value
<< property_x >>	actionType	instead
<< property_x >>	optional	true
<< property_x >>	ack	false
<< property_x >>	policyId	xName
<< property_x >>	priority	

need to generate the platform-specific one. Various alternatives can be chosen concerning non-functional properties: if we are going to use a platform which deals with this type of property we only have to generate the policy documents; on the contrary, if the platform does not deal with these properties or we want to tackle them ourselves, we could generate some code which performs the property behaviour plus policy documents. In this proposal, we focus on the second approach, which provides a complete final implementation of the property, independently from the properties the platform may deal with. Regarding target metamodels, we have two of them: our specific models will be based firstly on an aspect-oriented approach to specify the property behaviour and secondly on a policy-based one for property description. The details of these metamodels are provided in the following subsections.

Platform-Specific Metamodel for Non-Functional Properties

There are two fundamental aspects of properties which may be dealt with in a different manner depending on the final platform used or even according to the desired final results, which are functionality implementation and its description; this is the reason why we provide two different specific metamodels.

In regard to functionality implementation, properties imply certain non-functionality which has to be provided, be it by the host where the property is deployed, be it by the code implementation itself. Due to the fact that only a few middleware platforms currently deal with some of these types of property, we consider it appropriate to create the functionality code as part of the service itself. Currently the inclusion of the code related with the properties crosscuts the system main functionality code and therefore we find this intrusive code scattered all over the application. Thus, in order to maintain the main functionality decoupled from the property-related one and to avoid intrusive code in the main service functionality we propose an aspect-oriented approach. Consequently, this decision delimits our first metamodel to an aspect one.

Secondly, Web services are self-descriptive by definition: the Web service description language provides us with the way to describe services in such a way that the clients have entire information to invoke them. When adding non-functional properties it is essential to provide a description of them, even more so for optional properties since the client has to be aware of the property in order to decide on its inclusion or not (Ortiz, 2006). The WSDL document is not the most appropriate means to describe properties if we wish to maintain main and non-functionality decoupled,

but the WS-Policy document is. The proposed standards WS-Policy and WS-PolicyAttachment provide the way to describe service capabilities which do not belong to the main functionality. As a result, we conclude that we need a metamodel for property description to be modelled; the proposed metamodel will therefore be policy-based.

Aspect-Oriented Metamodel

As we said before, AOP establishes aspects as the way to implement crosscutting concerns. Aspects are units of encapsulation which incorporate two principal elements: *pointcuts* and *advice* (Elrad, 2001). On the one hand, through *pointcuts* we determine in which specific points of the implementation we wish to insert the new functionality; on the other, *advice* elements identify the new code to be injected, thus reflecting the desired new behaviour in the application.

The aspect metamodel is shown in Figure 4 and its corresponding code using the *Kernel MetaMetaModel* (KM3) syntax, provided by ATLAS (ATLAS was chosen as an available approach for defining metamodels and transformation rules;

Figure 4. Aspect-oriented metamodel

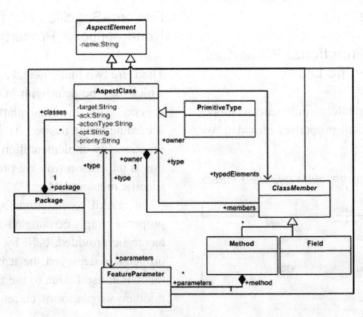

for further information see http://www.inria.fr/ rapportsactivite/RA2006/atlas/uid15.html), is shown in Box 3.

The metamodel represents pointcuts as the target attribute of *aspectClass*, the advice being the functionality of the said class. All the elements that constitute the Aspect package, which contains the necessary elements for the definition of the aspect metamodel are described in the following lines considering the elements in the figure from top to down and from left to right, that is, with the following order: *AspectElement*, *AspectClass*,

PrimitiveType, *Package*, *ClassMember*, *Method*, *Field* and *FeatureParameter*. A further description of their attributes can be found in (Ortiz, 2007).

- Abstract Class **AspectElement.** This class comprises the main base element in the aspect metamodel. In this sense, many of the elements later defined will extend this class.
- Class **AspectClass.** This class provides a way to define an aspect class, extending the *AspectElement* element.

Box 3

```
package ASPECT{
  abstract class AspectElement {
      attribute name: String;       }
  abstract class ClassMember extends AspectElement {
          reference type: AspectClass oppositeOf typedElements;
          reference owner: AspectClass oppositeOf members;       }
  class Field extends ClassMember {
      attribute value: String;       }
  class AspectClass extends AspectElement{
          reference typedElements[*]: ClassMember oppositeOf type;
          reference parameters[*]: FeatureParameter oppositeOf type;
          reference "package": Package oppositeOf classes;
          reference members[*] container: ClassMember oppositeOf owner;
          attribute target: String;
          attribute ack: String;
          attribute actionType: String;
          attribute opt: String;
          attribute priority: String;  }
  class Method extends ClassMember {
          reference parameters[*] ordered container. FeatureParameter
oppositeOf method;       }
  class Package extends AspectElement {
          reference classes[*] container: AspectClass oppositeOf "package";}
  class PrimitiveType extends AspectClass {       }
  class FeatureParameter extends AspectElement {
          reference type: AspectClass oppositeOf parameters;
          reference method: Method oppositeOf parameters;       }
}
```

- Class *PrimitiveType.* This class provides the primitive types which may be used in the models, extending the *AspectClass* element.
- Class *Package.* This class provides a way to define a package containing AspectElements and it itself extends *AspectElement.*
- Abstract Class *ClassMember.* This class provides a way to define the members of a class, this is, its fields and methods, and it also extends the class *AspectElement.*
- Class *Method.* This class provides a way to define a method, extending the *ClassMember* element.
- Class *Field.* This class extends *ClassMember* and provides a way to define the *Fields* in the classes.
- Class *FeatureParameter.* This class provides a way to define the parameters in the methods, extending the *AspectElement* element.

Policy-Based Metamodel

The policy metamodel is shown in Figure 5 and its KM3 code in Box 4.

The elements which constitute the Policy package, which contain the necessary elements for the definition of the Policy metamodel, and their attributes are described in the following lines, analysing the figure from top to bottom and from left to right (further details can be found at [Ortiz, 2007]):

- Abstract Class *PolicyElement.* This class comprises the main base element in the policy metamodel. In this sense, many of the elements later defined will extend this class.
- Class *PolicyClass.* This class provides a way to define a policy class, extending the *PolicyElement* element. It includes the signature of the *service* and *interface* affected by the property, as well as the *target* type and *name*, the *acronym* and *reference* given to the policy and if it is *optional* or not.
- Class *Package.* This class provides a way to define a package containing *PolicyElements* and it itself extends *PolicyElement.*
- Class *PrimitiveTypes.* This class provides the primitive types which may be used in the models, extending the *PolicyClass* element.

Platform-Specific Model for Non-Functional Properties

In order to convert platform-independent models into specific ones we have defined a transformation file, which establishes a correspondence between the elements in the source metamodel

Figure 5. Policy-based metamodel

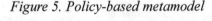
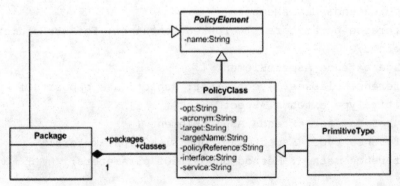

and those in the target one. In this case our source metamodel is UML –included the non-functional property profile and we have defined two sets of transformation rules –UML2Aspect and UML-2Policy–, based on the two different specific target metamodels: the Aspect one and the Policy one. Therefore, our current set of transformation rules will establish a correspondence between the UML element and the elements in the two named metamodels, generating two specific models for every independent model. An example of the transformation rules are shown in Box 5.

As shown in the previous code this rule applies to those properties whose *actionType* is other than *none* and which are applied to an operation. The first output is an *aspectClass*; its name is formed by the UML package name added to the operation name and property one. The remaining aspect attributes are obtained similarly, where helper rules may also be used. The second output –*out2*– is used for obtaining additional fields from the particular property to be included in the aspect. The third output provides the aspect with the action and its corresponding parameters. *Out4* will

provide us with the *soaptag* elements to be checked to apply the property when optional. Finally, policy information is found in *out5*.

Once we have applied the transformation rules to the UML source model, we obtain the specific models compliant to the Aspect and the Policy metamodels. In the following figures we will see a screenshot of the EMF models obtained from the previously examined example. Regardless of the EMF editor, these models could also have been edited by a general purpose text editor, although its format would be more difficult to understand.

Aspect-Oriented Model

The aspect model obtained when the transformation rules are applied to the Component_1 example is shown in Figure 6.

The elements which can be seen in the figure belong to those in the Aspect metamodel. This means that all represented packages are elements of the type *package* in the Aspect metamodel. Accordingly, *Package_1* also contains elements from the aspect metamodel: the illustration shows how an *AspectClass* element has been generated

Box 4.

```
package POLICY {
  abstract class PolicyElement {
        attribute name: String;      }
  class PolicyClass extends PolicyElement {
        reference "package": Package oppositeOf classes;
        attribute opt: String;
        attribute acronym: String;
        attribute targetType: String;
        attribute targetName: String;
        attribute policyReference: String;
        attribute interface: String;
        attribute service: String;      }
  class Package extends PolicyElement {
        reference classes[*] container: PolicyClass oppositeOf "package";}
  class PrimitiveType extends PolicyClass {      }
}
```

Box 5.

```
rule TV2AO {
from e: UML!TaggedValue (      (e.taggedValueType() = 'actionType')      and
    (e.taggedValueDataValue()<>'none')and (      e.modelElement.oclIsTypeOf(UML
!Operation))      )
to out: ASPECT!AspectClass(
name<-e.modelElement.owner.namespace.name+'_'
     +e.modelElement.name+'_'+      e.type.owner.name,
package <-e.modelElement.owner.namespace      ,
target <-'public '+e.modelElement.owner.namespace.name+ ' ' +
 e.modelElement.owner.name+'.'+ e.modelElement.name+'(..)',
actionType <- e.taggedValueDataValue(),
ack<-e.getAck()      ),
out2:distinct ASPECT!Field foreach(d in e.getFields())(
name <- d.type.name,
owner <- out,
type <- String      ),
out3: ASPECT!Action (
name <- 'action',
owner <- out,
type<-e.modelElement.parameter->select(x|x.kind=#pdk_return)->asSequence()
first().type,
parameters <- e.modelElement.getP()->
     collect (p |thisModule.P2F(p))      ),
out4:distinct SOAPTAGS!SoapTag foreach(d in e.optional='true')(
name <- d.type.name,
type <- String,
target <-'public'+e.modelElement.owner.namespace.name+' '+
 e.modelElement.owner.name +'.'+ e.modelElement.name+ '(..)',
value:<- true
side <-service,
package <-e.modelElement.owner.namespace      ),
out5: POLICIES!Policy(
name<-e.modelElement.owner.namespace.name+'_'
     +e.modelElement.name+'_'+      e.type.owner.name,
package <-e.modelElement.owner.namespace,
targetType<-'Operation',
targetName <- 'public '+ e.modelElement.owner.namespace.name      + ' '+
e.modelElement.owner.name +'.'+ e.modelElement.name+'(..)',
ack<-e.getAck(),
optional<-e.getOptional()      )      }
```

Figure 6. Component_1 example aspect models (edited by using the EMF editor)

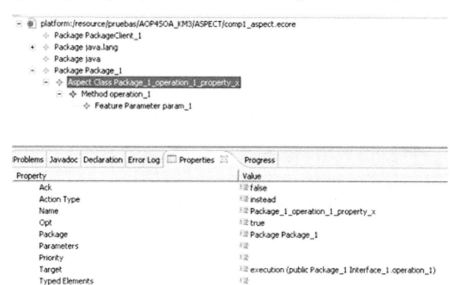

in *Package_1*. This aspect class corresponds to the *property_x* functionality, applied to *operation_1*. The aspect class attributes, described in the metamodel, are deployed in the bottom part of the figure, thus allowing us to see the name of the aspect (*name*), the element to which the property is applied (*target*), if the property is optional or not (*opt*), if it is well-known (*ack*) and its priority (*priority*), which can be added if not already present and necessary. *Package_1* also contains a Method element named *operation_1* with a *FeatureParamenter* called *param_1*. In order to see their attribute values, we would have to click on them in the editor.

Policy-Based Model

The policy model obtained when the transformation rules are applied to the *Component_1* example is shown in Figure 7.

The elements which can be seen in the illustration belong to the elements in the Policy metamodel. This means that all packages in the figure are elements of the type *Package* in the Policy metamodel. In the figure we can see how a policy class element has been generated in *Package_1*.

This policy corresponds to the *property_x* description, which refers to *operation_1*. The policy attributes, described in the named metamodel, are deployed in the bottom part of the figure, allowing us to see the name of the property (*name*), the type of element to which the property is applied (*targetType*), the name of the element to which the property is applied (*targetName*), the interface (*interface*) and the service (*service*), the acronym used in the policy description (*acronym*) and the URI where the policy is available (*policyReference*), which can be added at this point of development or even later.

Generating Code for Non-Functional Properties

Once we have our models for the case study it is time to generate code from them. For this purpose additional transformation rules will be created. From the aspect and policy specific models, where additional attribute values can be added or modified, we will generate the code motivated below:

From the aspect metamodel we will generate an AspectJ implementation; that is, an AspectJ

Figure 7. Component_1 example policy models (edited by using the EMF editor)

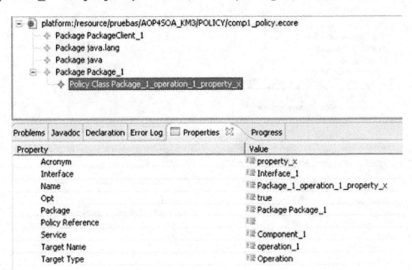

aspect will be generated for each aspect class in our model. This is because every aspect element in the model represents a property which should be applied to an operation or service interface and generating them into an AspectJ aspect allow us to maintain the code well decoupled and to keep the traceability from model to code and viceversa. AspectJ *pointcuts* will be determined by the *target* element. Concerning the *advice*, depending on the *actionType* attribute value, *before*, *after* or instead, the advice type will be *before*, *after* or *around*, respectively. Only affecting the server side, when *optional*, additional code will be generated in the advice in order to check whether or not the property was selected by the client. For *well-known* properties the functionality code will be automatically generated from a repository.

With regard to property description, it is proposed to generate a document which encapsulates the WS-Policy and WS-PolicyAttachment elements for each property. In this sense, an XML file where the policy is described and attached to the service is generated. The policy is attached to the stereotyped element in the PIM model, which is represented in the policy specific model by the attribute *targetName*, depending on the *target-*

Type we will need to specify the *port type* and the *operation* or only the first one.

An additional set of transformation rules is created in order to transform the Aspect and Policy specific models into code. Since the target to be obtained is based on strings, there is no target metamodel to be specified; the main code of the properties is generated by a set of rules. We show two representative examples of code generation rules, the first one used in order to generate an aspect class and the second to generate a policy document.

An AspecJ aspect is generated from every aspect element and a policy document containing the policy description and attachment from every policy element

AspectJ Code

Package_1_operation_1_property_x.java. The AspectJ aspect generated for *property_x* is shown below, where we can see the *pointcut Package_1_operation_1_property_x_P* referring to the execution of the operation affected by the property and the *around advice*, in which the necessary code to check whether this optional property

Box 6.

```
package Package_1;
public aspect Package_1_operation_1_property_x {
pointcut Package_1_operation_1_property_x_P(int param_1):execution(execution
(public Package_1 Interface_1.operation_1)(int) && args(param_1));
String around (int param_1):Package_1_operation_1_property_x_P(param_1){
    String result;
    try{
        if ((ServerHandler_ Package_1.Package_1_operation_1_property_x.
get("operationName").compareTo("operation_1")==0) &&
        (ServerHandler_ Package_1.Package_1_operation_1_property_x.
get("propertyName").compareTo("Package_1_operation_1_property_x")==0)) [Func-
tionality to be completed]
        else
            result=proceed(param_1);
    }catch(Exception e){System.out.println(e)}
    return result;
}}}
```

was chosen by the client is also included. If the property was not included the execution proceeds normally. (Box 6)

WS-Policy Code

Package_1_operation_1_property_x.xml. The policy generated for property_x is shown below, where we can see how it is attached to service *Component_1*, port type *Interface_1* and operation *operation_1*. The address where the service is deployed could be supplied. The policy description is also provided, where the namespaces to use are still to be included, depending on the specific policy; finally, the policy name is added and it is also indicated that it is an optional property. Additional content may be added to the property. (Box 7)

Evaluation

Concerning policy code, we are simply generating XML code to describe properties according to a proposed standard. It is known that XML is being used for providing a homogeneus and neutral description for Web services, therefore there is no question of why to use XML instead of other possible description types at code level. Besides, we chose to use WS-Policy compliant description instead of any other description proposal; however we think WS-Policy is the more mature option and is a recognized suitable candidate for a future standard. The validity of XML-based descriptions is widely proved in this area and thus there is no need for additional evaluation in this field.

Aspect-oriented programming may lead to some overhead in the applications' performance. This belief is probably originated by the first proposals of AOP; nevertheless, AOP weavers, and specifically AspectJ ones, have evolved considerably and the latter community aims for the performance of their implementation of AspectJ to be on par with the same functionality hand-coded in Java. In spite of this assertion, we are going to measure the performance of our aspect-oriented code to show how it does not suppose an over-

Box 7.

```
<wsp:PolicyAttachment >
    <wsp:AppliesTo>
        <wsp:EndpointReference>
        <wsp:ServiceName>Component_1</wsp:ServiceName>
        <wsp:PortType>Interface_1</wsp:PortType>
        <wsp:Operation>operation_1</wsp:Operation>
        <wsp:Address>...</wsp:Address>
    </wsp:EndpointReference>
    </wsp:AppliesTo>
    <wsp:Policy xmlns:wsp="..." xmlns:wsl="...">
    <wsl:Package_1_operation_1_property_x wsp:Optional=true/>
    </wsp:Policy>
</wsp:PolicyAttachment>
```

head for the system. Furthermore, we propose the use of an aspect-oriented implementation in this paper based on a search for better modularity and decoupleness of the system, therefore, these characteristics of our system will also be measured, together with some more aspect-related ones.

Concerning model-driven development, we are going to measure how much code is generated automatically and how much is still necessary to complete the system's behaviour. This metric will be realized both for services' code and for their properties. This way, we are able to measure how much effort we have avoided for the system developer by providing some of the code automatically generated from the models.

Aspect-Oriented Evaluation

The AOP metrics proposed in the literature allow the evaluation of separation of concerns, coupling, cohesion and size of aspect-oriented approaches [Ceccato, 2005; Garcia, 2006; Zhang, 2003CEC-CATO ET AL. [2004]GARCIA ET AL. [2006] ZHANG ET AL. [2003]]. To evaluate the proposal we developed a case-study, implementing the system both using and not using AOP and followed a set of metrics measurements. The case-study

consists on the inclusion of a set of extra-functional properties in a Web-service based system for the administration of the university in Spain. All the case-study details can be found in [Ortiz, 2007]. In Table 1 we describe the most common metrics used for AOP evaluation which are relevant for our scope; then metric results are discussed.

Separation of Concerns. In the test we conducted we found that concern diffusions are higher in object-oriented implementations compared to those where we have also used aspect-oriented techniques. Specifically, diffusion over classes is slower in aspect-oriented techniques since properties are encapsulated, avoiding references from the main implementation class of the service to side classes which implement the property functionality. Diffusion over operations is also lower for aspect-oriented approaches for the same reason, since they avoid invocations to the classes which implement the property functionality from the method in the main implementation class. Finally, diffusion over lines of code is also smaller for aspect-oriented implementations due to the fact that changes of context are avoided: when we have, for instance, an optional property, we will have to check whether the client decided to include it; if so, the property functionality code

Table 1. Metrics for the aspect-oriented implementation

Metric	Description
Concern Diffusion over Components (CDC)	Number of components in which there is code related to the implementation of the concern in question (Garcia, 2006).
Concern Diffusion over Operations (CDO)	Number of operations in which there is code related to the implementation of the concern in question (Garcia, 2006).
Concern Diffusion over Lines of Code (CDLOC)	Number of switches of concern through the lines of code (García, 2006).
Coupling on Intercepted Modules (CIM)	Number of modules named in the pointcut of a specific aspect (Ceccato, 2005).
Crosscutting Degree of Aspects (CDA)	Number of modules which may be affected by an aspect (Ceccato, 2005).
Performance	Response time of the system (Zhang, 2003).

is carried out, otherwise the regular functionality continues. If we do not use an aspect for that, then this implies at least two context changes in the main functionality code; with aspects, only one context change is done. Therefore, using aspect-oriented techniques in the implementation provides a better separation of concerns in the system than not using them, an expected result inasmuch as separation of concerns is one of the main purposes of aspect-oriented techniques.

Coupling and Crosscutting Degree. Coupling measurements provided the same values for the object-oriented implementation and the aspect-oriented one since we consider that a pointcut implies coupling to the target method. However, we must remember that even though the coupling is the same, the direction of the coupling is different, in the sense that the main system functionality is dependent on the non-functional property in the OOP implementation. On the contrary, when implementing properties using AOP, the dependence source is in the property itself, therefore avoiding any intrusive code being mixed with code in the system's main functionality. The measurements showed that coupling to intercepted modules is very low (one per aspect) which implies low coupling of the aspect regarding the application and therefore high aspect code reusability. Moreover, CDA measurements indicate that the aspects used in the system implementation indirectly affect a few more classes than those referred to in the

pointcuts. Therefore, with regards to coupling we can conclude that low CIM values and higher CDA values show low coupling and good crosscutting modularization of the system, which is the case of the system evaluated in this chapter.

Performance. We also measured the execution rate of service operations with the applied properties. The results showed the differences between the execution rates in the object-oriented implementation and the aspect-oriented one were below 10 percent, which in general can be regarded as insignificant, especially in systems where invocations are done though the Internet..

Code Generation Evaluation

Concerning the code generation process, we have to highlight that for well-known properties we generated the full aspect and description code and for properties unknown to the system, we generated their skeleton. It is important to mention that in the case of the aspect all the AspectJ code is generated, so, if functionality has to be added, it can be added in Java with no need to learn AspectJ. We also wish to analyze some additional characteristics of the model-driven process and the model-driven generated models and code:

- **Modularity:** thanks to the use of an approach in which properties remain separated from service models along all the process, we can see that our models and our generated code are modularized.

- **Encapsulation:** as a consequence of the modularity of the system, properties' implementation and description are completely encapsulated into a meaningful unit.
- **Traceability:** it is also a consequence of the previous characteristic that traceability of the systems is maintained along all the development process since any property located in a stereotype in the PIM is perfectly located in an aspect in the Aspect-oriented PSM, in a policy in the policy-based PSM and in a soap tag in the soap-tag-based PSM, when necessary. Moreover, these PSM elements are completely located in an AspectJ aspect and a WS-Policy description in the code, respectively. This process path can also be followed in the opposite direction, from code to PIM; therefore our properties are completely traceable from the platform independent model to the final implementation.
- **Simplicity:** once more as a consequence of prior statements, the transformation in the model-driven development is simpler than if properties were mixed with services at any stage, since independent elements can be generated separately.
- **Maintainability:** finally, it is also a consequence of previous characteristics that property models and code will be easily maintainable, since they remain separated from the main functionality; therefore, it is easier to add a new property, delete an old one or modify one of the existing ones without affecting the main service functionality at all.
- On the other hand, MDA provides us with faster development time by generating code rather than handwriting each file, and having the system well structured and modelled since early stages of develop-

ment. This implies a better consistency and maintainability of the code and from PIM we could increase portability across middleware vendors.

FUTURE TRENDS

Several trends could be considered for future work, which will be traced in the following lines.

The closer future work is the creation of a wide repository of predefined non-functional properties for which the full code, not only the skeleton, can be generated automatically. The repository should include well-known properties in the Web service domain, such as a digital signature or login. Due to the relative juvenility of Web services, there is not a wide set of well-known and well characterized non-functional properties other than security-related ones; however some additional properties could be provided too. In this regard, we could supply one property which would provide more or less detailed or specific information depending on the client's request, one which could provide real time values on a topic instead of a delayed or average value, etc.; this set should be defined in advance.

It could also be a task to research how a semantic description fits in the Web service model-driven development and especially in non-functional property development. The computer science community has been working hard on the semantic topic over the last years. However, it is still a long way until an agreement is reached, widely accepted and well settled. In this regard, one of the subtopics which could be investigated is how to integrate this semantic description of services and specially their non-functional properties in a model-driven development.

Bringing MDA into focus, it is important to remember reusability of platform-independent models for various platform-specific implementations is one of the main purposes of a model-driven approach. In this respect, immeasurable work can be pursued on this topic; in particular, we remark platform-specific models and implementations' development for mobile devices. Mobile devices are being more and more used every day and there is also demand for services by these types of device. In this regard we consider an important field to face how a model-driven development for Web services, and especially for their clients, are achieved in the scope of mobile devices. Moreover, non-functional properties which are specific to this domain, such as the way in which results obtained from a service invocation are represented in different types of device also suppose an interesting future research field.

Concentrating on the profile proposed for non-functional properties, the last issue that could be achieved in future work would be the extension of the named profile in order to cover traditional quality of service requirements (such as performance, reliability or availability) and exploring what type of specific model and code should be derived from these types of property. In this line of work, it should also be considered how this development would fit with standards such as WSLA (Ludwig, 2003), used in order to agree on the quality of service compromise which a service acquires with a specific client. This line of work is further explained in (Ortiz, 2008)

To conclude, the dynamic addition of software artefacts is a subject whose importance has increased in the last years in various disciplines. In this concern, future work could also consider the generation of a dynamic aspect-oriented implementation from non-functional property models in order to inject new behaviours even if services are already deployed. Furthermore, a dynamic description of property functionality could also be considered at platform-independent level and integrated through the remaining stages of development until the final code is obtained.

CONCLUSION

Some clear benefits of the contributions of this chapter are analysed below:

- It can be widely found in different discipline environments that non-functional properties should be decoupled from the main system functionality; besides, a loosely coupled environment is one of the main pillars of the Web service scope. The present proposal allows us to maintain non-functional properties in Web service development completely decoupled from the main functionality entities at all stages of development.

- In general, it is also widely known that model-driven development facilitates the development of applications from a platform-independent model until the final code implementation; furthermore, Web services may be modelled in a platform-independent manner and later transformed into a model specific to the platform in question, and finally into code. Properties are integrated in this development for non-functional properties from a platform-independent model, through a platform specific model in which implementation and description remain separated and finishing with a final code implementation for each of these types of model. In this model-driven development two relevant characteristics, desirable in an MDA process, are achieved: simplicity and traceability. Transformations between models are simpler when the different parts of the models remain decoupled, as is the case in our approach; traceability allows the exact location of every model element in other level models or in the code and vice versa; this is also achieved by our approach.

- Aspect-oriented techniques are also widely known by several disciplines as a good alternative when decoupling non-functional properties. We have demonstrated that this is also a good option for non-functional property implementation in the Web services scope and we have avoided the learning curve of using an additional programming language in development by automatically generating the property code. Furthermore, Web services are inherently self-descriptive elements; this is the reason why we have also generated the standard WS-Policy description for the implemented properties.

On the other hand, we mention what could be regarded as drawbacks of the proposal:

- In our chapter, Web service modeling is based on a component representation of services and on their offered interface and operations. There are several proposals which consider that service modeling has to be based on the WSDL document (Bezivin, 2004); these types of proposal try to represent all the elements in the standard way of describing Web services in XML by using the correspondent UML stereotypes. Although it is a very complete representation of services, it implies models of great complexity (Grommo, 2004) and may make their understanding and usability difficult, especially at PIM level. In this regard, we are neither against nor in favour of this alternative; however we consider that a simpler model is best, especially at PIM level, where services may be represented in models and may derive in an alternative PSM, different from a WSDL implementation. In any case, it is not our intention to establish how model-driven development of Web services has to be done, until a standard is provided to be

followed; we just provide an environment into which properties can be integrated. In any Web service modeling proposal the offered interface and operations will have a representation in the models, and this is enough for our proposal. This is the reason why we do not intend to provide a complete model-driven development approach for Web services.

- The proposed non-functional property stereotype has to be extended with every specific property to be used in the system in question. We are aware that the existence of a stereotype for each property may seem to complicate the modeling task. However, a set of common and well-known non-functional properties in the Web service domain, such as security related ones, logging, timing, etc., can be predefined and provided in an existent repository. Besides, the approach allows the possibility to define domain-specific properties and to specify well-known properties in a different manner than their usual form depending on the specific context.

- This approach provides an aspect-oriented implementation of non-functional properties. Aspect-based approaches may imply slower response times than when implemented without aspects. However, our evaluation shows that the response times of services which use an aspect-oriented implementation of properties or an object-oriented one are quite similar, thus this should not be a problem for the type of aspects we would have in our system.

- We chose the description of properties to be based on WS-Policy in our chapter, which we are aware is a standard proposal not approved to date. Due to the fact that there is no official standard for non-functional property description, we decided to adopt one which seemed to be mature enough and a suitable candidate for the standard.

WS-policy is already used by other standard proposals such as WS-Security, and we believe it may be approved in a short term. In any case, the transformation could be adapted to generate the description according to a different standard, if a new one were established.

REFERENCES

Bézivin, J., Hammoudi, S., Lopes, D., & Joault, F. (2004). *An experiment in mapping Web services to implementation platforms.* (Tech. Rep. No. 04.01), LINA: Université de Nantes.

Ceccato, M., & Tonella, P. (2005) Measuring the effects of software aspectization. In T. Tourwé, M. Bruntink, A.M. Marínn & D. Shepherd (Eds.), *Procedings of the First Workshop on Aspect Reverse Engineering. REPORT SEN-E0502,* (pp. 46-50). CWI: Stichting Centrum voor Wiskunde en Informatica.

Elrad, T., Aksit, M., Kitzales, G., Lieberherr, K., & Ossher, H. (2001). Discussing aspects of AOP. *Communications of the ACM, 44*(10), 33–38. doi:10.1145/383845.383854

Fensel, D., & Bussler, C. (2002). *WSMF in a nutshell.* Retrieved from http://www1-c703.uibk.ac.at/~c70385/wese/wsmf.iswc.pdf

García, A., Sant Anna, C., Figuereido, E. m., Uirá, K., Lucena, C., & von Sta, A. (2006). Modularizing design patterns with aspects: A quantitative study. In Tarr, P. (Ed.), *Transactions on aspect-oriented software development I.* Springer doi:10.1007/11687061_2

Grønmo, R., Skogan, D., Solheim, I., & Oldevik, J. (2004). Model-driven Web services development. In S. Yuan & J. Lu (Eds.), *International Conference on e-Technology, e-Commerce and e-Service 2004,* (pp. 42-45). IEEE Computer Society.

Hirsch, F., Yendluri, P., Orchard, D., Yalçinalp, U., Boubez, T., Vedamuthu, A. S., et al. (2007). *Web services policy 1.5 - framework.* Retrieved from http://www.w3.org/TR/2007/REC-ws-policy-20070904/

Lausen H., Polleres A. & Roman. (2005) *Web service modeling ontology.* Retrieved from http://www.w3.org/Submission/WSMO/

Ludwig, H., Keller, A., Dan, A., King, R. P., & Franck, R. (2003) *Web Service Level Agreement (WSLA) language specification.* Retrieved from http://www.research.ibm.com/wsla/WSLASpecV1-20030128.pdf

Orchard, D., Hondo, M., Yendluri, P. P., Boubez, T., Hirsch, F., Yalçinalp, U., et al. (2007). *Web services policy 1.5 – attachment.* Retrieved from http://www.w3.org/TR/2007/REC-ws-policy-attach-20070904/

Ortiz, G. (2007). *Integrating extra-functional properties in Web service model-driven development.* Unpublished doctoral dissertation, University of Extremadura, Spain.

Ortiz, G., & Bordbar, B. (2008) Model-driven quality of service for Web services: An aspect-oriented approach. In *Proceedings of International Conference on Web Services,* (pp 748-751). IEEE Computer Society

Ortiz, G., Hernández, J., & Clemente, P. J. (2005). How to deal with non-functional properties in Web service development. In Lowe, D., & Gaedke, M. (Eds.), *Web engineering* (pp. 98–103). Springer. doi:10.1007/11531371_15

Ortiz, G., & Leymann, F. (2006). Combining WS-policy and aspect-oriented programming. In P. Dini, P. Lorenz, D. Roman & M. Freire (Eds.), *IEEE Advanced International Conference on Telecommunications and International Conference on Internet and Web Applications and Services (AICT-ICIW'06),* (pp. 143-148). IEEE Computer Society.

Papazoglou, M., & Van Den Heuvel, W. (2006). Service-oriented design and development methodology. *International Journal in Web Engineering and Technology, 2*(4), 412–442. doi:10.1504/IJWET.2006.010423

Weerawarana, S., Curbera, F., Leymann, F., Storey, T., & Ferguson, D. F. (2005). *Web services platform architecture: SOAP, WSDL, WS-policy, WS-addressing, WS-BPEL, WS-reliable messaging, and more.* Prentice Hall.

Zhang, C., & Hans-Arno, J. (2003). Quantifying aspects in middleware platforms. In M. Akşit (Ed.), *Proceedings of the 2nd International Conference on Aspect-Oriented Software Development,* (pp. 130-139). ACM.

KEY TERMS AND DEFINITIONS

Aspect-Oriented Programming: A programming paradigm which complement object-oriented programming, in which transversal functions are isolated from the main program's business logic.

Extra-Functional Properties: They are properties of the system which provide additional functionality to the system, which is not part of the main functionality of the system.

Model-Driven Architecture: A software design approach, which provides a set of guidelines for the development of software systems expressed as models.

Model-Driven Development: A software development methodology which focuses on creating models of the systems, leaving implementation technologies for a later stage.

Service-Oriented Architecture: An architectural style based on services.

Unified Modeling Language: A standardized general-purpose modeling language for software engineering.

Web Service: Modular application that can be invoked through the Internet following some established standards.

Chapter 10
A Unified Deployment and Management Model for Dynamic and Distributed Software Architectures

Mohamed Nadhmi Miladi
Université de Sfax, Tunisia

Mariam Lahami
Université de Sfax, Tunisia

Mohamed Jmaeil
Université de Sfax, Tunisia

Khalil Drira
Université de Toulouse, France

ABSTRACT

Dynamic deployment of software components and services constitutes a solution for enhancing the addictiveness of distributed software systems. Such a property is necessary for the evolutionary systems that need to adapt their behaviour according to the changes in their application-level requirements or context situations. Therefore, this chapter looks for a modelling solution that can react in response to unpredictable changes in the communication and/or execution resources.

This chapter provides a generic model called Unified deployment and management Model of Dynamic and Distributed software architectures (UMoDD) based on the D&C standard proposed by the OMG. UMoDD has been designed to be suitable to dynamic deployment and management for both architecture styles: the service-oriented and component-based architecture style. The proposed model is based on a model-driven approach. It offers two levels of modelling: a generic level and a specific level to an architecture style.

DOI: 10.4018/978-1-60566-794-2.ch010

INTRODUCTION

Pervasive applications are generally composed of software entities that need to be deployed in various contexts which cannot be known in advance. For instance, a crisis management system includes software entities that need to be deployed in service-oriented or component-based architectures.

Modelling such applications needs to handle both architecture styles: the service-oriented and component-based architecture style. Several research and development works including Janssens, Joosen, and Verbaeten (2005), Janssens, Truyen, Sanen, and Joosen (2007), Keeney and Cahill (2003), Raverdy, Le, Gong, and Lea (1998), and Satoh (2005) propose such generic modelling. Most of these models are based techniques like aspect-oriented programming and reflective techniques. Such modelling still limited to the underling technique specificities. They do not support a high level modelling that enables dealing with unpredictable changes in the architecture context. Moreover, they do not support recent deployment and management standard including WSDM (Web Services Distributed Management) for Web Services (WS) (Bullard, Murray, & Wilson, 2006) and service-oriented architecture management, or the D&C (Deployment & Configuration) standard proposed by the OMG (OMG, 2006).

In order to ensure a standard based and a high level of abstraction modelling, we should establish a generic model that unifies the two architectural styles and drops research works weaknesses. Deploying and managing distributed architectures may also take benefit from the model-driven methodologies in order to master the complexity of deploying generic and reusable addictiveness properties.

The main purpose of this paper is to provide a modelling solution for the deployment and management of distributed architecture based on the

D&C standard. This solution is particularly beneficial for heterogeneous architectures that need to be dynamically adapted against unpredictable contexts changes, in order to meet non-functional requirements.

For that, we extend the D&C standard and we propose the UMoDD model (Unified deployment and management Model of Dynamic and Distributed software architectures) that provides, on the one hand, a platform-independent description. On the other hand, it provides the necessary generic description applicable for the deployment and the management of the two main software architecture styles: the Component-Based Architecture style (CBA) and the Service-Oriented Architecture style (SOA). In a more global view of the automated management and provisioning process supported by our approach, we consider also refining the generic model to obtain a specific model for each of the architecture styles: CBA and SOA. Moreover, we maintain the conformance with the notations of the most recent standards including SOARM (OASIS, 2006), SDD (OASIS, 2007) and WSDM (Bullard, Murray, & Wilson, 2006).

The paper is organized as follows. Section 2 presents an overview of a research related to the architecture deployment and its management. In order to introduce the major concepts of the D&C standard, we propose, in section 3, the basic principal of this standard. Section 4 introduces the proposed model. It stresses our approach vision and the various proposed parts. To illustrate the proposed model, section 5 describe crisis management case study. Section 6 presents our generic model called GeMoDE (Generic Model for Deployed Entity). While section 7 depicts the specific architecture style models: CBA and SOA based on a refinement process from the GeMoDE models. Section 8 presents a summary evaluation of our solution compared with some near research contributions. In Section 9 we conclude the paper and we point to future work.

DEPLOYMENT AND MANAGEMENT: THE STATE OF THE ART

This section addresses the state of the art of modelling the deployment and management of software architectures in general and especially in a distributed context. The objective is to provide not only an overview of different deployment and management concepts and notations but also a structured and synthesized description of the recent efforts of the community of deployment and management of software architectures.

This description includes an overview of the well known deployment and management standards. This part will be followed by a synthesis and a discussion of related work.

Deployment & Management Standards Overview

In this section we present an overview of the well known standard as well for software architecture deployment as for its management for both component-based and service-oriented architectures.

Standard for Architecture Deployment

JSR88 is a standard specification for the deployment of J2EE architectures (Searls, 2003). It allows a separation between J2EE middleware and the used tools to deploy applications on this middleware. This specification defines a set of interfaces that should implement the deployment tools and the J2EE middleware. The interaction between a deployment tool and the J2EE server is achieved through a component called "DeploymentManager" that each J2EE server must provide.

Standard for Architecture Management

In order to manage component-based architecture, JMX (Java Management eXtension) (Microsystems, 2002) provides four levels architecture and a set of services for managing java applications. It

ensures a remote access to the servers to be managed. Based on the JMX standard, JSR77 standard (Hrasna, 2002) presents a standard information model provided by each server to the administrator. It models all J2EE application server objects called "managed objects".

Web Services Distributed Management (WSDM) (Bullard, Murray, & Wilson, 2006) is a standard for web service resources management. It is proposed by the OASIS (Organization for the Advancement of Structured Information Standard). WSDM is based on two specifications:

- MUWS (Management Using Web Services) (Vambenepe, 2004): provides standard notations to manage any administered resource through web services. WS are used as a platform for exchanging messages within resources.
- MOWS (Management Of Web Services) (Sedukhin, 2004): focuses on the self-management of web services.

Standard for Architecture Deployment and Management

The OMG proposes a specification for the deployment and configuration (D&C) of distributed architecture (OMG, 2006). This specification follows the model driven architecture (MDA) approach trough the definition of two model levels. The first provides platform independent models (PIM). The second refines them into platform specific models (PSM). D&C divides its models into three areas that will be detailed latter:

- Component data and management model.
- Deployment target data and management model.
- Deployment execution data and management model.

Table 1 summarizes these standard characteristics. According to the deployment and

Table 1. Deployment and management standard

Standards	Generic granularity	Standard type	Model based
JMX	Specific to CBA and J2EE platform	Management standard	No
JSR77	Specific to CBA and J2EE platform	Management standard	No
JSR88	Specific to CBA and J2EE platform	Deployment standard	No
WSDM	Specific to SOA and Web services platform	Management standard	No
D&C	Specific to CBA And platform independent	Deployment and management Standard	Yes

management standard study, we noticed that numerous standards have proposed specification ensuring the deployment and management for both component-based such as JSR77, JSR88 and JMX and service-oriented architectures such as WSDM. However, these latter are often intended for specific platforms. This problem was partially resolved by the D&C standard which defines a generic support for deployment of component-based software.

This approach follows MDA concepts. It defines several PIMs, which are expected to be transformed to PSMs for concrete platforms. Whereas, this standard does neither support the dynamic management of software applications nor handle the deployment and the management of service oriented applications.

The model that we propose here extends this standard which includes the mainly required criteria such as an independent platform level, a model based approach and both deployment and management handling.

Deployment and Management Research Work Overview

The aim of this section is to provide an overview of works that handle the deployment modelling of software architectures and their management for ensuring a non-functional requirement adaptation. This study includes works handling both component-based and service-oriented architectures undependably of their deployment platforms

and their modelling techniques. These works can be sub-divided into three major classes. The first class includes works which are based only on a specific Platform deployment. In this class two sub-categories can be distinguished: those that adopt a component-based platform and those that adopt a service-oriented platform. The second class includes works that follow a platform independent approach. Whether architecture is component-based or service-oriented, the third class involves works that address the problem with a more generic approach and have proposed high-level descriptions disregarding not only the platform deployment but also the architecture style.

Component-Specific Platforms Works

These works target various component-based platforms such as EJB (Rutherford, Anderson, Carzaniga, Heimbigner, & Wolf, 2002) (Al Masri & Frénot, 2002), CCM (Deng, Balasubramanian, Otte, Schmidt, & Gokhale, 2005) FRACTAL (Hoareau, Abdellatif, & Mahéo, 2007), JavaPod (Marangozova & Hagimont, 2001). To be adaptive regardintg non-functional requirements, works including (Marangozova & Hagimont, 2001) (Grace, Coulson, Blair, & Porter, 2006) (Rutherford, Anderson, Carzaniga, Heimbigner, & Wolf, 2002) have proposed mechanisms for managing architecture structures. For instance, BARK (Rutherford, Anderson, Carzaniga, Heimbigner, & Wolf, 2002) is based on the EJB deployment descriptor "ejb-jar.xml" and proposes a management model for EJB beans through a set of XML scripts. Some other works follow a standard approach to achieve their architecture management. For instance, (Al Masri & Frénot, 2002) is based on the standard JSR77 specification. Other works including (Hoareau, Abdellatif, & Mahéo, 2007) (Pellegrini & Riveill, 2003) highlight a distributed context handling through the deployed architecture management. More specifically, (Hoareau, Abdellatif, & Mahéo, 2007) proposes a solution to deploy J2EE architectures on grids. It is based on "ZoneManager" entity for the deployment management process. DAnCE (Deployment and Configuration Engine) (Deng, Balasubramanian, Otte, Schmidt, & Gokhale, 2005) follows, in addition, a standard-based approach. It provides an implemented solution based on D & C meta-model for the deployment and the management of CCM components.

Despite research efforts, proposed description techniques for architectures deployment and management in this work class remain applied only on their specific platforms. Our specific component contribution part enhances these works and more specifically DAnCE works with a model-based and a generic description of component based architecture.

Services Specific Platforms Works

A first sub-class (Chen & Huangr, 2006) (Ruiz, Duenas, & Usero, 2004) proposes a framework-based solutions for the management of home gateway services. Other works focus on the dynamic management of service availability. In one hand, works including (Irmert, Fischer, & Meyer-Wegener, 2008) manages running services implementations. In the other hand, works including (Cervantes & Hall, 2004) focuses on the dependencies services management through the "ServiceBinder" which is implemented within the "Gravity" project. It provides an "InstanceMananger" for dynamically managing bundles dependencies as well as their creations and destruction.

However, only few works are based on standard specifications. AWSE (Autonomic Web Service Envirenement) (Martin, Powley, Wilson, Tian, Xu, & Zebedee, 2007) is one of these singular works but it rather manages the quality of services modelled as "Manageable resources". It is based on the OASIS WSDM standard (Bullard, Murray, & Wilson, 2006). In addition, works describing the deployment management of service-oriented architectures are not well handled. Despite (Cervantes & Hall, 2004) contributions, this work still limited to non-distributed context. The extension made here enhances these research efforts through a standard based modelling solution for describing the deployment management of service-oriented architectures in a distributed context.

Platform Independent Works

A first work subclass (Dowling & Cahill, 2001) (Bouchenak, Boyer, Cecchet, Jean, Schmitt, & Stefani, 2004) (Rosa, Lopes, & Rodrigues, 2008) follows a component-based approach. For instance, K-component (Dowling & Cahill, 2001) proposes context adaptation through a model separation between the deployment description and the management description. This latter is based on graph transformation techniques. This Platform independent modelling is sometimes refined to a specific platform. For example, (Bouchenak, Boyer, Cecchet, Jean, Schmitt, & Stefani, 2004) refines the proposed description to J2EE architecture specification.

Other studies enhance the previous work subclass through a standard-based description. DACAR (Distributed Component-based Autonomous Architecture) (Dubus & Mer, 2006), provides meta-model based on the specification D&C combined with ECA (Event-Condition-Action) rules. In this same class, other works enhance rather a model-based description that generally follows the MDA approach. We mention, for instance, CADeComp (Context Aware Deployment of Component-based Applications)

(Ayed, Taconet, Bernard, & Berbers, 2008) and DF (Deployment Factory) (Hnetynka, 2005). We noticed that most of these works opt for a D&C standard-based description.

Most research efforts achieved in this class focused on a component-based management on behalf of the service-oriented one. (Rosa, Lopes, & Rodrigues, 2008) is one of few works which models this management. It handles a services composition management with respect to adapt service-oriented architecture to the non-functional requirement change. However, this management is driven by the composition aspect. It is not suitable for the deployment architecture management.

Generic and Platform Independent Works

Several studies have been achieved in this class including (Janssens, Joosen, & Verbaeten, 2005), (Janssens, Truyen, Sanen, & Joosen, 2007), (Keeney & Cahill, 2003), (Raverdy, Le, Gong, & Lea, 1998), and (Satoh, 2005). More specifically, we distinguish the approaches presented in (Keeney & Cahill, 2003) (Raverdy, Le, Gong, & Lea, 1998) which are based on reflective techniques. The work in (Janssens, Truyen, Sanen, & Joosen, 2007) uses aspect-oriented techniques in order to ensure separation between the deployment description and the architecture management description. It extends JBOSS PDO through reconfiguration primitives. It is based on the NeCoMan (Janssens, Joosen, & Verbaeten, 2005) architecture that allows a reconfiguration operations modelling. DYVA (Ketfi & Belkhatir, 2005) provides "Deployment / Reconfiguration Manager" for a dynamic management based on a set of reconfiguration operations and adaptation policies. The proposed unified approach is refined to both a component-based architecture, and more specifically JavaBeans platform (Ketfi, Belkhatir, & Cunin, 2002), and a service-oriented architecture, and more specifically OSGi platform, (Ketfi & Belkhatir, 2003).

A second subclass, including (Satoh, 2005), ensures not only a software architecture management but also a deployment management. This subclass ensures both a generic description independent of the architecture styles and their related platform, and a description of the deployment and its management allowing them to integrate a distributed context. However, in this subclass, standard-based works are not well mastered.

Our contribution addresses the generic and platform-independent modeling solution enhanced with platform-independent models for both component-based and service-oriented architecture styles. This modeling solution is based on the D&C standard which is presented in the next section.

THE D&C STANDARD

The main purpose of this section is to familiarize the reader with standard concepts and to introduce the presentation of our contribution. The D&C standard (OMG, 2006) is sub-divided into two main parts. The first one focuses on the data deployment description and the second depicts the management of the described data. Each part includes three models detailed as follows.

Data Models

Component Data Model: The component data model focuses on the description of the component package configurations such as component package, ComponentPackageImport, Component-PackageReference, and properties. It basically includes the description of the component type and its various implementations. A component is either "assembly component" including some sub-components or "MonolithicComponent". The component implementation is delivered as an artefact (e.g. an executable file or library). Several implementations can be provided to the same component. The connection within component is achieved towards their several ports. D&C

standard is based on three connections types to model the component connections.

Target Data Model: The target data model describes all deployment context characteristics. More specifically, it describes the context in which the components are deployed and then executed. The D&C standard adopts a hierarchical target modelling. The domain notation is the top-level target entity. It is composed of a set of nodes that are inter-connected and can communicate using some bridges. A node models the host where the components implementations will be deployed. The bridge describes the communication path within nodes. The interconnection describes a connection link that can be established and even shared between two nodes.

Execution Data Model: All descriptions about the execution of an application deployment are provided by the data execution model. These descriptions are packed in the deployment plan notation. The Deployment plan involves all necessary informations to achieve the various application deployment executions.

Management Models

Component Management Model: The most basic notation in the Component Management Model is the "repository" that defines the host in which all component packages are stored. The management of this entity is achieved through the "RepositoryManager" notation. It maintains component packages hosted in a given Repository through some defined operations.

Target Management Model: This model focuses on managing the resources of the entity described in the target data model such as domain, node, bridges, etc. This management is achieved through some operations proposed in the "Target Manager" entity modelling.

Execution Management Model: The management of the applications deployment execution in D&C standard is based on the ExecutionManager entity. The main idea in this model consists in

dividing the ExecutionManager tasks into a set of sub-tasks. The whole application is sub-divided into sub-applications (components and connections). Each one is managed by a single node. The deployment of an application is achieved in two basic steps. The first prepare the execution plan through ExecutionManager.preparePlan() operation. The second step launches the application deployment execution which is in its turn divided into two phases: the first one, ApplicationManager. startLaunch() that provides port references to the available ports of the application. The second phase, Application.finishLaunch (), achieves the connections within the established components ports references. This operation creates an application object which allows the navigation within the various application ports and its introspection in the execution time.

This current work is based on D&C standard and it extends D&C power modelling by providing not only independent platform models, but also generic models for both architecture styles: component- based and service-oriented. Contrarely to the D&C standard, we handle a dynamic management ensuring to manage the deployment in response to requirements for adaptation.

THE PROPOSED MODEL: UMODD

The Unified deployment and management Model of Dynamic and Distributed Software Architectures (UMoDD), depicted in Figure 1 that we propose, here, extends the D&C standard model described in the previous section. It provides, in a high-level, the deployment of software entities and their management in a dynamic and distributed context.

UMoDD models are achieved in a platform independent level (PIM) following two fundamental layers as depicted in Figure 1. The first, allows the description of a deployment entity in a generic way independently of its related architecture style. This layer, called GeMoDE (Ge-

Figure 1. Representation of the UMoDD extension

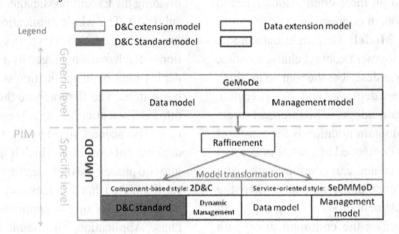

neric Model for Deployed Entity), follows the D&C standard and proposes two basic parts. The first focuses on data modelling. It describes explicitly data of the software entity to be deployed, the deployment context and the necessary data for the deployment execution. The second focuses on management modelling. It models how to manage the described software entity data, the deployment context and the deployment executions. The GeMoDE model straights also the dynamic management aspect.

In a further step, this generic layer will be refined towards a specific architecture styles either the service orientated architecture SeDMMod (Service Deployment & Management Model) or the component-based architecture 2D&C (Dynamic D&C) as depicted in Figure 1. These two specific architecture style models preserve a model independency upon the execution platforms while following, at the same time, the D&C decomposition vision on data and management models.

In order to illustrate the proposed models, throughout the UMoDD models descriptions, we will introduce a case study presentation in the next section that focuses on the deployment of IT solution for crisis management handling and execution.

CASE STRUDY DESCRIPTION

Crisis management (Mehrotra, Znati, & Thompson, 2008), (Gupta & Ranganathan, 2007) is one of large scale management challenges that need a structured organization and execution. In a crisis, many entities work together as a loosely coupled virtual organization to save lives, preserve infrastructure and community resources, and re-establish normalcy within the community. This virtual organization's operation can span multiple levels. Field-level operations such as crisis containment, evacuation, traffic management, decontamination, and medical services' provision are usually under the control of an on-site incident commander who reports back to a central Emergency Operations Center (EOC). EOCs, in addition to providing logistical support for immediate field level operations, focus on the evolving crisis. Driven by factors such as economics and communities usually design and manage software solutions for expected usage scenarios is quite difficult to be established. The challenge is to design IT solutions that should be at hand and efficient to react to these crisis events. Crisis management modeling techniques should take in consideration response involving the deployment and mobilization/ management of resource units and emergency equipment to the emergency locations once the situation is identified as a potential crisis.

To illustrate our contribution, we will focus on a special crisis situation: fire detection. In fact, since the situation has been identified, the fire management structure follows a hierarchical process for crises organization's operation. Various actors can be identified: (i) the investigators that are the nearest actors to the crisis scope. Their mission is to achieve the operations execution in response to the current situation feedbacks. (ii) The controllers that take the crucial decisions to restore a crisis situation. (iii) The coordinators that act as an intermediary between the investigators and the controllers. They enable the information dispatching and ensure the information delivery to the appropriate person and/or equipment.

With the diversity of actors requested in managing a crisis situation, several activities should be undertaken to cope with the fire crisis situation. For instance, we distinguish: fire extinction, area cleaning, and fire sources identification. In order to model such situation, we should establish hierarchical structures of the system architecture. First, the central controller of all the emergency operations is modeled using the principal entity "EOC". Second, affiliated coordinators to the "EOC" are modeled through several deployed entities. We distinguish:

- **Plane coordinator:** it models the structure for coordinating all aviation activities as an airport. Also, it manages others deployed entities such as canadairs and helicopters.
- **Firefighter coordinator:** it models the structure for rescue coordination as a civil protection center. It controls several deployed entities like fire chief and firefighter.
- **Walker coordinator:** it models the structure coordinating and supervising walker activities as control towers.
- **Robot coordinator:** it models the structure coordinating the activities of deployed

robots such as drone, ground-robot and amphibious-robot.
- **Policeman coordinator:** it models the structure coordinating the activities of police officers.

The diversity of actors requested in managing a crisis situation implies diversity on the transmitted data. These data can vary from simple notification on the progress of the crisis operation rescue to a much heavier data such as video surveillance. This diversity can be driven by the available deployment architecture styles.

For instance, for a heavy data such as multimedia streams, a service-oriented architecture is the most suitable architecture style. One or more multimedia service streams broadcasting can be established toward the related actors. However, others data kinds such as control instructions have different properties. They are lighter but their execution implies the success or the fail of a rescue operation. Thus, they often need to be traced. Tracing data allows a responsibility checking in case of a logistical error or a faulty situation judgment. It remains more interesting to take advantage of the maturity power of component-based architectures to handle state-full software entity tracing in order to establish a responsibility proof.

In order to deal with heterogeneous architecture styles and to reduce the complexity and the development cost of such applications that are characterized with their evolution and dynamic aspects, we are looking for giving a generic modelling independently of the architectures styles. This solution is presented in the next section.

GENERIC LEVEL: GEMODE

GeMoDE is introduced to increase the model generality and to provide a unified solution that is built on a top-level allowing the modelling of the common aspects of both services-oriented and component-based architecture. This solution enables the designer to model the deployment of an application and its management at run time without being limited to a specific architecture style.

The key to a best effort modelling for nonfunctional requirements handling and for a better crisis management is a modelling that enables an abstraction of both various techniques and deployment platforms as well as available architecture styles. GeMoDE models follow this directive and propose two basic parts: data and management following the D&C vision. Models of these two parts are presented in the next sections.

Deployable Entity Data Model

This section presents a generic model describing the various data concepts of a deployable entity. A deployable entity, either it models a component or a service, depicts some common notations including interfaces description, package description, and implementation description that are unified in a generic modelling. A deployable entity can be primitive or composite. It is described, as depicted in Figure 2, using:

- One or more software entity interfaces. They are described in a generic manner allowing them to be refined in further steps to specific architecture and platform types. For example, in a component-based archi-

tecture, software entity interfaces model can be refined such as facets and receptacles modelling: CCM platform. While in the service-oriented architecture, software entity interface models can be refined into a Bundle-Activator through the OSGi platform.

- One or more software entity implementations. It describes common implementation information for both architecture styles such as UUID, implementation name and implementation type.

- A software entity package that includes mainly the description of the software entities interfaces and their implementations. It is modelled in a generic way allowing its possible further refinement. For instance, in the OSGi platform, it will be refined into an OSGi bundle model. While in the EJB platform, it will be refined into an EJB Bean model (OSGi Alliance, 2003).

As depicted in the Figure 2, all established models are described through UML notations with respect to the D&C specification. This UML description ensures a modeling solution based on graphical notations. However, such notations are not suitable to be applied in a concrete context or to achieve a refinement process. Therefore, the proposed UMoDD models should be trans-

Figure 2. Generic model of data deployable entities

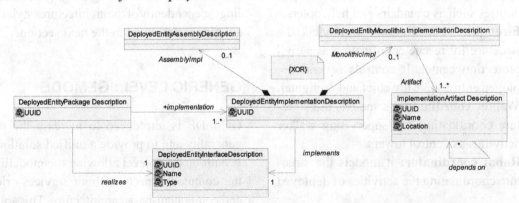

lated towards a textual format. This translation is achieved through the XML Metadata Interchange (XMI) (OMG, 2003) which is an OMG recommendation specifying, with a Document Definition Type (DTD), how UML models are mapped into a XML notation. Therefore, the illustration of our UMoDD models will be made through an XMI production through the crisis management case study.

An Application on the Scenario

In a crisis situation, the notification on the crisis status is crucial for monitoring the progression of such a situation. Deploying notification entities can be useful in several situations. For instance, such entities can be deployed on walker's PDA in order to send periodic notifications to his walker coordinator. Furthermore, it can be deployed on robots that are made to take climatic conditions measurements such as humidity, temperature, etc. In this case, the notification entity sends periodically these measurements to the robot coordinator. With the purpose of describing this notification entity without being limited to a given context and a specific architecture style, we are based on the generic data model as depicted in Figure 3.

Deployable Entity Management Model

In order to manage the deployment entities described in the Deployable Entity Data Model, we provide a generic notation allowing the modelling of management tasks such as: the installation, the search and the uninstalling of the software entity packages. This model is inspired from the D&C specification as depicted in Figure 4. Since both service-oriented and component-based architectures are based on the package notation, we generalize the "RepositoryManager" tasks defined in the D&C standard to be able to manage software entity package independently of the architecture style.

An Application on the Scenario

The packaging of software entities is a fundamental step in the deployment process. That's why, we provide management operations in order to create and install packages of all entities that are required in a crisis situation. This enables a faster architecture deployment. The Figure 5 illustrates the necessary operations to create and install a notification entity that was described in the previous section.

Figure 3. Notification entity data model

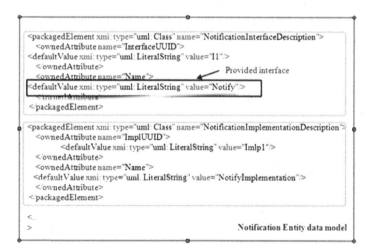

Figure 4. Generic model of data management

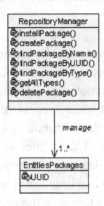

Deployable Entity Execution Data Model

This model describes a deployment plan following D&C standard concept entities as depicted in Figure 6. This plan provides a description of the entities to be deployed, their connections, their localizations (i.e. node on which to store this entity) as well as the basic resources for the deployment.

An Application on the Scenario

In some period and under special climatic conditions, the probability of a crisis situation occurrence increases. For instance, a camping season with a very low humidity and a high temperature. In such period, vigilance is heightened. Helicopters, ground-robots, and police officers are deployed in suspicion of a possible crisis. Drones, walker and their coordinators are in investigation status

for detecting a possible fire. In order to achieve a more efficient cooperation within deployed entities, some communications should be established. We distinguish a communication between policeman's chief and helicopters to better guide the direction of their deployment, communications between helicopters and drones in order to coordinate their deployment activity and obviously a communication between the walker and his walker coordinator. The description of these entities, their connections, their localizations as well as the basic resources for the deployment was regrouped on a deployment plan. Especially, the communication between the walker and his walker coordinator is illustrated in the Figure 7. It is established between the notification entity deployed on the PDA of the walker and a supervising entity deployed on the walker coordinator unit which is responsible to collect and analyse the various walker notifications.

Deployable Entity Execution Management Model

The deployment plan execution is achieved in two basic steps. The first achieves the initial execution of the deployment plan. The second ensures the dynamic adaptation of the executed deployment plan in response to non-functional requirements.

D&C standard proposes the following actors that achieve the application deployment as depicted in Figure 8:

Figure 5. Notification entity management model

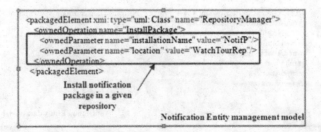

Figure 6. Generic deployment plan

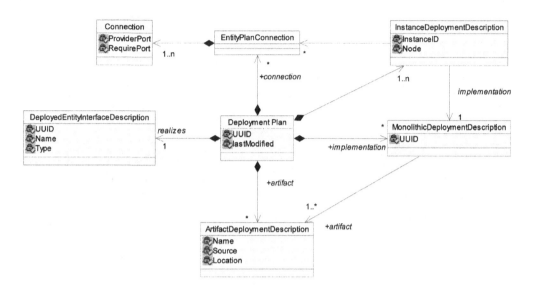

Figure 7. A part of the generic deployment plan

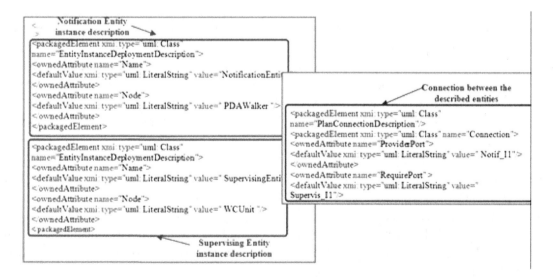

- Packager is the actor that handles repository creation.
- Repository Administrator: receives components packages from the Packager and installs them in the local repository using the RepositoryManager interface.
- Planer creates the application deployment plan.

- Executor uses the deployment plan in order to execute the deployment and launches the application.

To handle the generic dynamic deployment of the architecture application, we model a new actor called the "*Manager*". It manages at run time

Figure 8. Deployment actors

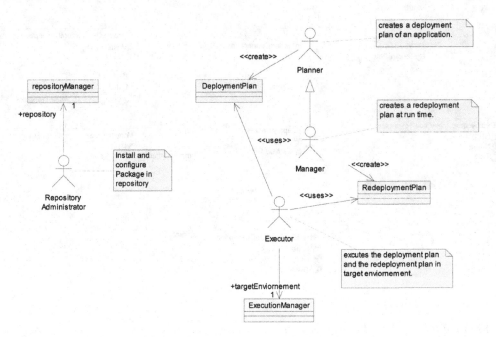

the application deployment plans in response to adaptive needs of the application on the fly.

In the first step, we focus on the deployment plan execution. In general, the deployment process, as presented in the D&C specification affects several nodes. To manage this distributed deployment, we rely on management entities proposed in the standard D&C. We extend the modelling scope of these entities: *ExecutionManager*, *NodeManager*, *NodeApplicationManager* and *NodeApplication* to enable the modelling of generic software entities. The Executor achieves the *preparePlan* method trough the *NodeManager* entity related to each node. The latter receives its deployment sub-plan and creates the *NodeApplicationManager* entity. A package entity search is achieved through the *RepositotyManager* entity to handle the deployable entities of each deployment sub-plan. The execution, in each deployment node, is achieved through the execution of the two methods: *Start* and *finish* launch.

In a second step, we focus on providing a dynamic management of the deployment execu-

tion. This dynamic requires the establishment of a set of generic management primitives that enable to adapt the deployed architecture to meet non-functional requirements and the not expected context variation.

In the second step, GeMoDE ensures the dynamic management of architecture deployment missed in the D&C standard. Relaying on the study presented in the state of the art, we provide the modelling of the generic redeployment primitives. These latter are achieved in a generic way to model the dynamic management despite of their architecture styles and their underling platforms:

- **DeployEntity** < Plan ID> <EntityID> <Node ID>: allows deploying a software entity in a given node.
- **UndeployEntity** < Plan ID> < Entity ID> <Node ID>: allows stopping the execution of a software entity and the uninstallation of the given node.
- **addConnection** <Plan ID> <Source Entity ID: Port Name> <Dest Entity ID: Port

230

Figure 9. Redeployment actions for a walker PDA failure event

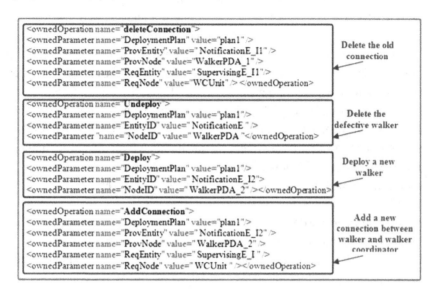

Name>: adds a connection between two software entities.

- **deleteConnection** <Plan ID> <Source Entity ID: Port Name> <Dest Entity ID: Port Name>: removes a connection between two software entities.
- **addEntity** <repository URL> < Entity ID>: adds an entity to a repository
- **deleteEntity** <repository URL> < Entity ID>: removes an entity from a repository
- **addRepository** <repository URL>: adds a repository
- **deleteRepository** < repository URL >: removes a repository

An Application on the Scenario

As presented in the previous section, to cope with a crisis situation, many entities have to coordinate together. Thus, we should relay on the proposed primitives to ensure the dynamic adaptation of the deployed architecture regarding to the context evolution. For instance, when the walker PDA autonomy become at a lower level, a walker could not continue his mission that consists to super-

vise and send periodic notifications to his walker coordinator about a current situation. Therefore, he should be substituted immediately by another walker. For this reason, some redeployment actions should be executed in order to preserve the continuity of the supervision in the related area. In this situation, the connection between the walker and his walker coordinator should be removed through the execution of "deleteConnection" action as depicted in Figure 9. In addition, the "undeployEntity" action will be executed to remove the defective walker. To deploy a new walker and establish communications with his walker coordinator, the "deployEntity" and "addConnection" actions are respectively executed.

In this section, we focused on the generic modelling of an application with an illustration through an initial fire crisis management solution. We have described the coordination between the deployed entities without being limited with their appropriate architecture style. In the next section, we introduce the specific level and we model this case study with both service oriented architecture and component based architecture.

SPECIFIC LEVEL: SOA AND CBA MODELLING

In this section we propose structured models that describe as well the deployment of service-oriented architecture as their management. These models follow the D&C approach in general and more specially the GeMoDE one. These models are subcategorized into three main parts: service data and management models, service deployment target data and management models, service execution data and management models. It is worth to note that the models of the service deployment target data and management model are those proposed in the D&C deployment target data and management models since they can be applied to any software entity styles.

SOA Specific Modelling: SeDMMod

Achieving SOA deployment and management models results, in a first step, to a model transformation refining those proposed in GeMoDE. Nevertheless, service-oriented architecture has its own specificity and sometimes a special deployment or a management process. Specific models will be proposed to take advantage of the recent proposed standards and related researches. In general, the deployment entity described in GeMoDE will be transformed towards the service concept. We will focus on the description of the various service deployment data models as well as the related models of its management.

Service Data Model

In the Service Data model, we focus only on the description of stateless service architecture. In order to build the fundamental concepts, we are based on the W3C standards (W3C, 2004) and the specifications suggested by OASIS (OASIS, 2006).

A service, as depicted in Figure 10, is a software entity which its description (*ServiceDescription*) realizes a contact between the provider and the consumers (OASIS, 2006). This description is achieved through a model refinement process of the deployable data entity model and handling

Figure 10. Service data model

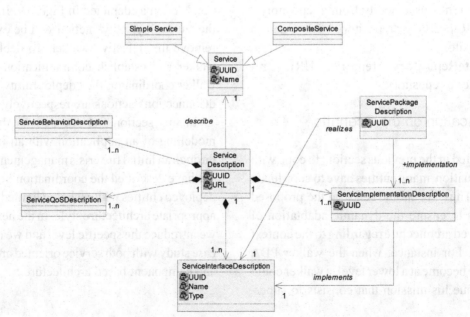

the specificity of the service-oriented approach. In SOA, a service data description driven by the contact interfaces and a description of its implementation can be a key for a suitable management.

The service data description is achieved through a model refinement process of GeMoDE *DeployedEntityInterfaceDescription*, *DeployedEntityImplementationDescription* and *DeployedEntityPackageDescription* model. They are transformed respectively to *ServiceInterfaceDescription* model which is based on the (W3C, 2004) (OASIS, 2006) standards, *ServiceImplementationDescription* models that follows the (Papazoglou, 2003) work and *ServicePackageDescription* that merges the two previous models.

Other specific SOA models are also established. They describe the service behaviour (*ServiceBehaviorDescription*) and also its qualities of service (*ServiceQoSDescription*) (Papazoglou,2003).

Moreover, a service can be simple or composite. A service is called composite (i.e. composed) when its execution implies interactions with other services in order to take advantages of their common functionalities. The services composition defines the services that should be called, in which order and how to manage the exception condi-

tions. For example, for web services WSBPEL (OASIS, 2007) provides a standard language to model WS composition.

In the present work, we especially focus on the description of the structural aspects of services deployment. The behavioural, non-functional and composition aspects are handled in others standard or works. The proposed models can easily integrate these latter thanks to the highly extensible power provided by our models.

The *ServiceInterfaceDescription* class is modelled in the Figure 11. An interface describes all interactions provided by the service and dependences within these interactions. An interface, in service-oriented architecture style, describes the communication actions of the given service, i.e. at sending and messages receptions (Papazoglou, 2007). An interface can be either required or provided and it should be called through an endpoint (W3C, 2005). It is modelled thanks to two basic notations:

- *Address*: the address identifying an *endpoint* and providing the service localization.

Figure 11. Service interfaces description model

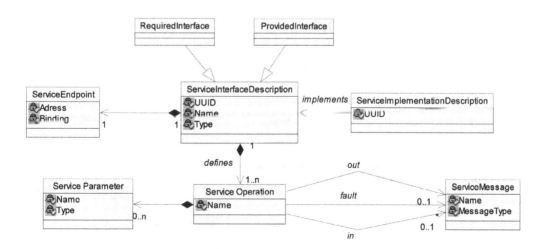

- *Binding*: models the communication protocol between two *endpoints* (for example TCP, HTTP…) and the messages coding used such as textual or binary.

Moreover, one interface may have many operations.

A *ServiceOperation* is an abstract description of an action ensured by the service provider that implements the interface operation signature. The modelling of an operation signature is based on three parameters: *input* for the entry message, *output* for the released message and *fault* for the exception message transmitted by service (UPMS, 2007) (Emig, Krutz, Link, Momm, & Abeck, 2007).

ServiceImplementationDescription, as depicted in Figure 12, describes the possible service implementations (Papazoglou, 2003). A service can have one or more implementations and each implementation can use imported packages and has some properties (Derler & Weinreich, 2007).

The description of the service as well its implementations will be wrapped in the *ServicePackageDescription* as depicted in the Figure 13. This model follows the SDD (Solution Deployment Description) standard presented by the OASIS comity (OASIS, 2007). It models the package descriptor in a standardized way.

An Application to a Scenario

As introduced before, for a multimedia notification which should be accessible to several actors implied in the crisis management activities, a service-oriented architecture is the most suitable architecture style. Therefore the notification entity modelled in the last section with a generic manner, should be refined to various multimedia types including an audio streaming service or video streaming service or even a picture notification service. The diversity of this refinement is due to the heterogeneity and the resources variety of the equipments. To improve their accessibility, each service should be described in a service descriptor that includes an overview of its provided and required interfaces, its implementations, and its package location. For example, the video streaming service data, depicted in Figure 14, is obtained by refining the generic description illustrated in Figure 3 and by providing some specificities of the service oriented architecture such as the service descriptor and the service endpoint.

Service Management Model

Since the registry notation persists in the service-oriented architecture (Orriëns, Yang, & Papazoglou, 2003). The registry model proposed in the GeMoDE will be maintained. However, managing

Figure 12. Service implementation description model

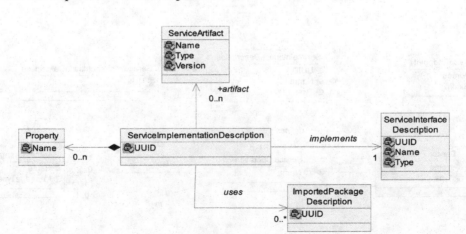

data of service-oriented architecture has also its specificity including the publishing of deployable service in the Registry.

The *RegistryManager* entity, as depicted in Figure 15, is modelled to ensure the management of the services descriptors handled by the related

directory. The operations provided for registry management are modelled as follows:

- *Publish (svcDescription, ref.):* publishes a service descriptor in the registry and grants it a single reference.

Figure 13. Service package description model

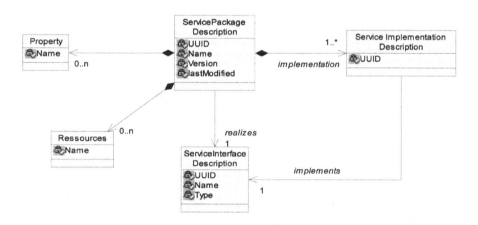

Figure 14. Video notification service data model

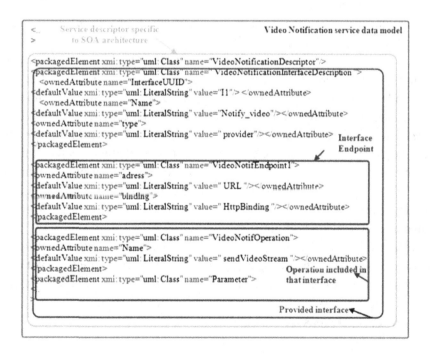

Figure 15. Service management model

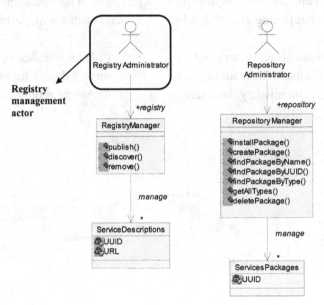

- *Remove (svcDescription, ref.):* removes a service descriptor from the registry.
- *Discover (svcDescription):* this operation allows the discovery of a service published in the registry using its descriptor.

The concept of *RepositoryManager* is preserved in SOA architecture since we need to manage the services descriptions as well as their implementations.

In order to support service-oriented architectures, a new actor called "*RegistryAdministrator*" is added as depicted in Figure 15. It operates on a set of *RegistryManagers*. This actor will publish, discover or remove descriptions of services in one or more directories.

An Application to a Scenario

The mangement of the serveral kinds of notification services is obtained by refining the generic management of the notification entity package. In addition, it includes some operations for publication, discovery and delete of service descriptors in a given registry. These operations are strongly coupled to the service oriented architecture style. As depicted in Figure 16, the video notification package will be installed in a given repository established for example in a watch tour. In addition, the descriptor of this service will be published in a given registry established in the same location.

Service Data Execution Model

Following the deployment plan concept proposed by the D&C standard, we refine in this section the GeMoDE DeploymentPlan modelling concepts to achieve the description of service deployment plan (*ServiceDeploymentPlan*) as depicted in Figure 17. This modelling is based on the SDD (Solution Deployment Description) standard proposed by the OASIS (OASIS, 2007). It models the following informations to achieve a service deployment:

- The service interface description.
- The service implementations description
- Properties and basic resources to achieve the deployment

Figure 16. Audio notification service management model

```
<packagedElement xmi:type="uml:Class" name="RepositoryManager">
  <ownedOperation name="InstallPackage">
    <ownedParameter name="installationName" value="VideoNotifP"/>
    <ownedParameter name="location" value="WatchTourRep"/>
  </ownedOperation>
</packagedElement>
                              Package installation on
                              a repository installed in
                              the watch Tour
<packagedElement xmi:type="uml:Class" name="RegistryManager">
<ownedOperation name="publish">
<ownedParameter name="svcDescription" value="VideoNotificationDescriptor"/>
<ownedParameter name="location" value="WatchTourReg"/>
</ownedOperation>
</packagedElement>
                              Publication
                              action specific to
                              SOA architecture
                    Video Notification service management model
```

Figure 17. Deployment plan service description

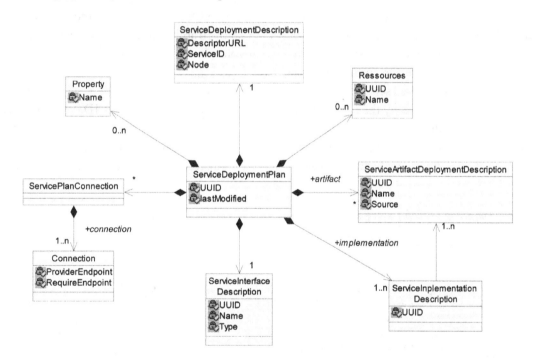

- The plan connection describes a set of connections made within services in the application.
- The description of the unique instance of the deployed service and its location (node).

An Application to a Scenario

The generic deployment plan presented in section 6.3 illustrates an invistigation status of the architecture while expecting a possible crisis situation. For instance, a walker in investigation discovers a fire situation. The architecture deployment of the system should be dynamically adapted to deal with the new situation. Thus, we refine entities that need multimedia streaming transmission to services. For example, investigators like walkers, firefihters and policemans are modeled through a service oriented style. While the controllers must take benefits of the component based architecture stytle in order to have a trace of all decisions made by these entities. As depited in Figure 18, we describe a part of the service deployement plan obtained by refining the generic one. It illustrates the notification sended by a walker to his walker coordinator through a video streaming service.

Service Execution Model Management

Based on the D&C execution approach and refining the GeMoDE execution management model, this model ensures two major tasks: the deployment plan execution and the dynamic deployment management tasks. Deployed services in the first task should be consolidated by the new services and/or replaced by others.

Starting from the refinement of the three operations for the initial applications deploy-

ment, we establish: the *ServicePreparePlan*, the *ServiceStartLaunch* and the *ServiceFinishLaunch* operations. *ServicepreparePlan* provides the sub-deployment plan to the suitable NodeManager entity of each node. Following the invocation of the *ServiceStartLaunch* operation, not only the services deployment is achieved but also their publication *publish (svcDescription)* contrarily to the other architecture styles. The deployed services will be operational with the *ServiceFinishLaunch* operation execution.

In the second task, the dynamic service deployment is achieved thanks to the refinement of the generic reconfiguration operations already described in GeMoDE. The execution of the provided primitives ensures the adaptation of the deployed architecture with respects to the context evolution:

- **Deploy** < Plan ID> <DescriptorID > <Service ID> <Node ID>: deploy a service in the given node. It is achieved by publishing its description in the registry and installing its package in the related node.

Figure 18. Deployment plan service description

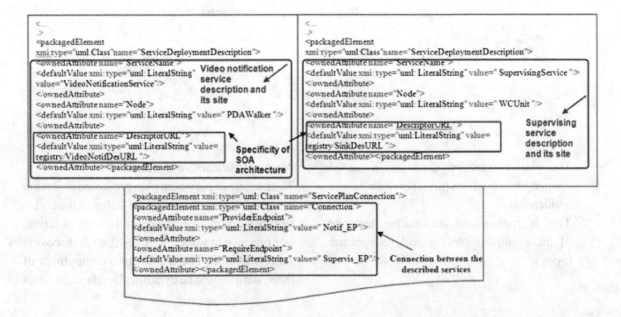

- **Undeploy** < Plan ID> <DescriptorID > <Service ID> <Node ID>: undeploy a service the given node. It is achieved by removing its service package from the related node and removes its description from the registry.
- **Attach** <Plan ID> <Source Service ID: EndPointReference> <Dest Service ID: EndPointReference >: this operation establishes a connection between two services. Thus it modifies the deployment plan and more specifically the composition services descriptor.
- **Detach** <Plan ID> <Source Service ID: EndPointReference > <Dest Service ID: EndPointReference >: this operation removes a connection between services and also modifies the deployment plan.
- **addService** <repository URL> <Service ID>: this operation adds the given service in the repository.
- **deleteService** <repository URL> <Service ID>: this operation removes the given service from the repository.

It is worth to note, that all the operations including a service state transfer or state duplication are not handled in our model since it focuses only on stateless services.

An Application to a Scenario

In order to highlight the dynamic management aspect, we consider a fire detection event. More specifically, starting with the architecture described in the previous section, a walker in investigation discovers a fire situation. He is equipped with limited PDA resources in which a message notification service was deployed. Thus, such walker has sent a notification message to his walker coordinator in order to inform him with the new situation. However, a message notification wasn't enough to give a clear idea about the danger and the difficulty of the situation. Therefore, the walker coordinator proceeds to search in the registry services descriptors of video notification services or picture notification services that may be deployed on others walkers closed to the affected area. This search is done with the execution of the "Discover" operation with specifying some criteria such as the location of the walker and the capacity of his PDA. In the case of the walker coordinator doesn't find the suitable service, she/he proceeds to deploy for example a video notification service on the nearest walker that has sufficient resources to execute this application by executing "Deploy "action. As depicted in Figure 19 a new connection was established between this deployed service and the walker coordinator by executing "addConnection" action.

Figure 19. Redeployment actions for the walker replacement event

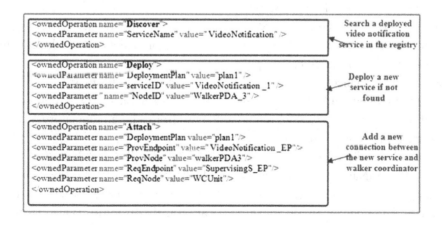

CBA Specific Modelling:2D&C

As already presented in the section above, the D&C standard provides models for data components deployment, as well as models of component management description. In the following we extend this standard specification to describe the dynamic component deployment. Moreover, this model follows a search achieved in the DAnCE works (Deng, Balasubramanian, Otte, Schmidt, & Gokhale, 2005) by proposing a generic and top_level models for the operations proposed for CCM platform.

Thus, we model the following generic reconfiguration operations that can be applied to any components platform. These operations ensure the dynamic deployment of CBA architectures. All these operations executions modify the given deployment plan:

- **Deploy** < Plan ID> <Component ID> <Node ID>: it deploys a component in a given node. This operation returns a new deployment plan.
- **Undeploy** < Plan ID> <Component ID> <Node ID>: it removes a component of a given node. This operation returns also the new deployment plan.
- **Duplicate** < Plan ID> <Component ID> <Node ID> <Target>: it duplicates a component identified and localized by the provided entry parameters.
- **addConnection** <Plan ID> <Source Component ID: PortName> <Dest Component ID: PortName>: it connects two compatible ports of the given component instances. This connection is achieved between the provided and the required component instance ports.
- **deleteConnection** <Plan ID> <Source Component ID: PortName> <Dest Component ID: PortName>: it disconnects two compatible ports of the given component instances. This connection is achieved

between the provided and the required component instance ports.

However, the dynamic management of component-based architectures recognizes its own characteristics.

Thus, during the execution of these reconfiguration operations, we should be sure that the given component instances are in a stable state. Thus, we turn the given component instances in a passive state. Once reconfiguration is finished, we switch them in their initial state. This state transformation is achieved through two components management operations: *passivate* and *activate* operations.

- **Activate** <Node ID> <Component ID>
- **Passivate** <Node ID> <Component ID>

Once we manage state full components, we should save their states during the dynamic deployment operation execution (Ketfi & Belkhatir, 2005). To achieve this task, we propose two operations allowing the return and the modification of the component state:

- **getState** <Component ID>: return the attributes value of a component.
- **setState** <Component ID><Value>: change the attributes value of a component.

In order to manage the repository we provides the following operations

- **addComponent** <repository URL> <Component ID>: adds a component in a given repository.
- **deleteComponent** <repository URL> <Component ID>: removes a component from a given repository.

An Application to a Scenario

In the last section, we distinguished some entities cooperating in the crisis management system that are modelled using a service-oriented architecture style. Other entities that achieve some crucial decisions or deliver some critical information need often to be traced. In fact, tracing data allows a responsibility checking in case of a logistical error or a faulty situation judgment. In this case, it remains more interesting to take advantage of the maturity power of component-oriented architectures to handle state-full software entity tracing in order to establish a responsibility proof or to recuperate missed information.

For instance, during an exploration operation in a forest, some robots are devoted for tracing some measurements like temperature and humidity evolution. They notify their robot coordinator periodically with the obtained measurements. The entities deployed on these robots ensure not only the notification but they also backup the context status. Thus in this situation the generic notification entity presented in GeMoDE was refined to a measurement notification component. If one of the deployed robots falls, then it is necessary to substitute the defective robot by another in order to continue the interrupted mission. Therefore, we execute dynamically the "Duplicate" action in order to recuperate the state of the defective robot as depicted in Figure 20. This duplication consists in deploying a new measurement notification component on the nearest robot or on a walker PDA if it is equipped with the necessary options

to measure temperature and humidity. Then, the state of the old component will be transferred to the new one. If the replacement process was finished and the component status was restored, we execute the "Undeploy" action in order to remove the faulty component. Finally, we add the communication between this component and the robot coordinator through the "addConnection" action.

MODELS EVALUATION

The aim of this section is to compare our contributions against some research works that propose such generic modelling including CADeComp. In fact the proposed solution is a standard and model based approach that takes advantages of both MDA and D&C standards. It provides the latter standard to achieve deployment and management of software architectures with two fundamental issues: the distributed execution environment and its dynamicity. Although it was based on the D&C standard and MDA by offering a generic level and a refinement to a specific level especially CCM platform, CADeComp focus only the management of the initial deployment architecture of context aware applications. While DAnCE work, extends the D&C standard with redeployment actions that can be applied only to CCM components.

Figure 20. Redeployment actions for the failure of robot event

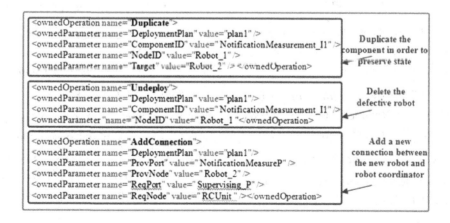

Our contribution enhances the D&C modelling power in order to support dynamic management of more generic software entities all over the context evolution.

CONCLUSION

In this chapter, we presented a unified deployment and management model called UMoDD based on the OMG Deployment & Configuration standard. This model-driven approach aims to establish a generic model for unifying two architectural styles: the service-oriented and component-based styles. Models defined by UMoDD are achieved in a platform independent level following two fundamental layers: the generic layer presented by GeMoDe and the specific layer presented by both 2D&C and SeDMMod. This modelling solution adapts dynamically the architecture deployment according to the changes in their non-functional requirements or context situations. The proposed models are illustrated through a crisis management case study based on an XMI translation.

We plan refining the proposed models in order to be mapped to a specific platform including OSGi.

REFERENCES

W3C. (2004). *Web Service Architecture*. Récupéré sur http://www.w3.org/TR/ws-arch.

W3C. (2004). *Web service management: Service life cycle*. Récupéré sur http://www.w3.org/TR/2004/NOTE-wslc-20040211/

W3C. (2005). *Web service addressing 1.0 - core(WS-Addressing)*. Récupéré sur http://www.w3.org/TR/2005/WD-ws-addr-core-20050215

Al Masri, N. & Frénot, S. (2002). *Dynamic instrumentation for the management of EJB-based applications*. INRIA RR-4481.

Ayed, D., Taconet, C., Bernard, G., & Berbers, Y. (2008). CADeComp: Context-aware deployment of component-based application. *Journal of Network and Computer Applications*, 224–257. doi:10.1016/j.jnca.2006.12.002

Bouchenak, S., Boyer, F., Cecchet, E., Jean, S., Schmitt, A., & Stefani, J. (2004). A component-based approach to distributed system management: A use case with self-manageable J2EE cluster. *EW11: Proceedings of the 11th workshop on ACM SIGOPS European workshop.*

Bruneton, E., Coupaye, T., & Stefani, J. (2004). *The fractal component model*. The ObjectWeb Consortium.

Bullard, V., Murray, B., & Wilson, K. (2006). *An introduction to WSDM*. OASIS Committee Draft.

Cervantes, H., & Hall, R. (2004). A framework for constructing adaptive component based applications: Concepts and experiences. *Proceedings of 7th International Symposium on Component Based Software Engineering, CBSE 2004*, (pp. 130-137).

Chen, I., & Huangr, C. (2006). An SOA-based software deployment management system. *Proceedings of the 2006 IEEE/WIC/ACM International Conference on Web Intelligence.*

Deng, G., Balasubramanian, J., Otte, W., Schmidt, D., & Gokhale, A. (2005). DAnCE: A QoS-enabled component deployment and configuration engine. In *Proceedings of the 3rd Working Conference on Component Deployment*, (pp. 67-82).

Derler, P., & Weinreich, R. (2007). Models and tools for SOA governance. *Proceedings of the International Conference on Trends in Enterprise Application Architecture.*

Dowling, J., & Cahill, V. (2001). The K-component architecture meta-model for self-adaptive software. *REFLECTION '01: Proceedings of the Third International Conference on Metalevel Architectures and Separation of Crosscutting Concerns*, (pp. 81-88).

Dubus, J., & Mer, P. (2006). Applying OMG D&C specification and ECA rules for autonomous distributed component-based systems. *Proceedings of MoDELS Workshop*, (pp. 242-251).

Emig, C., Krutz, K., Link, S., Momm, C. & Abeck, S. (2007). *Model-driven development of SOA services.*

Grace, P., Coulson, G., Blair, G., & Porter, B. (2006). A distributed architecture meta-model for self-managed middleware. *ARM '06: Proceedings of the 5th workshop on Adaptive and reflective middleware (ARM '06).*

Gupta, S., & Ranganathan, F. (2007). Multievent crisis management using noncooperative multistep games. *IEEE Transactions on Computers*, 577–589. doi:10.1109/TC.2007.1023

Hiers, C. (2005). *A2.3.1.1 fire investigator positions.*

Hnetynka, P. (2005). A model-driven environment for component deployment. *SERA '05: Proceedings of the Third ACIS Int'l Conference on Software Engineering Research, Management and Applications*, (pp. 6-13).

Hoareau, D., Abdellatif, T., & Mahéo, Y. (2007). Architecture-based autonomic deployment of J2EE systems in Grids. *Proceedings of International Conference on Grid and Pervasive Computing (GPC'07).*

Hrasna, H. (2002). *Javatm 2 platform, enterprise edition management specification JSR-77.* Récupéré sur Sun Microsystems.

Irmert, F., Fischer, T., & Meyer-Wegener, K. (2008). Runtime adaptation in a service-oriented component model. *SEAMS '08: Proceedings of the 2008 international workshop on Software engineering for adaptive and self-managing systems*, (pp. 97-104).

Janssens, N., Joosen, W., & Verbaeten, P. (2005). *NeCoMan: Middleware for safe distributed-service adaptation in programmable networks.* IEEE Distributed Systems Online.

Janssens, N., Truyen, E., Sanen, F., & Joosen, W. (2007). Adding dynamic reconfiguration support to JBoss AOP. *MAI '07: Proceedings of the 1st workshop on Middleware-application interaction.*

Keeney, J., & Cahill, V. (2003). Chisel: A policy-driven, context-aware, dynamic adaptation framework. *POLICY '03: Proceedings of the 4th IEEE International Workshop on Policies for Distributed Systems and Networks.*

Ketfi, A., & Belkhatir, N. (2003). Dynamic interface adaptability in service oriented software. *Proceedings of Eighth International Workshop on Component-Oriented Programming (WCOP'03).*

Ketfi, A., & Belkhatir, N. (2005). Model-driven framework for dynamic deployment and reconfiguration of component-based software systems. *MIS '05: Proceedings of the 2005 symposia on Metainformatics, Esbjerg, Denmark.*

Ketfi, A., Belkhatir, N., & Cunin, P. (2002). *Dynamic updating of component-based applications.* SERP'02, Las Vegas.

Marangozova, V., & Hagimont, D. (2001). Availability through adaptation: A distributed application experiment and evaluation. *Proceedings of European Research Seminar on Advances in Distributed Systems (ERSADS'2001).*

Martin, P., Powley, W., Wilson, K., Tian, W., Xu, T., & Zebedee, J. (2007). The WSDM of autonomic computing: Experiences in implementing autonomic Web services. *ICSEW '07: Proceedings of the 29th International Conference on Software Engineering Workshops.*

Mehrotra, S., Znati, T., & Thompson, C. (2008). Crisis management. *IEEE Internet Computing*, 14–17. doi:10.1109/MIC.2008.7

Microsoft. (1995). *COM: Component Object Model technologies*. Récupéré sur http://www.microsoft.com/com/resources/comdocs.asp

OASIS. (2006). *OASIS reference model for Service Oriented Architecture*. Récupéré sur http://www.oasisopen.org/committees/download.php/19679/soa-rm-cs.pdf

OASIS. (2007). *Solution deployment descriptor specification 1.0*. Récupéré sur http://docs.oasis-open.org/sdd/v1.0/pr01/sdd-spec-v1.0-pr01.p

OASIS. (2007). *Web services business process execution language version 2.0*. Récupéré sur http://docs.oasis-open.org/wsbpel/2.0/CS01/wsbpel-v2.0-CS01.pdf

OMG. (2002). *CORBA component model specification, version 4.0*.

OMG. (2003). *Xml Metadata Interchange (XMI), version 2.0*.

OMG. (2006). Deployment and configuration of component-based distributed applications specification.

Orriëns, B., Yang, J. & Papazoglou, M. (2003). *A framework for business rule driven Web service composition. Conceptual modeling for novel application domains*.

OSGi Alliance. (2003). *OSGi service platform, release 3*. Amsterdam: IOS Press.

Papazoglou, M. (2003). Service-oriented computing: Concepts, characteristics and directions. *WISE '03: Proceedings of the Fourth International Conference on Web Information Systems Engineering*.

Papazoglou, M. (2007). *What's in a service?* (pp. 11–28). ECSA.

Pellegrini, M., & Riveill, M. (2003). Component management in a dynamic architecture. *The Journal of Supercomputing, 24*(2), 151–159. doi:10.1023/A:1021798709301

Raverdy, P., Le, H., Gong, V., & Lea, R. (1998). DART: A reflective middleware for adaptive applications. In *Proceedings of OOPSLA '98 Workshop #13: Reflective programming in C++ and Java*.

Rosa, L., Lopes, A., & Rodrigues, L. (2008). Modelling adaptive services for distributed systems. *SAC '08: Proceedings of the 2008 ACM symposium on Applied computing*.

Ruiz, J., Duenas, J. & Usero, F. (2004). *Deployment in dynamic environments*. DECOR04.

Rutherford, M., Anderson, K., Carzaniga, A., Heimbigner, D., & Wolf, A. (2002). Reconfiguration in the enterprise JavaBean component model. *CD '02: Proceedings of the IFIP/ACM Working Conference on Component Deployment*, (pp. 67-81).

Satoh, I. (2005). Dynamic deployment of pervasive services. *Proceedings of IEEE International Conference on Pervasive Services (ICPS'2005)*.

Searls, R. (2003). *JavaTM 2 enterprise edition deployment API specification, version 1.1*. Récupéré sur http://jcp.org/jsr/detail/88.jsp

Sedukhin, I. (2004). *Web services distributed management: Management of Web services distributed management*. OASIS Commitee Draft.

Sun Microsystems. (2002). *Enterprise JavaBeansTM specification, version 2.1*. Récupéré sur http://java.sun.com/products/ejb/

Sun Microsystems. (2002). *Java management extensions (JMX) specification version 1.2*. Récupéré sur http://-java.sun.com/products/ejb/

UPMS. (2007, June 4). *UML profile and metamodel for services for heterogeneous architectures*. Récupéré sur http://www.omg.org/cgibin/doc?ad/07-06-02.pdf

Vambenepe, W. (2004). *Web services distributed management:management using web services (muws 1.0) part 1*. Récupéré sur http://docs.oasisopen.org/wsdm/2004/12/wsdm-muws-part1-1.0.pdf

Section 3
Methods for Implementing Non–Functional Properties in SOA

The final section discusses practical application of methods for implementing non-functional properties in SOA environments. Methods such as aspect oriented programming (AOP), model driven architecture (MDA), and control theory are presented and applied to diverse properties (e.g., security) in various domains (e.g., biomedicine).

Chapter 11

An Aspect–Oriented Framework to Model Non–Functional Requirements in Software Product Lines of Service–Oriented Architectures

Germán Harvey Alférez Salinas
Universidad de Montemorelos, Mexico

Edward Mauricio Alférez Salinas
Universidade Nova de Lisboa, Portugal

ABSTRACT

Non-functional requirements (NFRs) are of primary importance in Software Product Lines (SPLs) of Service-Oriented Architectures (SOAs) as they specify the quality characteristics of a software system within a SPL. However, they are difficult to manage because they are found in many contexts with varying concerns and crosscut multiple concerns along the software lifecycle.

Existing variability management techniques in the context of SPL engineering tend to concentrate at the code level and do not address NFRs in SOAs. The analysis of variability from the beginning benefits the management of services from requirements to design and vice versa.

Also, there is a need for a navigation chart to help practitioners to model NFRs in SPLs of SOAs while separating difficult to modularize and maintain crosscutting concerns.

This chapter presents and applies an extended version of an aspect-oriented framework for SPLs that exploits aspect-oriented software development (AOSD) techniques in order to model variability of NFRs

DOI: 10.4018/978-1-60566-794-2.ch011

in SPLs of SOAs from early development stages. The aspect-oriented framework for SPLs is related to the Core Asset Development and Product Development activities in product line development proposed by the Software Engineering Institute (SEI) of Carnegie Mellon University. The analysis is driven by a SPL where metrics were applied in order to assess the performance of the framework.

INTRODUCTION

Software Product Line (SPL) engineering is about exploiting commonalities among a set of systems while managing their variabilities in order to shorten time to market, achieve systematic reuse goals, and improve product quality (Clements & Northrop, 2002).

There is a close relationship between SPLs and Service-Oriented Architectures (SOAs) because both of them have similar goals: to implement, integrate and maintain software with reused artifacts in order to reduce costs (Bichler & Lin, 2006; Papazoglou, 2003).

Aspect-Oriented Software Development (AOSD) is a paradigm that has a direct relationship with SPL and SOA because one of its main objectives is to separate concerns to promote flexibility and configurability; these two objectives are also vital when constructing SPLs and SOAs. In addition, AOSD can improve the way in which software is modularized by means of the encapsulation of variabilities in functional requirements (FRs) and non-functional requirements (NFRs) into aspects that crosscut various services.

Our previous research (Alférez & Poonphon, 2007) presents a framework that uses AOSD to manage variability from the early stages of the SPL lifecycle in order to improve the traceability of variations throughout the development of SPLs of Web applications. The current research extends the aspect-oriented framework focusing on managing variability of NFRs at initial stages (requirements, architecture, and design) in the lifecycle of SPLs of SOAs. The success of a SPL approach depends on early variability management, not only at the implementation level (Voelter & Groher, 2007).

Also, this chapter briefly describes variability implementation with AspectJ.

Existing requirements engineering techniques such as goals, scenario, and use case modeling support the analysis of requirements but they do not focus on crosscutting concerns. As a result, research on aspect-oriented requirements engineering complements these approaches by providing systematic means for handling such crosscutting concerns (Chitchyan et al., 2005).

In addition, practitioners need an easy-to-follow framework to model NFRs with aspects in SPLs of SOAs to manage difficult to modularize and maintain crosscutting concerns.

The framework is closely related to the Core Asset Development and Product Development activities in product line development proposed by the SEI (Clements & Northrop, 2002). Also, it is designed as a process description and recommendation to use Unified Modeling Language (UML) models with extension mechanisms.

The analysis of the proposed framework is driven by a SPL of a SOA for help desks where metrics are applied in order to assess its performance in early stages.

The remainder of this chapter is structured as follows. Section 2 presents the background where three software engineering techniques are covered and related: SPL, AOSD, and SOA. Section 3 presents the aspect-oriented framework to model NFRs in SPLs of SOAs. Section 4 shows the application of the proposed framework in a SPL of help desks for plant services departments. Section 5 outlines the future trends and finally, section 6 provides some conclusions of this chapter.

BACKGROUND

The concept of SPL awakens a special interest because an increasing number of organizations are realizing that they cannot meet the expense of developing various software products one product at a time (Bergey, Fisher, Gallagher, Jones, & Northrop, 2000; Pohl, Böckle, & Van der Linden, 2005). Organizations are realizing that using a SPL approach can yield notable improvements in time to market, product quality, productivity, customer satisfaction, cost schedule enhancements, and mass customization (Clements & Northrop, 2002; Northrop, 2006; Carnegie Mellon University, Software Engineering Institute, n.d.; Krueger, n.d.). It is because of the strategic and predictive software reuse of commonalities and the management of variations among the products in the product line (Krueger, n.d.).

Many new technology initiatives have a direct relationship with SPLs. A promising emerging approach in both research and industry communities that can contribute to achieve SPL's goals is AOSD. One of the purposes of the separation of crosscutting concerns provided by aspect-orientation is to promote flexibility and configurability; this is also true when constructing SPLs (Colyer, Rashid, & Blair, 2004). AOSD can improve the way in which software is modularized, localizing its variability in independent aspects as well as improving the definition of complex configuration logic to customize SPLs.

Moreover, it is important to manage variability from the early stages of the SPL lifecycle (it is known as "early aspects" (Rashid, Moreira, & Araújo, 2003; Baniassad et al., 2006)) in order to improve the traceability of variations throughout every stage and to benefit the understanding of each SPL feature separately to avoid ultimately errors in their implementation.

SOA is an emerging style of software architectures. SOA has a close relationship with SPL because both of them are useful to implement, integrate and maintain software with reused artifacts.

Aspects can be used to encapsulate variabilities of FRs and NFRs that crosscut multiple services.

This chapter is divided into three main sections. The first one is about SPLs, the second is related to AOSD, and the third to SOA.

Software Product Lines

A SPL is defined as "a set of software-intensive systems sharing a common, managed set of features that satisfy the specific needs of a particular market segment or mission and that are developed from a common set of core assets in a prescribed way" (Clements & Northrop, 2002). SPL engineering is about exploiting commonalities among a set of systems while managing their variabilities to improve time to market, achieve systematic reuse goals and improve product quality.

The foundation of SPLs is reusing with strategies such as production plans to guide the creation of systems (Bergey, Fisher, Gallagher, Jones, & Northrop, 2000). The reuse is done on a wide variety of assets, such as requirements, software design (the architecture), documentation, code and test strategies. (Brownsword, Clemens, & Olsson, 1996; Pohl, Böckle, & Van der Linden, 2005).

SPLs are defined by their commonalities and variabilities. A commonality is a functionality or quality that all the applications in a product family share. In contrast, variability represents a capability to customize a system (Geyer & Becker, 2002). In SPLs, variability is made explicit through variation points which are places in a software asset at which the variation will occur (Brownsword & Clemens, 1996).

Aspect-Oriented Software Development

AOSD is a new paradigm to develop software that addresses limitations inherent in other approaches, including object-oriented programming. AOSD aims to address crosscutting concerns by encapsulating them in separated modules, known as aspects (Kiczales et al., 2001). The most important benefits of aspect-orientation are related to its main objectives: to separate concerns and to minimize the dependency among them.

At the beginning, the practices of aspect-orientation were mainly applied to the implementation activities (Kiczales et al., 1997). However, the software engineering community has been recently interested in its use from early stages in the namely "early aspects" (Rashid, Moreira, & Araújo, 2003; Baniassad et al. 2006).

Aspect-oriented modeling (AOM) has the potential to help to find and reason about diverse features of the system from a more abstract level perspective. Also, it is used to implement variability in models (Aspect-Oriented Modeling Workshop, n.d.; Clarke & Baniassad, 2005). Early aspects and AOM have the potential to help to identify and reason about diverse features and variability of the system from a more abstract level perspective, without the complexity of many implementation details.

The following sections explain fundamental concepts of aspect-orientation, such as separation of crosscutting concerns, crosscutting concerns, and the use of aspects to model variability in SPLs.

Separation of Concerns

The main objective of aspect-orientation is the separation of crosscutting concerns. A concern is defined as the primary motivation to organize and decompose software in manageable and comprehensive parts (Ossher & Tarr, 2000). Different kinds of concerns can be relevant to different developers in different roles, or in different stages of the software lifecycle (Ossher & Tarr, 2000). In addition, separation of concerns has been a constant issue in software engineering (Diskstra, 1976; Filman, Elrad, Clarke, & Aksit, 2004) and can be defined as the ability to identify, encapsulate and manipulate just the software parts that are relevant to a concept, goal or particular purpose (Ossher & Tarr, 2000).

Achieving the separation of concerns brings important benefits in software engineering such as: complexity reduction, reusability improvement, and evolution simplification (Tarr, Ossher, Harrison, & Sutton, 1999).

Crosscutting Concerns

"Crosscutting" denotes a concern that spans multiple units of modularity, thus resisting modularization using normal constructs. Aspect-oriented programs can be used to modularize such crosscutting concerns (Palo Alto Research Center, Xerox Corporation, n.d.).

Software which is not designed using aspect concepts reveals two problems; namely, scattering and tangling. "Scattering" happens when models or code related to similar FRs or NFRs span throughout many modules. It has the risk of misuse at each point and of inconsistencies across all points because changes to the software may require editing all the affected software artifacts. "Tangling" happens when a software artifact, such as a class, is difficult to understand because two or more concerns are implemented in the same body.

Aspect-oriented programming (AOP) makes it possible to program crosscutting concerns in a modular way and to reach the benefits of modularity improvement: simpler code that is easier to develop and maintain, and with a great potential for reuse (Kiczales et al., 2001).

Use of Aspects to Model Variability in Software Product Lines

The aspectual approach was chosen in order to model variability in SPLs of SOAs because one of the goals of the separation of crosscutting concerns provided by aspect-orientation is to promote flexibility and configurability, characteristics that are especially essential in SPL engineering (Colyer, Rashid & Blair, 2004). In addition, AOSD can empower software modularization with the localization of variability (crosscutting concerns) in aspects (Clements & Northrop, 2002; Pohl et al., 2007) and aspects are a viable way because they are a variation mechanism of fair monetary cost (Bachmann & Clements, 2005).

Various authors have shown aspects as a mechanism for achieving variability, for example: Anastasopoulos and Gacek (2004) show how AOP is especially suitable for variability across several components. In another research, Anastasopoulos and Gacek (2001) present a case study that was performed in order to evaluate AOP as a product line implementation technology. Heo and Man (2006) focus their research on the implementation phase with AspectJ, not in early stages (Kiczales et al., 2001). Pohl et al. (2007) show a framework for SPL engineering that incorporates the central concepts of traditional product line engineering, namely the use of platforms and the ability to provide mass customization. However, they propose a new graphical notation for variability models that may complicate its adoption in the industry. Voelter and Groher (2007) show an interesting MDSD-AOSD approach to support variability implementation, management and tracing throughout the product line development lifecycle. AOP is used on both code and generator level. Our research does not go deep into programming issues. Also, their approach uses Domain Specific Language (DSL) to bind variability; we use UML to model it.

Service-Oriented Architecture

SOA is a software architecture where functionality is built with reusable business processes and services (Newcomer & Lomow, 2004). Each business process defines how services act together to achieve a goal, and each service encapsulates the function of an application component (Wada, Suzuki, & Oba, 2008). SOA is a promising style of software architectures to build products using loosely coupled services and connections between them which define how services connect and exchange data.

In order to improve the reusability of services and connections among them in SPLs, we need a way to model NFRs of services and connections from early development stages. The answer to this matter is given by aspects that encapsulate non-functional requirements, which are a primary source of variabilities in SPLs (Alférez & Poonphon, 2007). The following sections extend the previous work (Alférez & Poonphon, 2007) with an aspect-oriented framework that models variabilities within NFRs in SPLs of SOAs.

AN ASPECT-ORIENTED FRAMEWORK TO MODEL NFRS IN SPLS OF SOAS

This chapter presents a framework that uses aspects in order to model variations of WNFRs from the early stages in the SPL lifecycle of SOAs using stereotypes in the Unified Modeling Language (UML) and contributing for the improvement of the traceability of variations by using mapping rules (see Table 2). The first version of this framework was presented in (Alférez & Poonphon, 2007).

This extended version of the aspect-oriented framework is also related to the Core Asset Development and Product Development activities in product line development proposed by the Software Engineering Institute (SEI) (Clements & Northrop, 2002) but including support for aspect-oriented NFRs modeling in SPLs of SOAs.

This section presents the issues that motivated the extension of the aspect-oriented framework. Then it shows the solutions and recommendations.

Issues

In SOA, services should ideally represent a self-contained business function with a well-defined behavior. However, in practice, services are found in many contexts with varying concerns (Huntley & San Filippo, 2006). As a result, the first issue is about variability management. Variability management has been addressed in the context of SPL but it tends to concentrate on the code level instead of doing it from the early stages of the software lifecycle.

It is difficult to trace some services because they are present in various modules, making it hard to maintain and evolve the software. Without traceability, it is difficult to link the implementation of the services with the models that explain their intended behavior and structure. Besides, traceability of services from early stages helps to reason about features without having to deal with implementation details. Also it facilitates thinking about the crosscutting impact of NFRs implementation in a group of services. That is why this chapter specifies mapping rules to improve traceability of models to describe concerns.

The second issue is the lack of a navigation chart, a framework, to help practitioners to model NFRs with aspects in SPLs of SOAs. In fact, there are no easy-to-follow frameworks for SPLs of SOAs to address variability of FRs and NFRs while separating difficult to modularize and maintain crosscutting behavioral modules.

Finally, software companies need concrete ways to materialize the SEI's Framework for SPL Practice in order to accelerate its implementation and obtain its benefits. The proposed framework helps them to exploit it by means of the use of AOSD techniques.

Solutions and Recommendations

This research exploits AOSD and UML in SPLs of SOAs to manage variability in NFRs from early stages. Variability management from early stages (requirements, architecture, and design) can benefit traceability of artifacts (i.e. services) and as a result, it helps to reduce the effort in the configuration of new products (Alférez & Poonphon, 2007).

An aspect-oriented framework for SPLs of SOAs is presented in this section. It is related to the Core Asset Development and Product Development activities in product line development proposed by the SEI for modeling variability of NFRs. Even when this research is focused on early stages, brief hints about implementation are given. The following sections explain each one of the foundations for the aspect-oriented framework for SPLs of SOAs.

Relationship with the SEI's Core Asset Development and Product Development Activities

The proposed framework is related to the Core Asset Development and Product Development essential activities described in the Framework for SPL Practice (Clements & Northrop, 2002) of the SEI. The Core Asset Development activity represents the activity of developing the product line's core asset base. Its outputs are the core assets used by the family of products, and a production plan that specifies how to use the core assets to produce a product. The Product Development essential activity represents the engineering activity of creating products using the core assets as given by the production plan. There are several reasons for choosing the SEI's approach:

- This is a mature effort: its information has been collected from studies of organizations that have built product lines, from direct collaborations on SPLs with customer organizations, and from leading practitioners in SPLs (Clements & Northrop, 2002).
- Important companies have been using it successfully (Carnegie Mellon University, Software Engineering Institute, n.d.).
- It eases and accelerates the adoption and implementation of the proposed framework in real cases because the SEI's framework is a well-established approach.
- The Software Engineering Practice areas of the SEI's framework are carried out in the Core Asset Development and Product

Development essential activities. These practice areas are necessary for the application of the appropriate technology to create and evolve both core assets and products (Clements & Northrop, 2002).

- It is possible to base the proposed framework on the SEI's framework because the latter does not prescribe that organizations must adopt a specific practice (Clements & Northrop, 2002); it gives a good level of flexibility.

Use of Aspects to Model NFRs' Variability

Variability in NFRs often crosscuts various services. This is why AOSD techniques are natural candidates to manage the crosscutting nature of variabilities of NFRs in SPLs of SOAs with a non-invasive strategy. Using aspects to model variability at early development stages brings the following benefits:

- Clear separation of variable and crosscutting SPL features starting at early stages, i.e., using early aspects (Rashid, Moreira, & Araújo, 2003; Baniassad et al., 2006).
- Some crosscutting features can be modeled as aspects.
- Models and code which are easy to understand and evolve due to the separation of crosscutting concerns.

Forward and Backward Traceability through the Stages of the Lifecycle

The framework enables forward (from requirements to design) and backward (from design to requirements) traceability by means of mapping rules (see Table 2). The provided forward and backward traceability in turn, allows the analysis of change impact along the software lifecycle phases. See Figure 6 for an example.

An Iterative, Architecture-Centric, and Use-Case Driven Approach

The proposed framework is based on the following three principles that have been borrowed from the Unified Process: iterative, architecture-centric, and use case-driven (Jacobson, Booch, & Rumbaugh, 2002):

1. *Iterative:* The iterative approach consists of a sequence of incremental steps or iterations.
2. *Architecture-centric:* Product line architecture is a description of the structural properties for building a group of related systems, typically the components and their interrelationships (Clements & Northrop, 2002). AOP is among the specific practices proposed by the SEI to implement architectures of SPLs: "AOP is an architectural approach because it provides a means of separating concerns that would otherwise affect a multitude of components that were constructed to separate a different, orthogonal set of concerns" (Clements & Northrop, 2002).
3. *Use-case driven:* The use case model is a widely known technique to structure and evolve requirements. It represents the wire that guides the tasks of the project from requirements to implementation. Use cases are first class concerns that facilitate the analysis about crosscutting concerns.

Use of the UML and its Extension Mechanisms

The proposed framework uses UML and its extension mechanisms to model aspects because: (i) it is one of the most accepted standard modeling language for the specification, visualization, construction, and documentation of software among the software engineering community; (ii) UML is a general-purpose modeling language with extension mechanisms such as stereotypes that let it to be adapted to specific technologies like SOA.

Figure 1. Aspect-oriented product line framework for SOAs

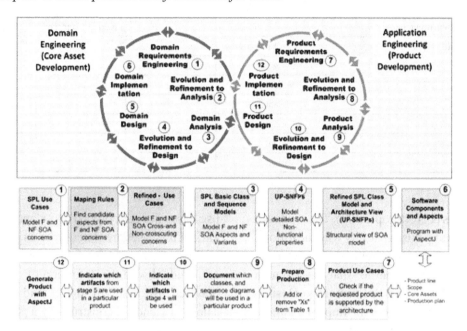

The UML views within each stage of the proposed framework are based on the multiple-view meta-model of SPLs given by (Gomaa & Shin, 2002). The following UML views are used in our approach: use case model view in the Requirements Engineering stage; class and sequence views in the Analysis stage; and subsystem architecture and refined class model views in the Design stage.

It is important to mention that this work only covers the most essential UML views for simplicity in the application of the approach and the chosen views are sufficient to show the benefits of the proposed framework.

Finally, even when other authors like (Gomaa & Shin, 2002) propose the use of collaboration models, sequence models are employed in our framework because they facilitate the view of crosscutting concerns in collaborations with a clear diagram through time.

Activities of the Aspect-Oriented Framework for SPLs

Figure 1 shows the two main activities of the aspect-oriented framework, namely Domain

Engineering and Application Engineering. Each activity has its own development cycle. The arrows indicate that it is an iterative process and that traceability can be done between any stage and between the two activities.

Domain Engineering is the process of SPL engineering in which the commonality and the variability of the product line are defined and realized. Application Engineering is the process of SPL engineering in which the applications of the product line are built by reusing domain artifacts and exploiting the product line variability. Even when Domain Implementation and Product Implementation are shown in Figure 1, they are not deeply explained in this chapter because it is focused on the early development stages.

The following sections explain in detail the Domain and Application Engineering activities and the stages inside them.

Domain Engineering

The Domain Engineering activity maps to the SEI's Core Asset Development activity; its goal is to establish a production capability for prod-

Table 1. Kernel concerns vs. candidate crosscutting concerns

Candidate Crosscutting Concerns		Kernel Concerns		
Optional FRs and NFRs	Variants	*Service 1*		*Service 2*
		Concern 1	*Concern 2*	*Concern n*
Optional use case 1 (FR)	Variant 1		X	
	Variant 2			X
Optional use case 2 (FR)	Variant 3		X	X
NFR1	Variant 4	X	X	
NFR2	Variant 5	X	X	X

ucts (Clements & Northrop, 2002). The proposed framework sets up this capability with the following stages: Domain Requirements Engineering, Evolution and Refinement to Analysis, Domain Analysis, Evolution and Refinement to Design, Domain Design, and Domain Implementation. These stages are explained in the subsequent sections.

Domain Requirements Engineering: Product line's FRs and NFRs define the products and the features of the products in the product line. Requirements common to the entire product line are written with use cases using extension points that can be employed to create product-specific requirements. For example, a use case may extend or include another use case at an extension point.

In addition, the framework uses the following notation for use cases given by (Gomaa, 2004): *Kernel use cases* are those use cases required by all members of the product line. *Optional use cases* are those use cases required by some but not all members of the product line. Some use cases may be *variant*, that is different alternatives of the use case are required by different members of the product line.

The use case categorization among kernel, optional, and variant use cases is depicted using the UML stereotype notation. A stereotype is a classification that defines a new building block that is derived from an existing UML modeling element but is tailored to the specific problem (Booch, Rumbaugh, & Jacobson, 2005). Kernel use cases are stereotyped as <<kernel>>, optional use cases are stereotyped as <<optional>>, and variant use cases are stereotyped as <<variant>>.

In the framework, variation points in use cases are handled with the definition of dependencies between use cases by the extend relationship. The <<extend>> construct is a stereotype of dependency.

Even when it is not common to employ use cases in order to document NFRs, the proposed framework does it because it facilitates the visibility of <<kernel>>, <<optional>>, and <<variant>> NFRs and their impact in the FRs. NFRs have the stereotype <<non-functional>>.

In summary, in the aspect-oriented framework for SPLs, the <<optional>> and <<variant>> use cases extend the <<kernel>> use cases using the <<extend>> stereotype in specific extension points or variation points. If an optional or variant use case is selected for a given member of the product line, then that functionality will be inserted in the use case at the location(s) specified by the variation point.

Evolution and Refinement to Analysis: The first step in this stage is the creation of a kernel concerns vs. candidate crosscutting concerns table (Table 1). Among the crosscutting concerns we include the optional use cases that were recognized in the previous step and NFRs because they crosscut or span multiple services, i.e. the kernel use cases (kernel concerns). In addition, some optional FRs and NFRs have variants that are represented in the Variants column.

Table 2. Mapping rules from domain requirements engineering to domain analysis, and vice versa

1. If an optional use case crosscuts several kernel use cases (kernel concerns), then an aspectual functional case is defined. In other words, a <<functional aspect>> represents an <<optional>> use case
2. If a NFR crosscuts several kernel use cases (kernel concerns), then an aspectual non-functional case is defined. In other words, a <<non-functional aspect>> represents a NFR
3. A <<variant>> use case continues using its representation as <<variant>>
4. When there is a relationship between a <<non-functional aspect>> with a <<kernel>> use case, or between a <<functional aspect>> with a <<kernel>> use case, it is represented with the stereotype <<crosscut>> in the refined use-case model. In a crosscut relationship, a functional or non-functional aspect crosscut the behavior of a kernel concern (base use case). The extending functional or non-functional aspect accomplishes this by inserting additional action sequences into the kernel use case sequence. The crosscutting use cases continue the activity sequence of a kernel use case when the appropriate extension point is reached in the kernel use case and the extension condition is fulfilled. When the extending use case activity sequence is fulfilled, the kernel use case continues.
5. When there is a relationship between a <<variant>> with a <<non-functional aspect>> or <<functional aspect>>, this relationship keeps the <<extend>> relationship

The objective of this stage is to create a bridge between the Domain Requirements Engineering stage and the Domain Analysis stage. It is done with the use of mapping rules (Table 2) to map the concerns (modeled as kernel, optional, and variant use cases) identified in the previous stage with functional aspects, non-functional aspects, and variants in the analysis stage. Use cases can be analyzed as concerns because a concern is the primary motivation for organizing and decomposing software into manageable and comprehensible parts (Ossher & Tarr, 2000).

Table 1 works as a production plan because it shows the kernel and candidate crosscutting concerns from which the products can be produced. This table works as a configuration model to specify products of SPLs with services. In other words, systems analysts can add or remove "Xs" from this table to indicate if a specific feature (optional use case, non-functional requirement, or variant (crosscutting concerns)) is applicable to a specific product during the Application Engineering activity. This table also helps to do forward and backward traceability among stages of the software lifecycle because it shows in a direct way which concerns are involved in the architecture.

After discovering crosscutting concerns, the next step is to define aspects from the established crosscutting concerns and create a refined use case

diagram with them. To do this, the *mapping rules* in Table 2 are proposed:

Domain Analysis: In this stage, the SPL class and sequence models are created. A class model view addresses the static structural aspects of a multiple-view model with classes. A sequence model view is used to determine the interactions in time of collaborations.

The class diagram maps to the Table 1 of kernel concerns vs. candidate crosscutting concerns (it indicates a group of features) and as a result, it is also supported by the use case model view. This is why classes keep the stereotypes of the supporting use cases that were built in the Evolution and Refinement to Analysis stage. Here again, we use the stereotype <<crosscut>> to indicate crosscutting relationships. The class diagram in this stage only shows the attributes of each class; methods are shown in the refined class diagram of the design stage. Supporting classes, such as the ones related to persistence have stereotypes that indicate their role in the diagram; for example, <<techServ.persistence>>.

The sequence diagram illustrates how aspects crosscut the execution of a method. These crosscutting concerns have a <<crosscut>> relationship with the message. The stereotype <<pointcut>> taken from AspectJ (Kiczales et al., 2001), is used to define the points where the aspects crosscut the execution of the program. A pointcut is a name

Figure 2. Notation for sequence diagrams

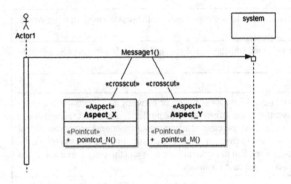

that identifies a set of join points that in turn are well-defined points in the execution of a program (Kiczales et al., 2001). Figure 2 shows the notation to model sequence diagrams in the proposed framework.

Evolution and Refinement to Design: UP-SNFPs (Wada, Suzuki, & Oba, in press), a UML profile to visually detail non-functional properties in UML's class and composite structure diagrams, is used in this stage. UP-SNFPs is designed over two concepts in SOA: *services* and *connections* between services. Services in UP-SNFPs encapsulate subsystems' functions. Each connection defines how services are joined with each other and how messages are exchanged throughout the connection.

In this stage, services, message exchanges, messages, connectors and filters are identified and stereotyped using classes with the following stereotypes respectively: <<service>>, <<messageExchange>>, <<message>>, <<connector>>, and <<filter>>. Relationships and classes inside services and connectors are modeled in the following stage.

Domain Design: In this stage, two model views are built: the refined class model view with attributes and methods, and the subsystem architecture model view which addresses the structural relationships between subsystems.

The following considerations are followed in the refined class model view:

- Aspects are declared using classes with the stereotype <<functional aspect>> or <<non-functional aspect>>.
- Attributes and pointcuts are also shown in every aspect.
- In order to define a pointcut, the following notation is used: +<<*pointcut*>> *pointcutN()*.

The subsystem architecture model view is implemented using UP-SNFPs. These are the considerations in the UP-SNFPs:

- UP-SNFPs is built with the stereotyped classes that were defined in the previous stage.
- Related classes in the refined class diagram with the same target (for example, Request and PersistentRequest where both of them work closely together to manage the requests in a help desk application) are encapsulated into a service.
- If at least one of the classes inside the service has the <<kernel>> stereotype, then the service will have the <<kernel service>> stereotype.
- All the connectors connecting two or more kernel services are also stereotyped with the <<kernel>> stereotype because kernel services cannot interact without them.
- Aspects have <<crosscut>> relationships with the connectors they affect.
- Aspects keep the stereotypes from the previous stages.

Domain Implementation: In this stage, software components and aspects are developed incrementally for systematic reuse across the product line. Incremental software implementation begins with the kernel use cases followed by the optional and variant use cases. The transition from design to implementation is part of future work.

Outputs of the Domain Engineering Activity: The three outputs of this activity are the same outputs of the SEI's Core Asset Development activity (Clements & Northrop, 2002). They are:

1. ***Product line scope:*** It is a description of the products that will constitute the product line or that the product line is capable of including. In general, this description is given in terms of the things that the products all have in common and the ways in which they vary from one another. The UML models and the kernel concerns vs. candidate crosscutting concerns table (Table 1) show commonalities in terms of kernel services, and variabilities in terms of functional and non-functional aspects.

2. ***Core assets:*** Core assets are the basis for the construction of systems in the product line. These assets include the architecture that the products in the product line will share, as well as software components and aspects that are developed for systematic reuse (it is mainly modeled with UP-SNFPs).

Each core asset has an attached process that indicates how it will be used in the development of products. These attached processes are also core assets that are mixed into the production plan for the product line. The kernel concerns vs. candidate crosscutting concerns table (Table 1), the UML models, and the results of the mapping rules in the stages of the proposed framework indicate the way in which the architecture can be used to develop products in terms of aspects.

3. ***Production plan:*** The production plan describes how the products are produced from the core assets. The UML models and the kernel concerns vs. candidate crosscutting concerns table (Table 1) form the production plan for specific products.

Application Engineering

During Application Engineering, individual applications that are members of the SPL are developed. Instead of starting from scratch, the application development makes full use of the artifacts developed during the Domain Engineering activity.

In this activity, product builders use the production plan and recognize the variation points for building a specific product depending on the variabilities that were discovered and defined as functional and non-functional aspects in the Domain Engineering activity.

The following sections describe each one of the stages inside the Application Engineering activity.

Product Requirements Engineering: This stage receives the three outputs from the Domain Engineering Activity: the product line scope, the core assets, and the production plan. It also has extra input that are the requirements for a particular product.

It is possible to know with the product line scope if the requested product can be supported by the architecture that was defined in the Domain Engineering activity. Also, the documentation of the specific product must indicate which use cases that were defined in the Domain Requirements Engineering stage are used in its construction.

Finally, the use case diagram and the documentation that were created in the Domain Requirements Engineering stage are taken as core assets in this stage.

Evolution and Refinement to Analysis: The main element in this stage is the kernel concerns vs. candidate crosscutting concerns table (Table 1). It works as a production plan that describes which products can be produced from the core assets. "Xs" can be added or removed from this table to indicate if a specific optional use case, NFR, or variant is applicable in a specific product.

Product Analysis: Documentation must be given to indicate which classes in the class diagram and sequence diagrams will be used in a particular product. Incompatibilities among a specific set of features can be solved with the analysis of dependencies among features in the kernel concerns vs. candidate crosscutting concerns table (Table 1).

Evolution and Refinement to Design: Documentation is created to indicate which classes, aspects, services, message exchanges, messages, connectors and filters created in the Domain Engineering's Evolution and Refinement to Design stage are going to be used in a particular product.

Product Design: Documentation must indicate which classes, aspects, services, message exchanges, messages, connectors and filters from the Domain Design stage are used in a particular product.

Product Implementation: Classes are woven with aspects in order to generate a particular product. We chose to use the aspect-oriented extension to the Java™ programming language called AspectJ (Kiczales et al., 2001) to exemplify the use of our framework because it is currently the most mature tool in terms of technical development, documentation, and IDE support (The Eclipse Foundation, n.d.).

Case Study: Software Product Line of Help Desks

We illustrate our approach with a SPL of a SOA for help desks used in plant service departments.

There are three roles: Director - he/she is the director of the help desk department. He/she only lists requests; Operator – he/she inputs requests and their specific services, lists requests and services, and updates requests and services; and Solicitant - he/she can submit requests using a Web interface and list his/her requests with their respective services. These three actors must log into the system to do operations over requests and services.

Some products of the product line require the calculation of the operational costs when there is an input request or input service operation. Some products require concurrency control for the input request and input service operations (this is a NFR).

On the other hand, some products of the product line measure the performance of the input request, list requests, input service, and list services operations (this is a NFR). In order to take this measure, some products calculate the execution time of these operations in milliseconds and others in microseconds. The analysis of these calculations can be employed to implement modifications to help to improve the levels of service quality.

In addition, some products notify by e-mail to the solicitant when a new request or service has been input or updated, or to the operator when a solicitant has input a request from the Web interface. These e-mails can be generated in plain text or in enriched formatting.

In brief, the SPL must contain the following services: *Location*, which manages information about buildings, rooms, and departments; *User*, which manages information about users and their roles; *Request*, which manages information about requests and their status; and *Service*, which manages information about services, service types, and technicians who carry out the service.

The following sections briefly present the implementation of the proposed aspect-oriented framework for SPLs in the SPL of help desks for plant service departments.

Domain Engineering

Domain Requirements Engineering: Figure 3 shows the use case diagram for the architecture of help desks with kernel, optional, and variant stereotypes for FRs and NFRs. For example, the Notify by E-mail optional use case (using the <<optional>> stereotype) extends the Input Request kernel use case (using the <<kernel>> stereotype). It means that *some* products of the product line will notify by e-mail to the solicitant when a new request has been input, or to the operator when a solicitant has input a request from the Web interface. Besides, the product can have any of two variants for e-mail generation: plain

Figure 3. Use case diagram for the architecture of help desks with kernel, optional, and variant stereotypes

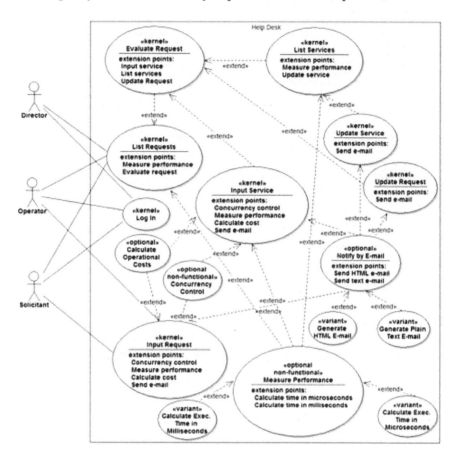

text or enriched formatting (they use the <<variant>> stereotype).

Evolution and Refinement to Analysis: Table 3 shows the kernel concerns vs. candidate crosscutting concerns with variants for two services, *Request* and *Service*, in the SPL of help desks. For example, the *Notify by E-mail* optional functional requirement (use case) has two variants, *Generate HTML E-mail* and *Generate Plain Text E-mail*. These two variants crosscut four kernel concerns of two services; it is indicated by putting "Xs" where the candidate crosscutting concern crosscuts the kernel concern. Figure 4 shows the refined use case diagram with the definition of aspects after applying the mapping rules of Table 2. For example, because the *Notify by E-mail* optional use case crosscuts four kernel concerns,

then the *Notify by E-mail* aspectual functional case is defined (as <<functional aspect>>. The variant use cases continue using their representation as <<variant>>.

Domain Analysis: The class and sequence diagrams were built in this stage. The class diagram kept the stereotypes of the supporting use cases at the Evolution and Refinement to Analysis stage. Sequence diagrams showed the aspects which crosscut the execution of certain methods using pointcuts.

Evolution and Refinement to Design: As an example, when the operator creates a new request, the following artifacts were identified:

- Two services: *User* and *Request*.
- A message exchange: *newRequestMsg*.

Table 3. Kernel concerns vs. candidate crosscutting concerns with variants for the "request" and "service" services in the SPL of help desks

Candidate Crosscutting Concerns		Kernel Concerns						
Optional FRs and NFRs	Variants	*"Request" Service*				*"Service" Service*		
		Input Request	*List Requests*	*Evaluate Request*	*Update Request*	*Input Service*	*List Services*	*Update Service*
Calculate Operational Costs		X				X		
Notify by E-mail	Generate HTML E-mail	X			X	X		X
	Generate Plain Text E-mail	X			X	X		X
Measure Performance	Calculate Exec. Time in Milliseconds	X	X			X	X	
	Calculate Exec. Time in Microseconds	X	X			X	X	
Concurrency Control		X				X		

Figure 4. Use case diagram for the architecture of help desks with aspectual cases

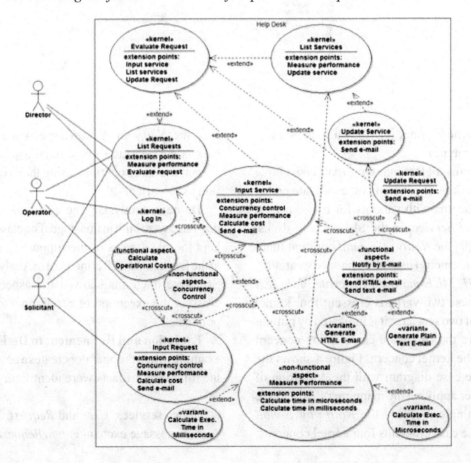

Figure 5. Model with UP-SNFPs when a new request is created by the operator in the SPL of help desks

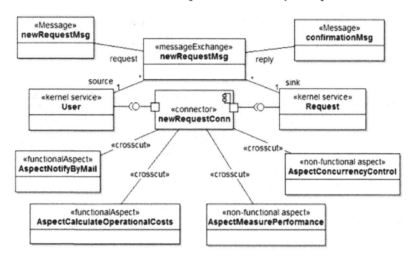

- Two messages: *newRequestMsg* (it demands a new request) and *confirmationMsg* (it replies a confirmation message after the operation has been completed).
- A connector between the two services: *newRequestConn*.
- Two functional aspects which crosscut the execution of *newRequestConn* connector: *AspectNotifyByMail* which sends an e-mail to the solicitant with the information about the new request; and *AspectCalculateOperationalCosts* which calculates the monetary cost of creating a new request.
- Two non-functional aspects which crosscut the execution of *newRequestConn* connector: *AspectMeasurePerformance* which measures the execution time of the operation; and *AspectConcurrencyControl* which controls the concurrency in the operation.

Domain Design: The refined class diagram for the SPL of help desks was drawn at this stage. In addition, the model with UP-SNFPs was created with the message exchanges, messages, connectors, filters, aspects, and classes inside services that were discovered in the previous stage.

Figure 5 shows an example of an UML model defined with UP-SNFPs to depict when the operator creates a new request. In this example, two services (*User* and *Request*) exchange messages. Each service is represented by a class stereotyped with <<kernel service>> because these two services are essencial for all the products in the SPL. Four aspects crosscut the *newRequestConn* connector because there is communication between the *User* service and the *Request* service when a new request is created. The relationship between an aspect and a connector is stereotyped with <<crosscut>>.

Services exchange two messages with the stereotype <<message>>. A class with the stereotype <<messageExchange>> indicates a pair of a request and reply messages (*newRequestMsg* in our example). <<connector>> represents a connection that transmits messages between services.

Domain Implementation: Four aspects (*AspectNotifyByMail*, *AspectCalculateOperationalCosts*, *AspectMeasurePerformance*, and *AspectConcurrencyControl*) were developed in this stage using AspectJ.

Example of Forward and Backward Traceability: Figure 6 summarizes the stages described above with an example showing that it is possible to do forward and backward traceability through

Figure 6. Traceability example with two features

Domain Engineering Stages	Traceability Example of Two Features: Notify by E-mail and Request
Domain Requirements Engineering	<<optional>>Notify by E-mail use case **<<extend>>** <<kernel>>Input Request use case (See Figure 3)
Evolution and Refinement to Analysis	(see table below) (See Table 3 and Figure 4)
Domain Analysis	<<functional aspect>>Notify by E-mail **<<crosscut>>** <<kernel>>Input Request
Evolution and Refinement to Design	List of artifacts which contains: *Request* service and *AspectNotifyByMail* functional aspect
Domain Design	Model with UP-SNFPs which contains <<kernel service>>Request and <<functionalAspect>>AspectNotifyByMail (See Figure 5)

Candidate Crosscutting Concerns		Kernel Concern
Optional FRs and NFRs	Variants	"Request" Service
Notify by E-mail	Generate HTML E-mail	X
	Generate Plain Text E-mail	X

the domain engineering stages of an optional use case (Notify by E-mail, in red) and a kernel use case (Input Request, in blue). Double-head arrows indicate traceability in both directions.

Application Engineering

In the creation of an application named "App1" based on the SPL architecture for help desks, we had to find out if this product could be built according to the product line scope. In order to do that, we had to list the use cases that App1 requires: Log In, Input Request, List Requests, Evaluate Request, Update Request, Input Service, List Services, Update Service, Calculate Operational Costs, Notify by E-mail (with only one variant: Generate Plain Text E-mail), and Measure Performance (with only one variant: Calculate Execution Time in Milliseconds). The Concurrency Control use case was not required. We concluded that all of the required use cases with their variations and extensions were supported by the architecture.

In the Evolution and Refinement to Analysis stage, the following "Xs" were removed from the variant's column: Generate HTML E-mail and Calculate Execution Time in Microseconds. Besides, the "X" related to the NFR Concurrency Control was also removed. These "Xs" were taken away because they are not required by App1.

In the Product Analysis stage, it was found that the following features did not have to be used in App1: Generate HTML E-mail, Calculate Execution Time in Microseconds, and Concurrency Control. Also, *AspectConcurrencyControl* was not used in App1 and as a result *Concurrency* and *ConcurrencyPer* were not used. Also, only the sequence diagrams related to the use cases used in App1 had to be considered.

In the Evolution and Refinement to Design stage, *AspectConcurrencyControl* was not included in the list of artifacts of the model with UP-SNFPs for App1. In the Design stage, the refined class model and the model with UP-SNFPs for App1 did not have *AspectConcurrencyControl*.

Table 4. Framework's goals, metrics, explanation of the metrics, and results (NF = No-Framework. UF = Using Framework)

Framework Goals	Metrics	Explanation	Results
Low Coupling: An object X is coupled to object Y if and only if X sends a message to Y	Coupling between object classes	A count of the number of other classes to which a class is coupled	NF = 4.08 UF = 1.06
	Response for a class	A count of the number of local methods of a class plus the number of methods called by local methods	NF = 11 UF = 9.48
High Cohesion: The degree to which the methods within a class are related to one another	Cohesion due to cross-cutting	The number of concerns for each module (class or aspect)	NF = 1.4 UF = 1
Low Complexity: The degree to which a system has a design that is difficult to understand and verify	Weighted methods per class	A count of the methods within a class	NF = 6.92 UF = 6.6

Performance Metrics

In order to measure the effectiveness of the framework, four metrics were applied on the SPL of help desks, one using the framework and another without the framework. Table 4 shows the framework's goals, performance metrics to measure the achievement of these goals, the explanation of each metric, and the results after applying the metrics. The metrics were measured at the design level. The definitions of the metrics were taken from (Benn et al., 2005).

The following paragraphs explain the results of each one of the metrics used in this study:

- **Coupling between Object Classes:** The average coupling among object classes for the no-framework approach is 4.08 (102 method calls to other classes / 25 classes) and the average coupling among object classes using the framework is 1.06 (40 method calls to other classes / 25 classes). In brief, the coupling between object classes is reduced by 74.01%. It is because various method calls were placed in the four aspects (*Aspect Notify By Mail, Aspect Calculate Operational Costs, Aspect Measure Performance*, and *Aspect Concurrency Control*).

- **Response for a Class:** The average response for a class is 11 in the no-framework approach ((173 methods + 102 method calls) / 25 classes) and 9.48 for the framework approach ((165 methods + 40 method calls from classes + 70 method calls from aspects) / (25 classes + 4 aspects)). It means that, with the framework, the number of methods and the number of methods called by local methods can decrease. This result is because various methods and method calls were encapsulated in the four aspects.

- **Cohesion Due to Crosscutting:** According to Benn (2005), cohesion of each class can be determined by looking at how many concerns it implements. For the no-framework approach it is 1.4 (35 concerns in 25 classes); some classes even encapsulated 5 concerns. Cohesion was improved with the framework because only one concern was encapsulated by class. It is a 28.57% improvement (one concern per class is the 71.43% of 1.4; so, 100% minus 71.43% equals 28.57%).

- **Weighted Methods per Class:** This metric was used to measure the complexity of the system by counting the methods within a class. There is an average of 6.92 weighted methods per class for the no-framework approach (173 methods / 25 classes) and an average of 6.6 weighted methods using the framework (165 methods / 25 classes). The small difference in the results is because not so many methods were affected by the aspects.

FUTURE WORK

The first area of future work is to address model-to-code traceability. The second area is to work on extending the framework to support the testing of SOAs in SPLs. We will also improve the scalability of the current notation for larger SPLs. In the current version of the framework, a model engineer must manually add the crosscut extension to all of the associations (see for example Figure 2). This manual tagging of modeling elements is difficult to scale and as a result it makes it important to build an automation tool. With this tool, we will apply model-driven development techniques to automatically generate models and code for specific products by means of transformation rules.

Also, we will formalize a way to model aspects' dependencies at the Domain Analysis phase; for example, an aspect providing encryption and an aspect providing digital signatures for messages have inter-dependencies and should be executed in correct order.

We will also work on a method for composing aspectual models which will be based on the use of UML. This work will be supported by (Whittle, Araújo, & Moreira, 2006).

Finally, in the current proposal, concerns are identified within a single SOA (i.e. a SPL where each product share the same architecture). However, non-functional features, such as the "Notify by Email" and "Measure Performance" concerns from the example case, are quite typically reusable also in a wider context, i.e. between different SOAs and SPLs. That's why a mechanism to manage concerns among different SOAs and SPLs will be built.

CONCLUSION

This chapter presented a framework that uses AOSD in order to manage variability of NFRs from the early stages of the SPL lifecycle of SOAs. It is related to the Core Asset Development and Product Development essential activities described in the Framework for SPL Practice of the SEI and uses the UML to model variability.

These are the conclusions after analyzing the framework and applying the metrics:

- The framework supports early development stages by easy-to-follow instructions.
- The framework provided traceability support from the very beginning in the construction of the case study. Forward and backward traceability was easily done with the UML models, conversion rules, and the table of concerns vs. candidate crosscutting concerns (Table 1). Figure 6 shows a traceability example.
- It was simple to analyze and modularize crosscutting concerns because the framework allows the encapsulation of variability in FRs and NFRs using aspects.
- The framework provides reuse support because it makes it flexible to reuse kernel, optional, and variant artifacts throughout the lifecycle.
- Variability is easily managed using aspects that can be plugged or unplugged from the SPL in order to create new customized products.
- The use of aspect-orientation in the framework has the following advantages: greater facility to analyze concerns because they are separated and have a minimal dependency among them; greater facility to evolve and make modifications in the software; modifications in a concern have a minimal impact on other concerns; more reusable artifacts that can be coupled and decoupled whenever it is necessary.

- The use of early aspects in the framework allows to get the benefits of aspect-orientation not just at the implementation stage, but also in the activities of requirements, analysis, and design. Also, early aspects help to anticipate the reasoning about aspects and their impact in the software development.
- Finally, the coupling between object classes can be dramatically decreased, the average number of methods and methods called by local methods can decrease, and cohesion is improved using the framework as shown in Table 4.

REFERENCES

Alférez, G. H., & Poonphon, S. (2007). An aspect-oriented product line framework to support the development of software product lines of Web applications. *International Journal of the Computer, the Internet and Management, 15*(SP4), 13.1-13.5. Retrieved February 14, 2008, from http://www.ijcim.th.org/v15nSP4.htm

Anastasopoulos, M., & Gacek, C. (2001). Implementing product line variabilities. In N. David (Ed.), *Symposium on Software Reusability: Putting Software Reuse in Context, 2001. ACM SIGSOFT software engineering notes,* (pp. 109-117). New York: ACM.

Anastasopoulos, M., & Muthig, D. (2004). An evaluation of aspect-oriented programming as a product line implementation technology. In D.C. Schmidt (Ed.), *8th International Conference, ICSR 2004. Software reuse: methods, techniques and tools,* (pp. 141-156). London: Springer-Verlag.

Bachmann, F., & Clements, P. (2005). *Variability in software product lines.* (Tech. Rep. No. CMU/SEI-2005-TR-012, ESC-TR-2005-012). Carnegie Mellon University, Software Engineering Institute. Pittsburgh, Pennsylvania.

Baniassad, E., Clements, P., Araújo, A., Moreira, A., Rashid, A., & Tekinerdogan, B. (2006). Discovering early aspects. *IEEE Software, 23*(1), 61–70. doi:10.1109/MS.2006.8

Benn, J., Constantinides, C., Padda, H. K., Pedersen, K. H., Rioux, F., & Ye, X. (2005). Reasoning on software quality improvement with aspect-oriented refactoring: A case study. In Tsai, W. T., & Hamza, M. H. (Eds.), *Software engineering and applications, 2005.* Phoenix: ACTA Press.

Bergey, J., Fisher, M., Gallagher, B., Jones, L., & Northrop, L. (2000). *Basic concepts of product line practice for the DoD.* (Tech. Rep. CMU/SEI-2000-TN-001). Carnegie Mellon University, Software Engineering Institute. Pittsburgh, Pennsylvania.

Bichler, M., & Lin, K. (2006). Service-oriented computing. *IEEE Computer, 39*(6), 99–101.

Booch, G., Rumbaugh, J., & Jacobson, I. (2005). *The unified modeling language user guide* (2nd ed.). Upper Saddle River, NJ: Addison-Wesley Professional.

Brownsword, L., Clemens, P., & Olsson, U. (1996). *Successful product line engineering: A case study.* Paper presented at the Software Technology Conference, Salt Lake City, UT.

Carnegie Mellon University, Software Engineering Institute. (2008). *Product line hall of fame.* Retrieved July 16, 2008, from http://www.sei.cmu.edu/productlines/plp_hof.html

Chitchyan, R., Rashid, A., Sawyer, P., Garcia, A., Pinto, M., Bakker, J., et al. (2005). *Survey of analysis and design approaches.* (Tech. Rep. No. AOSD-Europe-ULANC-9). AMPLE Project.

Clarke, S., & Baniassad, E. (2005). *Aspect-oriented analysis and design. The theme approach.* Amsterdam: Addison-Wesley Longman.

Clements, P., & Northrop, L. (2002). *Software product lines: Practices and patterns.* Boston: Addison-Wesley Professional.

Colyer, A., Rashid, A., & Blair, G. (2004). *On the separation of concerns in program families.* (Tech. Rep. COMP-001-2004). Bailrigg, Lancaster: Lancaster University, Computing Department.

Diskstra, E. (1976). *A discipline of programming.* Englewood Cliffs, N.J.: Prentice-Hall.

Filman, R. E., Elrad, T., Clarke, S., & Aksit, M. (2004). *Aspect-oriented software development.* Reading, MA: Addison-Wesley Professional.

Geyer, L., & Becker, M. (2002). On the influence of variabilities on the application-engineering process of a product family. In J. Bosch, F. Van der Linden, C.W. Krueger, & M. Becker (Eds.), *2nd International Conference on Software Product Lines. Software product line.* (pp. 1-14). London: Springer-Verlag.

Gomaa, H. (2004). *Designing software product lines with UML: From use cases to pattern-based software architectures.* Boston: Addison-Wesley Professional.

Gomaa, H., & Shin, M. (2002). Multiple-view meta-modeling of software product lines. In S. Liu (Ed.), *8th IEEE International Conference on Engineering of Complex Computer Systems. Proceedings of the Eighth International Conference on Engineering of Complex Computer Systems,* (pp. 238-246). Washington: IEEE Computer Society.

Heo, S., & Man, E. (2006). Representation of variability in software product line using aspect-oriented programming. In S. Kawada (Ed.), *Proceedings of the 4th International Conference on Software Engineering Research, Management and Applications,* (pp. 66-73). Washington: IEEE Computer Society.

Huntley, K., & San Filippo, D. (2006). Enabling aspects to enhance service-oriented architecture. *The Architecture Journal,* 7. Retrieved July 28, 2008, from http://msdn.microsoft.com/en-us/arcjournal/bb245654.aspx

Jacobson, I., Booch, G., & Rumbaugh, J. (2002). *The unified software development process.* Upper Saddle River, NJ: Addison-Wesley.

Kiczales, G., Hilsdale, E., Hugunin, J., Kersten, M., Palm, J., & Grisworld, W. G. (2001). An overview of aspectJ. In J.L. Knudsen (Ed.), *Proceedings of the 15th European Conference on Object-Oriented Programming.* (pp. 327-353). London: Springer-Verlag.

Kiczales, G., Lamping, J., Mendhekar, A., Maeda, C., Lopes, C., Loingtier, J., et al. (1997). Aspect-oriented programming. In M. Aksit & S. Matsuoka (Eds.), *European Conference on Object-Oriented Programming. Proceedings of the European conference on object-oriented programming* (pp. 220-242). Berlin, Heidelberg & New York: Springer-Verlag.

Krueger, C. W. (2008). *Benefits of software product lines.* Retrieved July 20, 2008, from http://www.softwareproductlines.com/benefits/benefits.html

Newcomer, E., & Lomow, G. (2004). *Understanding SOA with Web services.* Upper Saddle River, NJ: Addison-Wesley Professional.

Northrop, L. (2006). *Software product lines: Reuse that makes business sense.* Paper presented at the Australian Software Engineering Conference, Sydney, Australia.

Ossher, H., & Tarr, P. (2000). *Multi-dimensional separation of concerns and the hyperspace approach.* (Tech. Rep. No. 21452). Yorktown Heights, NY: IBM, T.J. Watson Research Center.

Palo Alto Research Center. Xerox Corporation. (2008). *Frequently asked questions about AspectJ.* Retrieved July 21, 2008, from: http://www.eclipse.org/aspectj/doc/released/faq.html

Papazoglou, M. (2003). Service-oriented computing: Concepts, characteristics and directions. In T. Catarci, M. Mecella, J. Mylopoulos & M.E. Orlowska (Eds.), *Proceedings of the 4th International Conference on Web Information Systems Engineering.* (pp. 3-12). Washington: IEEE Computer Society Press.

Pohl, C., Rummler, A., Gasiunas, V., Loughran, N., Arboleda, H., & Fernandes, F. A. (2007). *Survey of existing implementation techniques with respect to their support for the requirements identified in M3.2. (Tech. Rep. No. AMPLE D3.1).* AMPLE Project.

Pohl, K., Böckle, G., & Van der Linden, F. (2005). *Software product line engineering, foundations, principles, and techniques.* Berlin: Springer-Verlag.

Rashid, A., Moreira, A., & Araújo, J. (2003). Modularization and composition of aspectual requirements. In W.G. Griswold (Ed.), *Proceedings of the 2nd International Conference on Aspect-Oriented Software Development.* (pp. 11-20). Boston: ACM.

Tarr, P., Ossher, H., Harrison, W., & Sutton, S. M. (1999). N degrees of separation: Multi-dimensional separation of concerns. In B. Boehm (Ed.), *Proceedings of the 21st International Conference on Software Engineering.* (pp. 107-119). Los Alamitos: IEEE Computer Society Press.

The Eclipse Foundation. (2007). *AspectJ, crosscuting objects for better modularity.* Retrieved July 23, 2008, from: http://www.eclipse.org/aspectj/

Voelter, M., & Groher, I. (2007). Product line implementation using aspect-oriented and model-driven software development. In K. Chul Kang (Ed.), *Proceedings of the 11th International Software Product Line Conference (SPLC 2007).* (pp. 233-242).

Wada, H., Suzuki, J., & Oba, K. (2008). *Early aspects for non-functional properties in service oriented business processes.* Paper presented at the IEEE Congress on Services, SOA Standards Symposium, Hawaii, USA.

Wada, H., Suzuki, J., & Oba, K. (in press). A model-driven development framework for non-functional aspects in service oriented architecture. *Journal of Web Services Research.*

Whittle, J., Araújo, J., & Moreira, A. (2006). Composing aspect models with graphs and transformations. In P.C. Clements (Ed), *Proceeding of the 2006 International Workshop on Early Aspects at ICSE International Conference on Software Engineering.* (pp. 59-65). New York: ACM.

Workshop, A.-O. M. (2007). *Aspect oriented modeling.* Retrieved July 20, 2008, from http://www.aspect-modeling.org/

Chapter 12
Model–Driven Approach for End–to–End SOA Security Configurations

Fumiko Satoh
IBM Research – Tokyo, Japan

Yuichi Nakamura
IBM Research – Tokyo, Japan

Nirmal K. Mukhi
IBM Research – Thomas J. Watson Research Center, USA

Michiaki Tatsubori
IBM Research – Tokyo, Japan

Kouichi Ono
IBM Research – Tokyo, Japan

ABSTRACT

The configuration of non-functional requirements, such as security, has become important for SOA applications, but the configuration process has not been discussed comprehensively. In current development processes, the security requirements are not considered in upstream phases and a developer at a downstream phase is responsible for writing the security configuration. However, configuring security requirements properly is quite difficult for developers because the SOA security is cross-domain and all required information is not available in the downstream phase. To resolve this problem, this chapter clarifies how to configure security in the SOA application development process and defines the developer's roles in each phase. Additionally, it proposes a supporting technology to generate security configurations: Model-Driven Security. The authors propose a methodology for end-to-end security configuration for SOA applications and tools for generating detailed security configurations from the requirements specified in upstream phases model transformations, making it possible to configure security properly without increasing developers' workloads.

DOI: 10.4018/978-1-60566-794-2.ch012

INTRODUCTION

Service-Oriented Architecture (SOA) is an important concept that is useful for building applications for enterprise business processes, because an application based on SOA can change its business processes flexibly. Unfortunately, the processes for secure configurations have not been discussed sufficiently, even though security is one of the most important concerns for enterprise applications. Currently, the security properties tend to be ignored until the downstream development phases, and the developers in the downstream phases must manage the configurations. The resulting problems are that the downstream developers do not have sufficient information to create correct configurations and that the configurations themselves are too complex for developers who are not security experts.

This chapter discusses a security configuration process and defines the responsibilities of developers. To configure security correctly, various kinds of information are required, such as business security requirements and platform information. This information is not available at any single downstream development phase, so this chapter defines the developer's roles from the perspective of the information that is available during each development phase. Thanks to the chapter's proposed process, all of the developers can concentrate on their own responsibilities for the configuration.

Even if the configuration process is defined clearly, configuring security correctly is quite difficult because SOA security is so complex and the security domain federation must be considered. This chapter also proposes a supporting technology to create concrete configurations: Model-Driven Security. This contributes to generating correct configurations while reducing developers' workloads.

The remainder of this chapter is structured as follows. The background of and problems in the current configuration processes are discussed in the next section, and then the End-to-End security configuration process is proposed. The supporting technology is discussed; the security configuration process is demonstrated, and related work is discussed.

SOA SECURITY CONFIGURATION PROCESS

Security Domain Federation

The SOA approach develops applications by assembling computing system components called *services* which may be located on various platforms. These platforms may support their own security technologies, such as Kerberos or PKI, so the different security technologies should be integrated to secure all of the SOA application. This integration is called a security domain federation.

Web Services Security (WS-Security) (Web Services Security, 2006) is one of the security technologies that is typically used for SOA applications. WS-Security proposes a framework for a security federation (IBM and Microsoft, 2002) in which we can integrate various security technologies. Figure 1 shows a typical security federation framework. To exchange secured messages using WS-Security, a requester and a provider should share a common key as a security token. Suppose the service requester provides a username token that includes its own ID and password, but the service provider requests some another kind of token such as a SAML token. The WS-Security federation framework can exchange these different kinds of security tokens using an intermediary server called a security token service (STS). The requester sends a request for a security token exchange and its username token to the STS, and then the STS authenticates the requester and issues the SAML token for the requester to connect to the provider. Then the requester can send a secured message to the provider by using the issued SAML token.

Figure 1. Security domain federation by WS-security

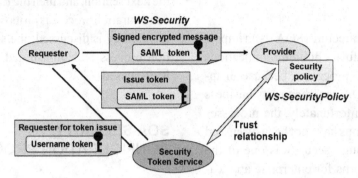

The federation model is the simplest one, but other extensible federation models have been proposed. The configuration for a security domain federation can be quite complex, because developers must fully understand the federation platforms including the STS. The difficulties of the security configurations are the focal issues in this chapter, and we clarify these problems in the next section.

Motivating Example: Travel Reservation Service

In order to explore the features of security federation with WS-Security, we have investigated a sample application for Supply Chain Management (SCM) as proposed by a Web services interoperability organization (WS-I, 2003). The SCM application is a typical multi-party business transaction where buyers, retailers and manufacturers interact with each other. When we applied WS-Security to the SCM application to secure it, we found that identity (ID) propagation is one of the most difficult aspects. For example, after receiving a buyer ID, a retailer has to propagate it to a manufacturer by transforming it so that the manufacturer can process it. The transformation is not simple because the retailer has to perform various tasks such as ID transformation by invoking STS, and use message protection with digital signatures and encryption.

In this chapter, we use the simple travel agency application in Figure 2 to simplify the SCM application, while retaining the key features of federation with WS-Security. This application is a composite application which consists of two services: Travel Agency service and Airline service. A customer asks the travel agency to reserve a travel, and then the agency transfers customer's information such as frequent flier account number (FFAN) to the airline to get the flight reservation. Then the airline reserves a seat on a flight for the customer. Here are the security requirements.

- The exchanged messages should be signed and encrypted.
- The travel agency authenticates each customer with an ID and password.
- The airline requires the customer's FFAN to reserve a flight.
- The airline only trusts the customer information that was transferred from a trusted travel agency.

In this service, the airline delegates the customer's authentication to the travel agency, which is an intermediate service, and then receives the customer's FFAN transformed from the customer's authenticated ID. We call this authentication mechanism "ID propagation". The airline asks for the travel agency's signature to check if the agency can be trusted. In this application,

Figure 2. Travel reservation service

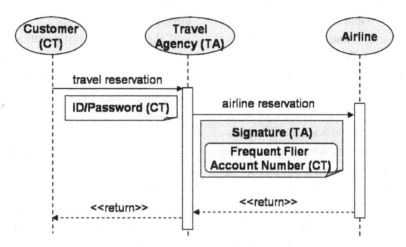

the customer's FFAN is sent by embedding it in an SAML token, and therefore the travel agency should sign the customer's SAML token with its own X.509 certificate.

To implement these requirements for the travel agency, the security configuration should be correctly configured, but it is quite difficult. Here we show the architecture of the travel agency service

executed in WebSphere Application Server (WAS) V6.1 (IBM, 2005a) in Figure 3. The WS-Security messages are processed by the WS-Security handler in WAS. The inbound WS-Security message is received by the inbound WSS handler to validate the signatures and encryptions. In this example, the username token including the customer's ID and password is authenticated using the associated

Figure 3. WebSphere WS-security runtime architecture

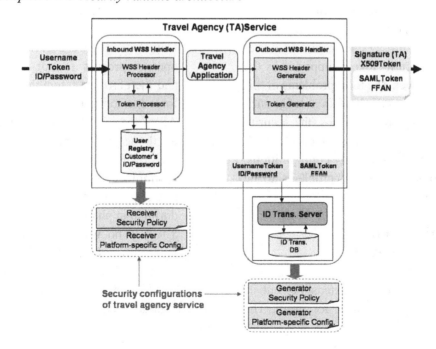

user registry. The outbound WSS Handler sends the authenticated username token to the external ID transformation server, and the server returns the transformed SAML token. The agency service receives the SAML token and signs it, and then transfers it to the airline service.

The security configuration for WS-Security includes both the security policies and the platform-specific configuration files required by WS-Security handlers. The security policy is standardized based on WS-SecurityPolicy by OASIS (OASIS, 2007), and the platform-specific configuration files are Deployment Descriptors and Binding Configurations which are configuration files for WAS V6.1. They describe more detailed information rather than the security policies. The difficulties of the security configuration do not come from the complexity of the configuration descriptions. The main cause of the difficulties is that the required knowledge and information are complicated and located in different development processes. For example, we need to know which user registry is used for customer's authentication by the travel agency. Also, we should know the types of security tokens and signatures required by the airline. Not only the information about the infrastructure for the travel agency, but external information is required, such as an URI of the ID transformation server and the types of security tokens supported by the transformation server. The focal problems of this article are that various kinds of knowledge such as the WS-Security specifications, the security platforms, and the security requirements for each service are required for security configurations. The next section clarifies the problems to be considered here.

Problems of Current Security Configuration

WS-Security is flexible and extensible, but its configuration is quite difficult for users. The methodology of security configurations for SOA applications has not been sufficiently discussed, and the security configuration is not included in the current application development process that follows the recommended steps (Chessell, & Schmidt-Wesche, 2006; High, Kinder, & Graham, 2005):

1. A business analyst clarifies the business requirements and creates a business process model.
2. A software architect designs service assemblies to satisfy the business requirements and creates a service model.
3. A developer develops and tests the atomic services.
4. An assembler assembles the atomic services to implement the application according to the service model created by the software architect.
5. A deployer deploys the application on the target platform.

The security requirements are not considered in the upstream phases, but are left to the downstream phases. The current configuration process creates the following problems:

*   How to configure security in the development process is not clearly defined, and therefore an assembler or deployer is forced to configure it.
*   All of the information required to configure the security correctly is not available in the downstream development phases. An assembler cannot obtain all of the information required for the security configuration during that phase.
*   There is no way to know what security is required from the business requirements and if the security-related business requirements are satisfied in the final configuration.

We present a methodology for security configuration and define roles for developers from the perspective of what information is available at each phase in the development process. In addition, we describe supporting technologies to generate complex security configurations automatically.

MODEL-DRIVEN SECURITY

End-to-End Security Configuration

In an SOA development process, developers handle data with granularities corresponding to the associated phases. For example, a service architect deals with composite services that are used to build a business process and does not know the details of the service implementations and execution environments. At a downstream phase, an assembler is responsible for the atomic services and implementations, which are the components of the composite services.

For the security configuration, various kinds of information are required and not all of it can be handled in one development phase. Therefore, we clarify the security configuration process by considering what information should be handled in each phase.

1. A business analyst is responsible for clarifying the business-level requirements, so the security requirements should be clarified as business-level policies defined by the business processes.
2. A software architect creates a concrete service model to satisfy the business process model, and hence the security requirements for the composite services should be specified in the service model.
3. An assembler should create security configuration files for each atomic service to meet the security requirements from Phase (2).

4. A deployer sets up the platform that runs the services for the secure service execution, and deploys the configuration to the target platform.

The developer has no role in configuring security because WS-Security specifies that the service will be secured by deploying security configuration files with a non-secured service implementation. Therefore, the developer who implements the non-secured services has no role in configuring the security.

The security configuration for WS-Security is quite complicated so that it is difficult for developers to configure it correctly even if the configuration process is defined. Therefore we propose a supporting technology named Model-Driven Security that service architects and assemblers can use in generating the complicated configuration files.

Model-Driven Security (MDS) is a technology to generate the concrete security configuration files by model transformations from the abstracted security requirements specified by a software architect. A software architect can specify the security requirements using keywords called "security intents", such as "integrity" and "confidentiality". The security intents can be transformed into the security configurations which should be created by an assembler using model-driven technologies. This model transformation requires the platform information that comes from a deployer, and therefore we propose a new model for the platform information. Each security configuration is created from a model of the platform information. In the following sections, the details of these technologies are discussed.

Model-Driven Configuration Process

In the previous section, we clarify the developers' roles in the security configuration. To support their roles, we propose a security configuration process based on Model-Driven Security, as shown in Figure 4. Here we suppose a software architect models an application to meet application requirements from business-level requirements. This model is assumed to be a platform-independent model, and hence the model has no information related to the security platform or technologies. Also, an assembler is responsible for creating concrete security configurations with the platform-specific information such as whether or not the security platform can support SAML tokens. Hence the security configuration can be regarded as a platform-specific model, and this model should satisfy the requirements of the platform-independent model created by the architect. The Model-Driven Security configuration process can support the creation of a correct platform-specific model.

In Model-Driven Security, a business analyst first defines the business-level security requirements. Then a software architect creates a service model and adds intents, which are abstract keywords representing security requirements, to each service in the model. The intents are transformed into the concrete security configurations by

model transformations executed by an assembler. To generate concrete configurations from the abstract intents, detailed information is required, such as the security technologies supported in the platform and the business-level requirements for the platform. The required platform information is modeled as a security infrastructure model (SIM) which is created by a deployer, and the SIM is referred to when the concrete configurations are generated. MDS can generate security configurations semi-automatically by just adding intents to a service model created by a software architect.

In the SOA application development process a software architect deals with a service model that is independent of the platform infrastructure. There are several model definitions which can be used as service models. The "UML 2.0 Profile for Software Services" (ServiceProfile) (Johnston, 2005) is the UML profile for software services and provides a common language for describing services. The Service Component Architecture (SCA) (OASIS, 2007a) defines a component model to describe how to assemble service components.

Figure 4. Model-driven security configuration

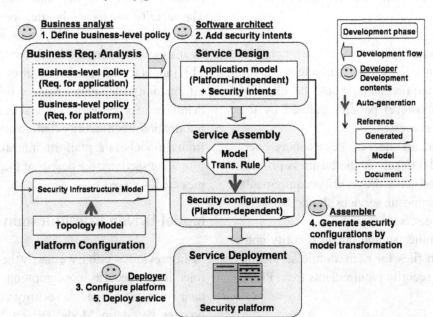

In this chapter, we assume these two models will be used as service models by software architects.

In the following, we explain the business level policy, the security intents, and the platform model called the security infrastructure model.

Business Level Policy

The Business Level Policy expresses the security requirements for the application based on the business requirements, and we assume that it is described in documents such as the Service Level Agreement (SLA). The Business Level Policy is also assumed to specify any requirements or restrictions for the platform defined from the application characteristics, not just the security requirements for the application itself. Hence, we define two kinds of requirements that make up the Business Level Policy:

Requirements for the application

- Requirements for service authentication, signatures, or encryptions
- Requirements for signature or encryption on data

Requirements for the security platform

- Requirements for the keys, such as key type or key length
- Algorithms for signatures and encryptions
- Trusted certification organization
- User registries used for authentication

Here are some concrete examples of possible security platform requirements: The messages of the application should be encrypted with a 256-bit AES algorithm and require signatures using X.509v3 certification authorized by Verisign, because the application needs to be secured to handle customer IDs and passwords. The platform requirements will be referred to when the Security Infrastructure Model (SIM) is generated, and the generated SIM will include these platform require-

ments. The concrete security configurations are generated automatically from the requirements for the application and the generated SIM, and hence the generated configurations will satisfy the requirements of the Business Level Policy.

This chapter assumes that the business level policies are translated by a domain expert who has expertise in the methods of applying the business requirements to service implementations. The methods for translation from business level policies into the security requirements are beyond the scope of this chapter. There are many existing reports on how to create security configurations from business level requirements, and we can use any of these methodologies. Therefore we do not concretely define how to describe the Business Level Requirements in this chapter and simply accept that the SLA document is written in a natural language. A business analyst should interpret the SLA and translate the requirements defined in the SLA into the security requirements for the application. Then the security requirements are passed to the next development phase and a software architect can create the application model satisfying those security requirements.

Security Intents

A software architect applies the security requirements in abstract form to a service model. Here we assume the use of the "UML 2.0 Profile for Software Services" (ServiceProfile) (Johnston, 2005) and the Service Component Architecture (SCA) (OASIS, 2007a) as a service model. The SCA model has a mechanism to specify security requirements using abstract keywords, but ServiceProfile has no mechanism for applying security requirements, and therefore we define the UML profile for WS-Security for security intents. WS-Security assures the following security requirements: *authentication*, *integrity*, and *confidentiality* (IBM and Microsoft, 2002). We define the security intents for WS-Security for ServiceProfile as shown in Table 1. The

Table 1. Security intents for ServiceProfile

Requirements	Stereoptype	Attribute
Authentication	authentication	userType
Integrity	integrity	userType
Confidentiality	confidentiality	userType

authentication stereotype means that a security token for a user authentication is required, and the *integrity* and *confidentiality* stereotypes specify the requirements for message signature and encryption, respectively. A software architect can apply authentication requirements to a service by adding an *authentication* stereotype and certified subject name as a value of a *userType* attribute.

SCA has a policy specification (OASIS, 2007b) that specifies security policies for an SCA model. The SCA policy has policy intents that are the same as the intents for ServiceProfile, and they can be applied to elements in an SCA model. Applying policies to SCA models seems easy, but there are some difficulties in specifying policies correctly, because a service component of an SCA may have a recursive structure and the intents may be applied recursively. A software architect should watch out for any inconsistent intents. This is hard for the architects, so we propose a technology to support software architects in the section "Pattern-based Intent Configuration."

Security Infrastructure Model

In MDS, security intents are transformed into concrete security configurations. When WebSphere Application Server (IBM, 2005a) is used as the application server, two kinds of configuration files are required: a security policy and a platform-specific binding configuration. Security intents are platform-independent, but the concrete configurations are dependent on the platforms. Therefore detailed platform-related information is required in the model transformation. We assume that the platform information is modeled by a deployer as a topology model which represents

the physical connections of the nodes. We use the Security Infrastructure Model (SIM) to hold the platform information required for concrete configuration generation.

Figure 5 shows a meta-model of the SIM. We assume that a deployer configures the WS-Security parameters for each node, and the SIM can be generated semi-automatically from these parameters. The generation rules for the SIM are different for different types of nodes, but the generation rules can be defined as simple mapping rules between the SIM elements and the node parameters, except for the Mapping element and the TrustMethod element of the SIM. The Mapping element and the TrustMethod element need to be specified by a deployer who manually references the platform requirements in the business level policies. The principal elements of the SIM are:

- A TokenAssertion element is an abstract element to specify the security token types supported by a node. The relationship between the TokenAssertion element and the MachineNode element shows how to use the security token in that node, such as for "inboundAuthentication", "outboundAuthentication", or "inboundSignature".
- A Mapping element connects two security tokens which can be exchanged by an ID transformation. This element should be specified by a deployer by referring to the information in the user registries for the security token authentication.
- A TrustMethod element specifies how to trust a transferred security token. In the travel reservation service, the transferred customer's SAML token is trusted because of the travel agency's signature on the SAML token. In this case, the trust method is called a "Signature", so the TrustMethod element has a "Signature" value in the method attribute. We have other kinds of trust methods, such as the "Basic" trust method that signifies basic authentication

Figure 5. Security infrastructure meta-model for WAS 6.1

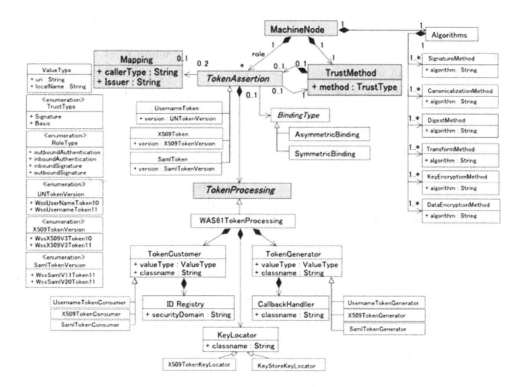

of the travel agency service is required for the transferred customer token. This type of element is specified manually by a deployer.

- TokenProcessing element specifies the parameters used to process a security token specified by a TokenAssertion element. The child elements of the TokenProcessing element depend on the types of nodes. Figure 5 models the WebSphere Application Service V6.1 (IBM, 2005a) as a node type. A security token is generated by a class specified by a classname attribute of the TokenGenerator element. EachTokenConsumer element specifies

- A classname that is invoked when a security token is processed at the receiver side. The TokenGenerator and TokenConsumer classes are invoked for a security token with a type specified by a valueType attribute. The TokenGenerator and TokenConsumer

elements are specialized by types of security tokens, such as X509TokenGenerator. If any custom input (such as random values) is required to generate a security token, the information is modeled by attributes of each specialized token generator and its consumer elements. KeyLocator element specifies a classname which implements methods to get cryptographic keys for generating signatures and for doing encryption. The user information used for authentication is stored in an ID registry element and returned by the CallbackHandler element class.

The model transformation from security intents into security configurations requires information about the execution node. The security intents are mapped to the SIM which corresponds to the execution platform of the services as shown in Figure 6, and then the intents can be transformed into concrete security configurations. The SIM is used to get the required information instead of referring to the specific configuration of each node, and therefore we can define model transformation rules for security policies that are independent of the node types. In contrast, the transformation rules for platform-specific configurations depend on the node types. In the next section, we will show how to generate the configurations by reducing the platform dependencies of the transformation rules.

MODEL TRANSFORMATION

This section discusses the details of model transformations from the platform-independent model (PIM) into the platform-specific model (PSM), the transformations from security intents into security policies, and from security policies into platform-specific configurations.

The security policies for WS-Security are standardized as WS-SecurityPolicy (OASIS, 2007), so the security requirements specified by the intents should be transformed into security policies written in WS-SecurityPolicy. Security policies can be executed on various platforms such as WebSphere Application Server V6.1 (IBM, 2005a) or Apache Rampart (Apache Software Foundation, 2008) that support WS-SecurityPolicy. This means that security policies should be independent of the ex-

ecution platforms. However the platform-specific configurations of the detailed PSM are needed to sign and encrypt according to the security policies. The transformation rules from security intents into the security policies are independent of the execution platforms, but the rules from security policies to the platform-specific configurations depend on the execution platforms. We describe the transformation rules in the following two sections.

Transformation from Security Intents into Security Policies

The security policy is described as a set of security policy assertions, which are XML element fragments specifying security requirements such as signatures or encryption and the required algorithms. The model transformation should generate a proper combination of multiple security policy assertions. The security policy assertions are combined in parallel and with nested structures. So we use template-based policy generation to create proper combinations, as shown in Figure 7.

Our transformation needs one security policy template and four kinds of security assertion templates. Some example templates are shown in Figure 8. The model transformation for policy generation has the following steps: (1) The required security assertion templates are selected for the security intents, (2) Variables in each se-

Figure 6. Mapping between security intents and security infrastructure model

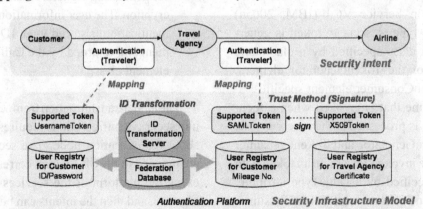

Figure 7. Template-based model transformation

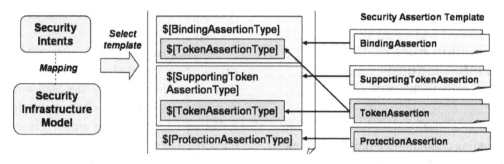

Figure 8. Template example

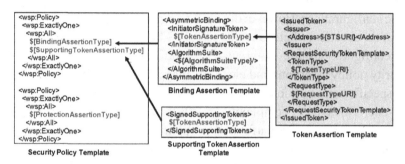

curity assertion template are assigned values extracted from the SIM of the platforms where the application will be deployed, and (3) A security policy is generated by filling in the parameters of the security policy template from the security assertion templates with their assigned values.

A security policy template has parameters such as $[BindingAssertionType] that are filled in by security assertions. Each parameter has a type corresponding to a type of security assertion template. A security assertion template has a nested structure, so a binding assertion template has a parameter $[TokenAssertionType] that should be filled in by using a token assertion template. Security assertion templates have other variables that should be assigned values that are extracted from the SIM. For example, a binding assertion template can have a variable ${AlgorithmSuiteType} that is assigned algorithm suite names extracted from the SIM.

The parameters of a security policy template that must be filled in are determined from the security intents. For example, if a service model has an *authentication* intent, a $[SupportingTokenAssertionType] parameter should be filled in using a supporting token assertion template. A supporting token assertion template also has a $[TokenAssertionType] parameter, so this should be also filled in with a security token assertion that is supported in the platform and extracted from the SIM. When an *integrity* intent is specified in a service model, $[BindingAssertionType] and $[ProtectionAssertionType] parameters should be filled in. The algorithm suite names extracted from the SIM are assigned to a variable ${AlgorithmSuiteType}.

The concrete security policy is generated by selecting the necessary security assertion templates based on the types of the security intents, and by assigning values extracted from the SIM to the variables in the security assertion templates.

Transformation from Security Policies into Platform-Specific Configurations

The model transformation also generates platform-specific binding configuration files for each platform environment. The transformation rules for platform-specific binding configurations depend on the environment. We need to define how to map between policy assertions and the elements of platform-specific configurations. However the description levels of the security policies and the platform-specific configurations are different, and hence the security policy assertions and elements of platform-specific configurations cannot be mapped one-to-one. This creates complexity in the mapping rules. For example, in platform-specific configurations, multiple signatures and encryptions are not distinguished and may be treated in the same way. In contrast, security policies regard signatures and encryptions on a SOAP Body as "message signatures and encryptions", and other signatures and encryptions are regarded as additional ones. Hence, multiple signatures are represented in the same way in platform-specific configurations, but they are represented by different policy assertions in the security policies. These assertions for signatures and encryptions are not mapped one-on-one to elements of the platform-specific configurations. This kind of difference in the description levels leads to complicated mapping rules between policy assertions and configuration elements.

Also, there are many platform environments, such as WebSphere Application Server V6.1 (IBM, 2005a), Apache WSS4J (Apache Software Foundation, 2004), and Apache Rampart (Apache Software Foundation, 2008). The mapping rules should be defined independently for each platform environment. Therefore, we must switch to appropriate transformation rules when the execu-

tion environment of an application is changed. A detailed discussion is provided in Satoh and Yamaguchi (2007).

We proposed a method to transform a security policy into a platform-specific binding configuration while reducing the platform-specific dependencies of the transformation rules (Satoh & Yamaguchi, 2007). An intermediate model is introduced for the model transformation, and the transformation is executed in two steps, as shown in Figure 9. The security policies and the platform-specific configurations have different description levels, but both are designed to represent a SOAP message structure by using WS-Security. Hence the security policies and platform-specific configurations can easily be mapped to the WS-Security message structure. We introduced an intermediate model based on the WS-Security message structure. To generate the platform-specific configurations, a security policy can be mapped to an intermediate model and then the model is transformed into the platform-specific configurations. By introducing this intermediate model, the complicated mapping rules between security policies and configurations can be discarded. We need two kinds of mapping rules for generating platform-specific configurations, but the implementation of model transformation is easier than the direct transformation from security policies into configurations.

The platform-specific configurations consist of two parts: one part is for representing security requirements based on security policies, and other part is for binding information required in each platform. For example, WAS V6.1 has a Deployment Descriptor (DD) that represents the security requirements corresponding to the security policies, and the Binding Configuration has the binding information required by the WAS platform to execute WS-Security. The binding information can be obtained from the TokenProcessing element of the SIM, and they are transformed into the Binding Configuration.

Figure 9. Model transformation into platform-specific configurations

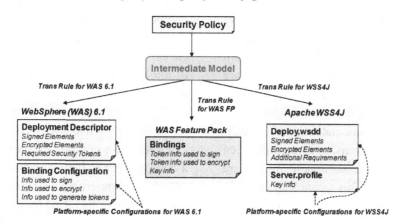

The advantages of simplifying the mapping rules using the intermediate model is that we can reduce the costs to implement the model transformations to support the various execution platforms. The mapping rules of the security policy and the intermediate model are independent of the type of execution platform, and so we can support configuration generation for a new platform by simply adding a new transformation rule from the intermediate model into a new configuration. We only need to implement a half of the configuration generation to add a new execution platform and this can reduce the costs of the implementation.

We prototyped this approach and compared the implementation costs of the direct transformation with the costs of this proposed transformation using WAS V6.1. The proposed approach increased the amount of code by only half of what was required in the direct transformation approach, and the implementation was simplified because the definitions of the transformation rules were simplified. Also, we found that the size of the implementation code was about half for the transformation into a new configuration for Apache WSS4J (Apache Software Foundation, 2004). This shows that the two-step transformation reduces the dependency of the model transformation rule on the execution platform.

Even if a methodology for security configuration is defined and roles for the security configuration are assigned to each developer, the security configuration is quite complicated and difficult. Model-Driven Security can generate the concrete and detailed security configurations for platform environments without writing the configurations by hand, greatly helping the assemblers, who no longer need detailed knowledge of the configuration description and can focus on their specific responsibilities.

PATTERN-BASED INTENT CONFIGURATION

An SOA application is a composite service which consists of assemblies of service components, and the components may also consist of other service components. This means that an application has a recursive structure. In the Model Transformation section, we explained this using ServiceProfile as a service model, and we also have an alternative to the UML profile: Service Component Architecture (SCA) (OASIS, 2007a). SCA can model services recursively. It is not easy for a software architect to add intents to a service model with a recursive structure, because the architect needs to pay attention to the intents applying to lower-level components when adding intents to higher-level components. As a solution to this difficulty, we propose a technology for pattern-based intent application, which is a framework to define intent patterns for component assemblies. A software architect can apply a pattern instead of directly adding the intents, and the pattern applies the intents to the components, including the lower-level components. In patterns, constraints between intents can be specified, so invalid intents are detected and corrected. This technology can help a software architect in applying correct intents to service assemblies even if an architect does not have detailed knowledge of the security-related specifications and their constraints.

SCA and SCA Policy

SCA has a specification that defines security intents to specify the abstracted security requirements (OASIS, 2007b). In contrast to the ServiceProfile model, an SCA model can assemble a service with a recursive structure. Here we briefly introduce the service model in SCA and its intents.

SCA provides solutions for building applications based on a Service-Oriented Architecture, and describes the content and linkages of an application in assemblies called *composites*. Composites consist of *components*, *services*, and *references*. Figure 10 shows an example SCA diagram of a composite that can be used as a service model by a software architect. Components are the

basic units of composition and are wired to create a composite where the externally visible portions of the components are provided by services and references. The components are configured instances of implementations. Implementations consist of pieces of code that provide business functions. SCA supports various kinds of implementation technologies such as Java or BPEL. A composite can itself be a component implementation, and a component can have a recursive structure. An SCA composite structure is represented in an XML serialization as specified by the grammar of the Service Component Definition Language (SCDL). Listing 1 is an example of part of the SCDL for the SCA composite of Figure 10.

SCA elements can have policies attached to them so that they exhibit desired non-functional properties, such as security and transactional properties. The SCA Policy Framework (OASIS, 2007b) specifies two kinds of SCA policies: interaction policies and implementation policies. The interaction policies can be applied to services and references to specify properties for component invocation. Thus, they impact communication with the component in some concrete way. The implementation policies are applied to component implementations to specify properties for a component itself, and are used to drive the behavior of the runtime container within which a component executes.

Policies are represented in two forms: policy intents and policy sets. Policy intents are declara-

Figure 10. SCA composite diagram

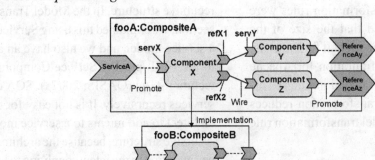

Listing 1. XML representation for SCA composite in Figure 10 (SCDL)

```
<composite name="CompositeA" targetNamespace="http://foo.com">
<service name="ServiceA" promote="componentX"/>
<component name="ComponentX" requires="authentication">
<service name="servX">
<implementation.composite name="fooB:CompositeB"/>
<reference name="refX1"/>
<reference name="refX2"/>
</component>
…..
<wire source="refX1" target="servY"/>
<reference name="ReferenceAy" promote="ComponentY"/>
……
</composite>
```

tions of abstract policy requirements, and policy sets specify more concrete security policies than intents. For the security intents, *authentication*, *integrity*, and *confidentiality* are defined and can be applied to any elements, such as *services* or *references* on *components,* in SCDL by a *requires* attribute. Some policy sets for security are also defined as special XML elements, such as an *allow* element with a *roles* attribute that specifies an access control policy. The policy set can specify more detailed requirements than intents, but here we deal with policy sets in the same way as intents because they specify platform-independent requirements for security domains and both can be used by a software architect. In Listing 1, an *authentication* intent is attached to the component element for *ComponentX* by a *requires* attribute.

SCA policies seem quite simple and easy to use, but users should apply them carefully. Figure 11 is an example SCA model for the Travel Reservation service. Here, we suppose that the Airline Service component (AS) is specified with an *authentication* intent on servAS, and this means that the AS requires information for user authentication. However AS is invisible to a user who invokes the Travel Reservation service composite

(TR), because the AS is an inner component of the composite. Therefore the user cannot know that AS requires authentication information. To inform a user about the authentication requirement, the servTR on TR should have an *authentication* intent, and then the authentication information will propagate to AS. If a component is implemented by another composite, similar problems may occur. Suppose that the Travel Agency service composite has an *authentication* intent on the service, and it implements a higher-level component as Travel Agency component. The servTR, and refTR of Travel Reservation service composite are visible to a user who invokes the application, so all of the information required by the inner components should be exposed by these elements. A software architect must explicitly add the intents to avoid such problems.

Figure 11 is an example of a simple composite, so it might seem that this problem is easy to avoid. However, a practical composite consists of many components linked to each other, so it is quite difficult for a software architect to manually avoid these problems. Though policy intents are supposed to allow a person who is not an expert in security to configure the security policies, it calls for a deep understanding of the

Figure 11. Travel reservation service composite

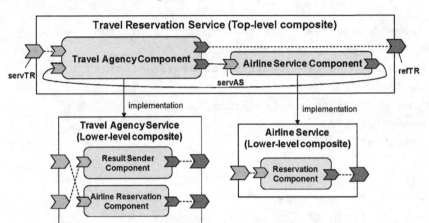

policy specifications and domain knowledge to apply the intents properly. Pattern-based intent configuration is a technology to support adding intents without these difficulties even when the components are implemented by another composite.

Pattern-Based Intent Configuration

Figure 12 shows an overview of the pattern-based intent configuration. We suppose that the policy intent patterns and pattern application rules are defined in advance by a policy administrator who is a domain-expert in security. A software architect

can apply intent patterns according to the corresponding application rules instead of applying a series of intents themselves. An intent pattern may have some constraints, so intent validation is done to make sure the application conforms to the constraints.

The policy intent patterns work on the policy application from a compositional perspective. To satisfy the end-to-end requirements of the composite, each component needs to be configured in a particular manner. We define each component configuration as a *role*, and the intent pattern consists of a set of roles, along with constraints on how the roles relate to each other. For example,

Figure 12. Pattern-based SCA policy configuration

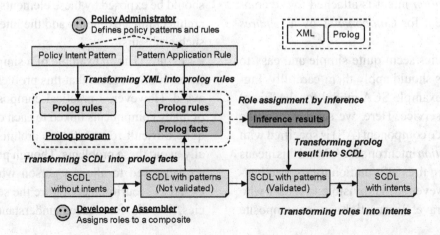

a component which requires user information is assigned an *idRequester* role, defined by the intents for authentication. Pattern application thus involves first assigning a pattern to the composite and then assigning roles to components within the composite. The alternative to manually assigning roles is to use a pattern application rule.

Our policy patterns are defined declaratively and mapped to predicate logic, so it is possible to validate role assignments by Prolog inference. The validation mechanism is based on a Prolog program which consists of the following two parts: (1) Prolog facts that are automatically transformed from SCDL, and (2) Prolog rules that are transformed from XML representations of the patterns and rules. The program infers elements which should be assigned roles, and the inference results can be used to update the original SCDL. Thus our system gives assurances about the validity of the applied policy. Finally, the roles in the updated SCDL are translated into a series of intents based on the role definitions when the composite is deployed to an SCA runtime, so there is no requirement for the runtime to be aware of the intent patterns. We also define an XML representation for the patterns, so policy administrators can define custom domain-specific policy patterns. A policy administrator works on a pattern in XML, and it is transformed into Prolog rules when the pattern is validated.

We describe the intent pattern definition in predicate logic, and propose various pattern application scenarios in the next sections.

Security Intent Patterns

The policy intent pattern defines how to specify policy intents for SCA elements by associating roles with those elements such as the "ID requester" role. The role assignment is made if that element is required to behave like a customer's ID requester. An intent pattern is defined based on the desired composite behavior. This approach thus allows developers to translate high-level require-

ments ("this composite authenticates a requester by ID") into a pattern ("this can be done by using the authentication pattern for the composite"). The developer will specify the pattern and then the roles played by individual components in the composite.

Here we show an example pattern which has two roles: *roleA* and *roleB*. This pattern is defined by the following predicate using Prolog syntax:

```
pattern:- roleA(X), roleB(Y),
constraints(X, Y),
```

Where X and Y are SCA elements which can have intents, such as components, services, references, and implementations. Here we assume the constraints that all *roleA* elements should be linked from a *roleB* element, and the predicate for these constraints is defined as

$$\forall X \exists Y \ \text{path}(X, Y), \ \text{roleA}(X),$$
$$\text{roleB}(Y).$$

The predicate path(X, Y) returns true if the source element X can invoke the target element Y. Both X and Y have quantifiers, $\forall$ or $\exists$, so we can validate the role assignment by inference based on the constraint.

Here we show two patterns for a security domain: an Authentication pattern and an Authorization pattern.

Authentication Pattern

This pattern defines roles to apply authentication requirements to a composite. This role is defined by predicate logic:

```
idRequester(X):- componentService(X,
S), hasAuthentication(S).
```

The *idRequester* is a role for a component. The *idRequester* predicate means that a component X has an *idRequester* role if and only if a service S of X has an *authentication* intent. The role for a service of a composite is defined similarly:

```
extIdRequester(X):-
compositeService(C, X),
hasAuthentication(X).
```

The *extIdRequester* predicate means that service X of a composite C has an *extIdRequester* role if and only if X has an *authentication* intent.

These roles have a constraint between them:

$$\forall Y \exists X \; path(X, Y), extIdRequester(X),$$
$$idRequester(Y).$$

This constraint means that all of the components that have an *idRequester* role have a path to one or more services in the composite that have

an *extIdRequester* role. If a composite includes a component that requires an ID, the composite should expose that component's request to external composites. A composite service that has an *extIdRequester* role can expose an ID request to the outside, so an inner component of the *idRequester* role needs to have a path to a service with the *extIdRequester* role.

We defined the XML representation of pattern predicates. Listing 2 is part of an XML representation of an Authentication pattern. The pattern representation schema is an extension of the SCDL schema. The *role* elements were introduced to define roles and a *constraints* element provides constraints between the roles. The quantifiers of the constraints are introduced in the representation, where the *AllTargets* and *ExistSource* elements

Listing 2. Authentication pattern in XML

```
<pat:policyPattern patternName="AuthenticationPattern" ...>
<pat:compositePattern>
<!-- Role definitions -->
 <pat:role name="extIdRequester" max="unbounded" min="1">
   <pat:service requires="authentication"/>
 </pat:role>
 <pat:role name="idRequester" max="unbounded" min="0">
  <pat:component name="idReqComp">
  <pat:service requires="authentication"/>
  </pat:component>
 </pat:role>
<!-- Constraints -->
<pat:constraints>
  <pat:And>
<pat:AllTargets>
 <pat:ExistSource>
    <pat:path sourceRole="extIdRequester" targetRole="idRequester"/>
</pat:ExistSource>
  </pat:AllTargets>
 </pat:And>
 </pat:constraints>
</pat:compositePattern>
</pat:policyPattern>
```

correspond to $\forall$ for the target elements and $\exists$ for a source element, respectively.

Access Control Pattern

This pattern defines roles to limit access to a specified component. The access control can be specified by a policy set that is an *allowed* element with a list of allowed IDs. Using this pattern, a role is defined:

```
allowedIdRequester(X, ID):-
componentService(X, S),
hasAuthentication(S),
componentImplementation(X, I),
hasAllowedId(I, ID).
```

The *allowedIdRequester* predicate means that a component X has an *allowedIdRequester* role if and only if a service S of X has an *authentication* intent, and an implementation I of X has an *allowed* policy set with an allowed ID.

This pattern also has an *extIdRequester* role defined in the Authentication pattern, and there are constraints between these two roles in this pattern:

$$\forall Y \exists X \ path(X, Y), \ extIdRequester(X),$$
$$allowedIdRequester(Y, ID).$$

This constraint means that all of the components that have an *allowedIdRequester* role have a path to one or more services on a composite that has an *extIdRequester* role. Listing 3 is a part of an XML representation for the Access Control

Listing 3. Access control pattern in XML

```
<pat:policyPattern patternName="AcessControlPattern" …>
<pat:compositePattern>
<!-- Role definitions -->
 <pat:role name="extIdRequester" max="unbounded" min="1">
    <pat:service requires="authentication"/>
 </pat:role>
 <pat:role name="allowedIdRequester" allowed="ID" max="unbounded" min="0">
  <pat:component name="idReqComp">
   <pat:service requires="authentication"/>
   <pat:implementation allowed="ID"/>
  </pat:component>
 </pat:role>
<!-- Constraints -->
<pat:constraints>
  <pat:And>
<pat:AllTargets>
  <pat:ExistSource>
     <pat:path sourceRole="extIdRequester" targetRole="allowedIdRequester"/>
</pat:ExistSource>
</pat:AllTargets>
</pat:And>
 </pat:constraints>
</pat:compositePattern>
</pat:policyPattern>
```

pattern. In Listing 3, the allowed ID is specified by using the "allowed" attribute for the example. In practice, a concrete ID field, such as "customer", needs to be specified in the pattern definition.

We defined the patterns of security intents related to user authentication and authorization, but security patterns are not restricted to these two cases. In an SCA policy framework, custom policy intents can be defined and custom patterns can also be defined flexibly using the XML representation of a pattern.

Pattern Application Rules

In configuring security by applying an intent pattern, there are several possible role assignment scenarios based on the manner in which the composite applications are developed. Here we describe three typical scenarios for role assignments:

1. **Top-down role assignment:** If a composite has no existing intents and the software architect has the expertise to satisfy the security requirements, the roles can be manually applied to the elements in the composite. After that, the roles can be transformed into corresponding predicates and validated constraints by inference. If the role constraints are not satisfied, our system will provide a suggested set of changes.

2. **Bottom-up role assignment:** Our system can support a software architect who applies all of the intents manually, but who still wishes to check if the intents as applied comply with a known pattern. First, the roles will be assigned by inference from the existing intents, and then the role constraints will be validated, in the same way as in Scenario 1.

3. **Rule-based role assignment:** When a composite has no existing intents, there are many possibilities for role assignments that can be inferred from the role constraints. To assign the roles automatically, we need meta-rules

called pattern application rules to apply the patterns. Using a pattern application rule, we can automatically assign roles to a composite. The rules also allow us to specify pattern applications to recursive composites, since we can refer to lower-level composites in the rule definitions.

We explain the pattern application rule for Scenario 3. This pattern application can be customized, so a security expert could define a customer's special pattern application. Here we explain the two application rules for the security patterns for the example.

Recursive Authentication Rule

The Recursive Authentication Rule applies the roles of an authentication pattern to a composite that has a recursive structure. The application rules are expressed using predicate logic:

```
∀X idRequester(X):- component(X).
∀X extIdRequester(X):-
compositeService(C, X).
```

These are the rules for a role assignment to the elements in a top-level composite. The first rule says that all of the components in a composite should have the *idRequester* role, and the second rule says that all of the services of a composite should have the *extIdRequester* role.

The following rules are for a role assignment to a recursive component:

```
∀X,Y idRequester(X):- component(X),
hasLowerComposite(X, Y),
authenticationPattern(Y),
recursiveAuthenticationRule(Y).
```

In the rule, X is a component in the top-level composite, and the predicate *hasLowerComposite* will be true if X is implemented by another composite Y. When this is true, the composite also is subject to the authentication pattern and the recursive authentication rule. Hence, all of the components in the lower-level composite will also have the idRequester role.

Recursive Access Control Rule

Recursive Access Control Rule is a rule for the access control pattern. Here are the rules for role assignments:

```
∀X allowedIdRequester(X, ID):-
component(X).
∀X extIdRequester(X):-
compositeService(C, X).
```

These rules say that all of the components in a composite should have an *allowedIdRequester* role with an *Id*, and all of the services of a composite should have an *extIdRequester* role.

Two additional rules are included for a component that has a recursive structure:

```
∀X,Y allowedIdRequester(X, ID):-
component(X), hasLowerComposite(X,
Y),
            accessControlPattern(Y),
recursiveAccessControlRule (Y).
```

If a component has an *allowedIdRequester* role and it is implemented by another composite, then the lower-level composite should be subject to the access control pattern and the recursive access control rule. All of the components in the lower composite should have the *allowedIdRequester* role with the same Id. All of the services of the lower composite should have the *extIdRequester* role to authenticate the user.

Here we present two pattern application rules as examples. The example rules apply the same pattern and rule to the lower-level composite, but in practice, the method for role assignments depends on the application's semantics or requirements. We provide an XML representation for a pattern

application rule that is similar to an intent pattern. By defining a custom rule using the XML representation, various kinds of pattern application rules are possible, and we can apply a different pattern and rule to the lower-level composite than is used for the top-level composite by defining custom rules. Listing 4 shows part of the Recursive Access Control Rule. The Access Control Pattern has the namespace URI (xmlns:acp="http://www..../accessControlPattern"), which is used to specify the roles in the rule (such as "acp:extIdRequester"). The predicates of hasLowerComposite are translated into attributes of the SCA element such as *component*. Just as with an intent pattern, we can use a quantifier element such as *All* and logical operations such as *And*. We stress that policy experts can define (in XML) their own application rules to express the behaviors that they desire. A custom application rule is transformed into Prolog rules before the role inferences are performed, as shown in Figure 12.

Such an application rule can specify a valid intent pattern for a lower-level composite and a corresponding role to be assigned to a higher-level component. We can validate the consistency of hierarchical roles from the application rules, which is one of the advantages of the pattern application rules. Our pattern-based approach not only reduces the costs of role assignments but also guarantees the validity of the roles for a component which has a recursive structure. We implemented our pattern-based policy application in Java and Prolog. The Prolog engine is SWI-Prolog (SWI-Prolog, 1987), and the Java interface for Prolog is JPL (JPL, 2004). Our implementation uses the extended SCDL to specify the intent patterns and pattern application rules applied to a composite as shown in Listing 5. The intent patterns and application rules are assigned their corresponding namespace URIs, and they are referred to by the *type* attributes of the *intentPattern* and the *applicationRule* elements. We can apply multiple roles to one element using the intent pattern namespaces. This extended SCDL

Listing 4. Recursive access control rule

```
<rul:applicationRule name="recursiveAccessControlRule"
xmlns:acp="http://www..../accessControlPattern">
<rul:And>
 <rul:All>
   <rul:compositeService role="acp:extIdRequester"/>
 </rul:All>
 <rul:All>
   <rul:component role="acp:allowedIdRequester" allowed="ID"/>
 </rul:All>
<rul:All>
<rul:component hasLowerComposite="true"
pattern="http://www..../accessControlPattern"
rule="http://www..../recursiveAccessControlRule"
role="acp:allowedIdRequester" allowed="ID"/>
</rul:All>
</rul:And>
</rul:applicationRule>
```

is transformed into Prolog facts and the role assignments are validated by Prolog inference.

The software architect may not have any security expertise, so this mechanism can support the addition of valid security intents and pass them to the downstream development phases without any problems in the intents.

APPLICATION EXAMPLE OF MODEL-DRIVEN SECURITY

We prototyped a tool that implemented Model-Driven Security using ServiceProfile, and evaluated our approach by configuring the security of the travel reservation service.

We developed the tool based on Rational Software Architect (RSA) V7.0 (IBM, 2005c) which is our platform for Model-Driven Development, and used the model transformation framework provided by RSA V7.0. RSA supports "UML 2.0 profile for Software Services" (Johnston, 2005) and can model an application using a UML class

diagram. Therefore, we developed the "WS-Security profile" for the UML model to specify the stereotypes and attributes for the security intents defined in the Security Intents section. The UML 2.0 profile (Johnston, 2005) has no topology model to model the platform-deployed application services, and so we used the UML deployment diagram as a topology model created by a deployer. The topology model specifies the WS-Security parameter configuration files that are deployed on each node. We defined a new stereotype <<sim>> in the "WS-Security profile" for the parameter configuration file in the topology model.

A screen image of the tool (with added red annotations) is shown in Figure 13. The tool supports rule definition for the model transformations that generate the security policies from the security intents specified in the service model. After preparing the service model with the intents and the topology model, the model transformation is invoked from the menu "Modeling" → "Transform" → "WSSecurity Policy Transformation".

Listing 5. Extended SCDL

```
<composite name="CompositeA" targetNamespace="http://foo.com"
xmlns:aup="http://www..../authenticationPattern"
xmlns:acp="http://www..../accessControlPattern">
<intentPattern type="http://www..../authenticationPattern">
<intentPattern type="http://www..../accessControlPattern">
<applicationRule type="http://www…/recursiveAuthenticationRule"/>
<service name="ServiceA" promote="ComponentX"
role="aup:extIdRequester"/>
<component name="ComponentX"
role="aup:idRequester, acp:allowedIdRequester">
<service name="servX">
<implementation.composite name="fooB:CompositeB"/>
<reference name="refX1"/>
<reference name="refX2"/>
</component>
…..
</composite>
```

Figure 14 shows the service model and the topology model for the travel reservation service. The service model is based on the "UML 2.0 profile for Software Services" (Johnston, 2005) for the travel agency service and the airline service. Here, *TravelAgency.jar* and *AirlineService.jar* are instances of the service implementation. A soft-ware architect creates this service model and adds security intents to specify the security requirements for each service from the business-level security requirements. In this example both the *ITravelAgencyService* and *IAirlineService* are specifying security intent <<authentication>> for customer authentication.

Figure 13. Model-driven security configuration tool

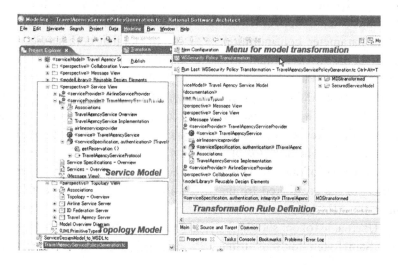

291

Figure 14. Service and topology model for travel reservation service

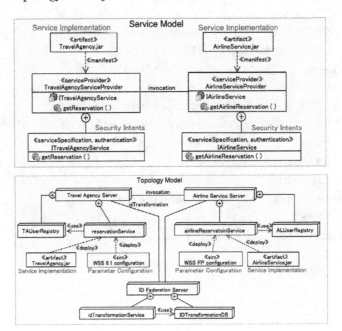

The topology model is created by the deployer and models the deployed services on the nodes. When the deployer specifies a node as a deployment target for TravelAgency.jar and AirlineService.jar, the service model and the topology model are linked by this deployment relationship. The required parameters for WS-Security are configured by the deployer and this parameter configuration is modeled as a *WSS 6.1 configuration* for reservationService in Figure 14. This WSS 6.1 configuration has a stereotype <<sim>> because the Security Infrastructure Model (SIM) is generated from this parameter configuration. Figure 15 shows a part of the SIM generated from this configuration for the travel agency service. The SIM specifies the supported security tokens in this execution environment. The *UsernameToken* is modeled as a security token for the authentication of inbound messages. The *SamlToken* is modeled for the authentication of outbound messages. These security tokens are linked by the *Mapping* element in the SIM because the customer's incoming UsernameToken should be transformed into a SamlToken for the airline

service. The Mapping element shows that the ID transformation is required between these security tokens. The service model and topology model are linked in Figure 14, and then an assembler selects the ITravelAgencyService in the model and does the model transformation, in which the security policies for the travel agency service are generated from the security intents and the SIM.

An important point is that we can specify the same security intents for the travel agency service and the airline service in the service model. We can model that both services have the same requirement for the customer's authentication, even though the required security token types are different. The concrete configurations, such as the required types of security tokens, can be generated from the SIM, and hence a software architect only needs to model the security requirements to meet the business requirements, which is an advantage of our security configuration process.

In the current security configuration process, the information about the topology and the application configurations on the topology are treated

Figure 15. Security infrastructure model for travel agency service

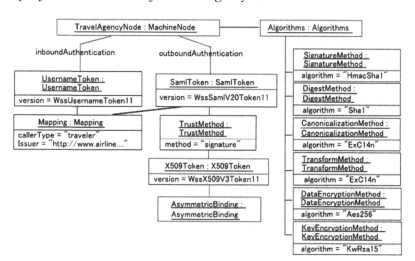

separately and they do not need to be coordinated in the security configuration process. This means that an assembler must write the security configurations manually from scratch, even though large parts of a security configuration can be specified based on information about the topology. To efficiently address this problem and to accelerate the security configuration process, we are proposing a methodology to generate configurations semi-automatically using information elicited from the topology model and supplemental information provided by a deployer and an assembler. The Security Infrastructure Model (SIM) is a model of the necessary information elicited from the topology information. Thanks to the introduction of the SIM, our technology can generate the security configurations as long as the business level requirements are modeled by an assembler and a deployer, breaking with the prior practice of writing the entire security configuration by hand.

There are several existing tools for editing the security policies or platform-specific configurations, but they require that an assembler have detailed knowledge of security requirements and how to configure them. Unfortunately, the required information for the WS-Security configuration is scattered within the business-level require-

ments and the platform-level information about the deployed services. If an assembler creates a configuration for a travel reservation application using an existing configuration tool, it requires manually specifying more than 50 parameters. In contrast, our Model-Driven Security allows the assembler to only add a few security intents on the service model for the security configuration generation. For this travel reservation application, only two stereotypes need to be specified in the service model. This is a significant reduction in the assembler's workload.

Considering the deployer's work, a deployer should have the skills for creating the topology model as a UML deployment model. The main contents of the topology model are just the physical connections of the nodes and the location of the WS-Security parameter files for the deployed nodes, and therefore learning of how to create the topology model should not be difficult. Also the SIM needs to be prepared by a developer, but almost all of the SIM can be generated semi-automatically from the topology model information. A deployer should manually specify only two elements in the SIM, which should not involve much work. Therefore, the model transformation in our Model-Driven Security can greatly reduce the developer's workload in creating complicated configurations.

We have assumed that the mapping between the business-level policies and security intents are defined by a software architect. Supporting technologies to map the business-level policies to the intents are future work. One possible approach might be to add functions to define the security requirements to the tool for the business requirements analysis used by a business analyst, such as WebSphere Business Modeler (IBM, 2005b). To further reduce the workload of a deployer, it may be possible to introduce patterns of typical topology models for security domain federations. A deployer would be able to create a topology model by selecting and modifying appropriate patterns instead of creating models from scratch, and this would be a great help. Another area for future work is supporting traceability between models, which is a desirable future for model-driven development. The traceability is especially important for security configurations, because it helps validate the security requirements available by checking the information in the SIM. We only discussed the top-down approach for security configuration in this chapter, and the bottom-up approach to define security requirements for existing platforms is also important for practical application development. In addition, we would like to improve the model transformation rules to handle new functions and future directions.

RELATED WORK

We are proposing a methodology to configure security based on Model-Driven Development as an extension of our work (Satoh, Nakamura, & Ono, 2006). In current development work, one developer, such as an assembler, handles the security configuration. There are some tools to write configurations (IBM, 2005c), but they do not support gathering the appropriate information or validating the configurations. We discussed not only the security configuration process, but also supporting technologies for the developers. We prototyped our approach as tools and we confirmed that they reduce each developer's work on the security configurations.

There is some previous work related to a security development process based on Model-Driven Development. Jürjens (2002) proposed a security extension of UML (UMLsec) to develop security-critical systems and Jürjens (2005) presented an extensible verification framework for verifying UMLsec models. Jürjens and Fox (2006) described tool support for checking the constraints associated with the UMLsec stereotypes against the security requirements. Configurations for authentication and access control policy were discussed in Basin, Doser, and Lodderstedt (2003), (Lodderstedt, Basin, and Doser (2002), Fink, Koch, and Pauls (2004), and Burt, Bryant, Raje, Olson, and Auguston (2003). Lodderstedt, Basin, and Doser (2002) also presented a modeling language for the development of a distributed environment system (SecureUML), and they discussed how to model constraints for role-based access control based on UML. Basin, Doser, and Lodderstedt (2003) proposed secure system generation from process models specifying the security requirements using SecureUML. Fink, Koch, and Pauls (2004) also discussed a model-driven development approach for the development of access control policies using View-based access control. Burt, Bryant, Raje, Olson, & Auguston (2003) proposed the unification of existing access control models and a platform-independent model for access control (AC-PIM). Alam, Breu, and Breu (2004) showed Model-Driven Development for security configurations for Web Services, but their target was a configuration for RBAC, which is different from our WS-Security configuration. Ortiz and Hernández (2006) discussed a configuration for WS-Security with a Model-Driven approach, but their policy was quite simple and they did not mention the development process or the developers' roles. Gutierrez, Fernandez-Medina, & Piattini

(2005) and Gutierrez, Fernandez-Medina, & Piattini (2006) proposed PWSSec (Process for Web Services Security) to integrate the development processes of Web-Services-based systems with security. Breu et al. (2003) discussed a security engineering process with modeling of business processes. They proposed methods to specify security requirements at a rough level corresponding to the business level. Their ideas are similar to ours, but involve attaching keywords such as public, confidential, or secret. In contrast, we discuss how to generate the platform-specific security configurations from the higher-level models, and also introduced the security patterns for applying keywords for security requirements consistently.

In this chapter, the methods of translating business-level security requirements into the service models is beyond our scope, but we have many related references that discuss business-level security. Huang (2005) proposed a policy-based security framework for business processed and an architecture similar to our model-driven approach. Model-driven security is mentioned as future work. Rodríguez, Fernández-Medina, and Piattini (2006) proposed a UML2.0 extension for the modeling of business-level security requirements. Rodríguez, Fernández-Medina, & Piattini (2007) presented a method of security requirement elicitation for business process descriptions. Sindre, & Opdahl (2005) also presented an approach to eliciting security requirements based on misuse cases. Heuvel, Leune, and Papazoglou (2005) proposed the Event-driven Framework for Service Oriented Computing (EFSOC) for developing business processes with Web services. They consider the security of the business processes in their framework and propose an access control model to enable event-driven delegation and retraction of authorizations. Herrmann & Herrmann (2006) analyzed how to fulfill the security requirements in a business process and proposed the MoSS$_{BP}$ (Modeling Security Semantics of Business Process) framework supporting domain experts in defining security requirements. Their research complements our approach.

As regards pattern-based intent applications, there have been many studies of security patterns (such as Halkidis, Chatzigeorgiou, & Stephanides, 2006; Fernandez, 2004; Arteaga, González, Álvarez, & Martín, 2006; Cheng, Konrad, Campbell, & Wassermann, 2003), but almost all of these patterns included platform-dependent security requirements. Rossebø and Bræk (2006) studied a pattern for authentication and authorization in SOA. Their motivation is similar to ours, but they proposed a pattern framework and discussed how to apply the patterns to UML models. Our policy patterns focus on the platform-independent requirements, and our patterns are abstracted at a higher level. Also our pattern framework can be applied to other domains, such as transactional properties. In earlier work, we discussed the transactional patterns for SCA policies (Satoh, Mukhi, Nakamura, & Hirose, 2008). This is a unique feature and useful for various kinds of platforms, which is important for SOA applications.

CONCLUSION

Handling the non-functional requirements for SOA applications pose important questions, but the configuration processes have not been well defined. We are proposing a methodology for the configuration of security requirements and for defining the roles of developers in the application development phases. Our configuration process is based on Model-Driven Development, called Model-Driven Security (MDS). MDS can assure that security requirements from the business level are satisfied in the concrete security configurations created during the model transformation, and the developers can concentrate on their own responsibilities while configuring for security. We assume two types of models as a service model, UML and SCA. Specifying the abstracted security requirements in the SCA model is supported by using security intent patterns and pattern application rules, and this will greatly help in generating concrete configurations correctly by using the model transformations in the downstream phases.

Our study will contribute to creating complex configurations properly while reducing the developers' workloads, even when the security domain is federated. We have a tool prototype for MDS, and we believe our approach will be a great help for SOA application development. We prototyped our approach and our evaluations are still ongoing. We need to continue comparing the current configuration processes. Various extensions are being considered as future work. For example, a method to extract business requirements to apply the approach to other domains would be useful.

REFERENCES

Alam, M., Breu, R., & Breu, M. (2004). *Model driven security for Web services (MDS4WS)*. 8th International Multitopic Conference, (pp. 498-505).

Apache Software Foundation. (2004). *WSS4J*. Retrieved September 1, 2008, from http://ws.apache.org/wss4j/

Apache Software Foundation. (2008). *Apache rampart*. Retrieved September 1, 2008, from http://ws.apache.org/rampart/

Basin, D., Doser, J., & Lodderstedt, T. (2003). Model driven security for process-oriented systems. *Proceedings of 8th ACM Symposium on Access Control Models and Technologies*, (pp. 100-109).

Breu, R., Burger, K., Hafner, M., Jürjens, J., Popp, G., Wimmel, G., et al. (2003). Key issues of a formally based process model for security engineering. *Sixteenth International Conference on Software & Systems Engineering & their Applications*.

Burt, C. C., Bryant, B. R., Raje, R. R., Olson, A., & Auguston, M. (2003). Model driven security: Unification of authorization models for fine-grain access control. *Proceedings of 7th International Enterprise Distributed Object Computing Conference*, (pp. 159-171).

Cheng, B., Konrad, S., Campbell, L. A., & Wassermann, R. (2003). Using security patterns to model and analyze security requirements. *Proceedinsg of IEEE Workshop on Requirements for High Assurance Systems*.

Chessell, M., & Schmidt-Wesche, B. (2006). *SOA programming model for implementing Web services, Part 10: SOA user roles*. Retrieved January 7, 2009, from http://www.ibm.com/developerworks/webservices/library/ws-soa-progmodel10/

Fernandez, E. B. (2004). Two patterns for Web services security. *Proceedings of International Symposium on Web Services and Applications*.

Fink, T., Koch, M., & Pauls, K. (2004). An MDA approach to access control specifications using MOF and UML profiles. *Proceedings of 1st International Workshop on Views On Designing Complex Architectures*, (pp. 161-179).

Gutierrez, C., Fernandez-Medina, E., & Piattini, M. (2005). *Web services enterprise security architecture: A case study*. 2005 ACM Workshop on Secure Web Services, (pp. 10-19).

Gutierrez, C., Fernandez-Medina, E., & Piattini, M. (2006). PWSSec: Process for Web services security. *Proceedings of International Conference on Web Services,* (pp. 213-222).

Halkidis, S. T., Chatzigeorgiou, A., & Stephanides, G. (2006). A qualitative analysis of software security patterns. *Computers & Security, 25*(5), 379–392. doi:10.1016/j.cose.2006.03.002

Herrmann, P., & Herrmann, G. (2006). Security requirement analysis of business processes. *Electronic Commerce Research*, 305–335. doi:10.1007/s10660-006-8677-7

Heuvel, W.-J. V. D., Leune, K., & Papazoglou, M. P. (2005). EFSOC: A layered framework for developing secure interactions between Web-services. *Distributed and Parallel Databases, 18*(2), 115–145. doi:10.1007/s10619-005-1400-1

High, R., Kinder, S., & Graham, S. (2005). *IBM SOA Foundation: An architectural introduction and overview.* Retrieved January 7, 2009, from http://www.ibm.com/developerworks/webservices/library/ws-soa-whitepaper/

Huang, D. (2005). Semantic policy-based security framework for business processes. Retrieved December 29, 2008, from http://www.csee.umbc.edu/swpw/papers/huang.pdf

IBM. (2005a). *Welcome to the WebSphere application server, version 6.1 information center.* Retrieved September 1, 2008, from http://publib.boulder.ibm.com/infocenter/wasinfo/v6r1/index.jsp

IBM. (2005b). *IBM WebSphere business modeler advanced documentation.* Retrieved January 7, 2009, from http://publib.boulder.ibm.com/infocenter/dmndhelp/v6r2mx/index.jsp

IBM. (2005c). *IBM rational application developer version 7.0.0.x information center.* Retrieved September 1, 2008, from http://publib.boulder.ibm.com/infocenter/radhelp/v7r0m0/index.jsp?topic=/com.ibm.help.doc/home.html

IBM & Microsoft. (2002). *Security in a Web services qorld: A proposal architecture and roadmap.* Retrieved September 1, 2008, from http://www.ibm.com/developerworks/webservices/library/specification/ws-secmap/

Johnston, S. (2005). *UML 2.0 profile for software services.* Retrieved September 1, 2008, from http://www.ibm.com/developerworks/rational/library/05/419_soa/

JPL. (2004). *A bidirectional Prolog/Java interface.* Retrieved Septermber 1, 2008, from http://www.swi-prolog.org/packages/jpl/

Jürjens, J. (2002). UMLsec: Extending UML for secure systems development. *Proceedings of 5th International Conference on The Unified Modeling Language,* (pp. 412-425).

Jürjens, J. (2005). *Sound methods and effective tools for model-based security engineering with UML.* 27th International Conference on Software Engineering, (pp. 322-331).

Jürjens, J., & Fox, J. (2006). Tools for model-based security engineering. *Proceedings of 28th International Conference on Software Engineering,* (pp. 819-822).

Lodderstedt, T., Basin, D., & Doser, J. (2002). SecureUML: A UML-based modeling language for model-driven security. *5th International Conference on The Unified Modeling Language,* (pp. 426-441).

Muñoz, J., Mendoza, R., Álvarez, F. & Vargas, M. (2006). A classification of security patterns for the transactions between a requester, an intermediary, and a Web service. *International Association of Science and Technology for Development,* 95-132.

OASIS. (2007). *WS-security policy 1.2.* Retrieved September 1, 2008, from http://www.oasis-open.org/committees/download.php/23821/ws-securitypolicy-1.2-spec-cs.pdf

OASIS. (2007a). *Service component architecture/assembly.* Retrieved September 1, 2008, from http://www.oasis-open.org/committees/tc_home.php?wg_abbrev=sca-assembly

OASIS. (2007b). *Service component architecture/policy.* Retrieved September 1, 2008, from http://www.oasis-open.org/committees/tc_home.php?wg_abbrev=sca-policy

Ortiz, G., & Hernández, J. (2006). Toward UML profiles for Web services and their extra-functional properties. *Proceedings of IEEE International Conference on Web Services*, (pp. 889-892).

Rodríguez, A., Fernández-Medina, E., & Piattini, M. (2006). *Towards a UML 2.0 extension for the modeling of security requirements in business processes*. Third International Conference on Trust, Privacy & Security in Digital Business, (pp. 51-61).

Rodríguez, A., Fernández-Medina, E., & Piattini, M. (2007). *M-BPSec: A method for security requirement elicitation from a UML 2.0 business process specification*. International Workshop on Foundations and Practices of UML, (pp. 106-115).

Rossebø, J. E., & Bræk, R. (2006). Towards a framework of authentication and authorization patterns for ensuring availability in service composition. *Proceedings of The First International Conference on Availability, Reliability and Security*, (pp. 206-215).

Satoh, F., Mukhi, N. K., Nakamura, Y., & Hirose, S. (2008). Pattern-based policy configuration for SOA applications. *Proceedings of IEEE International Conference on Services Computing*, (pp. 13-20).

Satoh, F., Nakamura, Y., & Ono, K. (2006). Adding authentication to model driven security. *Proceedings of IEEE International Conference on Web Services*, (pp. 585-594).

Satoh, F., & Yamaguchi, Y. (2007). Generic security policy transformation framework for WS-security. *Proceedings of IEEE International Conference on Web Services*, (pp. 513-520).

Sindre, G., & Opdahl, A. L. (2005). Eliciting security requirements with misuse cases. *Requirements Engineering, 10*, 34–44. doi:10.1007/s00766-004-0194-4

SWI-Prolog. (1987). *Homepage information*. Retrieved September 1, 2008, from http://www.swi-prolog.org/

Web Services Security. (2006). *SOAP message security 1.1 (WS-security 2004)*. Retrieved September 1, 2008, from http://www.oasis-open.org/committees/download.php/16790/wss-v1.1-spec-os-SOAPMessageSecurity.pdf.

Chapter 13
Control Engineering for Scaling Service Oriented Architectures

Yixin Diao
IBM, USA

Joseph L. Hellerstein
Google, USA

Sujay Parekh
IBM, USA

ABSTRACT

Scaling Service Oriented Architectures (SOAs) requires a systematic approach to resource management to achieve service level objectives (SLOs). Recently, there has been increasing use of control engineering techniques to design scalable resource management solutions that achieve SLOs. This chapter proposes a methodology for scaling SOAs based on control engineering. The methodology used here extends approaches used in scaling software products at IBM and Microsoft.

INTRODUCTION

Service Oriented Architectures (SOAs) provide a way to build applications that facilitate re-use and sharing. This is accomplished by using web services (or other similar techniques) to construct applications from services deployed in a computing infrastructure so that the applications are themselves services that can be used by other applications. For example, an email application could be structured to use services for message presentation, database look-up, and full text search.

Further, if the email application itself exposes a web services interface, this application might in turn be used by a workflow system to route work requests.

While appealing, SOAs present significant challenges, especially in scaling. A central concern is the extent to which an SOA application is assured that the services it depends on will deliver the performance required for the application to meet its service level objectives (SLOs). For example, an email server built on an SOA architecture may have SLOs for client access to their mailboxes, but achieving these SLOs requires that the database service provide suitably short

DOI: 10.4018/978-1-60566-794-2.ch013

response times for database queries. Although there are always concerns about the performance of embedded components in complex applications, SOAs present new challenges because the underlying services may experience rapid changes in resource demands due to concurrent use by multiple applications.

This chapter proposes an approach to engineering scalable resource management solutions for SOA environments. The proposed approach is forward thinking in that it is an extrapolation of our experience with building resource management solutions for software products, especially IBM's DB2 Universal Database Server and Microsoft's .NET. Our definition of scalability is quite broad. It encompasses the traditional perspective of solutions that scale to higher request rates. But it also includes scaling in terms of the diversity of requests and operating environments, such as the challenges faced by the .NET Thread Pool that is deployed on almost all of the one billion computers running the Windows Operating System. Because it is difficult to obtain accurate models of real world systems, our approach to scaling resource management does not depend on having detailed system models. Rather, we rely on simple performance models and employ feedback control to sense and correct for errors in modeling and control as well as changes in workloads and resources. Thus, our approach relies heavily on control engineering to design effective closed loop systems such as is done in mechanical, electrical, and aerospace engineering.

To illustrate the challenge of resource management in SOAs, we begin with an example of SOA scaling as reported in James (2008). The service described in this article automatically constructs professional video from still photographs and sound tracks. The service is deployed on a multi-layer SOA consisting of an Application Layer, a Management Layer, and a Cloud Layer. The Application Layer was developed by Animoto, a company founded in 2006. The animation application consists of services providing video analysis,

music analysis, customization, and rendering. The Management Layer, which is provided by RightScale, maps the application to the underlying computing and storage infrastructure. This requires considerations for application provisioning, load balancing, scaling the number of servers, and application deployment. The Cloud Layer, which uses Amazon.com EC2 and S3 services, provides the compute and storage infrastructure.

Each layer has its own set of resource management objectives, according to its purpose. At the Cloud Layer, the objectives are to maximize the utilizations of computing and storage resources. The objectives of the Management Layer are to minimize the cost of the deployment by minimizing the number of servers allocated and minimize application response times. The latter can be achieved through load balancing, but this objective is sometimes in conflict with the objective of minimizing costs. At the Application Layer, the objectives are to manage the trade-offs between resource demands (compute cycles and storage) and service quality. In this SOA, quality metrics include response time to produce the video and the quality of the rendering.

The foregoing illustrates the complex interactions that take place in multi-layer SOAs to achieve SLOs. Dealing with these interactions in an ad hoc way often results in scaling issues that degrade service quality and demand costly human interventions by service providers. Control engineering provides a systematic approach to dealing with these challenges. In particular, control engineering is a way to analyze complex dynamic systems and design robust feedback-based solutions to achieve scalable resource management in a dynamic and diverse environment like SOA (Astrom, 2006).

The approach we propose is forward thinking in that it is based on our experience with engineering resource management solutions of the component technologies of SOAs (e.g., databases and operating system concurrency), but not SOAs per se. However, our belief is that the same fundamentals apply to SOAs as well. Also, having scalable

Figure 1. Methodology for building scalable SOA solutions

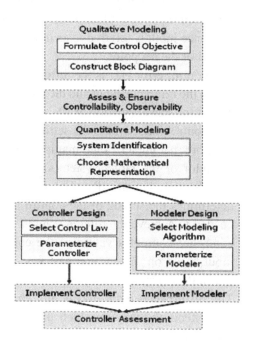

building blocks is fundamental to constructing scalable Service Oriented Architectures.

Figure 1 illustrates our methodology for building scalable SOA solutions. The first step, Qualitative Modeling, identifies the type of resource management problem that is being solved in an SOA environment and constructs a control block diagram to depict the overall SOA structure from the perspective of performance measurement and control. The second step, Assess and Ensure Controllability and Observability, analyzes the SOA dynamics and determines if the technologies under consideration for the SOA require extensions or enhancements to build a scalable resource management solution. The third step, Quantitative Modeling, uses formal modeling techniques to understand the performance of the assembled SOA components. The next steps, Controller Design and Modeler Design, address techniques employed to build the scalable SOA resource management solution. These two steps are coupled closely with the associated implementa-

tion steps, Implement Controller and Implement Modeler. Last, Controller Assessment addresses the testing of the resulting system to assess its ability to provide a scalable resource management solution.

Related Work

Designers of computing systems rarely approach feedback in a systematic way, which often results in poor handling of load surges and other changes in workloads. In mechanical, electrical, aeronautical and other areas of engineering, control theory is used to systematically design feedback control systems, which are also referred to as closed loop systems. This has motivated us and researchers elsewhere to explore how to apply control theory to computing systems. For example, researchers at the University of Virginia and Hewlett Packard (Abdelzaher & Bhatti, 1999) along with the University of Illinois have applied control theory to managing various aspects of the Apache™ Web Server (Sha, Liu, & Abdealzaher, 2002), and investigators at the University of Massachusetts have applied control theory to the Internet Transmission Control Protocol (TCP) (Hollot, Misra, Towsley, & Gong, 2001).

Our initial focus was the IBM Lotus Domino Server(Gandi, Hellerstein, Tilbury, Jayram, & Bigus, 2002; Gandi, Hellerstein, Tilbury, Jayram, & Bigus, 2002), a commercial email system. However, our connections with IBM product teams have allowed us to see if the techniques used in the science experiments have value in practice. This has resulted in several control-theory based features in IBM's Universal Database for Linux, UNIX, and Windows (hereafter, just DB2). Further, our work on the .NET Thread Pool provides insight into testing considerations in scaling the .NET Thread Pool Controller to the diverse workloads of computers running .NET (Hellerstein, 2009)(Hellerstein, 2009)(Hellerstein, 2009)(Hellerstein, 2009). Having seen the practical value of applying control theory to computing systems, we have commenced a third phase in our work—educating software engineers on the theory and practice of applying control theory to computing systems. Our efforts here have included co-authoring a book on this topic (Hellerstein, Diao, Parekh, & Tilbury, 2004) and teaching at Columbia University, Stanford University, and the University of California at Berkeley.

Control Theory Background

Here, we provide some motivation for and background on using control theory, the mathematical foundation for control engineering.

The central idea in control engineering is to enhance an existing system by adding a new element, the **controller**, which dynamically adjusts the behavior of one or more elements in the existing system based on the measured outputs of the system. We use the term **target system** to refer to the elements that are manipulated by controllers to achieve desired outputs. The integrated ensemble of the target systems and controllers is called a **closed loop system**, which is depicted in Figure 2.

The elements of a closed loop system are depicted in Figure 2. Below, we describe these elements and the information, or signals, which flow between elements. Throughout, time is discrete and is denoted by k. Signals are a functional of time.

- The reference input $r(k)$ is the desired value of the measured output (or transfor-

mation of it), such as CPU utilization. For example, $r(k)$ might be 66%. In SOAs, the reference input is a SLO. Sometimes, the reference input is referred to as the desired output or the set point.

- The control error $e(k)$ is the difference between the reference input and the measured output (or transformation of it).

- The control input $u(k)$ is the setting of one or more parameters that manipulate the behavior of the target system(s) and can be adjusted dynamically. The controller determines the setting of the control input needed to achieve the reference input. The controller computes values of the control input based on current and past values of the control error.

- The disturbance input $d(k)$ is any change that affects the way in which the control input influences the measured output (e.g., running a virus scan or a backup). Common disturbances in SOAs relate to changes in the services requested (e.g., "browse" versus "buy" requests at a commerce web site) or the resource demands imposed by service requests (e.g., the size of a catalogue query).

- The measured output $y(k)$ is a measurable characteristic of the target system. In SOAs, the outputs are service level metrics such as response time and throughput.

- The transducer transforms the measured output so that it can be compared with the

Figure 2. Architecture of a closed loop system

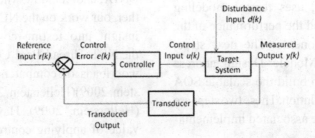

reference input (e.g., smoothing stochastics of the output).

Diagrams such as Figure 2 are interpreted in a very different way from workflow diagrams in software systems. The signals (or values associated with arcs) represent the flow of internal metrics and tuning parameters between the elements of the control architecture. Two kinds of signals are typically distinguished when defining the control objective: the system metrics (or measured output, such as response time, throughput, and buffer pool hit rate) and the system control parameters (or control input, such as thread pool size, buffer pool size, etc). In addition, although many control diagrams look like Figure 2, it is sometimes necessary to break down the system into smaller components. A common example is when it becomes necessary to model effects related to delays and noise in the control parameters or measurements.

In general, there may be multiple instances of any of the element of the control architecture. For example, in systems such as Amazon's EC2 and S3 there may be multiple load balancers which are controllers that regulate loads on multiple servers (target systems).

There are several properties of feedback control systems that should be considered when constructing controllers for computing systems.

- A system is said to be *stable* if for any bounded input, the output is also bounded. Stability is typically the first property considered in designing control systems since unstable systems cannot be used for mission critical work.
- The control system is *accurate* if the measured output converges (or becomes sufficiently close) to the reference. Accurate systems are essential to ensuring that control objectives are met, such as differentiating between "gold" and "silver" classes of service and ensuring that throughput is

maximized without exceeding response time constraints. Once a system is in steady state, its inaccuracy, or *steady state error* is the steady state value of the control error $e(k)$.

- The system has *short settling times* if the measured output converges quickly to its steady state value after an input perturbation. Short settling times are particularly important for disturbance rejection in the presence of time-varying workloads so that convergence is obtained before the workload changes.
- The system should achieve its objectives in a manner that the measured output *does not overshoot* the final value. The motivation here is that overshoot is typically accompanied by some oscillatory behavior which increases the variability in the measured output.

We use the term **SASO** properties to refer collectively to the properties of stability, accuracy, settling time, and overshoot. Control engineering provides design techniques for determining the values of control input (such as the number of servers) so that the resulting system is stable, achieves its service level objectives, responds quickly to changes (e.g., in request rates), and settles without much of oscillation. More details on control engineering and its application to computing systems can be found in Hellerstein, Diao, Parekh, and Tilbury (2004).

Running Examples

In this chapter, we use several SOA component technologies as illustrative examples of applying the methodology depicted in Figure 1. Below is a brief summary of the component technologies and the resource management problems addressed.

DB2 Utilities Throttling

The first example is the utilities throttling feature incorporated into the IBM DB2 Universal Database Server to regulate the impact of administrative utilities on production work. The problem addressed is common and crucial in an SOA environment, especially in the Cloud Layer for managing the underlying SOA platforms. Note that many platforms require the execution of administrative utilities to preserve the system's integrity and efficiency. For examples, on server nodes, programs for virus scanning and disk de-fragmentation are periodically executed. In Java Virtual Machines, garbage collection is an asynchronous administrative utility. In database systems, there are utilities for BACKUP, RESTORE, REBALANCE, and STATISTICS COLLECTION.

While it is essential that these utilities execute in order to maintain the health and performance of the services being provided, running these utilities can be extremely resource intensive, thereby resulting in reduced performance for user experienced services such as longer response times. To avoid service erosion, an automated utilities throttling feature is desired to control the trade-off between achieving good performance for SOA services while concurrently running utilities to maintain system health of the underlying SOA platforms.

Microsoft.NET Thread Pool

The second example is a controller for the .NET Thread Pool, a widely-used interface for the asynchronous execution of work items in the Microsoft.NET framework. The interface to this feature is QueueUserWorkItem(DelegateMethod), where the argument is a method that is invoked asynchronously. Each such call results in the creation of a work item that is queued until sufficient resources are available for its execution. The Thread Pool Controller tries to adjust the number of threads in the Thread Pool to maximize performance, where performance is measured in terms of throughput (the number of delegate completions per second). A simplistic approach to implementing the Thread Pool Controller is to create a thread for each work item so that concurrency is maximized. Unfortunately, this is not in general the best solution since excessively high concurrency levels often results in thrashing, a situation in which throughput degrades dramatically due to context switching and excessive paging. Thread pool management is also vital in the Cloud Layer of an SOA environment, so that a proper concurrency level can be maintained regardless of the dynamics of service calls.

DB2 Self-Tuning Memory Management (STMM)

The final example concerns automated memory pool sizing in the IBM DB2 Universal Database Server. In database management systems, such as the IBM DB2 Universal Database Server, there are multiple memory pools such as buffer pools that cache copies of data on disk, and sort areas used for in-memory sort operations. Properly sizing these pools is a significant challenge, which has typically required a human expert. This motivated the development of a DB2 feature called self-tuning memory management that determines the size of memory pools so as to reduce response times.

Figure 3 displays the target system of the IBM DB2 Universal Database Server for which self-tuning memory management was developed. The agents respond to database client requests to obtain data. Memory pool allocations are provided by a memory resource. Also, statistics are recorded for each pool including the time that would have been saved if additional memory had been provided to a pool.

While memory management solutions is useful for the Cloud Layer, the scalable load balancing techniques is as valuable in balancing the memory among various memory pools as in the Management Layer to balance the applications

Figure 3. Architecture of database memory management

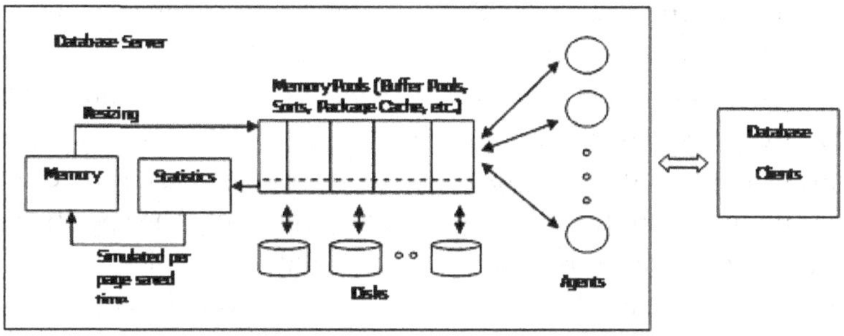

among the underlying computing and storage infrastructure.

QUALITATIVE MODELING

Control engineering of SOAs begins with the management problem to be addressed. Examples of the management problem include service level differentiation (e.g., if there are different grades of service to be provided in the Application Layer) and achieving target resource utilizations (e.g., to prevent resource overloads of the Cloud Layer). Ultimately, the nature of the management problem results in a control objective that forms the foundation for control engineering. In this section we will use all three running examples to illustrate how control objectives can be formulated for different management problems.

Control Objectives

We begin a top-down assessment with the management objectives, and decide how to map them into a control framework. The focus here is more on the nature of the problem than the specifics of the target system. Two principal types of control objectives are encountered in SOAs:

1. Regulation or tracking describes a scenario where a target (reference) value for specific system metrics is available or given, and the goal is to adjust the system parameters so that the metrics reach their targets. An example of this type of problem arises in the case of differentiated service. Here, user requests are grouped into classes (for example, by type such as 'buy' or 'browse') and the reference value is in terms of relative performance of the workload classes. A variation of this goal is disturbance rejection, wherein the actions are taken to counter the effect of extraneous factors on the system (shown as "disturbance" in Figure 2). This typically includes errors in the actuator, modeling inaccuracies or measurement noise. In both cases, the reference signal and the disturbance can vary over time, and the control system aims to keep the system operating in the desired regime.

2. Optimization, wherein there is no fixed or known target value for the metrics, and instead the objective is to obtain the best performance possible. Examples of this kind include maximizing the throughput in the .NET Thread Pool, minimizing response time for DB2, and minimizing cost in the "Cloud" layer of our example SOA scenario.

Consider the example systems described in the section entitled "Running Examples". In the case of utilities throttling, we translate the performance objective as follows. Suppose administrators can specify the amount of impact to the production work that they are willing to tolerate while the utilities are performing their work. The impact is quantified as the percent by which the performance of production work is reduced as a result of the utilities. This means that utilities are allowed to cause up to this limit of impact. Since we also want to maximize the progress of utilities, having less impact than the limit is not ideal. This means that the objective becomes to regulate the utility resource consumption to be at the level of the maximum permitted impact on production work.

In the case of the .NET Thread Pool Controller, there is no a priori target value. Rather, it is the controller's responsibility to determine a concurrency level that maximizes throughput. This is an optimization objective.

At first glance, self-tuning memory management (STMM) appears to be an optimization problem as well. While there is an entire field of optimal control, the techniques employed can be complex. For example, special control techniques are used in the .NET Thread Pool to address throughput optimization. Fortunately, in the case of STMM, the optimization problem can be reformulated into a regulation problem (Diao et al., 2004), which greatly simplifies control engineering. The key observation is that response times are minimized when the response time benefit across pools is equalized. This benefit is defined as the time saved due to having adding an additional byte of memory in a pool. By treating the mean response time benefit as a target value, this turns into a regulation problem in which all

memory pools are regulated to achieve the same mean response time benefit.

Once it is determined whether the problem addressed is a regulation problem or an optimization problem, we also determine if there are requirements related to accuracy, settling time, and overshoot. The specific system and domain can guide this choice, or it may be inferred from a service-level agreement (SLA) or administrative policy. For example, in the utilities throttling problem, a settling time of 5 minutes was deemed acceptable to the product team based on domain knowledge.

To the extent that these components (database, thread pool) are elements of an SOA, we can already see the applicability to SOAs. Moreover, SOAs will tend to combine these components into a composite that provides a particular service. These composites have their own performance management objective, which may even be similar to those discussed above. Thus, the translation of management objective to control objective is a broad concept, and can be applied either for individual components or when they are composed together to provide a service.

Block Diagram Construction

Once the control objective is determined, the next step is to identify the key components of the control architecture such as in Figure 2. This is a bottom-up process that utilizes system-specific knowledge. Note that these qualitative steps may be revisited later, for instance to construct an

Figure 4. Control architecture for DB2 utilities throttling

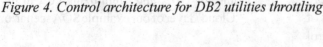

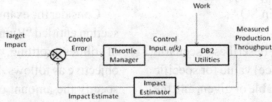

Figure 5. Block diagram for concurrency control in.NET thread pool

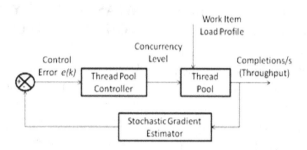

equivalent variation of the original problem that may be easier to analyze.

For DB2 utilities throttling, the main elements and the signals between them are shown in a block diagram in Figure 4. Here, the elements are the target system consisting of the DB2 utilities whose resource consumptions are controlled, the Throttle Manager which sets the control value to achieve a target impact, and a sensor (Impact Estimator) that measures the impact from system metrics. The need for the sensor is discussed later in Section 3. The signals of interest are the target impact value (given by the administrator), the throttle value to the utilities, the metric consisting of the workload throughput, and the impact estimate from the sensor.

A block diagram for the.NET Thread Pool Controller is shown in Figure 5. The main signals of interest are the throughput measure, which is the metric and the concurrency level, which is the control parameter. The Thread Pool Controller adjusts the concurrency level so that the slope of the concurrency-throughput curve goes to zero. This means that the reference input is zero, and so the control error indicates the direction of movement along the concurrency-throughput curve. Note that there is no explicit reference value in this case. The figure also shows the two key components that need to be modeled: the Thread Pool and the Controller. This is a relatively straightforward adaptation of the canonical feedback loop; there is no need to break down the system any further.

The DB2 self-tuning memory system diagram, shown in Figure 6, is slightly more complex. In this case, the signals of interest include the system metric y_i representing benefit-per-page for pool i, and the control parameters u_i denoting the buffer pool sizes. However, due to the system complexity, other signals need to be considered as well. Because the buffer pool size setting occurs asynchronously and opportunistically, it intro-

Figure 6. Block diagram for DB2 self-tuning memory controller

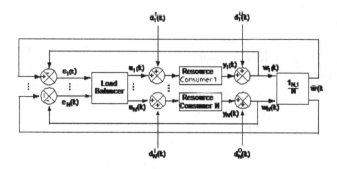

duces some uncontrolled variability in the control parameter. This is represented as an input disturbance d_i^I, where superscript 'I' denotes input. Similarly, the measurement of the response time benefit is done by a simulation component, which itself introduces some variability into the system. This variability is denoted by the output disturbance, and adding it to the actual benefit-per-page yields w_i, the *measured* value of the benefit-per-page metric. The disturbances d_i^I and d_i^O, and the actual response time benefit y_i are unmeasurable quantities. Finally, the average measured time $\bar{w}$ constitutes the feedback which serves as the reference value. The system elements (blocks) to be considered are the controller, the bufferpools, and the averaging computation. Note that in this case, we have some components which have multiple inputs and outputs, such as the controller. Such a controller is called a Multiple Input Multiple Output (MIMO) controller.

When modeling complex middleware such as web servers and databases, it is always a challenge to find the right level at which to construct the block diagrams and models. A general principle we have found useful is to start with as coarse (or simple) a breakdown of the target system as possible. For example, in the DB2 throttling case, we simply represent the utility program as a black box – we do not further model the structure of individual utilities, nor the interaction with the main database engine. We believe this principle extends to SOAs, which are an even larger aggregation of already-complex middleware components. In fact, such an approach may be even more necessary at the SOA level to make the solution tractable. The use of more complex models should be considered if deficiencies are discovered in the quantitative modeling or controller design steps. However, more complex models should be employed only after weighing the benefits of improved model accuracy against the cost of developing, calibrating, and maintaining more complex models.

ASSESSING AND ENSURING MEASURABILITY AND CONTROLLABILITY

Given the control architecture, we now examine the system metrics and control parameters in preparation for quantitative modeling. Again, all three running examples will be used in this section to illustrate different aspects of measurability and controllability analysis, since not all the behaviors in an SOA environment are measurable, and not all the SOA metrics are controllable.

To get qualified control parameters, we must be sure to choose parameters that will be effective in modifying the behavior of the system in a desirable way. For metrics, we must ensure they are measurable and they reflect the system properties that we wish to manage. Further, we evaluate whether the system sensors or actuators impose other restrictions or have behaviors that must be taken into account. These include:

- Limits on the rate of change, for example if the thread pool can only spawn some number of threads in a given timeframe
- Delays in terms of the control taking effect or measurements being available. This is very common, especially in distributed systems. In many cases our system metrics represent metrics on requests, so getting metrics such as response time is difficult until the request actually completes.
- Noise or disturbances in the measurements. As seen above for DB2, these effects can be a barrier for effective and resilient control, and so they must be modeled.

We say that a system is *measurable* if there are metrics exposed for system behaviors we wish to control, such as response time and throughput. A system is *controllable* if there are APIs (or other mechanisms) that allow us to control these behaviors. If suitable metrics or control parameters are not readily available, they can be added to the system to enable effective control. Note that these determinations are *qualitative*. It is also useful to do a quantitative evaluation in terms of what control theory calls *observability* and *controllability* (Hellerstein, Diao, Parekh, & Tilbury, 2004).

A *measurability* issue appears in the case of the.NET Thread Pool Controller, which needs a way to detect when new threads are needed. In.NET version 3.5, the controller uses CPU utilization as the indicator. However, this metric does not work well with non-CPU intensive workloads, since it leaves the CPU under-utilized even though there may be additional work performed by creating additional threads. Hence, the decision is altered to use the metric of throughput defined as work item completions per second. Moreover, this more closely matches the intention of doing automated control of the Thread Pool.

Now consider the case of the DB2 utilities throttling problem. The control objectives determined above do not explicitly consider which control knob should be used. A natural choice would be to control the OS priority of the background work since that usually determines how many resources it should receive. To assess the suitability of this parameter, we measured the throughput of foreground transaction work while setting the priority of the OS background work

to different levels. As shown in Figure 7(a), the priority does not actually have any impact on the foreground work. This is because the background task (BACKUP) is I/O-bound, and the OS priority only controls CPU contention. The system is therefore *not controllable* using the background task OS priority.

To address this, we implemented a control mechanism called self-imposed sleep (SIS) (Parekh, Rose, Hellerstein, Lightstone, Huras, & Chang, 2003) which employs the OS sleep() function call. SIS is a value between 0 and 1 which denotes a dynamically changeable fraction of time for which the background job is prevented from running, allowing the foreground work to continue unimpeded. At SIS=1, the foreground job has virtually no slowdown, whereas with SIS=0, the background job runs at its maximum speed, thereby having maximum interference on the foreground work. We can see from Figure 7(b), the sleep fraction is an extremely effective control knob, having a linear effect on the foreground work's throughput for its entire range.

This case also poses a *measurability* challenge because the management objective is stated in terms of the *impact* on the production workload, where *impact* is defined as the % deviation from the "normal" performance for that workload, that is, when the workload is running in the absence of

Figure 7. Evaluating the effect of different control parameters on the system metric

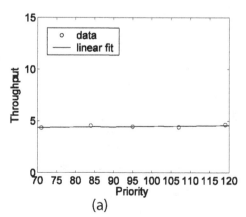
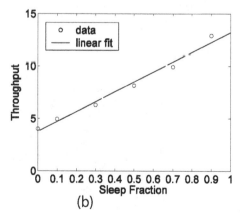

(a) (b)

the background task. This "normal" performance is not a directly knowable quantity. To obtain *measurability*, we devise a scheme to *estimate* the normal performance. This is done by leveraging the linear effect of the sleep fraction control parameter, seen above. Specifically, we introduce a *transducer* element (see Figure 2) that uses the throughput and sleep fraction information to build an online model of the slope of the line. Using a variant of the recursive least-squares technique, it is possible to estimate this slope using very few data points. When this line is projected to a sleep value of 100%, it yields a prediction of the system throughput when the utility is effectively not executing in the system. We use this prediction as the metric against which to assess the impact target. Thus, we have ensured both controllability and measurability for the DB2 throttling system.

In addition to the static properties of the actuators and metrics, one needs to consider any dynamics introduced by these components. Typically, sensor/actuator dynamics in computing systems typically manifest in terms of delays. Consider the case of the sleep fraction control knob in the case of DB2 utilities. An actuator with no delay or a known, fixed delay is desirable because fixed delays are easily modeled. To assess this, we change the throttling value (sleep fraction) in a discrete sinusoid pattern, where each value in the sinusoid is maintained for 60 seconds. Visual

inspection of the data shown in Figure 8(a) seems to indicate the absence of any noticeable delay. We numerically verify it by analyzing the cross-correlation between the control and throughput. The normalized correlation factors shown in Figure 8(b) have the highest peak at delay 0. This indicates that the sleep fraction is a good actuator for throttling since actuator dynamics are not significant: it has an effect on the utility impact without delay or overshoot.

In the case of DB2 self-tuning memory management (STMM), there is also a cost to changing the buffer pool size. The cost arises because resizing activity can cause pages to be flushed to disk, which consumes CPU and I/O resources. Another aspect of the cost is in the case where pages are being transferred from one pool to another, where we can end up with the situation where the total available memory for bufferpool use is reduced temporarily because the transferred memory is "in transit" between the pools.

In addition to the effectiveness and dynamics of the metrics and control parameters, a key issue that must be determined is that of *control intervals*. In the discrete-time control framework discussed in this paper, the control interval is the periodicity with which the control loop is activated – it determines both when a new sensor value is needed as well as when a new control value can be applied to the system. Its value must chosen

Figure 8. Evaluating the dynamic behavior of SIS

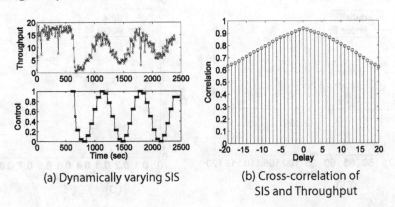

(a) Dynamically varying SIS

(b) Cross-correlation of SIS and Throughput

based on (a) application requirements, (b) sensor properties and semantics and (c) control parameter properties. The control interval cannot be too large since otherwise it limits the responsiveness obtainable from the controller. On the other hand, the sensors or actuators impose limits on how small the interval can be. For example, in computing systems, we often use metrics which are averages of multiple instantaneous measurements, such as response time and throughput. In this case, the control interval determines the averaging interval, which must be large enough to be meaningful. For the control knobs, there may be delays in implementing a particular control value. By choosing an appropriate control interval, such delays can be either exaggerated (short interval) or masked (long interval). To gain maximum responsiveness and avoid unnecessary oscillation, the STMM controller uses a dynamic control interval selection algorithm (Storm, Garcia-Arellano, Lightstone, Diao, & Surendra, 2006) that adjusts the control interval based on the observed variability in the sensor data. The goal is to pick the smallest interval where the noise is tolerable.

QUANTITATIVE MODELING

This section discusses the Quantitative Modeling step in our methodology. The section discusses the formal models used in control theory to describe the target systems. Although we use the DB2 self-tuning memory management as the running example, the underlying linear difference model is applicable to a wide range of SOA components.

Often, computing systems are modeled using first principles, typically based on queuing models (e.g. Kleinrock, 1976(Kleinrock, 1976)). However, considerable sophistication may be required to effectively use queuing models in control design, especially for complex systems. Also, queuing models almost always assume that the system being modeled is in steady state. In contrast, controllers must deal with dynamics.

Notwithstanding our concerns, some have shown success in applying queuing models to controller design, such as (Liu, Heo, & Sha, 2005)(Liu, Heo, & Sha, 2005).

These concerns motivate us to rely on empirical models, which are models based on data collected from running systems. Empirical models focus on the relationship between inputs and outputs, and require a less detailed knowledge of system internals than first principles models. The term black-box model is used in this case since only the inputs and outputs of the target system need to be known. We note in passing that while our models are black-box, the model structure often relies on insights into the system being modeled.

In control, a common approach to constructing black-box models is to use linear difference equations. These equations quantify the dynamic relationship between control inputs and measured outputs through relating current output to past inputs and outputs.

The following is a general form of linear difference equations

$$y(k+1) = a_1 y(k) + \cdots + a_n y(k-n+1) + b_1 u(k) + \cdots + b_m u(k-m+1)$$

which relates the current system output $y(k+1)$ to n past output values $y(k), \ldots, y(k-n+1)$ and m past input values $u(k), \ldots, u(k-m+1)$. This relationship is quantified through model parameters $a_1, \ldots, a_n$ and $b_1, \ldots, b_m$, whose values can be obtained by applying statistical techniques such as the least squares techniques.

One simple form of difference equation is called a first order model, a model in which the next output only depends on the control input and the previous output:

$$y(k+1) = ay(k) + bu(k)$$

This model is very useful in practice since it is general enough to represent the transient behavior of the system (the full effect of control input cannot be observed immediately and it requires a time lag for reaching the steady state) and also simple enough for model building (only two parameters) and controller design.

As noted previously, it is often the case that a black-box model is based on key insights into the behavior of the system being modeled. We illustrate this by describing the quantitative model used in DB2 Self-Tuning Memory Management (STMM).

The starting point for this model is some observations about the relationship between response times and the size of memory pools. Response times are short if the requested data is in the memory pool, and response times are long if a disk access is required. We consider the marginal reduction in response time to access data in a memory pool if there is a small increase in the size of the memory pool. This is referred to as the response time benefit. The observation is that the response benefit for a pool increases (or at least does not decrease) as we increase the size of the pool. However, the magnitude of this benefit declines as the memory pool grows, and it becomes zero if all data are in memory. This nonlinear relationship can be modeled as an exponential function

$$x_i = a_i \left(1 - e^{-b_i u_i} \right)$$

where x_i is the response time benefit for memory pool i, u_i is the memory size for memory pool i, and a_i and b_i are model parameters dependent on memory pool characterizations and workload access behaviors. While this is a black-box model in that we do not make assumptions such as those in employed in queuing models, the form of the black-box model is a consequence of the structure of the system being modeled.

We define the control objective as maximizing the total response time benefit over all memory pools, given the constraint that the total memory size is fixed. Thus, for a total of N memory pools, the control objective is

$$\max f = \sum_{i=1}^{N} x_i$$

subject to

$$\sum_{i=1}^{N} u_i = U$$

Here, f stands for the total response time benefit and U is the size of total available memory. According to constrained optimization theory, specifically, the Karush-Kuhn-Tucker conditions (Nocedal & Wright, 1999), the maximum total response time benefit can be achieved when the partial derivative for each memory size is equal, that is,

$$\frac{\partial f}{\partial u_i} = \frac{\partial f}{\partial u_j}$$

where $i,j = 1..N$. If these equations hold, then we have maximized the total response time benefit.

To achieve the STMM objective, it is vital to model the relationship between the memory size and the response time benefit value. Analytically this relationship can be derived from above as an exponential function

$$y_i = \frac{\partial f}{\partial u_i} = \frac{dx_i}{du_i} = a_i b_i e^{-b_i u_i}$$

where y_i stands for the response time benefit for memory pool i. In practice, the relationship may not be exact due to the significant noise in the system and also the interaction between different memory pools. Thus, we resort to a linear difference equation to represent a linearized model of the above. The linear model is initially constructed at the

Box 1.

$$benefit\_slope_i(k) = \frac{\sum\limits_{j=k-n+1}^{k}\Big(size_i(j) - mean\_size_i(k)\Big)\Big(benefit_i(j) - mean\_benefit_i(k)\Big)}{\sum\limits_{j=k-n+1}^{k}\Big(size_i(j) - mean\_size_i(k)\Big)^2}$$

current operating point, and continually updated to capture system and workload changes. Using linear models facilitates feedback control design using linear theory, which simplifies controller design and increases robustness to modeling uncertainties.

The linear difference model is of the form

$benefit_i(k+1) = benefit\_slope_i(k) \times size_i(k) + offset_i(k)$

which assumes a local linear relationship between the *i-th* memory pool size ($size_i$) at time interval k and its benefit ($benefit_i$) at time interval k. This is a zero order model since our experiments show that the transient behavior from changing the memory size is negligible compared to the observed noise level. From our experience, the models of most SOA components can be expressed as linear difference equations. Doing so, provides a formal structure, and it simplifies model building and controller design.

Essentially, building this quantitative model involves calculating the slope of the memory benefit curve generated from each of the memory pools. We compute the *benefit_slope* by fitting a line to the historic data: the data pairs of memory pool size and benefit value. This curve fitting is done using batch least squares, a statistical regression technique. Note that *benefit_slope* is negative because the larger the memory pool size, the smaller the benefit. Also note that *benefit_slope* may vary over time with workload fluctuations. As a result the model must be rebuilt frequently

in real time to maintain accuracy over potentially changing workloads.

Specifically, we calculate the *benefit_slope* value as follows. First, we compute the sample mean of the memory pool size *mean_size$_i$(k)*, and the sample mean of the benefit *mean_benefit$_i$(k)*. Once these values are determined, the *benefit_slope* can be computed using the least squares regression equation shown in Box 1. Which generates a best fit to the data in the moving window with a size of *n*.

For a database with *N* memory pools, the above modeling procedure generates a set of *N* independent linear difference models. Alternatively, we can extend the above single-input single output models into a multiple-input multiple-output model that captures the cross memory pool impact as well as the system dynamics

$Benefit(k+1) = A \times Benefit(k) + B \times Size(k) + Offset(k)$

where *Benefit* is a vector of *N* response time benefits, *Size* is a vector of *N* memory pool sizes, and *A* and *B* are *N* by *N* matrices containing the model parameters. Although this model is more comprehensive and can lead to more advanced controller design such as Linear Quadratic Regulation (Hellerstein, Diao, Parekh, & Tilbury, 2004), we found it is less practical in a commercial environment since there are more parameters that need to be estimated, which takes more time and reduces the controller robustness in general.

CONTROLLER DESIGN AND IMPLEMENTATION

This section describes how to construct the controller based on the quantitative models developed in the previous section. We also address implementation considerations. Again, we continue to use the DB2 memory management problem as the running example to simplify the illustration. Controllers can be constructed off-line using post-processed data or on-line using real time data. We give examples of controller design using linear, deterministic, time invariant (LTI) system theory. More details can be found in Hellerstein, Diao, Parekh, and Tilbury (2004).

A feedback controller computes the control input based on the control error. The objective is to drive the control error to zero. A generic and widely used feedback controller is the proportional, integral (PI) controller. Proportional control sets the control input *u(k)* proportional to the current control error *e(k)*

$$u(k) = K_p e(k)$$

where K_p is the controller gain determining the degree of this proportional action. The larger the control error, the larger the control action. However, proportional control alone cannot lead to zero steady-state error, because when the current control error is zero the control input will be zero too.

Integral control determines the control input based on the sum of all current and past errors. The integral control law generally has the form

$$u(k) = u(k\text{-}1) + K_I e(k)$$

where the controller parameter K_I defines the ratio of control change to the control error. Note that the above integral control law is in the differential form, which can be easily converted to show the control input is based on the sum of all current and past errors.

$$u(1) = u(0) + K_I e(1)$$
$$u(2) = u(1) + K_I e(2) = u(0) + K_I e(1) + K_I e(2)$$
$$\vdots$$
$$u(k) = u(k-1) + K_I e(k) = u(0) + K_I e(1) + \cdots + K_I e(k)$$
$$= u(0) + K_I \sum_{j=1}^{k} e(j)$$

As long as a non-zero control error exists, the control input from integral control continues to change. Since the control error can be nonzero when the current error is zero, integral control has the capability to drive the steady-state error to zero. However, integral control generally makes slow controller response, and thus is used together with the proportional control law.

Derivative control determines the control action based on the rate at which the control error has been changing. The derivative control law has the form

$$u(k) = K_D(e(k) - e(k\text{-}1))$$

where the controller parameter K_D defines the ratio of control input to the change in the control error. Since the derivative controller adjusts the control input according to the speed of error variation, it is able to make an adjustment prior to the appearance of even larger errors. Practically, the derivative controller is never used by itself since if the error remains constant, the output of the derivative controller would be zero. In addition, although derivative control provides a way to respond quickly, it is often too sensitive to measurement noise, and is used with caution.

For the database memory management problem, we only use the integral control law. The derivative control law is not used due to the high level of measurement noise. The proportional control law is also not used since the target system is fast enough (a zero order model without transient behaviors). Typically, the feedback control law operates to drive the measured output to a desired reference value. However, for the memory tuning problem, this reference value does not exist because we do not know in advance what each memory pool's benefit value should be when the system is in the optimal state. Instead, we compute the average benefit of N memory pools, and use it as the reference value. Then, when the difference between the individual memory pool's benefit and average benefit is zero, it would also equalize the benefits from all memory pools and thus maximize the total response time benefit.

To size the memory pool sizes the integral control law uses the following equation for the i-th memory pool

$$size_i(k) = size_i(k-1) + gain_i(k) \times (average\_benefit(k) - benefit_i(k))$$

which takes the benefit of added memory for memory pool i and compares that with the average benefit over all of the memory pools. The result of the above equation is the target size for the given memory pool from which we can easily generate the amount of memory to transfer in the current interval.

Next, we assess the stability of closed loop system using the integral controller, and analyze the transient response. First, we take the Z-transform of the above linear difference equation. Z-transform is a simple but powerful mathematical technique used in control theory for solving difference equations, connecting smaller systems (e.g., memory pool, integral controller) into larger systems (e.g., the closed loop system), and extracting key properties such as the steady state value of the control error and the settling time of the closed loop system.

The Z-transform encodes signals and describes systems by using the variable z to indicate time delays. Applying the Z-transform, the above integral control law is transformed to

$$U(z) = z^{-1}U(z) + K_I E(z)$$
$$\left(1 - z^{-1}\right)U(z) = K_I E(z)$$
$$\frac{U(z)}{E(z)} = \frac{K_I}{1 - z^{-1}}$$

where $U(z)$ is the Z-transform of the memory pool size, and $E(z)$ is the Z-transform of the control error. (Note that for simplicity of representation, we omit the subscript i. The result of applying the Z-transform is called the transfer function of the integral control law.

$$C(z) = \frac{U(z)}{E(z)} = \frac{K_I z}{z - 1}$$

Similarly, we take the Z-transform of the memory pool model from the previous section.

$$zY(z) = bU(z)$$

where $U(z)$ is the Z-transform of the memory pool size, $Y(z)$ is the Z-transform of the benefit, and b is the benefit slope. This gives the transfer function of the memory pool.

$$G(z) = \frac{Y(z)}{U(z)} = \frac{b}{z}$$

Note that the offset term does not appear here since it is a constant.

Afterwards, we can construct the closed loop transfer function. Figure 9 illustrates the components of the closed loop system and their relationships.

From the diagram, we see that $Y(z)=G(z)C(z)(R(z)-Y(z))$, where $R(z)$ is the Z-transform of the reference value. From this, we conclude that

$$F\left(z\right) = \frac{Y(z)}{R(z)} = \frac{bK_I}{z - 1 + bK_I}.$$

Figure 9. Control loop for database memory management

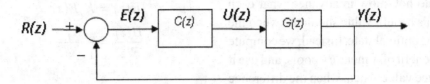

Using the closed loop transfer function, we can easily study system stability, steady state error, and transient performance. The closed loop system is stable if the pole (the root of the denominator polynomial) at $p=1-bK_I$ is within the unit circle. That is, $-1 \leq p \leq 1$ or $\frac{2}{b} \leq K_I \leq 0$. Note that the controller gain K_I is always negative because the benefit slope b is negative – increasing memory pool size results in decrease of benefit. Also note that the pole can be a complex value for a second or higher order system (i.e., the denominator polynomial has a second or higher order.)

To examine the steady-state error, we set $z=1$ for the above closed loop transfer function, that is, $F(1) = \frac{bK_I}{1-1+bK_I} = 1$. This gives the steady-state gain between the reference value and the measured output. Since the steady-state gain is equal to 1, regardless the choice of the controller gain, this implies a zero steady-state error for integral control as long as the closed loop system is stable.

Next, we study the transient behavior of the closed loop system. The settling time of the system depends on the magnitude of the dominant closed loop pole. In the memory management example, we only have one closed loop pole, so that $p=1-bK_I$ is the dominant pool. The settling time can be computed from the value of *pole* using equation

$$k_s = \frac{-4}{\log|p|}$$

For example, if $p=0.8$, then the setting time is $-4/log(0.8) = 17.9$ intervals. That is, the closed loop system will reach convergence after 20 control intervals. A larger (magnitude) pole means a longer settling time. For the memory management model described in the previous section, the pole is 0, which means that settling time is 0 as well. For the integral controller, the pole is 1, which is the slowest of all – the integral controller itself may never converge.

We use the pole placement technique to determine the integral controller gain based on the desired settling time and thus the desired pole location. Given the desired pole location, the controller gain can be computed as follows

$$K_I = \frac{1-p}{b}$$

That is,

$$gain_i(k) = \frac{1-p}{benefit\_slope_i(k)}$$

for memory pool *i*. The *gain* is then plugged into the integral control law to compute the new memory pool size.

After discussing how the feedback control algorithm determines the magnitude of memory resizing, we address several implementation considerations. First, memory reallocation is executed through the use of a greedy algorithm that resizes memory pools in pairs and ensures that total memory is unchanged. The memory pools are separated into two groups: those pools whose benefits are larger than the mean benefit and those equal to or smaller than the mean benefit. The memory pools are then sorted based on their expected benefit, and the memory exchange starts between the one that is most in need of memory and the one least in need of memory, in the amount of memory resizing value specified in the feedback control algorithm above, until no more pages can be transferred.

Second, although the feedback control algorithm determines the amount of pages transferable to or from a memory pool in the view of maximizing the total response time benefit. These values, however, are limited to further preserve system stability in the presence of rapidly fluctuating workloads. In addition to the restrictions placed on the maximum amount of memory that can be transferred in a given interval, the resizes are also restricted to the minimum transferable memory. This restriction helps to prevent the tuner from undertaking insignificant resizes that will likely have little effect on overall performance.

Finally, in many cases, if a memory pool is not given enough memory, the implications can be severe. Insufficient memory can result in failed transactions or utilities, essentially making the database appear off-line. In an attempt to mitigate out of memory conditions, each memory pool will specify a minimum amount of memory that the pool requires. This minimum size calculations are specific to each pool, and the memory tuner uses these minimum sizes prevent a further decrease if the pool is at its minimum size.

CONTROL SYSTEM ASSESSMENT

This section addresses how to assess controller implementations, the last step in the methodology depicted in Figure 1. The discussion focuses on the .NET Thread Pool because of the considerations made to address corner cases due to the large

diversity of .NET applications, which is common in an SOA environment.

The control system assessments herein considered address both controller correctness and controller performance. In particular, our experience with the .NET Thread Pool is that assessments of control systems must consider the following:

1. ***Reproducing error scenarios:*** Most errors in Thread Pool code result from unexpected event sequences due to the non-determinism introduced by parallelism. Reproducing these sequences is difficult.

2. ***Obtaining good test coverage:*** Having good test coverage for performance characteristics depends on having tests that cover a large fraction of the possible event orderings, which requires tests that run with high concurrency levels and time varying workloads. This in turn requires a flexible, scalable test infrastructure.

3. ***Assessing test outcomes:*** In functional testing, test outcomes are checked by predicates (Assert Statements) to determine if the proper value(s) is returned. In contrast, our main concern is with Thread Pool performance, and so assessing test outcomes requires prior knowledge of the ideal controller performance.

4. ***Ease of testing and debugging:*** There are requirements imposed on the controller itself so that it can be tested in an efficient manner and the cause of software errors can be easily identified.

Note that many of the foregoing considerations focus more on software engineering than control engineering. Our experience is that the emphasis on software engineering is essential to build scalable resource management solutions.

Reproducibility, coverage, and verification are concerns common to all correctness testing (Cooke, 2008). However, much like the challenges faced by shared services in SOA architectures, testing for performance in a low level service like the.NET Thread Pool presents unique challenges because of the wide range of users of the service. As such, the lessons learned in testing the.NET Thread Pool apply broadly to performance and scalability testing for SOA applications.

We employ the following principles to enhance testability of a controller implementation:

a. **Simplicity:** A simpler component has fewer conditions to check and so is easier to test.
b. **Test-Observability:** By exposing key information about the controller's operation, we can better detect when its behavior differs from expectation, and we can better determine the source of software errors.
c. **Test-Controllability:** This means being able to change the components internal state. With a test-controllable component, we can more easily test corner cases and resolve software errors.

Simplicity is achieved in two ways. First, we structure the Controller as two separate components—the Controller Adaptor and the Controller Logic. The Controller Adaptor deals with the multi-threaded environment in which the Thread Pool operates, especially measurement collection (e.g., computing throughputs from delegate completions) and timer management for invoking control logic. The Controller Logic implements the controller features in single threaded code. Second, we simplify the representation of the Controller Logic by using a finite state machine. Structuring the Controller Logic as a set of states and state transitions is a natural representation that enhances controller extensibility and greatly facilitates testing. For example, having a state machine representation means that we can quantify test coverage in terms of state transitions invoked.

The controller code is test-observable if we can observe all inputs and internal variables that affect state transitions. Key variables in the.NET Thread Pool include the previous concurrency level, new concurrency level, and the state machine transition. Our implementation includes a detailed logging facility that reports all material state. By material state, we mean that the logged information is sufficient so that the controller's execution can be reproduced from the log file.

Test-controllability means that we can force the controller into a desired state. Having this ability allows us to construct a log replay feature. This feature inputs a log of the controller transitions traversed, specifying a desired position in the log for which the controller is to be evaluated (e.g., where the controller behaved in an unexpected way). Then, the log reply feature sets the controller internal variables to values that correspond to those of the controller state for the desired position in the controller log.

The log replay feature improves testability in two ways. First, it allows us to use an Interactive Development Environment or IDE (i.e., Microsoft Visual Studio) to resolve controller software errors detected during test or production runs. This is accomplished by replaying the log up to the point of the error and then single-stepping in the IDE debugger. Second, the re-play feature allows us to validate that we have identified all material internal state since if there is missing state information, replay will not work.

Next we consider the infrastructure used for testing. Figure 10 displays the Test Infrastructure developed for unit testing the Thread Pool Controller. There are three parts: the implementation of the Thread Pool Controller, the Test Harness that interprets experiment descriptions and generates work items, and Services employed to run the experiments.

A key consideration in the Test Infrastructure is addressing thrashing scenarios efficiently. It is easy to create thrashing by injecting a workload that overcommits memory. However, this approach is problematic for several reasons. First, test results become highly variable because of the way virtual memory systems behave under high memory loads. Although the controller must

Figure 10. Test infrastructure for the.NET thread pool controller

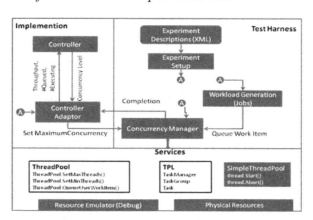

handle such variability in its operation, it is desirable to have a test environment with low variability to facilitate interpretation of test results. Put differently, with highly variable test results, a large number of test runs are required in order to detect performance improvements. Second, the test runs themselves take much longer since test machines must be re-booted to recover from memory overloads. These problems led to the creation of the ResourceEmulator, a component that provides efficient emulation of resource thrashing with sufficient fidelity to the characteristics of real resources so that we can test controller corner cases.

Thus far, we have discussed the test environment. We now consider test scenarios used to evaluate the controller. There are several requirements:

1. Scenarios should exercise the Thread Pool in ways that are similar to real workloads.
2. Scenarios should create load profiles for which the optimal concurrency level involves non-obvious trade-offs. In particular, it should not always be the case that the optimal concurrency level is the number of cores or the number of work items.
3. At least some of the scenarios should be simple enough so that we can determine analytically the optimal concurrency level,

thereby providing a way to assess the effectiveness of the controller.

Requirements 1 and 2 suggest that we should construct test scenarios that have a basis in practice, but the test scenarios need not be representative of real world applications. Test scenarios should stress the controller by presenting complex trade-offs in determining the optimal concurrency level. This led us to structure test scenarios using work items that consume resources as in the central server model, an abstraction that is widely employed in queuing analysis (Kleinrock, 1976) (Kleinrock, 1976). As displayed in Figure 11, the resources in our test scenario are memory, CPUs, and disks. There are multiple CPUs for which work items contend, and during the wait for and consumption of CPU resources, work items consume memory. If memory is over-committed, then nominal CPU execution time is expanded by the magnitude of the over-commitment of memory. There are also multiple disks. Disks are accessed in parallel without contention and without memory requirements. Thus, the controller must find a balance between (a) minimizing concurrency to reduce memory demands and (b) maximizing concurrency to achieve parallel access to disks.

The flow for a work item is: (a) wait in first-in-first-out (FIFO) order for one of the M threads; (b) acquire a fraction q of total memory; (c) wait

Figure 11. Diagram of scenario used for testing the thread pool controller

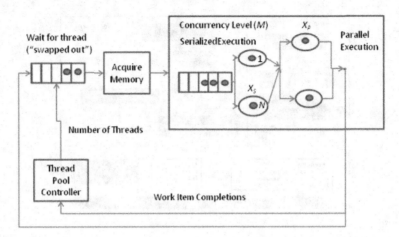

(in FIFO order) for one of the N CPUs; (d) execute on a CPU with a nominal time of X_S seconds; and (e) execute disk commands for a total of X_P seconds.

What follows is the derivation of a model to determine the optimal concurrency level for the test scenario in Figure 11. We emphasize that this model is not used in the Thread Pool Controller. Rather, the model is only used to provide a priori knowledge of the ideal concurrency level so that observed results from test cases can be evaluated.

The relationship between nominal and actual CPU time depends on memory contention. Memory contention exists if the set of active jobs consumes more memory than is physically available; that is, $qM > 1$. When memory contention exists, CPU execution expands to qMX_S.

The ideal Thread Pool Controller should find the optimal concurrency level M^*, the smallest concurrency level M such that throughput is maximized. It turns out that the test scenario in Figure 11 is sufficiently simple so that we can determine M^* analytically and hence have a priori knowledge of the ideal controller performance. Assuming that $M^* >> N$, we want M^* larger enough so that we obtain the benefits of concurrent execution of CPU and disk requests but without M^* so large that work items wait at the CPU since this over-commits memory and hence increases the nominal CPU execution times. Put differently, we want the flow out from the CPUs to equal the flow out from the disks. That is

$$\frac{N}{M^* q X_S} = \frac{M^* - N}{X_P} \approx \frac{M^*}{X_P}.$$

That is

$$M^* \approx \sqrt{\frac{rN}{q}}$$

where r is the ratio of the Disk execution time to the CPU execution time or $r = \dfrac{X_P}{X_S}$.

To assess how well our approximation for M^* estimates the optimal concurrency level for the test scenarios in Figure 12, we conducted several experiments. The experiments varied the ratio r of Disk execution time to CPU execution time as well as the fraction q of memory consumed. Figure 12 displays the results of three "open-loop" experiments in which we incrementally change the concurrency level to determine M^* after-the-fact. In all three plots, the horizontal axis is time (in seconds). The vertical axis represents both throughput (asterisks) and M or concurrency level

Figure 12. Results of experiments using the central server model. TP is throughput and Concur is the concurrency level

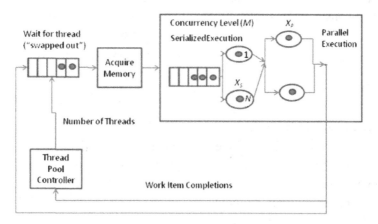

(dotted lines). Throughout, there are 20 work items, and $N=1$. The test cases considered are: $r=20$, $q=0$; $r=10$, $q=20$; $r=20$, $q=20$, as indicated by the file names in the titles of each plot. The horizontal dashed line is M^* as estimated by the above approximation. We see that there is a close correspondence between the measured concurrency level that maximizes throughput and the estimated M^*.

The ability to estimate the ideal controller concurrency level M^* from the parameters of the experiments has two benefits. First, it means that the performance of the Thread Pool Controller that is observed in tests using the above scenario can be assessed without the time-consuming process of running open-loop experiments such as those in Figure 1 to determine M^*. Second, being able to estimate M^* analytically allows us to construct a test matrix that obtains better coverage of the range of optimal concurrency settings, an important consideration in covering corner cases.

CONCLUSION

This chapter provides a forward thinking view of a methodology for scaling Service Oriented Architectures to achieve service level objectives (SLOs). We motivate this by the multi-layer SOA used by Animoto to deliver professional videos.

We claim that constructing scalable resource management solutions requires an effective approach to designing feedback control. Our approach is displayed in Figure 1, and we describe its application to several technologies that are used in SOAs, especially the DB2 Universal Database Server and the .NET Thread Pool.

Our approach begins with qualitative modeling in which the control objective is formulated (e.g., regulate administrative utilities) and an architecture is constructed that augments the existing system, or target system, with one or more controllers. Next, the target system is assessed and possibly enhanced to ensure that it exposes the measurements needed to effect control (e.g., response time measurements if the SLOs have response time objectives) and it includes tuning parameters that can regulate these measurements. In some cases, the desired measurements are unavailable and so a modeler component is included to estimate the unknown measured values. The controller is designed using techniques such as pole placement to determine if the closed loop system will be stable and settle quickly. Similar considerations are made for the modeler. Last, all components are implemented, and assessments are done. The last step, Controller Assessments, addresses engineering considerations related to controller testing.

FUTURE TRENDS

We see several trends that should motivate builders of SOA systems to make use of the techniques we have described. First, the growth in on-line data and the insatiable desire to access these data create huge scaling problems. Further, the competitive advantage of deploying new services to access these data strongly motivates businesses to use SOAs to facilitate re-use in their Information Technology (IT) infrastructure. This means that SOAs will be increasingly pressed to deploy quickly and scale rapidly. A final trend is that since SOA's have complex patterns of sharing and can experience rapid changes in workload characteristics, SOAs may well motivate a new wave of innovation in control engineering.

REFERENCES

Abdelzaher, T., & Bhatti, N. (1999). Adaptive content delivery for Web server QoS. *Proceedings of the International Workshop on Quality of Service.*

Astrom, K. (2006). *Challenges in control engineering.* Retrieved September 2008, from http://www.dia.uned.es/ace2006/plenaryspeakers.html

Babcock, C. (2008). Hyperic to monitor Amazon. com's Cloud Computing capabilities. Retrieved August 25, 2008, from http://www.information-week.com/news/hardware/utility_ondemand/showArticle.jhtml?articleID=208800360

Cooke, J. (2008). *Constructing correct software.* Lavoisier.

Diao, Y., Hellerstein, J. L., Storm, A., Surendra, M., Lightstone, S., Parekh, S., et al. (2004). Using MIMO linear control for load balancing in computing systems. *Proceedings of the 2004 American Control Conference.* Boston.

Fitzgerald, M. (2008, May 25). Cloud Computing: So you don't have to stand still. *The New York Times.*

Gandi, N., Hellerstein, J. L., Tilbury, D. M., Jayram, T. S., & Bigus, J. (2002). *Using control theory to achieve service level objectives in performance management.* Real Time Systems Journal.

Hellerstein, J. L. (2009). *Configuring resource managers using model fuzzing: A case study of the.NET thread pool.* IEEE/IFIP Integrated Management.

Hellerstein, J. L., Diao, Y., Parekh, S., & Tilbury, D. (2004). *Feedback control of computing systems.* Hoboken, NJ: John Wiley & Sons. doi:10.1002/047166880X

Hollot, C., Misra, V., Towsley, D., & Gong, W. (2001). *A control theoretic analysis of RED.* IEEE INFOCOM.

James, A. (2008, July 8). *Andrea James on Amazon.com and the business of online retail.* Retrieved September 30, 2008, from http://blog.seattlepi.nwsource.com/amazon/archives/142569.asp

Kleinrock, L. (1976). Queueing systems: *Vol. II. Computer applications.* Hoboken, NJ: John Wiley & Sons.

Liu, X., Heo, J., & Sha, L. (2005). Modeling 3-tiered Web applications. *Proceedings of IEEE International Symposium on Modeling, Analysis, and Simulation of Computer and Telecommunication Systems,* (pp. 307-310).

Parekh, S. S., Rose, K. R., Hellerstein, J. L., Lightstone, S., Huras, M., & Chang, V. (2003). Managing the performance impact of administrative utilities. *Proceedings of the 14th International Workshop on Distributed Systems: Operations & Management (DSOM 2003)*, (pp. 130-142). Heidelberg, Germany.

Sha, L., Liu, Y., & Abdealzaher, T. (2002). Queueing model based network server performance control. *Proceedings of IEEE Real Time Systems Symposium.*

Storm, A. J., Garcia-Arellano, C., Lightstone, S., Diao, Y., & Surendra, M. (2006). Adaptive self-tuning memory in DB2. *Proceedings of the 32nd International Conference on Very Large Data Bases.* Seoul, Korea.

Chapter 14
Addressing Non–Functional Properties of Services in IT Service Management

Vladimir Stantchev
Berlin Institute of Technology and FOM Hochschule für Ökonomie und Management, Germany

Gerrit Tamm
Humboldt-University at Berlin, Germany

ABSTRACT

The assurance of availability and dependability for distributed applications is a challenging and non-trivial task. Massively distributed architectures are becoming more prevalent with the convergence of the Internet of Services and the Internet of Devices. Flexible provider models like Cloud Computing allow for nearly limitless scalability of applications, together with an attractive pay-as-you-go investment model.

A key point that remains to be addressed is the assurance of service levels for end-user applications that rely on these provider models. This chapter describes an approach for addressing non-functional properties (NFPs) of services in service-oriented architectures (SOA). The approach is based on reference models such as the IT Infrastructure Library (ITIL) and the SOA life cycle model. It has been applied in several industrial settings in the telecommunications sector.

INTRODUCTION

The Internet of Services is emerging as a platform for the provision of software functionality. The web is becoming more and more a space where users interactively call services, instead of simply consuming existing information. Cloud Computing (Armbrust et al., 2010) amplifies this trend by allowing software as a service (SaaS) provision in a more granular way than traditional application service providing (ASP). The granularity of software offerings is now at the level of single

DOI: 10.4018/978-1-60566-794-2.ch014

application functions, respectively component operations. Web Services are the dominating technology for providing and combining such functionality in mobile (Wang et al., 2008) and distributed systems (Kumar, 2008).

Service-oriented architecture (SOA) is an architecture that combines elements of software architecture and enterprise architecture. It is based on the interaction with autonomous and interoperable services that offer reusable business functionality via standardized interfaces. Services can exist on all layers of an application system (business process, presentation, business logic, data management). They may be composed of services from lower layers, wrap parts of legacy application systems or be implemented from scratch. Typically, services at the business process layer are described as *business services*, while services at the lower implementation level are described as *technical services* (Stantchev & Schröpfer, 2009).

Two main aspects denote the successful provision of a service: it should provide the needed functionality, as well as the needed Quality of Service (QoS). QoS parameters are part of the non-functional properties (NFPs) of a service. The NFPs of a software system are those properties that do not describe or influence the principal task / functionality of the software, but are expected and can be observed by end users in its runtime behavior (Lohmann et al., 2005). Such properties can be design-time related or run-time related. Design-time related NFPs such as language of service and compliance are typically set during design time and do not change during runtime. Run-time related NFPs are typically performance oriented (e.g. response time, throughput, availability). They can change during runtime – when times of extensive usage by a big number of users are followed by times of unfrequent usage, or when failures occur.

In order to be successful in competitive and volatile settings, organizations require optimally designed business processes: Here, not one-time optimized business processes play the essential role, but rather the ability to quickly react to new developments and to flexibly adapt respective business processes are decisive (Borzo, 2005).

It is typical that these processes are supported through information technologies (IT) which consequently have been catalyzing increased interest in reference modeling for IT process management. Reference models such as ITIL and COBIT (Control Objectives for Information and related Technology) represent proven best practices and provide key frameworks for the design and control of IT services (Van Bon, 2008). On the one hand, utilization of reference models promises to enhance quality and facilitates better compliance according to statutes and contractual agreements. On the other hand, IT processes have to correspond to corporate strategy and its respective goals. Therefore, the question arises how best practices can be implemented in a particular corporate environment. Another challenge lurks in the checking of reference process execution as well as in assuring compliance to IT procedure in respect to new or altered business processes.

The application and the benefits of approaches such as COBIT and ITIL for the optimization of IT organizations are widely known. We recently introduced an approach for the continuous quality improvement of IT processes based on such models (Gerke & Tamm, 2009). Nevertheless, this approach is not directly applicable to NFPs in an intra-organizational SOA.

In this chapter we describe an approach that assures the continuous provision of service levels in such settings. It is based on our previous work with such reference models and our work in the area of service level assurance in SOA (Stantchev & Schröpfer, 2009; Stantchev & Malek, 2009; Stantchev & Malek, 2010). The approach has been implemented in several industrial settings.

The rest of this chapter is structured as follows: Section 2 presents the current developments in the area of Internet of Services and Internet of Devices. In Section 3 we describe governance approaches for IT and SOA as the context for our approach and then we describe our approach in more details. Section 4 contains a summary of our results and outlook on future trends.

THE INTERNET OF SERVICES AND THE INTERNET OF DEVICES

The Internet of Services is driven by the vision of providing functionality through the web. It major driving technologies are SOA and Software as a Service (SaaS) that extend the vision of older component technologies such as CORBA and .NET to a truly world-wide distributed applications. Cloud Computing provides an unprecedented elasticity of resources (without scale up premiums) (Armbrust et al. 2010) and thereby makes the combination of own and provided software functions, platforms, as well as hardware infrastructure even more attractive for a state of the art IT management.

On the other side, the Internet of Devices leads to a myriad of smart devices that can now consume functionality provided in such highly distributed architectures. Main driving forces there are the fields of Near Field Communication (NFC), Radio Frequency Identification (RFID), position and context awareness, as well as smart objects. Figure 1 visualizes the integration between the two fields.

While SaaS is a particularly challenging topic for IT departments it also opens some new possibilities for them. The integration of SaaS offering in an IT landscape is nontrivial – organizations need to adapt structure and processes. Furthermore, they need to tackle topics such as SaaS Identification, SaaS Assessment, SaaS Integration, and SaaS Risks. On the other side, IT departments can provide SaaS offerings themselves and thereby access new corporate and interorganizational markets.

One important prerequisite is the extension of the IT customer relationship management (CRM) with SaaS-related aspects. Tools for SaaS assessment can help organizations to better identify and select suitable SaaS offerings. Within the context

Figure 1. The integration between the internet of services and the internet of devices

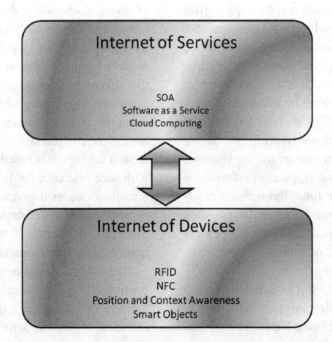

of SaaS quality management is regarded as an encompassing topic for identification, assessment, integration and management of SaaS offerings. It aims to cover the complete lifecycle up to SaaS decommissioning. Undefined responsibilities and requirements (particularly non-functional ones) are often the reason for failure of such SaaS integration projects. This is where approaches from IT governance and process mining can provide benefits – an organization can employ them to effectively assure continuous quality improvement and management of own and provided SaaS offerings.

NON-FUNCTIONAL PROPERTIES IN SOA AND IT SERVICE MANAGEMENT

IT Governance frameworks such as the IT Infrastructure Library (ITIL) (Van Bon, 2008) and Control Objectives for Information and Related Technology (COBIT) (Lainhart IV, 2000) aim to provide guidance for the design and implementation of dependable IT infrastructures.

The IT Infrastructure Library

ITIL Version 2 was developed between 2000 and 2004 as a Best Practice approach for structuring IT-related tasks and defining socio-technical services as the specific interface to the IT user. It emerged as a de-facto standard in the area of IT Service Management (ITSM). ITIL Version 3 was published in 2007 (Van Bon, 2008) and introduced an enhanced view of IT-related activities and a life cycle concept.

The life cycle concept is based on the following phases:

- Service design,
- Service transition, and
- Service operation.

These operational phases are preceded by service strategy, while continual service improvement provides the needed iteration aspects within the life cycle.

COBIT

COBIT was initially developed by the Information Systems Audit and Control Association (ISACA) in 1993. Since 2000 the standard is maintained by the IT Governance Institute. The version from 2000 (Version 3.0) was followed by Version 4.0 in 2005. As of 2009 current version is 4.1.

The standard includes four domains that are structured into 34 critical processes.

The domains are:

- **PO:** Plan and Organize,
- **AI:** Acquire and Implement,
- **DS:** Deliver and Support, and
- **ME:** Monitor and Evaluate.

There are 215 Control Objectives (COs) that are spread across the critical processes.

SOA Governance

ITSM has risen to the major challenge of aligning the IT services with the business and to produce high-quality IT services. The IT services are offered to customers and provided to users by an IT service provider. Within the last years, the number of organizations, which act as service providers, has increased due to the popularity of shared services and outsourcing. This in turn has strengthened the practice of service management and at the same time imposed greater challenges upon it. Today, IT service providers are on the one hand judged on their ability to deliver in time and at agreed service levels. The enormous pricing competition further puts pressure on them to reduce total costs of ownership in order to provide their services at an adequate cost-benefit ratio. The business environment on the other hand often increases the frequency, complexity, and the extent of changes and, thus, requests unprecedented flexibility with respect to the IT services and the customer requirements to ITSM.

Because of these pressures, quality enhancement and cost reduction have become mainstream thinking of IT service provider. Not only it is important that this commitment to quality and costs is targeted to the production processes, but also to the IT service management activities. A vivid demonstration of the importance of the quality of both IT services and ITSM processes is the internet service provider (ISP), which represents a special variant of an IT service provider. Since IT-based internet services are its products, IT processes include more than support processes. As a result of the relevant IT production processes and ITSM processes being the production processes of the ISP, the importance of IT services and ITSM processes is considerably higher. A similar observation can be made about service providers at the different levels of Cloud Computing – infrastructure, platform, or software.

ITIL and COBIT are not mutually exclusive. On the contrary - they are often applied together with a specific focus. ITIL provides the overall framework for defining and providing IT-related activities, while COBIT is best used to define the "measurement points" and the control processes for these activities.

These are two important aspects of IT Governance. With respect to SOA we can observe the particular applicability of these approaches for SOA Governance.

One important aspect of SOA Governance is the specification of service requirements. While there are a variety of methods to describe the functional requirements for a service, the field of the specification of NFPs is currently an emerging research area. In (Stantchev & Schröpfer, 2009) we proposed a structure for service level statements to formalize the requirements and capabilities of Web Services as depicted in Figure 2. We call it a Service Level Objective (SLO).

Figure 2 also contains sample service level statements about the NFPs response time, throughput and availability. With this statement, on the one hand the performance-related capabilities of the services used in the scenario can be described in a machine-readable form. On the other hand, the internal requirements of the service aggregator who is orchestrating the services can be specified in the same way, but on an aggregated level - better reflecting the user experience.

These statements are then stored with the service description (service capabilities) respectively with the process/scenario description (process requirements).

An example for a statement about the service capability is "The response time of the service is guaranteed to be less than 150 ms in 93% of the cases as long as transaction rate is less than 50 per second." An example for a requirement on an aggregated user experience level is "The response

Figure 2. Formalization of NFPs in a service level objective (SLO)

	NFP	Predicate	Metric (Value, Unit)	Percentage	Qualifying conditions (QC)		
					NFP	Predicate	Metric
SLO pattern							
SLO examples	Response time	less than	150 ms	in 93 % of the cases	if transaction rate	less than	50 transactions per second
	Throughput	higher than	900 kB/s	in 98 % of the cases	if transaction rate	less than	50 transactions per second
	Availability	higher than	99.9 %	-	if -	-	-

time of the aggregated services should be less than 1s in 96% of the cases while transaction rate is less than 50 per second."

The availability of formalized SLOs makes the comparison with actual service levels more transparent and straightforward. They can serve as reference points for service level assurance.

Service Level Assurance

To achieve service level assurance we should consider ways to represent and control NFPs at the level of a technical service. Formal representation can be generally realized in a structure similar to the SLOs. In (Stantchev & Malek, 2009; Stantchev, 2008b) we described several techniques to address availability and performance, particularly response time and throughput. We call the approach to apply such techniques at different levels of a service platform as architectural translucency (Stantchev, 2008a).

Bridging Service NFPs with IT Service Management

In order to connect NFP aspects in service-oriented infrastructures with NFP aspects in IT Service Management we should look at the life cycle approaches in these fields.

The SOA life cycle is an iterative process model that integrates software engineering and business process management approaches to deliver a holistic view of service creation, deployment and management (Cox & Kreger, 2005).

Figure 3 gives an overview of the approach. It consists of two general phases - the preproduction phase and the production phase. The preproduction phase includes two stages - the Model stage and the Assemble stage. In the first stage the business model of an organization is created. It includes business processes and business metrics (or key performance indicators - KPIs) that relate to them. A formalized business model is the starting point for the Assemble stage where the artifacts of the future information system (IS) that implements the business model are assembled. The use of the verb assembled rather than developed reveals the strong focus on reuse in a service-based system - needed functionality should be provided by existing services as far as possible. This includes functions of legacy applications that can be integrated (e.g., via EAI adapters or Web Service wrappers).

The production phase also includes two stages - the Deploy stage and the Manage stage.

Figure 3. The SOA life cycle

The Deploy stage is a combination of creating the hosting environment for the service-based applications and the actual deployment of those applications. Key objective is to find appropriate platform offerings for hosting user interaction components, business process workflows, business services, access services, and information logic. This involves the assurance of NFPs such as availability, reliability, integrity, efficiency, and service ability.

In the Manage stage key activities are: monitoring performance of service requests and timeliness of service responses; failure detection and localization; routing tasks around failures; recovering work affected by those failures; correcting problems; and restoring the operational state of the system. This stage also includes managing the business model, configuring the operational environment to meet the requirements of the business design, and measuring success or failure to meet those requirements (Cox & Kreger, 2005). The Manage stage also involves performing routine maintenance, administering and securing applications, resources and users, and predicting future capacity growth to ensure that resources are available when the business requires it.

These two phases of the SOA life cycle are similar to the two phases of the systems life cycle in the context of dependability - development and use (Avizienis et al., 2004). An important aspect is that in this second classification the acceptance and introduction activities are part of the development phase - it includes all activities from presentation of the initial user requirements to the successful pass of the acceptance test of the developed system. The use phase of a system in the second classification begins when it is accepted for use and starts the delivery of its services to the users. This phase consists of periods of correct service delivery, service outage, and service shutdown. A service outage (incorrect service delivery) is caused by a failure of a service. A service shutdown is an intentional halt of the service by an

authorized actor. Maintenance actions may occur during all three periods of the use phase.

We have recently evaluated the SOA life cycle and proposed a methodology and a structure to enhance it with dependability-related activities (Stantchev & Malek, 2010). Our assessment led us also to the idea of integrating IT Service Management approaches with the SOA life cycle.

Our approach for integrating IT Service Management within the SOA life cycle starts with the selection of a governance framework that we plan to apply within the cycle. After that selection we focus on a "bird-view" mapping of phases of the framework to phases of the SOA life cycle.

Figure 4 shows the result of such mapping for ITIL. The mapping is described in details in the following sections.

In the first mapping we integrate activities from the Model Stage of the SOA Life Cycle with the phase Service Strategy of ITIL. The model stage defines the business model of the enterprise and includes business processes and business metrics (or key performance indicators - KPIs) that relate to them.

Therefore, it is well suited for activities relevant to the phase Service Strategy of ITIL - defining service life cycle, demand estimation and the resulting development of the service portfolio.

In the second mapping we integrate activities from the Assemble Stage of the SOA Life Cycle with the phase Service Design of ITIL. In the Assemble stage the artifacts of the future information system that implements the business model are assembled. Activities there can be matched with the activities relevant to the phase Service Design of ITIL - definition of IT-Services with their functional requirements, resources and capabilities; technology architectures and design, transition and operation processes for the specific services.

In the third mapping we integrate activities from the Deploy Stage of the SOA Life Cycle with the phase Service Transition of ITIL. The Deploy stage is a combination of creating the hosting environment for the service-based applications

Figure 4. Integrating IT service management and the SOA life cycle

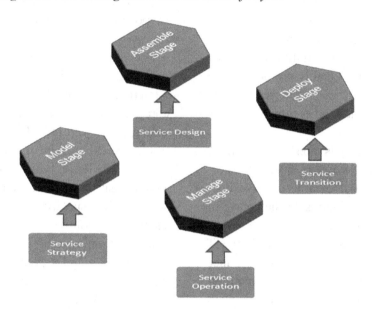

and the actual deployment of those applications. This correspond well with activities in the ITIL phase Service Transition – Transition Planning and Support, Change Management, Service Asset and Configuration Management, Release and Deployment Management, Service Validation and Testing, as well as Evaluation.

In the fourth mapping we integrate activities from the Manage Stage of the SOA Life Cycle with the phase Service Operation of ITIL. Key activities in the Manage stage include the monitoring performance of service requests and timeliness of service responses, as well as dependability-related actions such as fault handling and failure avoidance. It also includes managing the business model - configuring the operational environment to meet the requirements of the business design, and measuring success or failure to meet those requirements (Cox & Kreger, 2005). The Manage stage also involves routine maintenance - administering and securing applications, resources and users. Furthermore, it is responsible for the prediction of future capacity growth to ensure availability. These activities correspond to similar activities within ITIL Service Operation - Event Manage-

ment, Incident Management, Problem Management, Request Fulfillment, Access Management, Monitoring, and IT Operations.

In our evaluation of the SOA Life Cycle with regard to the introduction of dependability-related activities (Stantchev & Malek, 2010) we also observed the need of stronger focus on iteration-related aspects. There we also provided a structure to handle such iterations in the context of dependability. We regard ITIL Continual Service Improvement as a suitable framework to further specify concrete iteration activities.

Successful use of IT-services following SOA principles requires an integrative controlling and improvement model for risk and quality management. For such a new approach the composition use of IT controlling frameworks (e.g. COBIT), best practice reference models (such as ITIL), process monitoring tools and process mining is necessary. Through the aid of a SOA controlling model, an IT controlling department can achieve transparent oversight of information and service relationships between internal Cloud providers, external SaaS providers and the SOA customers. Information and service relationships may be continuously assessed based on accepted and agreed upon process controlling goals.

Through aforementioned service relationships, dependency structures and noninfluenceable factors become apparent. Quality-promoting and quality-reducing factors within the relationship network can be identified and eventually entirely controlled.

Maturity degree models integrated into SOA controlling model assess quality levels of respective processes on the basis of target quality values and provide recommendations on the course of action to improve process quality. The controlling model may act as decision support for the IT department in respect to monitoring performance quality of SaaS providers. By using a SOA controlling model, the process quality level of any SaaS provider can on the one side be assessed and be used to establish agreements on desired process quality targets.

Additionally, the model may provide action recommendations to the provider in order to achieve higher process quality. On the other side, information and communication relations between internal service departments, SaaS providers and customers may be assessed according quality

level and associated risk in order to yield basis for potentially necessary decisions for quality improvements.

Process mining is a specific data mining technique. The main goal of data mining is the extraction of process knowledge from large data storages. One very interesting field for process-mining analyses are recordings from goal-oriented process execution. Aim of analyses is to mine the process knowledge, which consists in raw data sets of what, how, when and where something was done in a specific process. Process mining results can optimize the as is process models of information system (IS) automatically. With the use of Mining Extensible Markup Language (MXML) recordings of the process execution can be stored and analyzed with data mining tools. The combination of ITIL, COBIT, monitoring and process mining allows a continual process quality improvement. Figure 5 represents an approach to continual process improvement. Fundamental is the composition of best-practice process models like ITIL or COBIT, process-monitoring and optimization tools and process mining tools.

Figure 5. Procedural model of service operations on the basis of process mining

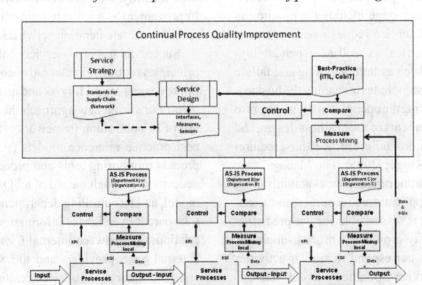

FUTURE RESEARCH DIRECTIONS

The definition and assurance of NFPs is still an open research field. The trends of SaaS and Cloud Computing exasperate the need for methodical frameworks that can address these topics. The integration of such frameworks with reference models such as ITIL and COBIT can make the introduction of NFP assurance in IT organizations more straightforward.

Future areas of research can be grouped in two sections - providing more detailed assessment of the quality of the currently provided NFPs, and automating service reconfiguration to adapt to changes in NFP levels.

In the first area we focus on the definition of application scenarios in the context of COBIT. Thus, we can more easily map between NFRs as defined in the COBIT phases, on the one side, and the NFP capabilities of the SaaS offerings, on the other.

Specific activities in the second area are the specification of KPIs and the extension of the monitoring infrastructure to accommodate aspects from related activities. Here, the presented method for process mining can be widely applied. We are currently working on its application in the preproduction phase.

CONCLUSION

The application and the benefits of approaches such as COBIT and ITIL for the optimization of IT organizations are widely known. In this chapter we described an approach to address NFPs based on ITIL and the SOA Life Cycle. We provided a specific set of activities that relate to ITIL and can be applied within the SOA Life Cycle. Furthermore, we described an approach for process mining that can provide insights about the quality and relevance of service operations. Our evaluation in several industrial settings demonstrates the feasibility and the benefits of the approach.

REFERENCES

Armbrust, M., Fox, A., Gri-th, R., Joseph, A. D., Katz, R., & Konwinski, A. (2010). A view of cloud computing. *Communications of the ACM, 53*(4), 50–58. doi:10.1145/1721654.1721672

Avizienis, A., Laprie, J.-C., Randell, B., & Landwehr, C. (2004). Basic concepts and taxonomy of dependable and secure computing. *IEEE Transactions on Dependable and Secure Computing, 1*(1), 11–33. doi:10.1109/TDSC.2004.2

Borzo, J. (2005). *Business 2010-embracing the challenge of change*. Technical report.

Cox, D. E., & Kreger, H. (2005). Management of the service-oriented-architecture life cycle. *IBM Systems Journal, 44*(4), 709–726. doi:10.1147/sj.444.0709

Gerke, K., & Tamm, G. (2009). Continuous quality improvement of IT processes based on reference models and process mining. *AMCIS 2009 Proceedings*, (p. 786).

Kumar, P. (2008). A low-cost hybrid coordinated checkpointing protocol for mobile distributed systems. *Mobile Information Systems, 4*(1), 13–32.

Lainhart, J. IV. (2000). COBIT: A methodology for managing and controlling information and Information Technology risks and vulnerabilities. *Journal of Information Systems, 14*, 21. doi:10.2308/jis.2000.14.s-1.21

Lohmann, D., Spinczyk, O., & Schröder-Preikschat, W. (2005). On the configuration of non-functional properties in operating system product lines. In Y. Coady, E. Eide, D.H. Lorenz & O. Spinczyk (Eds.), *Proceedings of the 4th AOSD Workshop on Aspects, Components and Patterns for Infrastructure Software* (AOSD-ACP4IS '05), NU-CCIS-05-03, (pp. 19-25). Boston: Northeastern University.

Stantchev, V. (2008a). *Architectural translucency*. Berlin: GITO Verlag.

Stantchev, V. (2008b). *Effects of replication on Web service performance in WebSphere. (ICSI tech report 2008-03)*. Berkeley, California: International Computer Science Institute.

Stantchev, V., & Malek, M. (2009). Translucent replication for service level assurance. In *High Assurance Services Computing* (pp. 1–18). Berlin, New York: Springer. doi:10.1007/978-0-387-87658-0_1

Stantchev, V. & Malek, M. (2010). Addressing dependability throughout the SOA life cycle. *IEEE Transactions on Services Computing, 99*.

Stantchev, V., & Schröpfer, C. (2009). Negotiating and enforcing QoS and SLAs in grid and cloud computing. In *GPC '09: Proceedings of the 4th International Conference on Advances in Grid and Pervasive Computing*, (pp. 25-35). Berlin, Heidelberg: Springer-Verlag.

Stantchev, V., & Schröpfer, C. (2009). Service level enforcement in Web-services based systems. *International Journal on Web and Grid Services, 5*(2), 130–154. doi:10.1504/IJWGS.2009.027571

Van Bon, J. (2008). *Foundations of IT service management based on ITIL V3*. Van Haren.

Wang, Y., Wong, D. S., & Wang, H. (2008). Employ a mobile agent for making a payment. *Mobile Information Systems, 4*(1), 51–68.

Chapter 15

Functional and QoS Semantics–Driven SOA–Based Biomedical Multimedia Processing

Shih-Hsi Liu
California State University – Fresno, USA

Yu Cao
California State University – Fresno, USA

Ming Li
California State University – Fresno, USA

Thell Smith
California State University – Fresno, USA

John Harris
California State University – Fresno, USA

Jie Bao
Rensselaer Polytechnic Institute, USA

Barrett R. Bryant
University of Alabama at Birmingham, USA

Jeff Gray
University of Alabama at Birmingham, USA

ABSTRACT

Although there have existed a wide range of techniques of biomedical multimedia processing, none of them could be generally satisfied by various domains. The main reason for such deficiency is due to the correlative nature between biomedical multimedia data and the techniques applied to them. This book chapter introduces an SOA-based biomedical multimedia infrastructure with a pre-processing component. Such an infrastructure adapts the concepts of requirements elicitation of Software Engineering as well as a training set of Machine Learning to analyze functional and QoS properties of biomedical multimedia data in advance. Such properties will be constructed as ontology and used for selecting the most appropriate services to perform data analysis, transmission, or retrieval. Two medical education projects are introduced as case studies to illustrate the usage of functional and QoS semantics extracted from a feature extraction service to improve the performance of subsequent classification service and searching service, respectively.

DOI: 10.4018/978-1-60566-794-2.ch015

INTRODUCTION

In the area of biomedical multimedia processing, there are many existing techniques for different applications. Each of these techniques has their own advantages as well as limitations. A common scenario is that a highly successful technique for a particular problem domain may not work properly for another. Even in the same domain, due to a wide variety of biomedical multimedia data under different conditions (e.g., different capturing devices, different decoding/encoding methods, different illuminations, scales, and viewing angles), a wide range of techniques may be utilized together or separately to achieve the best performance of processing such heterogeneous data. However, how to best leverage the composition/decomposition, rearrangement, or improvement of these techniques to tackle tight correlation between multimedia processing techniques and its data is an open problem. Most of the existing approaches perform preliminary analysis of the problem domain and manually inspection of the raw biomedical multimedia data in order to determine the best practice for later multimedia processing. Unfortunately, such manual trial-and-error procedures to analyze and inspect raw data are tedious and error-prone. The common nature of huge-volume in multimedia data also increases difficulties of the preliminary procedures as well as multimedia processing. Besides, software systems composed by existing or new techniques for biomedical multimedia processing usually have very specific and stringent yet sundry functional and Quality of Service (QoS) requirements. For example, OpenEHR (OpenEHR Foundation, 2010) and HL7 (Health Level 7 International, 2010) standards, HIPAA policies (U.S. Department of Health and Human Services, 2010), and FDA regulations (U.S. Food and Drug Administration, 2010) are mandatory privacy and security requirements that biomedical systems should guarantee. All such problems (i.e., tight correlation, huge-volume data, and stringent functional

and QoS requirements) make the determination of the best practice of multimedia processing a challenging task.

Service-Oriented Architecture (SOA) (Erl, 2005; Papazoglou et al., 2007) is a software engineering paradigm that creates, composes and interoperates homogeneous/heterogeneous services (i.e., individual units of logic autonomously perform specific functionalities conforming industry standards and principles (Erl, 2005)) in loosely coupled manners. Such a paradigm may also enable service rearrangements in accordance to specific functional or QoS needs (Papazoglou et al., 2007). This book chapter reviews the semantics-driven and data-driven SOA infrastructure for biomedical multimedia software development introduced in (Liu et al., 2008). The book chapter specifically concentrates on how the proposed SOA-based infrastructure, relying on the multimedia data, stringent multimedia software requirements, and communication protocols as functional and/or QoS contracts with services (Barreto et al., 2007), solves the abovementioned multimedia processing problem (i.e., the correlation problem).

Our infrastructure comprises five main aspects: (i) Services development for biomedical multimedia software. These services include, but not limit to, data analysis, transmission, and retrieval. Data pattern discovery, reliable and secure data transmissions, and efficient data access are the objectives of the three respective services; (ii) Multimedia data annotations, comprising both automatic and manual annotations, are introduced. Content analysis such as edge detection or corner detection may be performed when automatic annotations are invoked. Such an analysis is lightweighted and executed before the actual data processing stage. A few insights of the characteristics of the data sets could be revealed to guide on how to choose the most appropriate services/service combinations later. For example, QoS annotations (e.g., bone measures of a skull image) may be elicited by content analysis algorithms; (iii)

Ontology building. Biomedical multimedia data ontology will be built by extracting and organizing data annotations. Service and domain ontologies will be also described. Additionally, to help later semantics matching and better management, ontology associations between functional and quality of service requirements are also introduced. The association relationships include one-to-one (i.e., bijective; see Wolfram MathWorld, 2008), one-to-many, and many-to-one (i.e., non-injective and surjective; see Wolfram MathWorld, 2008). QoS requirements are also classified into strict, non-strict, static, dynamic, orthogonal and non-orthogonal, where non-orthogonal ones may also have association relationships similar to functional and QoS; (iv) Service discovery and selection. Appropriate services will be discovered and selected reasoned from the semantics matching among data, service and domain ontologies. The semantics matching aims at both functional and QoS requirements: Functional requirements act as mandatory matching rules of discovery criteria, and QoS requirements are used as selection criteria to determine how appropriate a service can be provided to a multimedia artifact.; and (v) QoS optimization. For a biomedical multimedia system to accomplish data analysis, transmission, and retrieval tasks in compliance to specific use cases, orchestration languages (Erl, 2005) (e.g., WS-BPEL (Barreto et al., 2007)) are needed to specify business process behavior based on services. However, many QoS are dynamically determined by the data processed by services as well as the execution status and deployment environments of services at runtime. Introducing monitoring, learning, and adaptation mechanisms (Papazoglou et al., 2007) may help tune up QoS or replace services dynamically. By achieving the five aspects, it is expected that the introduced semantics-driven and data-driven SOA infrastructure may not only solve the aforementioned problem but also overcome the interoperability and scalability issues. Due to space consideration, only the first four aspects are discussed.

The book chapter is organized as follows: QoS in SOA is summarized in the next section; Section 3 introduces the infrastructure, followed by two case studies presented in Section 4; Section 5 summarizes three other SOA approaches for biomedical domain; and finally, the concluding remarks and future directions are outlined in Section 6.

BACKGROUND

This section introduces major QoS supports for SOA/Web services provided by Windows Communication Foundation (WCF) (Bustamante, 2007) platform and Java EE 5 (Sun Microsystems, 2008).

WCF is a distributed messaging platform under the .NET Framework 3.0 or later. It advocates SOA by supporting interoperability across different processes, machines, protocols, and non-WCF web services (Bustamante, 2007). In order to provide satisfactory QoS, WCF introduces some advanced features to control throughput, security, and reliability. For throughput, *PerCall* or *PerSession* of *instancing mode* determines the lifetime a service allocated to requests. *Concurrency mode* and *throttling behavior* respectively determine if a service instance allows concurrent calls and control the load of each service by restricting the number of concurrent calls, sessions or service instances. For reliability, WCF introduces *reliable session* to overcome network failures and guarantee transmitting messages in order. *Transactions* are also present in WCF to coordinate a series of activities in a consistent state. Lastly, *queued calls* enhance reliability by guaranteeing that transmitting messages will be durably stored in queues until the message receiver is back online. As for security, when standard bindings that establish communication channels between clients and services are selected, default security configurations will be set. These configurations include six security modes (e.g., *transport* and *message*), four credential types (e.g., Windows Kerberos credentials), 16 encryption algorithms, and role-based authorization, to name a few (Bustamante, 2007). All of the default settings can be customized based on service needs.

Java EE 5 (Sun Microsystems, 2008) also provides QoS supports similar to the above-mentioned WCF features. Besides, implementing customized *javax.xml.ws.handler.Handler* optionally with *@HanlderChain* annotations is commonly seen under JAX-WS runtime (Hansen, 2007; Java Community Press, 2007). "Handlers are used to implement pre- and post-processing of a *MessageContext* before the invocation of a service implementation bean (Hansen, 2007)." For protocol-specific QoS requirements, a user-defined handler may implement *SOAPHandler* interface to operate the entire SOAP message and message context properties. For example, persistency for reliable message transmission and message authentication can be introduced using such an approach (Hansen, 2007). For protocol-independent QoS requirements, implementing *javax.xml.ws.handler.LogicalHandler* to access and operate message payload (SOAP body) facilitates the validation of QoS. *LogicalHandler* may be applied to regular as well as REpresentational State Transfer (REST) (Hansen, 2007) Web services while protocol-specific handlers are more appropriate to non-REST Web services.

Although both WCF and Java EE 5 platforms provide QoS supports to services in various aspects, QoS supports to solve the problems of abundant requirements, huge data size, and data/content-service correlation in biomedical multimedia systems should be also considered. By taking data, services and domain requirements into account and semantically describing them in ontologies, it may be easier to discover suitable services and adaptively tune services to optimal in accordance to specific data.

OUR APPROACH

This section reviews the four aspects of the semantics- and data-driven SOA-based infrastructure for biomedical multimedia data processing introduced in (Liu et al., 2008) but specifically focuses on QoS issues that may be influenced statically and dynamically by both multimedia data and services correlatively. Figure 1 shows the overview of the proposed SOA-based infrastructure. The figure can be interpreted bi-directionally: (i) Starting from the bottom, services for analysis (including automatic annotation), transmission, and retrieval are constructed with WSDL files automatically generated (Section 3.1). Service and domain ontologies, represented in OWL-S (Martin et al., 2004), is then generated based on WSDL files (Section 3.3); and (ii) Conversely, starting from the top, a user starts with annotating biomedical multimedia data, which will be converted into MPEG-7 format. Such results will be then used for data and domain ontologies establishment (Section 3.2). Followed by service, data, and domain ontology building, semantics matching can be performed to select suitable services for composition reasoned from data, domain and service ontologies (Section 3.4). Finally, the selected services can be composed together to perform analysis, transmissions, and retrieval, to name a few.

Service for Multimedia Data

Before introducing how our infrastructure processes biomedical multimedia data, the proposed SOA-based infrastructure is decomposed and classified into analysis, transmission, and retrieval services. This section briefly summarizes analysis and retrieval services mainly used in Section 4. (Liu et al., 2008) has experimented with six transmission services under WCF. The experimental results showed that HTTP-based concurrent transmission services performed better on small size (60MB) transmission while TCP-based

Figure 1. The overview of the proposed SOA-based infrastructure

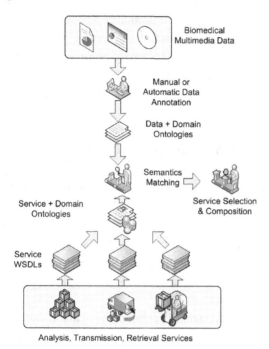

Biomedical Multimedia Data

Manual or Automatic Data Annotation

Data + Domain Ontologies

Semantics Matching

Service + Domain Ontologies

Service Selection & Composition

Service WSDLs

Analysis, Transmission, Retrieval Services

WCF-ChunCking (Tercom, 2008) outperformed others when transmitting 1.07GB files. For the details of transmission services, please refer to (Liu et al., 2008).

Analysis

The goal of analysis services is to develop data mining algorithms to discovery important patterns from biomedical multimedia data. Taking the project of developing new multimedia computing techniques for colonoscopy procedure in the health care domain as an example, interesting analysis algorithms include: (i) Audio-visual analysis approach for scene segmentation; (ii) Image/video analysis techniques for operation shot detection; (iii) Image analysis techniques for appendix image classification.

For (1), a scene is defined as a segment of visual and audio data that corresponds to an endoscopic segment of the colon. Since a typical colon has six different parts and as the terminal ileum is also reachable during endoscopy, in a complete colonoscopic procedure, a total of thirteen scenes are expected: Seven scenes from the insertion phase and six scenes from the withdrawal phase. Our algorithms comprise two stages. In the first stage, scene segmentation algorithm using audio analysis and finite state automata to recognize scenes and associated boundaries (Cao et al., 2004a) is developed. In the second stage of the proposed algorithms, a new visual model approach that employs visual features extracted directly from compressed videos together with audio analysis results from the first stage to improve the scene segmentation performance (Cao et al., 2004b) is implemented.

For (2), a new type of semantic unit called operation shot is defined, which is a segment of visual and audio data that corresponds to a diagnostic or therapeutic operation in a colonoscopy video. The problem of detecting operation shots is mapped to the problem of identifying instruments used in diagnostic or therapeutic operations, since the operations cannot be performed without these instruments. A new spatial-temporal segmentation approach for operation shot detection is introduced. The experimental results have shown the effectiveness of the proposed approach (Cao et al., 2004c; Cao et al., 2007). In our approach, spatial analysis methods are first applied to identify the presence of the instrument in each of the images extracted from the input colonoscopy video. Then the temporal analysis techniques are employed to determine the boundaries of operation shots by fusing the instrument detection results from stage 1 and the temporal information.

For (3), an image with a closely inspected appendicle orifice an "appendix image" is defined. Our purpose is to classify images in a colonoscopy video into two categories: appendix image class and non-appendix image class. Two different approaches to solve this problem (Cao et al., 2006; Liu et al., 2007a) have been developed. The first technique is based on new intermediate features extracted from each image, followed with different classifiers for image classification. The second approach is a new model based approach to capture both the local image parts and global spatial relations among the parts.

Note that because video segmentation and video classification algorithms may also generate metadata as annotations for multimedia data, these implementations can be regarded as annotation services described in Multimedia Data Annotation section. Additionally, besides the analysis services mentioned above, Case Study section also introduces light-weighted feature extraction analysis services for multimedia educational projects.

Retrieval

The objective of retrieval services is to efficiently assess large-scale biomedical multimedia databases using content-based image/video retrieve algorithms (Datta et al., 2008). However, due to a wide range of transforming, smoothing, and rendering, the same object in different videos may have totally different size, shape, and textures. How to design algorithms that are invariant to the object scale, illumination change, texture change, and transformation is a challenging problem. Our current focus is to investigate algorithms that can handle shape invariance, introduce new similarity measurements, and extend the measurements to handle other variances (e.g., texture and illumination changes). Adapting image retrieval algorithms from Lire (Lux, 2008b) and work in (Datta et al., 2008) into our infrastructure is also our plan.

Again, although there are only three types of services investigated, the loosely coupled design of autonomous services, interoperable message communications, and commonly agreed standards utilized in this infrastructure allow new services to be added and orchestrated easily in the future. All existing and new services should be described properly by WSDL (Erl, 2005), including their input and output formats, functionality provided, standards/policies/regulations followed, and QoS properties, to name a few. Finally, analysis and

retrieval services are usually considered as a joint component in the content-based image retrieval community. Our infrastructure decomposes them because of the definition of "service" (Erl, 2005). Such services can be easily composed together and considered as a single aggregator/composite service under our infrastructure following SOA principles.

Multimedia Data Annotation

In order to better annotate biomedical multimedia data and potentially tackle the semantic interoperability problems (Tzouvaras, Troncy, & Pan, 2007), our SOA infrastructure classifies biomedical multimedia annotations into four categorizes: data properties, contents, QoS annotations, and regulations.

Data properties describe physical attributes of text, audio, video and image data. For example, file name, file size, file format, bit rate, sample rate, channels, and duration are regarded as low-level physical properties (Garcia et al., 2008) of an audio file. Such low-level properties can be described using MPEG-7 (Celma et al., 2007), a standard for describing formatting information. More examples of data properties of different kinds of multimedia data are available in (Liu et al., 2008).

Content annotations using image/video content analysis have been an important topic for years. Annotations are obtained by either performing analysis services (e.g., video segmentation and classification) to automatically generate useful analysis results or manually updating useful content information. Important automatic and manual annotation approaches for images and videos can be respectively found at (Yan, Natsev, & Campbell, 2005) and (Tseng et al., 2008). In our infrastructure, a MPEG-7-based (Celma et al., 2007) manual annotation service adapted from the Caliph & Emir project (Lux, 2008a) has been introduced in (Liu et al., 2008). Such a service provides an interface to annotate data, contents,

Figure 2. The WSDL file of the annotation service

```
<definitions targetNamespace="http://arthemis/" name="AnnotateWSService"
xmlns="http://schemas.xmlsoap.org/wsdl/" xmlns:tns="http://arthemis/"
xmlns:xsd="http://www.w3.org/2001/XMLSchema"
xmlns:soap="http://schemas.xmlsoap.org/wsdl/soap/" xmlns:wsu="http://docs.oasis-
open.org/wss/2004/01/oasis-200401-wss-wssecurity-utility-1.0.xsd">
  <types>
    <xsd:schema>
      <xsd:import namespace="http://arthemis/"
schemaLocation="AnnotateWSService_schema1.xsd"/>
    </xsd:schema>
  </types>
  <!-- skipped some messages -->
  <message name="getVEllipsePoolAnnotation">
    <part name="parameters" element="tns:getVEllipsePoolAnnotation"/>
  </message>
  <message name="getVEllipsePoolAnnotationResponse">
    <part name="parameters" element="tns:getVEllipsePoolAnnotationResponse"/>
  </message>
  <message name="getNum4AnnotatedEllipse">
    <part name="parameters" element="tns:getNum4AnnotatedEllipse"/>
  </message>
  <message name="getNum4AnnotatedEllipseResponse">
    <part name="parameters" element="tns:getNum4AnnotatedEllipseResponse"/>
  </message>
  <message name="setEllipsePoolAnnotation">
    <part name="parameters" element="tns:setEllipsePoolAnnotation"/>
  </message>
  <message name="setEllipsePoolAnnotationResponse">
    <part name="parameters" element="tns:setEllipsePoolAnnotationResponse"/>
  </message>
  <portType name="AnnotateWS">
    <!-- skipped some operations -->
    <operation name="getVEllipsePoolAnnotation">
      <input message="tns:getVEllipsePoolAnnotation"/>
      <output message="tns:getVEllipsePoolAnnotationResponse"/>
    </operation>
    <operation name="getNum4AnnotatedEllipse">
      <input message="tns:getNum4AnnotatedEllipse"/>
      <output message="tns:getNum4AnnotatedEllipseResponse"/>
    </operation>
    <operation name="setEllipsePoolAnnotation">
      <input message="tns:setEllipsePoolAnnotation"/>
      <output message="tns:setEllipsePoolAnnotationResponse"/>
    </operation>
  </portType>
  <binding name="AnnotateWSPortBinding" type="tns:AnnotateWS">
    <soap:binding transport="http://schemas.xmlsoap.org/soap/http" style="document"/>
    <!-- skipped some operation binding -->
    <operation name="getVEllipsePoolAnnotation">
      <soap:operation soapAction=""/>
      <input>
        <soap:body use="literal"/>
      </input>
      <output>
        <soap:body use="literal"/>
      </output>
    </operation>
    <!-- skipped: soap setting for "getNum4AnnotatedEllipse" and "setEllipsePoolAnnotation"
are the same -->
  </binding>
  <service name="AnnotateWSService">
    <port name="AnnotateWSPort" binding="tns:AnnotateWSPortBinding">
      <soap:address location="REPLACE_WITH_ACTUAL_URL"/>
    </port>
  </service>
</definitions>
```

QoS, and regulations and converts the annotated results into MPEG-7. This section presents an annotation service, extended from the annotation portion of Arthemis (Liu et al., 2007b), not only specifically for colonoscopic procedures but also generically for domain-independent annotations. Figures 2 and 3 respectively show the WSDL files of the annotation service and its conversion

Figure 3. The WSDL file of the XML parsing and conversion service

```
<definitions targetNamespace="http://kxml/" name="KXMLDocumentService"
xmlns="http://schemas.xmlsoap.org/wsdl/" xmlns:tns="http://kxml/"
xmlns:xsd="http://www.w3.org/2001/XMLSchema"
xmlns:soap="http://schemas.xmlsoap.org/wsdl/soap/" xmlns:wsu="http://docs.oasis-
open.org/wss/2004/01/oasis-200401-wss-wssecurity-utility-1.0.xsd">
  <types>
    <xsd:schema>
      <xsd:import namespace="http://kxml/"
schemaLocation="KXMLDocumentService_schema1.xsd"/>
    </xsd:schema>
  </types>
  <!-- skipped some messages -->
  <message name="parseXMLFile">
    <part name="parameters" element="tns:parseXMLFile"/>
  </message>
  <message name="parseXMLFileResponse">
    <part name="parameters" element="tns:parseXMLFileResponse"/>
  </message>
  <message name="printToFile">
    <part name="parameters" element="tns:printToFile"/>
  </message>
  <message name="printToFileResponse">
    <part name="parameters" element="tns:printToFileResponse"/>
  </message>
  <portType name="KXMLDocument">
    <!-- skipped some operations -->
    <operation name="parseXMLFile">
      <input message="tns:parseXMLFile"/>
      <output message="tns:parseXMLFileResponse"/>
    </operation>
    <operation name="printToFile">
      <input message="tns:printToFile"/>
      <output message="tns:printToFileResponse"/>
    </operation>
  </portType>
  <binding name="KXMLDocumentPortBinding" type="tns:KXMLDocument">
    <soap:binding transport="http://schemas.xmlsoap.org/soap/http" style="document"/>
    <!-- skipped some binding (they are the same as parseXMLFile -->
    <operation name="parseXMLFile">
      <soap:operation soapAction=""/>
      <input>
        <soap:body use="literal"/>
      </input>
      <output>
        <soap:body use="literal"/>
      </output>
    </operation>
  </binding>
  <service name="KXMLDocumentService">
    <port name="KXMLDocumentPort" binding="tns:KXMLDocumentPortBinding">
      <soap:address location="REPLACE_WITH_ACTUAL_URL"/>
    </port>
  </service>
</definitions>
```

service. The conversion service converts the annotated results into two major modularized parts: MST (Minimal Standard Terminology) comprises domain-specific terms of European Gastrointestinal Society for Endoscopy (Liu et al., 2007b) (Figure 4); and MPEG-7 is a standard for not only formatting information but also comprehensive descriptions of the organizational and audio, visual and audiovisual features of multimedia content (Celma et al., 2007) (Figure 5). The advantage of such a modularized conversion is two-folds: (i) Both domain-specific and domain-independent

Figure 4. Domain-specific annotation for MST

```
<Arthemis xsi:schemaLocation="http://localhost/Arthemis combination2.xsd"
xmlns="http://localhost/Arthemis" xmlns:mst="http://localhost/mst"
xmlns:xsi="http://www.w3.org/2001/XMLSchema-instance"
xmlns:mpeg7="urn:mpeg:mpeg7:schema:2001">
 <?xml version="1.0" encoding="utf-8"?>
<mst:AnnotationProperities>
  <mst:NormalHeadings>...</mst:NormalHeadings>
  <mst:LumenHeadings>
   <mst:Dilated Site="Rectum"/>
   <mst:Stenosis Site="Peri-Anal">
     <mst:Apperance>Extrinsic</mst:Apperance>
     <mst:Length>80</mst:Length>
     <mst:Traversed>Yes</mst:Traversed>
   </mst:Stenosis>
   <mst:EvidenceOfPreviousSurgery Site="Cecum">
     <mst:Type>Colo-colonic</mst:Type>
     <mst:Value>Yes, describe</mst:Value>
     <mst:Location>hfg</mst:Location>
   </mst:EvidenceOfPreviousSurgery>
  </mst:LumenHeadings>
  <mst:ContentsHeadings>...</mst:ContentsHeadings>
  <mst:MucosaHeadings>...</mst:MucosaHeadings>
  <mst:FlatLesionsHeadings>...</mst:FlatLesionsHeadings>
  <mst:ProtrudingLesionsHeadings>...</mst:ProtrudingLesionsHeadings>
  <mst:ExcavatedLesionsHeadings>...</mst:ExcavatedLesionsHeadings>
  <mst:OtherHeadings>...</mst:OtherHeadings>
</mst:AnnotationProperities>
```

Figure 5. Domain-independent annotation for multimedia contents

```
<mpeg7:Mpeg7 mediaTimeBase=":" mediaTimeUnit="P" timeBase=":" xml:lang="en-us"
timeUnit="P">
   <mpeg7:Description xsi:type="mpeg7:SummaryDescriptionType">...</mpeg7:Description>
   <mpeg7:Description xsi:type="mpeg7:ContentEntityType">...</mpeg7:Description>
   <mpeg7:Description xsi:type="mpeg7:ContentEntityType">
     <mpeg7:MultimediaContent xsi:type="mpeg7:ImageType">
       <mpeg7:Image>
         <mpeg7:SpatialDecomposition>
           <mpeg7:StillRegion>
             <mpeg7:TextAnnotation>
               <mpeg7:KeywordAnnotation xml:lang="en">
                 <mpeg7:Keyword>20080923_12.25.58_192.168.1.2_1914.png</mpeg7:Keyword>
               </mpeg7:KeywordAnnotation>
             </mpeg7:TextAnnotation>
             <mpeg7:TextAnnotation>...</mpeg7:TextAnnotation>
             <mpeg7:TextAnnotation>
               <mpeg7:KeywordAnnotation xml:lang="en">
                 <mpeg7:Keyword>AnnotatedObject</mpeg7:Keyword>
                 <mpeg7:Keyword>Ellipse</mpeg7:Keyword>
                 <mpeg7:Keyword>ID=1</mpeg7:Keyword>
                 <mpeg7:Keyword>LineColor=-1250856</mpeg7:Keyword>
                 <mpeg7:Keyword>LineWidth=1</mpeg7:Keyword>
                 <mpeg7:Keyword>LineType=1</mpeg7:Keyword>
                 <mpeg7:Keyword>Visible=false</mpeg7:Keyword>
                 <mpeg7:Keyword>Location</mpeg7:Keyword>
                 <mpeg7:Keyword>Top=69.0</mpeg7:Keyword>
                 <mpeg7:Keyword>Left=146.0</mpeg7:Keyword>
                 <mpeg7:Keyword>Right=316.0</mpeg7:Keyword>
                 <mpeg7:Keyword>Bottom=154.0</mpeg7:Keyword>
                 <mpeg7:Keyword>Orientation=0.0</mpeg7:Keyword>
               </mpeg7:KeywordAnnotation>
             </mpeg7:TextAnnotation>
           </mpeg7:StillRegion>
         </mpeg7:SpatialDecomposition>
       </mpeg7:Image>
     </mpeg7:MultimediaContent>
   </mpeg7:Description>
</mpeg7:Mpeg7>
```

annotations require MPEG-7 part for describing images/video. This part could be left unchanged and treated as source of constructing data ontology.

Conversely, if a new domain-specific annotation is requested, changes to be made are isolated in the MST annotation. Such a domain-specific annotation could be later considered as the source of building domain ontology.

In order to solve the data/content-service correlation problem, QoS requirements for data and contents should be also annotated (i.e., QoS annotation). For example, if a skull image is expected to be transmitted to a remote site in a secure way, QoS annotations (e.g., minimum requirements of encryption algorithms) for such an image should be described. With QoS annotations, discovering and selecting appropriate services configured by WCF or Java EE 5 platforms may be easier. Additionally, because most of the users of biomedical multimedia software have biomedical background and may know specific standards to follow, manually annotating biomedical regulations for multimedia data is also needed (i.e., regulation annotation). If data to be processed require specific and stringent HL7/OpenEHR standards, HIPAA policies, and FDA regulations, the services to be selected for data process also need to follow them. An interface for users to manually input QoS and Regulation annotations has been introduced in (Liu et al., 2008). For security options, users can determine the security level of data from six security modes provided by WCF. Similarly, reliability, latency, and segmentation requirements can be also decided based on data's needs.

In order to conform to data and content annotations, QoS and regulation annotations are also expressed in MPEG-7. To our best knowledge, the current MPEG-7 schema does not offer suitable types to describe such annotations. Hence, *KeywordAnnotation* that is similar to Figure 5 is used to describe both QoS and regulation requirements. Other QoS or regulation requirements that are not listed by our interface by default (e.g., maximum file process size for an annotation service and encryption algorithm for a transmission service) may either use the same representation as in Figure 5 or investigate MPEG-7 schema in more details (e.g., (Bailer & Schallauer, 2008)).

Annotating data, contents, QoS and regulations is our first step for orchestrating biomedical multimedia software out of appropriate services. Such a step can be treated as data requirements elicitation either by automatic analysis services or by manual end user input. It can be also regarded as an extraction step "that supports acquisition of domain ontology from textual sources (Sabou et al., 2005)." Followed by annotations, ontology building is the next step.

Ontologies

"Successful employment of semantic Web services depends on the availability of high quality domain and service ontologies (Datta et al., 2008)." Building high quality domain ontology require following features: Generic enough to be used in many service descriptions; and rich enough to describe the complex relationships existing in a specific domain (Datta et al., 2008). To reflect such generality and specificity, we have built and integrated data and domain ontologies that contain both domain-independent and domain-specific descriptions (Bao et al., 2004). Figure 6 (Figure 3 of (Bao et al., 2004)) shows a part of OWL file that defines class *Scene* and *View*, where a data type property represents a simple property (e.g., *shotID* and *shotAnnotation*) of an entity and an object property implies a relationship between two entities (e.g., *subClassOf* and *partOf*). Figure 7 (Figure 5 of (Bao et al., 2004)) shows the integration of domain-independent and domain-specific ontologies.

For building service ontology, OWL-S (Martin et al. 2004) has been widely applied to describe service semantics, which facilitates service discovery, composition and invocation. Because of the correspondence between OWL-S and WSDL (Martin et al. 2004; Martin et al., 2003), XSTL can be used to transform from OWL-S to WSDL or vice versa. Some existing tools also support such transformation (e.g., OWL-S editor (Scicluna, 2004)). Note that because our infrastructure

Figure 6. The ontology of multimedia contents written in OWL (Figure 3 of Bao et al., 2004)

```
<owl:Class rdf:ID="View">
    <rdfs:subClassOf>
       <owl:Class rdf:about="#VideoClip"/>
    </rdfs:subClassOf>
    <rdfs:subClassOf>
       <owl:Restriction>
         <owl:onProperty>
           <owl:FunctionalProperty rdf:about="#hasStart"/>
         </owl:onProperty>
         <owl:allValuesFrom>
           <owl:Class rdf:about="#Scene"/>
         </owl:allValuesFrom>
       </owl:Restriction>
    </rdfs:subClassOf>
    ...
</owl:Class>
<owl:Class rdf:ID="Scene">
    <rdfs:subClassOf rdf:resource="#VideoClip"/>
    <rdfs:subClassOf>
       <owl:Restriction>
         <owl:onProperty>
           <owl:FunctionalProperty rdf:about="#hasStart"/>
         </owl:onProperty>
         <owl:allValuesFrom rdf:resource="#Shot"/>
       </owl:Restriction>
    </rdfs:subClassOf>
    ...
</owl:Class>
```

Figure 7. Integration of domain-independent and domain-specific ontologies (Figure 5 of Bao et al., 2004)

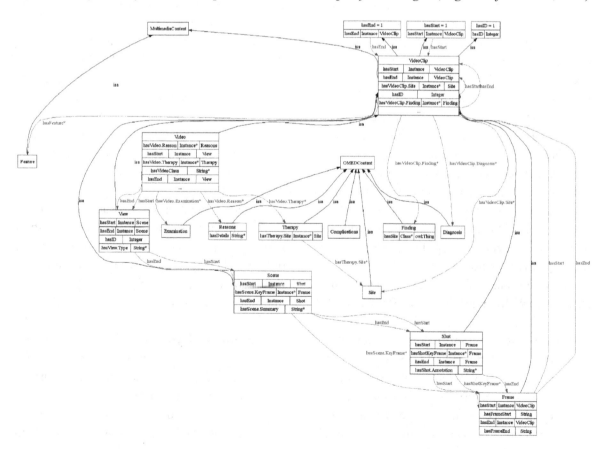

specifically concentrates on using data and domain ontologies to discover and select most suitable services based on service and domain ontologies, the expandable *serviceParameter* and *serviceCategory* profile attributes of OWL-S should offer sufficient information (e.g., the HL7 standards supported by and Quality Rate provided by a service), so that semantics matching among the three ontologies for the discovery and selection purpose can be achieved.

No matter which ontologies the infrastructure is building, each of them comprises both functional and QoS properties/requirements of domains, services, and data. For example, the domain ontology for HL7 standards may contain specific functional requirements of appointment and corresponding QoS requirements constraining scheduling (Chapter 10 of HL7); the service ontology for WCF transmissions may describe encryption algorithms as functional requirements for a specific transmission service and the secure levels of encryption (e.g., 64-bit or 128-bit) as its QoS requirements; and for data ontology, the coordinates of an abnormal polyp in a colon image from the health care project or the classification, facial features and bone measures of a skull image from the digital forensics project may be regarded as QoS properties. Analysis, retrieval, and transmission of these data can be treated as their functional requirements. In order to better ontology management and help for later semantics matching, ontology associations between functional and QoS requirements are introduced. The association relationships include one-to-one (i.e., bijective (Wolfram MathWorld, 2008)), one-to-many, and many-to-one (i.e., non-injective and surjective (Wolfram MathWorld, 2008)):

1. **One-to-One:** One-to-one associations between functional and QoS requirements are rarely seen in biomedical multimedia systems. For data ontology, the main reason is that, as seen in data property annotation subsection, biomedical multimedia data

naturally comprise very rich QoS properties. For domain ontology, possible examples may include a unique medical record format to overcome heterogeneity issues among health care organizations or applying the highest privacy policy. For service ontology, an example may be that a parsing service is only allowed to parse XML instances following a specific XML schema (e.g., MPEG-7 (Celma et al., 2007)).

2. **One-to-Many:** One-to-Many associations between functional and QoS requirements are commonly seen in the biomedical multimedia and may other domains. Examples of such associations include: a health care organization obeying HL7 may follow different rules to query patients' medical records (Chapter 3 of HL7); and a transmission service may be requested to provide concurrent, secure and reliable services.

3. **Many-to-One:** The reason of introducing Many-to-One associations is to speed up the later semantics matching process. For example, when REST-ful Web services are constructed, HTTP-based transmission services may be needed. Backtracking from HTTP protocol binding support (QoS requirement) to transmission services (functional requirements) will help us reduce the solution space of appropriate services.

For component-based software development, QoS requirements can be classified into strict, non-strict, static, dynamic, orthogonal and non-orthogonal (Liu et al., 2005). Such a classification may be also applied to SOA-based biomedical multimedia systems:

1. **Static and Dynamic:** Static QoS are usually design-related, which means QoS properties/requirements that remain the same regardless the current status of Web services container, network, or deployment environments. Examples include data properties (metadata),

regulations to follow, and specific encryption algorithms a service provides. Conversely, dynamic QoS is substantially influenced by the containers, network status, or deployment environments. Transmission rates and latency of transmission services, execution time of analysis and retrieval services are such kind of QoS commonly used as statistics to tune up services or select alternative ones for optimization purpose.

2. **Strict and Non-Strict:** Strict QoS means those must-met requirements. For example, when developing biomedical multimedia systems, some HL7 standards need to be strictly followed: Transmission latency between two (end-to-end) nodes and Interchange protocols used within the organization must obey the specified standards. Conversely, some QoS do not need to be strictly followed. The "freedom" of such QoS is problem specific. For example, in order to transmit a skull image from a crime scene, secure transmission services may be required. Such a security QoS requirement may be satisfied by choosing any two of six secure modes from WCF or any service that provide 64-bit encryption.

3. **Orthogonal and Non-Orthogonal:** Similar to associations between functional and QoS requirements, there may also exist associations between QoS and QoS requirements. Orthogonal QoS associations mean that two QoS will not have mutual influence if one is changed by containers or deployment environments. For example, changes of skull's facial features will not affect the QoS of encryption algorithms needed for transmission. Conversely, non-orthogonal QoS substantially affects other QoS directly or indirectly. Examples include QoS of encryption algorithms versus transmission latency and skull facial feature versus skull classification. Lastly, non-orthogonal as-

sociations may also have one-to-one, one-to-many and many-to-one relationships.

Note that the above three QoS classes are not monotonic: They can be correlatively used to describe a (pair of) QoS requirement(s) together. For example, a skull's facial feature is static and non-strict and non-orthogonal to static and non-strict skull classification.

Figure 8 shows the QWL-S service profile for the XML parsing and conversion service introduced in Figure 3. Such a profile introduces a static, strict and orthogonal association between the service functionality (parsing and conversion) and its XML output format (MPEG-7). Because the service is one-to-one association, there is no QoS-to-QoS association and the value of the orthogonal classification is left blank. If the service is associated with more than one QoS requirement, both *serviceParameter* and *serviceCategory* can be expanded to describe such relationships. With functional and QoS associations as well as QoS classifications/associations introduced, ontologies are more manageable and matching and discovery of suitable services may be more efficient.

Semantics Matching

As mentioned before, one of the objectives of OWL-S is to facilitate service discovery. With expandable *serviceParameter* and *serviceCategory* (Martin et al., 2004), more informative functional and QoS properties and constraints that a service can provide or is limited to can be described. For example, an analysis service may describe maximum file size and file formats it can process. Also, this service may mention the specific kinds of contents it can track/segment/classify and if the contents should be audio-enabled or not. Lastly, a transmission service may describe specific encryption algorithms it provides. Conversely, data ontology comprises the elicited "QoS requirements" as well as data and content properties of biomedical multimedia

Figure 8. OWL-S file for XML parsing and conversion service

```
<owl:Ontology rdf:about="">...</owl:Ontology>
  <profile:Profile rdf:ID="KXMLDocumentService_Profile">
    <service:presentedBy rdf:resource="KXMLDocumentService_Service"/>
    <profile:serviceName>KDocument</profile:serviceName>
    <profile:textDescription/>
    <profile:hasInput
rdf:resource="http://localhost/KXMLDocumentService_ProcessModel1#KXMLDocument_parseXMLFile_
parameters_IN"/>
    <profile:hasOutput
rdf:resource="http://localhost/KXMLDocumentService_ProcessModel1#KXMLDocument_parseXMLFile_
parameters_OUT"/>
    <profile:qualityRating/>
    <profile:serviceParameter>
      <profile:serviceParameterName>XMLSchema</profile:serviceParameterName>
      <profile:sParameter>MPEG-7</profile:sParameter>
    </profile:serviceParameter>
    <profile:serviceCategory>
      <profile:categoryName>Func-QoS association</profile:categoryName>
      <profile:taxonomy>one-to-one</profile:taxonomy>
      <profile:value>MPEG-7</profile:value>
    </profile:serviceCategory>
    <profile:serviceCategory>
      <profile:categoryName>QoS category</profile:categoryName>
      <profile:taxonomy>static</profile:taxonomy>
      <profile:value>XMLSchema</profile:value>
    </profile:serviceCategory>
    <profile:serviceCategory>
      <profile:categoryName>QoS category</profile:categoryName>
      <profile:taxonomy>strict</profile:taxonomy>
      <profile:value>XMLSchema</profile:value>
    </profile:serviceCategory>
    <profile:serviceCategory>
      <profile:categoryName>QoS category</profile:categoryName>
      <profile:taxonomy>orthogonal</profile:taxonomy>
      <profile:value></profile:value>
    </profile:serviceCategory>
  </profile:Profile>
</rdf:RDF>
```

data either from users or analysis services. Such information can be used to match the semantics of a service described in *serviceParameter* and/ or *serviceCategory*.

For quantitative matching (e.g., latency and QoS rates), mathematical formulae computed along with the directions of a flowchart under given constraints are the most popular approaches (e.g., Yu et al., 2007; Zeng et al., 2004). However, for non-quantifiable matching (e.g., security) among data, service and domain ontologies, semantics matching with ontology reasoning may be more suitable. For example, supposed a biomedical multimedia video (1.07GB) that describes a fruit fly's flying motion requires a reliable message transmission, the semantic reasoning engine may infer to the most appropriate transmission service.

In order to perform semantics matching, SWRL, an OWL-based semantic Web rule language (Horrocks et al., 2004), is utilized. Figure 9 shows an SWRL code snippet for reasoning about finding a reliable TCP-based message transmission service supported by WCF (Liu et al., 2008)

whose average transmission rate is less than one minute for a one GB file.

Some observations found from the above figure are:

1. Inference rules for semantics matching are domain-specific and application-specific. Such efforts are unavoidable and require a great amount of time and support from domain experts.

2. For all the transmission services selected by this code snippet, how to rank them is questionable. Some services may be ranked based on the quantitative results. However, for those rule-based service selections without quantitative results, ranking of those services should be determined with the help of domain experts. Even worse, such ranking results may be applied case by case instead of just based on a specific domain;

3. For semantics matching based on more than one functional/QoS selection criterion, such criteria may be weighed differently based on the importance to specific domains. How to

Figure 9. SWRL code snippet for reasoning about a suitable transmission service

```
<ruleml:imp>
  <ruleml:_rlab ruleml:href="#TransmissionService"/>
  <owlx:Annotation>
    <owlx:Documentation>A reliable transmission service whose average
    duration is less than 1 min for 1 GB data gets selected</owlx:Documentation>
  </owlx:Annotation>
  <ruleml:_body>
    <swrlx:individualPropertyAtom swrlx:property="&tns;#hasServiceParameter">
      <ruleml:var>service</ruleml:var>
      <owlx:Individual owlx:name="&tns;#protocol"/>
    </swrlx:individualPropertyAtom>
    <swrlx:individualPropertyAtom swrlx:property="&tns;#hasProtocol">
      <ruleml:var>service</ruleml:var>
      <owlx:Individual owlx:name="&tns;#TCP"/>
    </swrlx:individualPropertyAtom>
    <swrlx:datavaluedPropertyAtom swrlx:property="&tns;#hasSizeLimit">
      <ruleml:var>service</ruleml:var>
      <ruleml:var>size</ruleml:var>
    </swrlx:datavaluedPropertyAtom>
    <swrlx:builtinAtom swrlx:builtin="&swrlb;#greaterThanOrEqual">
      <ruleml:var>size</ruleml:var>
      <owlx:DataValue owlx:datatype="&xsd;#long">1000000000</owlx:DataValue>
    </swrlx:builtinAtom>
    <swrlx:datavaluedPropertyAtom swrlx:property="&tns;#hasAverage">
      <ruleml:var>service</ruleml:var>
      <ruleml:var>average</ruleml:var>
    </swrlx:datavaluedPropertyAtom>
    <swrlx:builtinAtom swrlx:builtin="&swrlb;#lessThan">
      <ruleml:var>average</ruleml:var>
      <owlx:DataValue owlx:datatype="&xsd;#int">60</owlx:DataValue>
    </swrlx:builtinAtom>
  </ruleml:_body>
  <ruleml:_head>
    <swrlx:datavaluedPropertyAtom swrlx:property="&tns;#hasSelected">
      <ruleml:var>service</ruleml:var>
      <owlx:DataValue owlx:datatype="&xsd;#boolean">true</owlx:DataValue>
    </swrlx:datavaluedPropertyAtom>
  </ruleml:_head>
</ruleml:imp>
```

express such importance into specific inference rules is a challenging task;

4. A service usually has more than one associated *serviceParameter* and these parameters may also have orthogonal or non-orthogonal associations between each other. How to introduce and manage such tangled relationships is difficult.

All of above findings are domain-specific, which reflects the design and development of our SOA-based infrastructure: Horizontal separation of domain-specific and domain independent concerns and vertical bridge of annotations, ontologies, and semantics matching rules of such concerns. Table 1's rows and columns show such horizontal and vertical concerns, respectively.

CASE STUDY

This section introduces a three-step approach along with a medical education project to illustrate how our infrastructure utilizes a pre-processing service to elicit the functional and QoS information of medical educational video clips for the service of classification processed afterwards. A power spectrum analysis enhanced approach is also introduced to illustrate how a search service could be benefited from the functional and QoS information obtained by a feature extraction service.

Background of the Multimedia Education Project

An example to illustrate our approach is shown in this section. In this example, the problem of content-based medical image/video analysis is investigated. This problem consists of two separate but well integrated tasks: (a) content-based video event categorization; (b) content-based image retrieval. More specifically, the goal of task (a) (i.e., content-based video event categorization) is to automatically classify a given medical video clip into one of the video event categories, such as physician's presentation, diagnostic procedure, and surgery procedure. The objective for task (b) (i.e., content-based image retrieval) is to search for medical images from a large image database using the contents in the images (e.g., shape,

Table 1. Domain-independent and domain-specific concerns

	Domain-Independent Concern	**Domain-Specific Concern**
Annotations	Figure 5	Figure 4
Ontologies	Figure 6	Figure 7
Semantics Matching Rules	Not available	Figure 9

texture, and color, and other information) that can be extracted from the images.

Our focus in this project is educational medical images and videos, which have been widely used in schools and hospitals for the training of medical students, residents, and fellows. Generally, an educational medical video starts with introductory images. These images summarize the main contents of the video, and they are usually presented by a third party anchor. This kind of video segments is called "General Introduction" event. The majority of the images in this event are natural images such as hospital buildings in an urban scene or hospital rooms in an indoor scene. Some example images in this event are shown in the first row of Figure 10. After the "General Introduction" event, the video may show the presentations by physicians. The physicians introduce the overview of the medical procedure and the explanations of some technique concepts related to the procedure. This kind of video segments is called "Presentation" event. The images in this event are usually individual physician's images captured from different view angles. These images are illustrated by the second row of Figure 10. Another type of images that often appear in educational medical videos is the conversations among physicians and patients. Images in this type of event include the interactive scenes such as chatting between the physician and the patient. This type of video segments is called "Conversation" event. The third row of Figure 10 illustrates this event. The images in the fourth row of Figure 10 show some example images of "Surgery" event. Usually, the images in this event include multiple people (e.g.,

surgeons, nurses, and patients) and objects (e.g., operation tables, instruments, and etc.).

Three-Step Approach for Task (a)

The major challenge of content-based video event categorization in medical domain is that the content variations among different types of images are huge due to the large variety of medical procedures, human anatomies, and medical devices, to name a few.

To solve the challenges of content variations, a three-step approach is introduced. Such an approach comprises pre-processing step, feature

Figure 10. Illustrative images belong to the first four types of medical video events, with the rows from the top to the bottom indicating "General Introduction", "Presentation", "Conversation", and "Surgery"

extraction step, and classification step, each of which is regarded as a service in our SOA-based infrastructure. The insights gained during the pre-processing step can be used to guide the following two steps. As mentioned in the last paragraph, the content variations among the images of medical videos are huge. If the common characteristics for each video category can be learnt to guide the following steps, the performance may be potentially improved.

The feature extraction step and classification step are similar to many existing solutions for video event detection. Feature extraction component is a procedure of transform the input data into a reduced representation set of features. It is expected that the extracted features will contain the relevant functional and/or QoS information in order to perform the desired task using the reduced representation instead of the entire input data set. Classification component is a procedure to place an individual item (i.e., a video clip or a video segment in multimedia context) into groups. The classification decision is based on two important aspects: The quantitative characteristics of the features extracted from the individual item; and the training sets used for building the classification model.

Different from existing approaches, the service selection of feature extraction and classification are partially determined by the analysis results from the first step (i.e., pre-processing step). The goal of the pre-processing step is to perform light-weighted analysis and obtain the insights of the data sets. The insights gained from this step will be used to guide the following two steps (i.e., feature extraction step and classification step). This idea is hinted by the basic principle of Machine Learning (ML) research. In ML research, a large number of training sets are employed to build a sophisticated classification model and this model will be used for classifying a new data set. Different from the typical learning procedure in ML research, a small number of data sets are used and no mathematical or statistical model is built.

Instead, a light-weighted analysis is performed to gain some basic understanding about the visual features for different type of video categories. This type of understanding provides the guidance for further processing.

Specifically, the methods of light-weighted analysis in our pre-processing step include: Edge detection (i.e., the points where there is a boundary (or an edge) between two image regions), corner detection (i.e., the point-like features in an image, which have a local two dimensional structure), and salient points detection (i.e., location in an image where there is a significant variation with respect to a chosen image feature). There are a few reasons to choose these algorithms. First, all the three algorithms are light-weighted, which means the computation resources required by these algorithms are relative small. Secondly, each algorithm could produce different results for images from different medical procedures. This is a desirable property, because our ultimate goal is to differentiate the videos into different categories. Thirdly, the conclusions drawn from applying the simple algorithms to different images can guide us the services/service combinations for the following two steps. For example, the "edge detection" method excels other methods in images belong to "Presentation" video category (shown in Figure 11). This result indicates that the flow-based methods (Efros et al., 2003; Ke, Sukthankar, & Hebert, 2005; Shechtman & Irani, 2007) should be pursued due to its QoS. Namely, the flow-based methods operate directly on spatial-temporal sequences without segmentation. The specified pattern can be recognized by brute-force correlation) for the next two steps. The corner detection can produce the best results for the images in the "Conversation" category while salient points detection works best for images in "Surgery" type. Figures 12 and 13 illustrate the results of corner detection and salient points detection results for "Conversation" and "Surgery" images, respectively. These results suggest that tracking based methods (Ramanan & Forsyth, 2003; Sheikh, Sheikh, & Shah, 2005;

Figure 11. (Best viewed in color): (a) Original example image from the "Presentation" video category; (b) Edge detection results (labeled with blue color) overlap with the original example image; (c) Corner detection results (labeled with red color) overlap with the original example image. The number of points detected by this method is very small (two points in this image) and could not serve as effective features; (d) Salient point detection results (labeled with green color) overlap with the original example image. The number of points being detected using this method is very large and it is computation intractable if we use this method.

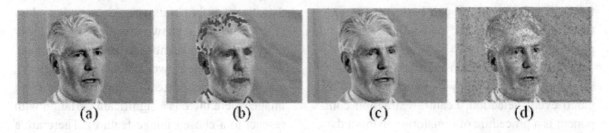

(a)   (b)   (c)   (d)

Figure 12. (Best viewed in color): (a) Original example image from the "Conversation" video category; (b) Edge detection results (labeled with blue color) overlap with the original example image. The number of points being detected using this method is very large and it is computation intractable if we use this method; (c) Corner detection results (labeled with red color) overlap with the original example image; (d) Salient point detection results (labeled with green color) overlap with the original example image. The number of points detected by this method is very small (about fifteen points in this image) and could not serve as effective features.

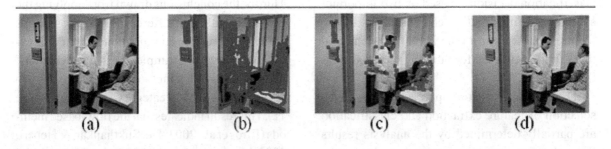

(a)   (b)   (c)   (d)

Yilmaz & Shah, 2005) (i.e., the methods follow the moving of the object and segment the objects of interests from the background. The trace of the model parameters are generated by tracking the movement of the object over time. The generated trace is compared with the target spatial-temporal pattern to determine the video event) maybe a good fit for "Conversation" images; and space-time interest points approaches (Laptev & Lindeberg, 2003; Dollar et al., 2005; Niebles, Wang, & Fei-Fei, 2008; Schuldt, Laptev, & Caputo, 2004), extending the traditional spatial interest points detection techniques to spatial-temporal domain for video event detection, may be suitable for "Surgery" images.

Power Spectrum Analysis Enhanced Approach for Task (b)

Most of the existing solutions for content-based image retrieval problem include two components: indexing and search. The "indexing" component generates mathematical descriptions of the images in the database and the "searching" component as-

Figure 13. (Best viewed in color): (a) Original example image from the "Surgery" video category; (b) Edge detection results (labeled with blue color) overlap with the original example image. The number of points being detected using this method is very large and it is computation intractable if we use this method; (c) Corner detection results (labeled with red color) overlap with the original example image. The number of points detected by this method is very small (about eight points in this image) and could not serve as effective features; (d) Salient point detection results (labeled with green color) overlap with the original example image.

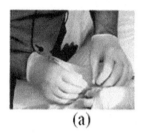 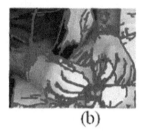 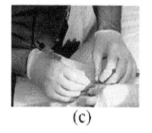 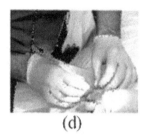

| (a) | (b) | (c) | (d) |

sesses the similarity between the query image and images in the database. Essentially, the "indexing" component is a feature extraction procedure. In our context, each visual feature extraction method is treated as an individual "indexing" service. Since each "indexing" service using a specific feature extraction algorithm must be performed for each image, the total cost of "indexing" service execution for the entire database is very high. This issue is particularly severe in the medical domain for two reasons. First, the number of medical images being indexed is huge (e.g., one day practice of the Radiology Department of the University Hospital of Geneva alone produced more than 12,000 images in 2002 (Müller et al., 2004)). The second reason is the wide range of the content variations of medical images. In order to handle the content variation issue, the majority of existing methods develops multiple "indexing" services and applies each service to each individual image, which is a very time-consuming procedure.

Different from the existing methods, a power spectrum analysis-based pre-processing step is introduced to identify the semantic category of each image before applying the "indexing" and "search" services. Our method is motivated by the observation that the image semantic category is a strong indicator for optimal "indexing" service. As a result, the image category information will greatly reduce the "indexing" time by indicating the optimal "indexing" services without the brute-force traverse of all the "indexing" services. In our context, the semantic category is defined as an important medical procedure (e.g., surgery procedure) or an event (e.g., presentation of the physician, conversations between the patient and the physician). This category is similar to the definition in the second paragraph of Section 4.1.

Our proposed power spectrum analysis-based pre-processing method is motivated by seminal studies in image science and cognitive science (Field, 1987; Tolhurst, Tadmor, & Chao, 1992) that the amplitude spectrum of natural images falls more or less monotonically with spatial frequency. Figure 14 illustrates our results. Images (a) to (d) of Figure 14 are the image examples for different semantic categories. Images (e) to (h) of Figure 14 show the corresponding power spectrum image of each semantic category. For example, image (e) of Figure 14 is the power spectrum of image (a), image (b) in Figure 14 is the power spectrum of image (f), and so on and so forth. To further explore the hidden patterns among these images, the spectral signature for each category is computed

Figure 14. (Images are best viewed in color) The first row of this figure (from image (a) to image (d)) are image examples for each semantic category: (a) "General Introduction" scene; (b) "Presentation" scene; (c) "Conversation" scene; and (d) "Surgery". The images in the second row are the corresponding power spectrum images while the images in the third row are corresponding spectrum signatures.

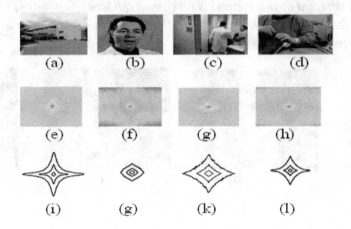

by averaging the power spectrum from a sequence of images per category. The results are shown in the third row of Figure 14. From these image examples, it is observed that different semantic categories exhibit different orientations and spatial frequency distributions. These differences can be captured by power spectrum analysis.

Specifically, most of the images in the "General Introduction" category are urban images with buildings (e.g., hospital buildings) captured from a far distance. Consequently, the energy of the power spectrum is concentrated mainly on high spatial frequencies shown in image (i) of Figure 14. Therefore, the optimal "indexing" service (feature extraction method) for this type of images is affine-invariant texture features (Mikolajczyk & Schmid, 2004; Kadir, Zisserman, & Brady, 2004). Most of the images belong to the "Surgery" category are objects (e.g., operation tables and instruments) and people (e.g., surgeons, nurses, and patients) with close-up view. Hence, the distance between the camera and the scene is short and the visual field is limited to a smaller space, and it is likely to produce images with flat and smooth surfaces, due to the close-up view of the objects. Additionally, the close-up view of the objects has a tendency of being isotropic in orientations. The spectral signature of "Surgery" scene (i.e., image (l) of Figure 14) verifies this discovery. This visual property indicates that the preferred "indexing" service for images in this category is the multi scale, multi orientation filter bank methods (Leung & Malik, 2001; Schmid, 2001; Geusebroek, Smeulders, & van de Weijer, 2003). The majority of images in "Presentation" scene are images with close-up view of physicians while the images in "Conversation" scene refer to images that shoot the conversations. Usually, the "Conversation" scene refers to the images with near view of people instead of close-up view of people. This explains the spectral signatures of these two types of images (i.e., image (g) and image (k) in Figure 14). As a result, texture thesaurus methods (Ma & Manjunath, 1998; Manjunath et al., 2001) maybe the optimal indexing techniques for "Presentation" and "Conversation" images.

RELATED WORK

Our work spans a wide spectrum of disciplines including functional, QoS and regulation requirements specific to biomedical domain, SOA for interoperability, and content-based image/video analysis, retrieval and transmission. This book chapter mainly focuses on functional and QoS-semantics for biomedical multimedia data processing under SOA. This section discusses the related work aiming at the same or similar focuses.

In Ma, Cao, and He (2008), a biomedical image storage, retrieval, and visualization project is implemented based on SOA. Such a project mainly concentrates on the processing of biomedical images related to Chinese human genetic resources. In order to fasten the retrieval performance, metadata of such images is introduced and stored in a database. The metadata information comprises ID, data type, distribution, provider, time and etc. (Ma, Cao, & He, 2008). Additionally, image queries are also utilized with the help of fuzzy query methods. Yet, which specific query methods/languages and if metadata can be treated as ontology semantically are not described in the paper.

An SOA-based health care platform and business modeling is introduced in Yang, Chang, and Chu (2008). Such a platform specifically concentrates on the domain of patient-centered health care and attempts to tackle domain's technical issues including: (i) Real-time bio-signal transfer between clients and providers; (ii) Heterogeneous bio-signal device integration; and (iii) Homogeneous provider integration. Conclusively, the main research focus is on SOA-based data transmission and integration in the realm of health care.

Lastly, Mayo Clinic College of Medicine demonstrated its eQuality solution in SOA consortium (OMG, 2008). Such demonstration concentrates on providing "health care practitioners and health care organizations with real time feedback (OMG, 2008)." Similar to Yang, Chang, and Chu (2008), the research focus is on data transmission and integration. The same affiliation also introduced

modular ontology techniques for biomedical domain (Pathak, Johnson, & Chute, 2008). Such techniques offer ontology decomposition and composition for ontology reuse, ontology alignment, distributed and incremental reasoning, and scalable querying, to name a few (Pathak, Johnson, & Chute, 2008). Regarding Web service selection and composition, labeled transition system is utilized to model functional service specifications and compose Web service through automatic reformulation of such specifications (Pathak, Basu, & Honavar, 2008). Dependency matrix is introduced to analyze the data and control dependencies of composition, which could potentially reduce the solution space of composed Web services and limit manual intervention.

As mentioned before, there is plenty of other related work focusing on different research challenges in the realm of SOA and biomedical multimedia/heal care domains. Due to space consideration and research focuses, a limited number of related projects are discussed in this section. For more information regarding other related work, please refer to OMG (2009).

CONCLUSION

In Software Engineering, correctly eliciting and extracting requirements from clients at the earlier stage of software lifecycle may assist software developers to design and implement products that satisfy clients' need. Similarly, in Machine Learning, a number of training sets are employed at the beginning to build a sophisticated classification model, which will be later used for classifying new data set. This book chapter adapts such a pre-processing concept from both realms and utilizes semantics and ontologies as main representations of data, domain, and service under SOA paradigm. With such representations, most appropriate services for processing these specific data may be discovered, performed, tuned up or replaced as needed. Besides introducing data semantics, *serviceParameter* and *serviceCategory* of OWL-S is expanded to fit into our needs of specifying services in more details with respect to the data semantics. Such service semantics provide support to match data semantics. Additionally, our infrastructure may be regarded as a generic framework for constructing biomedical multimedia systems and as a domain-specific one with customized services developed and orchestrated due to the advantages of SOA as well as the separation of domain-independent and domain-specific concerns. Our current focus is on consolidating the ontology reasoning along with functional-to-QoS associations as well as QoS-to-QoS associations/classifications. Additionally, how to utilize such associations and classifications to perform rule-based domain-specific semantics matching is our future work. All of the aspects are also being continuously improved with new features/algorithms.

REFERENCES

Bailer, W., & Schallauer, P. (2008). An MPEG-7 extension for describing visual impairments. In *Proceedings of International Workshop on Image Analysis for Multimedia Interactive,* (pp. 118-121).

Bao, J., Cao, Y., Tavanapong, W., & Honavar, V. (2004). Integration of domain-specific and domain-independent ontologies for colonoscopy video database annotation. In *Proceedings of the International Conference on Information and Knowledge Engineering,* (pp. 82-88).

Barreto, C., Bullard, V., Erl, T., Evdemon, J., Jordan, D., Kand, K., et al. (2007). *Web services business process execution language*. Retrieved from http://www.oasis-open.org/committees/wsbpel/

Bustamante, M. L. (2007). *Learning WCF*. O'Reilly.

Cao, Y., Li, D., Tavanapong, W., Oh, J., Wong, J., & Groen, P. C. (2004c). Parsing and browsing tools for colonoscopy videos. In *ACM Multimedia*, 844-851.

Cao, Y., Liu, D., Tavanapong, W., Wong, J., Oh, J., & Groen, P. C. (2006). Automatic classification of image with appendiceal orifice in colonoscopy videos. In *Proceedings of the IEEE International Conference of the Engineering in Medicine and Biology Society,* (pp. 2349-2352).

Cao, Y., Liu, D., Tavanapong, W., Wong, J., Oh, J., & Groen, P. C. (2007). Computer-aided detection of diagnostic and therapeutic operations in colonoscopy videos. *IEEE Transactions on Bio-Medical Engineering, 54*(7), 1268–1279. doi:10.1109/TBME.2007.890734

Cao, Y., Tavanapong, W., Kim, K., Wong, J., Oh, J., & Groen, P. C. (2004a). A framework for parsing colonoscopy videos for semantic units. In *Proceedings of the IEEE International Conference on Multimedia and Expo,* (pp. 1879-1882).

Cao, Y., Tavanapong, W., Li, D., Oh, J., Groen, P. C., & Wong, J. (2004b). A visual model approach for parsing colonocsopy videos. In *Proceedings of the International Conference on Image and Video Retrieval,* (pp. 160-169).

Celma, O., Dasiopoulou, S., Hausenblas, M., Little, S., Tsinaraki, C., & Troncy, R. (2007). *MPEG-7 and the Semantic Web*. Retrieved from http://www.w3.org/2005/Incubator/mmsem/XGR-mpeg7/

Datta, R., Joshi, D., Li, J., & Wang, J. Z. (2008). Image retrieval: Ideas, influences, and trends of the new age. *ACM Computing Surveys, 40*(2), 1–60. doi:10.1145/1348246.1348248

Dollar, P., Rabaud, V., Cottrell, G., & Belongie, S. (2005). Behavior recognition via sparse spatio-temporal features. In *Proceedings of IEEE International Workshop on Visual Surveillance and Performance Evaluation of Tracking and Surveillance,* (pp. 65-72).

Efros, A. A., Berg, A. C., Mori, G., & Malik, J. (2003). Recognizing action at a distance. In *Proceedings of IEEE International Conference on Computer Vision,* (pp. 726-733).

Erl, T. (2005). *Service-Oriented Architecture: Concepts, technology, and design.* Prentice Hall.

Field, D. J. (1987). Relations between the statistics of natural images and the response properties of cortical cells. *Journal of the Optical Society of America. A, Optics and Image Science, 4,* 2379–2394. doi:10.1364/JOSAA.4.002379

Garcia, R., Tsinaraki, C., Celma, Ó., & Christodoulakis, S. (2008). Multimedia content description using Semantic Web languages. *Semantic Multimedia and Ontologies, 2,* 17–54. doi:10.1007/978-1-84800-076-6_2

Geusebroek, J. M., Smeulders, A. W. M., & van de Weijer, J. (2003). Fast anisotropic Gauss filtering. *IEEE Transactions on Image Processing, 12,* 938–943. doi:10.1109/TIP.2003.812429

Hansen, M. D. (2007). *SOA using Java Web services.* Prentice Hall.

Health Level 7 International. (2010). *Health Level 7.* Retrieved from http://www.hl7.org

Horrocks, I., Patel-Schneider, P. F., Boley, H., Tabet, S., Grosof, B., & Dean, M. (2004). *SWRL: A Semantic Web rule language combining OWL and RuleML.* Retrieved from http://www.w3.org/Submission/2004/SUBM-SWRL-20040521.

Java Community Press. (2007). *JSR 224: Java API for XML-based Web services (JAX-WS) 2.0.* Retrieved from http://jcp.org/en/jsr/detail?id=224

Kadir, T., Zisserman, A. & Brady, M. (2004). An affine invariant salient region detector. In *Proceedings of European Conference on Computer Vision,* (pp. 404-416).

Ke, Y., Sukthankar, R., & Hebert, M. (2005). Efficient visual event detection using volumetric features. In *Proceedings of IEEE International Conference on Computer Vision,* (pp. 166-173).

Laptev, I., & Lindeberg, T. (2003). Space-time interest points. In *Proceedings of IEEE International Conference on Computer Vision,* (pp. 432-439).

Leung, T., & Malik, J. (2001). Representing and recognizing the visual appearance of materials using three-dimensional textons. *International Journal of Computer Vision, 43*(1), 29–44. doi:10.1023/A:1011126920638

Liu, D., Cao, Y., Kim, K., Stanek, S., Doungratanaex-Chai, B., & Lin, K. (2007b). Arthemis: Annotation software in an integrated capturing and analysis system for colonoscopy. *Computer Methods and Programs in Biomedicine, 88*(2), 152–163. doi:10.1016/j.cmpb.2007.07.011

Liu, D., Cao, Y., Tavanapong, W., Wong, J., Oh, J., & Groen, P. C. (2007a). Mining colonoscopy videos to measure quality of colonoscopic procesure. In *Proceedings of the International Conference on Biomedical Engineering,* (pp. 409 - 414).

Liu, S.-H., Bryant, B. R., Gray, J., Raje, R., Olson, A., & Auguston, M. (2005). QoS-UniFrame: A petri net-based modeling approach to assure QoS requirements of distributed real-time and embedded systems. In *Proceedings of the 12th IEEE International Conference and Workshop on the Engineering of Computer Based Systems,* (pp. 202-209).

Liu, S.-H., Cao, Y., Li, M., Kilaru, P., Smith, T., & Toner, S. (2008). A semantics- and data-driven SOA for biomedical multimedia systems. In *Proceedings of IEEE International Symposium on Multimedia,* (pp. 533-538).

Lux, M. (2008a). *Caliph and Emir.* Retrieved from http://www.semanticmetadata.net/features/

Lux, M. (2008b). *Lire*. Retrieved from http://www.semanticmetadata.net/lire/

Ma, L., Cao, Y. & He, J. (2008). Biomedical image storage, retrieval and visualization based-on open source project. In *Proceedings of 2008 Congress on Image and Signal Processing* (pp. 63-66).

Ma, W.-Y., & Manjunath, B. S. (1998). A texture thesaurus for browsing large aerial photographs. *Journal of the American Society for Information Science American Society for Information Science, 49*, 633–648. doi:10.1002/(SICI)1097-4571(19980515)49:7<633::AID-ASI5>3.0.CO;2-N

Manjunath, B. S., Ohm, J.-R., Vasudevan, V. V., & Yamada, A. (2001). Color and texture descriptors. *IEEE Transactions on Circuits and Systems for Video Technology, 11*, 703–715. doi:10.1109/76.927424

Martin, D., Burstein, M., Hobbs, J., Lassila, O., McDemott, D., McIlraith, S., et al. (2008). *OWL-S: Semantic markup for Web services*. Retrieved from http://www.w3.org/Submission/OWL-S/

Martin, D., Burstein, M., Lassila, O., Paolucci, M., Payne, T., & McIlraith, S. (2003). *Describing Web services using OWL-S and WSDL*. Retrieved from http://www.daml.org/services/owl-s/1.0/owl-s-wsdl.html

Mikolajczyk, K. & Schmid, C. (2004). Scale and affine invariant interest point detectors. *International Journal of Computer Vision, 60*, 63–86.

Müller, H., Michoux, N., Bandon, D., & Geissbuhler, A. (2004). A review of content-based image retrieval systems in medicine-clinical benefits and future directions. *International Journal of Medical Informatics, 73*(1), 1–23. doi:10.1016/j.ijmedinf.2003.11.024

Niebles, J. C., Wang, H., & Fei-Fei, L. (2008). Unsupervised learning of human action categories using spatial-temporal words. In *Proceedings of British Machine Vision Conference*, (pp. 1249).

OMG. (2008). *Case study from Mayo clinic added to SOA in healthcare qorkshop: Realizing quality of care*. Retrived from http://www.omg.org/news/releases/pr2008/03-31-08.htm

OMG. (2009). *SOA in Healthcare Conference: Value in a time of change*. Retrived from http://www.omg.org/news/meetings/HC-WS/index.htm

OpenEHR Foundation. (2010). *OpenEHR*. Retrieved from http://www.openehr.org/

Papazoglou, M.P. & Heuvel, W.-J. (2007). Service oriented architectures: Approaches, technologies and research issues. *The Very Large Data Bases Journal, 16*(3), 389–415.

Pathak, J., Basu, S., & Honavar, V. (2008). Composing Web services through automatic reformulation of service specifications. In *Proceedings of IEEE International Conference on Services Computing,* (pp. 361-369).

Pathak, J., Johnson, T. M., & Chute, C. G. (2008). Modular ontology techniques and their applications in the biomedical domain. In *Proceedings of IEEE International Conference on Information Reuse and Integration,* (pp. 351-356).

Ramanan, D., & Forsyth, D. A. (2003). Automatic annotation of everyday movements. In *Neural Information Processing Systems*. NIPS.

Sabou, M., Wroe, C., Goble, A., & Mishne, G. (2005). Learning domain ontologies for Web service descriptions: An experiment in bioinformatics. In *Proceedings of International Conference on World Wide Web,* (pp. 190-198).

Schmid, C. (2001). Constructing models for content-based image retrieval. In *Proceedings of IEEE Conference on Computer Vision and Pattern Recognition,* (pp. 39-45).

Schuldt, C., Laptev, I., & Caputo, B. (2004). Recognizing human actions: A local SVM approach. In *Proceedings of International Conference on Pattern Recognition,* (pp. 23-26).

Scicluna, J. (2004). *OWL-S Editor: To semantically annotate Web-services.* Retrieved from http://staff.um.edu.mt/cabe2/supervising/undergraduate/owlseditFYP/OwlSEdit.html

Shechtman, E., & Irani, M. (2007). Space-time behavior-based correlation-or-how to tell if two underlying motion fields are similar without computing them? *IEEE Transactions on Pattern Analysis and Machine Intelligence, 29*(1), 2045–2056. doi:10.1109/TPAMI.2007.1119

Sheikh, Y., Sheikh, M., & Shah, M. (2005). Exploring the space of a human action. In *Proceedings of IEEE International Conference on Computer Vision,* (pp. 144-149).

Sun Microsystems. (2008). *Java EE 5 tutorial.* Retrieved from http://java.sun.com/javaee/5/docs/tutorial/doc/

Tercom, L. (2008). *WCF chunking.* Retrieved from http://wcf- chunking.sourceforge.net

Tolhurst, D. J., Tadmor, Y., & Chao, T. (1992). Amplitude spectra of natural images. *Ophthalmic & Physiological Optics, 12*(2), 229–232. doi:10.1111/j.1475-1313.1992.tb00296.x

Tseng, V. S., Su, J.-H., Huang, J.-H., & Chen, C.-J. (2008). Integrated mining of visual features, speech features, and frequent patterns for semantic video annotation. *IEEE Transactions on Multimedia, 10*(2), 260–267. doi:10.1109/TMM.2007.911832

Tzouvaras, V., Troncy, R., & Pan, J. (2007). *Multimedia annotation interoperability framework.* Retrieved from http://www.w3.org/2005/Incubator/mmsem/XGR-interoperability/

U.S. Department of Health and Human Services. (2010). *Health Insurance Portability And Accountability Act.* Retrieved from http://www.hhs.gov/ocr/privacy

U.S. Food and Drug Administration. (2010). *FDA Website.* Retrieved from http://www.fda.gov

Wolfram MathWorld. (2008). *Bijective.* Retrieved from http://mathworld.wolfram.com/Bijective.html

Yan, R., Natsev, A., & Campbell, M. (2005). An efficient manual image annotation approach based on tagging and browsing. In *Proceedings of International Multimedia Conference,* (pp. 13-20).

Yang, C.-L., Chang, Y.-K., & Chu, C.-P. (2008). Modeling services to construct service-oriented healthcare architecture for digital home-care business. In *Proceedings of International Conference on Software Engineering & Knowledge Engineering,* (pp. 351-356).

Yilmaz, A., & Shah, M. (2005). Recognizing human actions in videos acquired by uncalibrated moving cameras. In *Proceedings of the IEEE International Conference on Computer Vision,* (pp. 150-157).

Yu, T., Zhang, Y., & Lin, K.-J. (2007). Efficient algorithms for Web services selection with end-to-end QoS constraints. *ACM Transaction on the Web, 1*(1), 6. doi:10.1145/1232722.1232728

Zeng, L., Benatallah, B., Ngu, A. H. H., Dumas, M., Kalagnanam, J., & Chang, H. (2004). QoS-aware middleware for Web services composition. *IEEE Transactions on Software Engineering, 30*(5), 311–327. doi:10.1109/TSE.2004.11

Compilation of References

Aagedal, J. O. (2001). *Quality of service support in development of distributed systems*. Unpublished doctoral dissertation, University of Oslo, Norway.

Abdelzaher, T., & Bhatti, N. (1999). Adaptive content delivery for Web server QoS. *Proceedings of the International Workshop on Quality of Service.*

Abramowicz, W., Zyskowski, D., Suryn, W., & Hofman, R. (2007). SQuaRE based Web services quality model. In [IAENG]. *Proceedings of IMECS, 08*, 827–835.

Aburub, F., Odeh, M., & Beeson, I. (2007). Modelling non-functional requirements of business processes. *Information and Software Technology, 49*(11), 1162–1171. doi:10.1016/j.infsof.2006.12.002

Achilleos, A., Georgalas, N., & Yang, K. (2007). *An open source domain-specific tools framework to support model driven development of OSS*. (LNCS 4530), (pp. 1-16).

Achilleos, A., Yang, K., & Georgalas, N. (2008). *A model-driven approach to generate service creation environments*. IEEE Globecom, Global Telecommunications Conference, (pp. 1 – 6).

Adamopoulos, D. X., Pavlou, G., & Papandreou, C. A. (2002). Advanced service creation using distributed object technology. *IEEE Communications Magazine, 40*(3), 146–154. doi:10.1109/35.989777

Adopted Specification, O. M. G. (2004). *UML profile for modeling quality of service and fault tolerance characteristics and mechanisms*. Retrieved from http://www.omg.org

Al Masri, N. & Frénot, S. (2002). *Dynamic instrumentation for the management of EJB-based applications*. INRIA RR-4481.

Alam, M., Breu, R., & Breu, M. (2004). *Model driven security for Web services (MDS4WS)*. 8th International Multitopic Conference, (pp. 498-505).

Alférez, G. H., & Poonphon, S. (2007). An aspect-oriented product line framework to support the development of software product lines of Web applications. *International Journal of the Computer, the Internet and Management, 15*(SP4), 13.1-13.5. Retrieved February 14, 2008, from http://www.ijcim.th.org/v15nSP4.htm

Al-Masri, E., & Mahmoud, Q. H. (2008). Toward quality-driven Web service discovery. *IT Professional, 10*(3), 24–28. doi:10.1109/MITP.2008.59

Amir, R., & Zeid, A. (2004). A UML profile for Service Oriented Architectures. In *Proceedings of the 19th Annual ACM SIGPLAN Conference on Object-oriented Programming Systems, Languages, and Applications*, (pp. 192-193).

Amouzegar, H., Mohammadi, S., Tarokh, M. J., & Hidaji, A. N. (2008). A new approach on interactive SOA security model based on automata. In *Proceedings of the Seventh IEEE/ACIS International Conference on Computer and Information Science*, (pp. 667-671).

Amyot, D. (2003). Introduction to the user requirements notation: Learning by example. *Computer Networks, 42*(3), 285–301. doi:10.1016/S1389-1286(03)00244-5

Amyot, D., & Mussbacher, G. (2003). *URN: Towards a new standard for the visual description of requirements*. 3rd SDL and MSC Workshop (SAM02), (pp. 21-37).

Amyot, D., Becha, H., Bræk, R., & Rossebø, J. E. Y. (2008). *Next generation service engineering*. ITU-T Innovations in NGN Kaleidoscope Conference, Geneva, Switzerland.

Anastasopoulos, M., & Gacek, C. (2001). Implementing product line variabilities. In N. David (Ed.), *Symposium on Software Reusability: Putting Software Reuse in Context, 2001. ACM SIGSOFT software engineering notes,* (pp. 109-117). New York: ACM.

Anastasopoulos, M., & Muthig, D. (2004). An evaluation of aspect-oriented programming as a product line implementation technology. In D.C. Schmidt (Ed.), *8th International Conference, ICSR 2004. Software reuse: methods, techniques and tools,* (pp. 141-156). London: Springer-Verlag.

Anderson, J. P. (1972). *Computer security technology planning study* (Tech. Rep. ESD-TR-73-51), L. G. Hanscom Field, Bedford, MA, USA: U.S. Air Force, Electronic Systems Division, Deputy for Command and Management Systems, HQ Electronic Systems Division (AFSC).

Andreozzi, S., Montesi, D., & Moretti, R. (2003). Web services quality. In [IEEE Press.]. *Proceedings of CCCT, 03,* 252–257.

Antón, A. (1997). *Goal identification and refinement in the specification of software-based Information Systems.* Unpublished doctoral dissertation, Georgia Institute of Technology, Atlanta, GA, USA.

AOSD. (2008). *Homepage information.* Retrieved from http://www.aosd.net.

Apache Software Foundation. (2004). *WSS4J.* Retrieved September 1, 2008, from http://ws.apache.org/wss4j/

Apache Software Foundation. (2008). *Apache rampart.* Retrieved September 1, 2008, from http://ws.apache.org/rampart/

Armbrust, M., Fox, A., Gri-th, R., Joseph, A. D., Katz, R., & Konwinski, A. (2010). A view of cloud computing. *Communications of the ACM, 53*(4), 50–58. doi:10.1145/1721654.1721672

Astrom, K. (2006). *Challenges in control engineering.* Retrieved September 2008, from http://www.dia.uned.es/ace2006/plenaryspeakers.html

ATL. (2008). *Homepage information.* Retrieved from http://www.eclipse.org/m2m/atl

Avizienis, A., Laprie, J.-C., Randell, B., & Landwehr, C. (2004). Basic concepts and taxonomy of dependable and secure computing. *IEEE Transactions on Dependable and Secure Computing, 1*(1), 11–33. doi:10.1109/TDSC.2004.2

Ayed, D., Taconet, C., Bernard, G., & Berbers, Y. (2008). CADeComp: Context-aware deployment of component-based application. *Journal of Network and Computer Applications,* 224–257. doi:10.1016/j.jnca.2006.12.002

Azmoodeh, M., Georgalas, N., & Fisher, S. (2005). Model-driven systems development and integration environment. *British Telecom Technical Journal, 23*(03), 96–110.

Babcock, C. (2008). Hyperic to monitor Amazon.com's Cloud Computing capabilities. Retrieved August 25, 2008, from http://www.informationweek.com/news/hardware/utility_ondemand/showArticle.jhtml?articleID=208800360

Bachmann, F., & Clements, P. (2005). *Variability in software product lines.* (Tech. Rep. No. CMU/SEI-2005-TR-012, ESC-TR-2005-012). Carnegie Mellon University, Software Engineering Institute. Pittsburgh, Pennsylvania.

Bailer, W., & Schallauer, P. (2008). An MPEG-7 extension for describing visual impairments. In *Proceedings of International Workshop on Image Analysis for Multimedia Interactive,* (pp. 118-121).

Baldwin, C. Y., & Clark, K. B. (2000). *Design rules: The power of modularity (Vol. 1).* Cambridge, MA: MIT Press.

Baniassad, E., Clements, P., Araújo, A., Moreira, A., Rashid, A., & Tekinerdogan, B. (2006). Discovering early aspects. *IEEE Software, 23*(1), 61–70. doi:10.1109/MS.2006.8

Bao, J., Cao, Y., Tavanapong, W., & Honavar, V. (2004). Integration of domain specific and domain-independent ontologies for colonoscopy video database annotation. In *Proceedings of the International Conference on Information and Knowledge Engineering,* (pp. 82-88).

Baresi, L., Guinea, S., & Plebani, P. (2007). Policies and aspects for the supervision of BPEL processes. In *Proceedings of CAiSE '07,* (LNCS 4495), (pp. 340-354). Springer.

Barreto, C., Bullard, V., Erl, T., Evdemon, J., Jordan, D., Kand, K., et al. (2007). *Web services business process execution language*. Retrieved from http://www.oasis-open.org/committees/wsbpel/

Basili, V. R., Caldiera, G., & Rombach, H. D. (1994). The goal question metric approach. In Marciniak, J. (Ed.), *Encyclopedia of software engineering*. Wiley.

Basin, D., Doser, J., & Lodderstedt, T. (2003). Model driven security for process-oriented systems. *Proceedings of 8th ACM Symposium on Access Control Models and Technologies*, (pp. 100-109).

Bass, L., & John, B. E. (2003). Linking usability to software architecture patterns through general scenarios. *Journal of Systems and Software*, 66(3), 187–197. doi:10.1016/S0164-1212(02)00076-6

Bass, L. J., Klein, M., & Bachmann, F. (2002). Quality attribute design primitives and the attribute driven design method. In F. van der Linden (Ed.) *Software product-family engineering, 4th International Workshop, PFE 2001, Revised Papers,* (pp. 169-186). Berlin: Springer.

Bauer, J. (2003). *Identification and modelling of contexts for different information scenarios in air traffic*. Diplomarbeit, Faculty of Electrical Engineering and Computer Sciences, Technische Universitat Berlin.

Bengtsson, P., Lassing, N., Bosch, J., & van Vliet, H. (2004). Architecture-level modifiability analysis (ALMA). *Journal of Systems and Software*, 69(1-2), 129–147. doi:10.1016/S0164-1212(03)00080-3

Benn, J., Constantinides, C., Padda, H. K., Pedersen, K. H., Rioux, F., & Ye, X. (2005). Reasoning on software quality improvement with aspect-oriented refactoring: A case study. In Tsai, W. T., & Hamza, M. H. (Eds.), *Software engineering and applications, 2005*. Phoenix: ACTA Press.

Bergey, J., Fisher, M., Gallagher, B., Jones, L., & Northrop, L. (2000). *Basic concepts of product line practice for the DoD*. (Tech. Rep. CMU/SEI-2000-TN-001). Carnegie Mellon University, Software Engineering Institute. Pittsburgh, Pennsylvania.

Bertoa, M., Vallecillo, A., & Garcia, F. (2006). An ontology for software measurement. In Calero, C., Ruiz, F., & Piattini, M. (Eds.), *Ontologies for software engineering and software technology* (pp. 175–196). Springer. doi:10.1007/3-540-34518-3_6

Bézivin, J., Hammoudi, S., Lopes, D., & Joault, F. (2004). *An experiment in mapping Web services to implementation platforms*. (Tech. Rep. No. 04.01), LINA: Université de Nantes.

Bhansali, P. V. (2005). Complexity measurement of data and control flow. *ACM SIGSOFT Software Engineering Notes*, 30(1), 1–2. doi:10.1145/1039174.1039191

Bichler, M., & Lin, K. (2006). Service-oriented computing. *IEEE Computer*, 39(6), 99–101.

Birk, A., & Heller, G. (2007). Challenges for requirements engineering and management in software product line development. International Conference on Requirements Engineering, (pp. 300-305).

Bode, S., & Riebisch, R. (2009). Tracing quality-related design decisions in a category-driven software architecture. In Liggesmeyer, P., Engels, G., Münch, J., Dörr, J., & Riegel, N. (Eds.), *Proceedings of Software Engineering 2009* (pp. 87–98). Bonn, Germany: Köllen.

Bode, S., Fischer, A., Kühnhauser, W., & Riebisch, M. (2009). Software architectural design meets security engineering. In *Proceedings of the 16th Annual IEEE International Conference and Workshop on the Engineering of Computer Based Systems (ECBS)*. (pp. 109-118). USA: IEEE.

Bondi, A. B. (2000). Characteristics of scalability and their impact on performance. In *Proceedings of the 2nd International Workshop on Software and Performance (WOSP '00)*, (pp. 195-203). New York: ACM.

Booch, G., Rumbaugh, J., & Jacobson, I. (2005). *The unified modeling language user guide* (2nd ed.). Upper Saddle River, NJ: Addison-Wesley Professional.

Borzo, J. (2005). *Business 2010-embracing the challenge of change*. Technical report.

Bosch, J. (2000). *Design and use of software architectures*. New York: Addison Wesley.

Bouchenak, S., Boyer, F., Cecchet, E., Jean, S., Schmitt, A., & Stefani, J. (2004). A component-based approach to distributed system management: A use case with self-manageable J2EE cluster. *EW11: Proceedings of the 11th workshop on ACM SIGOPS European workshop.*

Brcina, R., & Riebisch, M. (2008). Architecting for evolvability by means of traceability and features. In *Proceedings of the 4th International ERCIM Workshop on Software Evolution and Evolvability (Evol'08) at the 23rd IEEE/ACM International Conference on Automated Software Engineering,* (pp. 235-244). USA: IEEE.

Breu, R., Burger, K., Hafner, M., Jürjens, J., Popp, G., Wimmel, G., et al. (2003). Key issues of a formally based process model for security engineering. *Sixteenth International Conference on Software & Systems Engineering & their Applications.*

Brownsword, L., Clemens, P., & Olsson, U. (1996). *Successful product line engineering: A case study.* Paper presented at the Software Technology Conference, Salt Lake City, UT.

Bruneton, E., Coupaye, T., & Stefani, J. (2004). *The fractal component model.* The ObjectWeb Consortium.

Buhr, R. J. A., & Casselman, R. S. (1996). *Use case maps for object-oriented systems.* Prentice Hall.

Bullard, V., Murray, B., & Wilson, K. (2006). *An introduction to WSDM.* OASIS Committee Draft.

Burt, C. C., Bryant, B. R., Raje, R. R., Olson, A., & Auguston, M. (2003). Model driven security: Unification of authorization models for fine-grain access control. *Proceedings of 7th International Enterprise Distributed Object Computing Conference,* (pp. 159-171).

Bustamante, M. L. (2007). *Learning WCF.* O'Reilly.

Cai, Z., & Yu, E. (2002). *Addressing performance requirements using a goal and scenario-oriented approach.* International Conference on Advanced Information Systems Engineering, (pp. 706-710).

Candolin, C. (2005). *Securing military decision making in a network-centric environment.* Unpublished doctoral dissertation, Helsinki University of Technology.

Candolin, C. (2007). A security framework for Service Oriented Architectures. In *Proceedings of the IEEE Military Communications Conference,* (pp. 1-6).

Candolin, C., & Kiviharju, M. (2007). A roadmap towards content based information security. In *Proceedings of the Eight European Conference on Information Warfare and Security.*

Cao, Y., Liu, D., Tavanapong, W., Wong, J., Oh, J., & Groen, P. C. (2007). Computer-aided detection of diagnostic and therapeutic operations in colonoscopy videos. *IEEE Transactions on Bio-Medical Engineering, 54*(7), 1268–1279. doi:10.1109/TBME.2007.890734

Cao, Y., Li, D., Tavanapong, W., Oh, J., Wong, J., & Groen, P. C. (2004c). Parsing and browsing tools for colonoscopy videos. In *ACM Multimedia,* 844-851.

Cao, Y., Liu, D., Tavanapong, W., Wong, J., Oh, J., & Groen, P. C. (2006). Automatic classification of image with appendiceal orifice in colonoscopy videos. In *Proceedings of the IEEE International Conference of the Engineering in Medicine and Biology Society,* (pp. 2349-2352).

Cao, Y., Tavanapong, W., Kim, K., Wong, J., Oh, J., & Groen, P. C. (2004a). A framework for parsing colonoscopy videos for semantic units. In *Proceedings of the IEEE International Conference on Multimedia and Expo,* (pp. 1879-1882).

Cao, Y., Tavanapong, W., Li, D., Oh, J., Groen, P. C., & Wong, J. (2004b). A visual model approach for parsing colonocsopy videos. In *Proceedings of the International Conference on Image and Video Retrieval,* (pp. 160-169).

Cappiello, C., Pernici, B., & Plebani, P. (2005). Quality-agnostic or quality-aware semantic service descriptions? In *Proceedings of W3C Workshop on Semantic Web Service Framework.*

Carnegie Mellon University, Software Engineering Institute. (2008). *Product line hall of fame.* Retrieved July 16, 2008, from http://www.sei.cmu.edu/productlines/plp_hof.html

Carr, N. G. (2004). *Does IT Matter? Information Technology and the corrosion of competitive advantage.* USA: Harvard Business School Press.

Casola, V., Fasolino, A. R., Mazzocca, N., & Tramontana, P. (2007). A policy-based evaluation framework for quality and security in Service Oriented Architectures. In *Proceedings of IEEE International Conference on Web Services*, (pp. 1181-1190).

Ceccato, M., & Tonella, P. (2005) Measuring the effects of software aspectization. In T. Tourwé, M. Bruntink, A.M. Marínn & D. Shepherd (Eds.), *Procedings of the First Workshop on Aspect Reverse Engineering. REPORT SEN-E0502,* (pp. 46-50). CWI: Stichting Centrum voor Wiskunde en Informatica.

Celik, D., & Elci, A. (2008). Semantic QoS model for extended IOPE matching and composition of Web services. In [IEEE CS Press.]. *Proceedings of COMPSAC, 08, 993–998.*

Celma, O., Dasiopoulou, S., Hausenblas, M., Little, S., Tsinaraki, C., & Troncy, R. (2007). *MPEG-7 and the Semantic Web.* Retrieved from http://www.w3.org/2005/Incubator/mmsem/XGR-mpeg7/

Cervantes, H., & Hall, R. (2004). A framework for constructing adaptive component based applications: Concepts and experiences. *Proceedings of 7th International Symposium on Component Based Software Engineering,CBSE 2004,* (pp. 130-137).

Chaari, S., Badr, Y., Biennier, F., BenAmar, C., & Favrel, J. (2008). Framework for Web service selection based on non-functional properties. *International Journal of Web Services Practices, 3*(1-2), 94–109.

Chappel, D. A. (2004). *Enterprise service bus.* USA: O'Reilly Media.

Charfi, A., Khalaf, R., & Mukhi, N. (2007). QoS-aware Web service compositions using non-intrusive policy attachment to BPEL. In *Proceedings of ICSOC '07,* (LNCS 4749), (pp. 582-593). Springer.

Chau, T., Muthusamy, V., Jacobsen, H., Litani, E., Chan, A., & Coulthard, P. (2008). Automating SLA modeling. In *Proceedings of the 2008 Conference of the Center for Advanced Studies on Collaborative Research,* (pp. 126-143). Ontario, Canada.

Chen, I., & Huangr, C. (2006). An SOA-based software deployment management system. *Proceedings of the 2006 IEEE/WIC/ACM International Conference on Web Intelligence.*

Cheng, B., Konrad, S., Campbell, L. A., & Wassermann, R. (2003). Using security patterns to model and analyze security requirements. *Proceedinsg of IEEE Workshop on Requirements for High Assurance Systems.*

Cheng, B.H.C., de Lemos, R., Giese, H., Inverardi, P. & Magee, J. (2009). *Software engineering for self-adaptive systems.* (LNCS 5525).

Chessell, M., & Schmidt-Wesche, B. (2006). *SOA programming model for implementing Web services, Part 10: SOA user roles.* Retrieved January 7, 2009, from http://www.ibm.com/developerworks/webservices/library/ws-soa-progmodel10/

Chitchyan, R., Rashid, A., Sawyer, P., Garcia, A., Pinto, M., Bakker, J., et al. (2005). *Survey of analysis and design approaches.* (Tech. Rep. No. AOSD-Europe-ULANC-9). AMPLE Project.

Choi, S. W., Her, J. S., & Kim, S. D. (2007). *QoS metrics for evaluating services from the perspective of service providers.* IEEE International Conference on e-Business Engineering (ICEBE 2007), Hong Kong, China. IEEE Computer Society, (pp. 622-625).

Choo, K.-K. R., Smith, R. G., & McCusker, R. (2007). *Future directions in technology-enabled crime: 2007–09.* (p. 78).

Chung, L., Nixon, B. A., Yu, E., & Mylopoulus, J. (2000). *Non-functional requirements in software engineering.* Norwell, MA: Kluwer Academic Publishing.

Chung, L. (1993). *Representing and using non-functional requirements for Information System development: A process-oriented approach.* Unpublished doctoral thesis, Department of Computer Science, University of Toronto.

Chung, L., Supakkul, S., & Yi, A. (2002). *Good software architecting: Goals, objects, and patterns.* Information, Computing & Communication Technology Symposium (ICCT- 2002), UKC'02. Seoul, Korea.

Clancy, W. J. (1985). Heuristic classification. [Elsevier Science Publishers.]. *Artificial Intelligence, 27,* 289–350. doi:10.1016/0004-3702(85)90016-5

Clarke, S., & Baniassad, E. (2005). *Aspect-oriented analysis and design. The theme approach.* Amsterdam: Addison-Wesley Longman.

Cleland-Huang, J., Settimi, R., Zou, X., & Solc, P. (2006). *The detection and classification of non-functional requirements with application to early aspects* (pp. 36–45).

Cleland-Huang, J., Settimi, R., BenKhadra, O., Berezhanskaya, E., & Christina, S. (2005). Goal-centric traceability for managing non-functional requirements. In *Proceedings 27th International Conference on Software Engineering,* (pp. 362-371). New York: ACM.

Clements, P., Bachman, F., Bass, L., Garlan, D., Ivers, J., & Little, R. (2003). *Documenting software architectures: Views and beyond.* Amsterdam: Addison-Wesley Longman.

Clements, P., & Northrop, L. (2002). *Software product lines: Practices and patterns.* Boston: Addison-Wesley Professional.

Codd, E. F. (1979). Extending the database relational model to capture more meaning. *ACM Transactions on Database Systems, 4*(4), 397–434. doi:10.1145/320107.320109

Colyer, A., Rashid, A., & Blair, G. (2004). *On the separation of concerns in program families.* (Tech. Rep. COMP-001-2004). Bailrigg, Lancaster: Lancaster University, Computing Department.

Cooke, J. (2008). *Constructing correct software.* Lavoisier.

Cox, D. E., & Kreger, H. (2005). Management of the service-oriented-architecture life cycle. *IBM Systems Journal, 44*(4), 709–726. doi:10.1147/sj.444.0709

Cysneiros, L. M., & Yu, E. (2005). Non-functional requirements elicitation. In Leite, J. C. S. P., & Doorn, J. H. (Eds.), *Perspectives on software requirements: An introduction* (pp. 115–138).

Cysneiros, L., & Leite, J. (2002). Non-functional requirements: From elicitation to modelling languages. In *Proceedings of the 24th International Conference on Software Engineering,* (pp. 699- 700),

Czarnecki, K., & Eisenecker, U. (2000). *Generative programming: Methods, tools and applications.* Addison-Wesley.

Dardenne, A., van Lamsweerde, A., & Fickas, S. (1993). Goal-directed requirements acquisition. *Science of Computer Programming, 20*(1-2), 3–50. doi:10.1016/0167-6423(93)90021-G

Darimont, R., & Lemoine, M. (2006). *Goal-oriented analysis of regulations.* REMO2V06: Int. Workshop on Regulations Modelling and their Verification & Validation, Luxemburg.

Datta, R., Joshi, D., Li, J., & Wang, J. Z. (2008). Image retrieval: Ideas, influences, and trends of the new age. *ACM Computing Surveys, 40*(2), 1–60. doi:10.1145/1348246.1348248

Deng, G., Balasubramanian, J., Otte, W., Schmidt, D., & Gokhale, A. (2005). DAnCE: A QoS-enabled component deployment and configuration engine. In *Proceedings of the 3rd Working Conference on Component Deployment,* (pp. 67-82).

Department of Defense (1985). *Trusted computer system evaluation criteria.* DoD 5200.28-STD.

Derler, P., & Weinreich, R. (2007). Models and tools for SOA governance. *Proceedings of the International Conference on Trends in Enterprise Application Architecture.*

Dey, A. K., & Abowd, G. D. (2000). *The context toolkit: Aiding the development of context-aware applications.* ICSE Workshop on Software Engineering for Wearable and Pervasive Computing.

Diao, Y., Hellerstein, J. L., Storm, A., Surendra, M., Lightstone, S., Parekh, S., et al. (2004). Using MIMO linear control for load balancing in computing systems. *Proceedings of the 2004 American Control Conference.* Boston.

Diskstra, E. (1976). *A discipline of programming.* Englewood Cliffs, N.J.: Prentice-Hall.

Dobson, G. (2004). *Quality of Service in Service-Oriented Architectures.* Dependability Infrastructure for Grid Services Project.

Dobson, G., & Sanchez-Macian, A. (2006). Towards unified QoS/SLA ontologies. In [IEEE CS Press.]. *Proceedings of SCW, 06,* 169–174.

Dollar, P., Rabaud, V., Cottrell, G., & Belongie, S. (2005). Behavior recognition via sparse spatio-temporal features. In *Proceedings of IEEE International Workshop on Visual Surveillance and Performance Evaluation of Tracking and Surveillance,* (pp. 65-72).

Dowling, J., & Cahill, V. (2001). The K-component architecture meta-model for self-adaptive software. *REFLECTION '01: Proceedings of the Third International Conference on Metalevel Architectures and Separation of Crosscutting Concerns*, (pp. 81-88).

Duboc, L., Rosenblum, D., & Wicks, T. (2006). A framework for modelling and analysis of software systems scalability. In *Proceedings of the 28th International Conference on Software Engineering ICSE '06*, (pp. 949-952). New York: ACM.

Duboc, L., Rosenblum, D., & Wicks, T. (2007). A framework for characterization and analysis of software system scalability. In *Proceedings of the 6th Joint Meeting of the European Software Engineering Conference and the ACM SIGSOFT Symposium on The Foundations of Software Engineering ESEC-FSE '07*, (pp. 375-384). New York: ACM.

Dubus, J., & Mer, P. (2006). Applying OMG D&C specification and ECA rules for autonomous distributed component-based systems. *Proceedings of MoDELS Workshop*, (pp. 242-251).

Dueñas, J. C., & Capilla, R. (2005). The decision view of software architecture. In *Proceedings of the 2nd European Workshop on Software Architecture* (LNCS 3527), (pp. 222-230). Berlin: Springer.

Dumas, M., Van der Aalst, W., & ter Hofstede, A. (2005). *Process-aware Information Systems*. Wiley-IEEE. doi:10.1002/0471741442

Eden, A., & Mens, T. (2006). Measuring software flexibility. *IEE Proceedings. Software*, *153*(3), 113–125. doi:10.1049/ip-sen:20050045

Efros, A. A., Berg, A. C., Mori, G., & Malik, J. (2003). Recognizing action at a distance. In *Proceedings of IEEE International Conference on Computer Vision*, (pp. 726-733).

Egyed, A. (2001). A scenario-driven approach to traceability. *In Proceedings of the 23rd International Conference on Software Engineering ICSE'01*, (pp. 123-132). Washington, DC: IEEE.

Elrad, T., Aksit, M., Kitzales, G., Lieberherr, K., & Ossher, H. (2001). Discussing aspects of AOP. *Communications of the ACM*, *44*(10), 33–38. doi:10.1145/383845.383854

EMF. (2008). *Homepage information*. Retrieved from http://www.eclipse.org/modeling/emf/

Emig, C., Krutz, K., Link, S., Momm, C. & Abeck, S. (2007). *Model-driven development of SOA services.*

Endrei, M., Ang, J., Arsanjani, A., Chua, S., Comte, P., Krogdahl, P., et al. (2004). *Patterns: Service Oriented Architecture and Web services*. USA: WebSphere Software, IBM RedBooks.

Erl, T. (2007). *SOA: Principles of service design*. Upper Saddle River, NJ: Prentice Hall.

Erl, T. (2008). *SOA design patterns*. Upper Saddle River, NJ: Prentice Hall.

Erl, T. (2005). *Service-Oriented Architecture: Concepts, technology and design*. USA: Prentice Hall PTR.

Erl, T. (2007). *SOA principles of service design*. Prentice Hall PTR.

Erl, T. (2005). *Service-Oriented Architecture: Concepts, technology, and design*. Prentice Hall.

Erradi, A., Maheshwari, P., & Padmanabhuni, S. (2005). Towards a policy-driven framework for adaptive Web services composition. In *Proceedings of the International Conference on Next Generation Web Services Practices*, (p. 33).

Evans, J., & Filsfils, C. (2007). *Deploying IP and MPLS QoS for multiservice networks: Theory and practice*. Morgan Kaufmann.

Fensel, D., & Bussler, C. (2002). *WSMF in a nutshell*. Retrieved from http://www1-c703.uibk.ac.at/~c70385/wese/wsmf.iswc.pdf

Fernandez, E. B. (2004). Two patterns for Web services security. *Proceedings of International Symposium on Web Services and Applications.*

Field, D. J. (1987). Relations between the statistics of natural images and the response properties of cortical cells. *Journal of the Optical Society of America. A, Optics and Image Science*, *4*, 2379–2394. doi:10.1364/JOSAA.4.002379

Filman, R. E., Elrad, T., Clarke, S., & Aksit, M. (2004). *Aspect-oriented software development*. Reading, MA: Addison-Wesley Professional.

Fink, T., Koch, M., & Pauls, K. (2004). An MDA approach to access control specifications using MOF and UML profiles. *Proceedings of 1st International Workshop on Views On Designing Complex Architectures*, (pp. 161-179).

Finkelstein, A., & Dowell, J. (1996). A comedy of errors: The London ambulance system case study. In *Proceedings of the Eighth International Workshop on Software Specification and Design*, (p. 2).

Firesmith, D. G. (2003a). Engineering security requirements. *Journal of Object Technology*, *2*(1), 53–68. doi:10.5381/jot.2003.2.1.c6

Firesmith, D.G. (2003b). Security use cases. *Journal of Object Technology*, 53-64.

Fischer, A., & Kühnhauser, W. E. (2008). Integration von Sicherheitsmodellen in Web Services. In P. Horster (Ed.), *D.A.CH security 2008*. Hannover, Germany: eMedia.

Fitzgerald, M. (2008, May 25). Cloud Computing: So you don't have to stand still. *The New York Times*.

Fliedl, G., Kop, C., Mayerthaler, W., Mayr, H. C., & Winkler, C. (2002). The NIBA approach to quantity settings and conceptual predesign. In *Proceedings of NLDB '01*.

Folmer, E., & Bosch, J. (2003). Usability patterns in software architecture. In *Proceedings of the 10th International Conference on Human-Computer Interaction HCII2003 vol. I*, (pp. 93-97).

Fowler, M. (2003). *Patterns of enterprise application architecture*. Boston: Addison Wesley.

Franch, X. (1998). Systematic formulation of nonfunctional characteristics of software. In *Proceedings of the Third International Conference on Requirements Engineering*, (pp. 174-181).

Frankel, D. S. (2003). *Model Driven Architecture: Applying MDA to enterprise computing*. Indianapolis: Wiley Publishing Inc.

Galle, D., Kop, C., & Mayr, H. C. (2008). A uniform Web service description representation for different readers. In [IEEE CS Press.]. *Proceedings of ICDS*, *08*, 123–128.

Galster, M., & Bucherer, E. (2008). *A taxonomy for identifying and specifying non-functional requirements in service-oriented development*. International Workshop on Methodologies for Non-functional Properties in Services Computing (MNPSC), Honolulu, USA. IEEE CS, (pp. 345-352).

Galster, M., Eberlein, A., & Moussavi, M. (2006). Transition from requirements to architecture: A review and future perspective. In *Proceedings Seventh ACIS International Conference on Software Engineering, Artificial Intelligence, Networking, and Parallel/Distributed Computing (SNPD '06)*, (pp. 9-16). USA: IEEE.

Gamma, E., Helm, R., Johnson, R., & Vlissides, J. (1995). *Design patterns*. Addison-Wesley Professional.

Gandi, N., Hellerstein, J. L., Tilbury, D. M., Jayram, T. S., & Bigus, J. (2002). *Using control theory to achieve service level objectives in performance management*. Real Time Systems Journal.

Garcia, R., Tsinaraki, C., Celma, Ó., & Christodoulakis, S. (2008). Multimedia content description using Semantic Web languages. *Semantic Multimedia and Ontologies*, *2*, 17–54. doi:10.1007/978-1-84800-076-6_2

García, A., Sant Anna, C., Figuereido, E. m., Uirá, K., Lucena, C., & von Sta, A. (2006). Modularizing design patterns with aspects: A quantitative study. In Tarr, P. (Ed.), *Transactions on aspect-oriented software development I*. Springer. doi:10.1007/11687061_2

Gasser, M. (1988). *Building a secure computer system*. New York: Van Nostrand Reinhold Co.

Geet, J. V. (2008). Reverse engineering in the world of enterprise SOA. In *Proceedings of the 15th Working Conference on Reverse Engineering*, (pp. 311-314).

Gerber, A., & Raymond, K. (2003). MOF to EMF: There and back again. In *Proceedings of the OOPSLA Workshop on Eclipse Technology eXchange*, (pp. 60–64).

Gerke, K., & Tamm, G. (2009). Continuous quality improvement of IT processes based on reference models and process mining. *AMCIS 2009 Proceedings*, (p. 786).

Geusebroek, J. M., Smeulders, A. W. M., & van de Weijer, J. (2003). Fast anisotropic Gauss filtering. *IEEE Transactions on Image Processing*, *12*, 938–943. doi:10.1109/TIP.2003.812429

Geyer, L., & Becker, M. (2002). On the influence of variabilities on the application-engineering process of a product family. In J. Bosch, F. Van der Linden, C.W. Krueger, & M. Becker (Eds.), *2ⁿᵈ International Conference on Software Product Lines. Software product line.* (pp. 1-14). London: Springer-Verlag.

Ghezzi, C., Jazayeri, M., & Mandrioli, D. (2003). *Fundamentals of software engineering.* USA: Prentice Hall.

Glitho, R. H., Khendek, F., & De Marco, A. (2003). Creating value added services in Internet telephony: An overview and a case study on a high-level service creation environment. *IEEE Transactions on Systems, Man and Cybernetics. Part C, Applications and Reviews*, *33*(4), 446–457. doi:10.1109/TSMCC.2003.818499

GMF. (2008). *Graphic Modelling Framework.* Retrieved from http://www.eclipse.org/gmf/

Goguen, J. A., & Meseguer, J. (1982). Security policies and security models. In *Proceedings IEEE Symposium on Security and Privacy,* (pp. 11-20). Washington, DC: IEEE.

Gomaa, H. (2004). *Designing software product lines with UML: From use cases to pattern-based software architectures.* Boston: Addison-Wesley Professional.

Gomaa, H., & Shin, M. (2002). Multiple-view metamodeling of software product lines. In S. Liu (Ed.), *8ᵗʰ IEEE International Conference on Engineering of Complex Computer Systems. Proceedings of the Eighth International Conference on Engineering of Complex Computer Systems,* (pp. 238-246). Washington: IEEE Computer Society.

Gotel, O. C. Z., & Finkelstein, A. C. W. (1994). An analysis of the requirements traceability problem. In *Proceedings of the First International Conference on Requirements Engineering,* (pp. 94-101). USA: IEEE.

Grace, P., Coulson, G., Blair, G., & Porter, B. (2006). A distributed architecture meta-model for self-managed middleware. *ARM '06: Proceedings of the 5th workshop on Adaptive and reflective middleware (ARM '06).*

Grau, G., & Franch, X. (2007). A goal-oriented approach for the generation and evaluation of alternative architectures. In F. Oquendo (Ed.), *Software architecture, Proceedings First European Conference, ECSA 2007.* (pp. 139-155). Berlin: Springer.

Grønmo, R., Skogan, D., Solheim, I., & Oldevik, J. (2004). Model-driven Web services development. In S. Yuan & J. Lu (Eds.), *International Conference on e-Technology, e-Commerce and e-Service 2004,* (pp. 42-45). IEEE Computer Society.

Gross, D., & Yu, E. (2001). From non-functional requirements to design through patterns. *Requirements Engineering Journal*, *6*(1), 18–36. doi:10.1007/s007660170013

Gross, D., & Yu, E. (2001). Evolving system architecture to meet changing business goals: An agent and goal-oriented approach. *Proceedings of the First International Workshop From Software Requirements to Architectures (STRAW 2001) at the International Conference of Software Engineering.* Toronto, Canada.

Guceglioglu, A. S., & Demirors, O. (2005). Using software quality characteristics to measure business process quality. In *Proceedings of BPM'05,* (LNCS 3649), (pp. 374-379). Springer.

Gupta, S., & Ranganathan, F. (2007). Multievent crisis management using noncooperative multistep games. *IEEE Transactions on Computers,* 577–589. doi:10.1109/TC.2007.1023

Gutierrez, C., Fernandez-Medina, E., & Piattini, M. (2005). *Web services enterprise security architecture: A case study.* 2005 ACM Workshop on Secure Web Services, (pp. 10-19).

Gutierrez, C., Fernandez-Medina, E., & Piattini, M. (2006). PWSSec: Process for Web services security. *Proceedings of International Conference on Web Services,* (pp. 213-222).

Halkidis, S. T., Chatzigeorgiou, A., & Stephanides, G. (2006). A qualitative analysis of software security patterns. *Computers & Security*, *25*(5), 379–392. doi:10.1016/j.cose.2006.03.002

Hansen, M. D. (2007). *SOA using Java Web services.* Prentice Hall.

Harrison, N., & Avgeriou, P. (2007). Pattern-driven architectural partitioning: Balancing functional and non-functional requirements. In *Proceedings Second International Conference on Digital Telecommunication (ICDT'07)*, (pp. 21-26). USA: IEEE.

Hassine, J., Dssouli, R., & Rilling, J. (2005). Applying reduction techniques to software functional requirement specifications. *Proceedings of System Analysis and Modeling - Fourth International SDL and MSC Workshop, SAM 2004*, Ottawa, Canada. (LNCS 3319), (pp. 138-153). Springer.

Health Level 7 International. (2010). *Health Level 7*. Retrieved from http://www.hl7.org

Heitmeyer, C. L. (2007). Formal methods for specifying, validating, and verifying requirements. *Journal of Universal Computer Science, 13*(5), 607–618.

Hellerstein, J. L. (2009). *Configuring resource managers using model fuzzing: A case study of the .NET thread pool*. IEEE/IFIP Integrated Management.

Hellerstein, J. L., Diao, Y., Parekh, S., & Tilbury, D. (2004). *Feedback control of computing systems*. Hoboken, NJ: John Wiley & Sons. doi:10.1002/047166880X

Henricksen, K., & Indulska, J. (2006). Developing context-aware pervasive computing applications: Models and approach. *Pervasive and Mobile Computing Journal, 2*(1), 37–64. doi:10.1016/j.pmcj.2005.07.003

Henricksen, K., & Indulska, J. (2004). A software engineering framework for context-aware pervasive computing. *Proceedings of the 2nd IEEE International Conference on Pervasive Computing and Communications*, (pp. 77–86).

Henricksen, K., Indulska, J., & Rakotonirainy, A. (2002). *Modeling context information in pervasive computing systems*. (LNCS 2414), (pp. 79 – 117).

Heo, S., & Man, E. (2006). Representation of variability in software product line using aspect-oriented programming. In S. Kawada (Ed.), *Proceedings of the 4th International Conference on Software Engineering Research, Management and Applications*, (pp. 66-73). Washington: IEEE Computer Society.

Herrmann, P., & Herrmann, G. (2006). Security requirement analysis of business processes. *Electronic Commerce Research*, 305–335. doi:10.1007/s10660-006-8677-7

Heuvel, W.-J. V. D., Leune, K., & Papazoglou, M. P. (2005). EFSOC: A layered framework for developing secure interactions between Web-services. *Distributed and Parallel Databases, 18*(2), 115–145. doi:10.1007/s10619-005-1400-1

Hiers, C. (2005). *A2.3.1.1 fire investigator positions*.

High, R., Kinder, S., & Graham, S. (2005). *IBM SOA Foundation: An architectural introduction and overview*. Retrieved January 7, 2009, from http://www.ibm.com/developerworks/webservices/library/ws-soa-whitepaper/

Hill, M. D. (1990). What is scalability? *SIGARCH Computer Architecture News, 18*(4), 18–21. doi:10.1145/121973.121975

Hirsch, F., Yendluri, P., Orchard, D., Yalçinalp, U., Boubez, T., Vedamuthu, A. S., et al. (2007). *Web services policy 1.5 - framework*. Retrieved from http://www.w3.org/TR/2007/REC-ws-policy-20070904/

Hnetynka, P. (2005). A model-driven environment for component deployment. *SERA '05: Proceedings of the Third ACIS Int'l Conference on Software Engineering Research, Management and Applications*, (pp. 6-13).

Hoareau, D., Abdellatif, T., & Mahéo, Y. (2007). Architecture-based autonomic deployment of J2EE systems in Grids. *Proceedings of International Conference on Grid and Pervasive Computing (GPC'07)*.

Hobbs, C., & Storrie, J. (2007). Time-sensitive Service-Oriented Architectures. *Nortel Technical Journal, 5*, 20–32.

Hobbs, C., Becha, H., & Amyot, D. (2008). *Failure semantics in a SOA environment*. 3rd Int. MCeTech Conference on eTechnologies, Montréal, Canada. IEEE Computer Society, (pp. 116-121).

Hofmeister, C., Nord, R., & Soni, D. (2000). *Applied software architecture*. New York: Addison Wesley.

Hollot, C., Misra, V., Towsley, D., & Gong, W. (2001). *A control theoretic analysis of RED*. IEEE INFOCOM.

Horkoff, J. (2006). *Using i* models for evaluation*. MSc thesis, Toronto, Ont, Canada.

Horrocks, I., Patel-Schneider, P. F., Boley, H., Tabet, S., Grosof, B., & Dean, M. (2004). *SWRL: A Semantic Web rule language combining OWL and RuleML*. Retrieved from http://www.w3.org/Submission/2004/SUBM-SWRL-20040521.

Hrasna, H. (2002). *Javatm 2 platform, enterprise edition management specification JSR-77*. Récupéré sur Sun Microsystems.

Huang, D. (2005). Semantic policy-based security framework for business processes. Retrieved December 29, 2008, from http://www.csee.umbc.edu/swpw/papers/huang.pdf

Hughes, C., & Hillman, J. (2006). *QoS Explorer: A tool for exploring QoS in composed services*. International Conference on Web Services (ICWS'06), Chicago, USA. IEEE Computer Society, (pp. 797-806).

Hündling, J. (2005). Modelling properties of services. In *Proceedings of 1st European Young Researchers Workshop on Service Oriented Computing*.

Huntley, K., & San Filippo, D. (2006). Enabling aspects to enhance service-oriented architecture. *The Architecture Journal*, 7. Retrieved July 28, 2008, from http://msdn.microsoft.com/en-us/arcjournal/bb245654.aspx

IBM & Microsoft. (2002). *Security in a Web services qorld: A proposal architecture and roadmap*. Retrieved September 1, 2008, from http://www.ibm.com/developerworks/webservices/library/specification/ws-secmap/

IBM. (2005a). *Welcome to the WebSphere application server, version 6.1 information center*. Retrieved September 1, 2008, from http://publib.boulder.ibm.com/infocenter/wasinfo/v6r1/index.jsp

IBM. (2005b). *IBM WebSphere business modeler advanced documentation*. Retrieved January 7, 2009, from http://publib.boulder.ibm.com/infocenter/dmndhelp/v6r2mx/index.jsp

IBM. (2005c). *IBM rational application developer version 7.0.0.x information center*. Retrieved September 1, 2008, from http://publib.boulder.ibm.com/infocenter/radhelp/v7r0m0/index.jsp?topic=/com.ibm.help.doc/home.html

IEEE. (1998). Recommended practice for software requirements specifications.

IEEE. (1998). *Standard for software requirements specification*. Retrieved from http://ieeexplore.ieee.org/stamp/stamp.jsp?arnumber=720574&isnumber=15571

INCOSE. (2008). *The INCOSE requirements management tools survey*. Retrieved from http://www.incose.org

Irmert, F., Fischer, T., & Meyer-Wegener, K. (2008). Runtime adaptation in a service-oriented component model. *SEAMS '08: Proceedings of the 2008 international workshop on Software engineering for adaptive and self-managing systems*, (pp. 97-104).

ISA. (2000). *ISA–95.00.01–2000 Enterprise-control system integration. Part 1: Models and terminology*. North Carolina: ISA.

ISO. (2001). ISO/IEC 9126-1 International standard. Software engineering–product quality –part 1: Quality models.

ISO. (2005). ISO/IEC 27001:2005 Information technology–security techniques–information security management systems–requirements.

ISO/IEC. (2004a). Security techniques-management of information and communications technology security.

ISO/IEC. (2004b). Security techniques-guide for the production of protection profiles and security targets.

ISO/IEC. (2005a). Security techniques-evaluation criteria for IT security.

ISO/IEC. (2005b). Security techniques-code of practice for information security management.

ISO/IEC. (2005c). Security techniques-information security management systems requirements.

ISO/IEC. (2006). Security techniques-information security management systems requirements.

ITU-T. (2003). *User Requirements Notation (URN)–language requirements and framework*. Geneva, Switzerland.

ITU-T. (2007). *Framework and methodologies for the determination and application of QoS parameters*. Geneva, Switzerland.

ITU-T. (2008). *User Requirements Notation (URN) language definition*. Geneva, Switzerland: International Telecommunications Union.

ITU-T. (2008a). *User Requirements Notation (URN)– language definition*. Geneva, Switzerland.

ITU-T. (2008b). *Definitions of terms related to quality of service*, Geneva, Switzerland. jUCMNav. (2008). *Version 3.2*. University of Ottawa. Accessed October, 2008, from http://jucmnav.softwareengineering.ca/jucmnav/

Jacobson, I., Booch, G., & Rumbaugh, J. (2002). *The unified software development process*. Upper Saddle River, NJ: Addison-Wesley.

James, A. (2008, July 8). *Andrea James on Amazon.com and the business of online retail*. Retrieved September 30, 2008, from http://blog.seattlepi.nwsource.com/amazon/archives/142569.asp

Janicki, R., Parnas, D. L., & Zucker, J. (1997). Tabular representations in relational documents. In Brink, C., Kahl, W., & Schmidt, G. (Eds.), *Relational methods in computer science*. Berlin: Springer.

Janssens, N., Joosen, W., & Verbaeten, P. (2005). *NeCo-Man: Middleware for safe distributed-service adaptation in programmable networks*. IEEE Distributed Systems Online.

Janssens, N., Truyen, E., Sanen, F., & Joosen, W. (2007). Adding dynamic reconfiguration support to JBoss AOP. *MAI '07: Proceedings of the 1st workshop on Middleware-application interaction*.

Java Community Press. (2007). *JSR 224: Java API for XML-based Web services (JAX-WS) 2.0*. Retrieved from http://jcp.org/en/jsr/detail?id=224 Kadir, T., Zisserman, A. & Brady, M. (2004). An affine invariant salient region detector. In *Proceedings of European Conference on Computer Vision*, (pp. 404-416).

JGoodies. (2008). *JGoodies: Java user interface design*. Retrieved October 13, 2008, from http://www.jgoodies.com/

Jiang, H., Nguyen, T. N., Chang, C. K., & Dong, F. (2007). Traceability link evolution management with incremental semantic indexing. In *Proceedings 31st Annual International Computer Software and Applications Conference (COMPSAC 2007)*, (pp. 309-316). USA: IEEE.

Jin, L.-J., Machiraju, V., & Sahai, A. (2002). *Analysis on service level agreements of Web services*. (Technical Report HPL-2002-180). HP Laboratories Palo Alto.

Jingbai, T., Keqing, H., Chong, W., & Wei, L. (2008). A context awareness non-functional requirements metamodel based on domain ontology. In *Proceedings of IEEE International Workshop on Semantic Computing and Systems,* (pp. 1-7). IEEE CS Press.

Johnson, P., & Ekstedt, M. (2007). *Enterprise architecture: Models and analyses for Information Systems decision making*. Studentlitteratur.

Johnson, P., Lagerström, R., & Narman, P. (2007). Extended influence diagram generation. In *Enterprise Interoperability II* (pp. 599–602). New Challenges and Approaches.

Johnson, P., Lagerstrom, R., Narman, P., & Simonsson, M. (2006). Extended influence diagrams for enterprise architecture analysis. In *Proceedings of the 10th IEEE International Annual Enterprise Distributed Object Computing Conference*, (pp. 3-12).

Johnston, S. (2005). *UML 2.0 profile for software services*. Retrieved September 1, 2008, from http://www.ibm.com/developerworks/rational/library/05/419_soa/

JPL. (2004). *A bidirectional Prolog/Java interface*. Retrieved Septermber 1, 2008, from http://www.swi-prolog.org/packages/jpl/

Jureta, I.J., Herssens, C. & Faulkner, S. (2008). A comprehensive quality model for service-oriented systems. *Software Quality Journal.*

Jürjens, J. (2002a). *Automated verification of UMLsec models for security requirements* (pp. 365–379).

Jürjens, J. (2002c). *Using UMLsec and goal trees for secure systems development* (pp. 1026–1030).

Jürjens, J. (2002). UMLsec: Extending UML for secure systems development. *Proceedings of 5th International Conference on The Unified Modeling Language,* (pp. 412-425).

Jürjens, J. (2002b). *UMLsec: Extending UML for secure systems development*. (LNCS 2460), (pp. 412-425).

Jürjens, J. (2005). *Sound methods and effective tools for model-based security engineering with UML*. 27th International Conference on Software Engineering, (pp. 322-331).

Jürjens, J., & Fox, J. (2006). Tools for model-based security engineering. *Proceedings of 28th International Conference on Software Engineering*, (pp. 819-822).

Kang, K., Cohen, S., Hess, J. A., Novak, W. E., & Peterson, S. A. (1990). *Feature-Oriented Domain Analysis (FODA) feasibility study*. Software Engineering Institute, Carnegie-Mellon University.

Kaschek, R., Kop, C., Shekhovtsov, V. A., & Mayr, H. C. (2008). Towards simulation-based quality requirements elicitation: A position paper. In *Proceedings of REFSQ 2008*, (LNCS 5025), (pp. 135-140). Springer.

Kassab, M., Ormandijeva, O., & Daneva, M. (2008). A traceability metamodel for change management of non-functional requirements. In *Proceedings of International Conference on Software Engineering Research, Management, and Applications*, (pp. 245-254). IEEE CS Press.

Kazman, R. (2005). From requirements negotiation to software architectural decisions. *Journal on Information and Software Technology*, 47(8), 511–520. doi:10.1016/j.infsof.2004.10.001

Kazman, R., Klein, M., & Clements, P. (2000). *ATAM: Method for architecture evaluation*. (Tech. Rep. CMU/SEI-2000-TR-004). Pittsburgh: Carnegie-Mellon University, Software Engineering Institute.

Ke, Y., Sukthankar, R., & Hebert, M. (2005). Efficient visual event detection using volumetric features. In *Proceedings of IEEE International Conference on Computer Vision*, (pp. 166-173).

Kealey, J., & Amyot, D. (2007). *Enhanced use case map traversal semantics*. 13th SDL Forum (SDL'07), Paris, France. (LNCS 4745), (pp. 133-149). Springer.

Keeney, J., & Cahill, V. (2003). Chisel: A policy-driven, context-aware, dynamic adaptation framework. *POLICY '03: Proceedings of the 4th IEEE International Workshop on Policies for Distributed Systems and Networks*.

Keller, A., & Ludwig, H. (2003). The WSLA framework: Specifying and monitoring service level agreements for Web services. *Journal of Network and Systems Management*, 11(1), 57–81. doi:10.1023/A:1022445108617

Keller, S. E., & Kahn, G. H. (1990). Specifying software quality requirements with metrics. In Thayer, R. H., & Dorfman, M. (Eds.), *Tutorial: System and software requirement engineering* (pp. 145–163). IEEE Computer Society Press.

Ketfi, A., & Belkhatir, N. (2003). Dynamic interface adaptability in service oriented software. *Proceedings of Eighth International Workshop on Component-Oriented Programming (WCOP'03)*.

Ketfi, A., & Belkhatir, N. (2005). Model-driven framework for dynamic deployment and reconfiguration of component-based software systems. *MIS '05: Proceedings of the 2005 symposia on Metainformatics, Esbjerg, Denmark*.

Ketfi, A., Belkhatir, N., & Cunin, P. (2002). *Dynamic updating of component-based applications*. SERP'02, Las Vegas.

Kiczales, G., Hilsdale, E., Hugunin, J., Kersten, M., Palm, J., & Grisworld, W. G. (2001). An overview of aspectJ. In J.L. Knudsen (Ed.), *Proceedings of the 15th European Conference on Object-Oriented Programming*. (pp. 327-353). London: Springer-Verlag.

Kiczales, G., Lamping, J., Mendhekar, A., Maeda, C., Lopes, C., Loingtier, J., et al. (1997). Aspect-oriented programming. In M. Aksit & S. Matsuoka (Eds.), *European Conference on Object-Oriented Programming. Proceedings of the European conference on object-oriented programming* (pp. 220-242). Berlin, Heidelberg & New York: Springer-Verlag.

Kim, E., & Lee, Y. (2005). *Quality model for Web services 2.0*. OASIS.

Kim, H. M., Sengupta, A., & Evermann, J. (2007). MOQ: Web services ontologies for QoS and general quality evaluations. *International Journal of Metadata. Semantics and Ontologies*, 2(3), 195–200. doi:10.1504/IJMSO.2007.017612

Kimball, R., & Ross, M. (2002). *The data warehouse toolkit: The complete guide to dimensional modeling* (2nd ed.). Wiley.

Kleinrock, L. (1976). Queueing systems: *Vol. II. Computer applications*. Hoboken, NJ: John Wiley & Sons.

Kleppe, A., Warmer, J., & Bast, W. (2005). *MDA explained: The Model Driven Architecture: Practice and promise.* Boston: Addison-Wesley.

Kop, C., & Mayr, H. C. (2002). Mapping functional requirements: From natural language to conceptual schemata. In *Proceedings of SEA, 02*, 82–87.

Kop, C., Mayr, H. C., & Zavinska, T. (2004). Using KCPM for defining and integrating domain ontologies. In *Proceedings of Web Information Systems - WISE 2004 Workshops,* (LNCS 3307), (pp. 190-200). Springer.

Kotonya, G., & Sommerville, I. (2000). *Requirements engineering process and techniques.* John Willey & Sons.

Kritikos, K., & Plexousakis, D. (2007). OWL-Q for semantic QoS-based Web service description and discovery. In *Proceedings of SMRR '07.*

Krueger, C. W. (2008). *Benefits of software product lines.* Retrieved July 20, 2008, from http://www.softwareproductlines.com/benefits/benefits.html

Kuloor, C., & Eberlein, A. (2003). Aspect-oriented requirements engineering for software product lines. *Proceedings of the 10th IEEE International Conference and Workshop on the Engineering of Computer-Based Systems* (ECBS'03).

Kumar, P. (2008). A low-cost hybrid coordinated checkpointing protocol for mobile distributed systems. *Mobile Information Systems, 4*(1), 13–32.

Lagerström, R., & Ohrstrom, J. (2007). A framework for assessing business value of Service Oriented Architectures. In *IEEE International Conference on Services Computing,* (pp. 670-671).

Laguna, M. A., & Gonzalez-Baixauli, B. (2005). *Goals and MDA in product line requirements engineering.* Department of Computer Science, University of Valladolid.

Lainhart, J. IV. (2000). COBIT: A methodology for managing and controlling information and Information Technology risks and vulnerabilities. *Journal of Information Systems, 14*, 21. doi:10.2308/jis.2000.14.s-1.21

Lamanna, D., Skene, J., & Emmerich, W. (2003). SLAng: A language for defining service level agreements. *Proceedings of The Ninth IEEE Workshop on Future Trends of Distributed Computing Systems.*

Lampson, B., Abadi, M., Burrows, M., & Wobber, E. (1992). Authentication in distributed systems: Theory and practice. *ACM Transactions on Computer Systems, 10*(4), 265–310. doi:10.1145/138873.138874

Lamsweerde, A. (2001). Goal-oriented requirements engineering: A guided tour. In *Proceedings of the Fifth International Symposium on Requirements Engineering,* (pp. 249-262).

Laptev, I., & Lindeberg, T. (2003). Space-time interest points. In *Proceedings of IEEE International Conference on Computer Vision,* (pp. 432-439).

Lara, R., Polleres, A., Lausen, H., Roman, B., de Bruijn, J. & Fensel, D. (2005). *A conceptual comparison between WSMO and OWL-S.* (WSMO Deliverable 4.1).

Larman, C. (2004). *Applying UML and patterns, an introduction to object-oriented analysis and design and iterative development.* USA: Prentice Hall PTR.

Larrucea, X., & Alonso, R. (2008). ISOAS: Through an Independent SOA Security Specification. In *Proceedings of the Seventh Composition-Based Software Systems,* (pp. 92-100).

Lausen H., Polleres A. & Roman. (2005) *Web service modeling ontology.* Retrieved from http://www.w3.org/Submission/WSMO/

Lee, Y., Bae, J., & Shin, S. (2005). Development of quality evaluation metrics for BPM (Business Process Management) system. In [IEEE CS Press.]. *Proceedings of ICIS, 05*, 424–429.

Lee, Y., & Yeom, G. (2007). A research for Web service quality presentation methodology for SOA framework. In [IEEE CS Press.]. *Proceedings of ALPIT, 07*, 434–439.

Lennox, J., & Schulzrinne, H. (2000). *Call processing language framework and requirements.* Retrieved from http://www.ietf.org/rfc/rfc2824.txt

Letelier, P. (2002). A framework for requirements traceability in UML-based projects. In *1st Int. Workshop on Traceability in Emerging Forms of SE (TEFSE'02),* (pp. 32-41). Edinburgh, UK.

Leung, T., & Malik, J. (2001). Representing and recognizing the visual appearance of materials using three-dimensional textons. *International Journal of Computer Vision, 43*(1), 29–44. doi:10.1023/A:1011126920638

Littlefair, T. (2001). *An investigation into the use of software code metrics in the industrial software development environment.* Unpublished doctoral dissertation, Faculty of Communications, Health and Science, Edith Cowan University.

Liu, Y., Ngu, A. H. H., & Zeng, L. (2004). QoS computation and policing in dynamic Web service selection. In [ACM Press.]. *Proceedings of WWW, 04,* 66–73.

Liu, D., Cao, Y., Kim, K., Stanek, S., Doungratanaex-Chai, B., & Lin, K. (2007b). Arthemis: Annotation software in an integrated capturing and analysis system for colonoscopy. *Computer Methods and Programs in Biomedicine, 88*(2), 152–163. doi:10.1016/j.cmpb.2007.07.011

Liu, D., Cao, Y., Tavanapong, W., Wong, J., Oh, J., & Groen, P. C. (2007a). Mining colonoscopy videos to measure quality of colonoscopic procesure. In *Proceedings of the International Conference on Biomedical Engineering,* (pp. 409 - 414).

Liu, L., & Yu, E. (2001). From requirements to architectural design–using goals and scenarios. In *From Software Requirements to Architectures Workshop (STRAW 2001),* (pp. 22-30). Toronto, Canada.

Liu, S.-H., Bryant, B. R., Gray, J., Raje, R., Olson, A., & Auguston, M. (2005). QoS-UniFrame: A petri net-based modeling approach to assure QoS requirements of distributed real-time and embedded systems. In *Proceedings of the 12th IEEE International Conference and Workshop on the Engineering of Computer Based Systems,* (pp. 202-209).

Liu, S.-H., Cao, Y., Li, M., Kilaru, P., Smith, T., & Toner, S. (2008). A semantics- and data-driven SOA for biomedical multimedia systems. In *Proceedings of IEEE International Symposium on Multimedia,* (pp. 533-538).

Liu, X., Heo, J., & Sha, L. (2005). Modeling 3-tiered Web applications. *Proceedings of IEEE International Symposium on Modeling, Analysis, and Simulation of Computer and Telecommunication Systems,* (pp. 307-310).

Liu, Y., Zhu, L., et al. (2008). *Non-functional property driven service governance: Performance implications.* ICSOC Workshop on Non Functional Properties and Service Level Agreements in Service Oriented Computing.

Lodderstedt, T., Basin, D., & Doser, J. (2002). SecureUML: A UML-based modeling language for model-driven security. *5th International Conference on The Unified Modeling Language,* (pp. 426-441).

Lohmann, D., Spinczyk, O., & Schröder-Preikschat, W. (2005). On the configuration of non-functional properties in operating system product lines. In Y. Coady, E. Eide, D.H. Lorenz & O. Spinczyk (Eds.), *Proceedings of the 4th AOSD Workshop on Aspects, Components and Patterns for Infrastructure Software* (AOSD-ACP4IS '05), NU-CCIS-05-03, (pp. 19-25). Boston: Northeastern University.

Ludwig, H., Keller, A., Dan, A., King, R. P., & Franck, R. (2003) *Web Service Level Agreement (WSLA) language specification.* Retrieved from http://www.research.ibm.com/wsla/WSLASpecV1-20030128.pdf

Lux, M. (2008a). *Caliph and Emir.* Retrieved from http://www.semanticmetadata.net/features/ Lux, M. (2008b). *Lire.* Retrieved from http://www.semanticmetadata.net/lire/ Ma, L., Cao, Y. & He, J. (2008). Biomedical image storage, retrieval and visualization based-on open source project. In *Proceedings of 2008 Congress on Image and Signal Processing* (pp. 63-66).

Ma, W.-Y., & Manjunath, B. S. (1998). A texture thesaurus for browsing large aerial photographs. *Journal of the American Society for Information Science American Society for Information Science, 49,* 633–648. doi:10.1002/(SICI)1097-4571(19980515)49:7<633::AID-ASI5>3.0.CO;2-N

MacKenzie, C.M., Laskey, K., McCabe, F., Brown, P. & Metz, R. (2006). *Reference model for Service-Oriented Architecture 1.0.* OASIS Public Review Draft 1.0.

Mäder, P., Gotel, O., & Philippow, I. (2008). Rule-based maintenance of post-requirements traceability relations. In *Proceedings of the 2008 16th IEEE International Requirements Engineering Conference (RE '08),* (pp. 23-32). USA: IEEE.

Mäder, P., Philippow, I., & Riebisch, M. (2007). Customizing traceability links for the unified process. In *Proceedings of the Third International Conference on the Quality of Software-Architectures (QOSA2007)* (LNCS 4880). (pp. 47-64). Berlin: Springer.

Mäder, P., Riebisch, M., & Philippow, I. (2006). Traceability for managing evolutionary change. In *Proceedings of the 15th International Conference on Software Engineering and Data Engineering (SEDE-2006),* (pp. 1-8). USA: ISCA.

Manjunath, B. S., Ohm, J.-R., Vasudevan, V. V., & Yamada, A. (2001). Color and texture descriptors. *IEEE Transactions on Circuits and Systems for Video Technology, 11,* 703–715. doi:10.1109/76.927424

Marangozova, V., & Hagimont, D. (2001). Availability through adaptation: A distributed application experiment and evaluation. *Proceedings of European Research Seminar on Advances in Distributed Systems (ERSADS'2001).*

Marinescu, R., & Ratiu, D. (2004). Quantifying the quality of object-oriented design: The factor-strategy model. In *Proceedings 11th Working Conference on Reverse Engineering (WCRE 2004),* (pp. 192-201). USA: IEEE.

Martin, D., Burstein, M., Lassila, O., Paolucci, M., Payne, T., & McIlraith, S. (2003). *Describing Web services using OWL-S and WSDL.* Retrieved from http://www.daml.org/services/owl-s/1.0/owl-s-wsdl.html Mikolajczyk, K. & Schmid, C. (2004). Scale and affine invariant interest point detectors. *International Journal of Computer Vision, 60,* 63–86.

Martin, D., Burstein, M., Hobbs, J., Lassila, O., McDemott, D., McIlraith, S., et al. (2008). *OWL-S: Semantic markup for Web services.* Retrieved from http://www.w3.org/Submission/OWL-S/

Martin, P., Powley, W., Wilson, K., Tian, W., Xu, T., & Zebedee, J. (2007). The WSDM of autonomic computing: Experiences in implementing autonomic Web services. *ICSEW '07: Proceedings of the 29th International Conference on Software Engineering Workshops.*

Maßen, T. d., & Lichter, H. (2004). *RequiLine: A requirements engineering tool for software product lines* (pp. 168-180).

Maximilien, E. M., & Singh, M. P. (2004). A framework and ontology for dynamic Web services selection. *IEEE Internet Computing, 8*(5), 84–93. doi:10.1109/MIC.2004.27

Mayr, H. C., & Kop, C. (1998). Conceptual predesign-bridging the gap between requirements and conceptual design. In [IEEE CS Press.]. *Proceedings of ICRE, 98,* 90–100.

Mayr, H. C. (2006). Conceptual requirements modeling–a contribution to XNP (eXtreme Non Programming). In *Proceedings of APCCM'06,* (CRPIT, Vol. 53). Australian Computer Society.

Mayr, H. C., Kop, C., & Esberger, D. (2007). Business process modeling and requirements modeling. In *Proceedings of ICDS'07,* (p. 8). IEEE CS Press.

McFadden, T., Henricksen, K., & Indulska, J. (2004). Automating context-aware application development. In *Proceedings of UbiComp, 1st International Workshop on Advanced Context Modelling, Reasoning and Management,* (pp. 90 – 95).

McIlraith, S. A., Plexousakis, D., & van Harmelen, F. (2004). The Semantic Web. In *Proceedings of the Third International Semantic Web Conference.* (LNCS 3298), Springer.

McKnight, D. H., & Chervany, N. L. (2000). *The meanings of trust.* MISRC Working Papers Series.

Mehrotra, S., Znati, T., & Thompson, C. (2008). Crisis management. *IEEE Internet Computing,* 14–17. doi:10.1109/MIC.2008.7

Mellado, D., Fernández-Medina, E., & Piattini, M. (2007). A common criteria based security requirements engineering process for the development of secure Information Systems. *Computer Standards & Interfaces, 29*(2), 244–253. doi:10.1016/j.csi.2006.04.002

Mellado, M., Fernández-Medina, E., & Piattini, M. (2008c). Towards security requirements management for software product lines: A security domain requirements engineering process. *Computer Standards & Interfaces, 30,* 361–371. doi:10.1016/j.csi.2008.03.004

Mellado, D., Fernández-Medina, E., & Piattini, M. (2006). *Applying a security requirements engineering process.* 11th European Symposium on Research in Computer Security (ESORICS 2006). (LNCS 4189), (pp. 192-206). Springer.

Mellado, D., Fernández-Medina, E., & Piattini, M. (2008a). *Security requirements engineering process for software product lines: A case study.* The Third International Conference on Software Engineering Advances (ICSEA 2008), (pp. 1-6).

Mellado, D., Rodríguez, J., Fernández-Medina, E., & Piattini, M. (2009). *Automated support for security requirements engineering in software product line domain engineering*. The Fourth International Conference on Availability, Reliability and Security (ARES 2009).

Mellado, M., Fernández-Medina, E., & Piattini, M. (2008b). *Security requirements variability for software product lines*. Symposium on Requirements Engineering for Information Security (SREIS 2008) co-located with ARES 2008, (pp. 1413-1420).

Microsoft. (1995). *COM: Component Object Model technologies*. Récupéré sur http://www.microsoft.com/com/resources/comdocs.asp

Milanovic, N., Milic, B., & Malek, M. (2008). *Modeling business process availability*. International Workshop on Methodologies for Non-functional Properties in Services Computing (MNPSC), Honolulu, USA. IEEE CS, (pp. 315-321).

Ministry for Public Administration of Spain. (2005). *Methodology for Information Systems risk analysis and management*.

Mohamed, M., Romdhani, M., & Ghedira, K. (2007). EMF-MOF alignment. *Proceedings of the 3rd International Conference on Autonomic and Autonomous Systems*, (pp. 1–6).

Morgan, G. (2006). *Design for flexibility*. Retrieved October 13, 2008, from http://blogs.msdn.com/gabriel_morgan/archive/2006/10/03/Design-for-Flexibility.aspx

Müller, H., Michoux, N., Bandon, D., & Geissbuhler, A. (2004). A review of content-based image retrieval systems in medicine-clinical benefits and future directions. *International Journal of Medical Informatics, 73*(1), 1–23. doi:10.1016/j.ijmedinf.2003.11.024

Muñoz, J., Mendoza, R., Álvarez, F. & Vargas, M. (2006). A classification of security patterns for the transactions between a requester, an intermediary, and a Web service. *International Association of Science and Technology for Development*, 95-132.

Mussbacher, G., Amyot, D., & Weiss, M. (2007). *Formalizing patterns with the user requirements notation* (pp. 304–325). Hershey, PA: IGI Global.

Mussbacher, G. (2008). Aspect-oriented user requirements notation. In Giese, H. (Ed.), *Models in software engineering: Workshops and symposia at MODELS 2007. (LNCS 5002)* (pp. 305–316). Springer.

Mussbacher, G., Amyot, D., & Weiss, M. (2007). Visualizing early aspects with use case maps. In Rashid, A., & Aksit, M. (Eds.), *Transactions on Aspect-Oriented Software Development III* (pp. 105–143). Springer. doi:10.1007/978-3-540-75162-5_5

Mussbacher, G., & Amyot, D. (2008). Assessing the applicability of use case maps for business process and workflow description. *3rd International MCeTech Conference on eTechnologies Proceedings*, Montréal, Canada. IEEE Computer Society, (pp. 219-222).

Mussbacher, G., Amyot, D., Araújo, J., Moreira, A., & Weiss, M. (2007a). *Visualizing aspect-oriented goal models with AoGRL*. Second International Workshop on Requirements Engineering Visualization (REV'07), New Delhi, India.

Mussbacher, G., Amyot, D., Whittle, J., & Weiss, M. (2007b). *Flexible and expressive composition rules with Aspect-oriented Use Case Maps (AoUCM)*. 10th International Workshop on Early Aspects (EA 2007), Vancouver, Canada. (LNCS 4765), (pp. 19-38).

Mylopoulos, J., Chung, L., & Nixon, B. (1992). Representing and using non-functional requirements: A process-oriented spproach. *IEEE Transactions on Software Engineering, 14*(6), 483–497. doi:10.1109/32.142871

Mylopoulos, J., Borgida, A., et al. (1997). *Representing software engineering knowledge*. Automated Software Engineering.

Nano, O., & Zisman, A. (2007). Realizing service-centric software systems. *IEEE Software, 24*(6), 28–30. doi:10.1109/MS.2007.166

Nelson, K., Nelson, H., & Ghods, M. (1997). Technology flexibility: Conceptualization, validation, and measurement. In *Proceedings of the Thirtieth Hawaii International Conference on System Sciences, Vol. 3*, (pp. 76-87). Washington, DC: IEEE.

Newcomer, E., & Lomow, G. (2004). *Understanding SOA with Web services*. Upper Saddle River, NJ: Addison-Wesley Professional.

Niebles, J. C., Wang, H., & Fei-Fei, L. (2008). Unsupervised learning of human action categories using spatial-temporal words. In *Proceedings of British Machine Vision Conference*, (pp. 1249).

Nielsen, J. (1993). *Usability engineering*. Boston: Academic Press.

Nikander, P. (1999). *An architecture for authorization and delegation in distributed object-oriented agent systems*. Unpublished doctoral dissertation, Helsinki University of Technology.

Nixon, B. (1994). Representing and using performance requirements during the development of Information Systems. *Proceedings of the 4th international conference on extending database technology: Advances in database technology*, (p. 187).

Northrop, L. (2006). *Software product lines: Reuse that makes business sense*. Paper presented at the Australian Software Engineering Conference, Sydney, Australia.

O'Sullivan, J., Edmond, D., & ter Hofstede, A. (2002). What's in a service? Towards accurate description of non-functional service properties. *Journal on Distributed and Parallel Databases, 12*(2-3), 117–133. doi:10.1023/A:1016547000822

OASIS. (2006). *OASIS reference model for Service Oriented Architecture*. Récupéré sur http://www.oasisopen. org/committees/download.php/19679/soa-rm-cs.pdf

OASIS. (2006). *Reference model for Service Oriented Architecture 1.0*. OASIS Standard. Retrieved October 2008, from http://www.oasis-open.org/specs/index. php#soa-rmv1.0

OASIS. (2007). *OASIS Web services business process execution language*. Retrieved from http://www.oasis-open.org/committees/tc_home.php?wg_abbrev=wsbpel

OASIS. (2007). *Solution deployment descriptor specifi cation 1.0*. Récupéré sur http://docs.oasis-open.org/sdd/ v1.0/pr01/sdd-spec-v1.0-pr01.p

OASIS. (2007). *Web services business process execution language version 2.0*. Récupéré sur http://docs.oasis-open. org/wsbpel/2.0/CS01/wsbpel-v2.0-CS01.pdf

OASIS. (2007). *WS-security policy 1.2*. Retrieved September 1, 2008, from http://www.oasis-open.org/committees/ download.php/23821/ws-securitypolicy-1.2-spec-cs.pdf

OASIS. (2007a). *Service component architecture/assembly*. Retrieved September 1, 2008, from http://www.oasis-open.org/committees/tc_home.php?wg_abbrev=sca-assembly

OASIS. (2007b). *Service component architecture/policy*. Retrieved September 1, 2008, from http://www.oasis-open.org/committees/tc_home.php?wg_abbrev=sca-policy

OASIS. (2008). *Homepage information*. Retrieved October 2008, from http://www.oasis-open.org/home/ index.php

oAW. (2008). *User guide v4.3.1*. Retrieved from http://www.openarchitectureware.org/pub/documentation/4.3.1/openArchitectureWare-4.3.1-Reference.pdf.

OECD. (2005). The promotion of a culture of security for Information Systems and networks in OECD countries.

Öhrström, J. (2007). *Business value using Service Oriented Architecture*. Unpublished Master thesis, Royal Institute of Technology.

Ollson, T., & Grundy, J. (2002). Supporting traceability and inconsistency management between software artifacts. In *Proceedings of IASTED International Conference on Software Engineering and Application*.

Oman, P., Hagemeister, J., & Ach, D. (1991). *A definition and taxonomy for software maintainability* (pp. 91–108). Software Engineering Test Lab, University of Idaho.

OMG. (2006). Deployment and configuration of component-based distributed applications specification.

OMG. (2004). *Reusable Assets Specification*. RAS.

OMG. (2002). *CORBA component model specification, version 4.0*.

OMG. (2003). *Model Driven Architecture (MDA) specification guide v1.0.1*. Retrieved from http://www.omg. org/docs/omg/03-06-01.pdf

OMG. (2003). *Xml Metadata Interchange (XMI), version 2.0*.

OMG. (2005). *Meta Object Facility (MOF) core specification v2.0*. Retrieved from http://www.omg.org/docs/formal/06-01-01.pdf

OMG. (2005). *Object Constraint Language (OCL) specification v2.0*. Retrieved from http://www.omg.org/docs/formal/06-05-01.pdf

OMG. (2008). *Case study from Mayo clinic added to SOA in healthcare qorkshop: Realizing quality of care*. Retrived from http://www.omg.org/news/releases/pr2008/03-31-08.htm

OMG. (2009). *SOA in Healthcare Conference: Value in a time of change*. Retrived from http://www.omg.org/news/meetings/HC-WS/index.htm

Opdahl, A.L. & Sindre, G. (2008). *Experimental comparison of attack trees and misuse cases for security threat identification*.

OpenEHR Foundation. (2010). *OpenEHR*. Retrieved from http://www.openehr.org/ Papazoglou, M.P. & Heuvel, W.-J. (2007). Service oriented architectures: Approaches, technologies and research issues. *The Very Large Data Bases Journal*, *16*(3), 389–415.

Orchard, D., Hondo, M., Yendluri, P. P., Boubez, T., Hirsch, F., Yalçinalp, U., et al. (2007). *Web services policy 1.5 – attachment*. Retrieved from http://www.w3.org/TR/2007/REC-ws-policy-attach-20070904/

Orriëns, B., Yang, J. & Papazoglou, M. (2003). *A framework for business rule driven Web service composition. Conceptual modeling for novel application domains*.

Ortiz, G., Hernández, J., & Clemente, P. J. (2005). How to deal with non-functional properties in Web service development. In Lowe, D., & Gaedke, M. (Eds.), *Web engineering* (pp. 98–103). Springer. doi:10.1007/11531371_15

Ortiz, G. (2007). *Integrating extra-functional properties in Web service model-driven development*. Unpublished doctoral dissertation, University of Extremadura, Spain.

Ortiz, G., & Bordbar, B. (2008) Model-driven quality of service for Web services: An aspect-oriented approach. In *Proceedings of International Conference on Web Services*, (pp 748-751). IEEE Computer Society

Ortiz, G., & Hernández, J. (2006). Toward UML profiles for Web services and their extra-functional properties. *Proceedings of IEEE International Conference on Web Services*, (pp. 889-892).

Ortiz, G., & Leymann, F. (2006). Combining WS-policy and aspect-oriented programming. In P. Dini, P. Lorenz, D. Roman & M. Freire (Eds.), *IEEE Advanced International Conference on Telecommunications and International Conference on Internet and Web Applications and Services (AICT-ICIW '06)*, (pp. 143-148). IEEE Computer Society.

OSGi Alliance. (2003). *OSGi service platform, release 3*. Amsterdam: IOS Press.

Ossher, H., & Tarr, P. (2000). *Multi-dimensional separation of concerns and the hyperspace approach*. (Tech. Rep. No. 21452). Yorktown Heights, NY: IBM, T.J. Watson Research Center.

O'Sullivan, J., Edmond, D., & ter Hofstede, A. (2002). What's in a service? Towards accurate description of non-functional service properties. *Distributed and Parallel Databases*, *12*, 117–133. doi:10.1023/A:1016547000822

Padmanabhuni, S., Majumdar, B., Chawla, M., & Mysore, U. (2006). A constraint satisfaction approach to non-functional requirements to adaptive Web services. In *Proceedings of the International Conference on Next Generation Web Services Practices*, (pp. 109-116).

Palo Alto Research Center. Xerox Corporation. (2008). *Frequently asked questions about AspectJ*. Retrieved July 21, 2008, from: http://www.eclipse.org/aspectj/doc/released/faq.html

Papazoglou, M. P., & van den Heuvel, W. J. (2006). Service-oriented design and development methodology. *International Journal of Web Engineering and Technology*, *2*(4), 412–442. doi:10.1504/IJWET.2006.010423

Papazoglou, M. P., & van den Heuvel, W. J. (2007). Service Oriented Architectures: Approaches, technologies, and research issues. *The VLDB Journal*, *16*(3), 389–415. doi:10.1007/s00778-007-0044-3

Papazoglou, M., & Van Den Heuvel, W. (2006). Service-oriented design and development methodology. *International Journal in Web Engineering and Technology*, *2*(4), 412–442. doi:10.1504/IJWET.2006.010423

Papazoglou, M. (2007). *What's in a service?* (pp. 11–28). ECSA.

Papazoglou, M. (2003). Service-oriented computing: Concepts, characteristics and directions. In T. Catarci, M. Mecella, J. Mylopoulos & M.E. Orlowska (Eds.), *Proceedings of the 4ᵗʰ International Conference on Web Information Systems Engineering.* (pp. 3-12). Washington: IEEE Computer Society Press.

Parekh, S. S., Rose, K. R., Hellerstein, J. L., Lightstone, S., Huras, M., & Chang, V. (2003). Managing the performance impact of administrative utilities. *Proceedings of the 14th International Workshop on Distributed Systems: Operations & Management (DSOM 2003)*, (pp. 130-142). Heidelberg, Germany.

Parnas, D. L. (1972). On the criteria to be used in decomposing systems into modules. *Communications of the ACM, 15*(12), 1053–1058. doi:10.1145/361598.361623

Pastor, O. (2006). From extreme programming to extreme non-programming: Is it the right time for model transformation technologies? In *Proceedings of DEXA'06,* (LNCS 4080), (pp. 64-72). Springer.

Pathak, J., Basu, S., & Honavar, V. (2008). Composing Web services through automatic reformulation of service specifications. In *Proceedings of IEEE International Conference on Services Computing,* (pp. 361-369).

Pathak, J., Johnson, T. M., & Chute, C. G. (2008). Modular ontology techniques and their applications in the biomedical domain. In *Proceedings of IEEE International Conference on Information Reuse and Integration,* (pp. 351-356).

Pavlovsky, C. J., & Zou, J. (2008). Non-functional requirements in business process modeling. In *Proceedings of APCCM'08 - Vol 79,* (pp. 103-112). Australian Computer Society.

Pellegrini, M., & Riveill, M. (2003). Component management in a dynamic architecture. *The Journal of Supercomputing, 24*(2), 151–159. doi:10.1023/A:1021798709301

Perrey, R., & Lycett, M. (2003). Service-Oriented Architecture. In *Proceedings of the Symposium on Applications and the Internet Workshops*, (pp. 116-119).

Petriu, D. B., & Woodside, M. (2005). Software performance models from system scenarios. [Elsevier.]. *Performance Evaluation, 61*(1), 65–89. doi:10.1016/j.peva.2004.09.005

Petriu, D. B., & Woodside, M. (2007). An intermediate metamodel with scenarios and resources for generating performance models from UML designs. [Springer.]. *Software and Systems Modeling, 6*(2), 163–184. doi:10.1007/s10270-006-0026-8

Pinheiro, F. A. C. (2004). Requirements traceability. In Leite, J. C. S. P., & Doorn, J. (Eds.), *Perspectives on software requirements* (pp. 91–113). Norwell, MA: Kluwer Academic Publishers.

Pohl, C., Rummler, A., Gasiunas, V., Loughran, N., Arboleda, H., & Fernandes, F. A. (2007). *Survey of existing implementation techniques with respect to their support for the requirements identified in M3.2. (Tech. Rep. No. AMPLE D3.1).* AMPLE Project.

Pohl, K., Böckle, G., & Van der Linden, F. (2005). *Software product line engineering, foundations, principles, and techniques.* Berlin: Springer-Verlag.

Pohl, K. (1996). PRO-ART: Enabling requirements pre-traceability. In *Proceedings of the Second International Conference on Requirements Engineering ICRE'96,* (pp. 76-84). Washington, DC: IEEE.

Pohl, K. Böckle, G. & Linden, F.v.d. (2005). *Software product line engineering. Foundations, principles and techniques.* Berlin, Heidelberg: Springer.

Pourshahid, A., Chen, P., Amyot, D., Forster, A. J., Ghanavati, S., & Peyton, L. (2009). Business process management with the user requirements notation. [Springer.]. *Electronic Commerce Research, 9*(4), 269–316. doi:10.1007/s10660-009-9039-z

Pourshahid, A., Chen, P., et al. (2007). Business process monitoring and alignment: An approach based on the user requirements notation and business intelligence tools. 10th International Workshop on Requirements Engineering. (pp. 149-159).

Pure Systems. (2008). *Pure variants.* Retrieved from http://www.pure-systems.com/Variant_Management.49.0.html

Raibulet, C. (2008). Facets of adaptivity. In *Proceedings of the 2ⁿᵈ European Conference on Software Architecture*, (LNCS 5292), (pp. 342-345).

Ramanan, D., & Forsyth, D. A. (2003). Automatic annotation of everyday movements. In *Neural Information Processing Systems*. NIPS.

Ramesh, B., & Jarke, M. (2001). Toward reference models for requirements traceability. *IEEE Transactions on Software Engineering, 27*(1), 58–93. doi:10.1109/32.895989

Ran, S. (2003). A model for Web services discovery with QoS. *ACM SIGecom Exchanges, 4*(1), 1–10. doi:10.1145/844357.844360

Rashid, A., Moreira, A., & Araújo, J. (2003). Modularization and composition of aspectual requirements. In W.G. Griswold (Ed.), *Proceedings of the 2ⁿᵈ International Conference on Aspect-Oriented Software Development*. (pp. 11-20). Boston: ACM.

Raverdy, P., Le, H., Gong, V., & Lea, R. (1998). DART: A reflective middleware for adaptive applications. In *Proceedings of OOPSLA'98 Workshop #13: Reflective programming in C++ and Java*.

Regev, G., & Wegmann, A. (2005). Where do goals come from: The underlying principles of goal-oriented requirements engineering. In *Proceedings of the 13th IEEE International Requirements Engineering Conference*, (pp. 353-362).

Reiff-Marganiec, S., Yu, H.Q. & Tilly, M. (2009). *Service selection based on non-functional properties*. Service-Oriented Computing - ICSOC 2007 Workshops: ICSOC 2007.

Rodríguez, A., Fernández-Medina, E., & Piattini, M. (2006). *Towards a UML 2.0 extension for the modeling of security requirements in business processes*. Third International Conference on Trust, Privacy & Security in Digital Business, (pp. 51-61).

Rodríguez, A., Fernández-Medina, E., & Piattini, M. (2007). *M-BPSec: A method for security requirement elicitation from a UML 2.0 business process specification*. International Workshop on Foundations and Practices of UML, (pp. 106-115).

Rosa, L., Lopes, A., & Rodrigues, L. (2008). Modelling adaptive services for distributed systems. *SAC '08: Proceedings of the 2008 ACM symposium on Applied computing*.

Rossebø, J. E., & Bræk, R. (2006). Towards a framework of authentication and authorization patterns for ensuring availability in service composition. *Proceedings of The First International Conference on Availability, Reliability and Security*, (pp. 206-215).

Roy, J., Kealey, J., & Amyot, D. (2006). Towards integrated tool support for the user requirements notation. In R. Gotzhein & R. Reed (Eds.), *System analysis and modeling: Language profiles*. (pp. 198-215). Fifth International Workshop, SAM 2006. Berlin: Springer.

Roy, J.-F., Kealey, J., & Amyot, D. (2006). Towards integrated tool support for the user requirements notation. *Proceedings of SAM 2006: Language Profiles - Fifth Workshop on System Analysis and Modelling*, Kaiserslautern, Germany. (LNCS 4320), (pp. 183-197). Springer.

Ruhe, G., & Eberlein, A. (2003). Trade-off analysis for requirements selection. *International Journal of Software Engineering and Knowledge Engineering, 13*(4), 345–366. doi:10.1142/S0218194003001378

Ruiz, J., Duenas, J. & Usero, F. (2004). *Deployment in dynamic environments*. DECOR04.

Rutherford, M., Anderson, K., Carzaniga, A., Heimbigner, D., & Wolf, A. (2002). Reconfiguration in the enterprise JavaBean component model. *CD '02: Proceedings of the IFIP/ACM Working Conference on Component Deployment*, (pp. 67-81).

Saaty, T. L. (1990). How to make a decision: The analytic hierarchy process. *European Journal of Operational Research, 48*(1), 9–26. doi:10.1016/0377-2217(90)90057-I

Sabou, M., Wroe, C., Goble, A., & Mishne, G. (2005). Learning domain ontologies for Web service descriptions: An experiment in bioinformatics. In *Proceedings of International Conference on World Wide Web*, (pp. 190-198).

Sahai, A., Machiraju, V., Sayal, M., Moorsel, A. P., & Casati, F. (2002). Automated SLA monitoring for Web services. In M. Feridun, P.G. Kropf & G. Babin (Eds.), *Proceedings of the 13th IFIP/IEEE International Workshop on Distributed Systems: Operations and Management: Management Technologies For E-Commerce and E-Business Applications* (October 21 - 23, 2002). (LNCS 2506), (pp. 28-41). London: Springer-Verlag.

Satoh, F., & Yamaguchi, Y. (2007). Generic security policy transformation framework for WS-security. *Proceedings of IEEE International Conference on Web Services*, (pp. 513-520).

Satoh, F., Mukhi, N. K., Nakamura, Y., & Hirose, S. (2008). Pattern-based policy configuration for SOA applications. *Proceedings of IEEE International Conference on Services Computing*, (pp. 13-20).

Satoh, F., Nakamura, Y., & Ono, K. (2006). Adding authentication to model driven security. *Proceedings of IEEE International Conference on Web Services*, (pp. 585-594).

Satoh, I. (2005). Dynamic deployment of pervasive services. *Proceedings of IEEE International Conference on Pervasive Services (ICPS'2005)*.

Schek, H., & Pistor, P. (1982). Data structures for an integrated database management and information retrieval system. In *Proceedings of VLDB, 82*, 197–207.

Schilit, B., Adams, N., & Want, R. (1994). Context-aware computing applications. In *Proceedings of the IEEE Workshop on Mobile Computing Systems and Applications*, (pp. 85 – 90).

Schmid, C. (2001). Constructing models for content-based image retrieval. In *Proceedings of IEEE Conference on Computer Vision and Pattern Recognition*, (pp. 39-45).

Schröpfer, C., Schönherr, M., Offermann, P., & Ahrens, M. (2007). A flexible approach to service management-related service description in SOAs. In *Emerging Web Services Technology, Part II.* (pp. 47-64). Basel: Birkhäuser.

Schuldt, C., Laptev, I., & Caputo, B. (2004). Recognizing human actions: A local SVM approach. In *Proceedings of International Conference on Pattern Recognition*, (pp. 23-26).

Scicluna, J. (2004). *OWL-S Editor: To semantically annotate Web-services.* Retrieved from http://staff.um.edu.mt/cabe2/supervising/undergraduate/owlseditFYP/OwlSEdit.html

Searls, R. (2003). *JavaTM 2 enterprise edition deployment API specification, version 1.1.* Récupéré sur http://jcp.org/jsr/detail/88.jsp

Sedukhin, I. (2004). *Web services distributed management: Management of Web services distributed management.* OASIS Commitee Draft.

SEI. (2007). *A safety extension to CMMI-DEV V1.2.* Software Engineering Institute, Carnegie Mellon University.

Sha, L., Liu, Y., & Abdealzaher, T. (2002). Queueing model based network server performance control. *Proceedings of IEEE Real Time Systems Symposium.*

Shah, N., Iqbal, R., James, A., & Iqbal, K. (2008). An agent based approach to address QoS issues in Service Oriented Applications. In *Proceedings of 12th International Conference on Computer Supported Cooperative Work in Design,* (pp 317-322).

Shechtman, E., & Irani, M. (2007). Space-time behavior-based correlation-or-how to tell if two underlying motion fields are similar without computing them? *IEEE Transactions on Pattern Analysis and Machine Intelligence, 29*(1), 2045–2056. doi:10.1109/TPAMI.2007.1119

Sheikh, Y., Sheikh, M., & Shah, M. (2005). Exploring the space of a human action. In *Proceedings of IEEE International Conference on Computer Vision*, (pp. 144-149).

Shekhovtsov, V. A., Kop, C., & Mayr, H. C. (2008). Capturing the semantics of quality requirements into an intermediate predesign model. In *Proceedings of SIGSAND-EUROPE'2008 Symposium*, (pp. 25-37). GI.

Shneiderman, B. (1992). *Designing the user interface: Strategies for effective human-computer interaction* (2nd ed.). Boston: Addison-Wesley.

Siedersleben, J. (2004). *Moderne Software Architektur: Umsichtig planen, robust bauen mit Quasar.* Heidelberg, Germany: dpunkt.verlag.

Simons, C., & Wirtz, G. (2007). Modelling context in mobile distributed systems with the UML. *Journal of Visual Languages and Computing, 18*, 420–439. doi:10.1016/j.jvlc.2007.07.001

Sindre, G., & Opdahl, A. L. (2005). Eliciting security requirements with misuse cases. *Requirements Engineering, 10*(1), 34–44. doi:10.1007/s00766-004-0194-4

Singhera, Z. U. (2004). Extended Web services framework to meet non-functional requirements. In *Proceedings of the International Symposium on Applications and the Internet Workshops*, (pp. 334-340).

Sommerville, I. (2004). *Software engineering*. USA: Pearson Addison-Wesley.

Song, X. (2007). Developing non-functional requirements for a service-oriented software platform. In [IEEE CS Press.]. *Proceedings of COMPSAC, 07*, 495–496.

Song, X., Hwong, B., et al. (2009). *Experiences in developing NFRs for the service-oriented software platform*. Technical Report.

Sousa, G. I., & Castro, J. (2003). Adapting the NFR framework to aspect-oriented requirement engineering. In *Proceedings of the XVII Brazilian Symposium on Software Engineering*.

Speck, A. (2003). Reusable industrial control systems. *IEEE Transactions on Industrial Electronics, 50*(3). doi:10.1109/TIE.2003.812274

Sperling, W. & Lutz, P. (1997). Enabling open control systems: An introduction to the OSACA system platform. *Robotics and Manufacturing, 6*.

Standards Coordinating Comittee of the Computer Society of the IEEE. (1990). *IEEE standard glossary of software engineering terminology*. IEEE Std 610.12-1990.

Stantchev, V. (2008a). *Architectural translucency*. Berlin: GITO Verlag.

Stantchev, V. (2008b). *Effects of replication on Web service performance in WebSphere. (ICSI tech report 2008-03)*. Berkeley, California: International Computer Science Institute.

Stantchev, V., & Malek, M. (2009). Translucent replication for service level assurance. In *High Assurance Services Computing* (pp. 1–18). Berlin, New York: Springer. doi:10.1007/978-0-387-87658-0_1

Stantchev, V., & Schröpfer, C. (2009). Service level enforcement in Web-services based systems. *International Journal on Web and Grid Services, 5*(2), 130–154. doi:10.1504/IJWGS.2009.027571

Stantchev, V. & Malek, M. (2010). Addressing dependability throughout the SOA life cycle. *IEEE Transactions on Services Computing, 99*.

Stantchev, V., & Schröpfer, C. (2009). Negotiating and enforcing QoS and SLAs in grid and cloud computing. In *GPC '09: Proceedings of the 4th International Conference on Advances in Grid and Pervasive Computing*, (pp. 25-35). Berlin, Heidelberg: Springer-Verlag.

Storm, A. J., Garcia-Arellano, C., Lightstone, S., Diao, Y., & Surendra, M. (2006). Adaptive self-tuning memory in DB2. *Proceedings of the 32nd International Conference on Very Large Data Bases*. Seoul, Korea.

Strang, T., & Linnhoff-Popien, C. (2004). A context modelling survey. In *Proceedings of UbiComp, 1st International Workshop on Advanced Context Modelling, Reasoning and Management*, (pp. 34–41).

Sturm, R., Morris, W., & Jander, M. (2000). *Foundations of service level management*. Indianapolis: Sams.

Sun Microsystems. (2002). *Enterprise JavaBeansTM specification, version 2.1*. Récupéré sur http://java.sun.com/products/ejb/

Sun Microsystems. (2002). *Java management extensions (JMX) specification version 1.2*. Récupéré sur http://-java.sun.com/products/ejb/

Sun Microsystems. (2008). *Java EE 5 tutorial*. Retrieved from http://java.sun.com/javaee/5/docs/tutorial/doc/ Tercom, L. (2008). *WCF chunking*. Retrieved from http://wcf- chunking.sourceforge.net

SWI-Prolog. (1987). *Homepage information*. Retrieved September 1, 2008, from http://www.swi-prolog.org/

Tarr, P., Ossher, H., Harrison, W., & Sutton, S. M. (1999). N degrees of separation: Multi-dimensional separation of concerns. In B. Boehm (Ed.), *Proceedings of the 21st International Conference on Software Engineering.* (pp. 107-119). Los Alamitos: IEEE Computer Society Press.

Taylor, R. N., Medvidović, N., & Dashofy, E. M. (2009). *Software architecture: Foundations, theory, and practice.* John Wiley & Sons, Inc.

The Eclipse Foundation. (2007). *AspectJ, crosscuting objects for better modularity.* Retrieved July 23, 2008, from: http://www.eclipse.org/aspectj/

Tolhurst, D. J., Tadmor, Y., & Chao, T. (1992). Amplitude spectra of natural images. *Ophthalmic & Physiological Optics, 12*(2), 229–232. doi:10.1111/j.1475-1313.1992.tb00296.x

Toma, I., Foxvog, D., & Jaeger, M. C. (2006). Modeling QoS characteristics in WSMO. In *Proceedings of MW4SOC'06* (pp. 42–47). ACM Press. doi:10.1145/1169091.1169098

Tondello, G. F., & Siqueira, F. (2008). The QoS-MO ontology for semantic QoS modeling. In *Proceedings of 2008 ACM Symposium on Applied Computing,* (pp. 2336-2340). ACM Press.

Trinidad, P., Benavides, B., Ruiz-Cortés, A., Segura, S., & Jimenez, A. (2008). *FAMA framework.* Software Product Line Conference, 2008. SPLC '08. 12th International. (pp. 359-359).

Trujillo, S., Kästner, C., & Apel, S. (2008). Product lines that supply other product lines: A service-oriented approach. In S. Cohen & R. Krut (Eds.), *Proceedings of the First Workshop on Service-Oriented Architectures and Software Product Lines.*

Tsai, W. T., Fan, C., & Chen, Y. (2006). DDSOS: A Dynamic Distributed Service-Oriented Simulation framework. In *Proceedings of the 39th Annual Simulation Symposium,* (pp. 1-8).

Tsai, W. T., Xiao, B., Chen, Y., & Paul, R. A. (2006). Consumer-centric Service-Oriented Architecture: A new approach. In *Proceedings of the Fourth IEEE Workshop on Software Technologies For Future Embedded and Ubiquitous Systems, and the Second international Workshop on Collaborative Computing, integration, and Assurance,* (pp. 175-180).

Tseng, V. S., Su, J.-H., Huang, J.-H., & Chen, C.-J. (2008). Integrated mining of visual features, speech features, and frequent patterns for semantic video annotation. *IEEE Transactions on Multimedia, 10*(2), 260–267. doi:10.1109/TMM.2007.911832

Tzouvaras, V., Troncy, R., & Pan, J. (2007). *Multimedia annotation interoperability framework.* Retrieved from http://www.w3.org/2005/Incubator/mmsem/XGR-interoperability/

U.S. Department of Health and Human Services. (2010). *Health Insurance Portability And Accountability Act.* Retrieved from http://www.hhs.gov/ocr/privacy

U.S. Food and Drug Administration. (2010). *FDA Website.* Retrieved from http://www.fda.gov

UPMS. (2007, June 4). *UML profile and metamodel for services for heterogeneous architectures.* Récupéré sur http://www.omg.org/cgibin/ doc?ad/07-06-02.pdf

URN Virtual Library. (2008). *Case maps.* Retrieved October 2008, from http://www.usecasemaps.org/pub/

Vambenepe, W. (2004). *Web services distributed management:management using web services (muws 1.0) part 1.* Récupéré sur http://docs.oasisopen.org/wsdm/2004/12/wsdm-muws-part1-1.0.pdf

Van Bon, J. (2008). *Foundations of IT service management based on ITIL V3.* Van Haren.

Vanderfeesten, I., Cardoso, J., Mendling, J., Reijers, H. A., & van der Aalst, W. (2007). Quality metrics for business process models. In *2007 BPM and Workflow Handbook,* (pp. 179-190). Future Strategies Inc.

VDI. (2007). *VDI 5600: Fertigungsmanagementsysteme. Manufacturing Execution Systems (MES).* Berlin: Beuth.

Voelter, M., & Groher, I. (2007). Product line implementation using aspect-oriented and model-driven software development. In K. Chul Kang (Ed.), *Proceedings of the 11th International Software Product Line Conference (SPLC 2007).* (pp. 233-242).

W3C. (2004). *Web service management: Service life cycle.* Récupéré sur http://www.w3.org/TR/2004/NOTE-wslc-20040211/

W3C. (2004). *Web Service Architecture.* Récupéré sur http://www.w3.org/TR/ws-arch.

W3C. (2005). *Web service addressing 1.0 - core(WS-Addressing)*. Récupéré sur http://www.w3.org/TR/2005/WD-ws-addr-core-20050215

W3C. (2008). *Homepage information*. Retrieved October 2008, from http://www.w3.org/

Wada, H., Suzuki, J., & Oba, K. (in press). A model-driven development framework for non-functional aspects in service oriented architecture. *Journal of Web Services Research*.

Wada, H., Champrasert, P., Suzuki, J., & Oba, K. (2008a). Multiobjective optimization of SLA-aware service composition. *Proceedings of the International Workshop on Methodologies for Non-functional Properties in Services Computing (MNPSC)*, Honolulu, USA. IEEE CS, (pp. 315-321).

Wada, H., Suzuki, J., & Oba, K. (2008b). *Early aspects for non-functional properties in service oriented business processes*. 2008 IEEE Congress on Services - Part I, Honolulu, USA. IEEE CS, (pp. 231-238).

Wada, H., Suzuki, J., & Oba, K. (2006). Modeling non-functional aspects in Service Oriented Architecture. In *Proceeding of the IEEE International Conference on Service Computing*, (pp. 222-229).

Wada, H., Suzuki, J., & Oba, K. (2007). A feature modeling support for non-functional constraints in Service Oriented Architecture. In *Proceeding of the IEEE International Conference on Service Computing*, (pp. 187-195).

Wada, H., Suzuki, J., & Oba, K. (2006). Modeling non-functional aspects in Service Oriented Architecture. In *Proceedings of SCC'06*, (pp. 222-229). IEEE CS Press.

Wada, H., Suzuki, J., & Oba, K. (2007). A feature modeling support for non-functional constraints in Service Oriented Architecture. In *Proceedings of SCC'07*, (pp. 187-195). IEEE CS Press.

Wada, H., Suzuki, J., & Oba, K. (2008). Early aspects for non-functional properties in service oriented business processes. In *Proceedings of 2008 IEEE Congress on Services - Part I*, (pp. 231-238). IEEE CS Press.

Wada, H., Suzuki, J., & Oba, K. (2008). *Early aspects for non-functional properties in service oriented business processes*. Paper presented at the IEEE Congress on Services, SOA Standards Symposium, Hawaii, USA.

Wang, Y., Wong, D. S., & Wang, H. (2008). Employ a mobile agent for making a payment. *Mobile Information Systems, 4*(1), 51–68.

Wang, X., Vitvar, T., Kerrigan, M., & Toma, I. (2006). A QoS-aware selection model for Semantic Web services. In *Proceedings of ICSOC'06*, (LNCS 4294), (pp. 390-401). Springer.

Web Services Policy Framework. (2006). *Policy outline*. Retrieved from http://www.w3.org/Submission/WS-Policy/

Web Services Security. (2006). *SOAP message security 1.1 (WS-security 2004)*. Retrieved September 1, 2008, from http://www.oasis-open.org/committees/download.php/16790/wss-v1.1-spec-os-SOAPMessageSecurity.pdf.

Weerawarana, S., Curbera, F., Leymann, F., Storey, T., & Ferguson, D. F. (2005). *Web services platform architecture: SOAP, WSDL, WS-policy, WS-addressing, WS-BPEL, WS-reliable messaging, and more*. Prentice Hall.

Weiss, M., Esfandiari, B., & Luo, Y. (2007). Towards a classification of Web service feature interactions. *Computer Networks, 51*(2), 359–381. doi:10.1016/j.comnet.2006.08.003

Weiss, M., & Esfandiari, B. (2004). On feature interactions among Web services. In *Proceedings of the IEEE International Conference on Web Services*, (pp. 88-95).

Weiss, M., Esfandiari, B., & Luo, Y. (2005). Towards a classification of Web service feature interactions. *Proceedings of the International Conference on Service-Oriented Computing (ICSOC)*, Amsterdam, Netherlands. (LNCS 3826), (pp. 101-114). Springer.

Whittle, J., Araújo, J., & Moreira, A. (2006). Composing aspect models with graphs and transformations. In P.C. Clements (Ed), *Proceeding of the 2006 International Workshop on Early Aspects at ICSE International Conference on Software Engineering*. (pp. 59-65). New York: ACM.

Winkler, S., & von Pilgrim, J. (2010). A survey of traceability in requirements engineering and model-driven development. In *Software and Systems Modeling, 9*(4), 529-565.

Wohlfarth, S. (2008). *Entwicklung eines rationalen Entscheidungsprozesses für Architekturentscheidungen.* Unpublished doctoral dissertation, Ilmenau University of Technology, Germany.

Wolfram MathWorld. (2008). *Bijective.* Retrieved from http://mathworld.wolfram.com/Bijective.html

Workshop, A.-O. M. (2007). *Aspect oriented modeling.* Retrieved July 20, 2008, from http://www.aspect-modeling.org/

Wu, Z., & Weaver, A. C. (2007). Requirements of federated trust management for Service-Oriented Architectures. In. *Journal of Information Security, 6*(5), 287–296. doi:10.1007/s10207-007-0027-9

Xiping, S. (2007). Developing non-functional requirements for a service-oriented software platform. In *Proceedings of the 31st Annual International Computer Software and Applications Conference,* (pp. 495-496).

Yan, R., Natsev, A., & Campbell, M. (2005). An efficient manual image annotation approach based on tagging and browsing. In *Proceedings of International Multimedia Conference,* (pp. 13-20).

Yang, K., Ou, S., Azmoodeh, M., & Georgalas, N. (2005). Policy-based model-driven engineering of pervasive services and the associated OSS. *British Telecom Technical Journal, 23*(3), 162–174.

Yang, C.-L., Chang, Y.-K., & Chu, C.-P. (2008). Modeling services to construct service-oriented healthcare architecture for digital home-care business. In *Proceedings of International Conference on Software Engineering & Knowledge Engineering,* (pp. 351-356).

Yilmaz, A., & Shah, M. (2005). Recognizing human actions in videos acquired by uncalibrated moving cameras. In *Proceedings of the IEEE International Conference on Computer Vision,* (pp. 150-157).

Yu, T., Zhang, Y., & Lin, K.-J. (2007). Efficient algorithms for Web services selection with end-to-end QoS constraints. *ACM Transaction on the Web, 1*(1), 6. doi:10.1145/1232722.1232728

Yu, E. & Mylopoulos, J. (1996). Using goals, rules, and methods to support reasoning in business process reengineering. *Intelligent Systems in Accounting, Finance and Management, 5*(1-13), 1-13.

Yu, E. (1994). *Modeling strategic relationships for process re-engineering.* Unpublished doctoral thesis, Department of Computer Science, University of Toronto.

Yu, E. (1995). *Modelling strategic relationships for process reengineering.* Unpublished doctoral dissertation, Dept. of Computer Science, University of Toronto, Ontario, Canada.

Yu, E. (2001). Agent-oriented modelling: Software versus the world. *Agent-Oriented Software Engineering AOSE-2001 Workshop Proceedings.*

Yu, E. S. (1996). *Modelling strategic relationships for process reengineering.* PhD thesis, Toronto, Ont., Canada.

Zdun, U., Hentrich, C., & Van Der Aalst, W. M. P. (2006). A survey of patterns for Service-Oriented Architectures. In. *International Journal of Internet Protocol Technology, 1*(3), 132–143.

Zeng, L., Benatallah, B., Ngu, A. H. H., Dumas, M., Kalagnanam, J., & Chang, H. (2004). QoS-aware middleware for Web services composition. *IEEE Transactions on Software Engineering, 30*(5), 311–327. doi:10.1109/TSE.2004.11

Zeng, L., Benatallah, B., Ngu, A. H. H., Dumas, M., Kalagnanam, J., & Chang, H. (2004). QoS-aware middleware for Web services composition. *IEEE Transactions on Software Engineering, 30*(5), 311–327. doi:10.1109/TSE.2004.11

Zeng, L., Benatallah, B., Ngu, A. H. H., Dumas, M., Kalagnanam, J., & Chang, H. (2004). QoS-aware middleware for Web services composition. *IEEE Transactions on Software Engineering, 30*(5), 311–327. doi:10.1109/TSE.2004.11

Zeng, D., & Zhao, J. (2002). Achieving software flexibility via intelligent workflow techniques. In *Proceedings of the 35th Annual Hawaii International Conference on System Sciences, HICSS,* (pp. 606-615). Washington, DC: IEEE.

Zhang, C., & Hans-Arno, J. (2003). Quantifying aspects in middleware platforms. In M. Akşit (Ed.), *Proceedings of the 2nd International Conference on Aspect-Oriented Software Development,* (pp. 130-139). ACM.

Zhou, J., Niemelä, E., & Savolainen, P. (2007). An integrated QoS-aware service development and management framework. In *Proceedings of WICSA '07.* IEEE CS Press.

Zhu, L., Aurum, A., Gorton, I., & Jeffery, R. (2005). Tradeoff and sensitivity analysis in software architecture evaluation using analytic hierarchy process. *Software Quality Journal, 13*(4), 357–375. doi:10.1007/s11219-005-4251-0

Zscahler, S. (2004). Towards a semantic framework for non-functional specifications of component-based systems. In *Proceedings of the EUROMICRO Conference*, (pp. 92-99).

About the Contributors

Nikola Milanovic is co-founder and CEO of Model Labs. The Berlin-based company offers innovative model-based software product family for system integration and service availability assessment. Previously he was senior researcher at Berlin University of Technology (TU Berlin) and Hasso-Plattner Institute (HPI) in Potsdam. Milanovic received his PhD in computer science from the Humboldt University in Berlin.

* * *

Germán Harvey Alférez Salinas is a lecturer of undergraduate and graduate courses and director of the Center for Research and Technology Development at the Faculty of Engineering and Technology, Montemorelos University, Mexico. He is also an adjunct research associate at Asia-Pacific International University, Thailand. He finished a MSc in Information and Communication Technology at Assumption University, Thailand (President's Award for Academic Excellence) and a BSc in Computer Science Engineering at EAFIT University, Colombia. He has worked in industrial as well as on academic environments such as: the Software Engineering Research Group at EAFIT University; the Information Technology Department at Orbitel, Colombia, and at the Master of education, Avondale College, Australia. He has a deep research interest on the following areas: software product lines, model-driven software development, aspect-oriented software development, and software orchitectures. Additional information may be found on his personal Website: http://fit.um.edu.mx/harvey/

Edward Mauricio Alférez Salinas is a PhD candidate in Computer Science/Informatics at Faculdade de Ciências e Tecnologia, Universidade Nova de Lisboa, Portugal. His main research topics are requirements engineering, model-driven development, variability management and aspect-oriented software engineering. He worked in research as well as in the industry: EAFIT University, Colombia; West Indies Union, Jamaica; and Termopaipa Power Plant - STEAG A.G, Colombia. Since 2007 he has been working for the European Union's project for the improvement of development techniques for Software Product Lines – AMPLE. He is member of the Research Center for Informatics and Information Technologies (CITI) and the Software Engineering group at Universidade Nova de Lisboa since 2007. He publishes and participates as a reviewer of international events. More information can be found at http://citi.di.fct. unl.pt/member/member.php?id=80.

Achilleas Achilleos obtained recently his PhD from the School of Computer Science and Electronic Engineering at the University of Essex, having being awarded a studentship, co-funded by the UK Engineering and Physical Sciences Research Council (EPSRC) and British Telecom (BT). During that time he was also working as part-time researcher at BT. He received his M.Sc. with distinction from the same department and a B.Sc. with excellence from the Budapest University of Technology and Economics in Hungary. He is currently working as a post-doc researcher at the Department of Computer Science at the University of Cyprus. His research interests include model-driven development, pervasive service creation, mobile and service-oriented computing. He has published his research work in internationally refereed journals and conferences and as book chapters. He served also as a TPC member and referee in various conferences related to his research area. He is a member of the IEEE Computer Society and Cyprus Scientific and Technical Chamber (ETEK).

Daniel Amyot is Associate Professor at the University of Ottawa, which he joined in 2002 after working for Mitel Networks as a senior researcher in the Strategic Technology group. His research interests include requirements modeling and analysis with goals, scenarios, and aspects, business process modeling, software engineering, healthcare informatics, and feature interactions in emerging application domains. Daniel is Associate Rapporteur for formal languages at the International Telecommunication Union, where he leads the evolution of the User Requirements Notation (URN). He also leads the development of an open-source Eclipse plug-in (jUCMNav) for the creation, analysis, and transformation of URN models. Daniel has a PhD and a MSc from the University of Ottawa (2001 and 1994), as well as a B.Sc. from Laval University (1992), all in computer science. He is also a Professional Engineer in the province of Québec.

Francesca Arcelli Fontana has received her Master and PhD degrees in Computer Science at the University of Milano, Italy. She is currently in the position of Associate Professor at University of Milano-Bicocca. Her actual research activity principally concerns the software engineering field. In particular, her attention is focused on software evolution and reverse engineering, design patterns detection for reverse engineering, program comprehension, and system migration towards SOA architectures.

Jie Bao received his PhD in computer science from the Iowa State University in 2007. At ISU, his research interests included semantic data integration, modeling modular ontologies, collaborative ontology building and Web privacy protection. From 2008 to present, Dr. Bao has been a postdoctoral research associate at the Tetherless World Constellation, Rensselaer Polytechnic Institute, where he worked on a variety of topics in social Semantic Web, semantic wikis, ontology integrity constraint languages, policy formulation and scalable reasoning with Web ontologies. Currently he is visiting MIT as a Research Affiliate. He is a member of the OWL Working Group at W3C.

Hanane Becha received a MSc degree in the area of distributed computing from the University of Ottawa in 2004. While working as a key member of the Nortel Strategic Standards development team, leading the creation of Nortel-wide standards strategy for SOA and Web Services and contributing to the development of SOA-related international standards, she focused on identifying and filling gaps in standards for using SOA principles in telecommunications and mission critical applications. Hanane led the Object Management Group (OMG) Telecom Special Interest Group initiative and she is the editor of multiple documents at the International Telecommunications Union, Standardization Sector

(ITU-T). For her PhD studies at the University of Ottawa, Hanane is developing a framework to better handle non-functional properties (NFP) of services from the perspective of service consumers to enable advanced applications such as NFP-aware service selection. Hanane also taught several courses at the University of Ottawa.

Stephan Bode studied at Ilmenau University of Technology, Germany from 2002 to 2008 and received a diploma degree in computer science. Since 2008 he has been working on his PhD in computer science at the Department of Software Systems/Process Informatics at Ilmenau University of Technology under supervision of Matthias Riebisch. He got a doctoral scholarship from the federal state of Thuringia, Germany and is now working as a research associate. His research interests are on software architectural design methods, software evolution, software quality, and traceability. He already has several publications and is reviewing submissions to national and international workshops and conferences.

Barrett R. Bryant is Professor and Associate Chair of Computer and Information Sciences at the University of Alabama at Birmingham. His research interests include theory and implementation of programming languages, formal specification of software systems, and component-based software engineering, and he has authored or co-authored over 130 published papers in these areas. He received his MS and PhD from Northwestern University and his B. S. from the University of Arkansas at Little Rock, all in computer science. He is a member of EAPLS, and a senior member of ACM and IEEE. Further details are available at http://www.cis.uab.edu/bryant.

Daniele Cammareri is a former student of the Università degli Studi di Milano-Bicocca in Italy, where he received his Master degree in Computer Science in December 2009. His main academic interests concern software engineering, and in particular, object-oriented development, agile methodologies and project management. He is the co-author of three previously published papers related to the adaptivity aspects in software systems.

Yu Cao has been an Assistant Professor at the Department of Computer Science, California State University, Fresno (Fresno State) since August 2007. Prior to that, he was a Visiting Fellow of Biomedical Engineering at Mayo Clinic, Rochester, Minnesota. He received his MS and PhD degrees in Computer Science from Iowa State University in 2005 and 2007, respectively. He received the B.Eng. degree from Harbin Engineering University in 1997, the M.Eng. degree from Huazhong University of Science and Technology in 2000, all in Computer Science. His research interests span a variety of aspects of intelligent system and biomedical informatics, which include the areas of imaging and structural informatics, medical information retrieval, consumer health informatics and telemedicine. His research work has appeared in various prestigious journals, book chapters, and refereed conference proceedings. His research is being supported by both NSF and NIH.

Yixin Diao received his PhD degree in Electrical Engineering from Ohio State University in 2000. Since 2001, Dr. Diao has been a Research Staff Member at the IBM Thomas J Watson Research Center in Hawthorne, New York. His research interests include performance and systems management, service automation and complexity benchmark, and adaptive control and optimization of distributed systems. Yixin received the 2002-2005 IFAC Theory Paper Prize from the International Federation of Automatic Control for "Immunity-based hybrid learning methods for approximator structure and parameter adjustment" published in Engineering Applications of Artificial Intelligence. Dr. Diao is also a co-recipient of the 2002 Best Paper Award at IEEE/IFIP Network Operations and Management Symposium for "Using MIMO feedback control to enforce policies for interrelated metrics with application to the Apache web server." He has published more than 40 papers and is the co-author of the book "Feedback Control of Computing Systems" (Wiley 2004).

Khalil Drira received the Engineering and MS (DEA) degrees in Computer Science from ENSEEIHT (INP Toulouse), in June and September 1988 respectively. He obtained the PhD and HDR degrees in Computer Science from UPS, University Paul Sabatier Toulouse, in October 1992, and January 2005 respectively. He is since 1992, Chargé de Recherche, a full-time research position at the French National Center for Scientific Research (CNRS). Khalil Drira's research interests include formal design, implementation, testing and provisioning of distributed communicating systems and cooperative networked services. His research activity addressed and addresses different topics in this field focusing on model-based analysis and design of correctness properties including testability, robustness, adaptability, and reconfiguration. He is or has been involved in several national and international projects in the field of distributed and concurrent communicating systems. He is author of more than 150 regular and invited papers in international conferences and journals. He is or has been initiator of different national and international projects and collaborations in the field of networked services and distributed and communicating systems. Khalil Drira is or has been member of the programme committees of international and national conferences. He is member of the editorial board of different international journals in the field of software architecture and communicating and distributed systems. Khalil Drira has been editor of a number of proceedings, books and journal issues in these fields.

Eduardo Fernández-Medina has a PhD and MSc in Computer Science. He is Associate Professor at the Escuela Superior de Informática of the Universidad de Castilla- La Mancha at Ciudad Real (Spain). His research activities are security requirements, security in databases, data warehouses, Web services and Information Systems, and also in security metrics. He is the co-editor of several books and chapter books on these subjects, and has several dozens of papers in national and international conferences. He participates at the ALARCOS research group of the Department of Information Technologies and Systems at the University of Castilla- La Mancha, in Ciudad Real (Spain). He belongs to various professional and research associations (ATI, AEC, AENOR, IFIP, WG11.3, etc).

Nektarios Georgalas holds a Diploma in Electrical and Computer Engineering from the University of Patras, Greece, an MPhil in Computation from University of Manchester (UMIST) and a PhD in Computer Science from the University of London. He joined British Telecom (BT) in 1998 and is now a principal researcher in the company's Centre for Information and Security Systems Research. During his career with BT, he has participated and managed research projects in areas including active networks, market-driven data management systems, policy-based management, distributed Information Systems, Service-Oriented Srchitectures and Web services. His research is currently focused on product lifecycle management, particularly migration planning and concept-to-market, and rapid service assembly. Nektarios has led numerous international collaborations on the application of model-driven architecture and New Generation Operations Systems and Software (NGOSS) standards in telecoms operational support systems and has both led and contributed to the work of the TeleManagement Forum. He holds five patents, has authored more than 30 papers and has frequently been invited to speak at international conferences.

Jeff Gray is an Associate Professor in the Department of Computer Science at the University of Alabama. His research interests include model-driven engineering, aspect orientation, code clones, and generative programming. Jeff received a PhD in Computer Science from Vanderbilt University and both the BS and MS in Computer Science from West Virginia University. He is a member of the ACM and a Senior Member of the IEEE. Further details are available at http://www.cs.ua.edu/~gray.

Daniel Gross is completing his doctorate at Faculty of Information at the University of Toronto. His research focuses on applying goal and agent oriented modeling and analysis techniques to support architectural software design in organizational settings. Daniel holds a Dipl. Ing. Degree in informatics from the Technical University of Vienna, and a Bachelor degree in Computer Science and Industrial Control Systems from the Jerusalem College of Technology. Daniel has worked in various capacities related to workflow management at the IBM Vienna Software Development Laboratory in Austria, and on object-oriented meta and insurance business modeling at the IBM World Wide Insurance Solution and Delivery Center in La Hulpe, Belgium. Daniel has also worked as a freelance system analyst, and holds a UK and US patent on a method for Recipient controlled communication systems.

John Harris was born in Greece and came to the United States to pursue a higher education. He is now a U.S. citizen. He has gotten a B.S. degree in Computer Science from CSU Bakersfield in 2005 and an M.S. degree in Computer Science from CSU Fresno in 2009. His research has mainly focused on the merging of a proprietary XML schema with that of the MPEG-7 schema.

Joseph Hellerstein received the PhD from the University of California at Los Angeles (USA) in 1984. From 1984-2006, he was a researcher and senior manager at the IBM Thomas J. Watson Research Center in Hawthorne, NY (USA) where he founded the Adaptive Systems Department that contributed management and control technologies to IBM products. From 2006-2008, he was a Principal Architect at Microsoft Corp. in Redmond, WA (USA) where he contributed to Visual Studio and .NET. From 2008- present, he has been a software engineer and engineering manager at Google in Fremont, WA where he manages the Performance Analytics Department that provides performance modeling tools for the Google computing infrastructure. Dr. Hellerstein has published over 100 papers, is a Fellow of the IEEE, and received the IEEE/IFIP Stokesberry Award for outstanding contributions to the network management community.

Juan Hernández is a Full Professor of Languages and Systems and the Head of the Quercus Software Engineering Group of the Extremadura University (Spain). He received the BSc in Mathematics from the University of Extremadura and the PhD degree in computer science from the Technical University of Madrid. His research interests include component-based software development, aspect orientation and distributed systems. He is involved in several research projects as responsible and senior researcher related to these subjects. He has participated in many workshops and conferences as speaker and member of the program committee. He is currently member of the Spanish steering committee on Software Engineering, and organized several workshops and international conferences. He is a member of both the ACM and the IEEE Computer Society.

Mohamed Jmaiel obtained his diploma of engineer in Computer Science from Kiel (Germany) University in 1992 and his PhD from the Technical University of Berlin in 1996. He joined the National School of Engineers of Sfax (Tunisia) as Assistant Professor of Computer Science in 1995. He became an Associate Professor in 1997 and full Professor in January 2009. He participated in the initiation of many graduate courses at the University of Sfax. His current research areas include software engineering of distributed systems, formal methods in model-driven architecture, component oriented development, self-adaptive and pervasive systems, autonomic middleware. He published more than 100 regular and invited papers in international conferences and journals, and has co-edited four conferences proceedings and three journals special issues on these subjects. More details are available on his home page: http://www.redcad.org/members/jmaiel/

Roland Kaschek studied mathematics at the University of Oldenburg (Germany). His interest was in algebraic subjects such as semigroups and categories. In 1990 he received a PhD with a thesis in algebraic graph theory. As a fresh PhD holder he joined Heinrich Mayr's Information Systems research group at the University of Klagenfurt (Austria) where he worked on object oriented analysis methods, business process modelling, and database design. From 1999 to 2001 he was employed by UBS AG in Zurich (Switzerland). There he was involved in software architecture and data warehouse projects. From 2002 to 2008 he was an Associate Professor with Massey University in Palmerston North (New Zealand) working on various aspects of Information Systems design and its mathematical foundations. Until 2009 he was a Professor for Information Systems with the KIMEP in Almaty (Kazakhstan). Currently he works on aspects of the mathematical foundations of Information Systems design.

Christian Kop currently works as an Assistant Professor at Klagenfurt University and is a member of the German computer society "Gesellschaft für Informatik (GI)". He studied Informatics at the same university and received his PhD in 2002. His research interests cover the research areas of conceptual modeling, requirements engineering, natural language processing, and ontologies. Especially, he is interested in bridging the gap between natural language sentences and conceptual models as well as ontologies. The aim of his research activities is to make conceptual models and ontologies also understandable for persons with no technical background.

Mariam Lahami has obtained her diploma of engineer in computer science from National Engineering School of Sfax (Tunisia) in 2006. From the Faculty of Economics and Management of Sfax (Tunisia) she obtained her **Master's thesis in 2009.** She participated in the initiation of many graduate courses at the University of Sfax. Her current research works are concentrated on the runtime testing of distributed and evolvable real time systems. More details are available on her home page: http://www.redcad.org/members/meriam.lahami/

Ming Li has been a faculty in the Department of Computer Science, California State University, Fresno, since August 2006. He received his MS and PhD degrees in Computer Science from The University of Texas at Dallas in 2001 and 2006, respectively. His research interests include QoS strategies for wireless networks, robotics communications, and multimedia streaming over wireless networks. He is a guest editor of a special issue on Recent Advances in Sensor Integration for International Journal of Sensor Networks, a special issue on Data Semantics for Multimedia Systems in Springer Multimedia Tools and Applications, and a special issue in Journal of Multimedia. He has served as the TPC co-chairs and program committees in various international workshops and conferences in multimedia and networking areas. Ming Li is a member of ACM and IEEE.

Shih-Hsi "Alex" Liu is currently an assistant professor in the Department of Computer Science at the California State University, Fresno. He received his BS degree at National Chiao-Tung University, Taiwan in 2000, M.S. degree at University of Houston in 2002, and Ph.D. at the University of Alabama at Birmingham, all in computer science. Dr. Liu's primary research interests are in software product line engineering, model-driven engineering, domain-specific languages, service-oriented computing, and evolutionary computations. His research work has been published in the journals, book chapters, and refereed proceedings and he has co-edited, co-organized or committed in journals/conferences/workshops in the aforementioned areas. Dr. Liu is a member of ACM, IEEE, and Upsilon Pi Epsilon. More information about Dr. Liu is available at http://zimmer.csufresno.edu/~shliu.

Heinrich C. Mayr received his doctorate in applied mathematics from the University of Grenoble (France) in 1975. Until 1983 he was an assistant professor at the University of Karlsruhe (Germany) and a visiting professor in the domain of database technology and Information Systems at several universities. From 1984-1990 he was CEO of a German software company, since 1990 he is full professor of informatics at the Alpen-Adria-Universitaet Klagenfurt, Austria. For 10 years he was the Dean of the "Faculty of Economics, Business Administration and Informatics". Since 2006 he is the Rector of the AAU. His research is documented by more than 160 publications and includes Information Systems design methodologies, natural language processing in requirements analysis, knowledge management and case based reasoning in the context of service systems, and software project management. He has been, among others, Vice President of the Council of European Professional Informatics Societies (CEPIS), President of the Gesellschaft für Informatik (GI), Vice President of the Software Internet Cluster SIC, Carinthia. Currently he is editor in chief of the GI-Edition "Lecture Notes in Informatics", member of the board of the Austrian Computer society (OCG), chairman of the Council of the Carinthian College of Education, board member of Carinthia Tech Institute, and Fellow of GI.

Marco Massarelli is a former student of the Università degli Studi di Milano-Bicocca in Italy, where he received his Master degree in Computer Science in April 2010. His academic career covered various software engineering areas such as software architectures, software development, object-oriented methodologies, software test and analysis, software evolution, and reverse engineering and project management. As a personal interest he constantly studies Web design and Web-related technologies and trends. He is an avid reader of everything related to technology, including science-fiction.

Daniel Mellado has a PhD and MSc in Computer Science from the Castilla- La Mancha University (Spain) and Autonomous University of Madrid (Spain), and Certified Information System Auditor by ISACA (Information System Audit and Control Association). He is Assistant Professor of the Department of Information Technologies and Systems at the Castilla- La Mancha University in Toledo (Spain). He participates at the ALARCOS research group of the Department of Information Technologies and Systems at the University of Castilla- La Mancha. He is civil servant at the Spanish Tax Agency (in Madrid, Spain), where he works as IT Auditor. His research activities are security requirements engineering, security in Information Systems, secure software process improvement, and auditory quality and product lines. He has several dozens of papers in national and international conferences, journals and magazines on these subjects and co-author of several chapter books. He belongs to various professional and research associations (ASIA, ISACA, ASTIC, ACTICA, etc).

Mohamed Nadhmi Miladi obtained his diploma of engineer in Computer Science from the Faculty of Science of Tunis (FST) in 2003 and his **Master's thesis** diploma from National Engineering School of Sfax (ENIS) in 2005. He is now finalising his Ph.D. diploma in the Research Unit of Development and Control of Distributed Applications (ReDCAD) related to the ENIS School with the collaboration of the Laboratory of Analysis and Systems Architecture (LAAS) in Toulouse (French). He joined the High institute of Industrial Management of Sfax (ISGI) as Assistant Professor of Computer Science in 2009. He participated to the initiation of many graduate courses at the ISGI institute. His current research areas include design of software engineering of distributed systems, component based development, service oriented development, and self-adaptive systems. More details are available on his home page: http://www.redcad.org/members/miladi/

Alireza Moayerzadeh received his MSc in Computer Science from University of Toronto. His research interests include goal-oriented knowledge representation methods, analysis of Open-Source software from social and technical perspectives, and software architecture and design. Alireza is currently working at Facebook helping make the Internet more social for everyone.

Nirmal K Mukhi is a Senior Software Engineer at IBM T.J. Watson Research Center. At IBM, he has worked on Web services standards and was involved in development of a number of early Web service technologies including WSIF and BPWS4J. Nirmal also studied QoS issues for Web services and more recently has been researching methods for monitoring informal business processes. Nirmal has published a number of research articles in these areas. Prior to joining IBM, Nirmal worked on middleware for Grid infrastructures at Indiana University, where he completed his Masters degree in Computer Science in 1999.

Gunter Mussbacher received a MSc degree in the area of requirements engineering from Simon Fraser University in 1999. While working as a research engineer for the Strategic Technology department of Mitel Networks, he applied and taught User Requirements Notation (URN) concepts at Mitel. In 2008, Gunter co-edited with Daniel Amyot the URN standard of ITU-T. For his PhD studies at the University of Ottawa, Gunter is developing the Aspect-oriented URN (AoURN), a framework that enables goal-oriented, scenario-based, and aspect-oriented modeling in a unified way. His general research interests lie in requirements engineering, URN, aspect-oriented modeling and software development, and patterns. Gunter organized the Early Aspects (EA) workshop at AOSD 08 and is on the programming committee of the AOM and EA workshops. He taught URN and AoURN tutorials at RE, ICSE, UML, and AOSD and other venues and software engineering courses at Simon Fraser University and the University of Ottawa.

Yuichi Nakamura is a research staff member at IBM Research - Tokyo. He joined in IBM in 1990, and has worked on several areas such as object-oriented systems, multi-agent systems, B2B e-commerce and knowledge engineering. Between 1999 and 2007, he led several Web services projects such that he initiated Apache Axis project to implement a Web service engine, designed security and cache components for IBM WebSphere Application Server as a lead architect, and conducted security policy research including Model-Driven Security. After two year experience as an IT architect at IBM service division, he joined in the Research division again to work on a security management project. He received an MSc and a PhD in applied physics from Osaka University in 1987 and 1990 respectively.

Kouichi Ono received his B.S.E. and M.S.E. degrees, both in electronics from Waseda University, Japan in 1987 and 1989, respectively. From 1990 to 1992, he was a Research Associate in the Centre for Informatics, Waseda University. His research interests include formal methods for software verification, program analysis, mobile agent technology, software development support technology for Web/XML application, software reuse, computer security, model-driven development for embedded software, and reverse engineering. He was a board member of Japan Society for Software Science and Technology from 2003 to 2006. He is currently working at IBM Research - Tokyo. He is a member of the IPSJ, the JSSST, the ACM and the IEEE Computer Society.

Guadalupe Ortiz completed her PhD in Computer Science at the University of Extremadura (Spain) in 2007. Since graduating in 2001 and for the following eight years, she worked as an Assistant Professor as well as a research engineer at the University of Extremadura's Computer Science Department. She has recently joined the University of Cádiz as Professor in the Computer Science Language and Systems department. She has published numerous peer-reviewed papers in international journals, workshops and conferences, and she has been a member of various program and organization committees of scientific workshops and conferences over the last years. Her research interests embrace aspect-oriented techniques as a way to improve Web service development in various fields, with an emphasis on model-driven extra-functional properties and quality of service, as well as their adaptation to mobile devices.

Sujay Parekh is a Software Engineer at IBM T.J. Watson Research Center. He earned his BS in Computer Science and Mathematics from Cornell University and his PhD in Computer Science from the University of Washington. His interests are broadly in the performance, tuning and management of distributed computing systems. He has published papers in a variety of areas including feedback control, computer architecture, databases and systems management. He is co-author of a book on feedback control of computing systems.

Nicolò Perino is a PhD student in Computer Science at the University of Lugano since 2009 under the supervision of Prof. Mauro Pezzè. He is interested in software engineering and in particular in autonomic and self-healing systems area. His research is focused on detecting and healing techniques for functional failures in Web and desktop applications. He received his Bachelor and Master degree in Computer Science from Università degli Studi di Milano-Bicocca in 2007 and 2009 where he took an internship at STMicroelectionics about the interoperability issues among UML tools. During his Master and doctoral studies he taught as assistant for several courses in various computer science disciplines.

Mario Piattini has a MSc and PhD in Computer Science from the Politechnical University of Madrid. He is certified Information System auditor by ISACA (Information System Audit and Control Association). He is Associate Professor at the Escuela Superior de Informática of the Castilla- La Mancha University (Spain). He is author of several books and papers on databases, security, software engineering and Information Systems. He leads the ALARCOS research group of the Department of

Information Technologies and Systems at the University of Castilla- La Mancha, in Ciudad Real (Spain). His research interests are: advanced database design, database quality, software metrics, object-oriented metrics and software maintenance.

Claudia Raibulet is an Assistant Professor at the Universitá degli Studi di Milano-Bicocca in Italy. She received her Master degree in Computer Science from Politehnica University of Bucarest, Romania in 1997 and her PhD degree from Politecnico di Torino, Italy in 2002. She is involved in Software Engineering and Reverse Engineering courses. Her research interests concern various software engineering areas including software architectures, object-oriented methodologies, development of adaptive systems, mobile systems, distributed systems, software architecture reconstruction, and design pattern detection. Claudia Raibulet co-authored more than fifty research papers published in international journals, conferences, and workshops. She is involved in referee activities for various international journals, as well as in organizing and program committees for international conferences and workshops.

Matthias Riebisch received a diploma degree in automation engineering from Dresden University of Technology in 1988. In 1993 he earned a doctoral degree in computer science from the Ilmenau University of Technology, Germany for research on component-based software engineering and reusability. He is currently teaching and researching at the Ilmenau University of Technology, where he is leading a research group on software architectural design methods and software evolution. He spent three years in leading positions in industry as project leader and architect of large software projects. During his career in academia he worked in several international and national projects in a strong collaboration with industry. In 2005, he served one term at the Oldenburg University as a professor for software engineering. His research has spanned a range of topics in the fields of software engineering, systems engineering, software processes and quality, reusability and software architectures. He has also worked on software evolution and traceability, especially for model-driven design.

Jesús Rodríguez has an MSc in Computer Science from the Castilla- La Mancha University (Spain). He participates at the ALARCOS research group of the Department of Information Technologies and Systems at the University of Castilla- La Mancha. He works at the Department of Defense of Indra Software Labs (in Ciudad Real, Spain). His research activities are security requirements engineering, security in Information Systems, quality and product lines. He has some papers in national and international conferences.

Fumiko Satoh received her Master's degree in physics and Doctoral degree in computer science from Tokyo Institute of Technology in 2001 and 2010, respectively. She joined IBM Research - Tokyo in 2001. She has worked on metadata for video digest, security for SOA applications (Web Services security runtime and tooling, WS-Security related specifications, security policies, security configuration and validation), and model-driven development. She is an author of two Redbooks titled "WebSphere application server V6 security handbook" and "WebSphere version 6 Web Services handbook development and deployment." She started new research that focused IT technologies contributing to emissions trading and management. Her current research interests include non-functional requirements of business process management, Cloud Computing, emission management technologies, and eXtensible Business Reporting Language(XBRL).

Vladimir A. Shekhovtsov currently works as an Associate Professor at National Technical University "Kharkiv Polytechnical Institute", Kharkiv, Ukraine. He studied Information Systems at the same university and received his Candidate of Science degree (Ph.D. equivalent) in 1998. His research interests include stakeholder involvement in software process activities, human-computer interaction in software engineering, service-oriented computing, and software quality modeling. The aim of his research activities is to establish foundations for the software process driven by stakeholder opinions on quality of the prospective system.

Thell Smith is currently a graduate student in the Information Systems program at the University of Phoenix. He received his BS degree from the Department of Computer Science at the California State University, Fresno in 2008. His research has focused on the semantic annotation of biomedical multimedia as well as the merging of a proprietary XML schema with that of the MPEG-7 schema. He was the president of the Kappa Chapter of Upsilon Pi Epsilon.

Xiping Song is a senior consultant at the requirement engineering program at Siemens Corporate Research. In over a decade serving at Siemens, Dr. Song has been involved in a large number of software development projects. His research interests include non-functional requirements, platform requirements, medical workflows and software architecture. Dr. Song had published widely in the software engineering community. Dr. Song received a BS from Beijing Polytechnic University, China, a MS from University of Colorado at Boulder, and a PhD from University of California at Irvine, all in computer science.

Vladimir Stantchev is a senior scientist at the Berlin Institute of Technology where he heads the Public Services and SOA Group. He is also a senior lecturer at the FOM Hochschule für Ökonomie und Management in Berlin, Germany. Vladimir received a Masters Degree in Computer Science from the Humboldt University in Berlin, Germany in 2005 and a PhD in Computer Science from the Berlin Institute of Technology in 2007. In 2008 he was a visiting postdoctoral scholar - Fellow at the University of California, Berkeley and at the International Computer Science Institute in Berkeley. His research interests are in the areas of service-oriented computing, software engineering, and IT management.

Gerrit Tamm is affiliated with the Humboldt-University at Berlin. He is also a professor of Business Information Systems at the SRH University Berlin and CEO of Asperado GmbH. Gerrit received a Masters Degree in Industrial Engineering from the Berlin Institute of Technology and in 2003 a PhD from Humboldt University in Berlin. After a post-doc stay at the St. Gallen University in Switzerland he was a visiting professor in 2004 in Erfurt, Germany. He headed the Research Centers "InterVal - Internet and ValueChain" and "Ko-RFID -Kollaboration und RFID." Gerrit is founder and DEO of the Electronic Business Forum and Absolvent.de. He is an advisory board member of eco e.V. (Verband der deutschen Internetwirtschaft e.V) and member of the UDDI Advisory Board.

Michiaki Tasubori is a researcher at IBM Research - Tokyo in Japan. Since 1997, he has worked on advanced reflection technologies in Java (a.k.a. OpenJava and Javassist), and applied the technologies to aspect-oriented development for distributed computing (a.k.a. Addistant) at University of Tsukuba, Japan. Just after receiving a PhD degree in Engineering in 2002, he joined IBM Research in Japan. There he shifted his research focus to more application side, Web, and worked on XML and Web Services. He also led the Java zone in IBM developerWorks Japan during 2002-2003. In 2005, he started a research project on multiple programming languages situation with a few colleagues, the predecessor of the Dynamic Scripting Languages project, in which he is currently engaged.

Kun Yang received his PhD from the Department of Electronic & Electrical Engineering of University College London (UCL), UK, and MSc and BSc from the Computer Science Department of Jilin University, China. He is currently a Reader in the School of Computer Science and Electronic Engineering, University of Essex, UK. Before joining in University of Essex at 2003, he also worked at UCL on several European Union research projects such as FAIN, MANTRIP, CONTEXT, etc in the area of IP network management and service engineering. His current major research interests include wireless networks and communications, heterogeneous wireless networks, fixed mobile convergence, pervasive service engineering, IP network management and network virtualization, which are supported by externally-funded research projects from EPSRC, TSB, industries and EC. He has published more than 50 journal papers. He serves on the editorial boards of both IEEE and non-IEEE journals. He is a Senior Member of IEEE.

Eric Yu is Associate Professor at the Faculty of Information, University of Toronto. He received his PhD in Computer Science from the University of Toronto. His research interests are in the areas of Information Systems design, requirements engineering, knowledge management, and software engineering. He is a co-author of the book Non-Functional Requirements in Software Engineering (Springer, 2000). He is originator of the i* agent-oriented modeling framework. GRL (Goal-oriented Requirements Language), a variant of i*, has been approved as the international standard ITU-T Z.151, as part of the User Requirements Notation (URN). Prof. Yu serves on the editorial boards of the International Journal of Agent Oriented Software Engineering, the International Journal of Information Systems Modelling and Design, IET Software and the Journal of Data Semantics, and was program co-chair for ER 2008.

Index

A

acquire and implement (AI) 327

Airline Service component (AS) 283

air traffic management 148

analysis services 339, 340, 344, 348

annotations 336, 337, 338, 340, 341, 343, 344, 349

application-level requirements 217

application platforms 24, 25, 26, 30, 31, 40, 42, 43, 46

application service providing (ASP) 324

aspect maps 51

aspect-oriented extensions to URN (AoURN) 48, 49, 50, 51, 67, 68

aspect-oriented GRL (AoGRL) 51, 71

aspect-oriented modeling (AOM) 249

aspect-oriented programming (AOP) 104, 249, 250, 252

aspect-oriented software development (AOSD) 194, 195, 215, 246, 247, 248, 249, 250, 251, 252, 264, 265

aspect-oriented UCMs (AoUCM) 51, 65, 66, 67, 72

Atlas Transformation Language (ATL) 152, 160, 167

attack trees 89, 90, 92

Attribute-Driven Design (ADD) 2, 3, 4, 5, 13

automation technology (AT) 26, 27, 40, 41, 42

Autonomic Web Service Envirenement (AWSE) 221

B

biomedical multimedia data 335, 336, 338, 339, 340, 346, 347, 355

biomedical multimedia infrastructure 335

biomedical multimedia processing 335, 336

black-box model 311, 312

bookkeeping departments 177, 178, 180, 181, 182

building technology (BT) 26, 40, 41, 42

business infrastructures 97

business people 176

business processes 172, 173, 175, 181, 183, 188, 189, 190, 193

business services 97, 112, 325, 330

C

C# 82

Carnegie Mellon University 247, 248, 251, 265

Change of Input Values (COV) 31, 34, 35, 36, 39, 40, 41

classification 335, 339, 340, 346, 347, 349, 351, 355, 356

classification service 335

client server systems 28

closed loop system 302, 315, 316, 321, 322

Cloud Computing 324, 326, 328, 333

code writers 74

Common Criteria (CC) 75, 76, 78, 80, 81, 82, 83, 84, 85, 86, 87, 88, 89

communication protocols 336

Component-Based Architecture style (CBA) 218, 220, 232, 240

composition/decomposition 336

Computer-Aided Requirements Engineering (CARE) 73, 75, 81, 82, 88, 90

content-based image retrieval 340, 349, 352, 358

Context Modelling Framework (CMF) 147,